THE NEW POLITICAL ELITE

OTHER BOOKS BY THE AUTHOR

1. Women in Bihar
2. Altering Structures: Innovative Experiments at the Grassroots
3. Development with a Bang
4. The Tribal Experience: An Investigation into Poverty and Survival
5. The New Political Elite: MLAs v/s MPs
6. Poems

THE NEW POLITICAL ELITE

The Inconsequential MP?

Volume II

Gautam Vohra

1994

KAVERI BOOKS
DELHI - 110085

ISBN 81-7479-001-2

Published by : **Rakesh Goel**
Kaveri Books,
125, Kadambari,19/IX, Rohini,
Delhi-110085 (India). Phone: 7265687

Laser Typeset by : ShiKi Associates, New Delhi - 110058

Printed at: D.K. Fine Art Press, Delhi-110052

PRINTED IN INDIA

Preface

The Inconsequential MP? is the second volume of a three-part study on "The New Political Elite" that I undertook some years ago to get an idea of the nature and style of functioning of our political masters. My perception, as a member of the middle class who had taken up a profession, was that the politician had emerged as the more "powerful" actor on the stage of independent India than the members of either the administrative or industrial elites. He certainly arouses a great deal of interest which is evident from the preoccupation with his activities, as for instance, reflected in the media.

Even as I was completing the ICSSR supported study on the MLAs I discussed the idea of a similar project on MPs—like the previous one, a case study of Maharashtra—with Dr. Usha Thakkar, head of the department of political science, SNDT University. She thought it worthwhile and a proposal was sent to the University Grants Commission with whose support the current study was undertaken.

I am most grateful to Dr. Thakkar for her unstinted co-operation, and the facilities of the university she placed at my disposal. Through her I met Sharada Kokaty who accepted the onerous but essential task of condensing/paraphrasing the speeches/debates of the MPs reproduced in Annexure-IV. Some people maintain that the MP can still embarrass influential groups/people by raising inconvenient questions on the floor of the House. Whether this is so, it is for the reader to decide from the fairly extensive coverage that has been provided to the questions/debates/speeches. Research scholars may also find this section useful to negate or support their hypotheses.

I would like to thank my publisher for patiently putting up with the delay in the completion of the manuscript. As before, the Daya Publishing House has not made a fuss about the revisions that became necessary when the initial manuscript appeared inadequate or inappropriate in the light of the changed circumstances a couple of years later. In fact, Daya Publishing House has also undergone changes since the MLA study was published by it two years ago. It has now taken to bringing out publications on science and related material. This explains why its sister concern, Kaveri Books, is publishing my latest volume on the new political elite.

This study, like the previous one, was initiated because little or no material is available on the politician of the eighties and nineties, a politician vastly different from his predecessor of the sixties and seventies, let alone those who entered Parliament in the fifties dominated by Nehru and the leaders of the freedom struggle. It is possible that academics and research scholars will find the material presented in these two volumes of some use to refine their argument on the new political elite and offer fresh insights to enable us to understand its role and functions in India venturing into the twenty-first century.

New Delhi
January 1994

Gautam Vohra

Contents

	Preface	v
1.	Introduction	1
2.	The Role/Functions Of MPs	7
3.	Impact On Policy	19
4.	Change In The Nature Of Elected Representative	29
5.	The Reluctant MP	44
6.	Quality Of Debate	51
7.	Importance Of The MP	85
8.	Socio-Economic Background	89
9.	Conclusion	95
	Tables	
I	Socio-Economic Status	101
II	Political Profile	112
	Annexures	
I	MPs interviewed	127
II	Notes on early history and career of Vasant Sathe, V.S. Mahadik, M.P. Bopche, Baban Rao Dhakne, Uttam Rathod, Haribhau Mahale, Balasahib Vikhe Patil, Datta Samant, G.M. Banatwala, Murli Deora	129
III	Select bibliography	167
IV	Condensed versions of select debates/ speeches, as well as questions of MPs during the eighth Lok Sabha session	171
	Index	227

1

Introduction

What do we know about our MP. What manner of man is he. What lies behind the public face of the vote seeker we confront every few years during the elections. The answers to these questions, and related ones, are not available in the existing literature. An effort will be made to fill the gap by examining the careers and contributions of the protagonists of the ninth Lok Sabha from Maharashtra, many of whom have found a place in the tenth Lok Sabha.[1]

Unless a minister, an MP counts for little in Delhi (or his state, for that matter). His perks and privileges are few: residential accommodation, telephone facility and the right to travel first class by train.[2] In contrast, an MLA is a power in his own right, regardless of whether he makes it as a minister. He gets about Rs.20 lakhs each year to spend on his constituency. As chairman of the district development board his approval is needed for all development schemes. And as a result of his control over the co-operative structure and the 'downstream' benefits he is in a position to create (in terms of educational, technical and other institutions), the MLA disburses largesse.[3]

1.

Lok Sabha	*Constitution*	*Dissolution*	*Tenure*
1st (52-57)	17.4.1952	4.4.1957	60 months
2nd (57-62)	5.4.1957	31.3.1962	60 months
3rd (62-67)	2.4.1962	3.3.1967	59 months
4th (67-70)	4.3.1967	27.12.1970	45 months
5th (71-77)	15.3.1971	18.1.1977	70 months
6th (77-79)	23.3.1977	22.8.1979	29 months
7th (80-84)	10.1.1980	31.12.1984	59 months
8th (84-89)	31.12.1984	29.11.1989	59 months
9th (89-91)	2.12.1989	13.3.1991	15 months

2. A middle level IAS bureaucrat, or a corporate executive, receives similar perks; the MP is worse off as he does not enjoy a secure tenure of office, having to periodically seek re-election. A while ago his pension shot up considerably as the Lok Sabha decided to be generous to its members. This has, however, not altered his position in the scheme of things

3. Baviskar, B.S., *The Politics of Development; Sugar Co-operatives in rural Maharashtra* (OUP, 1980): There is now greater recognition than, say a

Some MPs are more equal than others. Murli Deora is more influential than 90 percent of the MPs. The position of former chief ministers turned MPs such as S.B. Chavan, A.R. Antulay and Sharad Pawar is exceptional, for the linkages they have established enable them to exercise influence. As noted, the ministers, or former ministers, such as Vasant Sathe and Shivraj Patil fall into the same category.

The rest of the Maharashtra MPs, or those from other states, remain faceless except during elections. For their speeches do not get reported in the newspapers; only those of the leaders of the opposition (and of course the ministers) get quoted. During parliamentary sessions, which are covered by Doordarshan, the names of a few more of the MPs may be announced for making this remark or the other, or participating in some debate. But the bulk of the 545 parliamentarians, who have entered politics[4] with certain expectations, their activities, their contributions, remain unreported, and for the members of the public at large they may not exist; and this is true even with regard to the voters in their constituency, for the parliamentary sessions and committees keep them in the capital for eight months in the year.

Lifestyle

Mahadik's home on Chamar Baugwala lane in Merwanji wadi, Parel is difficult to locate. One wanders through lanes, and by-lanes, into a clearing. And there it is, a hole in the wall, a poky little place. It can't be an MP's house, one feels. But it is. Mahadik's son asks us to await the elected representative in the visitors' room which is no larger than six feet by six feet, or a bit more. As three,

---

decade ago, that co-operatives have played, and continue to play a vital role in the politics and development of Maharashtra. The leaders of the opposition parties in Maharashtra are critical of the advantages which the Congress party enjoys through its control over the co-operatives and resent its consequent superior resources during the general elections.

4. Dhanagare, D.N., *Political Dynamics: a survey of research in political science, volume III* (Allied Publishers Pvt. Ltd., 1981): Pp 97— "Politics" here would mean not abstract ideological warfare but a concrete set of activities, strategic or otherwise, for seeking scarce power positions for decision-making and distributing rewards in a political system or in those spheres of social life which directly or indirectly influence political power relationships or get influenced by them.

four supplicants enter with requests for school admission and jobs, the room is already packed and I wonder how we will make space for the MP when he shows up.

If Mahadik's residence reflects a lower middle class ambience, Sharad Dighe's place is middle class. A fourth storey flat on Kashinath Dhuru Road in Dadar, it overlooks the sea. The breeze wafts through the open window while we listen to Dighe in his drawing room (sitting room, if you like) which is littered with a child's toys; there are a number of papers, magazines, and clippings on a coffee table which also has a copy of the 'American Review'. A number of potted plants adorn a corner, and from another Ganesh gazes at us.

Ram Naik's flat is on the second floor of Sonal Apartments in Jayaprakash Nagar, near the railway station in Goregaon East. The 15 feet by 20 feet visitors' lounge (which during the night can well be converted into a guest bedroom) boasts a television set, a video (National), and a Sanyo transistor. A plastic rose *guldasta* gathers dust on a glass show-case which has some shells, a clock, a metal replica of the Eiffel Tower and other curios. The sofas-cum-diwans are draped in dull mud-brown covers. The floor is plastered with a linoleum sheet. On the wall is a calendar (Mitsui Bank) and on the opposite one a portrait of a Hindu reformer of the previous century.

In the case of Mahadik and Dighe, their residences serve as their office as well. Datta Samant's office in Pantnagar, Ghatkopar East adjoins the single storey shack where he lives. The office can hold about 15 plastic lined chairs which are invariably all taken up as groups of workers are ushered into his presence. Outside, hordes of others await their turn to obtain *darshan*. And, as in Dighe's home, Samant's office too has a Ganesh idol but placed on top of a shelf so that it seems to cast a benign glance on the proceedings. All other walls are bare.

G.M. Banatwala's first floor flat is housed in a crumbling building on Meghraj Sethi Marg (formerly Souter Street) in Bombay Central and as one mounts the overused wooden steps, one tends to tred lightly for fear they may give way. The building has a deserted air; most of its tenants appear to have found alternative accommodation. Banatwala makes an entrance in a two piece suit to join me on a maroon-brown plastic-covered sofa set in the elongated drawing-cum-dining room. The glass table top has a couple of English dailies and an Urdu paper. The grandfather clock is in working order and the show-case is crammed with bric-a-brac. The maroon carpet is threadbare. The walls are bare but for a Paradise Housing Agency calendar.

Curiously the MPs' residences do not have photographs which show them posing with the P.M. (except Sathe's home and a couple of others). The MLAs' homes, almost all, have such photographs (if in the Congress), and with their respective party leaders (those in other parties).

Somewhat disturbing is the realisation that hardly any MP reads. There is not a bookshelf in sight to suggest that during a moment or two of relaxation, the MP may pull out a paper-back (let alone books on national policy, to bone up on an issue before his speech).

It was difficult to contact rural MPs at home/in their constituencies, as most of them spent a large part of the year in Delhi. Their lifestyle, however, was apparent from the way they maintained their residences in North or South Avenue or in the relatively more stately bungalows. Whether it was Y.S. Mahajan (Jalgaon constituency) at 175 North Avenue, Dr. K.P. Bopche (Bhandara constituency) at 91 South Avenue, or Babasahib Vikhe Patil (Kopargaon constituency) at bungalow number four on Dr. Bhishambar Das Marg (near Gol Dakhana), their living quarters radiated a dilapidated, uncared for ambience. The furnishings were shabby, the diwan covers frayed, the carpets old and cheap, with signs suggesting that the sitting room was converted by visitors from the district into a bedroom (alongside the sofas/diwans were hastily rolled up beddings). While the non-Maratha MPs display no photographs, the Maratha ones may have one of a Gandhi-capped individual in kurta-dhoti, either their father, or a regional leader.

Not all MPs live poorly. The houses of ministers like that of Sathe—when interviewed he was still occupying the bungalow assigned to him while a minister—radiate comfort, may be affluence, if not taste. The homes of some MPs, mostly Congress ones, are maintained in style: such as those of Sunil Dutt, or Murli Deora on Malabar hill. Deora's air-conditioned office in Khaitan Bhavan in South Bombay could be mistaken for a luxury suite in a five-star hotel. Antulay's Marine Drive apartment is no middle class deal either. Among the non Congress MPs living in affluence, only the name of Ram Jethmalani springs to mind.

But the well-off MPs are the exceptions. Most belong to the lower middle class, or the middle class. Like the MLAs, even the MPs, come from relatively humble backgrounds; they are men of the people, so to speak. The voters now seem to go in for men who are accessible, who will take up their cause, not the well-heeled men who live elite lifestyles, cut off from the realities of the common man. Or so it appears.

Gaps to be filled

It would have been most useful to go through all the speeches of the candidates interviewed for the study and trace, wherever possible, the impact, if any on policy. This has not been feasible and perhaps another researcher can take up the task. Here the available debates and contributions in the House of three MPs have been examined (The contribution of several others is presented in Annexure-IV).

Another lacuna that needs to be filled is the work of the parliamentary committees, the individual MP's contributions to them and the nature of influence that is exercised by the committees on the formulation of policy.

Unlike the MLA study[5], sufficient data was not collected on the socio-economic background of the type of man who gets elected as MP (except in so far as a mention has been made in 'Lifestyle' above). In the case of the MLA it was found that there was a perceptible change in favour of those candidates who were men of the people, small landowners, mofussil lawyers and teachers (i.e. small time professionals) in contrast to the major Maratha landlords and members of the urban elite who made it to the Vidhan Sabha in the past.

Methodology

The secondary sources consulted are mentioned in the select bibliography (Annexure-III). The focus has been on interviews; of the 48 MPs of Maharashtra, more than a third have been interviewed. Nine belong to the Congress, four to the BJP, three to Shiv Sena and two to the Janata Dal.

5. Vohra, Gautam, *The New Political Elite: MLAs v/s MPs* (Daya Publishing House, 1992)

In addition, some MPs of the previous Lok Sabhas have been interviewed because of their peculiar contributions: Datta Samant, a trade union leader, reflects what he could, or could not, achieve for the working class as a legislator and G.M. Banatwala expounds on what he has been able to deliver through the legislature to the Muslims.

The interviews were conducted in three phases, spread over almost the entire life of the ninth Lok Sabha.

* During the first phase Ram Naik, Murli Deora and others were interviewed in January 1990; they had been elected to the House a month or two earlier. These interviews were conducted in Bombay.
* The second phase spread through April-May 1990 was implemented in Delhi, the interviews being conducted in residential bungalows (Sathe), flats (Y.S. Mahajan), Parliament's chambers (Shivraj Patil, Uttam Rathod) and their rooms in Maharashtra Sadan (Ashok Deshmukh, Baban Rao Dhakne).
* The last round of interviews were conducted a year later, in April 1991 when the decision to dissolve the House was taken and dates of fresh elections announced. The focus, during this phase, was on those MPs who had been elected for the first time (S.N. Kale, P.P. Phundkar) and could discuss their experience and contribution as parliamentarians.

Significance of the study

The study brings to the fore the change in the nature of the MPs, who stand in sharp contrast to those elected to Parliament during the Nehru era.

The changes began to be reflected shortly thereafter and by the sixth-seventh Lok Sabhas, it may not be inaccurate to claim, the new man was in Parliament. He hardly differs from his successor in the ninth Lok Sabha and will have much in common with the MPs in the tenth and subsequent Lok Sabhas.

2

The Role/Functions Of MPs

The functions of the MP are as diverse as he may deign to choose. There are the legislative functions, not to mention his other duties in Parliament. There are others related to dealing with the demands made by his constituents, the voters who sent him to Parliament.

The duties in Parliament may involve (a) securing benefits for the constituency that the Centre alone can provide (railway track, heavy industry i.e. those pertaining to Central ministries) and (b) contributing to the debate on issues of national concern, issues affecting public life (See chapter entitled "Quality Of Debate").

An MP's functions with regard to fulfilling the demands of the voters are those that do not fall within the purview of the municipal councillor or the MLA. He need take up local issues only if and when the other elected representatives refuse, or fail, to perform their duties.

We find that MPs do not contribute significantly to the formulation of laws. With regard to other duties, some do secure concessions from Central government ministries. To the extent that they attempt to meet the needs of their voters, they are performing the tasks of the councillor, and less frequently, that of the MLA.

II

An MP may address himself to purely local issues (in the domain of the civic body or the state) or tackle that which are his mandate i.e. in the domain of the Centre.[6]

---

6. Maheshwari, Shriram, *Political Development in India* (Concept Publishing Co., 1984) — The variety of individual requests made to the MP can be put in the following categories:
   (a) employment
   (b) harassment by police and revenue officials
   (c) civil service matters
   (d) land disputes (in rural constituencies)
   (e) agricultural inputs, water, seeds, fertilizers, credit (also rural)
   (f) civil supplies such as foodgrains, coal, cooking oil

The Congress MP, Uttamrao Deorao Patil (Yavatmal constituency) is among those who has taken up issues with the Centre to benefit his constituency and these include:

- Installation of a T.V. centre at Yavatmal
- Installation of an Akashvani centre at Yavatmal
- A cooperative sugar factory has been set up at Yavatmal. Since this project cost over Rs.25 crores the Centre's sanction was needed; it issues the licence

He has continued to put pressure on the concerned ministers and ministries to

- Sanction a broad gauge railway line; since the British period Yavatmal has been connected by a narrow gauge track.
- Shift the Western Coalfield office from Chandrapur to Wani near Yavatmal.[7]

The provision of a broad gauge railway track appears to be a common issue that MPs take up with the Centre. The Shiv Sena MP, Ashok Deshmukh (Parbani constituency) appears to have a single

---

(g) certificate of character and residence

(h) admission to educational institutions, particularly medical, engineering, and technical, during the opening sessions.

In metropolitan cities like Calcutta and Delhi, a very large number of people approach their MPs for the allotment of houses or for stopping demolition of slums where they live. Interestingly, the cases of harassment by police have been reported to be much lower in sophisticated localities of a city such as Delhi.

To wealthy MPs, the constituents ask particularly for employment and even outright monetary assistance. It is not uncommon for a people perennially haunted by poverty, hunger, and unemployment to remain more concerned with their own individual problems. Only after the basic physical needs of a people are moderately satisfied do they venture into articulating demands of a more general, community-wide interest.

The very low constituents concern for community-wide needs must also be noted.

7. Having done a fair amount of work for his constituency at the Centre, Uttamrao says that he intends to concentrate on taking up other issues to develop his constituency such as the promotion of the co-operative sector, rural industrialisation, providing small irrigation projects and thus changing the cropping pattern and raising agricultural production as well as introducing more educational activities—in fact the whole gamut of development programmes. This is tantamount to confessing that since he cannot influence policy through (i) debates or (ii) even securing more benefits from Central ministries, he might as well concentrate on taking on issues at the local (i.e. constituency) level.

point programme, to install a broad gauge railway track from Manmad to Kachiguda (on Andhra border) linking Aurangabad, Parbani, Adilabad, Parli and Muthked. In fact, it will need to be constructed over a period of 10 years and in three stages: (1) Aurangabad to Parbani (ii) Muthked to Parbani and (iii) Adilabad to Parli.

As in the case of many MPs representing rural areas, serving the farmers is Deshmukh's priority. The broad gauge railway will enable their produce to be transported to (i) Bombay and (ii) the southern states and secure for them remunerative prices. At present they do not since the produce can go no further than Manmad; it is being dumped there, fetching the farmers poor returns.

The lack of a broad gauge track linking "Marathwada, comprising a third of Maharashtra and an important part too" according to Deshmukh, is particularly surprising in view of the fact that it has three jyotirlingas, one gurudwara and the famous Ajanta-Ellora caves. Yet only a narrow gauge links these centres to Bombay and consequently yatris (tourists) are inconvenienced, having to make do with putting up in Manmad.

In the past, the Centre usually gave a few lakh rupees for such projects, but Ashok Deshmukh met George Fernandes (the then minister of railways) and convinced him about its importance and he sanctioned Rs. 25 crores for the first stage and the state government, Rs.15 crores. "We are ready to go in for an agitation if there is delay in the implementation. We will get the broad gauge track by hook or by crook", says Deshmukh.[8]

The other schemes that Deshmukh mentions which will require the sanction of the Centre are the setting up of

- Agriculture-based industry. Being a cotton growing belt, cotton units (spinning, ginning, weaving, dyeing) can be set up
- Sugar factories (apparently Parbani region is within the command area of a dam and hence sugar co-operatives are possible)[9]

---

8. Now that the ninth Lok Sabha has been dissolved and a new one is serving its term, whether this project will get through, is a question mark.
9. A sugar co-operative appears to be a must regardless of whether the area is suitable for it, or needs one. Baban Rao Dhakne obtained the sanction in December 1989 when the V.P. Singh government was in power for a Rs.25/

- Paper mill: the site selected was between Nanded and Parbani, but the Centre had plans to shift it to Sholapur under S.B. Chavan's pressure.

If the sums of money required for the above are Rs.25 to Rs.30 crores, then clearance from the Centre will be needed. Else, as in the case of small units, such as agriculture-based ones, the issues can be taken up to better effect by the MLA who is in regular contact with the minister and bureaucrats dealing with these state subjects.[10]

Dr. K.P. Bopche, BJP MLA (Bhandara constituency) mentions a couple of projects that he intends taking up with the Centre for his constituency.

Rs.30 crore sugar co-operative in his family home of Pathardi in Ahmednagar district (though on this occasion he has contested from the adjoining district of Beed where he also has done much work for the people). The Congress government, he says, was not sanctioning the sugar co-operative. Perhaps, with good reason for Ahmednagar district where the sugar co-operative movement was launched has 18 sugar co-operatives. The most powerful politicians of Maharashtra have come from this district: Vikhe Patil, Shankar Rao Kole, Annasahib Shinde, Ramrao Adik, Govindrao Adik, Bahusahib Thorat, Rupavate and so on, and their control of the sugar co-operatives has played no small part in their emergence as leaders. At one stage, Ahmednagar district produced a number of Communist leaders (Datta Deshmukh, Raosahib Patwardhan, Achyutrao Patwardhan) but since it has become a Congress stronghold.

10. Subjects like law and order, police, agriculture, irrigation, electricity, education, co-operatives, small scale industries, and public health are under the direct control of the state government and as such come within the purview of state legislators.

However, constituents particularly in the rural areas, do not comprehend such functional differentiation. Therefore, they bring to their MP not only problems and matters that are the Centre's direct concern but also those that fall within the state's field.

Twenty-three of the 50 MPs interviewed by Maheshwari reported that over 80 percent of the problems brought to them by constituents fell within the jurisdiction of the states, and another 20 reported that more than 60 percent of the problems were in that category.

Thus, although an MP's constitutionally specified role is limited to the central sphere of functions, his major workload from his constituents relates to the state's field.

Even at the best of times, an MP is thus seen to engage in performing functions of an MLA without, of course, sitting in the state legislature and doing legislative work. The MLA's role devolves upon him completely, in a sense even formally, when the state happens to be brought under presidential rule under article 356 of the Constitution.

- Conversion of the narrow gauge track in Bhandara district i.e. the Jabalpur-Gondia-Chandrapur track, to broad gauge.
- Changing the provisions of the Forest Conservation Act.[11]

Bopche maintains (as do other MPs) that the forest act has put a stop to a number of development projects. In certain parts of Bhandara constituency belonging to the forest department, roads, tanks, electricity cannot be provided as they violate the provisions of the law. Let alone roads, even electric wires cannot be taken through the forest as it may involve the felling of trees. By the same token, irrigation projects (dams) cannot be initiated.[12]

The BJP MP, S.N. Kale (Buldana constituency) has sought to obtain the sanction of the following projects through his intervention at the Centre during the ninth Lok Sabha's short tenure:

- Through the state government, he got the go ahead for the installation of a sugar co-operative in Deolgaon Mahi, Buldana district. It is a Rs.30 crore project and the state is willing to put up Rs.8 crores. The Centre was to give Rs.22 crores, but since the V.P. Singh government was removed and the Chandrashekhar government was a caretaker one, the screening committee examining the proposal set it aside.
- He has followed up on a Rs.200 crore dam (irrigation) project at Kharakpurna also in Deolgaon. The work on it had stopped as it was encroaching upon eight hectares of forest land. In March 91, Maneka Gandhi, the concerned minister, gave the green signal. The proposal and the sanction were forwarded to the Maharashtra government and Kale expected the work on the project to commence shortly.
- He has had the STD facility sanctioned for Buldana district and residents from the area will shortly be in a position to make direct trunk calls.

---

11. Our concern is not whether the MP got the work done but what issues he perceives that only he as an MP can tackle for his constituency i.e. the issues he can take up at the Centre.
12. Dr. Bopche wrote to Maneka Gandhi, the then minister for environment, that the Forest Conservation Act had put paid to 132 irrigation projects.

- In 15 or so interior villages telephone facilities have been installed; electronic telephone exchanges have been established in each tahsil headquarters of Buldana district.
- The railway station is located at Malkapur, 50 km away from Buldana. Buldana residents had to go to Malkapur to book the tickets; now a booking office has been set up in Buldana thanks to Kale's intervention.

P.P. Phundkar, BJP MP (Akola constituency) like Kale, a first time MP, can claim to have provided several benefits as a consequence of his efforts in Delhi:

- The Centre's sanction has been obtained for the establishment of Doordarshan relay stations at Akot and Khandgaon.
- In three tahsil centres, electronic telephone exchanges have been set up. And as the Divisional Engineer Telephones (DET) office was located at a distance, the repairs and complaints took long to tackle. Now the DET office has been installed within Phundkar's constituency.[13]

The interventions at the Centre by the Congress MP, A.T. Kamble (Osmanabad constituency) may be looked at:

- He claims to have obtained a licence for a sugar co-operative for his constituency costing more than Rs.30 crores.
- He was instrumental in getting the Vayudoot to operate a service from Osmanabad. It did so for 3-4 months but because of low passenger traffic, it was discontinued.
- Two T.V. transmitters have been set up in the constituency.

---

13. Phundkar's unstarred question on February 28, 1991 to the minister of surface transport concerned the construction of a bypass on National Highway No.6 and the minister was asked to state (a) whether there was any proposal to construct a bypass near Ridhora village in Akola district of Maharashtra and a bridge on the river Ridhora on N.H.6. (b) if so, the estimated cost thereof; and (c) the time by which the construction work in this regard is likely to be started? Manubhai Kotadia, the minister, said "Yes, Sir" to (a) & (b) and observed that the work would cost Rs.8 crores and to (c) he stated "Since the Eighth Five Year Plan is not yet finalised, it is too early to indicate the date by which the construction work will start".

- STD facilities have been made available at Barshi, Bhoom, Paranda and Naldurg.
- The National Highway will be linked to Osmanabad.
- A demand has been forwarded to convert the narrow gauge railway track to broad gauge from Latur to Kurduvadi via Osmanabad.
- Kamble has obtained LPG distributorships and sanctions for setting up petrol pumps for any number of his constituents.

He has taken an interest in a broad range of issues. In an unstarred question on December 2, 1988 Kamble asked the minister of law and justice to state (a) the number of judges in the Aurangabad Bench of Bombay High Court (b) whether there is any proposal to increase the number of judges; and (c) if so, the details thereof and the time by which the additional appointment of judges is likely to be made. The minister, H.R. Bharadwaj, stated that as per the High Court of Bombay (Establishment of a permanent Bench at Aurangabad) Order, 1984 the Chief Justice of the Bombay High court could increase the number of judges at Aurangabad if and when he liked.

While Kamble may not have got anything much out of the law minister, with regard to the cancellation of the Sindhi play "Jhooley Lal" by Doordarshan, he succeeded in having it telecast by raising the issue in Parliament.[14]

III

The lamentations of the Shiv Sena MP and former journalist Vidyadhar Gokhale give an idea of the role an MP is expected to play by his voters. He is irritated with the tasks his constituents want him to perform. As an MP he has had to be in touch with them

14. Kamble stated in relation to matter under rule 377 "I wish to raise something which has aroused the sentiments of the Sindhi community in my state and the people of the community are losing their confidence. This happened with the cancellation of the Sindhi Play "Jhooley Lal", which was scheduled to be telecast on March 28, 1990 on the occasion of the Sindhi New Year Day, Chetti Chand. Doordarshan, Bombay had signed a contract to this effect with Priyadarshni Academy. The Academy went ahead with the preparations, engaged topmost artistes for the play.... The Doordarshan authorities abruptly cancelled the shooting without assigning any reason.....I request the Minister for Information & Broadcasting to ask Doordarshan to announce the telecast of the play at the earliest."

right from early morning to late at night. "In fact, so many come, there is hardly any time to take meals" he notes and says that they do not understand that the problems they bring are local ones that need to be redressed at the corporation level.[15]

Gokhale admits that he works as an additional councillor and relates the story of the woman "who wasted my time almost for an hour" insisting that a pipeline was needed against the wall of the building opposite her house.

Other issues that MPs have been asked to tackle include

- Shopkeepers' demand for an extension of the area of their retail outlets.
- Parents/students request for recommendations to enable them to secure admission to schools, colleges and other educational institutions (but primarily schools).
- Letters of recommendation for different schemes.[16]

The MP has to face his constituents not only while he is in his constituency, but when they land up in Delhi (where because of the parliamentary session he spends at least eight months, if not more, each year). And invariably the solution to the problem that confronts them is not in the hand of the MP. Yet he is entrusted with it.

To take an example: there was a dispute between a (state) government department and the employees' union and consequently 15 people were transferred to another department. They decided to visit their MP in Delhi and the delegation duly arrived. For a start, he had to arrange accommodation for its members. Next, they wanted to visit the Parliament, so passes had to be organised. Then they were keen to see the minister concerned, and accordingly the meeting was set up.[17] Not unexpectedly, the

15. Maheshwari: Currently, an MP can scarcely avoid meeting functionaries like the district collector, the superintendent of police, even the B.D.O. Indeed he would neglect this only at his peril. An MP observed: "*An MP has no effective power: he has to run to the district collector to get anything done. Moreover, the bureaucracy is so powerful that one has to handle it diplomatically; mere telephone talk is not enough (emphasis added).*"

16. Vidyadhar Gokhale says: he is "harassed" for securing for them the benefits of some scheme or the other. Of course, not all MPs adopt a testy approach. Some accept their voters requests as routine; certainly the professional politicians do.

17. I was, during the course of my discussions, witness to MPs making efforts to fix interviews/meetings for their constituents with ministers. Y.S. Mahajan

minister said the matter was not within his purview; and he could not do anything about it but obligingly he offered to write a letter to the chief minister to look into the matter. And he did. The delegation returned to Bombay.

What had it accomplished? Zilch. Why? Because the delegation went to the wrong person, the MP, who put them in contact with another gentleman, the minister, who was not in a position to redress the grievance.

Result: waste of energy all round, in particular that of the MP.[18]

The MP is a victim of the increasing awareness and consequently, the expectations of the voter.[19] Uncertain as to who will deliver the goods, he approaches all the elected representatives

---

made several efforts to get through to Maneka Gandhi, the then minister of environment, but it appeared the P.A. concerned was either being uncooperative or could not locate Ms. Gandhi.

To take another case: Vasant Sathe had signed copies of four of his books and presented them to me and who should walk in but the Speaker of the Maharashtra legislative assembly, M.D. Choudhary. Vasant Sathe excuses himself, I put paper/pen aside while there is hurried confabulation between former cabinet minister and visiting dignitary who is keen to meet the ex-P.M., can Sathe arrange it. Of course, no problem, an order is given to the P.S. to get George on the line. He appears and Sathe mentions that Choudhary Sahib has to rush back to Bombay to attend the session of the legislative assembly and needs to confer with Rahivji for a few minutes on an urgent matter, George at the other end of the phone is polite, understanding but he can't help as the ex-P.M. is away. Other attempts follow, but all the charm of Sathe is unable to secure an appointment for Choudhari Sahib.

Is this what MPs have been reduced to? Mere contact men! What price politics!

18. Maheshwari: The functions entrusted to the Central Government under the constitution are such that they do not touch directly and immediately the lives of ordinary men and women. The MP is offered more opportunities to work with national and international themes. The problems agitating the minds of the people in the constituency do not as a rule fall within his direct parliamentary responsibility. Also, it is not physically possible for an MP to spend as much time in his constituency as an MLA. Parliamentary sessions last for nearly seven months of the year, and an MP who is devoted to his parliamentary work must necessarily study the various problems very carefully and prepare himself adequately. He is also a member of at least a few parliamentary committees, which also require time and energy. Further, the MPs go abroad as members of parliamentary delegations when Parliament is not in session.

19. See Vohra, Gautam, *The New Political Elite: MLA v/s MPs.*

irrespective of whether the matter falls within their jurisdiction. He surmises that if the councillor cannot solve the problem and neither can the MLA, then the MP will be an additional force whose backing should be sought.[20]

Clearly then the expectations of the voters from their MP are broad-spectrum in nature, and which he is hardly in a position to fulfil. In the circumstances MPs tend to define their own role. They choose to perform tasks that suits their style of functioning. Whether these are such that an MP should perform i.e. whether they fall within his ambit of duties and functions, is another matter.

Take the case of an influential Bombay based MP[21] who performed several tasks:

- Provided protection to tenants by setting up the Bombay Repair Reconstruction Board that has made safe for habitation hundreds of buildings (Ultimate goal, says the MP, is to get legislation passed conferring occupation rights to the tenant).
- Provided ambulance service for riot affected victims (After Rajiv Gandhi visited the riot affected Bombay in 1984, he voiced his concern and the MP promptly collected funds and the Bombay Central Wireless, Ambulance system was created).
- Ensured the immunisation of children through creating awareness.[22]
- Reduced the drop-out rate in municipal schools in his constituency. (The MP felt that a major reason for this was lack of uniforms, so he regularly distributes them.)

But are these the functions of an MP? Should he be tackling issues best left to the municipal councillor? Or the MLA who has

---

20. As Vidyadhar Gokhale puts it: In our society there is a tendency to go to every level at a time. It is like our religious practice, one offers prayers to Shiv, Shanmukha, Jagathamba, and seven-eight other gods. This tendency has been transferred to politics.
21. Murli Deora. See the write-up on him in Annexure-II handed out at his business office premises which indicates that he is involved almost entirely in tackling local issues.
22. As the MP notes, the cost of awareness generation is nothing and cure prohibitive; in fact if there is no awareness, there is no cure. He claims that since he launched the campaign, the number of polio victims in schools and slums has dropped dramatically, if not disappeared altogether.

an annual grant of Rs.20 lakhs for undertaking any development scheme that affects the people?[23]

As the above indicates, not all MPs have renounced the development role to the MLA or the municipal councillor. The Congressman Uttamrao Deorao Patil (Yavatmal constituency) even believes that he can influence the overall development of the district if he maintains good relations with the MLAs (During the ninth Lok Sabha three MLAs in his constituency belonged to the Congress and three to the JD). Theoretically anything is possible.

IV

The role of MPs is not defined anywhere. They are people's representatives, and that is the central issue as far as they or the voters are concerned. The voter does not bother whether an issue is under the ambit of the councillor, the MLA, the MP. Whomever he approaches, he wants the job done and from his perspective any elected representative should be able to deliver the goods, else he is not worth it.

The MP dare not suggest to the voter that this or that is a councillor's function, or of the MLA. They would lose support, that's all, for the voter would think that he was trying to pass the buck.

Invariably the poorer voters, those from the hutment colonies (slums) approach the MP. They come several times; no longer are they reticent or reserved. But not the middle class or upper class voter, who does not ever, or hardly ever, take his grievance to the MP. Whether they are consumers, telephone subscribers, railway commuters, none from the relatively affluent sections of society contact their elected representative. They rather get their jobs done through their own associations.[24]

23. Murli Deora is quick to point out that he has taken part in debates in Parliament (and thus presumably influenced policy, or the issue under discussion) on the (i) Economy, in particular the balance of payments position and exports; and (ii) Foreign affairs. But this claim does not withstand scrutiny. A speech or two a year hardly constitutes a major contribution.

24. Congressman Sharad Dighe, MP during 1984-89 and MLA for two terms prior to that makes this point forcefully and observes that they don't invite the MP to intervene on their behalf because they fear losing their own control, or leadership, over the association, whether it is that of telephone subscribers, or consumers.

V

In brief, the MP has no legislative role left to perform. Or not a single MP talks of his contribution to the formulation of laws, (except for Uttam Rathod who has introduced private member's bills, covered under 'Impact On Policy'), for the good reason that most subjects have already been covered; the previous Lok Sabhas have legislated upon every conceivable topic. That leaves him with the benefits he can secure from the Central government ministries and in this regard though the MP makes various claims, what he can get done, deliver on the ground as it were, is not particularly impressive. We note that a considerable part of his time is spent on performing chores that is the responsibility of the municipal councillor or MLA. Some MPs prefer this function for they would rather not be in Delhi (see the chapter entitled 'The Reluctant MP'). But others have to take up local issues because of the pressure of the voters.

3

Impact On Policy

An MP can have an impact on policy formulation by extending advice through three forums:

(i) Party forums/meetings
(ii) Parliamentary committees[25]
(iii) Debates in the House

---

25 Broadly parliamentary committees are of two kinds—standing committees and *ad hoc* committees. The former are elected or appointed every year or periodically and their work goes on, more or less, on a continuous basis. The latter are appointed on an *ad hoc* basis as need arises, and they cease to exist as soon as they complete the task assigned to them and have submitted their reports. The Lok Sabha has 18 standing parliamentary committees with membership indicated against each:

1.	Business Advisory Committee	15
2.	Committee of Privileges	15
3.	Committee on Absence of Members from the Sittings of the House	15
4.	Committee on Estimates	30
5.	Committee on Govt. Assurances	15
6.	Committee on Papers Laid on the Table	15
7.	Committee on Petitions	15
8.	Committee on Private Members' Bills and Resolutions	15
9.	Committee on Public Accounts	22
10.	Committee on Public Undertakings	22
11.	Committee on Subordinate Legislation	15
12.	Committee on the Welfare of Scheduled Castes and Scheduled Tribes	30
13.	General Purpose Committee	29
14.	House Committee	12
15.	Joint Committee on Offices of Profit	15
16.	Joint Committee on Salaries & Allowances of MPs	15
17.	Library Committee	9
18.	Rules Committee	15

Among the standing committees, the three financial committees are:

Committee on Estimates
Public Accounts Committee
Public Undertaking Committee
} These constitue a distinct group and keep vigil over govt. spending and performance.

Parliamentarians get a chance to meet ministers at various party forums and these can be utilised by the MP to take up an issue under consideration. The MP can get his view across to a minister informally if he meets him in Parliament (as opposed to the floor of the House). As an MP stated: "It is difficult to say how far one has influenced policy. I spoke to the minister when the textile strike was on in full force in Bombay at a party (Congress) meeting, casually, may be I indirectly influenced him."[26]

While it is difficult to estimate the influence MPs' exercise, through party forums as there are no written records, parliamentary committees produce reports, and some are more powerful than others, these being the

- Public Accounts Committee
- Privileges Committee
- Joint Select Committees on FERA etc.

These committees undeniably influence policy and mould public opinion.

Y.S. Mahajan who has been on almost every committee including the Central Advisory Board of Education, Central Employment Committee, the Bofors Committee, considers the PAC to be the most powerful, remarking "It unearths a number of scandals."

Uttam Rathod has been a member of several committees during his decade in Parliament. He observes that the committees are an instrument of keeping a check on the all powerful bureaucracy, and can give direction to it. Another study can investigate into the extent this has been achieved.[27]

---

26. Sharad Dighe made this point with characteristic modesty. It will be useful here to quote Shivraj Patil: "In the present circumstances, no one can say `I did it'. All contribute to formulating policy, the newspapers, the bureaucracy, the MP, ministers, the PM, knowingly and unknowingly they influence policy."
27. Morris-Jones, W.H., *Parliament In India* (Pennsylvania Press, 1957): On the whole, however, the committees have proved valuable. In the first place, from the party point of view, the committees strengthen and improve its parliamentary performance; on any subject there is a team of party MPs who can be expected to have given some thought to the matter. The committees, that is, do something to reduce the big gap in ability and knowledge between Minister and member and perhaps a little to lessen the burden on Ministers of parliamentary debate; as one party office-bearer put it, "each member is able to contribute his mite to the second line of parliamentary

As has been argued elsewhere[28], the ministers in concert with the bureaucrats formulate policy. Or the kitchen cabinet and the PM's secretariat with the civil servants of the concerned government department. But we are discussing the self-perception of the MPs as to how they may have influenced policy, and this is duly recorded in the following pages.

II

The self-perceptions of MPs with regard to their impact on policy formulation is hereby stated:

Y.S. Mahajan

- As a student of economics he was among those who pressed upon the ministry (at the Centre) to adopt the

---

defence. It has been our experience that members of the party reply to criticisms levelled by the opposition without the intervention of the Minister." In their role as a training ground for MPs the committees can do a great deal—and there is certainly much to do. Up to the present, they have perhaps done more to raise the level of the really backward MP rather than to produce teams of advanced specialists; there no doubt are certain specialists in the party, but they have become so without the help of 'post-entry training.'.....There is no doubt that the keen party MP appreciates the standing committees. It gives him an important feeling of contributing to the process of government, especially if the Minister appears to be grateful for suggestions and is conscientious in his replies to complaints. If the MP makes use of opportunities wisely, it enables him to gain a reputation for a command over a particular subject. If he is ambitious, he will realise that it can be made into a route that leads to junior ministerial posts. The committees show up the lazy and the stupid; they also make it possible for the bright to shine....The Congress party in Parliament has organised its members not only into standing committees for the study of particular subjects but also into standing groups whose real importance is as a channel for special local representations to departments.

An MP may serve as a member of a number of bodies and committees of the Parliament, such as the Consultative Committee for the Ministry of Commerce, the Consultative Committee for Central Railway Zone, the Joint Committee on the Indian Veterinary Council Bill, the Hindi Advisory Committee of the Ministry of Civil Supplies, the Consultative Committee for the Ministry of Information and Broadcasting etc. He may be nominated as a Member representing the Rajya Sabha on the Kendriya Sainik Board of the Ministry of Defence and contribute to these bodies and committees with useful suggestions and guidance. He can also be nominated as a Member of the Library Committee of the Parliament and of the Executive Committee of the Indian Parliamentary Group where he can play a significant role.

28. Vohra, Gautam, *The New Political Elite: MLAs v/s MPs*

Maharashtra Employment Guarantee Scheme. The then minister of planning, N.D. Tiwari thought it was a good scheme, and others too were inclined towards it; hence the rural landless EGS was enacted.

- In 1985, there was a move to reduce the ceiling on agricultural land. As a member of the Parliamentary Farmers' Forum, Mahajan and others opposed the move. A committee was appointed to study the subject and it submitted its view to the PM who had specifically invited Mahajan to a meeting of the Forum. The suggestion to reduce the ceiling was dropped (Mahajan is modest enough to admit that there could be other reasons why the issue was dropped for in "matters of social policy it is difficult to take full credit", but he adds that the committee's recommendation did influence it.)
- Before the Eighth Lok Sabha, a bill dealing with the perks, privileges, salary etc. of judges of the High Court and Supreme Court was introduced. Mahajan was the first speaker and among other things suggested that women judges be appointed to the Supreme Court; all speakers following him supported the suggestion. A couple of months later, a lady was made a Supreme Court judge.[29]

Uttamrao Deorao Patil

- As a member of the Agriculture Price Commission and the Parliamentary Farmers' Forum U.D. Patil took an active part in their deliberations and held several meetings with the concerned ministers and their officials. Consequently their representations influenced Rajiv Gandhi's farm package programme such as (a) the APC which accepted farmers as representatives on its governing body (b) whereas previously agricultural labour was not taken into account while calculating the price of agricultural commodities, it has since been reflected in it as also (c) the cost of transport of the

29. "In the circumstances it is not unreasonable to presume I influenced policy" says Mahajan. Apart from being a student of politics, he also acquired a law degree from the Middle Temple in 1935.

produce to the market i.e. the APC price takes (b) and (c) into account.[30]

Ram Naik

In Parliament he raised several issues, among them the

- Re-constitution of the Price Index and
- D.A. be linked to the Price Index (on supplementary demand and since this was not a political issue, it presented no big hassle)

Uttam Rathod

- The farmers have not obtained remunerative prices. Rathod introduced a private member's bill to obtain a better deal for them, taking into consideration the "social needs". This has been accepted (in a general bill on the subject), differences arising on the definition of "remunerative".[31]

---

30. (a) *News Item, July 1984:* Thousands of farmers belonging to the Bharatiya Kisan Union (BKU) Punjab, led by Bhupinder Singh Mann, and from Maharashtra (led by Shetkari Sanghatana leader Sharad Joshi), Haryana, Karnataka, Gujarat, Madhya Pradesh and Uttar Pradesh will court arrest in several places in Punjab to protest against the government's efforts to exploit the present situation in the state by enforcing debt recoveries and payment of electricity bill arrears from the farmers....The BKU had recommended to the government an increase of a least Rs.38 per quintal in wheat price. The BKU leader maintained without giving effect to this recommendation, the government was unilaterally enforcing recovery of electricity bills as also loans....Mann said the farmers owed the govt. Rs.15 crores as electricity arrears and about Rs.1000 crores against loans. However, the government had procured wheat at below cost prices and thus owed the farmers Rs.1,400 crores.

    (b) Jha, Dayadhar, *State Legislature in India* (Abhinav Publications, 1977). Commenting on the 4th Bihar Vidhan Sabha, Jha says where self-interest or group interest of members is in conflict with the public interest, they try to safeguard their own interest and try to rationalise it in terms of public interest. The assembly is under the influence of land-owners. Hence the legislators would not want any change in the existing structure of land ownership, compulsory procurement of food and even lower land ceilings. Sometimes they support egalitarian policies simply to attract votes but they know that the obligation would not be binding. They support agricultural income tax because they know nobody is going to collect it.

31. (a) Mehta, Balraj, *Rich Farmers' Lobby in Full Cry* (EPW, Dec. 2, 1978): The demand put forward was for specific steps to arrest the fall in prices of agricultural commodities, especially of sugarcane and cotton. The suggested steps included take-over of sugar mills which refused to accept cane for

- The issue of setting up of the High Court office in Aurangabad, was introduced in Parliament by Rathod, which was later adopted by the government.
- Another private member's bill introduced by him and later adopted by government, suggesting changes in the Land Acquisition Act, provided relief to cultivators.

Babasahib Vikhe Patil

Babasahib maintains that he has "fought" for several issues in Parliament and hence has influenced policy formulation on the following:

- Rural industrialisation
- Expansion of technical and medical education in rural India
- Development of an integrated rural university
- Free education for women at all levels

---

crushing under the enabling powers assumed under the ordinance issued recently, exemption of khandsari units from excise duty, reduction of excise on mill made sugar and substantial export of sugar by providing necessary subsidy for the purpose. As regards cotton, ban on import of cotton and restrictions on import of polyester fibre was demanded in addition to increase in support prices for cotton as well as large scale purchase of cotton by official agencies.

(b) Mitra, Ashok, *Terms of Trade & Class Relations* (Frank Cass & Co. Ltd. 1977) Chap. 8: The weighted terms of trade between agriculture & industry have over a period moved by close to 50% in favour of the former. This shift in terms of trade towards the direction of agriculture reflects the extent of the decline of the relative unit value of non-farm output and, correspondingly, the rise in the relative unit value of farm product.

(c) Chattopadhyay, B. Sharma, S.C. Roy, A.K. *The Terms of Trade & The Rising Power of the Farm Lobby* (1982): The literature on agriculture in developing economies particularly in the Indian sub-continent, suggests that there are basically two trends of opinion: one trend represented, among others, by Papanek, Mason, Schultz, Millikan & Lipton has held that the terms of trade has generally moved against agriculture and constitute, as such one of the major weaknesses of Indian planning effort; the other trend represented among others by Chakraborty, Griffin, Dantwala, Kelkar, Mitra etc. have held quite the opposite view, that the problems of resource mobilisation in the Indian planning and fiscal set up derive, to a large measure, from the tendency of the terms of trade to move in favour of agriculture in a secularly inflationary situation.

One can safely take the position that the long-term trend in the movement of the terms of trade in the post-independence period, at least from 1950-51 to 1975-76 (especially between 1956-57 and 1975-76), has been on balance, significantly in favour of the agricultural sector.

- A model for rural development (as per the government's guidelines)
- Non aided technical education institutions in Maharashtra, for boys and girls, and extension of several concessions to them.
- Specialised training for rural youth to be integrated into the infrastructure of rural development.
- Making rural agro-based industry either a joint venture, or a co-operative one, with the farmer being made a partner.

Haribhau Mahale

As an MP from a tribal area, Haribhau has discussed issues concerning the welfare of his constituents, though he is aware, and says as much, that this is not tantamount to having impact on policy. The subjects he has raised on the floor of the House include

- Forests and forest produce
- Schemes for adivasis
- Predicament of neo-Buddhists (in his area)
- Agriculture related problems.[32]

Vidyadhar Gokhale

The MP's ideological proclivities, such as they are, may determine the type of policy impact he has; rather these will decide on the issues he would like to take up. Vidyadhar Gokhale stated that he was interested in

- Shaping the Hindutva movement (He says that he has always belonged to the Hindutva camp and when the opportunity arose to project it in its proper perspective he took it and accepted Bal Thackerey's offer to enter politics). He hoped to influence the Ramjanamabhoomi and masjid issue through participating in debates and committees.
- Taking a stand on the important matter of exhibiting Tipu Sultan on Doordarshan (As a member of the advisory committee to the Information and Broadcasting ministry his views would carry weight).

---

32. He makes a point of mentioning that he has brought to the fore the contribution of Babasahib Ambedkar for whom he has much admiration.

Vasant Sathe

- Introduced colour television and other revolutionary changes on AIR and Doordarshan when he was Information & Broadcasting minister and maintains that 80 percent of what the government media is today is due to his contribution in 1980.

Of particular interest is this claim of Sathe since he makes no others with regard to the numerous ministries he was in charge of, and important ones at that. Whereas his cabinet colleague as well as fellow MP from Maharashtra, Shivraj Patil, as the following list demonstrates, feels he has had impact on the policies of every ministerial portfolio he held (Though to be fair to Shivraj Patil, on reflection he admits that a minister *alone* cannot influence policy. See footnote 26)

Shivraj V. Patil

Patil has held several ministerial posts. His impact on policy will be considered, as per his perceptions, with regard to each ministry he has been in charge of, or as minister of state[33]

As *minister of state for defence*, 1980-82, Patil claims to have instituted measures to modernise India's defence in a systematic manner, which involved

- Making the teeth-to-tail ratio favourable
- Developing indigenous capacity to produce equipment so that the defence services were as self-sufficient as possible
- Emphasising R & D
- Promoting better co-ordination between the three defence services
- Helping ex-servicemen

As *minister of commerce* Patil attempted to

- Increase exports
- Reduce imports even as industries were enabled to import machinery for modernisation so as to enhance

33. I have met few ministers who take themselves as seriously as Shivraj Patil. When he was asked to provide an idea of his possible contribution to policy formulation, he rattled off at break-neck speed, with no 'perhaps', of his "enormous" impact. The list is elaborate, and it is given if only to highlight how impressed some politicians are with themselves.

exports (he held conferences within and outside the country with trade, industry and administration towards this end)
- Emphasise the production of quality goods so that they were competitive internationally
- Emphasise not merely the export of raw materials and basic commodities but finished goods (At international conferences tried to create an atmosphere/environment so that protectionism was reduced, leading to a new international economic order)
- Create conditions to meet the demand of developing countries not only for commodities, goods, services but appropriate and even sophisticated technologies.
- Develop trade and commerce between countries of the North and South, and within the South itself; took care of the suceptibilities of the developing countries so as to increase India's exports to them
- Bargain with developed countries to obtain terms mutually favourable and provide India with a footing as an equal partner

As *minister of science and technology* for three years and vice president of CSIR for two years
- Launched new departments; the department of genetics, and department for ocean development, to mention, two, and set up an administrative machinery for them and planned their future direction
- The department of electronics was created, new policies formulated and industry, trade encouraged to enter this sphere, even as R & D promoted
- Tried to develop space and science technology so as to strengthen India in the spheres of communication broadcasting, weather forecasting and so on
- Emphasis was laid on the indigenous production of atomic energy even as safety conditions were provided for; atomic science was sought to be applied to agriculture, health and industry while capability was developed to use atomic energy for peaceful purposes

As *minister for defence production*
- Saw to it that the plans prepared were implemented,

and new industries established (he made the claim that their productivity and efficiency reached "new heights")

- Developed the more (the most) sophisticated equipment and weapons systems

As *minister for civil aviation*

- Launched new airlines and departments: (i) Vayudoot (ii) Parvahans (iii) Indira Gandhi Udaan Academy and (iv) National Airport Authority (These institutions would give essential strength to civil aviation, for they aimed at creating capabilities to reach distant and inaccessible places even as new airports were set up, the old modernised, civil aviation personnel given training, their knowledge updated; training of ground and sky emphasised)
- The capacity of the different wings augmented through the acquisition of new aircraft
- Formulated a long-term plan (20 years) for the development of civil aviation and another one for the entire transport industry (roadways, railways, waterways, all were sought to be "jelled", integrated so as to provide maximum benefit and convenience to the travelling public)

III

In brief, the policy impact of MPs can be evaluated (i) through the influence they exercise during their informal contacts with the concerned ministers at party and parliamentary forums. Since no records are kept, it is difficult to assess the impact the MPs have had. Documentary records exist as to (ii) the work of parliamentary committees. This study has not gone into this issue; another one will be needed. As for (iii) i.e. impact through debates in the Houses, this is discussed in the chapter 'Quality Of Debate'. Thus we are left with the self-perceptions of MPs. In so far as they are members of various forums, such as the Parliamentary Farmers' Forum, there is evidence to indicate that they have influenced policy. But in so far as their claim is that they probably had impact on it by raising issues in the House, it is difficult to tell whether they did or not. Lastly, the ministers' claims, there is likely to be more substance to these, but as the nature of the decision making process has changed, so must their influence on it.

4

Change In The Nature Of Elected Representative[34]

A large number of Members of Parliament during the Nehru era had participated in the freedom struggle and were recognised leaders of their states. The stalwarts were not confined to the Congress. Ram Manohar Lohia, Ashok Mehta, Nath Pai (Socialits), Hiren Mukerjee (Communist), Shyama Prasad Mukerjee (Hindu Mahasabha) and Dr. Ambedkar are a few leaders who belonged to different political persuasions.[35] Among the galaxy of leaders with the Congress were Patel, Maulana Azad, Acharya Kripalani. Nehru was in Parliament all the time, guiding, participating and hence the attendance was high. Apart from being distinguished speakers, some were intellectuals. But even at that time, the remaining MPs, the rank and file so to speak, many from the rural areas, were unremarkable in terms of experience, education or ability. But because of the freedom struggle, and for the fact they had grown up under Gandhiji, they had a distinct stamp in dress, demeanour and behaviour.

During what can be termed as the second phase of Parliament, the transition from Nehru to Lal Bahadur and the early period of Indira Gandhi, stretching from 1962 to 1972, there was a shake up and a rebellion against the old guard, within the Congress and Parliament. The 1967 SVD ministries (influx of the rural feudal

---

34. One is tempted to use C.P. Snow's title for his book, "The New Men" as the heading for this chapter. But that has a positive connotation.

35. Baxter, Craig, *The Jana Sangh: A biography of an Indian political party* (University of Pennsylvania Press, Philadelphia, 1969): On March 28, 1952, a group of 45 Lok Sabha members met in New Delhi under the chairmanship of Mookerjee. These included, in addition to Jan Sanghis, members of the Hindu Mahasabha, Ganatantra Parishad, Akali Dal and Jharkhand Party and a number of independents. As the talks continued some of the smaller parties from the south joined the discussions including the Tamilnadu Toilers Party and the Commonweal Party, but the Ram Rajya Parishad stayed away throughout. Mookerjee attempted to enlarge the area in which he was negotiating and is reported to have met Asoka Mehta and Mrs. Kriplani.

elements) joined forces with an unusual mix of Young Turks, socialists and communists against the old leadership represented by Morarji Desai, Atulya Ghosh, Nijlingappa, Y.B. Chavan, Kamraj and S.K. Patil.[36]

Shortly after Nehru's death and that of Shastri, the old guard had consolidated, and Indira, to use Lohia's description, was passing through the "goongi gudiya phase", leaving everything to senior leaders, imbibing the art of politics and the means to manipulate. Even so, around her the younger lot rallied many of whom were "ideologically socialists," or left of Centre in their politics. Using the issues of abolition of privy purses, and bank nationalisation, she got rid of the old guard by 1969.

Some of them still remained with the Congress led by Indira Gandhi including eminent people like Govindvallab Pant, C. Subramaniam, T.A. Pai; as also Jagjivan Ram, Barooah, Swaran Singh and Y.B. Chavan. In the opposition were men like Vajpayee. But by this stage Indira had begun to emerge as the undisputed leader of the Congress. The Bangladesh war, the massive mandate (1971) and victory across the Vidhan Sabhas (1972), made her the dominant leader of Parliament and the country.

She was able to induct a number of younger people, those she liked, who were capable but not known leaders (of their state). Neither were they men steeped in Congress culture. At this stage, the Congress as an organisation began to stagnate: there was no fresh enrolment of members and neither were elections held within

---

36. Hangen, Welles, *After Nehru Who* (Rupert Hart-Davis, London, 1963): I remember asking him (S.K. Patil) if he thought that he hurt his chances by failing to conform to the Indian image of leadership. His answer was revealing. "Isn't the Indian image of leadership changing? Its true I'm not an ascetic. You can't reflect something you aren't. I want to serve the people, not just reflect asceticism. The people are very happy if their lot improves. That's the important thing to them... But as for frugal living, avoiding motion pictures, wearing khadi—that kind of thing—I don't practice and I don't ask any man to do that. (Morarji) Desai even turns of the ceiling fan when he goes to sleep. I can't live without air conditioning. He wears the dhoti. I don't because I don't believe a dhoti is necessary in the modern world where in an hour's time I may be asked to go to London."
..... His frequent forays abroad, especially during Delhi's hot season, have been criticised as ministerial globe-trotting. His fondness for movie actresses, home-grown or foreign, is viewed less favourably in traditionalist India than it woul be in most Western countries...

the Party. However, the rank and file, and the people, had full faith in Indira.[37]

The third phase, which may be said to begin after 1972, involved the induction of new members; during the Emergency (1975-77) and thereafter another, younger lot of MPs began to emerge to the fore: Sathe, Antulay, Unnikrishnan, Priyaranjan Das Munshi, Pranab Mukherjee. But the elections were a disaster for Congress, except in the south, where under Urs and Reddy it fared reasonably. This led to a shake up and the second split (1978) and the establishment of Congress (I). The stalwarts had begun disappearing such as Brahmanand Reddy, Swaran Singh while the hitherto unknowns such as Sathe, C.M. Stephen, Antulay began to make their mark.

However, the Congress party did not witness any growth in terms of membership or inner party democracy, a hallmark of the Indira Gandhi phase. Not surprisingly upstarts began to control the party machine. Some people maintain that Sanjay Gandhi brought in the lumpen element in politics and this view is resisted by the Congressmen with the argument that to deal with the onslaught and repression unleashed against the Congress by the Janata regime, a youth force or Youth Congress was created; it may have had some people with dubious backgrounds such as Arjun Das, but the others, it is maintained, were well educated sorts and included Jagdish Tytler, Rajesh Pilot, Lalit Mohan; no one could call them lumpen, and neither Kamal Nath, a Calcutta businessman

---

37. (a) Writing in the late fifties Morris-Jones said "The Congress party has, in the course of its 70 years existence, changed its character in radical fashion, and its constitution has had to try to reflect this changing nature.....The transformation of the Congress at the end of the First World War is reflected in the new constitution of 1920; a refined liberal pressure group of middle-class gentleman sets out to be a mass movement with a single clear aim: `the attainment of Swarajya (independence) by the people of India by all legitimate and peaceful means'."

(b) Brecher, Michael, *Political Leadership in India* (Vikas Publications, 1969): Congress MPs were preoccupied with the techniques of reconciliation: They focussed on the integrative role, not on the transforming role of the Congress party in the Indian political system. Their sensitivity to the scope and impact of regional variations in the election outcome, to shifts in the authority structure of the party, and to changes in the personal and institutional loci of decision-making—all these are consistent with the supreme value they placed on *political reconciliation* and their image of the Congress as its indispensable instrument (Emphasis added).

nor Kalpanath Rai, a "double graduate". They differed, as some of Indira Gandhi's nominees to Parliament, in so far as they did not have much experience in politics, let alone a background in Congress culture.

If the rot set into the Congress, it was because there were no party elections at the grassroots or elsewhere and hence no effort was made to mobilise fresh recruits to join the party.

II

Even as the type of men entering Parliament was changing reflecting new social forces, so were their values, their mores.[38]

---

38. (a) Erdman, Howard L., *The Swatantra Party and Indian Conservatism* (Cambridge University Press, 1967): There was no coherent, explicitly conservative response (to the Congress) at the party level during the first decade after independence..... The brief catalogue of challenge and response during the Nehru era suggests one important factor: the diversity of the social forces involved. In addition to inter-group cleavages, however, there were also intra-group cleavages, based in large part on the historic social fragmentation of Hindu society; and these also worked against the formation of a cohesive opposition force. ..... A brief glance at the historical record will show that even within a given group, viz. the aristocracy, landed peasantry, business communities, etc., unity was at best a remote possibility.

(b) The influx of aristocrats, through party mergers and individual entry, has certainly been the most important development, following the consolidation of the inner circle of the party. India's ex-princess and landed nobles either dominate or are very important in the Swatantra units in Bihar, Orissa, Rajasthan, U.P., the Punjab, and to a lesser extent, Gujarat; and in higher circles, first Ramgarh and then Gayatri Devi have served as Vice-Presidents of the party..... The entry of aristocrats, who in Swatantra were very heavily Rajput, introduced into the leadership cadres the element of aristocratic conservatism and the often overweaning pride of the Kshatriya group..... Of decisive importance, however, is the fact that in terms of electoral support and legislature strength, the critical element in the coalition was the aristocracy in the northern states. In the 1962 general elections, only one Swatantrite was elected from South of Vindhyas to serve in the Lok Sabha; and almost all the Swatantra MPs (Lok Sabha) were from aristocratic areas, and were either aristocrats themselves or handpicked followers thereof.—*Ibid*

(c) Rudolph, L.I. and Rudolph, S.H. *Transformation of Congress Party—Why 1980 was not a restoration* (Economic and Political Weekly, May 2, 1981): The most striking finding of their regional analysis is that the elections of 1967 and 1977 marked a deterioration of Congress heartland support that the 1971 and 1980 elections only partially reversed. The return of one-party dominance of the Congress in 1980 masks the fact first there has been a

Which is to be expected as they were and are, the products of their society, their environment. And society and environment differ now from that prevalent during the first Lok Sabha, or the second or third. Here it may be instructive to get the views on the nature of the change that has taken place from at least some of the MPs.

Y.S. Mahajan

— Over the 17 years that I have been in Parliament, the calibre of MPs that have become its members has been such that there has been a considerable fall in the standard of debate. (He entered Parliament during the fag end of the fourth Lok Sabha; the other two who have as much experience of Parliament are Babasahib Vikhe Patil and Vasant Sathe). A debate involves marshalling of facts and close argumentation. Now there is little effort to present an argument, a case for or against. There are only statements, no arguments. And if an argument is presented, it is poor, full of holes. It does not appeal to the reasoning of members. Democracy involves/means a government by persuasion. The effort to persuade, or the capacity, does not exist now. MPs just cite opinions and stick to them without giving arguments. The lack of intellectual discipline among the new crop of MPs is obvious. Yes, most have higher educational qualifications, but these days they don't count for much.

— Debates, such as they are, are boring also because the same points are repeated by the different speakers. This was not the case in the past. At least the repetition (of points) was not so frequent. If it is avoided, Parliament would take half the time it does to do its work (See chapter "Quality Of Debate").

— There is much greater indiscipline on the floor of the House now. When I first came to Parliament, if an MP created disturbance, the leader of his party would immediately request him to maintain order, or send a

---

signal shift in the regional distribution of party support. This has resulted in the Congress party, which had traditionally relied on its disproportionate support in the 'Hindi heartland' moving towards a 'southern strategy'. Secondly the minorities bloc support to the Congress can no more be taken for granted.

party leader to restrain him (from misbehaving). I have seen Indira Gandhi telling her party men to cool off. Now no such action is taken. In fact, they are encouraged to disrupt the proceedings of the House.

— The attendance in the House has gone down. With the result, we have an understanding that as far as possible the question of quorum should not be raised.

Uttam Rathod

— During the Nehru era, the elite were given tickets and they dominated Parliament; many were freedom fighters. After the first three, or first two elections, local forces started asserting themselves; they wanted to send their man, and hence the elected members whether at the state or the Parliament are closer to the people, more genuinely their representatives.

— At one time MPs (and MLAs) were largely Brahmins; if not that, they belonged to the upper castes. Now the majority castes (different castes and those larger in number) are represented in Parliament.[39]

– A consequence of greater democratic representation is that people without the right type of education or background are getting into Parliament. Degrees are

---

39. (a) Beteille, Andre, *Caste, Class & Power; Changing patterns of stratification in a Tanjore village* (OUP, 1966) Chap. VI: Today political power, whether in the village or outside it, is not as closely tied to ownership of land as it was in the past. New bases of power have emerged which are, to some extent, independent of both caste and class. Perhaps most important among these is the strength of numerical support.

(b) Kahane, Reuven, *Legitimation & Integration in Developing Societies; The case for India* (A Westview Replica Edition, 1982): In India of the 1980s, the harijans have aggregated more and more power and have diminished the political gap between themselves and the centre of society. Under the leadership of Jagjivan Ram, himself an untouchable, it has become clear that it is difficult to mobilize their voting power without catering to their interests and thereby increasing their bargaining position.

(c) Blair, Harry, *Rising Kulaks & Backward Classes in Bihar; Social Change in the late 1970s* (EPW Pg. 64 Jan. 12, 1980): During the Janata period in Bihar the Karpoori Thakur ministry's reservation policy, was indicative of a sea-change in the structure of Bihar's political economy: the 'Forwards' or 'twice-born' caste groups that had been dominant in Bihar since independence and before were replaced by 'Backward' castes as the dominant stratum in the state.

not education; neither a knowledge of the three R' s. There is no understanding or concern for the impact an individual's action will have on others, or his behaviour in the House. Hooliganism has become rampant.[40]

---

40. Uttam Rathod's speech at a seminar on corruption is worth quoting in some detail as it reveals the change in the nature of MPs. He begins by saying that Chimanbhai Patel, C.M. of Gujarat and others have compared the present times with the pre-Nehru and post-Nehru era which, according to them, was the best period in the life of our newly born nation. "The people were patriotic; they were prepared to sacrifice anything for the nation to win the freedom. Subsequently, after having won that, they wanted to maintain high standards in personal and social behaviour which were enunciated by Gandhiji. They were also prepared to do anything to keep the integrity and security of the country. Corruption was not this rampant.

"When we look at the scenario, I am reminded of the society, its leaders in those days. It was the Second World War which gave impetus to corruption among the Government servants and their god-fathers. Since the national struggle for freedom was going on, we did not see politicians protecting such people. During war days, I remember several cases were detected and the freedom fighters also condemned them as anti-social elements and the British Government also saw that they were booked and, in many cases, they were even punished.

"The chances of spread of corruption which were already in existence were limited and they were confined to a few. The amount also used to be meagre as the percentage of profit was also low. The main reason why corruption and casteism could not spread in India as you see today was because of the impact of Gandhiji's teaching on the society as a whole. Gandhiji always used to say during the Satyagraha Movement that for achieving any good thing, the means also had to be good. If means of achieving were not good, the quality of the goods that you would get will also be debased. This view was popularised by him throughout Indian society, be they patriots or the public in general. They all accepted and tried to practise it in their day-to-day life.

"After independence, the things were changed. During British days, businessmen, industrialists and others used to deal with the bureaucrats but, now in addition to these factors, a new factor came to be added and that was, some of the people who had influence in politics began to support anti-social elements; this support from powerful people was necessary. Unfortunately, it went on increasing day by day. Easy money had become the order of the day.

"It was difficult for a man of shady character to get elected in those days. The election also cost much more than the limit that was provided for by the Representation of the People Act. All this culminated in spread of corruption in the society.

"Gandhiji's preaching of Ahimsa, Satya, Asangraha and Aparigraha were fading. The people who were in upper strata were tempted to avail of this opportunity and collect more money and subsequently they spent it for bribing the people who came in their way. In a nutshell, this is the history of corruption in India.

— A salutary impact of greater grassroot level representation is that MPs cannot be imposed from the top. Earlier it was not difficult to dump people from the Centre on to the state. Or get those people elected from the state who did not belong to it. Or if they could not get elected, they were inducted into the Rajya Sabha. Even now there are MPs (and ministers) who have been taken in this manner:

* Narasimha Rao is from Andhra Pradesh; he has been elected from Ramtek in Maharashtra.
* Gulam Nabi Azad cannot get elected from Kashmir; so he has been given a safe seat in Gujarat.
* M.L. Fotedar, a Kashmiri has been elected from U.P.; earlier from Gujarat.
* R.K. Dhawan has been inducted through Andhra Pradesh.
* V.Shiv Shankar from Hyderabad has been assisted to obtain a seat from Gujarat.
* Vishwajit Prithvijit Singh from Punjab has got in through Maharashtra.

Most of the above cases indicate that they have been inducted into Parliament through nomination to the Rajya Sabha. At the Lok Sabha level few outsiders are finding a place due to people wanting their own man. But even at the Rajya Sabha level, people from outside the state are not being accepted. Karnataka refused Buta Singh and Mani Shankar Aiyar also could not find acceptance in any state (though in the tenth Lok Sabha elections another try is bound to be made on his behalf from a constituency in Tamil Nadu).

"Shri S.N. Dwivedy has written a book about political corruption in which he has tried to give the nature of corruption and he started with rice scandal in Kerala and in his next book he started with jeep scandal. According to him, the corruption in ruling party vis-a-vis corruption in Opposition Parties ruling in other States was of a different kind in nature. But it was there. A foreigner also wrote a book titled `The Dangerous Decade' where he accepted that there was political corruption. There was corruption in India. But it was not that rampant as the people see today. Both these books were written almost 20 or 25 years back and now there is a sea-change in the social outlook of our own people. They are becoming more materialistic. All this has led to increase in corruption."

Babasahib Vikhe Patil

— There has been a striking change in the lifestyle of MPs. A number openly live in style, entertain lavishly, flaunt their wealth. In the past, there were well-off men in Parliament, but they were low key. The MPs dressed, behaved, lived in a simple fashion.

— Previously, most MPs were (a) men of principles, (b) honest. This is not the case now.

— Debates then contributed to building national policies and at the same time ministers were most responsive to suggestions made by fellow MPs on the floor of the House. This is also a thing of the past now.

— Criticism in earlier Parliaments was not taken as a personal affront. What is more, there was much easier and relaxed mixing between members of different political parties, and firm friendships existed across the ideological barriers. This position has deteriorated sharply. Ministers take every criticism as a personal attack to be dealt with in like fashion. Friendships across party lines are a rare phenomenon as even an invitation to dinner leads to speculation of defection. I had good friends among CPI, CPM members, we dined often together but do not do so now.

A.T. Kamble

— People without money could get into Parliament in those days. My father was an MP between 1962 to 1977 (and an MLA from 1952 to 1962). In 1952 my father was elected unopposed and his election expenses could not have been more than Rs.200. During 1967 my father may have spent between Rs.5,000 to Rs.10,000. There was never a problem about money. All he used was a single vehicle for his electioneering campaign. Till 1962 MLA and MP elections were held at the same time, so the expenses, in particular of MPs, were limited. Even in the 1971 elections funds were not important thanks to the Indira wave.

Those days the public perception of politicians and in particular of MPs was of respect. This is no longer so.[41]

41. Sharad Dighe: Now rural people are playing a greater role in leadership. In Maharashtra, in particular, rural leadership dominates and the chief minister

Haribhau Mahale

— In Nehru's days MPs enjoyed the maximum respect. The decline in his status began during Indira Gandhi's period. She had no time for MPs' views; she imposed her own. Even Morarji had more time for the MP. I belong to the Scheduled Tribe, and am not very educated, yet he included me in various deliberations, "aur hamare saath khana pina bhi tha" (he ate meals with me). Morarji was very conscious of time, but with me he used to make special allowances (as with other MPs). V.P. Singh also seems to be a thinking man. I'm not saying this because he is in my party. He genuinely appears to be conscious of the right values.

Baban Rao Dhakne

Dhakne who has witnessed the political elite since Nehru's time (see his profile in Annexure-II) says there is a great difference between the MPs of the earlier Lok Sabhas and the last few ones.

— The MPs of the first few Lok Sabhas were nationalists, and many were into *samaj seva*; most of the MPs today do not consider the interests of the country, or that of society.

— Any issue, before being taken up for debate, was studied in depth by the MPs in the past.

— When public interest issues came up, opposition and ruling party MPs (and MLAs for that matter) got together and hammered out the best possible solutions. The opposition did not oppose for the sake of it.

— The elected representatives and the party membership were united on the basis of ideology whether they belonged to the RSS, Seva Dal or were Marxists. And they were propelled to work for the public on the basis of their ideology; there were distinct groupings. Only after they had put in some years of service were they selected by the party to stand as MLA or MP, in the

---

is always from a rural area. And as a consequence, urban problems are not properly appreciated and hence often neglected. At the Centre (Parliament), however, urban leadership dominates (Nehru family, V.P. Singh, Morarji Desai, Chandrashekhar) and rural leadership is put down (Charan Singh, Devi Lal).

tradition of Gandhiji who on the basis of the work done decided who was worthy of undertaking satyagraha. Now the service rendered to the people is of secondary consequence, often of no consequence. For often those candidates are selected by the party leadership to stand for elections who donate money, or obtain it for the party. The quantum of money brought in by the candidate, whether or not he has done any political work, decides his future.[42]

K.P. Bopche

— Corruption has certainly taken much deeper root among the MPs (and MLAs) since how could they spend the enormous sums they do during elections, especially the Congress elected representatives (We of the BJP have little money. That given by supporters are small grants. The BJP workers/supporters campaign for us without a fee).[43]

U.D. Patil

— The decline in the prestige of the MPs, according to Patil's perception (he refers to corruption among them only in passing) is a consequence of decentralisation and the emergence of new centres of power. The number of people's representatives have increased, beginning with the panchayat, the Z.P., the co-operative sector, the

42. Ashok S. Patil, former Maharashtra minister who was with Dhakne during the course of the interview, nodded vigorously while discussing the merits of the present day MPs and added "There are good MPs today also, but those who have money are manipulating the whole media, everyone, and getting into power, while the real party workers languish behind the scene. First (earlier MPs) public interest was to the fore, now self interest. Opportunism through flattery is the name of the game. That's why we have all the evils of communalism. Leaders are not chosen for character, integrity or the work they have done, the contribution they have made to strengthening of the party. The Congress Party itself has decayed, as no election has been held within it for the last 18 years; this was not the case when we were its members."

43. Not all MPs think there is a change for the worse among the elected representatives. Murli Deora says formerly Parliament (and Vidhan Sabhas) were dominated by uneducated topiwallas and now it has young, bright, well informed MPs who have so much to contribute. D.B. Shingda holds similar views. He points out that since the younger generation dominates, much more is achieved as the younger MP will meet the minister concerned

civic body, not to mention the MLAs, and they all vie with one another for influence and power.

P.P. Phundkar

— In the days of Nehru, the voter knew the MP only by name not by face. Not so now. The MP, if he is to survive, must visit each village, even though the jobs brought to his notice are those that the MLA or other elected representative are in a position to tackle. The people want him to visit them and see him. The elite MPs are no more; those who have direct contact with the people survive.

III

If MPs have changed, it is because the demands on them have changed; the expectations of them are different and hence the new type of MP has emerged.

During 1947-50, Indian leaders were busy setting up institutions, drafting the Constitution; ideas were rapidly being generated. Other important issues included the formulation of the Hindu Code Bill. The focus of the first phase was the establishment of democracy. Nehru, Ambedkar and others were taken up with laying the foundations of a political system new to India.

The second phase involved the creation of a new economic order, the socialist pattern of society: ceiling laws, tenancy laws, distribution of land, public sector (taking charge of big basic industries), the five year plans....

The next phase was to establish an ethos in administration considerate to the people at large.

Then came foreign policy, a foreign policy that introduced the concepts of Panch Sheel and Non-alignment.

Under Nehru then, the essential effort was to establish democratic norms. Indira Gandhi continued, by and large the policies of her father in politics, economic and social fields. This view is maintained by some Congress MPs, though few will offer any resistance to the idea that Indira Gandhi destroyed democratic institutions, flouted democratic norms and acquired enormous powers.

---

and get the job done whereas the elderly, who dominated previous parliaments, would fob people off with vague promises.

While not seeking to challenge this perspective, MPs who want to present her brighter side say she refused to accept street politics (railway strike), but gave in to moral force as expressed by the hunger strike (Morarji Desai). The principle of planning and the public sector were accepted by Indira Gandhi while the strengthening of the science and technology base of the country was dear to her: atomic power, electronics industry, genetic research, ocean exploration; two-thirds of the science and research laboratories were established during her term in power, and in the field of foreign policy she got on well with the non-aligned nations who made her the chairperson.

Rajiv Gandhi too has not deviated from the essential norms laid down by his grandfather; democracy, planning, modernisation, poverty alleviation and non alignment are key issues for him. But as in the case of his mother, so too in his case, new forces have emerged on the scene and his perception, influenced by them, has led to new emphasis. New technology, new sciences have come to the fore. A mix of the old and the new has been adopted even as the end product is somewhat different to the one accepted in Nehru's time but not that different to that in his daughter's.[44]

---

44. (a) The policies and programmes pursued by the Congress changed in response to the new forces represented in Parliament. Does this explain why non Congress parties too had to adopt them? The Janata Party pursued the same policies as the Congress, maintains C.P. Bhambhri in his book, *The Janata Party: A profile* (National Publishing House, 1980): All the major political parties in India which are staking their claim for governance represent the national alliance of the bourgeoisie and the rich peasantry. The Congress operated this alliance which was sought to be replaced by the Janata party in 1977. The Janata party also tried to work on the basis of a national alliance of the urban and the rural rich, and for this reason it was described by many sympathetic observers as the new Congress party minus the liability of the excesses of the Emergency and the evil consequences of the authoritarian system of Mrs. Indira Gandhi.

(b) The Janata party also projected a left-of-centre image and like the Congress party it had supporters of free enterprise co-existing with fire-brand socialists. Irrespective of the rhetoric of Gandhism and decentralisation of economic power, the Janata did not adopt any policy regarding industry and rich peasantry which was fundamentally different from that of the Congress. The Janata's slogan of rural development was essentially for the development of Indian capitalism. (Ibid)

(c) It is estimated that the Congress groups, the Congress (O), CFD and Independent Congressmen like Chandrasekhar, had a strength of 89 memebers; the Jana Sangh 90, the BLD 68, and the socialists 51 members in the Janata party tally of 298 Lok Sabha members.

The primacy of place in Rajiv Gandhi's time has been given to implementation. Towards this end he focussed on the dissemination of information. And in the development process he tried to introduce, as his MP supporters point out, new norms and ethos of management. "He was not looking to the country's history alone, but to its future, to that of the cosmos as such", explained one MP.*

Rajiv Gandhi was well aware of the new trends, the trends and forces of the 21st century whereby environment and ecology had become important concerns (a consequence of the too rapid industrialisation and the exploitation of nature). He was conscious that affluence too created its own problems (drug addiction among the youth, for instance) and that the world was not going to develop in departments. Parts of the world would not be entirely independent of each other, and some countries were in danger not because of the lack of weapons, but because of them, and hence his promotion of disarmament.

Thus, in a society which was once battling with the problems thrown up while installing democratic institutions, the socialistic pattern of society....to the one involved in space, computers, genetics.....the nature of the MP that is thrown up, or emerges, is bound to be different.[45]

IV

In brief, the Congress culture evolved with the induction of new MPs. Those elected to the fourth and subsequent Lok Sabhas

* Shivraj Patil.

45. Byres, T.J., *The New Technology, Class Formation & Class Action in the Indian Countryside* (The Journal of Peasant Studies, Vol. 8, Number 4, July '81, Pg. 405-54): Rich peasants are well on their way to becoming masters of the Indian countryside in the 'ryotwari' and 'mahalwari' regions (as contrasted with 'zamindari' and 'jagirdari' areas) in particular, and since these were the locations of the largest concentration of marketed surpluses, rich peasants had growing influence in the polity. They showed themselves to be eminently capable of exercising political power, not only in the village, but also at the level of district, state and centre. D.L. Sheth, in his article *Social basis of the political crisis* (Seminar, March 1980), indentifies the following new forces i.e. "support bases": (i) the peasant proprietors (not the feudal landlords) in the rural areas and the (ii) growing tertiary sectors in the urban areas (iii) agricultural labourers (iv) ethnic minorities (v) scheduled castes and scheduled tribes who were brought within the political fold partly through the governmental policy process and partly through the political mobilisation of these groups in the party structure.

differed in so far as they had not participated in the freedom movement, or were not steeped in the ethos of the party. The nature of the MPs has continued to change till the ninth Lok Sabha, which is not that different to the nature of those elected to the tenth Parliament, though the MPs of the latest three are unrecognisable when compared to those of the first three. Among the changes noted by MPs are that election expenses have sky-rocketed, hence Congress candidates who are well-heeled, or have access to funds, contest them. Whereas previously MPs maintained a simple lifestyle, now some are not above flaunting their wealth. Earlier the MPs were men of integrity, committed to the party's ideology, now commitment to self-promotion is the norm. Whereas earlier the party's nominees were those who had worked for the people, now those get the ticket who donate large sums to its coffers no matter if they have not had any previous connection with the party. The lack of interest in policy matters of the present generation of MPs and their inability to contribute anything of value to debates in the House stands out in sharp contrast to the members of the Lok Sabha during Nehru's days. The nature of the MP, being drawn to Parliament, is bound to have changed even as society has changed. In the earlier phase, laying the foundations of democracy was the prime concern of the newly elected members, and as these concerns altered, so did the elected representatives.

5

The Reluctant MP

It has been suggested that men of action prefer to be MLAs and men with a reflective cast of mind, MPs. For at the state level, the politician has the powers to get things done since he has (a) development funds (b) direct contact with the people and (c) access to ministers and bureaucrats.

An M.P., at best has a certain access to the powers that be at the Centre, but little else. But he has the most important forum in the country to take up issues that affect the nation, and focus on public grievances. Thus if he does his home work, informs himself on the various aspects of an issue, there is no reason why he cannot have impact on policy formulation, if indirectly (See profile of G.M. Banatwala in Annexure—II).

It is possible to argue that MPs have not had an impact on policy, even indirectly (direct impact on policy is possible when they become ministers) since suitable candidates have not been fielded by political parties:[46] those who get nominated are (i) strong regional/local leaders who pose a threat to other leader(s) of the state and hence are "kicked upstairs", so to speak, for example, Babasahib Vikhe Patil and also Vasant Sathe (See their profile in Annexure—II); (ii) MLAs who have served three terms or more i.e. the professional politicians and need to stay in politics such as Uttam Rathod; (iii) politicos who have no base of their own but because of loyalty to party bosses deserve a favour such as Damodar Barku Shingda; (iv) those who can win the election because of their work for the people (See profile of V.S. Mahadik in Annexure—II).

---

46. Naik, J.A., *From Total Revolution to Total Failure*, (National Publishing House, 1979): During the long 30 years of the Congress rule, Parliament was filled largely by unaccommodated men in district politics. Those who were not wanted in district politics were sent to Delhi and given Lok Sabha tickets. Their electability was the only criterion. This inevitably filled Parliament with men who never had any interest in national affairs and as a result the Indian Parliament did not develop as a forum for building capable national leaders. Such leaders sprang up largely from provincial legislatures in course of time and the control of national politics by such provincial leaders became inevitable.

The primary interest of such men has not been national policy, or the desire to influence it.

Even so, some unusual characters do slip through who have the capacity to function as an MP. They are the ones who prefer Parliament to the state legislature.

Y.S. Mahajan, who has been a Congress MP (Jalgaon District) for five terms since 1970 (he lost only the 1977-80 contest because of the anti-Emergency wave), observes that Parliament gives great scope for his "temperament and habits". He adds "here you can study and contribute as Laski said your `instructed judgement' to the solution of the socio-economic and political problems".[47] Consequently he maintains he has had an impact on policy formulation (See chapter, Impact On Policy).

Uttam Rathod (Congress), who in 1989 was serving his third term in Parliament (Hingoli constituency), is a professional politician and his reason for preferring it to the Vidhan Sabha differs from that of Y.S. Mahajan. At his age (62 years) he does not have the energy to take up the tasks of an MLA who is expected to do a lot of field work, or the time required, for an MLA has to meet any number of people and at all hours of the day. He admits that an MLA is more powerful than an MP though he points out several subjects on which he has influenced policy as an MP (See chapter Impact On Policy)[48]

Not unlike Uttam Rathod, Haribhau Mahale (Congress), a professional politician (or to put it another way, a man who has had a long innings in politics, joining Congress at the age of 16 and rising up the panchayat, zilla parishad, MLA ranks), is not unhappy being an MP as he sees the post as the top rung of the political ladder. But he was happiest as an MLA "because you can do a lot for the *chota mota log* (the small man) "with whom he is in constant touch. The MLA, Mahale observes, is much more powerful than

---

47. Y.S. Mahajan was a student of the LSE when Harold Laski was at the peak of his influence.
48. An MLA has more power maintains Rathod because (a) he is a chairman of the co-ordination committee of all the departments of the tahsil; he controls the administration and can get any work done if he, is active (b) gets Rs.20 lakhs for developing his tahsil; an MP gets no money, nor (c) a vehicle for 8-15 days to tour his constituency; not the MP. Uttam Rathod has been an MLA for four terms, an MLC for one term as well as a minister of Maharashtra State (See his profile in Annexure—II)

the MP, more effective "but he has to deal with party workers, keep them in order, keep them happy". An MP does not have to bother about all that, and at this stage in his career, Mahale rather not face the headaches of an MLA.

II

A handful of the politicians (as above) prefer being an MP. The majority would like to work in the state:

— V.S. Mahadik (SS) had no interest in going to Delhi. He bowed to party dictates.

— Dr. K.P. Bopche (BJP) was not keen on an MP's post. He contested it since his party commanded him to do so.[49] ("My constituents bring me a lot of work and I can do it well only if I was an MLA").

49. (a) The rightist parties can tell their members what to do and they behave as good soldiers by following orders. This cannot be said of Congressmen.

(b) Deshmukh, Nana, *RSS: Victim of Slander* (Vision Books, 1979): There has been discipline in both (the Jana Sangh and RSS) the organisations, generally speaking. The credit for that goes to the commitment to principles which motivates both of them, because it is this commitment which helps to maintain discipline and zeal among the workers. But in an organisation where there is a preponderance of leaders, the workers are conspicuous by their absence and the former are in the habit of maintaining themselves in that position by inciting the baser instincts of their followers. That has, generally, been the method popular among the political activists in other parties. Their belief being that all things can be done only through state power, they concentrate all their energies and their workers on the elections. In the leader-oriented political parties, discipline and harmony goes by the board.

(c) The swayamsewaks of the R.S.S. in Jana Sangh like me and the others have been taking part in the programmes of the RSS from time to time. During informal discussions we have, of course, mentioned the political activities that we are engaged in. The only common ground between the RSS and the Jana Sangh has been that both the organisations had bands of disciplined workers who were their mainstay. A causal observer, may, therefore, be misled into believing that the two organisations had a common cadre. *The RSS is a class organisation, whereas the Jana Sangh is a mass organisation.* How could they have a common cadre? The cadres have been separate. *The Jana Sangh has drawn its cadre from the common people* (Emphasis added)—*Ibid*

(d) Goyal, D.R, *Rashtriya Swayamsewale Sangh* (Radha Krishna Prakashan, 1979): Even today if the class character and composition of the RSS membership is analysed it will be found to be overwhelmingly middle class drawn from sections who ordinarily harbour fear about other classes and communities and seek security in group life. It is another matter that when

— Babasahib Vikhe Patil (Congress) would have preferred to be an MLA (did not became one like Mahadik and Bopche above) and had the potential of being a major regional/state leader but others opposed him, wanting him out of state politics and hence he became an MP straight after having contested (and won) only zilla parishad elections.[50]

— As in the case of men of action, Baban Rao Dhakne (Janata Dal) would rather be an MLA for he sees his voters as "people of my state, for whom I can work directly and produce direct results." And compared to those mentioned above, he has been in a position to have more of an impact as he has been a minister (albeit for brief periods).[51] Dhakne is not among those who feels he can do much in Parliament for his constituents, in particular the agriculture community whose welfare is his primary concern. As he notes "I can at best draw the attention of the government towards the lot of farmers as and when opportunity arises." (See his profile in Annexure-II)

— P.P. Phundkar (BJP) has no doubt that as an MLA he was much more powerful, even though he was not a member of the ruling party. He could get any job done; in case there was delay, it could be expedited by taking out a

---

occasion arises very few of them are found among the fighting battalion; whether it is communal confrontation, or political conflict, the RSS men concentrate on inciting others to violence and keep themselves safe in the background.

50. Vikhe Patil says "because of my popularity and my father's background (founder of the first sugar co-operative in Maharashtra) the local bosses feared I would become a powerful state leader and unanimously forced me to go to Parliament. I was known as a good organiser, a man of principle and honest and the local leaders considered me a challenge and a headache".

51. Dhakne mentions the suggestions he gave to his ministry (and which were accepted) related to giving priority to water scarcity areas. And where water was available and two crops were being grown, the supply should be reduced. In particular this should apply to sugar growing areas which receive water for 12 months in the year; they should get it for eight months and the water saved for four months can be directed to scarcity areas. Another policy issue Dhakne refers to influencing as MLA was to provide relief to uneducated unemployed. The government decided to give them a monthly grant of Rs.150 till such time as they secured a job.

morcha, and he always had 300-400 farmers ready for a procession, if one was needed. He accepted the MP's ticket as a loyal party worker would, but he finds the constituency too big to handle in the manner he functioned earlier. In theory, he says, an MP can influence policy by participating in debates or through parliamentary committees, but he asks, who listens.[52]

— Vidyadhar Gokhale, Shiv Sena MP representing a Bombay constituency, says he would have preferred being an MLA because of (a) age limitations; at the age of 68 he would not like to stay away from home; the physicial climate of Delhi does not suit him and (b) Hindi is not his language and parliamentary business is conducted essentially either in Hindi or English, whereas he is a good Marathi orator and would have been able to contribute much more to discussions/debates in the Maharashtra assembly.

III

Apart from lack of interest in national issues or the desire to influence them, there are other reasons why the candidate a party has fielded may not qualify:

— Unfamiliarity, or lack of adequate fluency in English or Hindi, the two main languages in which debates take place in Parliament.

— Inadequate experience of politics and political life.

Damodar Barku Shingda, Congress MP representing the constituency of Dahanu (Thane district), is handicapped on both these counts. Prior to his becoming an MP he had held no political party post except that of a village panchayat sarpanch (1978).[53] In

52. There is the odd exception though. The MPs were able to get the loans of farmers cancelled. But this was possible because all of them, across the party divide, were one on this issue. In fact, the political parties can be said to have joined hands on the question of overdues of agriculturists.

53. He was given a party ticket because local political bosses liked him and his subsequent support of Sanjay Gandhi whose backing he obtained enabled him to continue securing the MP ticket from the area despite his lacklustre performance, rather non-performance in Parliament. For the 1980 ticket, Antulay backed him; for the 1984, Vasantdada did while Kesari and

1980 he was suddenly flung into Parliament at the age of 25, to his surprise, perhaps bewilderment, a condition that persists to this day, for why else during his third term in office, should he find it difficult to list his contribution to Parliament. When prodded, rather prompted, he mentions schemes that relate essentially to an MLA's functions, and appears unfamiliar with even the anti-poverty programmes of the government, looking perplexed when IRDP or ITDP are mentioned.[54]

IV

In brief, because of the compulsions of political parties, suitable candidates do not get selected, i.e. those who by experience, training, temperament can contribute to issues concerning the nation. Politicians who have nowhere else to go or those who are not wanted in the state, and those whose primary interest is state politics, cannot be expected to be of much use in Parliament. Yet such men form the bulk of the MPs. There are even some who despite having served a couple of terms in the Lok Sabha are still not clear about their role—they are vague about what they can contribute and how they can go about it. How can such men be effective parliamentarians at any level. About their duties as law makers, we have already discussed in an earlier chapter. As men who can secure benefits for their voters, the ministries in Delhi are

---

Moopanar came as observers from the High Command. Shingda appears to be ambiguous about when he made the acquaintance of Sanjay Gandhi. At one point he says he began working actively since Sanjay Gandhi's days when the Youth Congress of Wada was set up in 1978 and he was appointed its vice president. Then he observes that he came close to Sanjay after he became an MP (in 1980) and was made the MPCC Youth Congress vice president with his support. But his loyalty to him cannot be questioned. Shingda implemented the 20 point programme with vigour and was one of the 80 Congress MPs in Parliament who formed Sanjay's main support base. And in 1977 when the Janata party came to power, many Congress party workers deserted in droves; Shingda went from village to village doing *prachar* on behalf of Congress with the help of the remaining *chota mota* Congress workers and enabled 29 of the 63 people to win seats on the Thane Z.P.

54. Shingda makes the valid observation that the tribals—a tribal himself, the majority in his constituency are tribals—have to be often reminded to apply for the schemes meant for them, else the funds/grants made available for these have to be returned to the government. Anyone, or any organisation, that is working among tribals is often confronted with this problem.

hardly likely to be impressed by them and hence will be reluctant, or lackadaisical, to give in to their demands for their constituencies. As for influencing national policy through debates, let us turn to the next chapter.

6

Quality Of Debate

Some MPs maintain that the general level of debate has declined because the parliamentary system has become ineffective.[55] During the first three Parliaments, the MPs propounded ideas that led to the formulation of laws and laid the foundation of the "socialist pattern of society". Since then most laws have been enacted (All that becomes necessary from time to time is their amendment). Hence the legislative function of Parliament is over.

What other function is left? What role can the MPs play? They should, theoretically speaking, be able to influence policy by participating in debates on the floor of the House. This was possible perhaps during the Nehru era. With increasing specialisation, policy is formulated by the concerned ministry (bureaucracy), the minister and the Cabinet, the first being the major contributor.

When an issue affecting policy is debated in the House few, if any, MPs have the requisite expertise to make significant suggestions to have an impact on it. (Nevertheless there are some who feel they are influencing issues through debates.)[56]

---

55. Which is why MPs like Vasant Sathe, and others like R. Venkataraman and Bahuguna before him, campaigned for the Presidential system.
56. A brochure on J.K. Jain, setting out what he achieved during the six years he was an MP from Madhya Pradesh, gives an indication of the range of topics an MP may take up on the floor of the house: "Shri Jain has voiced many public issues and grievances in the Rajya Sabha through various avenues of parliamentary practice and business viz. Questions (Oral and written), Call Attention Notices, Short Notice Questions, Special Mentions of matters of urgent public importance, resolutions and motions on a variety of topics and subjects and by actively participating in debates on the working affairs of various Ministries and Departments as also in the Railway Budget and the General Budget of the Union Government. Numerically speaking, Shri Jain has, in course of these six years of his Parliamentary career, put up 654 questions, given notices of 67 Calling Attention, 125 Special Mentions and short notice questions and nine resolutions and motions out of which a majority of these were admitted and granted. He took part in parliamentary debates on a variety of topics like Export and Import Bank, Working Journalists and Newspaper Employees Bill, Paper crisis, sick mills, proposal of holding Parliament Session in the South, Pay and Allowances to MPs, Affairs of Public Sector Undertakings, Assam, Punjab, National Security, improvement in Railways, industrial growth, Bills relating to Finance

In any case they have to vote in accordance with the party whip, on party lines. Men of conscience who differ with the policy as presented and consequently tender their resignation, have not been seen or heard of in recent parliamentary history. Or those who can present an alternative formulation to the existing one and win some adherents.

Parliamentary procedures are against debates of any importance. What can an MP contribute in the seven minutes that is allowed him.[57] Many are content with ritual speeches; in fact are most capable of anything else?

The level of education of MPs has steadily been increasing; many more MPs are better qualified than those in previous Parliaments. Surely this should improve the quality of debate.

It should. But what of the quality of education being imparted? Few can deny that it has been steadily, some say rapidly, deteriorating. The so-called centres of higher learning, many of them, are mere centres with no learning let alone of the "higher" variety. The education imparted by them is at best shoddy. In the circumstances, higher qualifications hardly mean anything. The debates in the House do not indicate how these have been of any use.

Corporations, Declaration of assets, Cane Development, Transport permit system, Bhopal Gas Tragedy, 20 point programme, Expansion of hospital and medical facilities in Delhi and their modernisation, Assam-Nagaland Border problems etc. etc. With a record number of Special Mentions and Call Attention Motions to his credit, Shri Jain raised issues like irregularities in Imports, inaccuracy in the map of the World Hockey Cup, Obscenity in Cabaret shows, self-styled sexologists and Sex specialists, Hooliganism in Holi, Ranjy Trophy, Tented schools in Delhi, shortage of coins, Accommodation in college, Expansion of Vocational Studies, Security in Air Traffic, Fate of Indians in Sri Lanka, Problem of Milk supply, Violence Vulgarity etc. in films, and *a baffling range of other topics* (emphasis added)."

57. A Member desiring to notify the Speaker of his intention to take part in a debate or discussion in the House may have his name communicated to the Speaker through the Parliamentary Party or Group to which he belongs. Actually, in all important debates, each Party or Group forwards a list to the Speaker containing the names of the Members who would be their spokesmen in such debates. The Speaker gives due consideration to such lists while calling upon Members to speak but he is not bound by the list or the order in which names have been given. A Member wanting to speak may also write directly to the Speaker or the Secretary-General without having to go through the machinery of Parliamentary Party or Group, or he may try to catch the Speaker's eye by rising in his place when he wishes to take part in a debate.

Lack of opportunity to study the subject that is going to be taken up by the House also explains the decline in standards of debate. This is so because of the overwhelming pressure on the MP (itself a consequence of the rising expectations of the voter) which leaves him little time to devote to issues that interest him.[58]

Thus the MP is handicapped because of

— the allotted seven minutes
— the lack of time to study an issue
— the need to focus on his constituency whenever opportunity permits

Unable to make much of an impact because of these limitations, a consequence of the fault of the system as it has evolved, the focus, the concentration of the elected representatives has become the Zero Hour, which during the days of Speakers P.G. Mavalankar and Hukum Singh was a non-hour.

Zero Hour is known for the

— exhibition of lung power; MPs begin shouting the moment it is announced
— spreading of sensational stories with the hope of catching the eye of the pressmen and getting these reported

The zero hour behaviour of the MPs would not have been tolerated by Mavalankar or Hukum Singh. Rowdy MPs would be disciplined immediately. Now MPs think nothing of moving into the well of the house (as is the case with MLAs and Vidhan Sabhas).

But the new ethos is a result of the evolving mores of society which are reflected in Parliament (as in other institutions). Since the MP cannot influence policy, or rather his capacity to do so has declined, he tries to make a mark by speaking out, being controversial so that the media picks up his views. Once this is achieved the MP

58. Vidyadhar Gokhale, Y.S. Mahajan and a few others with similar temperaments and a "studious bent of mind", make this point. Sharad Dighe with a sense of helplessness exclaims "We get no time to study" and goes on to observe that the ideal thing would be if an MP is not expected to keep much contact with his constituents, but represent views. But first "we should get a chance to study them; physically this is at present impossible. When you get 50 letters a day, you don't get time to reply to them, let alone study them". And then, he says people waste a lot of our time (refrains of Gokhale) and expect us to tackle the gutter problem, the shortage of water......

feels his constituents at least will be aware that their man in Parliament is doing something.[59]

So who is a good parliamentarian in a Parliament where, as an MP puts it, erudition, learning, intelligence are at a discount, but lung power and the capacity for sensationalism are being given primacy.[60]

That in short is the new MP. Our man in Parliament: he has strong lungs; he is all set to make newspaper headlines.

One other point may be made. Since he has little or no time to study an issue, or no inclination to do so, he can take up any number of them without going into the pros and cons. He feels no hesitation in doing so, dealing with subjects in Parliament as diverse as the price of wheat and the cost of nuclear energy. (See footnote 56 on J.K. Jain's contributions)

II

The bulk of an MP's contribution in Parliament may well consist of the questions he raises and the clarifications he seeks. Speeches, on behalf of an issue, could well comprise a minor part of his contribution (See Annexure—IV).

Here the contributions of three MPs are reproduced:

— Y.S. Mahajan's speeches on the KVIC bill, a part of the budget (1989-90) speech and that on the judiciary.
— Uttam Rathod's speech on the forest conservation act, upliftment of tribals, "one of my better speeches" says Rathod, and Hindu-Muslim unity.
— Sharad Dighe's questions and clarifications (which indicate the wide range of issues that an MP may raise) and two speeches, one on the report by the Thakkar Commission and the other on that of the Sarkaria Commission.

The three above are not representative of the average MP. They are among the more experienced and thoughtful ones. Yet their speeches/contributions could hardly be said to have affected policy. True, they may well have served some purpose or the other.

---

59. Sharad Dighe notes, an MLA may not speak on the floor of the House yet do a lot for his constituents. However, an MP can make a mark only by speaking, participating in debates, and how is his contribution to be recognised if the newspapers do not reflect it.

60. Vasant Sathe made this observation to me in a three hour interview at his house on 2, Krishna Menon Marg, New Delhi 110 011 on April 13, 1990.

But here we are concerned with an MP's impact on policy.

Y.S. Mahajan's speech on the budget is a ritual one, welcoming it like a loyal party man and attacking those who have opposed it. The khadi and village speech too falls into the ritual category. On the judiciary he highlights the ills afflicting it; these have been with us for as long as one can remember and Mahajan's speech could not have made an iota of difference.

Of the three speeches by Rathod, one is on the forest conservation act, which many MPs oppose since it prevents works on any project that passes through an area designated as a forest: it is not known whether Rathod's diatribe persuaded the minister concerned (Maneka Gandhi) to exempt his constituency from the purview of the act. The second speech deals with tribal uplift; being a tribal himself, he spoke knowledgeably about the neglect of the adivasis. But to what end? His ideas on Hindu-Muslim unity as reflected in the third speech, are laudable but to all intents and purpose they were so much hot air.

The Sharad Dighe selections (of speeches/questions), as noted, show the number of issues an MP may take interest in. But it is difficult to say what purpose this serves. The answers to his queries often conceal as much as they reveal; sometimes they are banal.

Y.S. Mahajan welcoming the Khadi and Village Industries Bill:

This is a small Bill but it has a great significance considering our historical development. We all have sentimental attachment to khadi and village industries. It speaks well for the Bill that our first speaker on this side, Prof. Ranga comes from Andhra Pradesh. It was at the Vijaywada Congress session that it was decided to launch a khadi production programme. Secondly, the Minister who is piloting this Bill is also from Andhra Pradesh. Sir, the production of khadi has increased considerably since those days. At that time they invested only Rs. 3 lakhs in the production of khadi and now the banks are providing Rs.80 crores to the different institutions producing khadi and even according to the committee that amount is not adequate.

Sir, this Bill is important not only from this point of view but also because it makes the khadi commission an important instrument for the rural industrialisation of this country. Sir, Gandhiji advocated village industries; which according to our new terminology, are included in the mini sector. Now, the scope of the work of the commission is going to be widened. It would cover not only village industries as conceived by Gandhiji but all industries in rural areas and whether they use power or not and whether they employ more than 10 people or not they will come under the Khadi and Village Industries Commission. Since the new industries that are coming up are going to be an important instrument in industrialising the country, the work of the Commission will be transformed and it will be completely different from what it was before. It is going to be the major instrument of industrialising the country. I think rural industrialisation is the only solution to the poverty in our country. After all, there are limitations to the number of people who can be engaged in agriculture; land is limited, but so far as industry is concerned, Sir, there is no limit to the growth of industries. That is the lesson that we can draw from the experience of the industrialised countries.

Then, Sir, some Members have said that the limit of Rs.10,000 per head on capital expenditure, that is, on land, labour and machinery is too small but the Act makes provision for increasing it. If experience shows that if this limit should be increased, it can be done later on. The provision is not rigid.

Then, Sir, the Act makes important changes. It extends the scope of the work of the Commission in another way and says that it should undertake to provide raw materials, set up raw materials bank and it should undertake science and technological development. Sir, in this matter the commission has done fairly good work in the last few years. It has set up thousands of new model charkhas, the Amber Charkha. The reason why people are not attracted to these village industries is that their productivity is low and they are forced to maintain a low standard of living. The work is not very productive and, therefore, the imposition of this duty under the Bill, namely, that it should make for technological development, would increase the productivity of workers and enable us to raise their wages. Sir, members have complained that they do not get enough wages, that the wages are even less than the minimum wages prescribed by the state governments in their respective areas. Sir, wages could be increased if productivity is increased. It is very important that along with productivity there should be an increase in the quality of the work that is done in the village industries. Widening the definition of village industry, increasing productivity and the scope of the work of the commission, and improving the quality of work are the most important provisions of attaining the objectives of the Seventh Five Year Plan. In the Seventh Five Year Plan period, the value of the output of this sector is targeted to be increased from Rs.929 crores to about Rs.2000 crores. Employment coverage is likely to increase from 40 to 50 lakhs. Well, an increase of 10 lakhs is not much. Sir, it cannot solve the problem of poverty in this country unless we are in a position to fully tackle the root-cause of the problem, i.e. the rapidly increasing population. Anyway, I will not go into that aspect now.

Gandhiji had regarded khadi and village industries as a major instrument for liberating this country and making it economically self-reliant. But this object cannot be achieved unless we also improve upon the quality of work, increase productivity, increase the wages of the workers and attract more and more people towards these industries.

I want to mention another factor which is very important and necessary. There must be linkages between khadi and village industries and other programmes in the Seventh Five Year Plan which aim at increasing employment and productivity of the people. I am referring to programmes such as the Integrated Rural Development Programme, Rural Landless Employment Guarantee Programmes and so on. If these programmes are linked to the work being done by the Khadi and Village Industries Commission, it will be much more effective. I need not say anything further on this aspect.

I would like to make just one more remark, which is about the members of the KVIC. It is stated in the Bill that six members will be taken from six areas of the country. I feel that if there are only six areas, each region will be very big. These should at least be increased from 6 to 10 or 12 so that the areas would be manageable. If you have just six areas, the whole of Maharashtra and Gujarat will be one area and if you take just one person from that area, how can you expect the work to be really effective? I believe the number of members of the commission is too small for the work contemplated. So please increase it to 10 or 12. With these remarks, I support the Bill and hope that rural industries and the work of the KVIC will prosper.

Budget 1989-90

Shri Y.S. Mahajan (Jalgaon): Mr. Deputy Speaker, Sir, I rise to congratulate The Hon. Minister of Finance for the budget of 1989-90. The Hon. Member Shri Madhav Reddi made certain astounding statements. Some of the statements made by him are: that the hon. Minister of Finance is not concerned with economic development, that there is virtually stagnation of economic growth in this country; the statistics about economic growth and development and other figures are dressed-up figures. He is also pessimistic about the rise in prices of commodities. He feels certain that prices will again show a steep rise. Finally, he wound up his speech by saying that India is the sick man of Asia. His marathon speech reminded me of the great politician of this House Shri V.K. Krishna Menon, who was once reported to have made a speech for 16 hours in the United Nations. I hope the hon. Minister will answer most of his points. During my speech I will try to answer some of the general points mentioned by him.

Sir, the Budget has been framed keeping in view the long-term objectives of our economic policy viz. growth, modernisation, self-reliance and social justice. As a result of the substantial progress made in these fields in the recent years, the economy has reached the take-off stage. The reason is due to our sustained efforts. Even during the year 1987-88 when the country had to face the most serious famine of the century, even during that year, foodgrains production was 138 million tonnes, only marginally lower than in the previous years. Our national income registered a growth rate of 3.7 percent. That shows the great resilience of the economic system. This year, as a result of good monsoons, as the hon. Member has pointed out, and success of developmental efforts such as Special Foodgrains Production Programme in areas where the development could be quickly exploited, the production is expected to go to 166 million tonnes, only slightly less than 170 million tonnes, the production expected during the last year of the Seventh Five Year Plan.

Sir, agriculture is the backbone of our economy. Already, the hon. Finance Minister has stated in his Budget speech, the mainstay of our population for a number of years till now, the average growth of agricultural production could not go beyond 2.5 percent per year. As a result of the Green Revolution, due to the application of high yielding varieties of seeds, expansion in irrigation facilities, use of chemical fertilizers and pesticides etc. agriculture promises to register now a higher rate of growth in the immediate future. It not only contributes to the resilience of our economy but also gives hope of rise in the standards of living of millions of people of our country. Agriculture has always had the highest priority in our planned development. Maximum possible resources have been allocated. This year more than about Rs.5000 crores have been set apart for the development of agriculture and spread the Green Revolution to areas to which it had not spread so far, by the usual method of irrigation, the high-yielding varieties of seeds, pesticides and fertilizers. This strategy has yielded results over the last ten years and has built up the strength of our economy which nobody can deny.

There is, however, one aspect of agricultural development which, I think, has not received the attention it deserves, namely, dry land farming, that is, farming on rainfed areas. Its significance can be assessed from the fact that 70 percent of agriculture is under dry land farming and 42 percent of the total food production comes from this area. Almost the entire production of coarse grains, pulses and most of the cotton and oil seeds are produced in the rain-fed areas. I think, this aspect of agricultural planning needs greater attention. Many of the agricultural development schemes now in operation have a bearing on this subject. I think, the hon. Finance Minister could have mentioned it during the course of his speech. He has sharply increased the allocation for agriculture and fertilizer subsidy to the level of Rs.5,173 crores. I believe, this will enable us to push the agricultural revolution to new areas, to diversify it and make for better post-harvest technology and processing of agricultural goods.

Industry is the second important leg of our economy. The sustained growth of industrial sector, improved performance of infrastructure have been very encouraging factors of the economy during the last years. The rate of growth has been about eight per cent continuously for the first four years of the Seventh Five Year Plan. This has been reflected in the generally good performance of the corporate sector and buoyant conditions in the capital market also. Particularly helpful in maintaining this high rate of growth were the steady increase in electricity generation and productivity in the power sector, improvement in the performance of the basic materials industries and the load carrying capacity of the railways.

In this upward improvement, the public sector has its share. It has not lagged behind. During the first six months of this year, the result of the 179 operating undertakings have shown a profit of Rs.694 crores as against Rs.597 crores during the corresponding period of last year. This does not, however, fulfil our expectations as regards generation of resources. The management of the public sector units must be given free hand and held responsible for the results achieved. Mr. L.K. Jha once said: "they should not be held responsible for compliance with governmental procedures, a multiplicity of guidelines and adhoc instructions written or verbal from the Government department under which the enterprise is placed." Our industrial policy resolution of 1956 made it quite clear that speedy decision and willingness to assume responsibility are essential if these enterprises are to succeed. For this, wherever possible, there should be decentralisation of authority and their management should be along business lines....

The Judiciary 1989

Shri Y.S. Mahajan (Jalgaon): Mr. Speaker, Sir, I rise to support the High Court and Supreme Court Judges (Conditions of Service) Amendment Bill. In financial terms, the Bill is not important. It's object is to rationalise some fringe benefits such as to raise the ceiling of carry forward leave, to raise the leave allowance of Judges and to fix the minimum family pension at Rs.375/- per month to the families of High Court Judges who have not held a pensionable post prior to their appointment as such and who retire within less than seven years of service.

The Judiciary is the third pillar of the realm and the importance of its function cannot be exaggerated. Thousands of learned persons with a judicious bent of mind have contributed to the building up of the system of legal dispensation in the country and many of our Judges have distinguished themselves as jurists in the world. The system has grown up gradually over the last 150 years. But never was it in such a dangerous position as it is today. It is likely to collapse soon unless steps are taken immediately to strengthen and revitalise it. The dispensation of justice has become almost impossible because delay is endemic in our system. Justice delayed is justice denied is a truism which is neglected by us completely. The number of cases pending in the High Courts is more than 1.6 million apart from the 10 million cases pending in the lower Courts. This was the situation as on 31st March, 1989. In the

Supreme Court and High Courts, cases remained pending for 15 to 20 years. This means that if the case is filed in one generation, the verdict is given in the next generation. The reason for this serious situation is the inadequacy in the number of Judges. The previous Law Commission had recommended an increase in the number of Judges in the Supreme Court and High Courts. But steps have not yet been taken to fill the vacancies. Therefore, steps should be taken immediately to increase the strength of Judges. There is no dearth of talented and able advocates in our country. If necessary, their salary and emoluments should be raised sufficiently to attract able and efficient people from the profession.

The Government should also deal with inefficiency at the lower levels which is mainly due to the fact that law degrees like other degrees can be obtained easily by dubious means. The minister should consider or explore the possibility of holding a Central examination for those who are aspirants for jobs in the judicial services. Legal procedures should also be streamlined to provide justice expeditiously. I do not wish to underestimate the significance of procedure. Every student of law or practitioner will admit the truth of Henry Maind's statement that justice is secreted in the interstices of procedure. Sir, in our country, there is no denying the fact that procedural law is abused to defeat the ends of justice, through interminable arguments, frequent adjournments, and excessive liberal attitude towards grant of leave to appeal. Government is the trustee of the national interest and Government is the biggest litigant in the High Courts and the Supreme Court. Therefore, apart from the interest of the people, the Government itself is interested in seeing that justice is dispensed expeditiously.

In this matter, I would like to recommend strengthening of the Lok Adalat system. I myself attended many Lok Adalats in my district. Many contentious cases can be decided immediately, when both the parties are present and those cases are examined by the people who are not judges, who are not professional lawyers.

Then I would like to bring to your notice the question of appointing women as judges. We have been giving a certain percentage of reservations for women in the lower levels, in the Taluka panchayat, district panchayat. But the number of women judges in the High Courts and the Supreme Court is very low. I hope, the hon. Minister will consider the possibility of raising the number of women judges in all the courts.

And then, there is one more thing, it is small yet very important. When judges are transferred at the district level, they go about looking for houses. Considering the housing situation, it is very difficult to get proper quarters. Therefore, I recommend that housing for judges should be improved so that transfer does not cause any inconvenience or have any adverse effects on their efficiency.

With these few recommendations and suggestions, I recommend the acceptance of the Bill.

The comments on the Forest Conservation Act by Uttam Rathod

Shri Uttam Rathod (Hingoli): I welcome this Bill introduced by Shri Haribhau Shankar Mahale, a man representing a tribal constituency. All the three Gandhis who have ruled this country, knowingly or unknowingly, have played havoc with the tribals and their lives. Madam Gandhi introduced the 1980 Amendment to the Forest Act. Unfortunately I also supported it. Shri Rajiv Gandhi had tightened it and I am sure hon. Madam Maneka Gandhi is going to strangle our lives and the lives of tribals because of her love for environment and eco balance. I represent a constituency which is a tribal constituency where even the laying of telephone lines was not allowed, and where the branches were not allowed to be cut. I am telling you from my experience. (Sir, we are neighbours.) I took up this matter with the Prime Minister but no use. "We are looking into it," was the answer I got. When Shri Ansari was there 145 cases were referred to him by the Maharashtra Government. All these things were just kept in abeyance. Everytime there used to be a query, so that it got delayed. I have myself been writing to Madam about a canal which is close to a sugar factory, if allowed will irrigate the lands. I have been receiving her acknowledgements. I would just request her to come and see the area which require water. It is really dying for water. Unless you give us water, we cannot grow more food. You will be requiring food more and more every day. I can understand the importance of environment. Mr. Mehbool Haq, the Planning Minister of Pakistan says in `Poverty Curtain' that at some point of time, the developing countries will have to draw a line when they decide what should be the ratio of forest and cultivable land. You cannot have international ratio as far as forest and other land is concerned.

The developing countries have got their own problems. Recently we had come across such an incident. When Mr. Seshan was incharge of Environment Department, he turned down a request by the Defence Ministry. They wanted to have an arms testing range. But when he took over Defence, the same person had to request the Environment Ministry to allow him to have this testing range. I do not know why it be so. I am just coming to my point.

Mr. Deputy-Speaker: For your information, Ministers change but Ministries do not change.

Shri Uttam Rathod: Sir, why I support this Bill is because construction of roads in my constituency has been completely stopped. Construction of dams have been completely stopped. Unless we have water for our agricultural lands, we cannot give more work to our people. You will be able to give work to the people in the rural areas if you have got intensive agriculture. That is why I say that it is better to concentrate on this. So many states have adopted different measures. For example, the old Madhya Pradesh (CP & Berar province) used to have forest villages. There some land was demarcated for agriculture. People who used to cultivate these lands were expected to look after the interests of the Forest Department. Since they were connected with that, they always took precautions. Whenever they came across somebody illicitly trying to fell trees, they used to stop them. Why don't we adopt that method? In Orissa, you must have seen that on the canals poor people who do not own lands were given lands and asked to plant coconut trees. They have been asked to plant trees very close to the canal so that they can draw water and water those plants. Whenever they get fruits they can utilise them. Why don't we find out some such thing? In the State of the old Madhya Pradesh area people were given land and they were asked to plant certain number of trees. That is how they protected forest and tribals. In Old Madhya Pradesh, this Forest portfolio was always held by the Finance Minister so that he could pay more attention. Will you please look into all these things? Will you please see that some justice is done to the tribal area. You want to take these people to the 21st century. For heaven's sake don't take them without education. Otherwise, again in the 21st century you will be treating them as slaves for they will be poor, they will be uneducated. I do not want you to do that again. They will be the most unfortunate people. Do not strangle our tribal people and their development. I have already raised this issue through Matters Under Rule 377 only two days back. I am sure you will be replying soon.

Finally, I would request you to visit my constituency and see the plight of my people there. When the area actually concerned for construction of canals is only about two-and-a-half hectares, your Department is coming in the way. Why do you forget one thing? It was in Maharashtra where one Secretary used to hold charge of the Departments of Forest and Revenue.

In 1975-77, lands were distributed to the people though they were forest lands. The Forest Department people are forcibly evicting people from their land which was legally given to them. And now those people are the members of cooperative societies and they have loans against their names. Who will pay their dues? Are you prepared to take the responsibility of that? At least do that, when you are taking the land. They were rightly given by the Government. You know that. They were given by Shri Sharad Pawar. And now those people are being deprived of that. I want the hon. Minister to do something with regard to that. In case, she comes to my constituency, I can take her across and show her all these problems and see that she does not become the instrument of strangling the development of the tribals. Thank you.

Upliftment of tribals

Shri Uttam Rathod (Hingoli): Mr. Deputy Speaker, Sir, I think it was Dewan Chaman Lal who addressed the tribals as forgotten children of India. These forgotten children were remembered by my colleague, Shri Bhuria, through this Resolution and I am happy to see that many hon. Members are participating in this debate giving new ideas for the promotion of overall development of the tribals.

Benefits for the betterment of tribals and Harijans were there during the British time also but when we drafted our Constitution....

Mr. Deputy Speaker: The time allotted for this Resolution, that is, two hours is exhausted. So how much time we may extend for this Resolution.

Some hon. Members: Another two hours.

Mr. Deputy Speaker: Is it the pleasure of the House to extend the time of this Resolution by another two hours?

Some hon. Members: Yes.

Shri Uttam Rathod: The framers of the Constitution say that there were different sections of people in this country who were at different stages of development. So Articles 340, 341 and 342 for the benefit of the backward classes were introduced and accordingly the lists were prepared. Even these lists were prepared in a hurry. Therefore, it was suggested when the Governor feels that a certain caste or tribe is left out and it is socially, educationally and economically backward then the Governor would suggest the name, of course, with the consent of the State Government to the President and through a Constitutional amendment they could be included in the scheduled caste or scheduled tribes list.

Unfortunately when we see the progress that has been achieved by the Welfare Department, we find again the pathetic condition of these tribals. With the advent of so many new things, development of roads and infrastructure even the people who would not have gone to the tribal areas they are going there and there they find that the tribals are there where they were earlier. There is a greater degree of frustration among them. For this you will have to see wherever the revolutionary movements have cropped up; wherever they have gone militant you will invariably find that they have their fort in a tribal area. Take the example of our Hon'ble Minister for Industries. He will tell us. In Hyderabad State, it was again Nalgonda, Suryapet and Warrangal districts where the communists took over. Again in Karimnagar, Srikakulam, Gadchiroli, Chandrapur tribal areas the Naxalites are flourishing for the simple reason that the tribals have been badly exploited. The tribals look after the interests of these revolutionary people. Sir, I remember when I was a child, the old Hyderabad State had promulgated an ordinance known as Hyderabad Tribal Protection Act. Under the Act, the collector was supposed to be the agent, and one who had done his MA in anthropology was his deputy agent. Dr. Baron Heimandorff did not teach in classrooms. He taught his students not in the classrooms but in the tribal settlements. Students were introduced to the people and their aspirations. Simultaneously, he was taught the tribal dialect. I would like to know how many development officers working in the tribal areas know the tribal dialect. It is a pathetic scene. On the contrary, the Christian missionaries, before they are sent to any area, have to know the regional language. Our development officers do not know tribal dialects. Let us understand one thing. The tribal dialects are always short of terminology. Their vocabulary is very limited. Their grammar is limited. If the development officers want to say something, he has to use the regional word which is again new to the tribals. The regional words are difficult for the tribals to learn. But that is a reality.

In the north-eastern sector, for example, in Nagaland, Arunachal Pradesh, etc., the Christians organised to teach the tribals their dialect in the Roman script. One of the Garos told me "if we are grateful to the Christian missionaries, we are grateful to them not for Christianity, not for giving us this religion, but we are grateful to them for having given us the Roman script because this script has brought us all together." Garos, Nagas, Jaintias—all have different dialects. But all these people can write to each other in the Roman script. Dr. Heimandorff did the same thing in the Marathi-speaking areas for the tribals by accepting Devnagari script. So, the tribals could learn the Devnagari script in the tribal dialect. When Dr. Heimandroff went to the Telugu-speaking area, he took the Telugu script and the tribal dialect to teach them the primer. The equivalent of Telugu word was written along with the tribal dialect. That is how they could learn.

Sir, under the above regulation, the tribals could enjoy forests. They could bring whatever they liked from the forests for their consumption but not for sale. At that time, denudation of forests was not there. It is only a subsequent development that denudation of the forests is on the increase.

The tribals were governed by their own customs. Even their own criminal cases, civil cases, revenue cases were tried by the deputy agent and the collector. If a Gond caught the hand of a lady, it would not be molestation. But he will be tried under their own customs, as they have their different customs and different ethics.

We select the boys for service in the tribal areas without considering his aptitude for that work. We put him in the tribal area even if he does not know the tribal dialect. When you make it compulsory for IAS and IPS people to know one regional language of the area where they are being posted, how is it that you do not compel the development officers to know the tribal dialect of that area? Why not about tribals? Do not think that the tribals are in any way less intelligent. The main thing is that we are short of our political determination. We send wrong types of people. Go and see Maharashtra. In Maharashtra there is a GR. In 1948 they said that officers of doubtful character would never be posted in a tribal area and his stay would not exceed more than two years. Do you have such things? No, we do not have. That is why we see that in spite of thirty-nine years of independence, we have hardly been able to create another Jaipal Singh, who is known as Roshanara or Jahanara or whatever it is. He was a Deputy Minister here and he led our hockey team. Panditji used to say: I want Indian tribals to rise to his height. How did they rise? At that time we had Christian missionaries, who could send them abroad. We do not have people to send out now, nor can we give them something from here. We have the 5th and 6th Schedules of our Constitution. Except the North-Eastern sector, all the tribals in our country are there in Schedule 5 and what are the provisions for the development of these people? They will have a Tribal Committee at their District level or Taluka level and there would be one Tribal Advisory Committee presided over by the Chief Minister at the State level. The President, as and when he feels, shall get a report from the Governor about the development of these tribals. I would like to know on how many occasions, any Governor has made a point to send weekly, even six-monthly or an yearly report to the Home Department. Even I will ask Mr. Gomango if he has received any such report. Is there any difference in what they have said in the first report and the thirty-ninth report? Has the Parliament ever discussed it? We have not. We are busy with Bofors, we are busy with submarines and so many other things.

If there is a small thing against a minority, it becomes an international news; if there is some injustice against Harijans, it becomes an all-India news, but if there is some injustice against a tribal, it does not become even a taluka news. That is the fate of these people.

As I said earlier, there are many communities which are yet to be listed as tribals. We have been postponing that. Twice Select Committees were nominated, but unfortunately on both these occasions, the House was dissolved and it could not be taken up. Somewhere in 1976-77, the Area Restriction Act was revoked and some benefits could be extended. There are certain people who are neither living the life of scheduled castes nor scheduled tribes, and who are living the life much worse than that and they are ex-criminal tribes. We do not have any scheme to settle them. The

Minister says: I do not think there are any ex-criminal tribes. Good, Madam. How is a Rajkumari supposed to know about these people? In this unfortunate country, we have the census of tigers. Even Mr. Gorpade will tell you how many tigers are there in our country, because every year we have a census. But we do not have the census of the nomadic tribes. See the condition in this country. This is the country of Panditji and Gandhiji. So, we have to fight for it.

What is the character of those people who are working for it (tribals)? They go regularly on tour. You are aware that the tribals do not have vegetables as their diet. Very few consume pulses also.

If they have a big feast, generally they will bring chicken and eat it. Invariably when this great man comes, the man who is connected with the tribal welfare work, he has to be offered a chicken. One day, I remember, a big officer came—a senior officer—and his district level officer thought that he must take him to certain tribal villages. Somehow, this man knew the regional language and some of the words of the tribal dialect. After having seen the work of the tribals he asked them, "Well, my dear tribals, I find that you have made very good progress. Please tell me what do you want me to do. Now, I am in a position to do something for you." One intelligent tribal—of course there are intelligent people among tribals also; intelligence is not our own forte alone—got up and asked for a big clock. When asked whether they could tell time, the tribal answered that they may be given a chiming clock. When asked how it will help them, the tribal replied that they could not know when the sun rises, for all the cocks (chicken) were eaten away by the corrupt officers. That is the fate of the tribals. Do not forget that. Our officers indulge in such practices and the poor tribal people do not know whom to approach to get redressal.

Sir, I will say only one thing at the end, do something drastic for these people. Frustration is creeping among them. Naxalite or some other movement will take place and they will not keep quiet. So, do something. Secondly, Sir, do something for those castes and tribes which have not been enlisted so far, which we are avoiding every time. Whether it is Mandal Commission or anything, you should not avoid (this task).

Lastly, I shall say, Sir, why is it that the tribals welfare ministry is always given to the people who somehow cannot run it. I remember, it is said that in old Madras State when somebody like me was after Rajaji requesting him to provide him a berth in the Cabinet. Rajaji was a big man. He was a magnanimous man. He made him a Minister of Stamps. In our country generally tribal welfare ministries in different States are manned by such people.

Sir, you have been prolonging our trouble for 40 years. You must put an end to that. For that I will say a determined effort should be made by Government to bring these people on par with the other people by having a dedicated bureaucracy, a devoted band of workers and of course with the Chief Minister in charge at the State level and the Prime Minister at the national level in charge of the tribal welfare. When the Prime Minister can take such portfolios as Planning and so many other ministries, why cannot he take over this tribal welfare department? It is an important department as the tribals constitute 7.76 per cent of the total population. Tribals are displayed like mummies in a museum and are not recognised as human beings.

Hindu Muslim Unity

Shri Uttam Rathod (Hingoli): Mr. Chairman, Sir, I am really ashamed that during the last 10 years, we must have discussed this problem of communal riots not less than 20 times. Even during the last Monsoon Session, it was Prof. Saifuddin Soz who had initiated a debate on this and I happened to be third or fourth speaker. When he started speaking, I thought, he could be much more mature after the elections that we had faced this time. Instead of quoting the incidents in Bhagalpur, I suggested to him to give some concrete suggestions where we could have national integration.

Today I want all of you to read the Preamble.

> "We the people of India, having solemnly resolved to constitute India into a sovereign, socialist, secular, democratic republic and to secure to all its citizens....."

It is a sovereign, socialist, secular, democratic republic.

When we said secular, I think, the first thing we should have decided is what type of education we have to give to our people. We cannot forget that it was Hindu-Muslim disunity that brought partition of India. I was a boy. I have seen Hindu-Muslim riots. I have heard about the Calcutta riots and I felt at least after the martyrdom of Gandhiji, we may not have to face all these things. But again we saw in 1984, Indiraji was murdered and we saw that in spite of that, the Hindus and Sikhs have not been able to come closer.

It is high time that we all think about it, how we can have national integration. I was happy that the Prime Minister yesterday said that very soon he is going to call a meeting and he is going to discuss. I wish him well. As far as integration is concerned, I can say in the words of Brig. Dalvi:

> "It has been Himalayan blunder and it has been the greatest failure of our times."

We were the ruling party. We were the first people to segregate the nationalist Muslims and that is why we have to face today this plight. I feel that hereafter we should not denigrate, we should not try to push aside the nationalist Muslims who are trying to come into the national mainstream. Unless we do not, no other Muslim would feel that he should join the national mainstream.

I know the psychology of the minorities. They are afraid, hesitant and it is here that the majority community will have to assure them "Don't worry. We will safeguard your interests. We are here to safeguard your life." But if this does not happen, then there will be trouble. Shri Arif Beg Khan spoke about the role of his party. I was really very happy about the `positive secularism' of which Shri L.K. Advani speaks. But what happened in Maharashtra? They joined their forces with the Shiv Sena. What is the harm? I come from a downtrodden community. Do you expect us to go over and bow our head at somebody's feet? We are not prepared to do so. We will go and request and appeal to the Mussalman to come and join the national mainstream. There is no other way out. If we want to live together, we will have first of all to define what is communalism. I was sorry, during the last Session, there was a question which was put by some people and both of them were unfortunately absent, and at that time the Deputy Chairman allowed me to put that question as it was very important and it was "What is a communal party?". I was shocked to know that the Government has replied that even to that day they had not defined the word `communal party'. Are you prepared? I am asking this Government, the Government which is headed by Mr. Vishwanath Pratap Singh, the Government which has the first Muslim Home Minister. Will you define it? Please define it soon. If the Government does that, then also ask the educationists to teach our boys about `tolerance'. In this country we have to live by the side of other communities. So many things between you and the other man may not tally. But still we will all have to live together. Therefore, a sense of tolerance will have to be taught. Unless we do that, no secularism will survive in this country. We will have to accommodate the views of others. If I speak something against other groups, if they get offended and start fighting, it will be difficult for anybody to control it. The main thing is that the `rule of law' should prevail in this country. I find that people who create all these confusions, people who are responsible for all these things are not punished by the law. They are allowed to go scotfree. That is where we are committing mistakes. Arifji, do not praise your Government or do not denigrate our Government. We have all failed on some or the other count. It has been the total failure of Indian citizens that we have not been able to organise our education, we have not been able to organise our judiciary and we have not been able to implement the rule of law. That is why we have to face all these things.

Sir unfortunately we have also used the word 'democracy'. We say we want democracy. Democracy entails election and election entails majority—may be simple majority. When we want to win votes, naturally we try to appease the people, we try to associate ourselves and we want to take people on our side in the name of religion, caste if not on language or region or something like that. Please do not get surprised that this also invariably happens in America. I was shocked when I read one of the issues of the *Indian Post* that there also the ethnic group, the race that has played a great role. What I want to suggest is that we must have an understanding between all the political parties that we will not do these things. Unless we have some restriction on us, it is very difficult. We can all do this in the National Integration Council and we can decide about it there. But let us have some understanding between us that we shall not exploit these things. Then only we will be able to have a real secular democracy.

Mr. Chairman: Please conclude. You are a good friend of mine. Kindly help others also. Will you conclude in a minute?

Shri Uttam Rathod: That is exactly what I am doing.

Shri Somnath Chatterjee (Bolpur): With the last sentence of about 10 lines....

(*Interruptions*)

Shri Uttam Rathod: I only pray that wisdom prevails not only on the people of India but also on the Government which will try to implement the rule of law, which will try to teach our boys a sense of tolerance and thereby we will have secularism in this country.

Sharad Dighe's Contributions

In this section, some questions raised by Sharad Dighe are noted, followed by extracts from his speeches on the Thakkar Commission and the Sarkaria Commission.

Talks with British Secretary of State for Foreign Affairs

Shri Sharad Dighe: Will the Minister of External Affairs be pleased to state:

(a) the outcome of the subjects discussed with British Secretary of State for Foreign Affairs during his recent visit to India;

(b) whether the subject of taking effective steps to curb terrorist activities against India from the British soil was also discussed; and

(c) if so, the outcome thereof?

Answer

The Minister of External Affairs
(Shri P.V. Narasimha Rao)

(a) During the visit of the British Secretary of State for foreign and Commonwealth Affairs, both sides exchanged views on East-West Relations, Middle-East, South Africa, China, Afghanistan and Kampuchea. Indo-British bilateral relations were also covered.

(b) & (c) Yes, Sir. The question of taking effective measures to curb terrorist activities in the UK was also discussed.

Likely major quakes in April, 1989

Shri Sharad Dighe: Will the Prime Minister be pleased to state:

(a) whether according to some scientists major quakes are likely in April, 1989 in Italy, Armenia, Turkey, India, Tibet and China belt as reported in the *Times of India* dated the 1st April, 1989; and

(b) if so, the precautions taken by Government in this regard?

Answer

The Minister of State in the Ministry of Science and Technology and the Minister of State in the Departments of Ocean Development, Atomic Energy, Electronics and Space (Shri K.R. Narayanan).

(a) Yes, Sir. Such reports have appeared in newspapers, but prediction of earthquakes has not been found to be possible in the present state of knowledge.

(b) Does not arise.

Preparations for launch of Agni

Shri Sharad Dighe: Will the Minister of Defence be pleased to state:

(a) whether preparations are complete for the test launch of India's first long-range missile "Agni", at Chandipur, Orissa;

(b) if so, whether such preparations includes a scheme under which villages in and around Chandipur will be temporarily evacuated;

(c) if so, the details thereof?

(d) whether the villagers are not willing to be temporarily displaced and instead demand compensations for permanent displacement; and

(e) if so, the decision of Government in this regard?

Answer

The Minister of Defence (Shri K.C. Pant).

(a) Yes, Sir.

(b) & (c): Yes, Sir; a scheme has been drawn up to temporarily shift the local population for a few hours on the day of launch from the safety zone area of 3.5 km radius around the Agni launch point to camps set up outside this area. The affected people are adequately compensated. Payments are made at the rate of Rs.80- per adult and Rs.40/- per child of 12 years or below. At the camp sites, provision has also been made for drinking water, adequate health care and entertainment etc.

(d) No formal request from the local people for permanent displacement from the safety zone area has been received.

(e) Does not arise.

Technology transfer to a private firm by B.A.R.C.

Shri Sharad Dighe: Will the Prime Minister be pleased to state:

(a) whether Bhabha Atomic Research Centre (BARC) has transferred technology of producing Zirconium oxide and oxychloride from zircon sand developed by its chemical engineering division to M/s. C.S. Zircon products; and

(b) if so, the reasons for transferring this technology to a private firm?

Answer

The Minister of State in the Ministry of Science and Technology and Minister of State in the Departments of Ocean Development, Atomic Energy, Electronics and Space (Shri K.R. Narayanan):

(a) Yes, Sir, but on a non-exclusive basis.

(b) M/s. Indian Rare Earths Ltd. supplied the commercial grade Zirconium oxide and oxychloride till 1980 by which time sufficient indigenous demand developed for these products. It was then decided to transfer this technology to organisations outside the Department of Atomic Energy for their production to meet the indigenous demands for non-nuclear applications. The transfer of this technology was effected by following the existing procedure for the transfer of technologies from BARC to outside organisations on a non-exclusive basis.

Meeting between defence secretaries of India and Pakistan

Shri Sharad Dighe: Will the Minister of Defence be pleased to state:

(a) whether there is any move between India and Pakistan to consider any bilateral defence co-operation between the two countries;

(b) if so, the details thereof; and

(c) if not, the purpose of the forthcoming meeting between the two defence secretaries of Pakistan and India?

Answer

The Minister of State in the Department of Defence Production & Supplies in the Ministry of Defence (Shri Chintamani Panigrahi):

(a) & (b) No. Sir.

(c) The purpose of the forthcoming talks is to discuss the Siachen issue.

Conference on protection of Ozone layer

Shri Sharad Dighe: Will the Minister of Environment and Forests be pleased to state:

(a) whether India refused to sign the Montreal Treaty of 1987, seeking to half the use of chloroflurocarbon gases by the year 2000 as suggested at the international conference on the protection of the Ozone layer which concluded in London on 7 March 1989;

(b) if so, the reasons thereof;

(c) whether India proposes to develop substitutes for CFCS which are used in refrigerators, among other appliances; and

(d) if so, the details thereof?

Answer

Minister of Environment and Forests (Shri Z.R. Ansari):

(a) & (b) The issue is under consideration of the Government and a final decision is yet to be taken.

(c) There is no such proposal at present.

(d) Does not arise.

MOU between BEL & Samtel

Shri Sharad Dighe: Will the Minister of Defence be pleased to refer to reply given on 3 August, 1988 to Unstarred Question No.1179 regarding joint ventures of BEL with Samtel India and state:

(a) whether the examination of the MOU between BEL and Samtel India and Corning Glass Works of USA for bringing Taloja project in Maharashtra under a joint venture with these companies as partners has been completed;

(b) if so, the outcome thereof;

(c) whether the Government of Maharashtra has requested the Union Government not to privatise the Taloja project as per the demand of the employees; and

(d) if so, the reception of the Government thereon?

Answer

The Minister of State in Department of Defence Production & Supplies in the Ministry of Defence (Shri Chintamani Panigrahi):

(a) & (b) After careful consideration of all aspects, it has been decided not to pursue the joint venture proposal between BEL, Samtel India, and Corning Glass Works of USA.

(c) & (d) The Maharashtra Government had forwarded a representation from the workers of Taloja unit with the request that it be sympathetically considered. The Government of India is not considering any proposal for the privatisation of the Taloja unit of BEL.

Safeguarding people of Indian origin in Jalalabad

Shri Sharad Dighe: Will the Minister of External Affairs be pleased to state:

(a) whether Government's attention has been drawn to recent reports about the killing of persons of Indian origins near Jalalabad in an intensified attack on that city by Afghan rebels;

(b) if so, the reaction of Government in the matter; and

(c) the steps taken by Government for the safety and security of the Indians living there?

Answer

The Minister of State in the Ministry of External Affairs (Shri K. Natwar Singh):

(a) Yes, Sir.

(b) & (c) Government have received these reports with anguish. Our concern at the security and safety of the persons of Indian origin, as well as Indian nationals presently in Afghanistan, has been conveyed to the Government of Afghanistan who have assured us of their co-operation in this regard.

Leave to I.A. pilots

Shri Sharad Dighe: Will the Minister of Civil Aviation and Tourism be pleased to state:

(a) the details of existing facilities of privilege leave to the Indian Airlines pilots;

(b) whether Indian Airlines pilots have been barred from taking privilege leave during this year; and

(c) if so, the reasons thereof?

Answer

The Minister of State of the Ministry of Civil Aviation and Tourism (Shri Shivraj Patil):

(a) Under the service regulations of Indian Airlines, employees of Indian Airlines (including pilots) are allowed 30 days privilege leave for every 11 completed months of service which can be accumulated upto 240 days.

(b) & (c) No, Sir. However, considering the fact that quite a number of pilots are being sent for training to France in connection with induction of 19 Airbus A 320 aircraft, pilots have been advised to avoid taking privilege leave, to the extent possible. It has been agreed that the privilege leave in excess of 240 days, which would have otherwise lapsed, if not availed of, would be allowed to be accumulated as a special case. In urgent cases, pilots are also being granted privilege leave.

Excerpt from the Thakkar Commission speech by Sharad Dighe where he defends R.K. Dhawan:

His (Mark Tully's) allegation was that a "close member of the Prime Minister's staff", however, vouched for his integrity. "His integrity" means assassin's integrity. After saying so, the Commission immediately said:

> "It is generally known that the expression 'close member of the PM staff' was being widely used when it was desired to refer to Shri Dhawan."

I submit that this inference is drawn on a very weak assumption and we cannot rely upon it at all.

Some diary entries are there. What would be the motive for a gentleman who was with the Prime Minister for a major number of years of his life and was loyal to her even in her bad days? What motive can it be? What would he achieve by helping the assassination of his own boss? He had all the powers. Everything was with him. He was not stripped of the power at all. What was the necessity?

Who would commit this heinous crime? It is no probability at all from a person of his standing.

Not only that. Then the motive shown is, he was reprimanded some time in September, 1984. He was reprimanded by the Prime Minister in September, 1984 for the alleged acts of Andhra Pradesh politics. Now, I do not know exactly but, several other people are also alleged to be involved in this advice.

Prof. N.G. Ranga: We do that too.

Shri Sharad Dighe: So, there is no possibility that it was because of this and when he was there for several years with the Prime Minister, I think, there must have been several occasions when she must have reprimanded him. When he was so close in advising and helping the Prime Minister of this country, is it possible that because he was reprimanded only once in September, 1984 so that he got so much attitude of vengeance that he must assassin his boss to whom he was loyal all these years? All these things are absolutely based on weak evidence and inferences cannot be drawn by even a reasonable man from all these things. Therefore, what I submit is that this report, as far as this aspect is concerned, is merely speculative, is only a conjecture and I do not know whether anything can be alleged but, as far as he being a very high authority, a Supreme Court Judge for several years,.... we may merely say that he has not used his usual sense of judgement in assessing the evidence, in coming to conclusions, which was expected of a judge of this type and with great confidence such an inquiry we entrusted to a sitting Judge of the Supreme Court. Why do we do so? We are confident that his mind is trained and he can assess and he can come to proper conclusions and he bases everything on evidence and absolutely unbiased judgement is given by a Supreme Court Judge. But, somehow or the other, I must say we are not getting the benefit of those qualities as far as this Report is concerned. From this point of view, I am glad that thereafter SIT has exonerated Mr. Dhawan from all these allegations. The Government has thought it fit to restore him in his own position. The Government has also, acting on the report of the SIT, charge-sheeted those who were concerned in the broader and larger conspiracy, as far as this assassination is concerned. So, the Government has taken proper steps. The Commission itself was expecting that after this pre-inquiry investigation, something would be done by the Government, further investigations would be made and then only steps would be taken. This has been done by the Government. I am happy about it. Therefore, again I would like to say that it would have been better if the Opposition had participated in this discussion and put forth their own arguments here so that they could have been replied to here and the whole Parliament would have been satisfied that this report is merely based on inferences and conjectures. That would have satisfied even our Members of the Opposition. I hope so. But they knew that an embarrassing position would come after this discussion and they would have nothing to say on this report. Therefore, they have chosen this course of action of boycotting the participation on this discussion of the report.

With these words, I conclude.

Extract of the speech on the Sarkaria Commission Report

Shri Sharad Dighe (Bombay North Central): Mr. Deputy-Speaker, Sir, I rise to express some of my views on this Sarkaria Commission's report.

This Commission was appointed as far back as 9th June, 1983 and it has produced a beautiful report as far as the various provisions of the Constitution are concerned. Our Constitution came into force on the 26th January 1950, and during all these years as many as 61 amendments have been moved to our Constitution. And when I see a list of even the Private Members' Bills, I find that 90 per cent of the Private Members' Bills are also regarding the amendment of the Constitution.

So, as per the experience we gain, several suggestions come to the mind of the people and particularly the elected representatives and various (state) governments that certain amendments are necessary to this Constitution. Therefore, having due regard to the scheme and framework of the Constitution, the Sarkaria Commission was appointed to review and examine the arrangements between the Union and the States. A broad spectrum of recommendations has been made on various concepts, and different constitutional provisions have been examined by the Commission and also the issues raised by the various State Governments and the authorities on the Constitution have also been considered by them. Therefore, it may be said that it is a very valuable document produced by the Commission in which the present issues have been practically listed and discussed and the solutions have also been suggested by the Commission.

Within this short time it is not possible to examine and comment upon each and every recommendation of the Commission. Therefore, I will restrict myself only to the legislative relations and also to the role of the Governor and the various suggestions made with respect to them.

Considering the various provisions of the Constitution one has mainly to keep in mind the main framework of the Constitution and as was stated by the Second Report of the Union Powers Committee on the 5th July, 1947, the soundest framework of our Constitution is a federation with a strong Centre and that is true in view of the Constitution. After the partition of this country the Constituent Assembly came to the conclusion that we should have a very strong Centre to defend this country and to keep the unity and integrity of this country intact. So also, from the historical point of view, they were also aware that undue centralisation has often proved counter-productive and triggered a chain reaction of divisive forces. Therefore, keeping both these principles in mind, a balance has been struck while framing the Constitution, namely, to have a strong Centre as well as to give as much autonomy as possible to the States which have been carved out. The whole scheme of the Constitution also shows that even the States have been carved out under the Constitution by Parliament itself. Articles 2 and 3 are also clear that even the States can be formed, their boundaries can be changed and all these things are within the powers of Parliament itself.

Similarly there is supremacy of the legislative powers of Parliament. Even there is power given to legislate any State subject under Article 249 if the Rajya Sabha passes a resolution to that effect. Therefore the whole scheme is to have a strong centre, but at the same time give autonomy in the normal times to various States which have been formed. From this point of view, we must test the various proposals that have been made by the Sarkaria Commission itself. As far as the legislative relations are concerned, I was a little bit surprised when after discussing the whole point, the Sarkaria Commission comes to the conclusion that as far as the residuary powers are concerned, the residuary powers should be divided into two parts and the provisions relating to the taxation should be left to the Parliament, and as far as other residuary items are concerned, they should be kept in the Concurrent List. And then it has also been stated that consultations should be made with respect to any legislation that would be brought on a subject under the Concurrent List. Sir, I feel that these two recommendations are very dangerous and are not in conformity with the views expressed before them and are not in conformity with the scheme of our Constitution. For example, they have themselves stated at Page 29 Para 2.6.04—I quote:

> "Most State Governments do not seek any change in the existing provisions relating to the residuary powers. However, four State Governments have suggested that the residuary powers should be vested in the States, and two State Governments have proposed that Entry 97 of List I be transferred to the Concurrent List."

Therefore, only two State Governments have suggested that Entry 97 of List I be transferred to the Concurrent List. Further, they have themselves stated at Page 31—I quote:

> "For reasons mentioned in the preceding paragraphs, we are unable to accept the suggestions that residuary powers should be vested in the States."

At this stage, they have come to the conclusion after considering all the views which were expressed before them. But then, further it states in the next paragraph—I quote:

> "We are of the view that residuary power of legislation in regard to taxation should advisedly remain with Parliament. But, the residuary field other than that of taxation may be transferred to the Concurrent List."

Therefore, having come to the conclusion that nothing should be given from the residuary powers to the States, it is surprising that in the next paragraph, the Commission without giving any justification further, in a short paragraph summarily changes the views and says that except taxation, the rest of the residuary powers should go to the Concurrent List. That means, they should be shared by the Centre as well as the States. Therefore, my submission is that this is basically contrary to the views expressed by them earlier, contrary to all the evidence before them and also contrary to all the arguments which they themselves have made in the same Chapter itself.

This is what I want to submit as far as the legislative aspect is concerned. Now I would like to take some time as far as the recommendations regarding Governors are concerned. I will not go into the details as far as the role of the Governor is concerned.

I shall merely say that the role of a Governor is not merely that of a Constitutional Head of that State but, according to me, the role is that of a sentinel of the Constitution and he is also a live link between the State and the Union. Therefore, he not only performs his function as the Constitutional Head, with the aid and advice of the Council of Ministers, but several powers are there which he has to exercise in his discretionary capacity, and while exercising his powers in his discretionary capacity, he is the sentinel of the Constitution. He has to see that the Government of State is being run in accordance with the provisions of the Constitution. He has also to keep the Central Government informed about the various activities, various legislations that are passed and about the political activities also in that State because ultimately whether the Government is being conducted in accordance with the Constitution or not is to be informed by the Governor to the State. That is very important from the point of view of our central idea of a strong Centre. He has also to supervise implementation of the provisions of the Constitution and of the laws, maintenance of law and order, implementation of the developmental plans and everything. So, that role also has to be performed by the Governor. Therefore, from this point of view, my submission is that....(Interruptions).

Prof. N.G. Ranga: Unity and integrity of the nation also.

Shri Sharad Dighe: Yes, unity and integrity of the nation also. Several border States are there where the Union Government has to keep a vigil as far as these things are concerned. From that point of view, I do not agree with two suggestions which have been made by them and, therefore, I say that they should not be accepted. Firstly, I do not agree with the suggestion that a person who is very much in politics, should not be appointed a Governor. That appears to be the trend of the whole discussion. The recommendation says that he should be a person who has not taken great part in politics generally, and particularly in the recent past. For that purpose, of course, they rely upon our first Prime Minister, Pandit Jawaharlal Nehru. But I submit that those days were quite different. At that time several freedom fighters and very respectable personalities were available and they commanded respect. So, wherever they were appointed Governor, there was no problem. Practically everywhere there were no problems which we are facing today. Now, from today's point of view, I submit that if the Governor has to perform his function as a sentinel of the Constitution and has to keep a live line with the Centre, then I feel that it is purely a political role and for that purpose you cannot say that you must have merely men of letters and very learned people and that they should be great personalities in some walks of life. It is no use saying that. It is a political role and that has to be performed by a politician only. You can, of course, say that he must be acceptable to the State. You cannot send persons who are inimical with that State and will create problems for that State. That should not be the idea. That I understand and agree to. But politically he is the sentinel of the Centre and he has to see that the functioning of the State is going on in accordance with the Constitutional provisions and that everything is being done according to the national policies which we are promulgating.

Therefore, Sir, from that point of view, I say that it is time now that we have to emphasise that he shall be a politician, he must know his role and from that point of view he should be selected. Of course, good people who are acceptable and who also command respect from the public, from all the political parties, may be considered. If these things are there, then there is no use saying that he should not have taken active part in politics, etc. etc. Then, Sir, a very very dangerous suggestion made is that while selecting Governors, Vice President of India and the Speaker of Lok Sabha should be consulted. I do not understand what link the selection of Governor has with the Speaker of Lok Sabha and the Vice President of India. It has nothing to do with the rights of the Members of Parliament. It has nothing to do with the procedure of parliamentary functioning. Therefore, in this onerous task of selection of Governor, the Speaker of the Lok Sabha and the Vice President of India should not be involved at all. They have got enough onerous responsibility here and after the passing of the anti-defection law, we have put one more responsibility of finding out whether a Member is qualified or disqualified under the anti-defection law. So, this thing should not be done at all and it is a very dangerous proposition. With all respect to the Speaker and the Vice President of India, I say that they should not be involved in the selection of the Governor at all....

III

In brief, the parliamentary system as it has evolved in the country has not been conducive to producing learned debates.

Besides, the new men in Parliament are not inclined either by temperament or training to contribute to debates. Even though the educational qualifications of the parliamentarians has steadily been increasing, the standard of education has been declining and hence they are not a reliable indicator of an MP's learning; in any case the debates do not reflect it. What we get in the House are essentially ritual speeches in support of the party line. These are in essence time-fillers (using up the time allotted to discuss a topic) re-iterating the by now familiar points related to an issue. Speeches apart, an MP's contribution can also be evaluated by the information he elicits from the ministers (bureaucracy) on matters of public concern. But in this regard too he fails to impress (as evident from the questions and answers reproduced above and in Annexure—IV).

7

Importance Of The MP

Since the Nehru era, the prestige of the MPs has declined and two reasons that may be cited are as follows:[61]

— As a consequence of the reputation for probity and sacrifice earned during the freedom movement (and Nehru's commitment to strengthening democracy) the views of MP of the Congress as well as the Opposition (as expressed during debates in the House) were treated seriously and hence they can be said to have influenced

---

61. The perks and privileges that have over a period of time become available to an MP are not likely to arouse envy. In his book *Parliament of India*, (1988) Subhash C. Kashyap describes the *perks* of an MP as follows: A member of Parliament, who represents a population of over 8,00,000, is provided with an official residence in Delhi for which he is charged a moderate rent. He is paid a salary of Rs.500/- per month and, when the Lok Sabha is in session or when he is on parliamentary duty, he receives a daily allowance of Rs.51/-. He is entitled to a first class railway pass with which he can travel throughout the country without any payment. The estimate of expenditure on MPs for the financial year 1974-75 is as follows: salaries—Rs.2.9 million, and travel expenses — Rs. 10.1 million. The total expenditure on the Lok Sabha amounted to Rs.31 million a year. *Privileges*: The term 'privilege' refers to certain rights and immunities enjoyed by each House of Parliament and its committees collectively, and by members of each House individually without which they cannot discharge their functions efficiently and effectively. Some of the most important privileges are

* freedom of speech in Parliament
* immunity to a member from any proceedings in any court in respect of anything said or any vote given by him in Parliament or any Committee thereof
* immunity to a person from proceedings in any court in respect of the publication by or under the authority of either House of Parliament of any report, paper, vote or proceedings
* prohibition on the courts to inquire into proceedings of Parliament
* freedom from arrest of members in civil cases during the continuance of the session of the House and forty days before its commencement and forty days after its conclusion

Parliamentary privileges do not, however, place a member on a footing different from that of an ordinary citizen in the matter of application of laws, unless there are good and sufficient reasons in the interest of Parliament itself to do so.

policy. Since then (the Sixth Lok Sabha onwards) few MPs have an untarnishd reputation.[62] Equally significant, hardly any have expertise in any field to make a contribution to policy formulation.

— An increasing tendency for the kitchen cabinet to take the decisions, so much so that whereas previously at least the MP was consulted over projects in his area, now he is often ignored with regard to them as well.[63]

The decline in the quality of the MP (and at a remove or two, his powers) can partly be attributed to the political party which not only fails to select suitable candidates for the post (as noted), but does not bother to see to it whether they are doing the job expected of them; this is, in particular, true of the Congress party.

There is no system of accountability. The MP may disappear for the whole five year term, the political party (the Congress is here

---

62. In a statement issued on April 16, 1991 resigning from the Congress (I), the former Union minister, K.R. Ganesh stated 'In this period 1972-89 the country also witnessed the lowering and debasement of the institutions of democracy and administration. Moral standards and probity in public life were thrown overboard. The political structure was penetrated by money power and criminal and mafia elements. The economic model on which there was broad consensus was reversed in many spheres, leading to the present state of economic crises (*The Statesman*, April 17, 1991).

63. "It is painful to note that all avenues before radical Congressmen for bringing about policy shifts has been closed by the coterie type leadership which has taken control of the organisation. Failing in the task of bringing about democratic changes, many radical Congressmen remained in a state of political passivity.... We note with regret that today the Congress (I) has become a party of stagnation, status quo and authoritarianism. It has a command type leadership. It has ceased to be an instrument of radical social change. Its authoritarian and highly centralized rule had generated disintegrating and divisive forces. There is no opportunity of inner party struggle...The stagnation of the party led to the defeat of the Congress in 1967. The retrievable period of 1967-72 was brought about by the initiative and unity of left of centre and left forces. The period of 1972-77 saw the reversal of the direction and growth of authoritafianism leading to the break-up of the left of centre alliance system. The country had to go through the horrors of emergency leading to the second defeat of the Congress in 1977... Since then stagnation, status quo and authoritarianism have been the guiding characteristic of the Congress. The period from 1985-89 saw the consolidation of this regressive character of the party and its isolation from the oppressed and deprived sections of the population and from minorities. The follow-on was the defeat of the Congress in the ninth Lok Sabha election and the loss of its hegemonic character" (*ibid*).

being considered as it has held dominant sway all these years) would not bother to enquire why he did so.[64]

Enough evidence is available, through party circles, about MPs who indulge in corrupt practices (or MLAs and municipal councillors for that matter who have greater scope in this sphere), but no internal enquiry is ever instituted. The party does not stir even when allegations appear in the newspapers and other media, what to speak of urging the elected representative to clear his name if he was interested in securing the party nomination (ticket) for re-election. Small wonder that corruption is rampant among the politicos.

II

In brief, the decline in the importance of the MP set in once his legislative functions diminished. He could still have maintained his status had he contributed to debates in Parliament. But his contribution has not been of the quality necessary to influence

---

64. *Code of Conduct for MPs*: In 1967, a code was drafted for legislators by Union Minister of Home Affairs and adopted. It sought to bring together in one place the recognised principles and conventions which should regulate the relationship between MP, MLAs on the one hand with civil servants on the other. It enjoined upon every civil servant the duty to help all legislators who are expected to ask for information only about matters of public interest or national interest and should abstain from taking up individual cases concerning grants of permits and licences, recruitment, promotion, transfer or disciplinary action. They should not seek information to further private interests or for use in court litigation or for giving other undue advantages to certain individuals against others.

    Some important conventions:

    (i) Information given to members in confidence or by virtue of being members of a Committee, should not be divulged to anyone, nor used by them directly or indirectly in the profession in which they are engaged.

    (ii) A member should not receive hospitality of any kind for any work he desires or proposes to do from a person or organisation on whose behalf the work is to be done by him.

    (iii) A member should not in his capacity as a lawyer or a legal adviser or a counsel or a solicitor appear before a Minister or an executive officer exercising quasi-judicial powers.

    (iv) A member should not write recommendatory letters or speak to government officials for employment or business contacts for any of his relations or other persons in whom he is directly interested.

policy. However, the environment has changed as well, in so far as policy is not his to influence as power has been absorbed by the kitchen cabinet and the Prime Minister's secretariat.

8

Socio-Economic Background

Among the 18 MPs interviewed, eight of them profess to be agriculturists, making it the largest occupational group. The land they own varies in size between 24 and 35 acres; in some cases information on the extent of irrigated land has been provided. The holdings are not small, but it would have been possible to determine how lucrative they are if we had data on the areas irrigated in all cases (only then would questions on cropping pattern—Kharif June to October, Rabi November to March—cash crops grown, etc. would acquire significance.)

We have two teachers (one at primary school level, the other college) one doctor, one businessman, one journalist and a lawyer. One of the MPs was a farm manager, another a clerical employee of a civic body. A couple of the MPs can be said to be professional politicians since they devoted themselves to full-time politics on completing their education (See Table No.I).

Twelve of the MPs are graduates, three post-graduates, and at least five graduates have an additional degree, that of LL.B. Five MPs have not gone beyond secondary school and one has a diploma in homeopathy/biochemistry. Not one has a Ph.D.[65]

---

65. (a) Dutta, Ratna, *The Party Representative in the fourth Lok Sabha* (Economic & Political Weekly, January 1969): In the fourth Lok Sabha, those representing agrarian interests constituted 31% of the members. Now they constitute 35.9% as highlighted by Bhambhri, C.P., & Verma, P.S., in their article '*Social Background of Seventh Lok Sabha* (1980) and in Mainstream, July 4, 1981.

(b) Commenting on the increase in agriculturists in the Lok Sabha, Pai Panandikar, V.A. and Sud, Arun, *Changing Political Representation in India* (1983) note: The present trend is a clear indication that the political process unleased through free and democratic parliamentary elections, have started to bring about a major transfer of political power from the westernised and urban political elite to the rural classes.

Shrader, L.L., Sisson, R., in book edited by Joshi, Ram, and Hebsur, R.K., entitled *Congress In Indian Politics : A Centenary Perspective* (Popular Prakashan, 1987): The increase of agriculturists is a clear indication of the 'ruralization' of the Lok Sabha at a steady and gradual rate. Increasing number of MPs are not following such classic middle class liberal professions as lawyer, teacher, journalist and physician as in the past. These trends suggest that even as education levels have remained high, some erosion in the "cosmopolitan" character of the legislature has taken place. Though

The average age of the group of MPs is 52.5 years. Except for a couple, all the MPs have been born in a village, and their childhood years have been spent in a rural setting.

As for the caste composition, there are only three MPs who belong to the dominant Maratha caste (Among MLAs the Marathas are considerably better represented). Five MPs belong to the OBC,

---

agriculturists may be well educated, they are more likely to spend more time in rural areas than in the cities and to have fewer contacts with the more urbane and cosmopolitan influences of the city.

(c) In Maharashtra, agriculture steadily rose from 1952 to 1972 with 39% identified as agriculturists in 1972 with another 15% having agriculture as a secondary occupation (Sisson & Shrader).

(d) In a computer study "The Indian Legislators" by Dr. N. Bhaskara Rao, it is stated that the seventh Lok Sabha has better educated members. Those with specialised skills of beyond post graduate level, however, are lower than before. Dr. Rao makes a number of other observations saying that contrary to popular impression the current Lok Sabha is not younger than before. He adds: Between 1952 and 1982, the number of members with an agricultural background has doubled in the Lok Sabha from 86 to 201 and the number of lawyers has gone up from 106 in 1952 to 112 in 1982. But professionals like doctors, journalists and writers decreased from 56 to 25. The study has revealed that full-time politicians dominate the Rajya Sabha although the founding fathers of the Constitution hoped it would have a range of faculties, professionals and specialists rather than party-based politicians. In the Rajya Sabha, lawyers form the single largest group next to politicians while agriculturists, followed by lawyers and politicians, dominate the Lok Sabha. Young professionals and highly qualified specialists are not getting inducted into the Rajya Sabha. The study notes that over the years younger people have entered the State legislatures instead of the Lok Sabha. In State Assemblies over one-fifth of the members are below 35 as against 10 per cent in the Lok Sabha.

(e) Bhambhri, C.P.: The age composition of the Lok Sabha members belonging to the Janata party reveals a preponderant representation of those who have crossed the middle age group and have entered the old age category. On the basis of age, it is a party of 'seniors'. The largest age group consists of people who are between 46 and 65 years. Young members below 35 years are only 5.6 percent and those above 66 years are 11.5 percent. If we compare the age composition of the Janata party members with those of the Congress party in the Lok Sabha, we find a great similarity in both parties. The largest group in the Congress party belongs to the category 46 to 65 years. The majority of the Janata party members, that is 49.5 percent possesses qualifications which are above the graduation level. The profile of the Janata party members on the basis of their profession shows the dominance of 'agriculture'—about 40 percent—which is closely followed by those who are involved in the modern professions. The Janata has a negligible representation of members who are involved in industry and business. In the Congress, the representatives of modern professions have a little edge over agriculturists.

three are Brahmins, two Kunbis, two scheduled caste (one has become a neo Buddhist)[66], two tribals, and there is a lone Marwari.

Candidates continue to be selected on the basis of the numerical strength of the caste in their constituency.

In Y.S. Mahajan's constituency which has six assembly segments and 10-11 lakh voters, the caste-wise break-up is as follows:

Marathas	—	20 percent
OBC	—	20 percent
Leva-Patidars	—	25 percent
Muslims	—	15 percent
SC	—	10 percent
ST	—	5 percent
Brahmins	—	5 percent

Y.S. Mahajan is a Leva-Patidar, which falls under the OBC category. Together with the rest of OBCs, he has been promoted as a leader of a chunk of 45 percent of the voters of his constituency (During the 1989 elections, Mahajan says there were other Leva-Patidar candidates in the field, their vote was thus split between him and others.) The Leva-Patidars are also in Gujarat; the Maharashtra ones have no connection with them.

The break-up of Uttam Rathod's constituency of 9.5 lakh voters is

SC	—	2 lakhs
ST	—	1 lakh
Muslims	—	1 lakh
Marathas	—	1.5 lakhs/2 lakhs
OBC	—	2 lakhs
Vanjaris	—	70,000 to 80,000

Being a Vanjari, Rathod is able to capitalise on the OBC vote though considering the size of the Maratha vote, a Maratha candidate stands a good chance of winning. (However, Rathod

66. Narayana, G: *Social Background of Scheduled Caste Members 1962-71* (Economic & Political Weekly XIII, 37, 1978, 1603-1606): This study suggests that the background of the scheduled caste representatives is becoming similar to that of the general representatives i.e. there is a trend towards homogeneity among scheduled caste representatives in Parliament and those representing the general population between the third and fifth Lok Sabhas.

was vague about the number of Maratha voters; they could be less than indicated above.)

Uttam Deorao Patil who considers himself a Kunbi Maratha has 9.5 lakh voters in his constituency:

Maratha-Kunbis	—	30 percent
OBC (Mali, Teli, Dhangar)	—	30 percent
ST & SC	—	25 percent
Muslims	—	10 percent
Rest	—	5 percent

An OBC candidate too can be put up from this constituency.

K.P. Bopche's constituency of 10 lakh and more voters has

OBC (Dhangar, Mali, even Kunbis are classed in this category)	—	25 percent
Povar	—	20 percent
SC	—	30 percent
ST	—	20 percent
Muslims	—	1 percent

It is clear why Bopche, who is a Povar, an OBC, was nominated as its party's candidate.

Damodar Barku Shingda, a Warli tribal, whose reserved constituency has 10 lakh voters covers six MLA constituencies. Its caste component is

Tribals of which 60 percent are Warlis	—	4 lakhs
Kunbi	—	2.5 lakhs
Muslim	—	1.5 lakh
SC	—	50,000
Brahmin, Vani & others	—	The rest

Political Socialisation

Eleven of the 18 MPs have previously been MLAs. The seven who have not are Babasahib Vikhe Patil, D.B. Shingda, Y.S. Mahajan, Vasant Sathe, S.N. Kale, Ashok Deshmukh and Vidyadhar Gokhale. (See Table No.II)

Babasahib Vikhe Patil was kicked upstairs. He had, however, won zilla parishad elections and also co-operative society elections. D.B. Shingda's case is that of nomination, largely because of the

Sanjay Gandhi connection. He was elected sarpanch of his village and also won the Z.P. elections. After having a shot at the 1955 bye-election and the 1957 general election, Y.S. Mahajan entered electoral politics. He gave up his career, much like Vidyadhar Gokhale. The only suitable opening for them was Parliament. At least Mahajan did not have any desire to join the Vidhan Sabha. While Deshmukh and certainly Kale would have been happy in the state legislature, they contested MP elections on the directives of their respective parties, the Shiv Sena and BJP, presumably because these had no other candidates (unlike Congress which has several aspirants for each ticket). In Sathe's case, Indira Gandhi sought to get him an MLA ticket but the Maratha leaders ganged up against him.

A few MPs' parents were active politically. While Vikhe Patil's father, the founder of the co-operative movement, was not a member of any political party he was a PWP sympathiser, Shingda's father was an active Congress party worker, whereas U.D. Patil's father entered electoral politics prior to the first general election, later becoming an MLA and MP. Kamble's father enjoyed the distinction of serving as an MP for three terms. Vasant Sathe's parents inculcated in him the Tilakite philosophy since childhood. Dhakne's father, not unlike Vikhe Patil's, was a member of the co-operative movement and a member of the Left Agadhi peasants movement.

Thus a third of the MPs political socialisation began during childhood and about an equal number took to politics prior to graduation, or more accurately, after leaving studies (i.e. Dhakne, for instance, did not graduate).

Three MPs have served five terms each in Parliament; four have served three terms each. All belong to the Congress party. Of the three MPs who have served two terms each, two are Congress party members, one Janata Dal. For all the BJP candidates, it was their first term in the Lok Sabha, as also for the Shiv Sena candidates.

Those who made it as ministers at the Maharashtra level are Shivraj Patil, Uttam Rathod, A.T. Kamble, and Baban Rao Dhakne. Except for Dhakne, all else belong to the Congress Party.[67]

67. (a) Jha, Shree Nagesh, *The Union Council of Ministers in India 1952-71; A Study in Elite Composition* (Political Science Review, Vo. 13, Nos. 1-4, Jan-Dec 1974): In terms of age, while there is a general tendency of increasing percentage (i.e. over 60 years) almost 70% belong to the age group of 41-60. Arora, Satish K., *Social Background of the Fifth Lok Sabha* (EPW Special no.

Only three of the 18 MPs have secured ministerial births at the Centre: Vasant Sathe and Shivraj Patil of the Congress and Baban Rao Dhakne of the Janata Dal.

1973): The percentage of lawyers has decreased; a quarter of the membership of the first Lok Sabha were lawyers, compared to only a fifth of the present House (5th Lok Sabha). Lawyers formed the single largest occupational group in the first Lok Sabha; today they represent the second largest group, exceeded only by agriculturists. Bhambhri, C.P., & Verma, P.S., *Social Background of Seventh Lok Sabha* (1980) (Mainstream July 4, 1981): The largest group of the present Lok Sabha members have acquired a B.A. plus another qualification. It comprises 48.8% of the members. Those that have graduated comprise 21.9% and those that have not, 27.4%. This was generally the trend in the earlier Lok Sabhas as shown by studies of Ratna Dutta & Satish K. Arora.

(b) Arora, Satish K., *Social Background of the Fifth Lok Sabha* (EPW Special no. 1973); In this study Arora says that it is unfortunate that there is so little data to measure accurately just how economically powerful our legislatures are. Among the handful of national elite studies one looks in vain for data on economic class or parental background of our national representatives or for systematic analysis of their socio-economic past.

9

Conclusion

The MP is on a losing wicket. The right to legislate is no longer his, if only because most laws have been formulated. His capacity to influence policy through debates in the House, or parliamentary committees, began to decline since an ever increasing amount of power was arrogated by the Kitchen Cabinet and the PM's Secretariat. An MP who becomes a minister and makes it to the inner circle, has the power to influence decisions. With regard to his own ministry he needs to rely on the bureaucracy which makes available the necessary expertise.[68]

But how many make it to the inner circle.

In our sample of MPs, of the three who made it as ministers, only one can be said to have belonged to the inner circle (Sathe). Other Maharashtra Central ministers, after the Y.B. Chavan era, have exercised influence but for brief spells. They did not, however, belong to the exclusive coterie. Perhaps A.R. Antulay did while the Indira Gandhi-Sanjay Gandhi axis was around, but not since. No, even S.B. Chavan was not part of this power elite.

---

68. Maheshwari, Shriram, *Political Development in India*: On intermediaries, i.e. power brokers the author notes: All MPs in the present sample (50 MPs) report that, although many people approach them independently, some are accompanied by political workers who are known to the MPs or at any rate, who pretend to have known them and whose purpose is to enlist their support in the matter. The number of these intermediaries recently has been increasing. While many of them are activated by a desire to help and also to carve out for themselves a place of influence and respect in the local community, this practice is not entirely without risk and abuse.

The intermediaries initiate a process that tends to insulate the representatives from the citizens: they interpose themselves, thereby increasing the distance between the two.

Dependence on them is much more marked in the case of those MPs who do not live in the constituency they represent. Unfortunately, some of the intermediaries are nothing short of political touts. One, known for his probity commented: "Power has itself become a vested interest in India. At various levels of political life, right from the secretariat to the village level, there has spawned a class of brokers or procurers, go-betweens between the citizens and the wielders of power. As power has remained with the Congress Party all these years, it has attracted to itself all kinds of unsavoury persons. A parasitic class has emerged in India particularly in the Congress".

The harsh reality is that the MPs are no longer in a position to exercise much power, some may say any power. Which was not the case in Nehru's time. The MPs then were very much the political elite. Now this description can aptly be applied to the MLA.

The other issue is whether MPs can be entrusted with the responsibility of exercising power responsibly. The answer cannot but be in the negative. The candidates nominated to Parliament by political parties, whatever their compulsions, confirm this view. Most of them are temperamentally not suited to function in the Lok Sabha. They are men for whom state politics, often regional politics, is all. They have been able to maintain good contacts and fulfilled local needs. But after having served several terms, they have been supplanted by younger men and the party has tackled the problem by finding them a place in the Lok Sabha. This is the common scenario with regard to Congress Party candidates. As for rightist parties which have of late been making their presence felt in the Lok Sabha, their candidates are first time winners.

Thus it is either the reluctant MP, or one new to the House; what can you expect of them. Uninterested in national issues, or not sufficiently prepared on any one, they are a bunch unlikely to contribute to a debate concerning the nation.

The institutional arrangements within the Lok Sabha militates against the MP. With seven minutes at his disposal, he can get across only that much to the members (or the ministers), most of whom are frequently not to be found in their seats. Hence the focus of the MP is to get media attention by making the kind of statement that gets it. Often he may resort to unruly behaviour which reflects poorly on him and the House.

Uninterested in influencing, or unable to, the course of national policy, the MP focuses on taking care of his constituents. He contacts the various Central government ministries in a position to extend benefits to his constituency and obtains commitments. Some of these are fulfilled. But the major ones which involve heavy financial outlays from the Centre's treasury—industrial units and sugar co-operatives, for instance—needing Rs.25-30 crores and more, or conversion of lengthy portions of the railway track from narrow to broad guage, remain essentially on paper.

Ignored by the Centre, the MP may decide to tackle local problems: he takes on projects related to provision of water, electricity, better housing, tackles farmers' demands or the woes of slum dwellers, helps secure school admissions and signs innumerable character certificates and others that may provide the voter with a job. All this is very well since nowhere is it stated that an MP's role should be confined to the Centre, to dealing with issues in Delhi. But is this an MP's function? For by devoting himself to local matters he is performing the task of a municipal councillor, or the MLA, which they are better placed to tackle.

As the MP does not have the wherewithal to deal effectively with civic or state level issues, neither the discretionary funds, nor the contacts with state level bureaucrats and ministers (as he is most of the time required to be in Delhi), his prestige, such as it is, takes another blow. Add to this the impression that an MP cannot be honest and yet collect the huge sums of money to fight the elections,[69] small wonder the image of our man in the Lok Sabha is a badly tarnished one. It has no shine at all, which has gradually been rubbed off during the decline that set in after the disappearance of Nehru from the scene.

---

69. The licence raj was a phenomena which highlights how the political elite gave licences to those industrial groups which coughed up funds to the party; at the state level, MLAs of the ruling party are granted a whole series of favours (powers) by the Chief Minister so as to make money. Manor, James, *Where the Gandhi writ doesn't run* (The Economist, May 15, 1982): The Chief Minister of Haryana, Mr. Bhajan Lal, created a large number of boards to supervise state enterprises, and packed them with politicians. Some of these people proceeded to use their position for personal gain. Private firms—foreign and domestic—have been awarded state contracts in exchange for huge kickbacks. One car company provided a large number of legislators with a new car each and a generous monthly stipend to cover 'running costs.'

TABLES

Table I : Socio-Economic Status Of MPs

	Name	*Age*	*Caste*	*Place of Birth*	*Education*	*Occupation*	*Political Party*
1.	Shivraj V. Patil	56	Maratha	Chakur, Ahmadpur tahsil, Latur district	B.Sc. & LL.M. (Schooling in Latur & graduation & law degree from Hyderabad & Bombay Universities)	Professional politician (Joined Congress after college in 1962 & contested municipal elections in 1967)	Congress
2.	Babasahib Vikhe Patil	59	Maratha	Loni Bk, Shrirampur tahsil, Ahmadnagar district	Matric (Schooling in Pune & Nasik Military School & Ahmednagar)	Agriculturist (30 acres)	Congress

contd.......

	Name	Age	Caste	Place of Birth	Education	Occupation	Political Party
3.	Uttam Rathod	62	Vanjari (a denotified ex-criminal tribe)	In Adilabad district, then part of Hyderabad state	M.A., LL.B. (Schooling in Mandvi, Nanded dist. & Yavatmal B.A. from Hilsop College, Nagpur, MA in politics & law degree from Nagpur University)	Lawyer from 1953-58 and since then full-time politics (Owns 46 acres)	Congress
4.	Damodar Barku Shingda	36	Warli tribal	Posheri, Wada tahsil, Thane district	Class 10 (Schooling in Posheri & Wada)	Agriculturist (35 acres)	Congress

5.	Uttamrao Deorao Patil	45	Kunbi	Loni, Digras tahsil, Yavatmal dist.	B.Sc. in agriculture (Schooling in Loni and Amravati, and graduation from Nagpur University)	Agriculturist (His father divided 100 acres between 5 brothers.	Congress
6.	Y.S. Mahajan	78	Leva-Patidar (OBC)	Hingone, Yawal tahsil, Jalgaon dist.	B.Sc. & Bar-at-Law (Schooling in Hingone, economics from London School of Economics & law from the Middle Temple)	Professor/ teacher	Congress
7.	Murli Deora	54	Marwari	Bombay	B.A. (Schooling in Bombay; graduate of Bombay University)	Businessman (small scale industrialist	Congress

contd.......

	Name	Age	Caste	Place of Birth	Education	Occupation	Political Party
8.	Vasant Sathe	66	Chitpavan Brahmin	Khandala village, 12 km from Nagpur	B.A., LL.B. (Bhonsale Military School, Nasik and Nagpur Mahavidyalaya; graduate of Nagpur Univ.)	Practised as a lawyer for a while, till he joined the Congresss and has been a fulltime politico	Congress
9.	Arvind Tulshiram Kamble	40	Scheduled Caste (Chamar)	Udgir, Latur district	B.A. (Schooling in Udgir and graduation from Osmanabad college)	Agriculturist (in name alone; owned 24 acres, 14 of it irrigated but sold the irrigated land as no time to cultivate it; essentially a	Congress

						professional politician, joined Congress after graduation)	
10.	Ram Naik	57	Brahmin	Atpadi, Sangli district	B.Com. & LL.B (Schooling in village and graduation from Pune University)	Pracharak (paid worker) Full time party worker. But prior to that has held several jobs (i) upper divisional clerk in Accountant General's office (ii) Accounts Assistant in private company making steel furniture, bus body & later its chief accountant and company secretary	BJP

contd.......

	Name	Age	Caste	Place of Birth	Education	Occupation	Political Party
11.	K.P. Bopche	40	Povar (OBC)	Hirdamali, Goregaon tahsil, Bhandara dist.	Diploma in homeopathy, Biochemistry from Nagpur University (Schooling in Hirdamali & Bhandara; pre-university (biology, in Gonda city)	Doctor	BJP
12.	Sukhdev Nandaji Kale	36	Neo-Buddhist	Chincholi, Shindkheraja tahsil, Buldana dist.	SSC (Schooling in village and Shindkheraja)	Agriculture (25 acres; 15 acres irrigated)	BJP
13.	Pandurang Pundlik Phundkar	40	Kunbi	Narkhed, Nandura tahsil, Buldana distt.	B.A. (Schooling at Narkhed, Nimgaon,	Agriculturist (25 acres)	BJP

					Nandura & graduation from Khamgaon college in Buldana dist.)		
14.	Ashok Deshmukh	38	Maratha	Jintur, Jintur tahsil, Prabani dist.	B.Sc., M.Sc. (Schooling in Jintur and graduation from college of agriculture, Parbani)	Agriculture-related teaching & managerial jobs (After college became (i) Agriculture Officer, Parbani University (ii) Farm Superin-tendent, Parbani University (iii) lecturer at Gram Sevak Training Centre, Parbani University	Shiv Sena

contd.......

	Name	Age	Caste	Place of Birth	Education	Occupation	Political Party
15.	Vamanrao Shivram Mahadik	66	Hindu Shimpi (OBC)	Talere, Sindudurg district	B.A., Diploma in Local self-govt. (Schooling in Talere, matric from Ratnagiri & graduation from college in Bombay; he paid his way through higher education)	Worked as a clerk in the local body as he ran Mahadik coaching classes in Dadar till 1967. After that full-time politics	Shiv Sena
16.	Vidyadhar Gokhale	68	Brahmin	Amravati, Nagpur dist.	M.A. (Schooling in Amravati and graduation from Nagpur University)	Journalist (Editor, *Loksata*)	Shiv Sena

17.	Haribhau Mahale	51	Konkana (Scheduled tribe)	Ware, Dindori tahsil, Nasik dist.	Class, 10 (Schooling in Ware and Wani)	Primary school teacher & agriculturist (25 acres in Ware)	Janata Dal
18.	Baban Rao Dhakne	53	Vanjari OBC till 1960 a nomadic tribe (Same as Uttam Rathod)	Akola, Parthadi tahsil Ahmadnagar dist.	Class, 10 (Schooling in Akola & Parthadi)	Agriculturist in name alone; owns 20 acres of unirrigated land but not there to cultivate it; in 1960 startd a hotel in Parthadi which ran for two years; in 1965 bought a printing press & ran a Marathi weekly	Janata Dal[70]

70. The bio-data of 517 members as collected from the members themselves constitute the basis of the present analysis of the age profile, level of educational background, the socio-economic status and so on of the members of the *Ninth Lok Sabha* compiled by Subhas C. Kashyap, secretary-general of the Lok Sabha Secretariat.

— The Ninth Lok Sabha is younger than the Eighth Lok Sabha with the average age of its members being 47.8 years as against 51.4 years in case of its immediate predecessor. In fact, in terms of average age, the present Lok Sabha is the third youngest House after the First and the Second Lok Sabhas.

In the Ninth Lok Sabha, as has been the case in all the previous Lok Sabhas, the middle-age group (41-55 years) has the largest representation.

The oldest parliamentarian is Prof. N.G. Ranga (89 years) who at present is the oldest sitting member in any legislature in the world. The youngest male member of the Ninth Lok Sabha is Mohan Bhai Delkar (27 years). The oldest and youngest female members in the House are Mrs. Sheila Kaul (75 years) and Ms. Kumari Umabharati (30 years) respectively.

— The Ninth Lok Sabha has the distinction of being the highest educated Lok Sabha ever with the largest population of educated members (74.22 percent) belonging to the category of graduates and above. The representation of graduates was the lowest in the Third Lok Sabha (32 percent).

Yet another significant feature is that it has 4.1 percent members possessing doctoral degrees, surpassing all previous Lok Sabhas. The Fourth one held the previous record at 3.7 percent.

With regard to the representation of the category of matriculates, higher secondary or intermediate certificate holders, the percentage in the Ninth Lok Sabha (20.68) remains lmost the same as in the Eighth Lok Sabha (21 percent) with only negligible increase. The lowest ever representation of 16 percent was in the Fifth Lok Sabha. A welcome development of the Ninth Lok Sabha is the lowest ever representation of under-matriculates in any of the Lok Sabhas.

— Agriculturists constitute a majority of the membership in the Ninth Lok Sabha. Their strength this time, an all time record, is 40.4 percent as against 38.3 percent in the Eighth. Only in the First Lok Sabha, this category had the lowest representation (22.5 percent).

— Next to agriculturists come political and social workers with 16.83 percent representation in the Ninth Lok Sabha. This group was at its peak in the Fourth Lok Sabha with 22.9 percent of total membership.

— Lawyers constitute the third largest occupational group (15.64 percent). In the Eighth they constituted 19.1 percent of the membership.

— The strength of teachers and educationists in the Ninth Lok Sabha is 8.71 percent as against 7.7 percent in the Eighth Lok Sabha.

— The category of traders and industrialists, which constitutes 4.36 percent of the total membership of the Ninth Lok Sabha, has registered a decline compared to the previous House (6.8 percent).

— In the Ninth Lok Sabha, there are 27 women members (5.22 percent) compared to 44 members (8.1 percent) in the previous House which enjoyed the distinction of having the largest ever representation of women members.

* * * * * *

Members of 1st to 8th Lok Sabha: data complied by Subhash C. Kashyap

— There has been a steep decline in the percentage of members in the age group of 25.30 years. The representation of this category was the highest (6.0 percent) in the First Lok Sabha and fell to 1.3 percent in the Eighth.

— The post-graduates had the highest representation of members (25.8) in the Seventh Lok Sabha as compared to 17.8 percent in the First Lok Sabha. There has thus been a steady rise in this category since the First Lok Sabha except a slight decline in the Eighth Lok Sabha with 24.6 percent.

— Next to the agriculturists come lawyers with 19.0 percent representation. In the First Lok Sabha, they accounted for 35.6 percent of the membership.

— With 8.1 percent women representatives in the Eighth Lok Sabha, this is a record, surpassing that of the Third Lok Sabha which had 6.7 percent. (It is interesting to note that the achievement in U.K., so far, has been only 4.6 percent in 1964; the U.S. Senate and House of Representatives can't compare either, though Scandinavian countries have had a relatively larger proportion of women representatives which can be explained by their history and tradition).

— Among the legislative experience of members, there are three veteran parliamentarians: the late Jagjivan Ram, Prof. N.G. RAnga and Frank Anthony. All of them were members of the Central Legislative Assembly before Independence and the Constituent Assembly. Of them Prof. Ranga has the largest legislative innings at the Centre. He entered the Central Legislative Assembly in 1930. But for a break of membership during 1971-77, he has all along been a member of the national legislature... The three members thus have the distinction of putting in 35 years each in the service of the House.

— It would seem that as many as 44 members of the Seventh and 57 members of the Eighth Lok Sabha have had ministerial experience in the Union Council of Ministers. These include two former Prime Ministers and a Deputy Prime Minister.

105 members of the Seventh and 123 of the Eighth Lok Sabha occupied ministerial positions in the state cabinets, and included 21 and 14 former Chief Ministers in the States respectively.

Table II: Political Profile Of MPs (Political Socialisation)

	Name	*Constituency*	*Political Party*	*Previous political office/ experience*	*No. of terms as MP*	*Minister: State/Centre*
1.	Shivraj V. Patil	Latur, Latur district	Congress	– Municipal councillor 1962 – President of council 1968-69 – MLA in 1972 and served as MLA till 1980	(i) 1980-84 (ii) 1984-89 (iii) 1989-91	– deputy minister irrigation, law & judiciary Maharashtra (for one year) – Speaker, Maharashtra assembly (for two years) At the Centre: – minister of state for defence (1980-82) – minister of commerce – minister of science & technology(for 3 years) – minister of civil aviation

2.	Babasahib Vikhe Patil	Kopargaon, Ahmadnagar district	Congress	– In 1961-62 contested Zilla Parishad elections (at age 28 yrs.) and won the vice president of Z.P. – Won Z.P. election 5 yrs. later but declined to become its President – Contested and won the Pravara sugar co-op. elections (the first sugar co-op. in India and established by his father) and appointed its chairman (his father was a PWP sympathiser)	(i) 1971-77 (ii) 1977-79 (iii) 1980-84 (iv) 1984-89 (v) 1989-91	
3.	Uttam Rathod	Hingoli, Parbani district	Congress	– MLA, 1957, 1962, 1967, 1978 – MLC 1972	(i) 1980-84 (ii) 1984-89 (iii) 1989-91	– minister of state for revenue, Maharashtra (1977-78)
4.	Damodar Bakru Shingda	Dahanu, Thane district	Congress	– Sarpanch of Posheri in 1978 – elected Zilla Parishad	(i) 1980-84 (ii) 1984-89 (iii) 1989-91	

contd.......

	Name	Constituency	Political Party	Previous political office/ experience	No. of terms as MP	Minister: State/Centre
				member, 1979 (His father was an active Congress worker)		
5.	Uttamrao Deorao Patil	Yavatmal, Yavatmal district	Congress	– Sarpanch of Loni, 1968 – Member, panchayat samiti in 1969 – MLA in 1978 (Digras constituency) – Z.P. member, 1979 (U.D. Patil's father was politically active, a member of the Central Provinces legislative assembly (Independent candidate) in 1952 and in 1952, MLA of Bombay state legislature (Independent candidate) & a Congress MP in 1962 and 1967 & elected to Rajya Sabha in 1976.)	(i) 1980-84 (ii) 1984-89 (iii) 1989-91	

6.	Y.S. Mahajan	Jalgaon, Jalgaon district	Congress	– A member of the Congress Party since the days of the Simon Commission – Contested the 1955 bye-election and the 1957 general election to Parliament (and lost)	(i) 1970 (bye-election, May to Nov. for six months) (ii) 1971-77 (iii) 1980-84 (iv) 1984-89 (v) 1989-91	
7.	Murli Deora	Bombay South	Congress	– Municipal corporator, 1968-78 – Mayor; chairman of All India Mayors' Council – MLC (nominated by govt. in 1982)	(i) 1984-89 (ii) 1989-91	
8.	Vasant Sathe	Wardha	Congress	– Joined the freedom movement at the age of 17 & unfurled the tricolour – Trade Union work (leader) in Vidarbha (then a part	(i) 1972 (bye-election from Akola) to 1977) (ii) 1977-79 (iii) 1980-84 (iv) 1984-89	–Cabinet minister –Minister for Information & Boardcasting (1980) – Minister for Chemicals &

contd.......

Name	Constituency	Political Party	Previous political office/ experience	No. of terms as MP	Minister: State/Centre
			of Madhya Pradesh) – Member of the Socialist Party in Congress till its merger into Congress after Lucknow Conference (1948-64); chairman of Vidharbha unit of Socialist Party	(v) 1989-91	Fertilizers (1982) – Minister for Steel, Mines & Coal (84-86) – Minister for power, energy & coal (1986-89)
9. Arvind Tulshiram Kamble	Osmanabad, Osmanabad district	Congress	– Kamble's father an M.P. in 1962 to 1977 (three terms) & President, MPCC Marathwada region – Kamble campaigned for Congress candidates for 1978 Vidhan Sabha electioons & 1979 Parliamentary election	(i) 1984-89 (ii) 1989-91	– deputy minister of industry, irrigation, rural development & transport in Babasahib Bhosale's ministry for four months in 1982

				– MLA from 1980-84 Hair constituency, Osmanabad district	
10.	Ram Naik	Bombay North	BJP	– 1969-1978–organising secretary of the Jana Sangh of Bombay North (Goregaon, Borivli, Mulund) – President, Janata Party–Bombay/Maharashtra – President, BJP for two years – MLA for three terms	1989 to 1981, his first term
11.	K.P. Bopche	Bhandara, Bhandara district	BJP	– Joined Janata Party in 1977 essentially into opposition (to Congress) politics; in school & college class representative – As Independent won Hirdamali panchayat elections in 1978 &	1989-1991, his first term

contd.......

	Name	Constituency	Political Party	Previous political office/ experience	No. of terms as MP	Minister: State/Centre
				became deputy sarpanch – On Janata Party ticket he and his panel won 6 of 12 panchayat samiti seats – On split of Janata Party in 1980, Bopche joined BJP – Won as BJP MLA in 1985		
12.	Sukhdev Nandaji Kale	Buldana, Buldana district	BJP	– For the first time joined a political party in 1982, the Congress (S) – Contested on Congress (S) ticket, M.P. elections and lost to Mukul Wasnik, All India Youth Congress President in 1984 – Joined BJP in 1986 when Cong. (I) & Cong. (S) merged	1989-91, his first term	

13.	Pandurang Pundalik Phundkar	Akola, Akola dist.	BJP		– Member of ABVP during college days, till 1976 – Jailed during Emergency for 11 months – Joined Janata Party, at its inception – In 1978, MLA from Khamgaon constituency on Janata Party ticket – In 1980 left Janata Party, joined BJP and elected MLA for the second term 1980-84 – Contested from Akola constituency MP elections and lost in 1984 – Later in 1984 also contested MLA seat from Khamgaon, Buldana dist. and lost	1989-91, his first term (defeated) Prakash Ambedkar & former Maharashtra minister, Azar Hussain; won by 1.50 lakh votes)

contd......

	Name	Constituency	Political Party	Previous political office/ experience	No. of terms as MP	Minister: State/Centre
14.	Ashok Deshmukh	Parbani, Parbani dist.	Shiv Sena	– His father was member of Y.B. Chavan's old Congress & president of the taluka panchayat but Ashok says he was never influenced by his father, was totally independent, so much so he did not take college fees. – general secretary of college student body (which agitated for and established Marathwada agriculture univesity); organised athletics meet with Akola University – In 1984 joined Congress (S) – Left Cong. (S) when it	1989-91, his first term	

				merged with Cong. (I) in 1986 – Joined Shiv Sena in 1988	
15.	Vamanrao Shivram Mahadik	Bombay South Central	Shiv Sena	– RSS member between 1936-48 – Joined Shiv Sena 1968 and became municipal councillor, till 1984, winning subsequent civic body elections – Mayor in 1978 – First Shiv Sena MLA in 1971 – 1980-86 MLC	1989-91, his first term
16.	Vidyadhar Gokhale	Bombay North Central	Shiv Sena	– RSS volunteer from school college days	1989-91, his first term
17.	Haribhau Mahale	Malegaon, Nasik dist.	Janata Dal	– Joined Congress in 1952 under the influence of Morarji	(i) 1977-79 (ii) 1989-91

contd.......

	Name	Constituency	Political Party	Previous political office/ experience	No. of terms as MP	Minister: State/Centre
				Desai & local Congress workers Beedkar & Kachrubhau Rawat – Came under Dr. Ambedkar's influence since 1956, renounced liquor, took up khadi weaving – On Congress ticket contested panchayat samiti & Z.P. of Nasik in 1962. Was Z.P. member for 15 years (till '77) – Joined Janata Party when Morarji joined it in 1977 – MLA for two terms between 1980-89 as Janata Party man		
18.	Baban Rao Dhakne	Beed, Beed district	Janata Dal	– Joined Congress party at the age of 15 and	1989-91, his first term	– minister, PWD Maharashtra

participated in the Goa Freedom Movement (His father against Congress, member of the Left Aghadi peasant front at village level and member of tahsil co-op. sangh) – In 1962 became member of three taluka committees, co-op. sales, purchase and President of Co-op. Supervising Union – In 1967 on Congress ticket became member of the Zilla Parishad – In 1969 when Congress split, he left with Morarji Desai & joined Congress (O) – In 1970 left Congress (O) – In 1972 President of panchayat samiti and member of Z.P. again, as	– minister, rural development, Maharashtra – At the Centre: appointed minister of Energy in Chandra Shekar's government in November 1990

contd.......

Name	*Constituency*	*Political Party*	*Previous political office/ experience*	*No. of terms as MP*	*Minister: State/Centre*
			Independent candidate – In 1977 joined Janata Party and became its general secretary, Ahmadnagar district – MLA in 1978 for six months and then joined Sharad Pawar's PDF govt. – In 1978 Maharashtra Janata Party president till 1980 – 2nd term as MLA in 1980 and 1981 appointed leader of opposition – 3rd term as MLA in 1985 for Janata Party and became deputy speaker (for the opposition).		

ANNEXURES

MPs Interviewed

Congress Party

1. Shivraj V. Patil
2. Babasahib Vikhe Patil
3. Uttam Rathod
4. Damodar Barku Shingda
5. Uttamrao Deorao Patil
6. Y.S. Mahajan
7. Murli Deora
8. Vasant Sathe
9. Arvind Tulshiram Kamble

BJP

1. Ram Naik
2. K.P. Bopche
3. Sukhdev N. Kale
4. P. Pundalik Phundkar

Shiv Sena

1. Ashok Deshmukh
2. Vamanrao S. Mahadik
3. Vidyadhar Gokhale

Janata Dal*

1. Haribhau Mahale
2. Baban Rao Dhakne

---

* Of the 48 MPs, the Congress has 28, the BJP 10, the Janata Dal 5, Shiva Sena 3, CPI 1, Independent 1.

Former MPs

1. Datta Samant, Kamgar Agadhi Party (See profile in Annexure-II that shows why the interests of the working class are neglected by Parliament)
2. Mrinal Gore, Janata Dal
3. Sharad Dighe, Congress

MPs from Outside the State

1. G.M. Banatwala, Indian Union Muslim League (formerly an MLA from Bombay; and resident of Bombay though he gets elected to Parliament from a safe constituency in Kerala without knowing Malayalam). His interview is included as he sheds insight into the minority question, important to Maharashtra politics as to several other states.

Annexure II

Vasant Sathe (Congress)

Structural reorganisation of the Congress Party

Sathe's grandfather Raghunath shifted from Ratnagiri in the Konkan region, where the family owned some agricultural land, to Nagpur (then the capital of the Central Provinces & Berar) as the size of the family had increased. He was educated till B.L. (a qualification acquired after matriculation) and joined the then judicial service as Munsif (civil judge).

In Nagpur Raghunath acquired some land ("eight anna share in Malguzari rights") and again became a landowner (though Sathe refers to him as "landlord") in the village of Khandala 12 km from Nagpur. Since he retired from service early, he took to farming as he had done in the Konkan. At the age of 54 he died, leaving behind eight children, four sons and four daughters.

At that time, Sathe's father Purshottam, the eldest son (though the third child) was 17 years old and in the process of completing his matriculation in Nagpur. All his brothers and sisters had yet to be married.

"My grandmother Janaki was very courageous. She told my father to stay on in Nagpur and pursue his studies while she would take care of the family in the village in Khandala", Sathe said.

Purshottam bought a small piece of land in Dhantoli, built a cottage on it. The house adjoined that of his cousin (Sathe's granduncle) who helped (economically, among other ways) Purshottam and his entire family.

Sathe's father continued his education, acquiring a B.A. and then an LL.B. In those days the most prestigious thing was to join government service, so Purshottam jointed the judicial service retiring as a District and Session Judge in 1950, the highest post an Indian could aspire to in the fading period of the raj.

All of Purshottam's brothers had by then left Khandala in search of jobs in urban areas. No one was left to tend the wheat, cotton and orange orchards in the village so the land was sold in 1944.

Politically, the Sathes—Chitpavan Brahmins, Sathe says are descendants of a tribe from Greece who made India their home before the Parsis—were Tilak's followers. Purshottam's cousin, Achyut Rao Sathe, a successful lawyer, was the right hand man of Tilak in the Vidarbha region. But it was Sathe's mother's family that was politically more active. His mother's father was a lawyer and a Tilakite from the Konkan and he sent his daughter to a co-educational school. In those days she was one of few girls to get such an opportunity. She was brought up in Pune and Nasik and was deeply influenced by Tilak. She married Purshottam shortly after completing her matriculation and Vasant Sathe was born to them on March 5, 1925.

The Sathes were considered intellectually advanced and martial. The clan got absorbed into the Santana Vedic pantheon and adopted Parsuram as their deity who was a seer as well as a warrior. Sathe's great grandfather was named after him, a spiritually inclined person who took *samadhi* in a place called Malghar in the Konkan and part of the Sathe family still lives there, which also has a family temple housing the deity Parsuram.

Sathe's childhood could not but be influenced by theTilakite philosophy absorbed by his parents during their formative years. As well as a certain strain of Hinduism.

When he was no more than three-and-a-half-years old his father would take him out for morning walks, at 4 a.m., and Sathe says he has distinct memories of them. The stars would still be in the sky and Purshottam would tell his son their names even as he related stories from the Ramayan and Mahabharat. Purshottam had imbibed a strong spiritual streak from his father (Raghunath) and grand-father (Parsuram) and during the walks Sathe would be exposed to a commentary on the Gita which was interspersed with Sanskrit slokas—both his mother and father knew Sanskrit.

Sathe's mother would chide her husband that their son was too young to appreciate Tilak and the Gita, but the father would say that no matter, an impression could be left on the mind.

On the jacket of his book is noted: "Sathe had his early education at Bhonsala Military School, Nasik and then did B.A. and LL.B. from Nagpur University. He was popular student leader and eminent orator, and practised as a leading advocate and lawyer in Nagpur. He actively participated in the freedom struggle. In the 1942 Quit India Movement, he faced a firing squad after hoisting the tricolour on the District Court in Nagpur along with other students. Thereafter he remained in the forefront of the trade union movement and progressive politics. Widely travelled all over the world, Sathe was a senior adviser to the Indian delegation to the 25th Session of the U.N. General Assembly. He has also represented India in the Human Rights Committee of the U.N. and attended the World Peace Congress in Moscow. He led the Indian delegation to the General Conference of UNESCO in 1981 at Belgrade".

But this is running ahead of events. Sathe got drawn into politics at an early age. At 17, as noted, he unfurled the tricolour as a member of the freedom movement.

In independent India he began to take an interest in the trade union movement in the Vidarbha region, then part of Madhya Pradesh. He was a member of the socialist party (1948-64) within the Congress till its formal merger with the Congress after the Conference in Lucknow. (This was the Ashok Mehta/ Chandrashekhar group; Lohia had broken away from the Congress much earlier). Sathe was at that time chairman of the Vidarbha unit of the socialist party.[71]

---

71. (a) *Morris-Jones,* Parliament in India (Pennsylvania Press, 1957): The post-independence socialist party had a triumvirate leadership: Jaiprakash Narayan, the principal personality and formerly undisputed leader of the Congress Socialist Party days, but now having abandoned Marxism for the Bhoodan philosophy and politics; Ashoke Mehta, intellectual but also organiser feeling his way towards an anti-communist doctrine of 'constructive opposition'; Ram Manohar Lohia, individualist and even eccentric, following a doggedly middle line of no compromise with either Congress or Communists. The merger with the K.M.P. added the fourth leader, Acharya Kriplani. His Gandhian radicalism has not proved wholly undigestible since the socialist leaders were already in search of a philosophic alternative to Marxism. The divergencies in the leadership which manifest themselves sharply from time to time (as at the Nagpur convention of the party in Dec. 1954, when Kriplani rather wearily resigned the Chairmanship in favour of the socialist 'elder statesmen', Narendra Dev) would have been hardly less marked in the absence of the merger.

(b) The PSP was essentially dominated by Congressmen. After the 1951 general election, the Kissan Mazdoor Praja Party, founded by those Congressmen who did not get Congress tickets, joined with the SP, which had seceded from the Congress in 1948, to form the PSP. Thus the socialists, like the Swatantra Party, were dominated by former Congress leaders. To secure an insight into the leadership other than that discarded by Congress, the communist parties and the Jana Sangh leaderships have to be examined after independence.

(c) *C.P. Bhambri & P.S. Verma,* Social Background of Seventh Lok Sabha, 1980 (Mainstream, July 4, 1981): Party affiliation of the MPs show shifts, and the Congress party seems to be the main supplier of leadership to some of

In 1972 Indira Gandhi offered him an assembly seat. He told her he was not interested in state level politics, even through she "wanted me at a later stage as a minister, and then chief minister", Sathe said. Indria Gandhi could not get him an assembly ticket because Y.B. Chavan opposed her. And Sathe was not too perturbed as he felt that he had little future in the politics of the state as "I was in their (Maratha leaders) view not born in the right caste".

Sathe had long set his eyes on Parliament since this was where policies concerning the nation were made, and he was involved in national issues. "My dream was to build a new India" remarks Sathe.

Despite the opposition of the entire Maharashtra leadership Indira Gandhi secured a ticket for him to fight the MP's bye-election from Akola in 1972. Sathe won. He has been in Parliament

---

the major parties in the country. 66.7% of the members of Congress (Urs) & the Janata Party; 47.5% of the members of the Lok Dal and 23.9% of the members belonging to the two communist parties had been associated with the Congress party in the past.

(d) *Brass & Franda*: The bastions of the democratic socialist parties have been the two great north Indian states of Bihar & Uttar Pradesh. Kerala, West Bengal & Andhra ranked 7th, 10th and 15th respectively, in terms of PSP—SSP support in 1967. There is also a considerable difference in the character of the dispersion of socialist & communist strength in the Indian states. There is a somewhat more even distribution of socialist strength than of communist strength in the states. The average vote of the communist parties in Kerala, West Bengal & Andhra is between two & three times that of the next strongest communist support state, whereas there is no similar gap between the highest socialist support states and other states. If socialist strength is more evenly dispersed, however, communist strength is greater than that of the socialist parties in their respective regional strongholds. The communist parties in Kerala & West Bengal are more powerful & better institutionalised parties than the socialist parties in Bihar & Uttar Pradesh.

(e) Fifty percent of Bihar CPI leaders compared to only 10 percent of SSP leaders have been party professionals.

(f) *Brass & Franda*: The differences between the communist & socialist parties in organisation can be summarized as follows: Authority in the communist parties tends to be concentrated at the state level and in the organisational apparatus of the party, whereas authority in the socialist parties is more diffusely distributed & weighted more in favour of the parliamentary leaders. Although all radical left parties have suffered from factionalism & indiscipline, the communist parties have emphasized the need for discipline more than the socialist parties which place a higher value on inner-party controversy. The communist parties have also had greater success in imposing discipline in so far as they have lost fewer legislators by defection.

since then, continuously for 21 years; he has won six elections though the 1989 Lok Sabha was the 5th one he had been elected to: 1972 (bye-election from Akola); 1975 (Akola); 1977 (Akola); 1980 (Wardha; Gulam Nabi Azad was recommended for Akola); 1985 (Wardha) and 1989 (Wardha).

Among the present crop of political leaders, in Congress or any other party, there are few who have held as many ministerial and cabinet posts as Sathe. He was appointed the minister for information and broadcasting in 1980 and was responsible for introducing colour television, and a network system for AIR and Doordarshan that, he claims, revolutionised the government controlled media. He has been since then the minister for chemicals and fertilizers (October 1982), steel, mines and coal (1984-86), power (energy) & coal (1986-89).

Since 1989 along with other Congress leaders Sathe has been putting pressure on the party to reorganise it from the grassroot levels. And consequently firmly establish inner party democracy. All this has been discussed in the Congress Working Committee (CWC).[72] It helped to assess the party's mood, explained Sathe and listed the issues that emerged:

---

72. (a) *Kochanek* writing about the CWC in the sixties said that as a sub-committee of the AICC, it was the highest executive authority of the Congress. In practice this means that the CWC (he refers to it as the WC) is the chief policy maker of the organisation. Second, the CWC was the chief executive of the party, with power over individual members and over sub-units in the organisation. Third, the CWC was charged with co-ordinating party-govt. relations in the states by means of a sub-committee called the Parliamentary Board. Finally, through a second sub-committee called the Central Election Board (C.E.C.), the CWC played a significant role in the selection of candidates for the national and state legislators.

Myron Weiner, India at the 1980 polls pp 43: Before 1971 the District Congress Committees (DCCs) and the Pradesh Congress Committees (PCCs) had the dominant voice in the selection of parliamentary candidates, but after the Congress split of 1971 candidate selection had been centralised in the hands of the Congress Central Election Committee (CEC) controlled by Mrs.Gandhi.

(b) *Narendra Sharma*, Cong-I—Facing Realities (1984): The zonal committee is itself a new ad hoc formation introduced in the Cong-I structure after the Calcutta plenary session. Five zonal committees are supposed to look after all organisational-political problems of the zone states. They were required to hold interviews and prepare reports on the zone PCC & work out guidelines for action. That DCCs had ceased to function in large parts of the country was known to the High Command. This was the lesson drawn at the

(i) People said Congress lost the mandate because of the weakness of the organisation at all levels. The suggestion was made that primary membership (identifiable one) needs to be established, each member given an identity card with photographs. And beginning from grassroot, elections should be held at each level to the top so that a structural reorganisation of the party takes place.

(ii) Ad hocism was eating into the party like a cancer. It needed to be uprooted.

(iii) No discussion within the party, no sharing of views. Educative camps were required to be held.

(iv) On the leadership of Rajiv Gandhi, the advice was similar to that Indira received from Vinoba Bhave "Charai Veti, Charai Veti—Chalte Raho, Chalte Raho" so as to gain knowledge from the people; that Rajiv should mingle with the people, travel by rail and car, but no helicopter hopping (From the way Rajiv is establishing direct contact with the people during his 1991 election tour, he seems to have taken the advice to heart).

The extended CWC meeting, Sathe pointed out also observed that Rajiv should shed some of the snakes around his neck put there by people like Gundu Rao and Santosh Mohan Dev. Such people

---

Congress-I defeat in Andhra Pradesh assembly elections in 1983. Not to speak of DCCs, many of even the PCCs had stopped responding to AICC-I directives.

(c) *Paul R. Brass*, The Politicization of the Peasantry in a North Indian State, Part II (The Journal of Peasant Studies Vol. 8, Number 1, October 1980): During the past three decades, the dominant party in the north Indian state of Uttar Pradesh, the Indian National Congress, has undergone a secular decline in its support in state legislative assembly elections. The principal factor in its decline has been its inability to establish a stable basis of support among the middle peasantry, particularly among the so called 'backward castes' with landholdings ranging from 2.5 to 30 acres. Disaffected from the Congress since the 1950s, these middle proprietory castes, who together form the leading social force in the state, turned in large numbers to the BKD, the agrarian party of Chaudhuri Charan Singh in its first appearance in UP elections in 1969. They also provided the central core of support for the Janata party in its landslide victory in the 1977 state assembly elections. The politicization of the middle peasantry in this vast north Indian province is no transient phenomenon, but rather constitutes a persistent factor with which all political parties & all governments in UP must contend.

tendered bad advice. They should be banned even as those astrologers who gave wrong advice.[73]

The key suggestion of the CWC was that Congress should not bother to seek power until it has re-organized from the base upwards and the structural transformation had strengthened it.

Obviously, this suggestion made in 1990, has not been implemented for the Congress was fighting to get back to power within a year (i.e. in 1991), without the reorganisation. (However, to some extent the re-organisation had taken place. As one observer noted: "The process of holding of organisational elections initiated in 1990, which were postponed by its president, Rajiv Gandhi because of the Lok Sabha mid-term poll, May 1991, has enabled the Congress (I) to fill its coffers with membership fees running in crores of rupees"- K.S. Saxena in *The Pioneer*, Lucknow edition, of April 10, 1991).

Sathe mentioned that Rajiv knew (in 1990) that BJP would try to seek power within the year; that the V.P. Singh-BJP alliance thus could last only that long. Even so, the Congress Party's approach would be not to seek power (for five years so as to ensure structural reorganisation) even as the parliamentary party machine was strengthened.[74] (As noted, the compulsions of politics have decreed otherwise.)

---

73. Sathe observed that one of the unhappy characteristic of Congress culture was sycophancy and no one could beat a Congressman at that. Rajiv, he felt, had a number of Congressmen telling him "No one like you Rajivji" and this may put him off track and Congress Party re-organisation could again be shelved.

74. (a) *R. Kothari*, Voting In India (EPW Feb. 1973): There is a shift from the politics of manipulation of voters by party organisational machines to a type of politics in which the direct appeal of parties and poltical personalities, the election campaign, and the issues at stake will play a major role.

(b) *Ram Joshi & Kiritidev Desai*, (EPW Feb. 1973): After an interval between 1967 and 1971, there has been a re-emergence of one party dominance, though this does not quite amount to the restoration of the old familiar model. This new version of one party dominance faces several strains and challenges arising mainly from failures in competitive mechanics, in economic performance and in party-building. Given these problems, and in view of the changed national context and goals, how long will this remain functional for Indian politics.

(c) *R. Kothari*, Politics in India (1970): ... the arena of power is not limited to a ruling oligarchy or an aristocracy of birth; it is increasingly being spread to society as a whole by drawing new sections into its ambit. This differentiates the Indian case both from the European case where, during

At the time of the interview with Sathe (April 13, 1990), the Congress parliamentary machine was functioning effectively. The Shadow Cabinet met regularly deciding what issues could be raised, even as the Congress Forum has been set up, and another one by Anand Sharma and Tariq Anwar. (Sathe said that during his younger days there was the Nehru Forum and the Socialist Forum within the party and he was a member of both).

He mentioned that in the Shadow Cabinet he held the portfolios of industry and agriculture (Presumably Narasimha Rao, N.D. Tiwari, V. Shiv Shankar, R.K. Dhawan, M.L. Fotedar, V.N. Gadgil held the other key posts). Sathe said that among the B team were Harish Rawat, Kumaramangalam and M.J. Akbar.

Vasant Sathe: Write-up prepared by his office

He joined the Congress Party in 1964 and since then he took active part in the activities of the Congress. He was associated with various committees of the party at the State and Central levels. He is at present Member of All India Congress Committee, Vice-President of Maharashtra Congress (I) Committee, Member of Maharashtra State Congress (I) Parliamentary Board, Special Invitee to the All India Congress Committee's Working Committee and till recently President of Vidarbha Region Congress (I) Committee.

Shri Sathe was first elected to the Lok Sabha in 1972 from Akola Constituency (Maharashtra) with a thumping majority. He was again elected to the Lok Sabha in 1977 from Akola and was elected Deputy Leader of the Party.

As a trade unionist, Shri Sathe functioned as President of Madhya Pradesh Textile Worker's Federation (1956-60), President of Vidarbha Textile Federation (1960-65) and Member of Vidarbha Productivity Council.

Shri Vasant Sathe was appointed a Cabinet Minister incharge of the Ministry of Information & Broadcasting in Smt. Indira

---

the phase of rapid industralisation and social change, political participation was confined to the upper classes of society, and from the revolutionary experiments of communist and non-communist varieties where, barring intra-party feuds and military coups, political competition was generally not allowed to interfere with the process of development.

In India, politics is neither suppressed nor confined to a small aristocracy. On the contrary, politics provides the larger setting within which decision-making in regard to economic development and social change takes place.

Gandhi's Cabinet on 14.1.1980. During his stewardship of the Ministry, a number of important projects were conceived and executed for the improvement of the services of the media, such as introduction of colour transmission of Television, increasing the number of TV Centres/Relay Centres from 20 to 41 so as to cover all State Capitals and far-flung areas, networking of TV centres with a common National Programme, infusion of professional expertise in the working of official media, such as Films, Films Censorship, Children's Film Society, TV programming, Press Information Bureau, Indian Institute of Mass Communication, etc. and involvement of the general public in the form of Tele-Clubs, etc. The Gandhi film project was also conceived and executed during this period.

In the re-shuffle of the Cabinet on September 2, 1982, Shri Sathe was given the portfolio of Chemicals & Fertilizers.

After 1984 Lok Sabha elections, Shri Sathe was inducted in the Union Cabinet as Minister of Steel, Mines and Coal. In the re-shuffle of the Cabinet on September 25, 1985, Shri Sathe was made Minister of Energy, in which position he continued till Dec. 2, 1989.

Besides attending International Film Festivals at Tashkent, etc., Shri Sathe also addressed the last Convention of Asian Indians of North America held at Chicago and also visited Hollywood.

His special interests in sports are: Cricket, Boxing, Horse-riding and Swimming. He was the Cultural Secretary of the Constitution Club for Members of Parliament for seven years. His special interests are: music, folk dances and economics. Many of his articles on political and economic topics were published in well-known journals. He is President of Badminton Association of India.

Shri Sathe has travelled widely abroad. His visits included USSR, Czechoslovakia, USA, Japan, Germany, France, Finland and other European countries. He was a senior Adviser to the Indian delegation to the 25th Session of UN General Assembly. He also represented India in the Human Rights Committee of the UN. He attended World Peace Congress in Moscow. Shri Sathe also led the Indian delegation to the General Conference of UNESCO in 1981 at Belgrade.

Shri Sathe is Married to Smt. Jayashri Sathe and has three children (son Subhash and two daughters, Smt. Suhasini and Smt. Sunita, all married).

V. S. Mahadik (Shiv Sena)

At his best as Municipal Corporator

If there is a case of a reluctant MP, it is that of Vamanrao Shivram Mahadik, who had no interest in going to Delhi but bowed to the party's dictates. A village boy, he feels comfortable only when he is directly working for the people and with the people, and openly confesses he would any day prefer to be a municipal councillor, if not that, an MLA, but no, not an MP

Born in Talere village, Sindudurg district in 1925 he studied upto class four in the village school, winning a Rs.4 government scholorship to the taluka school and stood first calss first in the Ratnagiri district matric exam.

Mahadik's first job was that of a clerk in the Mamlatdar's office on a monthly salary of Rs.18. At the age of 20 he got another clerical post in Sachivalaya (Bombay) and subsequently worked in the postal department.

Even before he found a job, he had taken to politics and "social work", as at the age of 11 years he had become a member of the RSS and with which he remained till 1948. (Another SS member, Vidyadhar Gokhale, has been an RSS volunteer.)

He left politics in 1948 and for 19 years he ran Mahadik coaching classes (the Indian Union Muslim League leader and an MP, G.M. Banatwala also conducted coaching classes in Bombay) even as he worked as a "municipal servant" between 1948 to 1967. In this period he completed his B.A. and took up law "but did not appear for the exam as my father died".

In 1967 Mahadik resigned from his job with the civic body and the following year joined the Shiv Sena. He was elected to the BMC in 1968 from Sewri which has a sizeable (Mahadik says "majority") number of Muslim voters. He was elected again in 1973, and 1978 and remained a Councillor till 1984. He was elected chairman of the BMC Improvement's Committee, the Standing Committee and Mayor of Bombay in 1978.

Even as he was a Councillor, because of his "win-ability", he was asked by his party to stand for the 1969-70 bye-election for MLA from Parel (covering Lalbaug-Sewri area). He emerged the victor, defeating a union of nine all India parties, including the communists and become the first Shiv Sena MLA.

Between 1980 and 1986 he was an MLC and held no political post until 1986 when he became an M.P. by defeating the trade union leader Datta Samant, and Rupavate, in the Bombay South Central constituency.

This is not the first MP election he has contested; on previous occasions he has lost to Bhole and latter to Datta Samant for he claims he does not have the money to contest elections that cover 7.5 lakh voters.

Rupavate filed a case against Mahadik because during the 1989 election he resorted " to evoking Hindutva communalism, and nationalism of Hindustan". Other SS candidates have also been taken to court for communalising the elections.

Rupavate did not win the case, at least till the end of the ninth Lok Sabha, but when I met Mahadik on February 25, 1990 for the interview he claimed that he wanted to be disqualified so that he could take on "less strenuous work".

He says, as he lets loose a *patang tode* fart, "Really speaking I would like to be a municipal councillor, I don't want to leave Bombay". If not that, he'd rather be an MLA as at least he would be serving the people of Maharashtra.

As an MP, eight months in the year he will have to live away from Bombay. "Mental peace is gone. Family life is upset", he says. Mahadik has five daughters. Two are married, two are working in the J. Bai Wadia Hospital, and the fifth is employed with B.E.S. & T. Of his two sons, one has a mining lease in the family village in Sindudurg district and the second one he hopes to place in a transport company where he can run a tempo. He has completed class twelve and Mahadik says that his sons did not receive a decent education because "their father is a leader".

He was dreading the thought of going to Delhi as he felt he was not equipped for the work. To be a good parliamentarian, Mahadik observes "one has to have a sea of knowledge". He finds it difficult to devote time to any particular subject because daily he meets 200 people on an average, fifty percent of whom want jobs (This seems to be major demand placed on MPs; Murli Deora too states that most people come to him for jobs). And people will continue to visit him for he has been a councillor for 16 years and an MLC for eight. He is after all *"Maji Amdar hai"*.

His record as a people's representative is impressive. Hutment dwellers in Sewri and other places have been provided the basic amenities. As vice-chairman of the housing board for six years, he looked after the needs of his constituents. He is requested often to be personally present at the police station so as to prevent the victim from receiving a hammering.

The police listen to Mahadik since he helps them and their children. Even with regard to land problems, he is able to assist since he sends a chit to the Shaka Pramukh (head of the SS organisation) in the village and the work gets done.

Mahadik says he can't turn his back on such people, which he will have to once in Delhi, and who come from outside his area as well. "Sometimes from different states, like U.P.", he remarks.

He is famous for the medical services he is able to make available. Living in an area which has a cluster of hospitals—K.E.M.,Wadia, Orthopaedic hospital, Cancer hospital—Mahadik secures admission to them for the poor. For this he raises money from the MPs' fund, the CM's fund, the Lion's Club; in the main for heart operation whose cost is beyond the means of the average constituent.

Even as he talks he is issuing character certificates to people who come with various demands, such as passport identification, job and so on: A lame fellow, who wants to take care of a public telephone booth from MTNL, acquires one. "Some come to ask for a wheelchair, other items for the handicapped and I issue the requisite document", and adds "I don't take a penny", whereby the three people who have squeezed into the foyer/visitors' room-cum-office at his residence in Chamar Baugwalla Street in Merwanjiwadi in Parel, nod solemnly.

On SS ideology, Mahadik is keen to express himself. In the early phase, SS was intent that the Marathi speaking people, the sons of the soil, "should be saved", by being provided 80 percent of the facilities available, i.e. they should be given priority over outsiders. Then SS focussed on fighting injustice, all types of it, for the downtrodden. The latest objective/focus is to provide water, food, clothes, shelter. It also makes available various social services through blood banks, medical banks, organises balwadis for children, sports for the youth as well as library facilities and study groups.

"We should not be selfish, we should be self-sufficient", reminds Mahadik pointing out that Shiv Sena's central concern is developing patriotism.

He says that the SS appreciates that the states were created on a linguistic basis (i.e. each state should continue its tradition, culture, history, social life, language) but the problem arises because of the constitutional right to *mobility*, which is fine but its impact on the sons of the soil can be harmful, as in the case of Marathi-speaking people in Bombay who have been denied jobs; outsiders (those from other states) should flourish in their areas, but they ought to be allowed to take up no more than 20 percent of the jobs.

If there is a clash, as in a border region over language, priority should be given to the mother tongue than to the state language, followed by the national language and fourth (last) English—this relates to schools and the administration. He calls this the fourth language formula and has suggested that it be implemented in the Belgaum-Karwar area where the dispute has been simmering for the last 33 years.

His maiden speech on the issue in the House (Legislative Council) was on the border issue on which he spoke for 10 minutes. He observes there are two main types of speeches, those delivered in the streets and those in the House. In the streets, he claims he has spoken to an audience of 10,000, 1,00,000 and more, and people have listened to him in pin drop silence; he cites the example of his speech when Balasahib (Thackeray) was attacked while he was helping Congressman Ramrao Adik. In the House, he recalls, he created a record when he spoke for six hours on the budget. Another record was set when Mahadik paid homage to a Sanskrit scholar in Sanskrit. His other maiden speech as an MLC for 12 minutes asking for entry to temples for one and all "was so good the speaker forgot to ring the bell".

That's V.S. Mahadik for you.

K. P. Bopche (BJP)

Obeying the party's commands

Unlike Dhakne, Rathod and others, who entered politics while still in school, K.P. Bopche took to it after his midtwenties. For he was involved in his medical practice.

He completed primary school from his village Hirdamali in Goregaon taluka, Bhandara district; till matric he was in the school at Goregaon. He completed his pre-university in Biology from a college in Gondia city in 1969. He took another five years to acquire a DSB, a diploma in homeopathy and bio-chemistry from Nagpur University.

Dr. Bopche had three dispensaries: one at his home at Hirdamali, one at Gankhera and a night dispensary at Karanja. Till 1977 when he joined the Janata Party, the only election he had fought was for the post of class representaive at school and pre-university days. While managing his practice (1974-77), he had got marginally involved in what he called "opposition politics", which was essentially opposing the Congress. He had not joined any party as PSP in the area was defunct; Jana Sangh had fought there in the past; neither sakha nor sangh existed.

In the gram panchayat elections of Hirdamali in 1978, Bopche and his panel opposed the Congress panel as Independents. Out of nine members, five were Independents who appointed an adivasi lady as sarpanch and Bopche became deputy sarpanch.

Within six months, another election, that of panchayat samiti was held; on this occasion Bopche and his panel stood on the Janata Party ticket and won six out of the 12 samiti seats. The rest went to the Congress. Bopche lost the toss and the chairmanship of the Goregaon panchayat samiti went to a Congressman.

The Janata Party broke up in 1980, Bopche joined the BJP and the same year contested the MLA election and lost by 1,100 votes to the sitting Congressman, Girija Shankar Singh. In 1985, again on a BJP ticket he contested the election and defeated the "millionaire bidi king", Prafullabhai Patel.

As an MLA, he utilised fully the annual Rs. 17-20 lakh *amdar* fund to build roads: "we did not have any even to walk on"; electricity was not available in 50 percent of the villages, now all have them; and drinking water was provided.

In 1989 Bopche contested the MP election. As noted, like Mahadik and others, he is a reluctant MP. He would have preferred to be an MLA but his party told him to stand as an MP candidate and being a good soldier (as most BJP members are), he obeyed.

Bopche has identified the projects that can be taken up with the Centre to benefit his constituents. They are the usual ones that have been listed elsewhere:

— Railway line: the narrow gauge to Bhandara district, Jabalpur-Gondia Chandrapur, is to be converted into a broad gauge

— Work in many forest tracts has come to a standstill because of the Forest Conservation Act

Dr. Bopche's constituency is unusual in so far as there do not appear to be a significant number of Maratha voters; at least Bopche does not list them in the electoral profile:

OBC (comprising Kunbi, dhangar, mali)	—	25 percent
Povar (Bopche's caste; also OBC)	—	20 percent
SC	—	30 percent
ST	—	20 percent
Muslims	—	1 percent

Bopch's political socialisation may well have taken place after he began to practice medicine. For his family members were not into politics. His father was a gram sevak who owned 20 acres in Hirdamali. This has been divided between the three sons.

Baban Rao Dhakne (Janata Dal-S)

Creating history

B..R. Dhakne is perhaps the only Janata Dal MP who has been a minister at the state level as well at the Centre. He got drawn to politics, while at school and created a bit of a furore — he thinks he created history — in the state assembly when he jumped onto the floor of the House from the visitors' gallery to protest against the neglect of his region.

Dhakne's father was a farmer with about 50 acres (This has been distributed among the three sons, of whom Baban Rao is the eldest; he has received 20 acres of unirrigated land). His father was against the Congress at that time, and a supporter of the Left Aghadi, a peasant front, at the village level and a member of the taluka co-op. society. He is now in his late eighties.

On completing primary schooling at Akola village, Dhakne came to the tahsil town Pathardi to attend the secondary school in 1948. He came under the influence of the Congressman M.Niharle, who went to jail during the freedom movement and later became an MLA. Dhakne was staying in the student hostel he had set up for the village youth.

In 1951, Dhakne ran away in anger from the hostel — something that he repeated several times subsequently — because the superintendent beat him. Travelling ticketless he arrived in Bombay and the same day he left for his brother's place in Delhi. He had heard that Pandit Nehru loved children and so he landed up at his bungalow past midnight and was given a place to sleep under a tree in the compound.

He woke to find Panditji strolling in the garden and running towards him fell at his feet. On discovering that he was from Ahmadnagar where he had served a term in prison, Nehru put Dhakne in the care of Vijayalaxmi Pandit, and C.D. Deshmukh, then the finance minister and a Maharashtrian who was able to communicate with the runaway in Marathi and learn his full story.

Deshmukh put him in touch with Kakasahib Gadgil then staying at Jantar Mantar Road. Comfortable with the Marathi ambience of the household, Dhakne lived there for a fortnight. Gadgil gave him a letter to G.D. Tapase (the then minister of welfare in Bombay state) with whose help Dhakne got admitted to a school and hostel in Pune (then Poona).

Within a year he had returned to Pathardi and while in the 10th standard, left school again to join those fighting for the liberation of Goa. Senapati Bapat was there in the front ranks — "he was my leader" says Dhakne — and the veteran freedom fighter Shrubhau Limaye who fought alongside Raosahib Patwardhan. During the *sangarsha*, Dhakne got beaten up, sustained a head injury and fractured his hand. He never returned to school.

He is a hostel man. After he marrried in 1957, his father asked him to return to the village and taken up farming. Instead he left his wife there and began to stay in a hostel in Pathardi where he began organising the student wing. In 1960 he opened a hotel in Pathardi which he ran for two years.

In 1962 he took to full-time politics and stood for the election to the Agricultural Produce Cooperative Marketing Committee. He was elected and the same year he became a member of the taluka sale-purchase co-op. sangh and President of the taluka co-op. supervising union, a powerful body.

As a full time Congress worker he began organising morchas (at the drop a hat) and got used to the idea of having to go to jail.

In 1965 he bought a printing press in Pathardi and ran a weekly Marathi paper *Ganarajya*, which Dhakne says is still being printed, though not so regularly now.

He became a member of the Zilla Parishad in 1967; he was the sole Congressman, the three other Z.P. members were communists.

For some time Dhakne had been taking an interest in the plight of agicultural labourers in paticular the sugar workers, the largest group. His tahsil being a scarcity area, they lived in villages without water, roads, electricity. He launched an andolan and when it did not have the desired effect, he decided to pay the state rulers a visit. He went to the assembly, threw pamphlets from the gallery highlighting the condition of the workers. And, to everyone's surprise, he jumped into the well of the House.

This was the first incident of its kind in India and under the privileges committee rules he was penalised, being put in jail for seven days.

On this release, V.P. Naik then the chief minister, invited him for a discussion and offered to help his tahsil. He was as good as his word. Six months later he visited it, and sanctioned funds for the the provision of roads, electricity and even small irrigation projects, some of which he inaugurated.

Dhakne attempted to improve the educational facilities. There are two schools now, which have as many as 2,000 students each.

In 1969, the Congress split. Dhakne left with Morarji Deṣai, who along with the old guard set up the Congress (O). In this study we have another MP who owned personal loyalty to Morarji: Haribhau Mahale, the Janata Dal M.P. from a scheduled tribe constituency.

In 1970, the Cong. (O), Dhakne felt, was not functioning well, so he left it and continued to work for the tahsil without joining any party. The 1971 drought saw him leading agitations to provide employment. As many as 68,000 labourers, a record number, were provided jobs in the tahsil. Thanks to local level plans, they created productive assets such as drinking water wells and percolation tanks. These are in use to this day. Nala bunding works implemented ensure that monsoon water is absorbed by the fields. Roads and electric connections were made available to every village.

In 1972 Dhakne and his team stood as Independents for the zilla parishad elections and all four won. They also captured the panchayat samiti which has eight members. Dhakne became the President of the panchayat samiti.

During the course of his work for the tahsil that is drought-prone, Dhakne realised that if a week's supply of water from the big irrigation projects was periodically directed to the scarcity affected areas, they would be transformed. In 1976/77 he and his followers were instrumental in launching andolans to attain this objective and Dhakne and some others were put behind bars. Subsequently, S.B. Chavan accepted the demand and accordingly policy changes were introduced in relation to the big dams so that small farmers from scarcity areas gained.

Dhakne took up the sugar workers issue once again in 1977. The andolan drew attention to the neglect of the lakhs of sugarcane labourers, the cane cutters who migrated to work in the co-operative factories and received a shabby deal. He highlighted their economic demands, as also the educational needs of their children since these alone could provide them an opportunity to escape from the fate of their fathers.

In 1977 Dhakne joined the Janata Party when it was inaugurated and became its general secretary for Ahmadnagar district. The following year he was elected on its ticket to the assembly. A year later, when the second Congress split occurred, under Sharad Pawar's PDF government he was appointed a minister of state for the PWD. In 1979 he became minister for rural development and retained that portfolio till 1980 when the PDF government was dissolved and Congress came back to power.

In the internal elections of the party, Dhakne continued to climb the ladder. In 1978 he contested the post of the President and defeated Bapusahib Kaldate (Till '78 the President was nominated). He remained the Janata Party's state unit President till 1980.

That year he was re-elected as an MLA and in 1981 became the leader of the opposition in the Maharashtra assembly (enjoying a cabinet minister's rank). He also was a member of several committees including those for Panchayati Raj and Public Sector Undertakings. Till 1985, for three years, he was the Janata Party leader in the assembly.

In 1985 he was again elected to the assembly. Three years later he became deputy speaker for the opposition, a post reserved for members of the opposition.

For the 1989 MP contest Dhakne shifted to Beed constituency as he had done work for sugar cane cutters there: this constituency adjoins Pathardi. As a member of Janata Dal (S), he was appointed minister of energy.

Dhakne is among the few politicians whose career we have looked at, who adopted the agitationist path to politics. And this approach appears to have paid dividends.

Uttam Rathod (Congress)

Denied a ministerial berth

Until the induction of Baban Rao Dhakne (who became a minister in Chandra Shekhar's government) Rathod had been the only member in Parliament for a decade belonging to the Vanjaris, a de-notified ex-criminal nomadic tribe. His father was a social reformer, "a man with a vision", who started a school to educate the Vanjaras (and the Gond tribals), a revolutionary step. And he paid from his pocket for this facility.

Rathod's mother was equally progressive. To jolt the women out of those traditional ways that kept them bound to superstition, she sought to change their ways. One of them was to get rid of their way of dress, the *ghagara* and amulet. She set the trend by donning a Maharashtrian sari.

Rathod's father was a *zamindar* with 2,500 acres of land in Mandwi, Nanded district and two ginning factories. The land has been distributed between his five sons and three cousins, and the rest has gone under the ceilling law and Rathod has got 46 acres of unirrigated land.

His father, with the psychology of a *zamindar*, felt that the village (Mandwi) school would not be able to instil discipline in him so Rathod was sent to a school in Yavatmal which he left after completing matric and graduated from Hislop College in Nagpur; from Nagpur University he acquired an M.A. in politics, as well as an LL.B. in 1953.

After practising as a lawyer between 1953 and 1958, he gave up law to devote himself to full-time politics.

Since school days he had been involved in the student Congress, the official organ of the Congress Party before Independence, and through it the freedom movement at the district level in Yavatmal, Vidarbha region. From 1944, Rathod began to concentrate on constructive work and went to Sevagram to see what village development involved. This phase lasted till 1952 when the General Elections were held and politics underwent a complete change.

Rathod was offered the assembly ticket in 1957 from Kinwat assembly constituency in Nanded district (in the then Bombay state). He won, as also in the subsequent assembly elections of 1962 and 1967.

In 1972 he was given a Vidhan Parishad (MLC) seat; because of seat adjustment the MLA ticket went to someone else.

In 1978, Rathod was elected to serve a fourth term as MLA from Kinwat. Next year, he was offered the MP ticket from Hingoli parliamentary constituency which includes three talukas of Parbani district and three of Nanded. He accepted, and won with a margin of 1,18,000 votes. He won the 1984 election by 1,36,000 voters and 1989 won by 71,000 votes.

Some of his contributions as an MP have been noted in the section 'Impact On Policy'. Let us glance through what he considers he was able to achieve after having been an MLA "for over two decades".

Kinwat in the fifties was a tribal area with few amenities. Now it has asphalted roads, complete electrification (by 1977). In 1957, the area had one middle school, now there are 13 high schools, more than 150 primary schools, an ITI, an arts, science and commerce degree college, and even a blind school being run in a village.

Rathod says that MLA is more powerful "but I am not after power, at least not government posts". He gets the job done by instilling in the people the desire to work for themselves. As a consequence of this approach

(i) an airstrip has been constructed
(ii) a hospital (sanitarium) has been built
(iii) a natural and historical museum displaying"our inheritence" has been set up in Mahur, Kinwat tahsil, Nanded district, not far from Yavatmal.

Whatever his contributions at the state level, where he made it as a minister, he has not been given any ministerial post during the decade he has been in Parliament. This may be because, as he says, he does not want government posts. But it is more likely that from Maharashtra itself there are several other politicians whose claims cannot be ignored: S.B. Chavan, Vasant Sathe, Shivraj Patil. Then there is V.N. Gadgil (Narasimha Rao, though elected from Maharashtra, is an Andhra man). Presumably, among the MPs interviewed for this study, Vikhe Patil and Y.S. Mahajan could make a stronger case for a ministerial berth than Uttam Rathod who is unfortunate in so far as he does not belong to the "right" caste, though as the names of the Maharashtra ministers in Delhi shows this is not as much a handicap as it is in state politics. He won from his constituency because it has a large tribal population. The constituency break-down of his 9.50 lakh voters is SC 2 lakhs, ST 1 lakh, Vanjari[75] 70,000/80,000, Muslims 1 lakh, OBC 2 lakhs and Marathas 2 lakhs (he does not appear sure of the number of OBC and Maratha voters). Presumably the SC, ST and minority votes are garnered by Rathod. During the time of interview Rathod was one of the secretaries of the Congress Party whose function was to liaise between the hierarchy and the lower ranks, and lay the ground for them to speak in Parliament, and so on.

Haribhau Mahale (Janata Dal)

Influenced by Ambedkar

On a fateful day 35 years ago, Haribhau Mahale renounced alcohol and vowed that he would not wear mill made cloth, but don only khadi.

No, he had not come under the influence of a Gandhian leader. But of Babasaheb Ambedkar. Mahale had gone to listen to him at a meeting in Nasik which Ambedkar was addressing in support of the Ram Mandir satyagraha (to which he had been invited by the then MP, Bahurao Krishanrao Gaikwad).

Belonging to the Konkana tribe, Mahale was teaching in a tribal area (in 1956 the *ashram shala* exclusively for adivasis had not been set up) and as is the case among adivasis, drinking was a way of life. A brew made of mahua is commonly consumed, but as the

75. Vanjaris are a denotified tribe (in 1960 they were denotified) in Maharashtra but in U.P. they are listed as OBC, Karnataka as SC; they are still tribals in Andhra Pradesh.

tree bearing this fruit/flower has grown scarce, illicit stills in tribal areas manufacture liquor which contains a chemical.

As a teacher, which Mahale maintains is a "pavitra profession", he felt he should take a lead in curbing a widespread habit that had caused much harm to his people and kept them within the clutches of poverty.

Mahale who represents a reserved (tribal) constituency like his fellow adivasi MPs (Shingda, for instance) speaks mainly Marathi and Hindi. He knows no English though other adivasi representatives may have a working knowledge of it. Mahale, however, is more articulate than most of them

Born in the village of Ware (Dindori tahsil, Nasik district) he went to the village school where he says he completed the "vernacular final" and attended secondary school at Wani but did not complete matric.

On leaving school, aged about 16 years, Mahale took to farming. His father had died when he was no more than six months old. He had left to him and his brother 25 acres each in Ware.

He gave up farming to teach at the primary level; he also took adult education classes, or night schools. Apparently he made a bit of a mark in this sphere for he says that government officials and other visitors who had occasion to observe him at his chosen vocation would remark "If more teachers like Harishankar (Mahale) existed, the country's future would be in secure hands".

Mahale taught school for four years and left it when he entered the cooperative field, which he says he did because it would enable him to serve "more of his people". He set up 12 agricultural credit co-operatives.

In fact, when he left teaching around 1952, he joined the Congress Party. His mentors were Morarji Desai and local Congress workers Beedkar and Kachrubhau Rawat who had contributed considerably to tribal uplift in his area.

In 1962 Mahale contested the panchayat samiti election, his first one, and subsequently the Nasik Zilla Parishad election, on Congress ticket, and won. He was a member of the Z.P. for 15 years, till 1977.

When Morarji Desai (Bharat Ratna, no less) joined the Janata Party, so did Mahale "as I am his follower", he says with pride.

Mahale contested the parliamentary election in 1977 on the Janata Party ticket and won.

He served a couple of terms as an MLA, between 1980 and 1989 on the Janata Party ticket before going back to Parliament in 1989.

As I asked him his preference between the Vidhan Sabha and Parliament and whom he considers more powerful of the two, MLA or the MP (his reactions are noted in the relevant sections), he requested that we interrupt the interview to watch the Doordarshan telecast of the popular serial *Mahabharat* (the interview was conducted on April 15, 1990). He did not have a television set so even as he summoned his wife in *ghunghat* we trooped upstairs to a neighbour's flat (Mahale had been allocated 146 North Avenue). There, on a small black and white set, we viewed B.R. Chopra's creative endeavour.

Before the conclusion of the serial I returned to Mahale's flat and got a chance to survey the surroundings. His was much like other MP quarters on North and South Avenue. The drawing (sitting) room was given over to the visitors who sleep on the diwan, the sofa sets, most of which had faded covers, and frayed in some instances. Mahale's drawing room walls did not carry even any posters; usually those of the others have at least a couple of photographs with themselves and the leaders (Congress MPs, like MLAs invariably have one of themselves with either Indira Gandhi or Rajiv, depending on their vintage). Outside the flats were rows of chappals and shoes, as visitors took them off before meeting their elected representative (See the section 'Lifestyle' in the Introduction).

Babasahib Vikhe Patil (Congress)

Kicked upstairs

Babasahib Vikhe Patil has spent over 20 years in Parliament which makes him among the seniormost legislators interviewed for this study since he joined the fifth Lok Sabha at its inception while Vasant Sathe entered it during the 1972 bye-election. And as for Y. S. Mahajan, though he became a member of the fourth Lok Sabha at its fag end, he did not get elected to the seventh Lok Sabha because of the Janata Party wave (or anti-Congress wave, if you prefer).

Does Vikhe Patil feel as Eliot did, while in a sombre mood, that these 20 years have been largely wasted.[76] He has spent twice

76. Twenty years largely wasted....
Trying to learn to use words, and every attempt

as long as Uttam Rathod in Parliament and yet not been rewarded with a ministerial berth; and unlike Rathod he doesn't even have the satisfaction of having made it as minister at the state (Maharashtra) level. This despite the fact that Vikhe Patil is a Maratha.

Such senior members may have felt particularly bitter when "Sanjay's goons and Rajiv's cronies" became ministers without having any legislative experience whatsoever, or political one for that matter i. e. having worked for and with a political party. At least those who have been making it to the ministerial *gaddi* in the non Congress governments at the Centre (1989-91 for one) and the states have for long been devoted party apparatchiks.

But then a minister's post isn't everything to a parliamentarian. Or is it?

Vikhe Patil's case is a good example of a man who had the potential of making a powerful regional (state) leader, but because of the animosity (jealousy) of other regional bosses, he was not allowed to stay in Maharashtra since one day he may have emerged as a challenger to the chief minister's post. He was kicked upstairs. And he has remained upstairs ever since.

Nothing novel, for this has been the practice in all the states, ever since Nehru's reign, though, as is clear from this study, it was a prestigious affair being an MP during the 1952, 1957 and 1962 Lok Sabhas.

Vikhe Patil attended primary school at Loni B.K. (Srirampur tahsil, Ahmadnagar district). Instead of going to the tahsil secondary school, he went the one at Sangamner where his mother's family was settled. His father had three wives, "the elder, my mother, and the younger", explains Vikhe Patil and his mother went to live with her parents, so he spent three years at another secondary school in Pune and a year in the Nasik military school, returning for a year to Ahmadnagar to complete his marticulation.

Is a wholly new start, and a different kind of failure
.... And so each venture
Is a new beginning, a raid on the inarticulate
With shabby equipment always deteriorating
.... And what there is to conquer
By strength and submission, has already been discovered
.... by men whom one cannot hope
To emulate.

"I was supposed to go to college but my younger mother died, and my father fell sick". His father's friends advised him to take to farming and his plans for hinger education fell through. He had acquired a diploma in mechanical engineering in Pune and hence his knowledge of how to repair oil engines and so on came in handy for cultivating the land. His father had a 100 acres and it was distributed between two sons and two daughters.

Vikhe Patil maintains he "personally" cultivates the 30 acres (This is probable if after 6-8 months in Delhi he returns during the sowing and harvesting seasons; but these may not coincide with the Lok Sabha sessions. And what if Vikhe Patil grows more than one seasonal crop, which is most likely).

While Vikhe Patil took to farming he gradually got sucked into politics. At that stage, he came into contact with his father's associates and acquaintances. His father was an influential (and probably a powerful) man, having set up the first co-operative sugar factory, the Pravara Co-op., in Maharashtra and the country. Dhananjay Rao Gadgil (later the deputy chairman of the Planning Commission) was its first chairman — for 10 years — and his father the vice chairman who was a PWP sympathiser but not a member; "he was a pro-progressive" explains his son.

Vikhe Patil recalls that no one came to consult him on factory matters, as everyone knew that his father did not listen to him, and indeed often showed his anger towards him. As Vikhe Patil kept his own counsel "people thought I was a good boy", he says.

After 10 years of farming, the residents of the area felt he should stand for the first zilla parishad elections (1961-62) of Maharashtra. Balasahib Desai had repeatedly been asking his father to give him workers for the Congress, and his son as well.

Eventually Vikhe Patil stood on the Congress ticket at the age of 28; his father objected saying there would be no one to look after the land and the factory. In fact his father announced that his son was contesting the election against his will. Vikhe Patil won and was appointed vice-president of the Z.P. shortly thereafter.

Since then he has been in politics.

Five years later he again contested the Z.P. elections, and won. It was suggested he become the president, but he declined (On both occasions he received more votes than the man who became the president).

Vikhe Patil got drawn into the Pravara Co-op. elections. He was not initially interested, but those who were elected did not enjoy the confidence of the general body. Hence in 1964-65 he stood for the co-op. election, won it and was appointed its chairman. The communists, who had opposed the Vikhe Patil group, were also inducted on to the panel irrespective of party affiliations and ever since they have worked together with Vikhe Patil and managed the factory.

Vikhe Patil's father submitted his resignation when candidates belonging to political parties (the communists and Congressmen) made inroads into the co-op. He had all along been against politicians controlling the co-operative.

His son was not, and in fact, Vikhe Patil began directly to deal with the communists and in 1968 S.A. Dange and he became associates.

In 1971, he stood as a member of Parliament for the Kopargaon constituency, Ahmadnagar district, one which has long had a communist presence and has indeed produced several leaders (See footnote 9). Initially Vikhe Patil was not the Congress candidate. When he withdrew, unwilling to fight the communists, Vikhe Patil moved into the ring, and won. And has been the Congress candidate ever since winning in 1977, 1980, 1984 and 1989. He states "I've never lost a single election in my life".

And perhaps it is this faith in him of the electorate that frightened the state Maratha leadership. Not only his popularity "but my father's background, and I being known as a man of principle and a good organiser" enabled the powerful political bosses to come together and send him to Delhi.

He has held several Maharashtra party posts but has never been an MLA which he was keen on becoming. And not because he was set on obtaining a ministerial berth in Maharashtra, though during Y.B. Chavan's days "no one wanted to be MLA, but minister straightaway was their aim".

In fact, in 1971 when he contested his first election to the Lok Sabha, the intelligence report stated that Vikhe Patil would not win. So much for intelligence reports.

Datta Samant (Kamgar Agadhi Party)

Legislators ignore workers' issues

Datta Samant, a trade union leader who has been in politics for the last 25 years, has the image of a man who is responsible for labour violence, strikes and factory closures. An erroneous image, Samant believes, for his focus is to keep factories going so that the workers, whose interests he upholds, are not thrown out of jobs.

But it is a popular image. When the Shiv Sena supremo Balasahib Thackeray at a public rally introduced Samant as a man who closes factories, there was thunderous applause. For that represented to the workers, the common man, that one of them, (their leader) had the strength to take on the mighty capitalists, and if need be teach them a lesson.

Undeniably, Datta Samant is the most powerful trade union leader unaffiliated to any political party. Claims are made that with a membership of 15-20 lakh workers, Samant has the biggest union. Some of thee major ones under his control are Premier Auto and Crompton Greaves; he takes on the cause of the smaller unions to such as that of the Race Course (Mahalaxmi, Bombay) employees, and the buffalo owners.

So Samant wields power. So do other trade union leaders. Where has that got the workers? No where. Or hardly anywhere.

And that is Samant's grouse, his intense pre-occupation, though he is not an intense man, a soft-spoken semi-bald gent in his early fifties, may be late forties, somewhat fleshy but not plump. As he points out, 44 years after Independence there is still no law in the country providing for workers' share in the company's profits despite repeated pronouncements to this effect by all and sundry, in the government and out of it. There is no wage policy. All the labour laws are out-dated and confused.

Samant's agony is that as a labour leader in Parliament and the state assembly he could do next to nothing to better the lot of the working class. Though he has tried. And tried.

During the 17 years he has been an MLA, he repeatedly raised working class issues, but no one else appeared to be interested in supporting him on them. And all that the media focuses on is strikes and violence which his unions have occasionally had to resort to. These build up his image as a violent man and Samant is not averse to it; as he says it has helped him to get his work done.

In Parliament as well, other legislators have not been supportive of labour welfare measures that Samant says he has tried to take up. No wonder that during the 40 odd years Parliament has functioned workers issues such as, for instance, the plight of contract labourers has not once been even raised. If the politicians have the will, they can ensure the implementation of the minimum wages act, and this alone will benefit the 15 crores unorganised labourers (organised labourers are around 5 crores) of whom 10 crores live below the poverty line. Samant took up this issue with Rajiv Gandhi when he was prime minister, pointing out that if the minimum wage law is implemented, 50 percent of the poverty would be reduced. As a major trade union leader, Samant says he can achieve this for some workers, but fighting poverty is the government's job, an issue over which it continues to slumber. True, as a result of Samant's persistence, Rajiv Gandhi appointed a committee to study the problems of unorganised labour (Later V.P. Singh, under Samant's influence began promoting workers' participation in management). But to what purpose if Parliament is uninterested in ensuring that these issues are implemented and to begin with formulate laws towards that end. "What to speak of such new legislation", says Samant "existing schemes that seek to benefit the workers are set aside". The Fourth Pay Commission Report dealing with 80 lakh workers was not discussed in Parliament. Let alone the Congress, even opposition parties did not raise the subject.

The speaker told Datta Samant who wanted to take it up "How can I allow a discussion on the basis of a single man's request. No one else appears to want to participate in it".

The neglect of workers' issues is also because of the lack of people representing their interests in Parliament. The specific labour representation, i.e. those MPs who represent a particular type of working class issue, is zero. And those like Datta Samant who want to take up major labour schemes, are negligible in number. For those who have been elected to represent labour are members of unions of various political parties, and they bow to party wishes, and the party is not concerned with labour welfare.

The political party uses the union to (i) collect funds (through their members and industrialists) and (ii) to gather people to political (public) rallies. As such the trade union movement (i.e. linked to political parties) has become weak and is unable to obtain from the industrialists

(i) fair wages
(ii) security of jobs for the workers
(iii) bonus

In the circumstances, Samant's regret is his inability to convert his working class followers into a political force, for if it had become one, lot could have been done for the welfare of the workers. That workers' plight has not become a political issue is a frustrating experience for independent labour leaders like Samant.

Samant says that other independent labour groups are emerging even as his continues to attract more members who give him presents —he was given a new Fiat car — but don't give him support. Politics, religion and caste, in the workers' perception, is not linked to the trade union. Samant has sought to dispel this misreading of the power game and repeatedly told the workers that this weakness on their part has rendered him ineffective as a legislator. He has drawn their attention to the fact that each and every action unless seen in the political context, will prove infructuous. Once a factory closes, that is a political issue (RBI figures put the number of factories closed at 1,60,000 and 98 percent have been shut down by the industrialists). But the workers don't accept this.

As a consequence of the approach of political parties, the leadership of other large unions is averse to making the working class issue into a political one. Not surprisingly the working class continues to suffer. Though the workers may be aware of their exploitation, and some take out their ire on the capitalists, the trade union movement is weakening at large. For unless the workers are seen as a political force, no political party will take them seriously, and thereby reflect their interest in the legislature.

The lack of politicisation of workers has meant that even the number of their representatives, already infinitesimal, is declining. In 1989, because they did not give their full support, Datta Samant lost the parliamentary election (The Kamgar Agadhi Party has three labour MLAs but no MP at present). Of course, Samant also lost since even the women did not vote for him because of the Hindutva wave (even though Samant's is the only consituency in the country which has less women than men because workers, textile labourers, do not bring their families from the village). Samant is a Hindu from Konkan and an MBBS, he is not against religion. But he cannot and will not accept the communalisation of elections as Shiv Sena did in his area (and BJP does at a national level) he avows.

Above all, Samant laments the inability of the trade unions to transform the workers into a political force.

Bio-data of Datta Samant as presented by his party

Dr. Datta Samant was born in village Deobag in Sindhudurg District in November 1932. Son of a middle class villager, he studied upto Matriculate at Taluka, Place Malwan and upto MBBS degree in Bombay. During school and college days he used to lead the students as General Secretary. He was also captain of the team.

He started his medical practice in Industrial workers colony at Pantnagar, Ghatkopar in 1961. He was the founder of Co-operative Consumer Societies, Education Societies in the area. He was also the President of Housing Board Tenants Association. He led the first ever mass morcha of Housing Board Tenants in which the police made lathicharge. The demands of the tenants are now recognised and granted. Today there are eight small and big schools in Kurla to Bhandup under his social field and he also has been responsible for the development of many slums and hutment areas in this suburban.

In 1965 he started the Trade Union of the Stone Quarry workers, whose plight was the worst. Because of his efforts the stone quarry workers in Chandivali to Powai hills, are now getting monthly salary of Rs. 1,000/- to 1,500/- and an annual bonus of Rs. 5,000/- to Rs. 6,000/-.

He was elected to the Assembly in 1967 as independent candidate. In 1972 to 1979 he was in the Congress party and continued to be the MLA till 1985, when he got elected as Member of Parliament from South Central Bombay.

His next trade Unions were of Seimens, Premier, APT, Godrej where he had to face too much of old rivalry and the opposition from the employers and the police. In Godrej case he was charged with murder and was jailed for over one year. He was however acquitted by Senior Court.

His militancy in this case attracted the industrial workers in Bombay and other parts of Maharashtra and Gujarat.

He has the knack of negotiating with the small and big

employers who are known to be publishing false balance sheets and employers have given big wage rise through Dr. Samant's settlements.

Today he has his Union in almost all types of Factories, Shops, Stone Quarries, Buffalo Tabelas, BEST workers, Textiles Workers etc. He also has branches in almost all the MIDC areas in Maharashtra like Nasik, Jalgaon, Nagpur, Ahmadnagar, Aurangabad, Lonawala, Pune, Tarapur etc. and part of south Gujarat. After he become MP and went to Delhi, some of the workers like BHEL, Hardwar, Bhopal and other industries in Faridabad, Modinagar, etc.have been inviting him and electing as President of their internal Unions.

Dr. Samant was similarly made the leader by 2-1/2 lakhs textile workers in Bombay 1981. He led the biggest strike of these workers in January 1982. Through this movement the INTUC Union of textile workers, the Government and the Mill owners have got exposed in their collusion of corruption, election fundings and diverting the Mills' profits. Even the selling of land of the Mills has been stopped by the mass agitation of textile workers

Dr. Samant then founded Kamgar Aghadi a political party through which he himself was elected as MP and its three activists as MLAs and three others as Bombay Municipal Councillors.

He has been the main spokesman of the working class in Lok Sabha and has been instrumental in suggesting amendments to various bills on Labour Laws which have been discussed and passed.

It is Dr. Datta Samant and his large Trade Union organisation, who first supported Shri V.P. Singh and Shri Singh has also formalised his labour policies in consultation with him.

The right to work, workers real participation in the management, due share of the workers in the production and profits of a company, benefits to the workers as Bonus, Gratuity etc. beyond the ceiling in the Law have been the principles of his labour movement for which he has activated few lakh workers in his Union and Party. Today he holds the largest number of workers and still largest number in the country have an attraction and craze to hear him and know him as his way of working in Trade Unions.

G.M. Banatwala (Indian Union Muslim League)

Protecting Muslim interests

G.M. Banatwala is unique in so far as he is the only MP who discusses the role of a parliamentarian being that of resolving conflicts. Other MPs are not so much as aware of the "conflict resolution" function that they ought to perform.

Banatwala took to politics in 1959 with the "re-activisation" of the Indian Union Muslim League (IUML) in the then state of Bombay. Before that he had been involved in the student movement and general welfare activities.

He participated as a worker and polling agent in the first general election in 1952 for the Socialist candidate, the late Akbar Peerbhoy, the nephew of the Qaider-E-Azam, Mohammad Ali Jinnah. In those days the Muslim League had merged with the Congress.

Banatwala grew up in Bombay. He went to the Anjuman Islam High School of Commerce from where he completed his SSC and joined the Sydenham College. After obtaining a B.Com. and an M.Com., he took up a teaching job in the Anjuman Islam High School (in 1962). Later he acquired a B.Ed. degree.

Even as he launched on a career he contested the MLA election in 1962 from Dongri (now Umarkhadi) constituency, and was defeated by 450 votes by Mustafa Faqi, a sitting Congress candidate and a minister of state for revenue.

The school asked him to tender his resignation "as I had become deeply involved in politics", says Banatwala. He introduced coaching classes. The Banatwala & Patel Institute of Education functioned till 1977 when it was wound up.

In 1967 he was elected MLA from Umarkhadi, and re-elected in 1972 from the same constituency.

Since 1977, however, Banatwala has entered Parliament not from Bombay, but a safe seat in Kerala, the Ponnani Lok Sabha constituency. He admits he knows no Malayalam but the voters happily send him back to Delhi. He has served them during the 1980-84, 84-89 and 89-91 terms. And from all appearances, he will again be representing the Ponnani voters in Parliament.

Banatwala has been the general secretary of the IUML, Maharashtra, since 1959.

As the IUML is unlikely to win more than a couple of MLA

seats in the Maharashtra legislature, Banatwala prefers to be an MP which provides him with a better forum to represent the interests of the Muslims. As he puts it: "Parliament gives me a greater field to serve the people, to advance their cause". The "cause" being the interests of the Muslims.

"No, we are not into extra constitutional rights, no question about it. But we stand for a sincere implementation of the Constitution, the provisions relating to minority rights" says Banatwala and talks of "holding and promoting the religious and cultural identity of Indian Muslims". That too, he stresses in a "secular democracy, make no mistake IUML upholds the secular democracy of India".

He gives reasons as to why IUML, in contrast to other Muslim or secular parties, is best placed to serve the largest single minority in the country, and indeed has all along been doing so.

- There is no other Muslim political organisation at the national level, active since Independence, that was represented in the Constituent Assembly and which has sent elected representative to every Rajya Sabha and Lok Sabha Since 1952.
- The Ittehad-ul-Muslimeen of Hyderabad (Andhra Pradesh, if you like) has sent representatives to Parliament; but it has lacked continuity and its strength is confined to a couple of pockets in the capital of Andhra Pradesh. Whereas the IUML has not only two to five members in the Lok Sabhas and the Rajya Sabhas, but representatives in several state assemblies. Even now it has an MLA in Maharashtra, Karnataka and West Bengal Vidhan Sabhas. And in 1969-70, in coalition with the Indian National Congress the IUML had seven MLAs, of whom three were appointed ministers, in West Bengal, "a border state".
- The Indian Majlis is confined to U.P. And it has come up relatively recently. It had one member in Parliament from Allahabad during the Janata regime, but then the Indian Majlis merged its identity with the Janata Party.
- The IUML, which is not a regional party, has been in power in Kerala first with the Congress, later with the communists, for the last 14 years.
- Compared to the Congress, the IUML has smaller

representation of Muslims in the assemblies and Parliament, but it has a much better record of service with regard to the Muslim community. The Congress Muslims are "helpless, they can't raise their voice", says Banatwala.

To prove his point, Banatwala lists some of the issues that the IUML has tackled on behalf of the Muslims in India, issues that not even the Congress with its relatively larger Muslim representation has been able to handle either because of the ineffectiveness of the representatives or the secular principles of the party:

(1) IUML has ensured that the religious and cultural inheritance and identity of the Muslims is not upset. Their identity is inseparable from the Shariat (personal laws) and the IUML has vigorously protested against article 44 of the Constitution which by "directing the State to *secure* a common civil code negates the personal law of all communities", maintains Banatwala. As a result of the persistent protests the IUML was able to obtain "a historical commitment" from Nehru that there will be no interference with the Muslim Shariat, unless so desired by the Muslims.

(2) The Income Tax Act was changed so that all Trusts including Muslim Wakfs that had acquired property since 1971 were required to sell it and invest in prescribed government securities. This would mean that the Wakfs would begin to earn an interest. And this is prohibited by Islam: that Wakf activities be financed by interest was "totally unacceptable" and the IUML protested. As a consequence, the provision was amended to allow investment in properties. The then finance minister and the present President of the country, R.Venkatraman, said that the amendment was introduced because earning interest is prohibited by Islam.

(3) The IUML made it clear that the Supreme Court Judgment on the Shah Bano case was blatant interference with the Muslim personal law, the Shariat. Its leader, Banatwala moved a non-official Bill to this effect, and which remained under discussion for almost a year, creating legislative history. The government came up with the Muslim Women's (Protection of Rights on

Divorce) Bill, 1986, which allows the woman *Idat* (maintenance) for a period of three-and-a-half months from her ex-husband; thereafter the maintenance is extended by her relatives vis-a-vis the precedents laid down as per the Shariat. Hence the law reverted to the position prior to the Shah Bano case.

(4) The IUML (Banatwala) was the first party to approach the government, the then home minister, Buta Singh, and request him to impose a ban on the import and circulation of Salman Rushdie's book "Satanic Verses" in India. And the ban was imposed.

(5) With regard to the Ram Janmabhoomi issue, the IUML position is that let us have a law which stipulates that the places of religious significance, as they existed since Independence, should be protected and no further claims entertained: a temple, church, synagogue, mosque should continue to be what is was on August 15, 1947.[77]

In fact, Banatwala introduced a non official bill to this effect in the eighth Lok Sabha and if it had been taken up, Parliament would have played a conflict resolving role says Banatwala. But it failed to rise to the occasion.

The IUML has introduced several non official bills that seek to tackle the problem of unemployment and housing. Though national issues of the Muslims have been given priority, Banatwala has not neglected his constituents: development of railways and communications, among other things, have been taken up by him.

As an MLA he was all the more conscious of meeting the need of the voters. The IUML was a member of the Sampurna Maharashtra Samiti headed by D.B. Patil. Banatwala took particular interest in

77. "The Pioneer's" staff reporter in Allahabad (April 14, 1991) in a report headlined: "Congress alliance with IUML shameful, says Dr. Joshi" observes that the BJP president Dr. Murali Manohar Joshi made a frontal attack on Congress for joining hands with the Muslim League in Kerala. He said this alliance proved that the Congress "wanted that the religious premises should remain with those who possessed them on August 15, 1947, even if such possession was illegal". Charging the Congress with adopting a policy of appeasement, Dr. Joshi urged Mr. Gandhi to clarify his position as to whether he had promised to save the Babri Masjid in return for poll adjustment with the Muslim league. He said, in a desperate bid to woo the minority, Mr. Gandhi "has crossed the limits of reasonableness".

ensuring that Urdu medium schools were provided in his constituency. He adroitly handled the vexed issue of Vande Mataram, by projecting the Muslim point of view which was that whenever it is sung everyone should rise in deference to the sentiments of the people though Muslims should not be compelled to sing it. This view was endorsed by the state level national integration council headed by V.P. Naik.

Here is an example of a legislator playing the role of conflict resolution. For Vande Matram could have become an explosive issue dividing the two communities. And indeed a fierce controversy raged in the assembly. During a special sitting of the Vidhan Sabha it was decided that India being a "multiple society, lingual, cultural, religious", the sentiments of the minorities must be respected.

According to Banatwala, IUML is the only political party that is able to represent the essential interests of the Muslims. He argues that a number of Muslim leaders "believe" that their interests can be upheld, as well as promoted, through what are generally called secualr parties such as the Congress, Janata Party, Janata Dal, the communists. The IUML argues that this is a myth. According to it only an organisation of the Muslims can justly protect their interests and "safeguard them through appropriate political strategies".

Most of the secular parties (including Syed Shahabudin's Insaf Party; his Babri Masjid Action Committee, which wields considerable influence among the Muslims, is not registered as a political party) believe in a common civil code. This conflicts with IUML's belief that every minority should have its own personal law (as protected by Article 29 of the Constitution).

In relation to reservations, almost all non Muslim parties are against providing them for Muslims. The IUML seeks reservations, and has secured them in Kerala. If reservations are not anti-national in Kerala (or the interests of Keralites), IUML maintains, they cannot harm national interests either.

The demands of the IUML are the true mirror of Muslim sentiments in India, says Banatwala and observes "I don't remember IUML representatives joining hands with Muslims in the Congress. If they did so they would lose their seats".

Murli Deora (Write-up prepared by his office)

A well-heeled MP operating as a municipal corporator

Mr. Murli S. Deora, elected Member of Parliament from the prestigious South Bombay Constituency in the last Lok Sabha election, is also the President of the Bombay Regional Congress Committee (I). Appointed to this position in 1981, he is the youngest of the BRCC Presidents. He also has the distinction of having been the youngest Mayor of Bombay. Upon election as MP, he resigned his Membership of the Maharashtra Legislative council to which he was nominated by the Government in 1982.

Born and brought up in Bombay, Mr. Deora ia a graduate of the Bombay University. Even as a student, he took keen interest in social welfare and community development activities which benefited people in the city, especially the southern parts. To give definite shape to his abilities and aspiring to make important contributions to the society around him, Mr. Deora joined the Jaycee Movement through the North Bombay Jaycees. He moved up on the Jaycee rungs fast eventually to become a Vice-President of the Indian Jayceess in 1970. During this period he organised numerous useful projects which met with widespread attention in Bombay and elsewhere and saw him groom himself into a capable leader. He participated in the Jaycees' World Congress at Argentina, Holland and Japan.

The exposure to organisation work as a Jaycee and the experience he gained paved the way to his successful election as a Municipal Councillor on the Congress ticket for two successive terms from 1968 to 1978.

Mr. Deora rounded off his civic career by becoming the Mayor of Bombay after winning the Mayoral elections by the highest number of votes in Bombay's civic history. During the same year he was also the Chairman of the All India Mayors' Council.

As a Councillor, too, Mr. Deora distinguished himself with finding solutions to, and improvement in, several areas of civic working such as budgetting, etc. He took personal interest in the BMC's negotiations with the World Bank in securing substantial loans for the city's Water Supply & Sewage Disposal projects. During the same period, he was Treasurer of the Bombay Municipal Congress Party, its Deputy Leader and later, its Leader as also the youngest Leader of the House in the Municipal Corporation.

During the one year he was Mayor of Bombay, Mr. Deora launched the BMC's Save Water, Immunization Of Children and Conservation Of Energy Campaigns with considerable success and widespread appreciation.

Mr. Deora undertook visits to several Sister-Cities of Bombay as Mayor and acquainted himself with the latest civic administration and urban problems like transport, water supply, etc.

He also held several positions on Government and semi-Government controlled bodies, the most notable of them being that of a Director of the Life Insurance Corporation of India, Chairman of the Maharashtra Small Scale Industries Development Corporation and Member of the Small Scale Industries Board of the Government of India. As Chairman of the MSSIDC, he led a delegation of entrepreneurs to China.

In 1982, Mr. Deora had the honour of being invited to visit Pakistan by President Zia-ul-Haq which received widespread press coverage both here and in Pakistan. During his visits abroad, Mr. Deora has met several world leaders like Robert Kennedy, and also distinguished men like Dr. Jonas Salk.

He is a successful small scale idustrialist apart from being a Director of some companies.

As a member of Parliament, Mr. Deora is committed to making all efforts to find speedy solutions to some of Bombay's pressing problems such as tenants woes, old and dilapidated buildings, improvement in civic services and controlling pollution.

Married with two children, Mr. Deora occupies himself with a round of Bridge or a swim in his leisure hours.

Annexure-III

Select Bibliography

1. Arora, Satish K. : Social Background of the Fifth Lok Sabha (EPW, Special no. 1973)
2. Baviskar, B.S. : The Politics of Development: Sugar Co-ops in rural Maharashtra (OUP, 1980)
3. Baxter, Craig : The Jana Sangh: A biography of an Indian political party (University of Pennsylvania Press, Philadelphia, 1969)
4. Beteille, Andre : Caste, Class & Power: Changing patterns of stratification in a Tanjore village (OUP, 1966)
5. Bhambri, C.P. & Verma, P.S : Social Background of the 7th Lok Sabha (Mainstream, July 4, 1981)
6. Bhambri, C.P. : The Janata Party: A Profile (National Publishing House, 1980)
7. Blair, Harry : Rising Kulaks & Backward Classes in Bihar: Social Change in the late 1970s (EPW, Jan. 12, 1980)
8. Brass, Paul R. : The Politicization of the Peasantry in a North Indian State (The Journal of Peasant Studies, Vol. 1, No.1, Part II, Oct. 1980)
9. Brecher, Michael : Political leadership in India (Vikas Publications, 1969)
10. Byres, T.J. : The New Technology: Class Formation & Class Action in the Indian Countryside (The Journal of Peasant Studies, Vol.8, No.4, July '81)
11. Chattopadhyay, B. Sharma, S.C. & Roy, A.K. : The Terms of Trade & the Rising Power of the Farm Lobby (Cressida Transactions, Eco-science Vol.II, 1982, Special Issue Nos. 1 & 2)

12. Deshmukh, Nana : RSS—Victim of Slander (Vision Books, 1979)

13. Dutta, Ratna : The Party Representative In The Fourth Lok Sabha (EPW, Annual Number, Jan.1969)

14. Erdman, Howard L. : The Swatantra Party & Indian Conservatism (Cambridge University Press, 1967)

15. Franda, Marcus F. & Brass, Paul R. (Ed.) : Radical Politics in South Asia (The MIT Press, Cambridge, Massachusetts, 1973)

16. Goyal, D.R. : Rashtriya Swayamsewak Sangh (Radha Krishna Prakashan, 1979)

17. Hangen, Welles : After Nehru Who (Rupert Hart-Davis, London, 1963)

18 Jha, Dayadhar : State Legislature In India (Abhinav Publications, 1977)

19. Jha, Shree Nagesh : The Union Council of Ministers in India 1952-71: A study in elite composition (Political Science Review Vol. 13, Nos. 1-4, Jan-Dec 1974)

20. Joshi, Ram & Desai, Kiritidev : Dominance With A Difference : Strains and Challenges (EPW, Annual Number Feb, 1973)

21. Kahane, Reuven : Legitimation & Integration in Developing Societies: The Case for India (A Westview Replica Edition, 1982)

22. Kashyap, Subhash : Socio-Economic Background of Lok Sabha Members (Monograph Series No.10; Govt. of India Press 1987)

23. Kochanek, S. : The Congress Party in India (1968)

24. Kothari, Rajni : Politics In India (Little Brown & Co., 1970) & (New Delhi, Orient Longman Ltd., 1970)

25. Kothari, Rajni : Voting In India; Competitive Politics & Electoral Change—

			Four papers by CSDS staff based on 1967 elections (EPW Annual No. Jan 1971)
26.	Lok Sabha Secretariat	:	A study of the socio-economic background of first to eight Lok Sabha members (New Delhi, 1986)
27.	Maheshwari, Shriram	:	Political Development in India (Concept Publishing Co., New Delhi, 1984)
28.	Morris-Jones, W.H.	:	Parliament In India (Pennsylvania Press, 1957)
29.	Mehta, Balraj	:	Rich Farmers Lobby In Full Cry (EPW, Dec 2, 1978)
30	Mitra, Ashok	:	Terms of Trade & Class Relations (Frank Cass & Co. Ltd., 1977)
31.	Narain, Iqbal Pande, K.C. & Lal, Mohan	:	Rural Elite & Elections in one Indian State (1976)
32.	Narayana, G.	:	Social Background of Scheduled Caste Lok Sabha Members, 1962-71 (EPW 1978)
33.	Naik, J.A.	:	From Total Revolution to Total Failure (National Publishing House, 1979)
34.	Prasad, Nageshwar	:	Ideology & Organisation in Indian Politics (Allied Publishers Private Ltd, 1980)
35.	Rudolph, Susanne & Lloyd	:	Transformation Of Congress Party—Why 1980 was not a restoration (EPW, May 2,1981)
36.	Sathe, Vasant	:	Towards Social Revolution: A case for economic democracy (Vikas Publishing House Pvt. Ltd., New Delhi 1984, third edition, 1988)
37.	Sathe, Vasant	:	Two Swords in one Scabbard: A case for presidential form of parliamentary democracy (NIB Publishers, New Delhi, 1989)

38. Sathe, Vasant : Restructuring of Public Sector in India (Vikas, New Delhi, 1989)

39. Sathe, Vasant : The Challenge of Change: Key issues for a developing society (Allied Publishers Pvt. Ltd., New Delhi, 1989)

40. Sharma, Narendra : Congress-I: Facing Realities (Mainstream, June 9, 1984)

41. Sheth, D.L. : Social Basis of the Political Crisis (Seminar, March 1980)

42. Sheth, D.L. : Poverty, Social Consciousness & Radicalism (ICSSR Research Abstracts Quarterly, Vol. VI, Nos. 3 & 4)

43. Vohra, Gautam : The New Political Elite; MLAs, v/s MPs (Daya Publishing House, 1992)

Questions/Speeches/Debates

The question and speeches have been selected, as well as paraphrased/condensed and in some cases translated from Marathi, by Ms. Sharada Kokaty. The methodology applied by her for the selection of speeches/debates and the questions raised by members since 1985 is explained as under:

There are 10-12 volumes of speeches/debates for each year of the eighth Lok Sabha upto 1989. Thus nearly 50 volumes were available.

The index to Lok Sabha debates are of two types

(1) Subject index

(2) Name index (name of the MP and the questions he has asked). From this index, we get a general idea of the type of question and the subject the MP has raised. If the question is not important it has not been included here. After studying three volumes of debates we get a general idea about the interests of the MP and his perspective on issues.

(i) Some questions are asked by MPs to show that they are vigilant; some of these MPs belong to the opposition party

(ii) Some questions relate to current affairs and happenings during that particular time-frame

The answers given by the Ministers are in the form of:

(i) statements of statistical data and facts provided by the departments;

(ii) explanations and justifications of government policies, and

(iii) straight-away denials.

For the year 1989 debates upto February session had been printed but they had gone for binding and were not available for scrutiny.

The Lok Sabha debates covered are:

1985 : March 25 to March 29, Vol. 3

1985	:	Aug 25 to April 8, Vol. 9
1986	:	April 2 to April 8, Vol.15
1987	:	Nov. 30 to Dec. 3, Vol. 33
1988	:	April 8 onwards, Vol. 38
1989	:	April 4 onwards, Vol. 65
1989	:	April 4 to April 6, Vol. 68

The major participants, as the following pages reveal, are Madhu Dandavate, Vikhe Patil, Datta Samant, Banwarilal Purohit, D.B. Patil, Prakash Patil, Y.S. Mahajan and Sharad Dighe. The occasional question has been asked or comment made by Sunil Dutt, Murli Deora, Gurudas Kamat, Prataprao Bhosale, Hussein Dalwai and a few others.

Lok Sabha Debates *2nd session*
English Version 8th Lok Sabha
Vol. 3 No. 11
March 25, 1985 Col. 228.

Prof. Dandavate to Dy. Minister

Question: Demand for unconditional release of Swami Agniwesh and his colleagues before the tripartite meeting to settle quarry workers' dispute.

Answer: Deputy Minister:
If the minister wants to have a meeting, he can have. I cannot comply.

Col. 282

G.S. Gholap

Content of the speech: (1st speech) on general budget 1985-86. General discussion and supplementary demands for grants (general) 1984-85.

(1) Supports the budget. Central Government's appointment of a Pay Commission with a view to increase the salaries of the Central Govt.'s employees. The creation of a problem—the state govt. employee start agitation for increase. There should be co-ordination between the two about the policies.

(2) The delay in clearing the files about the backward and Adivasi areas. He urges the Govt. to expedite the matter.

(3) Shortage of water supply to the zopadpatti areas of Bombay. The damaged conditions of the roads in Bombay, the Railways etc.

(4) Bombay being the city of the whole nation Central Govt. should help the state to solve such problems.

(5) Fishermen, on a small scale basis should be exempted from sales tax duty.

These were the suggestions he made in this first speech.

Dr. Datta Samant

In his speech he observed:

(1) Number of sick mills is increasing. What remedial action is the Central Govt. taking to reduce the number? Three lakh mill workers are unemployed—and no decision is taken to solve the problem.

(2) Unemployment is increasing, on the whole 5 crores of youths are unemployed. What does the Govt. propose to do for them? The Govt. is merely issuing assurances about restructuring the policy regarding all textiles, but it means delay. The minister concerned should clarify the matter.

(3) Compulsory deposit scheme (Act 1974) and Compulsory Deposit Scheme Amendment Bill 1985 — cancellation of the bill — the deposited money should be repaid immediately to the deposit holders so that the Government will not lose its credibility in the minds of the middle class deposit holders.

Answer by the Minister of finance (*Poojari*)

The Government has reduced the taxes on income, people will get benefit of these reduction in taxes. CDS Bill is to be abolished. To meet the requirements of the weaker classes, welfare schemes, defence expenses, development activities, we need money for which the repayment of the deposited amount is postponed.

Statutory Resolution in respect of the state of Punjab—National Security (Amendment Bill)

S.B. Chavan, Minister of Home Affairs, begs to move the resolution

(1) National Security Amendment Bill

(2) Punjab budget 1985-86. General discussion

(3) Demands for Grants on account (Punjab) 1985-86, supplementary demands for grants 1984-85

Col. 351-371.

S.B. Chavan—regarding terrorist attacks and details of deaths. Supplies full statistical information and explains the Government's policy and action taken.

Questions by MPs and answers by S.B Chavan to explain the Government action and position.

Written answers given on 25-3-1985

Production of sugarcane in Maharashtra

Balasahib Vikhe Patil to the minister of food and civil supplies.

Q. I Whether sugarcane production has registered a decline

II The details if so

III What remedial measures Govt. is introducing to check the decline as Maharashtra is the premier sugar producing state. It is likely to affect the national economy.

Answer: Statistical data is provided of the decrease due to climatic conditions. Advice is tendered on the types of measures that the state government can implement and these could include:

(1) Production and distribution of quality seed.

(2) Demonstration of improved practice of cane cultivation.

(3) Plant protection measures.

(4) Training of cane workers.

(5) Construction of link roads.

Funds to the states under RLEGP Col. 86

893. *Prof. Madhu Dandavate* to the Minister of Agriculture and Rural Development

Q. (a) Statement of the amount released to major states for

Rural Landless Employment Guarantee Programme, statewise, yearwise.

(b) Whether the state schemes for RLEGP assistance require prior approval of Central Govt.

(c) If so, the prescribed approval procedure.

(d) The interval between the state programme and approval from Central Government in respect of Andhra Pradesh, Bihar Gujarat, Karnataka, Maharashtra, Orissa and U.P. for 83-84, 84-85

Answer:(a)The amount of funds made available under RLEGP is given in the Annexure.

(b) The states under RLEGP are required to prepare specific projects and submit them to the Department of Rural Development for approval and sanction by the Central Committee for NREP/RLEGP.

Interval approximately one month upto 4 months.

A statement of statewise release made under RLEGP is submitted.

Col. 149

Inquiry into the diversion of truck carrying sugar to Faridabad.

Q. 952. *Balasahib Vikhe Patil*

A few years ago an entire truck load of sugar belonging to the Super Bazar, New Delhi was diverted to Faridabad. Any inquiry was made? The details if so, and if not, the reasons.

Answer: By the minister of food and civil supplies:

The Super Bazar intimated that it is not aware of such a case. According to them, *The Hindustan Times* news item is incorrect.

Q. 953. Payment of subsidy for holding buffer stocks of sugar.

(a) Long delays in payment of subsidy for holding buffer stocks of sugar.

(b) If so, how many claims for subsidy since Oct. 82 are pending disposal—with names of the factories and the total amount against each

(c) Whether Government proposes to pay interest to the factories where the payments have not been made to compensate their loss

(d) What steps are taken to streamline the procedure for payment of subsidy?

Answer: Due to administrative and legal difficulties some delay had occurred. The factories furnish incomplete, incorrect data and wrong claims. The annexure gives the position. The procedure is under review and steps to expedite the matter are under way.

Q. 954. Rise in price index due to sugar and gur as sweetening agents.

Balasahib Vikhe Patil

Has the government any record to determine how the sweetening agents

(1) have pushed up the consumer price index,

(2) the particulars and how much it is due to sugar?

Answer: The Government maintains the record and gives a statement of monthwise impact on the all-India index.

Q. 1007 Consumption of fertilizers

Balasahib Vikhe Patil to the minister of agriculture and rural development .

(a) Any increase in the consumption of fertilizers during the last 3 years, statewise improvement if any

(b) If not the reasons for lack of growth in the consumption rate.

(c) The hike in price is a cause? What steps will the Government take to deal with the situation?

Answer: There has been an increase in consumption. The growth is 31 percent.

An increase in all states but Jammu and Kashmir, Manipur. This lack of growth in the above states is due to weather aberrations

Government has reduced the price by 7.5% and a further rebate of 10% to promote the use of fertilisers.

Prof. Madhu Dandavate Col. 216-219

He shows three precedents, the rulings given by the speaker during the 5th Lok Sabha that a minister cannot announce a policy outside the House. Mr. Gandhi made an announcement about Punjab outside the House which according to Dandavate is a wrong procedure. He is ready to substantiate his notice with the precedents in the past during 5th, 6th and 7th Lok Sabhas.

General budget 1985-86. Col. 253-254

Dr. Datta Samant's speech

Concessions given to industrialists and (hence) the employers must benefit the poor and unemployed.

The sick textile mills are increasing—Bombay, Gujarat, Kanpur, Delhi—and 3 lakh workers are reduced to unemployed position. If the Government does not take a decision about the textile policy, there will be further increase in resentment.

He is displeased with the policy of the government not to levy tax on agriculture. Small farmers should be exempted but big farmers should be under income tax levy. There is no relief for people—44% living below the poverty line.

What steps are being taken to solve the problem of unemployed youth: 5 crores approximately. Remunerative prices will be fixed for agricultural produce (Rajiv Gandhi & Sharad Pawar) but the budget does not reflect it. The Government should do something for the poor.

G.S. Gholap

Supports the budget for being progressive and offering many concessions to the public.

The increase in pay of the Central Government employees will lead to an agitation by the state employees for increase. There should be co-ordination between the centre and the states about pay and bonus. Clearing of files is delayed especially regarding the development of hill and forest areas. He requests the Government to delegate power to the states to distribute land and provide money for their projects of forest and rural development.

In Bombay 42 lakhs live in zopadpatti, water supply is scarce. Roads are damaged. All these problems cannot be solved by the State Government alone. Bombay is the city of the whole nation and Central Government should provide the wherewithal for the improvement projects for the city of Bombay.

Accidental death provision should be extended to snake-bites, electric shock deaths etc.

Sales tax on diesel engine, deep-sea fishery boats must be exempted. Small fishermen must also get the benefit.

Col. 298 *Dr. Datta Samant*

The tax structure reforms should be raised to Rs. 20,000 or Rs. 25,000 instead of Rs. 18,000.

The minister, V.P. Singh, shows inconsistency says Samant in his speech.

V.P. Singh

The general approach is for growth, productivity, savings, and better compliance of taxes. The approach was to lower the taxes but take away exemptions—we had a high marginal tax rate but many exemptions—virtually big companies paying no tax at all. They took the benefits, the exemptions helped them to avoid tax paying but at the same time we made it a tax rate which would be reasonable and which would be complied with.

Col. 329 *Dr. Datta Samant*

Complains that the textile policy has not been announced and asks what relief the workers will get?

Answer: V.P. Singh shares his concern over the matter; pros and cons of the policy will be considered and a balance between handloom, powerloom and organised sector, employment of workers, sickness and fibre policy will be struck. The Textile Advisory body has made its recommendations and soon the policy will be formulated.

Compulsory Deposit Scheme (Income tax payers)

Dr. Datta Samant

Col.348 to Col.371 The abolition of this scheme is a good move but because of the postponement of the payment on a particular day (one year) the government will lose its credibility. Your commitment made to the middle class must be honoured.

Answer: There is some reason for postponement. There is constraint on our resources and we have to look after the welfare schemes and defence expenditure and maintain our development activities, hence the delay of a year to repay.

March 26, 1985

Oral answers to questions

Col. 15, 16, *Prof. Madhu Dandavate*

Since everything said here is going on record for future generations, Section 62 of the Constitution says that all the reports, individual as well as administrative, will be placed on the table of the House

With reference to the context of violation of guarantee by manufacturers of consumer products:—

Q. (1) Does the manufacturer's guarantee have any legal status

(2) Any complaints about largescale violation of such guarantees

(3) Any enquiry has been held by MRTP Commission into such cases and what is the outcome?

Answer: No complaints for reference to the MRTP act. However, MRTP Commission had enquired in 1984 into 14 complaints. A statement about the position of the cases is laid on the table for scrutiny.

Dr.Datta Samant wants the Government to amend the MRTP Act to regulate the prices of the consumer items manufactured by the MRTP companies.

Use of Black Money in elections

The minister of law and justice.

Col. 27 The use of back money, including during elections, can be curbed only by preventing the generation and proliferation of black money itself.

Law does not permit even white money to be used in elections in excess of the ceiling fixed under section 77. He who exceeds the ceiling is disqualified.

Prof. Madhu Dandavate: There was consensus, total unanimity that there should be state funding of elections.

Workers' participation in management Col. 79

Q. 1056 *Prof. Madhu Dandavate* to the minister of chemicals and fertilisers.

Whether the of govt. policy of workers'

participation in the management and appointment of workers' representatives on the boards of management of chemical and pharmaceutical units has been implemented. If so, the (1) details (2) claims of any union rejected in this respect (3) names of the union.

Answer: The scheme (1983) envisages representation of workers through consensus to be arrived at in consultation with the concerned trade union leaders.

The implementation by the following Central Government undertakings:

(1) The Hindustan Organic Chemicals

(2) The Hindustan Insecticides Ltd., the Delhi unit

(3) The Indian Drugs and Pharmaceuticals Ltd. at Rishikesh, Gurgaon and Hyderabad.

The employees' participation at the board level — certain preparatory steps have been initiated.

Production of oil

1058. *Balasahib Vikhe Patil*

Q. The quantity of oil in the country other than the Bombay High oil.

(1) Centre-wise during the last 3 years

(2) Any centres recording steady decline, the reasons thereof.

Answer: Statistical data is put before the member. Some centres show steady decline due to water/gas cut and decline in reservoir pressure.

Co.183 *Prof. Madhu Dandavate*

Prime Minister Rajiv Gandhi in a press conference in Ahmedabad made a blanket allegation against the entire opposition for being responsible for the communal troubles in Gujarat. We protest strongly against this allegation. The govt. has failed to substantiate that statement. I urge the House to take up an adjournment motion.

Col.130 Border Dispute between Karnataka & Maharashtra

Q. 1241 *Prof. Madhu Dandavate & Husein Dalwai.*

Whether the Central Govt. proposes to explore solutions to the long pending Karnataka-Maharashtra dispute in a time-bound manner.

Answer: The dispute can be solved with mutual co-operation and goodwill, for which the Central government is ready to extend all possible assistance. A time limit is not possible in this respect.

Col. 132 Highlighting of small accidents in Indian Airlines by the press

Q. 1243 *Balasahib Vikhe Patil* to the tourism and aviation minister
(1) Is the press highlighting small accidents and casting doubts on the credibility of the airlines? I want the statistical data of accidents within the last 2 years and causes:
negligence of maintenance, seriousness of accident, whether safety measures are upto the international standard. If not, whether the government is looking into the matter of public safety.

Answer: True. Reports are appearing in the newspapers. Inquiries of six out of seven in the last two years have been completed and govt cannot be accused of negligence.

Q. 1260 *Balasahib Vikhe Patil* to the Prime Minister

Col.162 Whether
(1) the steel and cement plants are surrounded by habitation
(2) these units are fully equipped to control pollution caused by smoke, gas and effluents
(3) A thorough survey to check pollution is carried out.

Answer: They are fully equipped and are functioning satisfactorily. A survey and standards of effective control of pollution are prescribed.

Bhopal gas leak disaster, processing of claims bill

Col.247 *D.B. Patil*
Welcomes the bill, gives a long lecture about the sad events, and the current situation. Urges that precautions should be taken while implementing the provisions of the bill.

March 27, 1985

Development of Gir forest

D.B. Patil

Q. He wants to know whether the Central Government proposes to develop the Gir forest as a Safari Park for tourist promotion.

Answer: The Central Govt. gives a grant of Rs.9.24 lakhs for this purpose.

Adequate training for SC and ST staff:

Q. 1187 *Banwarilal Purohit*

A news item in *The Times of India* of Feb 8, 85 announces that the Commission for SCs and STs has said that not much is being done by the various ministries/ departments, public enterprises or banks in imparting extra in-service training to SC and ST employees, despite the Home Ministry's instructions.

Answer: The existing instructors are being asked to revert to the ministries and departments. So far as public banks and enterprises are concerned, the nodal agency is advised.

March 28, 1985.

Oral answers

Reservation in Medical Colleges

Balasahib Vikhe Patil and D.P. Yadav

Q. The Health minister with Home and Education ministers must see that the policy of reservation for the Scheduled Castes and Tribes is implemented in full not only in medical colleges but also in Central Universities and technical institutions. We have found that things are not upto the mark.

Answer: There is definitely reservation in medical colleges and 15% reservation for the backward classes also. It is basically the concern of the state Governments. Statistical data is provided

The Central Universities are expected to follow the Central Govt./U.G.C. guidelines regarding such reservations, and the universities in the state generally follow the reservation policy and instructions issued by the state governments.

Q. 1332 Economic independence of women

Col. 76 *Balasahib Vikhe Patil*

The slow progress in the economic emancipation of women in rural areas is due to the lack of vocational opportunities and social taboos which prevent them to take to modern education and avail of opportunities; if this is so, what steps will the Govt. take to improve the situation?

Answer: The ministry of social and women's welfare implements schemes to help rural women

(1) to set up production units, training, rehabilitation through voluntary organisations.

(2) The ministry of rural development has started two schemes (i) Development of women and children in rural areas (DWCRA) (ii) Training of rural youth for self-employment programmes (TRYSEM)

The above ministry will help to co-ordinate such schemes being implemented by other Ministries.

Col.122 Causes of high level of Thiocynate in urine of victims

Q. 1385 exposed to MIC gas

Prof. Madhu Dandavate to the Health and Family Welfare Minister.

(1) the veracity of the fact that ICMR was entrusted with the task of determining the causes of high level of Thiocynate in the Bhopal gas leak disaster?

(2) the results of the study

Answer: Scientific medical research was conducted by ICMR with the health department. The scientific data collected is explained

---

1396 Inadequate specialisation in the field of toxicology and medical colleges having specialised courses.

Prof. Madhu Dandavate

Q. Our specialisation in the field of toxicology is inadequate How many colleges have specialised courses on this subject and the plans of the Central Government to create more facilities.

Answer: The subject of toxicology and clinical toxicology is taught as a part of undergraduate and post graduate courses of pharmacology and forensic medicine by 23 medical colleges and institutions in this country. There is scope for greater specialisation in this field.

29th March 1985
Oral answers

Col.7 Sub: Illegal mining in Bengal, Bihar, Assam

Prof. Madhu Dandavate

What steps is the Govt. taking to prevent it.

Vasant Sathe replies :

Answer: (1) The state government of Bihar is informed that no mining lease for coal can be granted without the prior approval of Central Government. After nationalisation, there is no question of any private party doing coal mining — it has not come to our notice. The state govt. under law has to prevent any illegal mining.

(2) Answers questions about mining and explains the Government policy and furnishes the statistical data.

Col.91 Filling up of posts of heads of public undertakings

Balasahib Vikhe Patil to the finance minister

Q.1469 Whether the Govt. proposes to weed out inefficient heads of public sector undertakings.. any action taken so far? The number of posts in public undertakings lying vacant and the time fixed for filling these posts.

Answer: The Government is constantly reviewing the various aspects of the management of public enterprises, with a view to improve the personnel. The initial tenure is of 2 years and the performance is under close scrutiny. The extension of their tenure depends on satisfactory performance. Satistical data—19 public enterprises have full-time chief executives—13 posts will be soon filled — 6 vacancies for consideration.

Q. 1553. Discovery of gold in hilly regions of the country
Col.201 *Balasahib Vike Patil* to the Minister of Steel, Mines and
202 Coal.

The results of the Geological Survey of India in the hilly regions, the details of the areas and the commercial exploitation of the areas

Answer: Uttar Pradesh, Himachal Pradesh, Punjab, Haryana, Jammu Kashmir are the states where gold has been found. It is not economically significant.

Calling attention to matters of urgent public importance

Col.247 Reported confiscation by custom authorities at Bombay Airport of large amount of U.S. dollars and travellers cheques intended to be deposited in foreign banks.

Q. *Prof. Madhu Dandavate* to the finance minister

Can you enlighten as about the above report and the action taken by the Govt.

Answer: Describes the event. And gives statistical data. It involves violation of the Foreign Exchange Regulation Act and direct tax laws. Follow up action and investigation are in progress.

Madhu Dandavate

Calling attention notice is a powerful instrument in the hands of the members to unearth and expose corruption and disclose it to the concerned minister — he describes the event of the confiscation

Col.255 onwards Prominent Congress (I) leaders and their relationship with industrialists will prove harmful to the party. I can prove that.

Answer: The culprit will not go scotfree. The law has a long grip under the FERA and the direct tax laws. The Govt. can and shall act under these laws.

Constitution Amendment Bill

Y.S. Mahajan

Col.370 onwards — The Muslim Personal Laws and the Hindu Personal Laws deal with marriage, succession, inheritance and custody of children. He objects to Banatwala's contention about the Muslim Personal Laws.

Lok Sabha Debates (English Version) 1985 Vol.9

8th series Vol.IX No. 21 Aug. 21 to 28, 1985.

Free movement of smugglers/terrorists on Rajasthan-Pak border.

Q. 4313 *Sharad Dighe* to the Minister of Home Affairs:

Whether Rajasthan's border with Pakistan has no fence or wall and the border security posts are scattered, allowing unrestricted movement of smugglers, terrorists?

Answer: Total length of the border is 1035 kms and BSF have established 122 border outposts on Rajasthan border. Vigilance has been tightened. It is incorrect to say that there is unrestricted movement of smugglers and terrorists.

4323. *Y.S. Mahajan* to the Minister of External Affairs

Opening of Consulate in Milan (Italy)

Q. Whether the Govt. have decided to open a Consulate to strengthen Indo-Italian trade relations and their details

A. Yes, the details are under consideration.

Seizure of restricted area maps from AVARD

4378. *Prof. Madhu Dandavate* to Minister of Home Affairs

Q. Whether the Intelligence Bureau searched the office of the Association of Voluntary Agencies for Rural Development (AVARD) during the Emergency in 1975-76. Could you tell us about maps that were seized. What areas do they depict?

Answer: No. The question does not arise

Prof. Madhu Dandavate

4379. Q. After assessing the impact of communal riots the National Integration Council had recommended the restructuring of police and para-military forces reflecting a cross-section of society. If so, the steps taken, and the time-frame for implementation

Answer: Yes. Under the Constitution, law, order and police are state subjects and the restructuring is to be activated by State Governments. They are considering the matter.

4428. *Sharad Dighe* to the Minister for Planning
Subject: Allocation for poverty alleviation schemes

Q. Whether Planning Commission is restricting the above schemes to Rs. 8600 crores against Rs.15,000 crores originally fixed. Please gave the reasons.

Answer: The details are being worked out and will be placed before the National Development Council.

Ill-treatment of Indian girls by visiting tourists

4448. *Murli Deora*

Q. The Gulf countries tourists are tricking girls into marriages of convenience and ill-treating them afterwards.

Protection offered to them by the Government by emigration laws, how it is ensured that such marriages are lawful and not merely marriages of convenience.

Answer: Such marriages take place in the poor Muslim community due to economic compulsions and cosy life inducements abroad in Gulf countries. The emigration laws do not cover such cases as they are meant for safeguarding the interests of the labourers. The State Governments concerned are alive to the situation and are maintaining due vigilance in this matter.

4460. Works of art rotting in Academy store room
Balasahib Vikhe Patil to the Minister of Culture

Q. Nearly 1000 works of art are rotting in Lalit Kala Art

Academy. What steps are being taken to keep them in proper custody and storage?

Answer: The academy is making efforts to create additional storage space and anti-termite treatment of storerooms is regularly conducted.

4463. Q. Surreptitious acquisition of Indian passports by Bangladeshis

Banwarilal Purohit to the Minister of External Affairs

Is the Government aware of the fabrication of fake Indian passports with the help of unscrupulous agents in this country. Does it not propose to remedy the situation?

Answer: Two cases were notified. Authorities concerned in Bombay are instructed to file fresh reports on the individuals. Police authorities, state governments are informed to be extra vigilant in this regard.

4484. Inquiry into charges against Chief Minister of Haryana

Madhu Dandavate to the P.M.

Q. Whether an inquiry against Bhajanlal is to be held within a fixed time limit?

Answer: Justice Jaswant Singh, retd. Supreme Court Judge has been asked to complete the inquiry.

Permission for running passenger service on Bombay-Goa line with special vessels.

Q. 4623. *G.S. Gholap* to the Shipping Minister

The Mughal line passenger service is incurring losses. The total loss incurred and a statement whether another co. wants to run the service and the Government policy

Answer: Yes. Rs. 903.63 lakhs loss. We have not received any such proposal.

Assistance given to Maharashtra for women welfare schemes

Balasahib Vikhe Patil to the Welfare Minister

4641.Q. What is the amount given to the women's welfare schemes in Maharashtra and the nature of schemes, the assessment of such schemes, the performance and the benefits gained by women and future schemes in the 7th plan.

Answer: The assistance is given to voluntary organizations and local bodies and not to particular states. The 7th plan is in the process of being finalised.

4675. *Balasahib Vikhe Patil* to the Education Minister

The five day week in Delhi University is a proposal by the Vice-Chancellor and which is opposed by some of the students. The reaction of the Government.

Answer: The University of Delhi has constituted a committee of students, union leader and other departmental heads who have been asked to consider the matter for recommendation. The Government's views in this matter does not arise.

Measures to help in removal of dowry practice.

A discussion, a lengthy one, is conducted in which many take part and Madhu Dandavate expresses his views.

Matter's under discussion

Railway Protection Force Amend.Bill.

Prof. Madhu Dandavate opposes the bill at the introduction itself.

Legislation governing minimum wages for Bidi Workers and special attention to the welfare of women Bidi workers

Balasahib Vikhe Patil expresses his views and gives a

statement with factual data about the wages and the sorry plight of the workers especially women workers.

Policy on aspects of black money

Y.S. Mahajan discusses the report on Black Money. The points in the report and the omission from the estimates of black income generated through large scale smuggling activities. In this context the figures given by the committee is an under-estimate of the total situation.

(1) Simplification and rationalisation of the tax laws

(2 The complexity of tax laws and differing interpretations give rise to corruption and tax evasion.

(3) Financing of election expenses, widespread corruption in almost all the departments of Government. Corruption as the biggest source of black money generation etc. etc.

Col.699.

Sharad Dighe on the report of the study by National Institute of Public Finance and Policy. With some points he fully agrees, with some he disagrees and explains why he disagrees.

(1) Strict measures against smugglers.

(2) Clean administration

(3) Financing of election expenses by the state is a must.

Col.717-18

Balasahib Vikhe Patil on the same issue

Almost the same observation are made by him.

Because of the mixed economy, corruption is increasing. Before announcing any new policy and its implications, the finance department should visualise all the pros and cons and weak points. Here tax policy helps to generate black money. Income tax, sales tax—He gives statistical data about how many crores of black money is in circulation.

Lok Sabha Debates Vol.15
2nd to 8th April, 1986.

Q.534 Setting up of science and technology centres at district level.

Sunil Dutt to the Prime Minister.

Q. Whether the government proposed to set up science and technology centres at district or block levels in the country to avail the rural people of latest technical information in development work, please give the details and when they will be set up.

A. Minister of Science, Technology, Atomic Energy etc.
Shivraj Patil
We have a scheme to establish such centres, with appropriate technology relevant for rural development. Under this scheme 19 centres — demonstration-cum-training — are established but not at block or district level but at various states.

4890. *Balasahib Vikhe Patil*
Tree plantation of Nilgiri in Maharashtra.

Q. Whether the Government is aware of tree plantation of Nilgiri (Eucalyptus)
(1) One project is in Maharashtra for which underground water is exploited
(2) State government has advised to stop the plantation to save water for drinking purposes. What is the Central Government's proposal to avoid consequent difficulties?

A. Central government is aware and has advised to discourage the cultivation of Nilgiri plantations and discontinue the supply of seedlings to the farmers and create public awareness.

D.B. Patil to the Prime Minister

Q.4891. Contracts and grants for development of electronic products

Q. Is there a scheme for contracts and grants for research and development of technological know-how for electronic products? How many such benefits are given in 83-84, 85 and the outcome of such contracts and grants

A. Financial support, a statement of two pages with tabulated data is made available.

Keshavrao Pardhi to the Minister of Welfare.

4901 Hindi shorthand code for the blind.

Q. Whether it is a fact that the national institute for visually handicapped in Dehradun has devised Hindi shorthand code for the blind; the number of shorthand experts who helped in devising the code; the names of the institutes who are using it and the number of persons who have derived benefit

A. About 10 shorthand and Braille experts were consulted. Training was given to 24 and 11 are employed.

4969

Q. Hindi shorthand typing — the number of employees

A. English stenographers are trained for this and their services are utilised when necessary.

4906. *Y.S. Mahajan* to the Prime Minister.

Usefulness of space technology in increasing foodgrain production.

Q. How far is the space technology useful in increasing food production by identifying and spotting soil salinity and taking remedial measures? Is it useful for afforestation and checking floods and increase forest wealth? The success of the programme and the cost.

A. Gives a technical explanation —now it is utilised for mapping and operational use. Difficult to quantify the cost and research is continuously conducted.

4980. *D.B. Patil* to the Prime Minister

Q. Application projects of IRSSUP.

Whether the Indian Remote Sensing Satellite Utilisation Programme initiated the eight applications projects in collaboration with relevant state and central agencies, the names of the states and Central agencies and the achievements?

A. 16 application centres —details given (3 pages)

Drug Addicts

4999. *Sunil Dutt* and others to the Welfare Minister.

Q. Traficking in drugs is increasing? Any survey conducted? And the details of the statistical data, the steps taken to check this menace and rehabilitation of drug addicts and curing centres.

A. No such assessment is available. A Study Committee in 1985 was commissioned in four Metropolitan cities and five other towns. A statement is annexed.

D.B. Patil to Minister of Home Affairs.

5025. Assent to bill from Maharashtra.

Legislation passed by Maharashtra legislature regarding payment of house-rent to National Textile Corporation Mill workers is pending with the Central Government for President's assent — since when and the reasons?

A. The bill is under examination and final reply from the state government for certain exemptions for Central Govt. will be given shortly

---

Friday, April 4, 1986.

568. *Balasahib Vikhe Patil* to the Minister for Finance.

Q. Any proposals by Government for structural changes in LIC for good returns in old age, the salient features.

A. The Life Insurance Corporation is under constant scrutiny for increasing welfare programmes and annuity schemes for providing pension in old age.

Import of raw sugar

5259. *Madhu Dandavate* to Minister for Food & Civil Supplies

Is it a fact that a number of sugar factories have faced

closure for want of adequate sugarcane supply, if so, a clearance certificate to produce sugar from imported raw sugar —any decisions in the offing?

A. Four sugar factories in Maharashtra did not go into production in 85-86. The proposal has been considered but not practically possible to accept.

Banwarilal Purohit to the Minister of Tourism

5293. Q Ajanta-Ellora are not included in the development plan— is it a fact? The reasons, which important tourist places are included and what efforts are made to locate such centres?

A. Ajanta Ellora are included. Quotes the names of the centres. They are being developed by Centre, State and the private sector.

5305. New areas for cashew and rubber plantation

Hussein Dalwai to the Minister of Commerce.

Q. Which areas are earmarked for development of cashew and rubber plantations?

A. Tripura, Assam, Andaman and Nicobar, Orissa are the new areas. With World Bank assistance some projects are being implemented for expansion as well as improvement of existing area under cashew.

5348. *Sharad Dighe* to Minister of Food & Civil Supplies.

Q. Is it a fact that many sugar mills in U.P. and Maharashtra are closed due to lack of sugar cane? And there is a sharp rise in sugar prices and what steps are proposed by the Government?

A. A statement yearwise. The sugar price rise is not due to any declining trend in production. Government maintains a close watch on the prices, etc.

Q.5268. *Prakash Patil* to Minister of Food & Civil Supplies.

Q. The per capita consumption of foodgrains in 1983-84-85 among the rural poor, the steps taken to raise the intake and abolish starvation deaths

A. A statement yearwise.

Per capita net availability of foodgrains 477.9 per day 463.3 in 85.

Steps taken to increase food production, distribution

(1) foodgrains made available at a concessional price to the people;

(2) increased coverage under the nutrition programme of young children and pregnant women;

(3) expansion of the coverage of rural landless employment guarantee programme.

5290 *Murlidhar Mane* to the Minister of Tourism

Q. The steps taken by Government for promotion of tourism in Maharashtra in the 7th five year plan to develop tourist resorts in the state and details.

A. Yes. 17 places of tourist importance have been identified. Central assistance for individual projects, if funds are available.

Cornering of sugarcane by co-operative sugar factories in Maharashtra

5398. *R.M. Bhaye* to the Minister of Food & Civil Supplies

Q. Whether the above statement is true and what steps the Government intends to take?

A. Government has no information regarding this.

5421. *Balasahib Vikhe Patil* to the Minister of Finance

Q. The percent of population in the country which is insured under various policies—the details.

A. The corporation has a total number of 265 crores of policies in force—79 lacs have the benefit of group insurance scheme upto 1985.

Vijay Patil to the Minister for Food & Civil Supplies

5448. Q. The amount of sugar cess collected till 1985 by the union government from factories in Maharashtra, the amount utilised and the number of new sugar factories.

A. A statement to the effect that there were no new applications for loan from sugar development fund for modernisation. Two applications for cane development.

Modernisation of Textile Mills in Maharashtra.

5463. *Hussein Dalwai* to the Minister of Textiles.

Q. No. of textile mills which are nationalised.
No. of closed mills which are not yet nationalised.

A. A statement statewise—a very long one.

Oral answers

Banwarilal Purohit to the Minister of Agriculture

Q. Col.15, a number of camplaints regarding the substandard seeds supplied to the farmers

A. There are no complaints which are serious.

5513. *Banwarilal Purohit* to the Minister of Steel

Q. Any possibility of development of mines in Rajasthan to remove unemployment among the youths?

A. Surveys are regularly carried out for the location of mines and development is speeded to increase employment chances.

Banwarilal Purohit to the Minister of Agriculture

Q.5547. Rejuvenation of orange trees affected by hailstorm in Vidarbha region of Maharashtra.

Q. Whether scientists from Indian Horticulture Research Centre, Bangalore, have suggested certain measures for the above problem, if so the details?

A. Detailed measures are suggested by the Centre.

D.B. Patil to the Agriculture Minister

5576. Whether Government of Maharashtra has submitted proposals for remunerative prices for agricultural produce to the Central Government, for 83-84, 84-85 and the recommendations of Maharashtra considered while fixing support price?

A. A statement. The prices are based on the recommendations made by the Commission for agricultural costs and prices; they are considered as well in consultation with the state Government.

5591. *Balasahib Vikhe Patil* to the Ministry of Agriculture

Q. Statewise use of fertilisers—84-85, 85-86. Whether there is a wide disparity in the use of fertilisers in the country.

A. Yes. A statement is provided.

5600. Security deposits by workers taking jobs abroad

Hussein Dalwai to the Labour Minister.

Q. How much amount is collected as security deposit by the immigration offices from Indians seeking jobs in Gulf countries? The reasons and any proposal for withdrawing it?

A. Yes. Only those workers directly recruited by foreign employers have to deposit security equivalent to one-way return air-fare in order to meet repatriation cost in case they are stranded.

5646. *Y.S Mahajan* to the Minister of Steel and Mines

Q. Inadequate supply of iron and steel materials to the engineering units in the North has hit the factories—any proposals to solve the problem?

A. Government is not aware of it. The supply is less than last years.

Telephone connections in Maharashtra

5701. *G.S. Gholap* to the Minister of Communications.

Q. Maharashtra Telecommunication Circle is getting funds to provide 10,000 lines in a year while waiting list is of 60,000—the action taken so far

A. Yes—Inadequate plan allocation is the main constraint in our expansion programme. Backlog of demand will be met progressively as soon as things improve.

Gurudas Kamat to the Communication Minister

Q. Whether a postal agency scheme is introduced in Maharashtra, the details

A. A statement is made to this effect.

Balasahib Vikhe Patil to the Petroleum Minister

5830. Q. Norms for sanctioning of LPG Agencies in rural and urban areas—rural areas have more demand, and the details

A. Periodical surveys are taken and marketing plans are prepared on a year to year basis. Towns with 20,000 population offer potential for economically viable marketing of LPG.

D.B. Patil to the Industry Minister.

Q. Study of performance of district industries centres—any agency to study the above, and the outcome of such studies?

A. No such study has been done.

D.B. Patil

Q. Deceptive advertisements by MRTP Commission—in how many cases?

A. 176 cases. Legal action is taken in 142 cases.

D.B. Patil

Q. The quota for SC is not being filled by ONGC on the ground of non-availability of technical and skilled personnel? Any programme taken up by ONGC to impart technical education to SCs?

A. Yes—a statement is issued to this effect.

Lok Sabha Debates Vol.33.

Oral Answer 30th Nov. to 3rd Dec. 1987

30 Nov. 1987

335. *Banwarilal Purohit* to the Urban Development Minister

Q. Whether non-resident Indians are permitted by the Govt.

(1) to construct houses in the country— the details?

(2) any proposal to solve the acute housing problem?

A. Government have not permitted non-resident Indians to invest in housing construction. The impact of such involvement on the problem of housing does not arise.

Col.15. Bhanwarilal Purohit—Government answer is not correct. And gives a statement of facts and requests the Govt. to induce non-resident Indians to invest money in housing to solve the problem.
Madhu Dandavate participates.

---

349. *Madhu Dandavate* to the Minister of Agriculture and Supplies

Q. Plight of drought hit persons—what Government plans to do?

A. Investigations are going on.
A lengthy discussion follows and Madhu Dandavate shows the inefficiency of the Government.

---

317. *G.S. Gholap* to the Finance Minister
Extension of Bombay cheques clearing facility upto the Kalyan complex.

A. RBI does not find it feasible.

Sugarcane production
Yeshwant Rao Gadakh Patil to the Agriculture Minister

346.Q. The average productivity of sugarcane per hectare and recovery percentage—any research work to increase the productivity?

A. A statement is issued to this effect.

3156. Revival of sick units by BIFR.
Datta Samant to Finance Minister

Q. The number of sick units detected by the Board for Industrial and Financial Recostruction under Sick Ind. Corporation—the details and the action of BIFR.

A. The Board was set up for action in 1985. Its operation started in 1987. 270 cases have been detected. They are at different stages of investigation.

Loans from IMF

3186. *Uttam Rathod* to the Finance Minister

Q. The amounts paid by India yearwise, and in the current year, towards repayment of IMF loans and interest.

A. A statement is issued to this effect.

Balasahib Vikhe Patil to the Finance Minister:

3233. Seizure of Assets in Bombay (Income Tax)

A. A statement.

Q. Is the government planning to evolve a new credit system for hire purchase companies—the details

A. RBI has no proposal to evolve such a system.

Q. *Prof. Madhu Dandavate*—closure of powerlooms after the implementation of New Textile Policy

A. No precise answer about closures can be given. Non-availability of yarns, shortage of electric supply, rise in price of cotton yarns, less purchasing power of the people are some of the reasons.

3255. *Banwarilal Purohit* to the Textiles Minister
Help to Handloom Weavers in Drought Affected Areas

Q. What type of help to the weavers; details and assistance provided by State Government

A. All state governments are asked to assist, guidelines are given.
NABARD, RBI have liberalised the norms for provision of assistance. Specific programmes have been developed.

3293. Inflation in Metropolitan Cities
Prakash Patil to Finance Minister.

Q. The double digit inflation recorded, the rate of inflation, and the steps taken by the Government.

A. A statement about the Government policy on the public distribution system— strong action taken against defaulting traders, and black-marketeers.

Opium Export
Prakash Patil

Q. Whether there is a fall in export.

A. Countrywise export. A statement. India faces stiff competition from Turkey and Austria.

3299 Modernising of ordnance factories
3300 *Prataprao Bhosale* to Defence Minister

Q. Any modernisation programmes?

A. Modernisation of ordnance factories is an ongoing process. A statement on the investments made.
To the Finance Minister
District Credit Plans for Vidarbha, Rajasthan and Sihore districts.

Q. Whether credit plans are discussed with local MPs, MLAs, Zilla Parishad, Panchayat Samiti and District Advisory Committee of these district.

A. Yes. RBI has issued detailed guidelines.

3382. Central Aid for construction of rural roads.
Balasahib Vikhe Patil to Minister of Agriculture.

Q. Any central scheme for the above? And the total amount allocated

A. A statement on the subject as covered in the 6th plan, 7th plan.

3383. *Vijay N. Patil* to the Minister of Labour

Q. Coal Mine accidents and steps taken by the Government to avoid them.

A. A statement to this effect.

Y.S. Mahajan to the Minister of Agriculture

3386.Q. Supply of phosphatic fertiliser to farmers—is it less due to shortage? And the measures Government has taken.

A. No—it is supplemented by imported stocks. Production is resumed and in full swing.

S.G. Gholap to Minister of Agriculture
Diversification of cropping pattern in Maharashtra

Q. With foreign aid in Konkan Region this scheme is being operated, if so, the cost, and plantation of oil-palm in the Konkan region

A. No such scheme is being implemented.

Balasahib Vikhe Patil to the Labour Minister

3465.Q. Implementation of Child Labour Act. Any review of the existing legislation on child labour? And the details.

A. The Central Advisory Board on child labour was set up in 1981. Conferences and meetings are held to discuss the procedures.

Bonded Labour:

3477. *Prakash Patil* to Minister of Labour.

Q. Has the Government formulated any scheme to involve voluntary agencies in indentifying and rehabilitating the bonded labourers in the country?

A. Yes, in 1987. It is too early to assess it.

Discussion on rate of inflation in 1988

Datta Samant participates. And gives a statement of percentage in the rates of inflation of the staple goods, eatables etc.

Take over of Chembur Complex of Union Carbide

3597. *Datta Samant* to the industry Minister.

A. Certain proposals from the State Government have come. They are under consideration.

3616. *Banwarilal Purohit* to the Minister of Communications.

Q. Waiting list for Telephone connections in Nagpur.

A. Yes. A statement to this effect.

3617. Q. *S.G. Gholap* about the same in Kalyan

A. A technical answer—for non sanctioning of telephone connections.

3625. *Prof. Madhu Dandavate* to the Industry Minister

Q. Any constraints on the rate of industrial growth, what type of constraints?

A. No— the rate of growth is increasing. A special programme has been launched.

3642. *Hussein Dalwai* to the Food Minister.

Q. The steps taken to become self-sufficient in the requirements of edible oils, plantation of groundnut, sunflower and palm trees on commercial basis can enhance production of edible oils— any proposals?

A. Government has taken a number of measures to increase production—a statement.

Y.S. Mahajan to the Energy Minister

Q. What type of measures taken for tariff restructuring on electrical energy?

A. They are being considered.

3736. *Banwarilal Purohit* to the Minister of Petroleum.

Q. About LPG dealers in Nagpur district. Dealers' shortage and waiting lists for gas connections.

A. The necessary infrastructure is to be augmented.

3764. Additional demand for rice and wheat in Maharashtra

Prof. Madhu Dandavate to the Food Minister.

Q. Total monthly supply of rice and wheat to Maharashtra is inadequate—what steps are proposed?

A. It is the responsibility of the State Government. The allocation from the Central Government is only supplemented in the context of the open market availability, and made on a monthly basis.

3777. *Prakash Patil* to the Industry Minister.

Q. Multinational companies manufacturing medicines and life-saving drugs and the profit made by these companies

A. A wide range of essential drugs. The Ministry monitors the production of only 87 imported bulk drugs. Profits made by the companies are not monitored by the Ministry.

Dec. 2,1987

0376. Maharashtra-Karnataka Border Dispute.

Dr. Datta Samant to the Minister of Home Affairs.

Q. Any progress in solving the dispute?

A. The Central Government has the view that this dispute should be solved with the willing co-operation of both the states.

Datta Samant, Madhu Dandavate and others present the familiar arguments

---

R.M Bhoye, Prakash Patil, Balasahib Vikhe Patil ask questions about technical programmes in collaboration with foreign countries on

(1) Nuclear Power Generation

(2) Water resources and irrigation

(3) The issue of Bangladesh nationals staying in India; they refer to it as infiltration

A. Due to socio-cultural reasons this is unavoidable—strict instructions are given...

Banwarilal Purohit asks for the same information.

Amendment to SC/ST list.

Uttam Rathod to the Welfare Minister.

3899.Q. Is any proposal for addition and deletion of certain castes from the SCs and tribes list pending with the Government?

A. The proposals are being examined.

4027. *D.B. Patil* to the Minister of Environment & Forests.

Q. A proposal for use of forest land for non-forest use

A. A number of such proposals in Raigad (Maharashtra) were received. But essential details were not provided so this issue is closed for the time being. A decision can be taken after the requisite information from the state government is made available.

April 8, 1988. Vol.38
8th series Vol.XXXVIII 10th session 1988
No.31 April 8, 1988

Oral answers to questions
Prof. Madhu Dandavate
The Minister of State in the department of Economic Affairs in the Ministry of Finance.
The statement by the minister.
The total loans outstanding in Government A/c. computed on the exchange rates prevalent on the relevant rates—the statement.....Col.3.
The minister—our position of exports has improved, considerable increase in the exports—
Madhu Dandavate—wants to know—our currency is linked up to a number of European currencies because of devaluation, percentage increase in the export in terms of rupee value is more. The same with the US dollar—the progress as the minister tries to project is not correctly interpreted.
Minister—besides this point mentioned by you, in volume, our exports have gone up.

Q.6280. Reservation for SC/ST in NABARD.
Prof. Madhu Dandavate to the Finance Minister

Q. The reservation for SC and ST for promotion in the NABARD were at par with those in R.B.I. till 1986, if so the same will be restored to protect the weaker sections of society as per the accepted policy of Govt.?

A. Yes. The policy for the recruitment is the same, and at par with the R.B.I.

Withdrawal of excise concessions to large companies.

Q.6205. *Y.S. Mahajan* to Finance Minister.

Q. Whether the department of electronics has represented against withdrawal of excise concessions to large companies marketing electronic items, manufactured by small scale units as these items do not attract excise duty if marketed by small scale units themselves—if so the reaction of the Govt.—the steps to ensure that the small scale units produce more electronics items of requisite quality to increase their share in exports.

A. Government introduced a new scheme providing for full excise duty exceptions for specified excisable goods. In rural areas women's societies, khadi & village industries—government has liberal policy for promotion; infrastructure, facilities and development centres are provided.

6323. Proposal for development of poor villages by big industrial houses

Dr. Datta Samant to the Finance Minister.

Q. Any Government proposal to hand over economically poor villages to big industrial houses for their development and their details

A. There is no such proposal.

Q.6440. *Sharad Dighe* to the Minister of Water Resources.

Q. Any Government proposal under consideration to formulate a national policy for resettlement and development of the people who are affected by the irrigation and water resources development projects including the Sardar Sarovar project, the details thereof and the guidelines based on the decision taken.

A. Guidelines have been already issued to the state Governments. A national Policy on rehabilitation of displaced persons by major projects is also considered.

6463. Stoppage of iron ore export from Redi port in Sindhudurg district.

Prof. Madhu Dandavate to the Minister of Commerce

Is it a fact that about 2000 workers in the Redi port of Sindhudurg district in Maharashtra are deprived of work because of the stoppage of iron ore exports from the port. The steps proposed to avoid hardship to these workers.

Answer: Iron ore exports are affected due to non-availability of funds in the Indo-Romanian Rupee Trade. A ministerial delegation visited Romania and positive results are expected by May 1988.

Col.323-324 *Prof. Madhu Dandavate*

Ref. Mass killings and attack on para military camp by terrorists.

He wants to know about the situation in Punjab. Who is committing murders in Punjab...

The terrorists proclaim that this is being done at the instance of the Government and some minister. Please clarify.

Minister: This is baseless propaganda to defame the Government.

Madhu— the guilty are not punished by the police. The behaviour of the police is not upto the mark

Dr. Datta Samant—the behaviour of the Punjab state government is pro them; the behaviour of the Gujarat government against terrorists.

Demands for Grants: 88-89—Ministry of Agriculture

Balasahib Vikhe Patil

The relief given to farmers in the budget is insufficient. Instead of giving subsidy to farmers, Govt. should not charge interest on the loans provided to them.

Open wells for the farmers should be supplied and loans for purchasing electric motors must be supplied and no charges for these facilities.

Col.362. Kisan Vikas Patra for the development of farmers should be utilised. Setting up of agro-processing industries. A scheme for interest free loans to SCs and STs. Migration of villagers to the cities. Water scarcity in Maharashtra. Industries in Cooperative sector in backward areas should be promoted. Short term, medium term and long term policies should be worked out and some basic changes introduced towards this end.

For introduction of sprinkle and drip irrigation systems Govt. should give long term interest free loans. An incentive to agriculture to increase exports; and the middlemen system in transactions should be avoided.

Sharad Dighe:

Col.366 Govt. should fix the price of cotton. I got a negative reply about the progress of employment guarantee scheme in Maharashtra. Scarcity of drinking water in Maharashtra. To reduce the price of inputs so as to increase agricultural output. Supports Vikhe Patil in the debate.

Col.392 *Sharad Dighe*

Constitution amendment bill

Expresses his views regarding the amendment of the Constitution:

The fundamental right of employment; if an individual cannot secure employment, he has a right to an unemployment allowance. These are there in the directive principles—I am sorry to say but the fact remains that some of the very important salient directive principles are not put into practice.

upto

Col.399 A long discussion about Social Security etc.

8th series—Vol. XXXVIII 10th session.

April 11 Col.30

Incentives for sugar factories

Balasahib Vikhe Patil to the Minister of Food

Q.6144 Whether the Government is examining any proposal to grant incentives for new expansions of the existing sugar factories in the 7th Plan? Whether Government is also considering to prescribe certain norms of efficiency for functioning of the sugar industry and the details.

A. Proposals for grant of incentive and norms of efficiency are under examination.

Col.95

Q. 6544 Import of rice from Thailand

Sharad Dighe to the Minister for Food & Civil Supplies.

Q. Whether Government proposed to import rice from Thailand, the reasons and the quantity and the rate.

A. The quantity of rice to be imported will depend on its availability and the price offered.

6557 *Y.S. Mahajan* to the Minister of Agriculture

Col.103

Q. As a result of price hike of Naptha, the production cost of fertilizer is going up? What steps does the Government propose to take?

A. No increase in the price of Naptha, therefore, no price hike since 17-3-85.

Col.155

Q.6616. *Balasahib Vikhe Patil* to the Minister of Agriculture. Whether the use of chemical pesticides and the disposal of hazardous substance is posing threats to health, what alternatives to pesticides in agriculture?

A. All pesticides are required to be compulsorily registered under the Insecticides Act 1968. A survey and study is going on side by side.

The handling of industrial waste poses a problem to human health. Following measures are taken:

Popularising Integrated Management (PIM) which encompasses various components of pest control technology, and imparting training to field functionaries and farmers etc.

6618. *Balasahib Vikhe Patil* to Minister of Agriculture

Q. Jalashaktiboom to Indian farming (Indian Express 8.12.87) an organic polymer—to what extent can the use of this compound solve the problems of the farmers who are dependent on the rains—what action will the government take to popularise this compound?

A. Experiments on testing the effectiveness of the compound—no conclusive results are yet available.

6619. *Balasahib Vikhe Patil* to the minister of tourism

Col.159

Any long term master plan for the development of tourism in various states, the details of the schemes statewise, and implementation during the plan period?

A. No long term master plan has been formulated.

Madhu Dandavate on hunger deaths due to starvation in different parts of the country.

Col.257

261 Bhajan Lal rejected the facts. The report of the Osmania University experts' statement of 17 persons with names. Bhajan Lal is guilty of telling lies and thereby committing contempt of the House.

A. Dy. Speaker—waiting for the comments.
M. Dandavate wants to share the comments as he wants to pursue this issue before the Dy. Speaker gives the ruling. "*We have a right to raise the question*".

Written Answers 12th April, 1988

659. *Dr. Datta Samant* to the Minister of Industry
Closure of National Byele Corporation Ltd. & Cyelo Corporation.

Q. Whether the Government has taken a decision about the closure of the above industries, the reasons and the efforts the Government has made to revive these units in the past 5 years?

A. No decision to close down the industries. Govt. is extending financial assistance on a yearly basis and plan and non-plan loans for modernisation, replacement of machinery, etc.

6807. *Madhu Dandavate* to the Minister of Information

Q. All the services of All India Radio commence with the National Song—whether Urdu services follow a different practice and the reasons.

A. Yes. They start with the National Anthem.
The Urdu services are a part of the external service for the foreign audience so they do not include the National Anthem.

6808. From *Dandavate* to the Minister of Petroleum
Col.216

Q. In 1987-88 new sources of oil have been explored—where and the likely oil potential and the time by which the country will become self-sufficient in this respect?

A. A statement of locations, the prospects are still under exploration. Time factor cannot be specified as surveys are not yet complete.

Heavy losses sustained by State Electricity Boards.

6826. *Datta Samant* to the Energy Minister.

Q. Whether low tariff for the energy sector is the reason for heavy losses suffered by the state electricity boards during 86-87 and the amount of total losses?

A. Yes, it is so. On the basis of the provisional accounts received, the state electricity boards (except Assam) have generated an overall surplus of Rs.269.4 crores in 86-87 after capitalisation of interest during construction.

6839. Printing of Bombay Telephone Directory
Madhu Dandavate to the Commmunications Minister

Is it a fact that telephone directories are printed by posts & telegraph department. Prior to the formation of the MTNL these were given to private agencies on the basis of open tenders invited? Is it a fact —in Bombay a private agency has increased the price for bold and additional entries? Was it permitted and the reasons.

A. The contractor in Bombay & Delhi have fixed the prices for bold and additional entries.

Col.262 Manufacture of cables.

6851. *Banwarilal Purohit* to the Industry Minister.

Q. Whether union government have urged the cable manufacturers to ensure strict quality, reliability, and safety of the cables—whether Government are aware of inferior quality products which are hazardous to human life. Whether Government proposes quality control and the details of implementation

A. Government have introduced compulsory quality control for 40 household appliances in 1981. Specified standard of quality is examined by the Government Staff.

Tyre Industry

From the same to the industry minister.

Q. Whether the Director General of Technical Development has a proposal to expand and modernise the tyre industry, the time factor, and whether the public sector tyre industry will be benefitted?

A. No proposals are in the offing.

Col.271. Import of Carbon Black.

6873. *Y.S. Mahajan* to the Industry Minister.

Q. Production of Automobile Tyres is affected by shortage of carbon black? Imports of 3000 tonnes are granted or not? Any steps to supply the demand of tyre manufacturers?

A. From Germany it is to be imported and if need arises, more will be imported.

6882. Improvement of financial position of state electricity boards.

Balasahib Vikhe Patil to Energy Minister.

Q. Any schemes to help the state electricity boards to improve their financial position and its details.

A. Amendments have been introduced to increase their capital by the states

Q. Whether the programme for rural electrification is given priority and its details.

A. Yes. 7th 5 year plan invests Rs. 2108 crores in this programme.

6884. *Balasahib Vikhe Patil* to the Minister of Natural Gas.

Q. The places which are covered by the LPG facility till Jan. 1988 and expansion to cover the whole district.

A. Gives a statement of centres in Ahmednagar.

Eighth series Vol.25 Oral Answers

4th April, 1989

13th session

Col.16 *Banwarilal Purohit* to the Minister of Industry

4558.Q. He wants to know the total strength of the employees of the BHEL group of industries and training of foreign personnel and their total number and the norms in this regard.

A. 8,0000 employees in different units of BHEL

300 persons are trained (from underdeveloped countries)

Shri Purohit's suggestion—2000 personnel (Indians) should be trained—to which the Minister answers—Our BHEL people are already trained experts.

S.T.D. Facility in Maharashtra

Gurudas Kamat to the Minister of Communications.

Q. Please state the names of the cities in Maharashtra which are likely to be provided with STD facility in 1989?

A. Alibagh, Bhiwandi, Barshi, Ichalkaranji, Latur.

Muralidhar Mane to the Minister of Energy

4563.

Q. The extent of power generation of each thermal station after modernisation and the estimation of expenditure on the power schemes.

A. 7,000 million units after the completion of renovation and modernisation programmes.
The sanctioned cost—Rs. 1083.26 crores.

Functioning of National Film Development Corporation.

4573. *Shri R.M. Bhoye* to the Information Minister

Q. Is the above corporation incurring a loss, the reasons and the events, and the Govt. steps to reorient the policies.

A. Except in 1981-82 it has made profits.

4585 *Vijay N. Patil* to the Industry Minister.

Q. The number of licences granted to open new companies in collaboration with foreign countries
(1) during 1986-1988
(2) the number of multinationals within 6 months after applying in 87 and those whose cases are pending and the reasons for the delay

A. 1986 — 957; 1987 — 853; 1988—926

Computerised system in Telephone exchanges

4599. *Hussein Dalwai* to the Communication Minister.

Q. Is the computerised system of recording telephone calls in electronic telephone exchange successful and the places where it has been installed

A. It is successful in all the electronic exchanges.

4609. *Balasahib Vikhe Patil* to the Communication Minister.

Q. Opening of new post offices in Ahmednagar, Maharashtra—how many?

A. A statement is given to this effect

4630. Pending applications for telephone connections in Maharashtra.

Prakash Patil to the Communication Minister.

Q. The number of applications for new telephone connections pending in Maharashtra, duration of time in acquiring a phone, any proposal for development programme for Maharashtra and the other details

A. Gives a statement. Development programme is drawn up in the 7th Plan.

4657. Scheme to review the working of Monopolies and Restrictive Trade Practices Act.

Vijay Patil to the Industry Minister.

Q. The number of cases referred to MRTP. The names of big industrial houses referred to MRTP and the results. Whether Govt. has any proposal to revise the MRTP Act and if not, the reasons.

A. Explains in details the names of the companies. All the procedures of the MRTP Act are implemented while scrutinizing the expansions or setting up of industrial houses.

4695. Car telephones in cities

Hamid Dalwai to Minister for Communications.

Q. Allotment of car telephones in Delhi and what about other cities?

A. 77 in Delhi. The implementation in Delhi is under scrutiny and will be introduced in other cities later on.

4691. *Hamid Dalwai* to the Minister for Communications.

Q. About excessive billing and complaints and the payment

of excessive billing first and then the investigation in the matter.

A. Clerical errors, wrong computations, wrong feeding into computers, wrong transcription of meter-reading etc.

4705. *Vijay N. Patil* to Minister of Industry

Q. Whether BHEL is facing grim prospects of gross under-utilisation of its installed capacity for designing and manufacturing power plant equipment, the reasons and the steps Government intends to take.

A. The capacity of BHEL is fairly satisfactory during the current year. It is under constant scrutiny by the Government to ensure that the manufacturing capacities are adequately utilised.

4701. Q. The small entrepreneurs running cottage industries have demanded better facilities and financial assistance and supply of raw materials. What assistance does the Government propose to provide

A. Village and small scale industries are accorded high priority. Bank finance and institutional assistance is made available to them.

Power Generation by Captive Power Plants.

4727. *Murlidhar Mane* to the Minister of Energy.

Q. The total generation of power of the captive power plants during the last 3 years.

Whether it does relieve the power supply of the National Thermal Corporation and the State electricity boards and the estimated power generation.

The new power projects and foreign collaboration, etc.

A. A lengthy statement is issued.

Col.34 April 5, 1989—Oral Answers

Banwarilal Purohit to the Speaker

Q. Consumer Protection Act was passed in 1986. Still no protection to the consumer—implemented in 7 states but the other states have not yet implemented, please clarify what directives you are imposing on these states?

A. We are pursuing this matter with state governments.

Q.4792 Plots to Bangladesh Refugees

Vijay Patil to Minister of Urban Development.

Q. Whether plots have not been allotted to all the refugees from Bangla Desh under the East Pakistan displaced persons schemes—the reasons, the time frame.

A. To eligible persons allotment of plots is made but physical possession is not given due to the stay order given by the Delhi High Court. The development of the plots is not yet complete.

Introduction of Anti-leprosy vaccine

Gurudas Kamat to Minister of Health

4865.Q. Anti-leporsy vaccine developed by the Cancer Research Centre is put to test in district Solapur—the results of the test and when actual use will be started?

A. It is being assessed for immunity—the results are awaited, actual use will be started afterwards.

Gurudas Kamat to the Health Minister.

4866.Q. Whether government proposes to set up public health schools in different states. The number and the funds earmarked for the purpose.

A. No

Increase in land prices for institutional areas.

4873. *Vijay Patil* to the Urban Development Minister.

The increase of prices, the particulars and the reasons

A. Yes. Gives a statement to this effect

Persons suffering from iodine deficiency

Banwarilal Purohit, Ramkrishna More to the Health Minister

4884 Q. Whether the Union Government has made an assessment of persons suffering from iodine deficiency and the steps taken by the Government.

A. The assessment – 43 million people. Intake of iodised salt is the cheapest remedy.

Vijay Patil to the Urban Development Minister.

4405. Unauthorised constructions of DDA flats

Q. Whether it is a fact—and the steps taken by the Govt.

A. Yes. When these are identified, demolition orders are given.

Dr. Datta Samant to the Minister of Textiles.

4911. Assistance to Swan Mills

Q. The Swan Mills has reopened, assistance and concessions given to it; the reasons for closures of such mills, and any proposal for assistance?

A. No manufacturing operation has started, though it has reopened. A rehabilitation package for the revival of the Company has been formulated.

Sugarcane arrears

R.M. Bhoye to the Food Minister

4914.Q. Whether arrears of sugarcane dues to be paid to the farmers are mounting, the details.

A. Ensuring payment is the responsibility of the States. The government has advised for prompt payment.

Proposal to set up branches of National Institute of Naturopathy

4436. *Pratap Bhosale* to the Health and Family Welfare Minister

Q. Any proposal for the above institute?

A. No

4937. *Bhosale* to Minister of Environment and Forests

Q. Is there wide scope for low cost environmental restoration schemes without expensive technical processes. Any proposal for public participation?

A. Yes. Government is using in several programmes low cost restoration in Soil Conservation and Watershed Protection, alternative sources of energy such as bio-gas, water purification, Mass multiplication of tree saplings for afforestation.

Q.4955. *Prakash Patil* to Health Minister.

Q. Suggestion of Maharashtra Government to accord sanction for medical colleges

Whether the Medical Council of India accords sanction to the private medical institutions in India on a non-grant basis, the number of applications from different states pending for decision with Union Government, whether the Maharashtra state has any suggestions and when the decision will be taken

A. The Government Policy is not to permit new medical colleges in the country. There are sufficient number of qualified doctors. There is a proposal from a private institution in Maharashtra and it comes under the scrutiny of the Medical Council of India and the Central Government.

4956. *Prakash Patil* to the Health Minister.

Q. Detection of Aids cases.

A. The Minister states the names of the centres.

The State Government is establishing centres for screening of blood donors in Bombay:

LTMG Medical College, J.J. Hospital, Nair, Haffkine, Tata, Cooper, Rajawad, Red Cross

---

Thursday, April 16, 1989

Oral answers

512 *Balasahib Vikhe Patil* to the Agriculture Minister

Loss of Mango Crop— the mango growers' association

have urged for aerial sprayinǵ and the reaction of the Government.

A. Yes—no requests from the mango growers.

Q. Balasahib continues to furnish information about the mango crop, and requests for subsidy for aerial spraying of pesticides technical details

A. A statement. A technical explanation.

4970. *R.M. Bhoye* to the External Affairs Minister.
Indian workers in jails in foreign countries

Q. The number of Indian workers in jail— in the last 3 years, year-wise, country wise. The action taken by the Indian embassies

A. The information is being collected.

4973. *Prakash Patil* to the Agriculture Minister

Q. Whether the Technical Mission of Drinking Water was to submit its report in March 1989 about the availability of water, and the details of the findings

A. The mission is still coundcting the survey. No source problem villages (976) are yet to be provided with safe drinking water facilities

---

5012. *Banwarilal Purohit* to the Agriculture Minister.

Q. Orange crops in Nagpur have been destroyed completely. Whether Union Government have sent a deputation to assess the damage? What scientific measures have been taken to save orange crops

A. No reports from Maharashtra State have come to us, but long term measures for control of destruction by diseases, etc. are made available by the Research Centre at Nagpur.

Seismic Survey by Geological Survey of India.

5020. *Keshav Rao Pardhi* to the Minister of Steel & Mines.

Q. A technical question

A. Technical answer.

5029. Proposal to set up National Education Wage Board.

Hussein Dalwai to Human Resource Development Minister.

Q. In order to settle the wage disputes of the staff of educational institutions, is it proposed to appoint a National Education Wage Board? If not what other measures?

A. The states have their own mechanisms and arrangements to settle the matter. The centre is providing financial assistance to the extent of 80% of the additional expenditure to the States for revising the pay scale.

R.M. Bhoye to the Human Resource Development Minister.

5048. Criteria for construction of working women's hostels

Q. Details of financial assistance provided to Maharashtra Government for women's hostels during the last 3 years.

A. Grants are given— a statement to this effect.

5051.Q *R.M. Bhoye* to Agriculture Minister.

Any independent evaluation of IRDP since its inception if not—the reasons; and any proposal to set up a monitoring and evaluating board?

A. A number of studies have been conducted since its inception by PEO, IFMR, NABARD

Q. Operation Flood II

In 7th Five year Plan—iteam-wise, milk etc. targets, expenditure incurred—year-wise, state-wise, achievements, shortfalls etc., regional inequalities, whether Government have appointed a Committee to assess the achievements

A. No specific studies have been undertaken on the issue.

5069. *Madhu Dandavate & Balasahib Vikhe Patil* to Agriculture Minister.

Q. In the Konkan region has any fruit processing plant proposal been received? If yes, the details.

A. The ministry has not yet received any proposal as such.

5090. *Vijay Patil* to Agriculture Minister.

Q. Whether we are moving towards the goal of sustainable agriculture without pesticides. Biological control—any research going on in this sphere

A. A statement to this effect is made.

5103.

Q. Any new methods to set the targets of farm output—the details.

A. Yes. Working Groups are set up for agriculture and allied sectors.

Exodus of refugees from Tibet

5107. *Sharad Dighe* to the Minister of External Affairs.

Q. Government reaction to the reports about recent public outcry in Tibet. Any exodus to India?

A. Government is aware of reports. No exodus of refugees to India

---

5122. Shortage of text books published by National Council of Educational Research and Training.

Vijay Patil to Minister of Human Resource Development.

Q. Whether Government have received complaints of shortage of textbooks outside Delhi, published by NCERT? Why? The reasons and what remedial measures to solve the problem?

A. The NCERT text books are distributed by the Publication Division of the Ministry of Information. Wholesale agents in five more cities will be appointed and we are planning to expand the network of wholesale agents to supply the needs of the students.

Engaging an U.S. Public Relations Company by India
Sharad Dighe to the External Affairs Minister.

Q. Whether Government have a proposal for engaging a leading American P.R. Company to promote India's interests in United States and the details thereof?

A. An assessment of the steps required to optimise the projection of Government policies is underway. No decision has yet been taken.

5164. *Prataprao Bhosale* to the Minister of Agriculture.

Q. Sheep-rearing activity—statewise details

A. In some states it is more due to the sheep population. The state-wise statement is given.

Prataprao Bhosale to the Minister of External Affairs.

Q. Whether the National Buildings Construction Corporation has been awarded a contract for construction of a medical complex at Male in the memory of Indira Gandhi?

A. Yes, Rs. 16.967 crores with Indian assistance.

8th series Vol.25
Tuesday April 4, 1989.
Oral answers to questions

4800. *Prakash Patil* to Minister of Health

Q. Union Government nominates 11 candidates to Medical Colleges. The Union Government is late in communicating their decision.

A. Union Government eagerly requests the states with

medical colleges which are allocated to states/union territories without medical colleges. Sometimes the states delay the matter. Hence matters keep pending.

4911. *Datta Samant* to the Minister of Textiles.
Assistance to Swan Mills Bombay.
Q. Whether assistance will be given to other closed mills
A. The Board for Industrial and Financial Reconstruction will decides on the issue it after investigating matters.

4987. *Datta Samant* to Labour Minister.
Q. Consumer price index for industrial workers has fallen by 26 points. The names of the commodities and statistical data.
A. It has declined by 5 points only. Price increase in Rice, Wheat, Arhar Dal, Gram Dal, Groundnut Oil, Onions, Chillies, and vegetables.

5702. *Banwarilal Purohit* on import of ships from Rumania and East Germany which are defective.
A. Yes, some defects, but no inquiry has been held.

5156. *Prakash Patil* to the Agriculture Minister.
Q. Assistance to Maharashtra under *S.F.P.P.*—Special Foodgrain Production Programme. Targets fixed and the funds earmarked as Central assistance for 1989
A. Focus on Rice crop. Rs.268.76 crores assistance has been provided. The target is 108.00 lakhs tonnes of food. The allocation for 1989 is not yet finalised.

Index

Advani, L.K., 70
Aiyar, Mani Shankar, 36
Ajanta, Ellora Caves, 9
Ambedkar, 29
Ansari, Z.R., 62, 75
Antulay, A.R., 2, 4, 31, 95
Azad, Gulan Nabi, 36
Azad, Maulana, 29
Banatwala, G.M., 3, 6, 49
Barooah, 30
Bhabha Atomic Research Centre, 74
Bhardwaj, H.R., 13
Bhuria, 64
Bopche, K.P., 4, 10, 11, 39, 46, 47, 92
Buta Singh, 36
Chaman Lal, Dewan, 64
Chatterjee, Somnath, 71
Chávan, S.B., 2, 10, 95
Chavan, Y.B., 30, 95
Dalvi, 70
Das, Arjun, 31
Deora, Murli, 2, 4, 6
Desai, Morarji, 30, 38, 41
Deshmukh, Ashok, 6, 8, 9, 92, 93
Dhakne, Baban Rao, 6, 38, 47, 93, 94
Dhawan, R.K., 36, 77
Dighe, Sharad, 3, 54, 55, 72-79, 82
Dutt, Sunil, 4
Elected representative-change of nature, 29-43
    Congress culture, induction of new MPs, 42-43
    Congress led by Indira Gandhi, 30-32
        Control of party machine, 31
        Induction of young people, 30-32
    During Nehru era, 29
    Rebellion against old guard, 29-30
    Transition from Nehru to Lal Bahadur, Shastri, 29-30
    Type of men entring Parliament, 32-40
        Calibre of MP, 33
        Caste wise MPs, 34
        Corruption, 39
        Decline of status and respect, 38-40
        Educational background of, 34-35
        Election expenditure, 37, 39
        Indiscipline on floor, 33-34
        Lifestyle of, 37
        Members elected did not belong to that state, 36
        Mixing of different political party MPs, 37
        Nature of change, 32-33
        Nomination to Rajya Sabha for outsiders, 36
        Party members united, 38-39
        Public interest issue, 38
        Quality of debate, 33, 37
        Quorum, 34
    Type of MPs emerged, 40-42
        Democratic norms, 40
        Destroyed democratic institution, 40
        Moral forces, 41
        Rajiv norms, 41
        Rajiv on environment and ecology, 42
        Socialistic pattern of society, 42
Fernandes, George, 9
Fotedar, M.L., 36
Gandhi, Indira, 30-32, 38, 40, 41,62, 69, 93, 95
Gandhi, Mahatma, 29, 39, 55-57, 60, 68, 69
Gandhi, Maneka, 11, 55, 62
Gandhi, Rajiv, 16, 22, 41, 42, 62
Gandhi, Sanjay, 31, 93, 95
Ghosh, Atulya, 30

Gokhale, Vidyadhar, 13, 14, 25, 48, 92, 93
Gomango, 67
Gorpade, 68
Haq, Mehbool, 62
Heimandorff, Baron, 65, 66
Impact on policy formulation, 19-28
  Debate in House, 28
  Parliamentary forums, 28
  Party forums meeting, 20-21, 28
  Self-perception, 21-28
  Work on Parliamentary Committees, 28
Jethmalani, Ram, 4
Jha, L.K., 60
Kale, S.N., 6, 11, 12, 92, 93
Kamble, A. T., 12, 13, 37, 93
Kamraj, 30
Khan, Arif Beg, 70, 71
Kripalani, Acharya, 29
Krishna Menon, V.K., 58
Laski, 48
Lohia, Ram Manohar, 29, 30
Mahadik, V.S., 2, 3, 44, 46, 47
Mahajan, Y.S., 4, 6, 20-22, 33, 45, 54-55, 58, 60, 91-92
Mahale, Haribhau, 25, 38, 45, 46, 62
Mandal Commission, 68
Mavalankar, P.G., 53
Mehta, Ashok, 29
Mohan, Lalit, 31
MP-importance, 85-88
  Corrupt practices, 87
  Legislative functions diminished, 87-88
  No accountability, 86-87
  Prestige decline, 85, 97
  Quality decline, 86
MP-role and functions, 7-18
  Duties in Parliament, 7
  Fulfilling voters demand, 7
  Functions of, 7-18
  Role of, 13-18
    Development role, 17
    Not defined, 17
    Solution to voters problems, 14-15
    Victim of expectations of voters, 15-16
  Tackle local issue in domain of Centre, 7-11, 18, 96-97
Mukerjee, Hiren, 29
Mukerjee, Pranab, 31
Mukerjee, Shyama Prasad, 29
Munshi, Priyaranjan Das, 31
Naik, Ram, 3, 6, 23
Narasimha Rao, P.V., 36, 72
Narayanan, K.R., 73, 74
Nath, Kamal, 31
National Integration Council, 71
Natwar Singh, K., 76
Nehru, 29, 34, 38, 40, 41, 43, 51, 68, 85, 97
Nijlingappa, 30
Pai, Nath, 29
Pai, T.A., 30
Panigrahi, Chintamani, 74
Pant, Govindvallab, 30
Pant, K.C., 73
Patel, 29
Patil, Babasahib Vikhe, 4, 24, 33, 37, 44, 47, 92, 93
Patil, S.K., 30
Patil, Shivaraj, 2, 6, 26-28, 77, 93, 94
  As Minister of Civil Aviation, 28
  As Minister of Commerce, 26-27
  As Minister of Defence Production, 27-28
  As Minister of Science and Technology, 27
  As Minister of State for Defence, 26
Patil, Uttomrao Deorao, 8, 17, 22, 39, 92, 93
Pawar, Sharad, 2
Phundkar, P.P., 6, 12, 40, 47
Pilot, Rajesh, 31
Political elite-MP, 1-6
  Gaps to be filled, 5
  Influence of, 2, 95
  Lifestyle of, 2-5
  Methodology, 5-6
  Ministers, 95
  Perks and privileges, 1
  Responsibility of exercising power, 96
Quality of Debate, 51-84
  Decline of level, 51
  Expertise to make significant suggestions, 51
  Influence on policy by participation in, 51, 83-84

Lack of opportunity to study subject, 53-54
Media picks up views of controversial MP, 53-54
Parliamentary procedures against, 52
Questions raised and clarification seeking, 54-58
Budget 1989-90, 58-60
Comments on Forest Conservation Policy, 62-64
Earthquakes in April 1989, 72-73
Foreign Policy, 72
Hindu-Muslim Unity, 69, 72
Joint Venture of BEL with Samtal India, 75-76
Judiciary, 60-62
Khadi and Village Industry Bill, 55-57
Leave Priviledge to IA pilots, 76-77
Meeting between Defence Secretaries of India and Pakistan, 74-75
Preparation for launch of Agni, 73
Protection of Ozone layer, 75
Safeguarding Indians in Jalalabad, 76
Sarkaria Commission report, 79-83
Technology transfer to private firm by BARC, 74
Thakkar Commission, 72-79
Tribal uplift, 64-69
Vote in accordance with party whip, 52
Rai, Kalpanath, 32
Rajaji, 69
Ram, Jagjivan, 30
Ranga, N.G., 78, 82
Rathod, Uttam, 6, 18, 20, 23, 34, 44, 45, 54, 55, 62-65, 69, 70, 91, 93
Reddy, Brahmanand, 31
Reddy, Madhav, 58
Reluctant MP, 44-50, 96
Impact on policy for mulation, 44-45
Interest in national issues, 48, 96
Inadequate political experience, 48
Lack of adequate fluency in English or Hindi, 48
MLA more powerful than MP 45-46
MPs prefer to work in their state, 46-48
Powers at Centre, 44
Reflective cast of mind, 44
Selection of suitable candidate for, 49-50
Samant, Dutta, 3, 6
Sarkaria Commission, 54, 72, 79-83
Sathe, Vasant, 2, 4, 6, 26, 31, 33, 44, 92-94
Seshan, 63
Shastri, Lal Bahadur, 29, 30
Shingda, Damodar Barku, 44, 48, 92, 93
Shiv Shankar, V., 36
Singh, Hukum, 53
Singh, Jaipal, 67
Singh, Swaran, 30-31
Singh, V.P., 38, 70
Singh, Vishwajit Prithvijit, 36
Socio-economic background of MP, 89-94
Age of, 89
Agriculturist, 89
Caste composition of, 90-91
Education of, 89
Political Socialisation, 92-94
Selection on the basis of numerical strength of caste of voters, 91-92
Teachers, 89
Soz, Saifuddin, 69
Stephen, C.M., 31
Subramaniam, C., 30
Thakkar Commission, 54, 72, 77-79
Tiwari, N.D., 22
Tully, Mark, 77
Tytler, Jagdish, 31
Unnikrishnan, 31
Urs, 31
Vajpayee, 30
Young Turks, 30
Youth Congress, 31

विश्व का इतिहास

(3000 ई॰ पू॰ से 500 ई॰ तक)

रश्मि शर्मा
महेश शर्मा

अर्जुन पब्लिशिंग हाउस

विश्व का इतिहास (3000 ई॰ पू॰ से 500 ई॰ तक)

संस्करण, 2013

ISBN 978-81-8330-453-5

प्रकाशक :

अर्जुन पब्लिशिंग हाऊस

4831/24, प्रह्लाद गली,

अंसारी रोड, दरियागंज,

नई दिल्ली—110002

फोन : 23272541, 23257835

फैक्स : 91-011-23257835

e-mail : arjunbooks2001@gmail.com

टाइपसेटिंग :

डिम्पल कम्प्यूटर्स

दिल्ली—110092

प्रिन्टर्स :

रोशन आफसेट प्रिंटर्स

दिल्ली - 53

प्रस्तावना

प्रारम्भिक दौर में जब मानव ने पृथ्वी पर जन्म लिया था, तब यहाँ का वातावरण मानव के अनुकूल नहीं था। कहने का तात्पर्य यह है कि उस समय का वातावरण जो व्याप्त था। वह काफी असहनीय था। पूरी पृथ्वी पर बर्फ का आवरण छाया हुआ था परन्तु इस वातावरण में धीरे-धीरे बदलाव आने लगा और मानव अपना निवास स्थान बनाने लगा। ऐसे ही वातावरण में पाषाण युग का उदय हुआ। आगे चलकर विश्व के विभिन्न क्षेत्रों में भिन्न-भिन्न सभ्यताओं का जन्म हुआ।

विश्व की विभिन्न सभ्यताओं में मिस्र की भी एक प्राचीन सभ्यता है। मिस्र की सभ्यता का विकास उत्तरी अफ्रीका की एक नील नामक नदी में हुआ था। इसीलिए मिस्र को नील नदी का जन्म स्थान कहा जाता है। प्राचीन मिस्रवासी नील नदी को असीम श्रद्धा के साथ एक देवता की भांति पूजा करते थे। नील नदी का वहाँ की कृषि में बहुत ही अधिक महत्त्व था। इसलिए प्राचीन मिस्र की सभ्यता को नील नदी का श्रेय कहा जाता है। मिस्र के अलावा मैसोपोटामिया की सभ्यता भी महत्वपूर्ण रही है। प्राचीनकाल में इराक को मैसोपोटामिया के नाम से जाना जाता था।

इसके अलावा चीन की सभ्यता भी विश्व के इतिहास में प्रमुख स्थान रखती है। जब विश्व के कई देश सभ्यताओं का अन्वेषण कर रहे थे उस दौरान चीन की सभ्यता काफी प्रभावशाली थी। इसके अलावा यूनान की सभ्यता का भी विशेष स्थान था। विश्व की सभ्यता में यूनान का विज्ञान, कला एवं साहित्य

जगत में अद्वितीय योगदान है। प्राचीन एवं आधुनिक सभ्यताओं के मध्य रोम ने एक सीढ़ी का काम किया है। यूनानी सभ्यता की तरह ही रोम की सभ्यता, संस्कृति भी बहुत पुरानी है। पाश्चात्य देशों में यूनानी संस्कृति का अत्यधिक प्रसार रोम के कारण हुआ है।

सभ्यताओं के विकास से भारत की अछूता नहीं रहा है। यहाँ प्राचीन नदी-घाटी सभ्यता विकसित हुई। जिसे सिंधु घाटी सभ्यता तथा हड़प्पा सभ्यता के नाम से भी जाना जाता है। यह एशिया महाद्वीप के सबसे प्राचीनतम ज्ञात नगरीय संस्कृतियों में महत्त्वपूर्ण स्थान रखती है। इस सभ्यता में पांच विशाल नगर : हड़प्पा, मोहनजोदड़ो, कच्छ में धोलावीरा, पाकिस्तान में अब सूख चुकी हकरा नदी की निम्नभूमि के पास गनवेरीवल और सतलुज-यमुना विभाजन क्षेत्र में द्रष्डवती नदी के समीप राखी गढ़ी शामिल थे।

पुस्तक को प्रामाणिक बनाने के लिए कई लिखित व अलिखित स्रोतों से मदद ली गई है जिनके लेखकों व प्रकाशकों के प्रति मैं अपना विनम्र आभार प्रकट करता हूँ। आशा है, पुस्तक का अध्ययन कर पाठकजन विश्व के इतिहास को समझ सकेंगे। पुस्तक के संदर्भ में पाठकों के सुझाव सहर्ष रूप में स्वीकार हैं।

-लेखक

अनुक्रम

	प्रस्तावना	V
1.	पाषाणकाल	1
2.	मिस्र की सभ्यता	14
3.	मैसोपोटामिया की सभ्यता	49
4.	प्राचीन चीन की सभ्यता	94
5.	प्राचीन यूनान की सभ्यता	134
6.	प्राचीन रोम की सभ्यता	196
7.	भारत में नदी-घाटी सभ्यता	248
8.	वैदिककालीन सभ्यता	265

1

पाषाणकाल

प्रारम्भिक दौर में जब मानव ने इस मानव रूपी संसार में जन्म लिया था तब यहां का वातावरण मानव के अनुकूल नहीं था। कहने का आशय है कि उस समय का जो वातावरण व्याप्त था वह काफी सहनीय था। पूरी पृथ्वी पर बर्फ का आवरण छाया हुआ था परन्तु इस वातावरण में धीरे-धीरे बदलाव आने लगा और मानव अपना निवास स्थान बनाने लगा। ऐसे ही वातावरण में पाषाण युग का उदय हुआ। इस युग के सन्दर्भ में हमें पर्याप्त ज्ञान नहीं है फिर भी पंजाब, राजपूताना, गुजरात आदि कई भागों में हमें प्राचीन मानव के अस्तित्व के कुछ प्रमाण मिले हैं। इस समय के हथियार अत्यन्त भद्दे थे। प्राचीन मनुष्य के औजार यूरोप के पाषाण युग के हथियारों से मिलते-जुलते हैं। प्राचीन मानव ने प्रथम हिम युग में उत्तर-पश्चिमी में रहना आरंभ किया। इन हिम युगों की निम्नलिखित विशेषताएं हैं—

(क) प्रथम हिम युग—प्रथम हिम युग में वातावरण मानव के अनुकूल नहीं था। इस युग में सर्दी, गर्मी तथा वर्षा तीनों असहनीय थे। उस समय के मानव के औजार अनेक स्थानों से प्राप्त हुए हैं। सभी औजार चौकोर और भद्दे हैं। इन औजारों की धारें टूटी हुई हैं।

(ख) द्वितीय हिम युग—इस समय के कुछ हथियार हमें खुशहालगढ़ एवं अटक के दक्षिण-पूर्व में हारी नदी के पास मिले हैं। इन औजारों में प्रायः पत्थर के औजार हैं। उन्हें गोल और चिकने पत्थरों से बनाया गया है। यह बीच में से उभरे हुए हैं।

(ग) तृतीय हिम युग—इस युग के प्राप्त हुए कुछ प्रमाणों के अनुसार इस युग में मैदानों में पर्याप्त हरियाली आ गयी थी। इसके अलावा कुछ प्राचीन पत्थर के हथियार मिले हैं। इन औजारों में पत्थर की कुल्हाड़ी एवं लकड़ी चीरने आदि के हथियार हैं।

(घ) चतुर्थ हिम युग—इस युग के सील नदी एवं टोक पठार के इर्द-गिर्द पत्थर के बने कुछ औजार प्राप्त हुए हैं। इनके आधार पर ऐसा प्रतीत होता है कि प्राचीन मानव पंजाब में आरम्भ से ही रह रहा था। परन्तु औजारों के साथ मनुष्य की अस्थियां नहीं मिली हैं। इसलिए इस बात को दावे के साथ नहीं कहा जा सकता। इस काल के हथियार पहले से अच्छे और अच्छे बनने लगे थे।

पाषाण युग का विभाजन—पाषाण युग को प्रागैतिहासिक काल भी कहा जाता है। सामान्य रूप से इस काल को तीन भागों में बांटा गया है—

1. पुरापाषाण काल
2. मध्य पाषाण काल
3. नव पाषाण काल।

अतः इन तीनों कालों पर विस्तृत प्रकाश नीचे डाला गया है—

पुरापाषाण काल

पुरापाषाण काल की अवधि 400,000 से 1,50,000 ई. पू. माना जाता है। भारत में इसका विकास 8000 इ. पू. तक होता रहा। 20वीं शताब्दी के अंत में भारत-पाकिस्तान की दक्षिणी सीमा के आधे हिस्से पर फैले विशाल भारतीय रेगिस्तान (थार) में महत्त्वपूर्ण पुरातात्विक सामग्रियां उपलब्ध हुईं। डीडवाना, राजस्थान में पाई गई कुल्हाड़ियां, जो शिवालिक पहाड़ियों की कुल्हाड़ियों जैसी ही हैं, कुछ बाद के काल की, यानी लगभग चार लाख वर्ष पूर्व की हैं। मरुस्थलीय मिट्टी के स्तर-परीक्षण और अन्य प्रमाणों ने पुरापाषाण युग की विद्यमान जलवायु व तकनीक के उत्तरोत्तर स्तरों के बीच के संबंध को स्पष्ट किया है।

उदाहरणार्थ, एक लंबा आर्द्र काल, जैसा काफ़ी गहरी लालिमायुक्त भूरी मिट्टी से प्रमाणित है, लगभग एक लाख चालीस हज़ार वर्ष पूर्व आरंभ हुआ जान पड़ता है। यह काल अब से लगभग 25 हज़ार वर्ष पूर्व तक चला, जो लगभग मध्य पुरापाषाण काल के बराबर की अवधि है। इसी दौर में आजकल के मरुस्थलीय क्षेत्र शिकार हेतु अत्यन्त समृद्ध वातावरण उपलब्ध कराते थे। क्षेत्र में अब तक पाए गए सबसे प्राचीन शैल चित्र ऊपरी पुरापाषाण काल के हैं। अब तक उपमहाद्वीप में पाई गई प्राचीनतम

शिल्प कृतियां उस काल की हैं, जिसे भारतीय निम्न पुरापाषाण युग का प्रारंभ कहा जा सकता है। ये पाकिस्तान के उत्तरी क्षेत्र में रावलपिण्डी के समीप शिवालिक पहाड़ियों के पश्चिमी भाग के पास प्राप्त हुईं हैं। पुराचुम्बकीय विश्लेषण के अनुसार स्फटिक पत्थरों के ये औज़ार और पतले टुकड़े लगभग 20 लाख वर्ष पुराने हैं। ये हाथ की कुल्हाड़ी से पूर्व के औज़ार निर्माण के उस प्रकार को दर्शाते हैं, जो तब से लेकर बहुत लंबे समय तक प्रयोग में रहे। इन शिल्प कृतियों का अत्यंत समृद्ध अवसादीय प्रमाणों और जीवाश्मों से संबंध है, किंतु अब तक इससे जुड़े कोई भी मानव अवशेष नहीं मिले हैं। इसी क्षेत्र में प्राप्त प्राचीनतम कुल्हाड़ियां (जो फ्रांस में इससे भी पहले मिलने पर सामान्यतः एक्यूलियन कहलाईं) पुराचुंबकीय विश्लेषण द्वारा 5 लाख वर्ष पुरानी सिद्ध हुई हैं।

1990 के दशक में किए गए उत्खनन कार्यों से भारत के अन्य महत्त्वपूर्ण पुरापाषाण स्थलों में कर्नाटक राज्य में हुंस्गी और गंगा की द्रोणी को दक्कन के पठार से अलग करने वाली विंध्य पर्वतमाला शामिल है।

कालानुक्रम के मुताबिक देखा जाए तो मध्य पाषाण संस्कृतियां भारत में विस्तृत रूप से फैली हैं। उत्तरी अफ़ग़ानिस्तान में, हिंदुकुश की गुफ़ाओं में, 15000 से 10000 ई.पू. में मानव निवास के प्रमाण पुरापाषाण काल के एक चरण का प्रतिनिधित्व करते हैं, जिसे मध्यपाषाण काल का हिस्सा माना जा सकता है। समझा जाता है कि भेड़ और बकरियां पालना इस काल में आरंभ हुआ।

मध्य-पुरापाषाण काल में शुरू हुआ पाषाण शिल्पाकृतियों के घटते आकार का सिलसिला भारतीय मध्यपाषाण काल कहलाने वाले युग के छोटे समानांतर सतह वाले फलकों व सूक्ष्म पाषाण औज़ारों में पराकाष्ठा पर पहुंचा। मध्यपाषाण संस्कृतियों का संपूर्ण भारत में विस्तार प्रमाणित है, हालांकि इनके बारे में जानकारी का एकमात्र स्रोत ज़मीन से मिले औज़ार हैं। इस काल की संस्कृतियां भरण-पोषण के अत्यधिक विविध प्रतिमान प्रदर्शित करती हैं, जिनमें शिकार, भोजन इकट्ठा करना, मछली पकड़ना और कम-से-कम उस काल के कुछ भाग में थोड़ा बहुत पशुपालन व छोटे पैमाने पर कृषि शामिल हैं।

भारत के मध्य राज्यों में कई गुफ़ाओं और शैलाश्रमों में विविध विषयों को दर्शाते भित्तिचित्र हैं, जिनमें शिकारी पशु और शिकार, शहद एकत्रित करने और नृत्य जैसी मानव गतिविधियां भी शामिल हैं। यह कला ऊपरी पुरापाषाण काल के पूर्वजों से विकसित हुई प्रतीत होती है और उस काल के जीवन के बारे में बहुत कुछ बताती है। कला के साथ ही उत्तरोत्तर स्पष्ट संकेत मिले हैं कि कुछ गुफ़ाएं धार्मिक गतिविधियों का केंद्र थीं।

मेहरगढ़ (अब पाकिस्तान) स्थित पुरातात्विक स्थलों का समूह दो प्रमुख कालों के कोई पांच या छः हज़ार वर्षों तक निवास का प्रमाण प्रस्तुत करता है। पहला आठवीं से सोलहवीं सहस्राब्दी ई. तक और दूसरा पांचवीं से चौथी (और संभवतः तीसरी) सहस्राब्दी ई.पू. तक।

पहले चरण के मेहरगढ़ के प्रमाण एक प्रारंभिक कृषि बस्ती का स्पष्ट चित्रण करते हैं, जिनमें घरेलू शिल्पकला और प्रचलित कलाओं की विविधता दिखाई देती है। दूसरे चरण की विशेषता बड़े पैमाने पर परिवर्तन है। जान पड़ता है कि इस काल के आरंभ में (लगभग 5500 ई.पू.) कोई बड़ी भू-भौतिक गतिविधि हुई, जिससे मैदानों में भारी मात्रा में गाद जमा हुई और मेहरगढ़ का मूल टीला लगभग पूरी तरह दब गया।

चरण 1 जो आठवीं-सातवीं सहस्राब्दी ई.पू. का है, मिट्टी के बर्तनों से रहित नवपाषाण निवास था। पत्थर के पतले टुकड़े मुख्य औज़ार थे। पत्थर की कुल्हाड़ियां भी थोड़ी संख्या में पाई गई हैं। भेड़-बकरी पालन की ही तरह गेहूँ और जौ का घरेलू उपयोग इस क्षेत्र में इस चरण के दौरान किसी समय आरंभ हो गया था, किंतु पशुओं के अवशेषों में चिंकारे की हड्डियों की प्रचुरता शिकार पर निर्भरता जारी रहना दर्शाती है। मिट्टी की ईंटों के मकान इस चरण के आंरभ से लेकर पूरे समय में मिलते हैं। मानव अवशेषों के साथ दफ़नाई जाने वाली वस्तुओं में सीपी या पत्थर के मोतियों के कंठहार, टोकरियां और यदा-कदा छोटे पालतू पशु (जिसमें भेड़ें और बकरियां, दोनों शामिल हैं), जो इस उद्देश्य के लिए काटे जाते थे, शामिल थे।

पुरापाषण काल में मिट्टी के बर्तन के निर्माण तथा कृषि के क्षेत्र में विकास होने लगा। उस युग के प्रारम्भिक दौर में पालतू पशु (स्पष्टतः बो इंडिकस, कूबड़ वाली भारतीय प्रजाति) शिकार के जानवरों और साथ ही भेड़ों और बकरियों से अधिक महत्त्वपूर्ण हो गए थे। एक नए प्रकार का भवन, जिसके समान आकार के छोटे कोष्ठ इसे काफ़ी हद तक एक अन्न भंडार के रूप में दर्शाते हैं, बहुधा प्रचुर फ़सलों के उत्पादन को इंगित करते हैं। इस युग में शवों को दफनाने का अत्यधिक प्रचलन था। एक गड्ढे के एक छोर पर दफ़न-प्रकोष्ठ खोदा जाता था और मृतक के शरीर को उसमें रखने के बाद, ईंट की दीवार से बंद कर दिया जाता था।

विशेषताएँ

पुरापाषाण काल की कुछ प्रमुख विशेषताओं को निम्नलिखित पंक्तियों में स्पष्ट किया गया है—

1. पुरापाषाण काल में मानव ने कुछ धार्मिक अनुष्ठानों के आयोजन करने शुरू कर दिये थे। मनुष्य को प्रकृति से कई प्रकार से मदद मिलती थी। वृक्ष से पत्ते, छाया और फल मिलते थे। इसलिए वह वृक्ष को प्रसन्न करने का प्रयत्न करने लगा। सूर्य को भी वह आदर की दृष्टि से देखता था। वह नुकसान पहुंचाने वाली वस्तुओं जैसे सांप और आग आदि से डरता था, इसलिए उन्हें भी प्रसन्न रखना चाहता था। इस तरह पूजा करने की भावना पैदा हुई। गुफाओं से प्राप्त चित्रों का अध्ययन करने से यह पता चलता है कि देवी-देवताओं को खुश करने के लिए इस युग का मानव पशुओं की बलि भी करता था।

2. इस युग में मनुष्यों ने औजारों को विकसित कर अपने आपको जानवरों की श्रेणी से अलग कर लिया। अब मनुष्य अपनी रक्षा के लिए अपना भोजन प्राप्त करने के लिए और पशुओं को मारने के लिए पेड़ों की शाखाओं, पत्थर के टुकड़ों से प्राकृतिक रूप में ही हथियारों का काम लिया करता था। आगे चलकर मनुष्य ने अनुभव किया कि नुकीला पत्थर पशुओं को मारने में अधिक घातक हो सकता है। इससे उसे एक पत्थर से काटकर नुकीला बनाने की प्रेरणा प्राप्त हुई। यह छैनी जैसा पत्थर ही शायद मानव के हाथ का बना पहला औजार था। इसे कठोर पत्थर का औजार कहा जाता है। बाद में चलकर शल्कनुमा औजारों का निर्माण किया जाने लगा। ये पत्थर एक बड़े कठोर पत्थर पर दूसरे पत्थर द्वारा प्रहार करके बनाए जाते थे। इन शल्कों को काट छांटकर चाकू या कुल्हाड़ी जैसे औजार बनाये जाते थे। इन औजारों से पशुओं की चमड़ी उतारी जाती थी और मोरा काटा जाता था। इस काल के मानव ने एक नुकीले की धार को पैना करके उसे पेड़ का डाली में तोते से बांधकर भाला नामक हथियार बना लिया था। भाले को फेंककर दूर से ही पशुओं को मार सकता था। धीरे-धीरे उसने तीर और कमान बनाना भी सीख लिया। इस हथियार को आगे चलकर बहुत अधिक महत्त्व प्राप्त हुआ।

3. उत्खनन में इस युग के कई अवशेष प्राप्त हुए हैं। इस काल का प्रथम अवशेष उत्तर-पश्चिम भारत में सोहन घाटी (सिन्धु की सहायक नदी) से प्राप्त हुआ है। विद्वानों ने इस संस्कृति को सोहन संस्कृति का नाम दिया है। इस संस्कृति को दो भागों—पूर्व सोहन संस्कृति एवं उत्तर सोहन संस्कृति में बांटा गया है। उत्खन्न द्वारा इस स्थल से अनेक उपकरण मिले हैं। इस स्थल के समीप चौंतरा नामक स्थान के भी हस्त कुठार और शल्क मिले हैं। नर्मदा घाटी के नरसिंहपुर

में भी पुरापाषाण कालीन अवशेष प्राप्त हुए हैं। नर्मदा के पास भीमबेरका (मध्य प्रदेश) की गुफाओं से मानव निर्मित निवास स्थलों का पता चला है। महाराष्ट्र की प्रवरा नदी के साथ निवास में, आंध्र प्रदेश के करीमपुड़ी और गिद्दलुर एवं मद्रास के कई स्थलों से इस सभ्यता से अवशेष मिले हैं। कर्नाटक की दो नदियों—नालप्रभा एवं घाट प्रभा के आस-पास भी पुरापाषाण कालीन संस्कृति के कई अवशेष पाए गए हैं।

4. भारत के अलावा कई देशों फ्रांस, स्पेन और इटली की गुफाओं की दीवारों पर उस काल के बहुरंगी चित्र पाये गये हैं। इनमें से कुछ रंगीन चित्र थे एवं कुछ नक्काशी किये हुए थे। इन रंगीन चित्रों और नक्काशियों में दौड़ते हुए जंगली बैल, भैंसों, घोड़ों, रीछों और रेडियरों के झुंड एवं शिकार के दृश्य बनाये गये थे। प्रायः इन चित्रों में दैनिक जीवन सम्बन्धी, पशुओं का शिकार करने व मारने के दृश्य दिखाये गये थे। ये चित्र अंधेरी गुफाओं में मिले हैं। इन गुफाओं में प्राप्त चित्रों का जादुई महत्त्व रहा होगा। आज भी अफ्रीका और भारत की कुछ आदि जनजातियां जादू टोने में विश्वास रखती हैं और उनके दैनिक जीवन में जादू टोने का बहुत महत्त्व है। इस युग में मनुष्य साज-सज्जा से भी कम-अधिक परिचित हो चुका था। पत्थर व हड्डियों के बने हार और आभूषणों से इसकी पुष्टि होती है। इस काल के लोग जानवरों की खालों और वृक्षों के पत्तों से अपना शरीर ढकते थे।

5. भोजन मानव की मूल आवश्यकता है परन्तु पुरापाषाण युग में मानव का जीवित रहना अत्यधिक कठिन था। अतएव उसे जो कुछ भी मिलता था, उसे खाकर अपनी भूख शांत करता था। वह घास-फूस, फल-फूल, कंदमूल और जानवरों का मांस खाता था। हाल की खोजों से ज्ञात होता है कि वह भोजन का संग्रह भी करता था और आगे आने वाले दिनों में उसका इस्तेमाल करता था।

6. विगत कुछ वर्ष पहले पाए गए कुछ प्रमाणों से यह स्पष्ट होता है कि उस समय के मानव ने अग्नि के बारे में भी ज्ञान प्राप्त कर लिया था। सही मायने में वृक्षों की डालियों की आपसी टकराहट से जंगल में आग लग जाया करती थी। इसको देखकर मनुष्य को आग के सम्बन्ध में ज्ञान प्राप्त हुआ होगा। वह इससे मांस को भूनकर कर खाने लगा, क्योंकि यह सुपाच्य होता था। जाड़े में गर्मी प्राप्त करता था और अंधेरे में प्रकाश पाता था। जानवरों को डराने के लिए भी आग का इस्तेमाल करता था। धीरे-धीरे उसने यह जान लिया कि चकमक पत्थर से अग्नि उत्पन्न की जा सकती है।

7. आधुनिक विद्वानों का कहना है कि मनुष्यों ने प्रारम्भ में समूहों में रहना प्रारम्भ किया। विवाह प्रथा न होते हुए भी कुछ पुरुष, स्त्रियाँ और उसके बच्चे साथ-साथ रहते थे। इसी को आगे चलकर परिवार कहा गया। वे साथ-साथ भोजन की खोज करते थे। मनुष्य समूह बनाकर गुफा में रहा करते थे। इसे समुदाय कहा जाता है। सभी वस्तुओं पर सबको अधिकार होता था। उस समय व्यक्तिगत सम्पत्ति का प्रश्न नहीं था। यदि मनुष्य समूहों में नहीं रहता तो वह हिंसक पशुओं से बच नहीं सकता था। इसलिए परिवार मूलभूत और प्रधान इकाई बन गयी। ऋतुओं के अनुरूप परिवार अपने सामान के साथ एक स्थान से दूसरे स्थान पर चले जाते थे। धीरे-धीरे परिवार में लोगों की संख्या बढ़ने लगी। इसलिए परिवारों के समूह और कुल बन गये। प्रत्येक परिवार अथवा कुल का एक प्रधान या मुखिया होता था। मुखिया स्त्री अथवा पुरुष कोई शक्तिशाली और बुद्धिमान व्यक्ति होता था।

8. भोजन की आवश्यकता पूरी होने के बाद मानव की दूसरी आवश्यकता उसके निवास की होती है परन्तु पुरापाषाण युगीन मानव अत्यधिक पिछड़ी हुई अवस्था में थी। मनुष्य पशुओं के समान जीवन व्यतीत करता था। वह जंगलों, पर्वत की कन्दराओं, नदियों के किनारे एवं गड्ढों में निवास करता था। इस समय न तो वह मकान बनाना जानता था और न ही किसी निश्चित स्थान पर रहता था। उसका जीवन खानाबदोशों का था।

9. इस युग में मनुष्य पूर्ण रूप से प्रकृति पर निर्भर था। वह पौधों के पत्तों, जड़ों और फलों का संग्रह करता था। वह अपने भोजन के लिए पशु पक्षियों का शिकार करता था एवं मछलियाँ पकड़ता था। पशु-पक्षियों को पकड़ने के लिए उसने विभिन्न प्रकार के उपाय किये और हथियारों का निर्माण किया। भोजन संग्रह में उन्हें अनेक कठिनाइयों का सामना करना पड़ता था। वे समूह बनाकर वनस्पतियों और पशुओं की खोज में सारा दिन इधर-उधर घूमते रहते थे। संकट के दिनों के लिए अन्न और फल सुरक्षित रखते थे। इसीलिए पूर्व पाषाण काल को भोजन संग्रह काल के नाम से जाना जाता है।

मध्य पाषाण काल

इस युग का कालक्रम 8000 ई.पू. से 5000 ई. पू. तक माना जाता है। यह काल पुरापाषाण काल और नव पाषाण काल के मध्य आता है। इसलिए इसे मध्य

पाषाण काल कहा जाता है। इस काल की जलवायु में कुछ बदलाव आ गया था। वह पहले की अपेक्षा अधिक गर्म एवं कम आर्द्र हो गयी थी। इस काल में वनस्पतियों और जीव जन्तुओं में भी बदलाव आया। मनुष्य ने अपने औजारों को काफी हद तक परिष्कृत कर लिया। इस काल के हथियार पहले की अपेक्षा छोटे हैं। इनका आकार 2.5 से. मी. से लेकर 4 से. मी. है। इसमें लकड़ी के बेट को लगाकर इस्तेमाल करता था। इस काल में पत्ते के आकार के नुकीले औजार एवं छेद करने वाले हथियार भारी संख्या में प्राप्त हुए हैं।

इस युग में मनुष्यों का जीवन खानाबदोशों का था, लेकिन कुछ सीमा तक स्थिरता आ गयी थी। वह किसी स्थान पर उस समय तक प्रतीक्षा करता था जब तक उसे भोजन मिलता रहता था। वह कभी-कभी नदियों के किनारों या पहाड़ों के समतल भागों पर पेड़ों की टहनियों एवं घास-फूस आदि से झोंपड़ी भी बना लिया करता था। इस युग में मनुष्य पेट भरने के लिए गाय, भैंस, भेड़, बकरी, हिरण आदि का शिकार करके और मछली मार कर अपना जीवन व्यतीत करता था। वह कन्दमूल और फल आदि का उपयोग भी करता था। मारे हुए पशुओं की खाल से अपने शरीर को ढकता था। मनकों को आभूषण के रूप में इस्तेमाल करता था। सम्भवतः उसने मिट्टी के बर्तनों का निर्माण और कुत्तों को पालना भी आरंभ कर दिया था।

इस युग में मृत मानव को दफनाया जाता था। ये शव उत्तर-दक्षिण दिशा में दफनाए जाते थे। शवों के सिर के साथ पत्थर के हथियार भी प्राप्त हुए हैं। शायद उनका दफनाने की रस्म से ही कोई सम्बन्ध था। भारत में इस सभ्यता के कई स्थलों की खोज हुई है। इस सभ्यता के केन्द्र पेशावर से बिनेवली एवं कराची से बिहार तक सभी स्थानों से मिले हैं। पंजाब से उचाली, गुजरात में लंघतज, मध्य भारत में प्रवर नदी घाटी एवं मैसूर में ब्रह्मगिरी और कुर्तूल आदि इस सभ्यता के प्रमुख केन्द्र हैं।

नव पाषाण काल

विश्वस्तर पर इस काल की शुरुआत 9000 ई. पू. से मानी जाती है। यह मानव सभ्यता में क्रान्तिकारी युग था। इस काल में विभिन्न क्षेत्रों में अनेक बदलाव हुए। इस युग की प्रमुख विशेषताएँ निम्नलिखित थीं–

1. इस युग का मनुष्य कला के विकास में लगातार लगा हुआ था। अनाज के अलावा अनाज के साथ-साथ मनुष्य कपास की खेती भी करता था। उसने कपास से धागा बनाना आरंभ कर दिया। प्रारम्भ में धागा रस्सी की तरह गूंथकर बनाया गया। पहिए के आविष्कार के साथ तकली नामक औजार

बनाया गया। तकली से सुन्दर धागा बनने लगा। कई प्रकार के रेशे का प्रयोग धागा बनाने एवं कपड़ा बनाने के लिए किया जाने लगा था। आरंभ में उसने प्रतिकूल ऋतुओं से बचने के लिए कपड़े का इस्तेमाल किया, परन्तु धीरे-धीरे गुप्त अंगों को भी ढकना जरूरी हो गया। धीरे-धीरे रेशम और ऊन से भी कपड़े बनाये जाने लगे। शरीर की कुरूपता को छिपाने के लिए सुन्दर-सुन्दर कपड़ों का इस्तेमाल किया जाने लगा। इस तरह कताई और बुनाई कला का बहुत अधिक विकास हुआ।

2. पहिए का आविष्कार इस काल की प्रमुख विशेषता है, जिससे यातायात जैसी प्रमुख समस्या हल हो गयी। पेड़ों के बड़े-बड़े तने के टुकड़ों को लुढ़काकर वह अपने इच्छित स्थान पर ले जाता था। इस काल के मानव ने बिना पहिए की स्लेज गाड़ी बना ली थी। यह गाड़ी बर्फ पर चलायी जाती थी। धीरे-धीरे पहिए की गाड़ी बनायी गयी। इस घटना से आवागमन के क्षेत्र में महान क्रान्ति हो गयी। बाद में इन गाड़ियों को खींचने के लिए पशुओं की सहायता ली जाने लगी। गाड़ियों में लगाए जाने वाले इन पहियों की मदद से मानव तेजी से प्रगति करने लगी। शीघ्र ही बर्तन बनाने में पहिए का इस्तेमाल होने लगा। इस तरह पहिए के द्वारा महत्त्वपूर्ण कला का विकास भी हुआ। उपरांत में इसे एक उद्योग के रूप में अपना लिया गया।

3. इस काल में मानव मृत लोगों को दफनाने लगा। दफनाने का स्थान घर के पास होता था तथा प्रायः मरे हुए व्यक्ति के साथ हथियार, बर्तन तथा साज-सज्जा सम्बन्धी सामग्री रख दी जाती थी। सम्भवतः लोगों की यह अवधारणा थी कि मृत व्यक्ति भी विभिन्न सामानों का उपयोग करता है। उनका यह विचार था कि फसल पैदा करने में उनके पूर्वजों की भूमिका है। इस युग के मनुष्य-गण चिह्नों में विश्वास करने लगे थे। किसी कुल या साथ-साथ रहने वाले परिवारों के समूह के लिए संकेत के रूप में किसी पौधे अथवा पशु के सूचक को गणचिह्न कहा जाता है। इस काल में लोगों का विश्वास था कि पशुओं के पुरखे ही मानव के पुरखे थे और पशु भोजन के लिए मानव की मदद करते हैं। इसलिए पशु मानव के मित्र होते हैं। इस काल के लोगों का यह मानना था कि चन्द्रमा, तारे और प्रकृति की अन्य शक्तियों के पास अद्‌भुत शक्ति होती है और उनकी पूजा करके उनको प्रसन्न करने के प्रयत्न भी करने लगा। इस समय के लोग लघु मूर्तियों की भी पूजा करते थे जिनको देवी माँ कहा जाता था।

उनका विश्वास था कि देवी माँ की कृपा से पृथ्वी की उर्वरा शक्ति बढ़ सकती है।

4. नव पाषाण काल के स्थलों से कुछ ऐसे भी अवशेष मिले हैं जिनसे ज्ञात होता है कि उस काल में व्यापार आरंभ हो गया था। भूमध्य सागर के सीपिया फायूम झील में बनाये गये कंगन दक्षिणी जर्मनी की कब्रों में पाये गये हैं। फिर उस समय व्यापारिक सम्बन्ध बहुत अधिक कठिन था क्योंकि यातायात की बहुत अधिक कठिनाई थी।

   कृषि करने के परिणामस्वरूप लोगों के पास पर्याप्त समय बचने लगा। इस समय को लोग अन्य उद्योग-धन्धों में लगाते थे। लोग कुदाल, कीली, बर्तन, वस्त्र और पड़िया आदि बनाते थे। अपनी बनाई हुई वस्तुओं को देकर लोग बदले में अनाज प्राप्त करते थे। इस तरह श्रम विभाजन की प्रक्रिया आरम्भ हो गई थी।

5. भारत में नवपाषाण काल के विभिन्न स्थल पाये गये। पूर्व में चिरांड (पटना के पास), उत्तर में बुर्जहोम (श्रीनगर), दक्षिण भारत में गोदावरी नदी के दक्षिण में ग्रेनाइट की पहाड़ियों, कर्नाटक में मास्को, ब्रह्मगिरी, हल्लुर, कौड़कल, संगनकल्लु, बैक्कड कोट और तमिलनाडु में पैयामपल्ली, आंध्र प्रदेश में फिकलीहल, उतनूर और असम के पर्वतीय क्षेत्र आदि इस संस्कृति के प्रमुख केन्द्र हैं।

6. नव पाषाण काल में जलवायु मानव के लिए उपयुक्त थी। ऐसी जलवायु में जनसंख्या की वृद्धि हुई और मनुष्य की बुद्धि का विकास हुआ।

7. नवपाषाण काल के लोगों को धीरे-धीरे यह ज्ञान हो गया कि ऋतुओं में बदलाव सूर्य के कारण होता है। इसलिए वह सूर्य की पूजा करने लगा। कुछ खास नक्षत्रों की दिशा से सौर वर्ष के विषय में जानकारी मिल जाती थी। बाद में मानव को विश्वास हो गया कि ये नक्षत्र पृथ्वी पर होने वाले कार्यों को प्रभावित करते हैं। इस युग में चित्र बनाना जारी रहा, लेकिन अब शिकार के दृश्यों के स्थान पर खेतों व फसलों के दृश्य बनाये जाने लगे। इस युग में संगीत का भी उदय हुआ। जिस वर्ष फसल अच्छी होती थी उस वर्ष खुशी के गीत तथा फसल के खराव होने पर दुःख भरे गीत गाये जाते थे।

8. इस युग की विशेषता पशुपालन की शुरुआत है। बहुत से जानवर भोजन की खोज में प्राचीन मानव के समीप आया करते थे। वह मनुष्य द्वारा फेंके गए मांस को खाकर अपनी भूख मिटाते थे। ये जंगली जानवर धीरे-धीरे मनुष्य के

मित्र बन गये। ये जानवर खतरे में मानव को सचेत कर देते थे। जब मनुष्य को पशुओं की उपयोगिता का ज्ञान हुआ तो उसने पशु पालना आरंभ कर दिया। सर्वप्रथम उसने भेड़िये को पालना आरंभ किया जो बाद में कुत्ता कहलाया। जैसे-जैसे मनुष्यों का ज्ञान विकसित होता गया, वैसे-वैसे उन्होंने स्तनधारी जानवरों को पालना शुरू कर दिया। प्रारम्भ में पशु पालन का उद्देश्य शिकार न मिलने पर मांस प्राप्त करना था। बाद में मनुष्यों को पता चला कि कुछ पालतू पशुओं का दूध भी अच्छा भोजन है। ये दुधारू पशु प्रायः घास और वृक्षों के पत्ते ही खाते थे। इस उपयोगिता के कारण मनुष्य ने गाय, भेड़, बकरी जैसे जानवर को पालना आरंभ कर दिया। अपने बचाव और पालतू पशुओं की रक्षा के लिए मनुष्य के लिए समूह में रहना आवश्यक था। जब एक स्थान पर घास खत्म हो जाती थी तो ऐसे कबीले या कुल दूसरे स्थान पर चले जाते थे। कबीले के लोग प्रायः तालाब, झील या नदी के किनारे ठहर जाते थे। इस तरह सैकड़ों वर्षों तक मनुष्य ने चरवाहे के रूप में जीवन व्यतीत किया और घास की खोज में विभिन्न स्थानों पर जाता रहता था।

9. प्राचीन काल में मानव घुमक्कड़ी जीवन व्यतीत करता था। परन्तु उस युग में मानव घुमक्कड़ी जीवन छोड़कर स्थायी रूप से एक स्थान पर निवास करने लगा था। रहने के लिए मकान बनाना आरंभ कर दिया था। सम्भवतः ये घर पशुओं की खाल के तम्बू थे। आगे चलकर मनुष्य घास-फूस, नरकुल और मिट्टी की मदद से झोंपड़ियाँ बनाने लगा। इस तरह की झोंपड़ियों के अवशेष महाराष्ट्र में नासिक, नेवासा आदि स्थानों पर प्राप्त हुए हैं जिसका समय लगभग 1500 ई. पू. माना जाता है।

10. प्रारम्भ में तरल पदार्थ रखने के लिए नारियल के खोपड़े का प्रयोग किया जाता था। बढ़ईगिरी में चतुर हो जाने के पश्चात् लकड़ी के बर्तन भी बनाए जाने लगे। तिनकों, पत्तों से टोकरियां बनायी जाने लगी और उसके बाहर चिकनी मिट्टी का लेप कर दिया जाता था। धीरे-धीरे उसने बर्तन पकाना भी सीख लिया। रेखाचित्रों के द्वारा उनकी सजावट भी करता था। विभिन्न स्थलों से कई प्रकार के बर्तनों के टुकड़े प्राप्त हुए हैं।

11. यह सही है कि मनुष्य पूर्णरूप से पशुओं पर निर्भर नहीं रह सकता था। वह वृक्षों और पौधों के फलों, पत्तों इत्यादि को भी खाता था। मनुष्य ने अनुभव के द्वारा खेती करना भी सीख लिया। वह अनाज और वनस्पतियाँ बोने लगा और अन्य प्रकार का भोजन भी आसानी से प्राप्त करने लगा। मनुष्य को अनुभव

हुआ कि सिर्फ बीज बो देना ही काफी नहीं है अपितु फसल की कटाई तक उसकी देखभाल भी करनी चाहिए। इसलिए किसान को अपने खेत के समीप ही रहना पड़ा। इस तरह एक कुल के लोग पास ही रहने लगे और आस-पास की भूमि पर खेती करना आरंभ कर दिया। इससे गाँव बनने लगे। मनुष्य ने सिंचाई के लिए बड़े-बड़े प्राकृतिक तालाबों, झीलों और नदियों के किनारों पर वृक्ष की शाखाओं से घर बनाना आरंभ कर दिया।

कृषि और पशुपालन की शुरुआत से मनुष्य के जीवन में एक बड़ा परिवर्तन आया प्रारम्भ में मनुष्य भोजन संग्रह में ही लगा रहता था परन्तु अब वह पशुपालन और खेती करके भोजन उत्पादन की ओर ध्यान देने लगा। पशुपालन और खेती मनुष्य के लिए अत्यन्त उपयोगी सिद्ध हुए और ये दोनों एक-दूसरे के पूरक थे। इसलिए इस युग के खेती के कार्य को मिश्रित खेती के रूप में जाना जाता है। बचे हुए अनाज के पौधों और पत्तों से भोजन बनाया जाता था जो पशुओं को खिलाया जाता था। उत्पादन में मानव पशुओं की मदद भी लेता था। बाद में यातायात के लिए इन पशुओं का इस्तेमाल किया जाने लगा और उनका मलमूत्र ईंधन और खाद के रूप में इस्तेमाल किया जाता था।

12. कुलों का निर्माण पूर्व पाषाण काल में ही हो गया था। कालान्तर में इन्हीं कुलों को मिलाकर गांव का रूप दिया गया। फसल के लिए भूमि साफ करने, दलदली भूमि से पानी निकालने एवं फसल उगाने के लिए मिल-जुल कर कार्य करने की अधिक जरूरत महसूस हुई। इससे मानव जीवन अधिक संगठित हो गया। इसमें मुखिया और प्रधान की भूमिका अधिक होती थी। धीरे-धीरे पंचायत किया जाता था और उसे हल करने का प्रयत्न किया जाता था। पंचायत अपराध के लिए दण्ड भी देती थी। यह सजा सामाजिक निष्कासन और बहिष्कार के रूप में होती थी।

विवाह की पद्धति धीरे-धीरे प्रारंभ हुई माता-पिता और बच्चे साथ-साथ रहते थे। इस तरह परिवार नामक संस्था का विकास हुआ। परिवार की सभी समस्याओं को मुखिया हल करता था।

13. इस युग में तेज और पालिशदार औजारों का निर्माण किया जाने लगा। पिछले युगों की अपेक्षा नवपाषाण युग के औजारों में एक प्रकार की बड़ी भिन्नता देखने को मिलती है। इस समय भी परस्पर के औजारों और हथियारों का इस्तेमाल होता था परन्तु अब उनकी बनावट में बहुत कुछ बदलाव हो गया था। मनुष्य ने अपने औजारों को पत्थरों से रगड़ कर पालिश करना आरंभ कर

दिया। भूमि की सतह के नीचे पाये जाने वाले पत्थर प्रायः मजबूत और टिकाऊ होते थे। इनसे उसने मजबूत हथियार बनाए। इनके औजारों में कुल्हाड़ी, हैमर स्टान, एलिक स्टोन आदि विशेष रूप से प्रमुख हैं। उसने बढ़ईगीरी का भी काम आरंभ कर दिया। मनुष्य अब तख्ते के नाव, हल, पहिये और लकड़ी के घर आसानी से बना सकता था। इस काल में हंसुवा नामक औजार का प्रयोग व्यापक स्तर पर किया जाता था। यह कठोर पत्थर से बनाया जाता था और इसमें एक लकड़ी का हत्था लगा दिया जाता था। युद्ध के लिए भी हथियार बनने लगे। भाले और तीरों का शीर्ष नोंकदार और तेज बनाया जाता था। गुलेल नामक नया हथियार बनाया जाने लगा। सुई और मछली पकड़ने के कांटे जैसे छोटे-छोटे औजार बनाने के लिए हड्डियों और हिरन के सींगों का इस्तेमाल किया जाने लगा।

2

मिस्र की सभ्यता

विश्व की विभिन्न प्राचीन सभ्यताओं में मिस्र की भी एक प्राचीन सभ्यता है। इस सभ्यता का विकास उत्तरी अफ्रीका की एक नील नामक नदी में हुआ था। इसीलिए मिस्र को नील नदी का जन्म स्थान कहा जाता है। एक प्राचीन मिस्री आप्तवचन के शब्दों में "मिस्र वह भूमि है, जिसे नील नदी सींचती है तथा इसका पानी पीने वाले लोग मिस्री कहलाते हैं।" प्राचीन मिस्रवासी नील नदी की असीम श्रद्धा के साथ एक देवता की भांति पूजा करते थे। नील नदी का वहाँ की कृषि में बहुत ही अधिक महत्त्व था। इसलिए प्राचीन मिस्र की सभ्यता को नील नदी का श्रेय कहा जाता है। मिस्र की सभ्यता का कृषि की दृष्टि से अत्यधिक महत्त्व है। नील नदी की कृषि योग्य भूमि में इस सभ्यता ने अपना विस्तार किया था। नील नदी की बाढ़ से इस सभ्यता की मिट्टी ऊपजाऊ बनी रहती थी। इतिहासकारों की मानें तो नील नदी में प्रतिवर्ष लगभग 3 महीने के लिए ग्रीष्म ऋतु में बाढ़ आती थी। इस समय उपजाऊ मिट्टी नदी के तट पर जम जाती थी जो फसल के लिए काफी उपयोगी होती थी। इतिहासकार जॉर्ज ऐलेन ने यह प्रकाश डाला है कि मिस्र देश की सम्पन्नता और समृद्धि नील नदी की बाढ़ पर निर्भर करती थी। इसलिए इस नदी को मिस्र के लिए वरदान माना गया है। विश्व प्रसिद्ध इतिहासकार डेविड महोदय का मानना है कि, "नील नदी समस्त युगों में मिस्रवासियों के जीवन तथा उनकी सम्पन्नता का साधन रही है। इस नदी के कारण ही मिस्र जैसे रेगिस्तानी प्रदेश में भी सदा हरियाली छाई रहती है। यहाँ के निवासी इस नदी की उपासना करते हैं।" इस सन्दर्भ में **जे. एच. बेस्टेड** महोदय का मानना है कि, "नील नदी हमारे लिए एक विशाल

ऐतिहासिक ग्रन्थ है, जिससे हमें बर्बर असभ्यता से लेकर सभ्यता तक क्रमानुसार रूप से मानव के प्रथम उत्थान का ज्ञान होता है।"

प्राचीन यूनानी इतिहासकार हेरोडोटस ने मिस्र को 'नील नदी का वरदान' कहा है। **हेज व मून** ने मिस्र को 'नील नदी की पुत्री' माना है। **सरदेसाई** ने कहा है कि, "मिस्र नील नदी की भेंट है।" **जे. एल. मायर्स** का मानना है कि, "मिस्र नील नदी का वरदान है और नील नदी की समता पृथ्वी पर कोई नहीं कर सकता।" पं. जवाहर लाल नेहरू ने लिखा है, "नील की सभ्यता मानव विकास के हार का एक महकता हुआ फूल है।"

मिस्र की सभ्यता के विषय में बिल ड्यूरेन्ट ने कहा है, "अपनी सुदृढ़ता और एकता की दृष्टि से, अद्‌भुत निर्माण-शिल्प और कलागत सफलता की दृष्टि से मिस्र की सभ्यता संभवतः इस पृथ्वी पर स्थापित होने वाली सभ्यताओं में महानतम थी। यदि हम उसकी बराबरी कर सकें, तो यह बहुत बड़ी बात होगी।"

मिस्र में सभ्यता विकास की अनुकूल परिस्थितियाँ

विश्व की अन्य प्राचीन सभ्यताओं की भांति मिस्र भी एक प्राचीन सभ्यता है। अफ्रीका महाद्वीप के पूर्वोत्तर में नील नदी की घाटी में मिस्र देश अवस्थित है। नील नदी अपने उद्‌गम से डेल्टा तक लगभग 2450 मील लम्बी है, परंतु वह घुमाव खाती हुई लगभग 4000 मील लम्बा रास्ता तय करती है। इस के उत्तर में भूमध्यसागर, पश्चिम में सहारा का रेगिस्तान, दक्षिण में घने जंगल और पूर्व में लाल सागर का विस्तार है। उस समय मिस्र की जनसंख्या लगभग बीस करोड़ थी। आज से लगभग 5000 वर्ष पहले मिस्र की बंदरगाह विश्व की सर्वश्रेष्ठ बंदरगाह मानी जाती थी। नील नदी के मुहाने पर विश्व की सबसे उत्तम कपास की पैदावर होती है।

यहां की भौगोलिक स्थिति मिस्र सभ्यता के विकास के अनुकूल है। इस सन्दर्भ में बीच महोदय ने लिखा है कि "भौगोलिक प्रभाव से मिस्र का इतिहास कम खंडित और वहाँ के लोगों का रक्त दूसरे देशों से कम मिश्रित है, क्योंकि यह देश अंदर से बंद था।"

अनुकूल परिस्थितियों के कारण धीरे-धीरे यहाँ जनसंख्या में वृद्धि हुई और सभ्यता का विकास हुआ। सिकंदरिया, काहिरा, मेम्फिस (मिस्र की प्राचीन राजधानी) और कारनाक ये सभी मिस्र के नगर हैं जो नील नदी के तट पर अवस्थित हैं। इसकी पुष्टि इन नगरों से प्राप्त खंडहरों से होती है। प्रसिद्ध इतिहासकार सेवाइन का विचार है कि नील नदी के किनारे पर नमक के कई देशों में ऐसे अवशेष प्राप्त हुए हैं, जो

वहां पर निवास करने वाले व्यक्तियों की कहानी कहते हैं। विश्व में और कहीं एक महान सभ्यता के भौतिक अवशेषों को संजोकर रखने में कुदरत ने इतना बड़ा योगदान नहीं दिया।"

काल निर्धारण तथा अध्ययन के साधन

जैसाकि पहले बताया गया है कि मिश्र की सभ्यता को विश्व की प्राचीन सभ्यता कहा जाता है। इस सन्दर्भ में **पेरी** महोदय का मानना है कि–"मिस्र की सभ्यता विश्व की अति प्राचीन सभ्यता है।" इससे आगे इन्होंने लिखा है कि–"पृथ्वी पर मिस्र में ही सर्वप्रथम सभ्यता का विकास हुआ और वहाँ से दुनिया के अन्य लोगों ने सभ्यता सीखी थी।" अधिकतर विद्वान पेरी के मत को गतल मानते हैं, परंतु यह बात सभी इतिहासकार एकमत से स्वीकार करते हैं कि पश्चिमी देशों में मिस्र की सभ्यता सबसे प्राचीन है। इतिहासकार जे. सी. रेविल के अनुसार, "3000 ई. पूर्व से 2000 ई. पूर्व के बीच मिस्र ने रहने की कला तथा संस्कृति को अफ्रीका तथा पूर्वी भूमध्यसागरीय प्रदेशों मे फैलाने में सर्वाधिक सफलता प्राप्त की।"

अधिकांश विद्वानों का विचार है कि जिस समय पूर्व में चीन तथा भारत की सभ्यताओं का विकास हो रहा था, उसी समय मिस्र तथा मैसोपोटामिया की सभ्यता का भी विकास हो रहा था। फिर भी, यह तो निर्विवाद है कि मिस्र की सभ्यता विश्व की प्राचीनतम सभ्यता है।

साधन–प्राचीन मिस्र का इतिहास जानने के प्रमुख साधन अथवा स्रोत निम्नलिखित हैं–

(1) पुरातात्त्विक साक्ष्य–मिस्र के इतिहास के विषय में जानने में मिस्र के लक्सर नगर के विशाल मंदिर तथा मूर्तियाँ और काहिरा (प्राचीन मेम्फिस) के पास जा गिजा के पिरामिड प्रमुख साधन हैं।

(2) साहित्यिक स्रोत–अधिकांश विद्वानों का मानना है कि मिस्र वासियों को कविता प्रेमी भी कहते थे। अनेक कागजों और ताम्रपत्रों पर संचित मिस्र के साहित्य से वहाँ के इतिहास के बारे में महत्त्वपूर्ण जानकारी प्राप्त होती है।

(3) लेखक एव इतिहासकार–अनेकों लेखकों एवं विद्वानों ने इस क्षेत्र में अथक प्रयास किया। अपने प्रयासों के दौरान उन्होंने जो अनुभव किया तथा जिस निष्कर्ष पर पहुंचे, प्राचीन मिस्र की सभ्यता की जानकारी के महत्त्वपूर्ण स्रोत हैं। यहाँ कुछ प्रमुख योगदानों की चर्चा संक्षेप में की जा रही है।

शाम्पोल्यो—फ्रांसीसी विद्वान शाम्पोल्यो ने 20 वर्ष की अथक मेहनत करने के उपरान्त रोसेटा पत्थर पर अंकित शिलालेख को पढ़ने में सफलता प्राप्त की। इस पत्थर पर तीन भाषाओं में लेख खुदे हुए थे—यूनानी भाषा, मिस्र की साधारण भाषा एवं चित्रलिपि में। इनके अतिरिक्त थामस यंग तथा स्वीडन के **अकेट ब्लाद** भी मिस्री भाषा को पढ़ने में कामयाब हुए।

हावर्ड कार्टर—इन्होंने 1922 ई. में 18 वर्षीय बालक सम्राट तूताखामेन के पिरामिड के एक गुप्त द्वार को खोज निकाला। इससे प्राचीन मिस्र की सभ्यता एवं संस्कृति के बारे में जानकारी प्राप्त हुई।

नेपोलियन बोनापार्ट—1798 ई. में फ्रांस के शासक नेपोलियन बोनापार्ट ने मिस्र पर आक्रमण किया, तब उसे नील नदी के मुहाने पर रोसेटा नामक स्थान पर एक प्रस्तर शिलालेख मिला, जो 12 मी. लम्बा और 70 सेमी. चौड़ा था। इससे मिस्र के टोलमी राजा के शासनकाल के विषय में विशेष रूप से जानकारी मिलती है। इस शिलालेख को बोनापार्ट अपने साथ पेरिस ले गया। आज भी इस शिलालेख को पेरिस के संग्रहालय में देखा जा सकता है।

मेनेथो—यूनानी सम्राट टोलमी के दरबार में मेनेथो शाही इतिहासकार के रूप में कार्यरत था। जिसने मिस्र की लगभग सभी प्रमुख राजाओं की वंशावली बनायी थी। दुर्भाग्य से उसकी आधी सूची नष्ट हो गई, किंतु फिर भी जो प्राप्त हुई है, उससे मिस्र के इतिहास को जानने में महत्त्वपूर्ण सहायता मिली है।

हेरोडोटस एवं डायोडोरस—हेरोडोटस यूनानी तथा डायोडोरस रोमन इतिहासकार थे। इन दोनों ने मेनेथो को आधार मानकर मिस्र के इतिहास के बारे में लिखा है। इनके विवरण में सच के साथ कल्पना का मिश्रण भी मिलता है। अतः उन पर पूर्ण विश्वास नहीं किया जा सकता। फिर भी, इन इतिहासकारों का वर्णन मिस्र के इतिहास को जानने के लिए बहुत उपयोगी है।

राजनीतिक इकाइयाँ एवं शासन-व्यवस्था

मिस्र का राजनीतिक इतिहास काफी पुराना है। उस समय यहां की राजनीतिक स्थिति कुछ खराब थी। इस सन्दर्भ में प्रो. पिलण्डर्स पेट्री ने लिखा है कि मिस्र की सभ्यता का विकास ईसा से दस हजार वर्ष पूर्व हो गया। अत्यन्त प्राचीनकाल में मिस्र छोटे-छोटे राज्यों में विभाजित था, जो आपस में लड़ते रहते थे। लगभग 4000 ई. पूर्व में एक नगर मुहाने का राज्य और दूसरा दक्षिण मिस्र अथवा नील नदी की घाटी का राज्य था। उत्तर मिस्र का राज्य चिह्न मधुमक्खी था यहां का राजा लाल रंग का

मुकुट पहनता था तथा इसी रंग के भवन में रहता था। पेपाइरस के गुच्छे दक्षिण मिस्र का राजचिह्न माना जाता है। वह श्वेत रंग के महल में रहता था। अंत में उत्तर मिस्र और दक्षिण मिस्र ये दोनों राज्य मिलकर एक हो गये और इन्होंने मिस्र के इतिहास की रचना की।

मिनिस एक कुशल सेनानायक इन दोनों राज्यों को मिलाने वाला नेता व एक महान विजेता था। उसने 3400 ई. पूर्व में इन दोनों राज्यों को मिलाकर संपूर्ण मिस्र को अपने अधीन कर लिया। मेम्फिस को उसने मिस्र की राजधानी बनाया और वहाँ राजतंत्रात्मक शासन-व्यवस्था की स्थापना की। मिस्र की राजनीतिक एकता का जनक भी उसी को माना जाता है। इसी को प्रथम राजवंश का संस्थापक कहा जाता है। प्रसिद्ध विद्वान डेविस ने लिखा है कि "मिनिस से मिस्र में वंशीय शासन चालू होता है और वह इस वंश का पहला राजा था"

प्राचीन मिस्र पर मिनिस ने लगभग 62 वर्ष तक राज्य किया लेकिन दुर्भाग्यवश दरियाई घोड़े द्वारा उसे नील नदी में खींच ले जाने के कारण उसकी मृत्यु हो गई। मिनिस के समय से ही मिस्र का क्रमबद्ध इतिहास आरंभ होता है।

फराओ प्राचीन मिस्र के शासक को कहते थे जिसका अर्थ भव्य भवन से लगाया जाता है। जहाँ ईश्वर निवास करता है। तात्पर्य यह है कि मिस्र का फराओ शक्तिशाली तथा निरंकुश शासक था। मिस्र में लगभग 31 राजवंशों ने 3100 वर्ष तक राज्य किया और अंत में 332 ई. पूर्व में सिकंदर ने इस पर अधिकार कर इसे अपना उपनिवेश बना लिया।

(1) पिरामिड युग (3400 ई. पूर्व से 2160 ई. पूर्व)

इस युग में पिरामिडों की उत्पत्ति हुई थी जिससे मिस्र इतिहास में अमर हो गया। मिस्र के फराओ ने विशाल पत्थरों के गगनचुम्बी पिरामिडों (त्रिभुजाकार समाधियों) का निर्माण करवाया था। मिस्र की आधुनिक राजधानी काहिरा के दक्षिण में मेम्फिस नामक नगर के पास आज भी 70 पिरामिड मौजूद हैं, जिनसे मिस्र की कला के विषय में जानने की विशेष रूप से मदद मिली है।

सर्वप्रथम फराओ ने मिस्र में पिरामिडों का निर्माण किया था। तृतीय राजवंश के फराओ जोसेर का वजीर था। इमहोटेप का योग्य मंत्री, कुशल वैद्य, निपुण वास्तुकार, सुप्रसिद्ध वक्ता और लिपि शास्त्री था। सक्कारा के सीढ़ीदार पिरामिडों का निर्माण उसी के द्वारा कराया गया था जो 190 फुट ऊँचा तथा जिसे बनाने में पत्थर का प्रयोग किया गया है। यह प्रख्यात पिरामिडों की शृंखला में प्रथम स्थान रखता

है। जोसेर के उत्तराधिकारी स्नेफू ने 170 फुट लंबा जलपोत बनवाया था जिससे विदेशी व्यापार को बढ़ावा मिला था। उसने दशूर नामक स्थान पर एक विशाल पिरामिड भी बनवाया था।

पिरामिडों का निर्माण फराओ के शासनकाल में कराया गया था, जिसका प्रकृति भी कुछ नहीं विगाड़ सकती थी। **नेपोलियन** ने इन पिरामिडों को देखकर कहा था, "मनुष्य ने दैत्य का आकार धरती पर उतार दिया है।" **मैक्समूलर** ने लिखा है, "पिरामिड मिस्रवासियों के दीर्घजीवी विचारों के प्रतीक हैं।" पिरामिडों का निर्माण मुख्य रूप से फराओ के काल में कराया गया था। इस प्रकार उस युग को पिरामिड युग की संज्ञा दी जाती है। इस युग के राजा सुहरे ने जलशक्ति में वृद्धि की और नूबिया तथा फिनीशिया पर सफल आक्रमण किए। पिरामिड युग के अंतिम फराओ पेपी द्वितीय ने 14 वर्ष तक राज्य किया और इसके बाद इस साम्राज्य की स्थिति दिन-प्रतिदिन बिगड़ती ही चली गयी।

पिरामिड निर्माण के उद्देश्य—इस युग में पिरामिड निर्माण के पीछे कोई एक उद्देश्य नहीं छिपा हुआ था उसके कई उद्देश्य थे जिनपर संक्षिप्त में प्रकाश नीचे डाला गया है—

(1) *संस्कृति उद्देश्य*—मिस्र के फराओ का संस्कृति से काफी लगाव था तथा वे उसके स्थायित्व को भी सही मानते थे। अतः इस उद्देश्य की पूर्ति के लिए उन्होंने पिरामिडों की स्थापना की। **हर्बर्ट जे. मूलर** ने लिखा है कि, "पिरामिड मिस्रवासियों के दीर्घजीवी विचारों के प्रतीक हैं।"

(2) *धार्मिक उद्देश्य*—पिरामिडों का निर्माण धार्मिक उद्देश्य को पूरा करने के लिये किया जाता था। मिस्रवासियों के अनुसार प्रत्येक मनुष्य के शरीर में आत्मा ('का') रहती है, जो मनुष्य की मृत्यु के बाद भी नहीं मरती। 'का' को दीर्घजीवी बनाने के लिए ये लोग देह को भूख, हिंसा और क्षय से रक्षा करते थे। प्रत्येक मृतक के शव के साथ कब्र में उसके धन, हथियार और सामग्री को दफना देने की प्रथा थी। फराओ के साथ तो उसके दास और पत्नियों को भी दफना दिया जाता था, ताकि उन्हें किसी प्रकार के कष्टों का सामना न करना पड़े। मृतक फराओ के शव (ममी) को इन कब्रों में मसालों में रखा जाता था। फराओ की कब्रों पर विशाल भवनों को बनवाया जाता था जिसे पिरामिड की संज्ञा प्रदान की जाती है। पिरामिड में आत्मा ('का') को संतुष्ट करने के लिए दीवारों पर सुंदर चित्रों का निर्माण कराया जाता था, जो दरबार, खेतों, बैल, रोटी पकाते हुए, शराब पीते और भोजन करते हुए लोगों के होते थे। मिस्र के चौथे राजवंश के संस्थापक खुफ़ु ने काहिरा के पास गिजे नामक

स्थान पर सबसे ऊँचे पिरामिड का निर्माण कराया था। इस पिरामिड की ऊँचाई 480 फीट है।

हेरोडोटस का मानना है कि, "गिरजे के पिरामिड के निर्माण में बीस वर्ष लगे। एक लाख बीस हजार व्यक्तियों ने बीस वर्ष तक काम करके इसका निर्माण किया था।" गिजे का पिरामिड विश्व की सात आश्चर्यजनक चीजों में शामिल किया गया है। **बिल ड्यूरेन्ट** ने लिखा है कि, "कला ने मानव के लिए आज तक कभी इतना अधिक नहीं किया।" **सेवाइन** का मानना है कि, "प्रथम युग की विशेष प्राप्ति पिरामिडों का निर्माण है। यह केवल जनशक्ति के प्रयोग का नमूना मात्र न होकर फराओ के अधीन शक्ति का प्रतिबिम्ब है।"

सूर्य देवता (रा) की मिस्र के शासक इष्ट देवता के रूप में पूजा करते थे। अतः उन्होंने सूर्य को प्रसन्न करने के लिए विशाल पिरामिडों का निर्माण करवाया, ताकि पिरामिडों पर सबसे पहले सूर्य की किरणें आ सकें।

स्फिक्स—गिजे के पिरामिड के पास स्फिक्स (नर तथा सिंह की मिली-जुली मूर्ति) का निर्माण किया गया है। उसकी ऊँचाई 25 गज तथा लम्बाई 50 गज है। इसे प्राचीनकाल में 'हूँ' के नाम से सम्बोधित किया जाता था। हूँ का अर्थ होता है—'सुरक्षा का चौकीदार'। आधुनिक समय में मिस्रवासियों ने इसे 'अब्बुल होल' का नाम दिया है जिसका तात्पर्य होता है—'भय का पिता'। मूर्तिकला के संबंध में **चार्ल्स पैरी** ने लिखा है, "यह मानना होगा कि मिस्री कलाकारों ने ऐसी कृतियाँ दी हैं, जिनकी तुलना आधुनिक यूरोप की कलाकृतियों से की जा सकती है।"

(3) *आर्थिक उद्देश्य*—जनता को पिरामिडों के निर्माण से रोजगार भी प्राप्त होता था। फराओ सामान्यतः बाढ़ के समय पीड़ित जनता को रोजगार देने के लिए पिरामिड बनवाया करते थे। इस सन्दर्भ में बेनफिंगर ने लिखा है कि, "बहुत से मनुष्य पिरामिडों को झूठे अभिमान की स्मृति समझते हैं, परंतु संभवतः ये उन लोगों को रोजी देने के लिए बनाये जाते थे, जब नील नदी में बाढ़ होती थी और खेत पानी से पूर्ण रहते थे।" पिरामिडों का निर्माण कराने के लिए जनता से वेगार लिया जाता था परन्तु निरंकुश होने की वजह से जनता उससे काफी भयभीत रहती थी।

पिरामिड युग की शासन-व्यवस्था—सर्वप्रथम दो वंशों के द्वारा राजधानी की स्थापना मिस्र में की गई थी। तीसरे वंश ने मेम्फिस को अपनी राजधानी बनाया, जो अगले 500 वर्षों तक मिस्र की राजधानी बनी रही। इस समय फराओ शासक के अधिकार असीमित थे तथा वह निरंकुश था। मिस्र के लोग फराओ को ईश्वर का पुत्र मानते थे। फराओ न्याय और ईश्वर का प्रतिनिधि माना जाता था, परंतु न्याय

उस पर भी लागू नहीं होता था। राज्य की समस्त शक्तियाँ फराओ के हाथों में केन्द्रित होती थीं तथा वे कुलगत होते थे। फराओ का उद्देश्य राज्य में शांति बरकरार रखना तथा प्रजा के हित के बारे में सोचना था।

उस दौरान न्याय व्यवस्था काफी मजबूत थी। अपीलों को फराओ द्वारा सुना जाता था। नदी के किनारे-किनारे राज्य नोम (जिले) में बँटा हुआ था। प्रत्येक नोम का एक धर्म, एक देवता, एक सरदार और एक कबीला होता था। फराओ की सेना स्थायी नहीं थी। जरूरत पड़ने पर वह नोम से सेना मंगवा लेता था। प्लेट जीन ड्रमण्ड के अनुसार, "कानून व्यवस्था और समृद्धि के दृष्टिकोण से बहुत उन्नति हुई, अनेक मिस्रवासियों के रहन-सहन का स्तर उन्नत हो गया। फराओ ने अपने कृपापात्र कुलीन सामन्तों को बड़ी-बड़ी जागीरें देकर मानो पुरातन राजत्व के मृत्युदण्ड आदेश पर हस्ताक्षर कर दिये।"

(2) सामन्तवादी युग (2160 ई. पूर्व से 1580 ई. पूर्व)

सामन्तीयुग में पांच राजवंशों के पास किसी प्रकार की शक्ति नहीं थी वे उनके हाथ के कठपुतली मात्र थे। इस युग में मिस्र की राजधानी थीब्स थी। उस काल में मिस्र को छोटे-छोटे राज्यों में बांट दिया गया था, जिससे सामन्तों ने राज्य की शक्ति को अपने अधिकार में ले लिया फिर उनके बीच प्रतिस्पर्धा होने लगी जिससे जागीरों का चौतरफा विकास हुआ। जिससे कृषि, व्यापार का काफी प्रसार हो सका था। इस प्रकार सभ्यता की शुरुआत यहीं से हुई थी।

सामंतों के मध्य काफी युद्ध भी होते थे तथा ये लोग जनता को काफी प्रताड़ित भी करते थे। ऐसे समय में सीरिया के हिक्सास लोगों ने मिस्र पर अधिकार कर लिया और लगभग 200 वर्ष तक मिस्र पर अत्याचार किए, जनता का शोषण किया। आम जनता को हिक्सास लोगों से घृणा हो गई और अंत में थीब्स के सामन्त अमोसिस ने हिक्सास लोगों को मिस्र से मार भगाया। इस युग में भी सभ्यता का विकास हुआ।

(3) साम्राज्यवादी युग (1580 ई. पूर्व से 650 ई. पूर्व)

प्राचीन मिस्र का 1580 ई. पूर्व से 650 ई. पूर्व तक का काल साम्राज्यवादी युग के रूप में माना जाता है, क्योंकि इस काल में अमेनमहैट, अहमोज, थुटमोस आदि ने साम्राज्य की स्थापना की। इस युग में निम्न राजाओं ने शासन किया—

(1) अमेनमहैट प्रथम—अमेनमहैट को सामंतवाद के पतन का श्रेय जाता है। उसने मिस्र से सामंतवाद को जड़ से समाप्त कर दिया और उसके स्थान पर

सुसंगठित शासन-व्यवस्था की स्थापना की। उसके वंशजों ने दो सौ वर्षों तक उसकी मृत्यु के पश्चात् भी मिस्र पर शासन किया। इस काल में जनता सुखी और समृद्ध थी। अमेनमहैट के शिलालेख से इस बात की पुष्टि होती है, जिसमें वह कहता है–

"मैंने बहुत बड़े पैमाने पर खेती की तथा उपज के देवता को प्यार किया। हर घाटी में नील नदी ने मेरा स्वागत किया। मेरे राज्य में न तो कोई भूखा था, न प्यासा। सभी लोग शांति का जीवन बिताते थे।"

अमेनमहैट की हत्या का प्रयास 1580 ई. पूर्व उसके शयनागार में रात को किया गया परंतु यह प्रयास सफल नहीं रहा। उसने अपने पुत्र सेसोट्रीज प्रथम की सहायता से तीस वर्ष तक राज्य किया। उसकी मृत्यु 1570 ई. पू. में हो गई।

फराओ अमेनमहैट प्रथम ने अपनी मृत्यु से पूर्व अपने बेटे राजकुमार सेनवोसरेत्र को राजनीति के नंगे यथार्थ का परिचय भी कराया था।

फराओ ने अपने बेटे को गोपनीयता का पाठ पढ़ाते हुए कहा है कि रात्रि में सोते समय भी अपने हृदय पर काबू रखना कि कहीं तुम्हारा हृदय किसी शत्रु द्वारा भेजी गई जासूस सुंदरी के मोहपाश में फंसकर तुम्हारे हितों को खतरे में न डाल दे।

अमेनमहैट की मृत्यु के बाद शासन का भार उसके पुत्र सेसोट्रीज प्रथम को सौंपा गया। उसने नूबिया पर विजय प्राप्त की और साम्राज्य का विस्तार किया। 1535 ई. पूर्व में उसकी मृत्यु हो गई।

(2) अमेनमहैट द्वितीय–अमेनमहैट द्वितीय को सेसोट्रीज प्रथम की मृत्यु के पश्चात् राजगद्दी सौंपी गई। उसका शासनकाल पचास वर्षों का था जो उसके पुत्र सेसोट्रीज की सहायता से संभव हो सका था। 1507 ई. पूर्व में सेसोट्रीज द्वितीय की मृत्यु हो गई। उसके बाद उसका पुत्र सेसोट्रीज तृतीय शासक बना। उसका शासनकाल मात्र तीस वर्षों का था। उसमें योग्य शासक के सभी गुण विद्यमान थे साथ ही साथ वह एक सफल विजेता भी था। उसने अपने साम्राज्य का विस्तार किया, जो नील घाटी में हजारों मील तक फैला हुआ था। 1449 ई. पूर्व में सेसोट्रीज तृतीय की मृत्यु हो गई। बाद में उसका पुत्र अमेनमहैट उसका उत्तराधिकारी बना।

(3) अमेनमहैट तृतीय–वह चारों तरफ शांति की स्थापना करना चाहता था तथा वह युद्ध के पक्ष में विल्कुल भी नहीं था। राज्य का विकास करना ही उनका मुख्य उद्देश्य था। उसके काल में सिंचाई की सुविधाओं का विकास होने से कृषि के क्षेत्र में उन्नति हुई। उसका शासनकाल पचास वर्षों तक चला। इस काल में राज्य में शांति एवं व्यवस्था बनी रही और प्रजा सुखी तथा समृद्ध थी।

अमेनमहैट के काल में स्थापत्य कला का काफी विकास हुआ था। उसने एल्काब के पास स्थित पुरानी राजधानी के चारों ओर दीवार का निर्माण करवाया। इस दीवार के कुछ हिस्से आज भी खड़े हैं। थीब्स नगर में भवनों का निर्माण काफी संख्या में कराया गया था। इस युग में शानदार पिरामिडों का निर्माण करवाया गया।

मूर्तिकला का विकास भी अमेनमहैट में सबसे अधिक हुआ था। इस समय मूर्तिकारों ने अमेनमहैट की चालीस से पचास फीट तक ऊँची मूर्तियों का निर्माण किया। अमेनमहैट तृतीय ने अपने दरबार में साहित्यकारों को भी आश्रय दिया, जिन्होंने बहुत-सी रचनाएं रचीं। मिस्र का सर्वांगीण विकास उसी के शासनकाल में सबसे अधिक हुआ था। उसकी मृत्यु 1501 ई. पू. में हो गई थी। इसके बाद अमेनमहैट चतुर्थ गद्दी पर बैठा। उसका शासनकाल नौ वर्षों तक रहा। उसके पश्चात् उसकी पुत्री ने चार वर्ष तक शासन किया।

(4) अहमोज प्रथम—अहमोज को अठारहवें राजवंश में राजगद्दी सौंप दी गई थी। उसने मिस्र के राजाओं तथा सरदारों की सहायता से 1570 ई. पूर्व में हिक्सास जाति को पराजित कर मिस्र पर अधिकार कर लिया। उसने आंतरिक व्यवस्था में सुधार किया और सीरिया, सूडान, फिलिस्तीन तथा पश्चिमी एशिया आदि कई देशों पर अधिकार कर लिया। उसके शासनकाल में जनता को किसी प्रकार की परेशानियों का सामना नहीं करना पड़ता था। साथ ही साम्राज्य का विस्तार किया उसके शासनकाल को इतिहास में 'स्वर्णयुग' की उपाधि दी गयी।

(5) थुटमोस प्रथम—अहमोज प्रथम की मृत्यु 1557 ई. पूर्व में हो गई। उसके बाद उसका पुत्र अमेनमहैट प्रथम गद्दी पर बैठा, जिसने दस वर्षों तक शासन किया। थुटमोस प्रथम एक महान विजेता, कला-प्रेमी तथा निर्माता था। उसने 1545 ई. पूर्व से 1514 ई. पूर्व तक राज्य किया। उसने कई मंदिरों का निर्माण करवाया तथा कई पुराने मंदिरों का पुनरुद्धार भी करवाया।

पश्चिमी एशिया से प्राप्त धन से मिस्र में देवालयों तथा पिरामिडों का निर्माण करवाया। उसने अपने जीवनकाल में ही एक पिरामिड का निर्माण करवाया, जहाँ मृत्यु के बाद उसको दफना दिया गया। आगे चलकर थुटमोस प्रथम के उत्तराधिकारी भी वहीं दफनाये गये। परिणामस्वरूप वहाँ कई पिरामिड खड़े हो गये और उस स्थान को आगे चलकर 'राजाओं की घाटी' कहा जाना लगा।

(6) हातशेपसुत व मिस्र का विकास—थुटमोस प्रथम की मृत्यु के बाद उसकी पुत्री हातशेपसुत को मिस्र की शासिका बनाया गया। उसे विश्व की पहली महिला साम्राज्ञी भी कहा जाता है। उसने 1501 ई. पूर्व से 1479 ई. पूर्व (22 वर्ष) तक राज्य

किया। वह मर्दाना पोशाक पहनती थी और नकली दाढ़ी-मूँछें भी धारण करती थी। उसके दरबारी उसे 'ईश्वर की पत्नी' कहकर संबोधित करते थे।

हातशेपसुत एक महत्त्वाकांक्षी तथा प्रतिभाशाली महिला थी। उसे ही राज्य की वास्तविक शासिका माना जा सकता था। सभी अधिकार उसी के हाथ में केंद्रित थे। उसका पति थुटमोस तृतीय उसके सम्मुख मात्र कठपुतली बना रहा।

उसके शासनकाल में कला एवं व्यापार के क्षेत्र में भी उन्नति हुयी उसने एक नुकीली मीनार का निर्माण राजधानी कारनाक में कराया, जिसका शीर्ष भाग सोने और चाँदी के पतरों से बनवाया गया था, उसने पश्चिमी थीब्स में एक शानदार मंदिर का निर्माण करवाया, जिसे 'दर-एल-बहरी' कहा जाता है। यह मंदिर उस समय की भवन निर्माण कला का उत्कृष्ट नमूना है। रानी ने कारनाक के मंदिर का और अधिक सुंदर तरीके से निर्माण कराया। उसने अपने साम्राज्य में शांति एवं व्यवस्था बनाये रखी। उसके समय में व्यापार की उन्नति हुई तथा चित्रकला के क्षेत्र में भी विकास हुआ। रानी ने पुण्ट प्रदेश पर विजय प्राप्त की, जिसके कारण वहाँ से सोना, चाँदी, हाथीदाँत तथा अन्य बहुमूल्य धातुएँ प्राप्त हुईं। उसका शासनकाल मिस्र के इतिहास में स्वर्णकाल भी कहा जाता है।

(7) थुटमोस तृतीय–रानी हातशेपसुत 1479 ई. पूर्व में काल के ग्रास में समा गयी। उसके पश्चात् उसके पति थुटमोस को राजगद्दी सौंपी गई थी। उसका शासनकाल 1479 ई. पूर्व से 1447 ई. तक था। चूँकि उसे अपनी पत्नी रानी हातशेपसुत के शासनकाल में काफी दुःख सहना पड़ा था, अतः वह उसकी मृत्यु पर काफी प्रसन्न हुआ। उसने अपने शासनकाल में अपनी पत्नी से बदले की भावना से मंदिरों तथा इमारतों से उसका नाम हटवा दिया।

थुटमोस तृतीय को बिल ड्यूरेन्ट नेपोलियन मानता था। इसने सूडान, सीरिया, फिलिस्तीन और अन्य पड़ौसी देशों को जीतकर अपने साम्राज्य का विस्तार किया। विश्व-इतिहास में इससे पहले इतना विशाल व संगठित साम्राज्य और कोई नहीं था। विजित प्रदेशों में उसने नेपोलियन की भाँति कुशल शासन-व्यवस्था की स्थापना की। थुटमोस की मृत्यु 27 मार्च, 1447 ई. में हो गई थी।

थुटमोस के राज्यकाल में प्रजा को किसी प्रकार की परेशानियों का सामना नहीं करना पड़ता था तथा उसने मिस्र के साम्राज्य को उसकी ऊँचाइयों पर पहुँचा दिया था। उसके प्रधानमंत्री शेख मीर ने उसकी प्रशंसा करते हुये लिखा–

"हमारे सम्राट ऐसे थे, जिन्हें सब कुछ मालूम था। जहाँ कहीं कुछ ऐसा होता था, उसकी खबर उन्हें हो जाती थी। वे ज्ञान के देवता थे। कोई ऐसा काम नहीं था,

जिसे वे नहीं कर सकते थे।" थुटमोस तृतीय ने अपने साम्राज्य को 55 सूबों में बांट दिया था तथा प्रत्येक सूबे के शासन-प्रबंध का संचालन करने के लिए एक सूबेदार की नियुक्ति की एवं कई सैनिक छावनियों की स्थापना की। थल सेना को शक्तिशाली बनाने के साथ-साथ नौसेना का भी काफी विकास हुआ था। इसके अतिरिक्त भूमि के सर्वेक्षण के आधार पर राजस्व कर निश्चित किया गया।

थुटमोस तृतीय को मिस्र के प्राचीन इतिहास में काफी प्रसिद्धि प्राप्त थी। उसे विश्व-इतिहास में प्रथम सेनानायक पुकारा जाता था। उसे विश्व-इतिहास का प्रथम सेनानायक माना जाता है, जिसने सर्वप्रथम एक वास्तविक साम्राज्य की स्थापना की। उसे प्रथम विजेता तथा प्रथम साम्राज्य निर्माता की भी संज्ञा दी जाती थी। उसका नाम मिस्र के इतिहास के पन्नों में स्वर्णाक्षरों में लिखा गया है। थुटमोस तृतीय की उपलब्धियों के कारण बाद के दो सौ वर्षों तक मिस्र तत्कालीन सभ्य संसार का सबसे शक्तिशाली तथा समृद्ध देश बना रहा। उसकी मौत के बाद भी उसके त्याग और बलिदान को मिस्रवासी आज भी भूला नहीं सके हैं।

(8) अमेनहोटेप द्वितीय तथा थुटमोस चतुर्थ—उसके पुत्र अमेनहोटेप द्वितीय को थुटमोस तृतीय के पश्चात् राजा बना दिया गया था। वह एक सफल विजेता एवं निर्माता था। उसने कारनाक के मंदिर की मरम्मत करवाई तथा उसमें कुछ नये भाग भी जुड़वाए। वस्तुतः वह एक सुयोग्य पिता का सुयोग्य पुत्र था। उसने 26 वर्ष तक शासन किया। उसकी मृत्यु 1420 ई. पूर्व में हुई। वह एक प्रतिभा सम्पन्न राजा था, जिसमें तैराकी, नाविक एवं घुड़सवार, तीरंदाजी जैसी विलक्षण प्रतिभायें थीं। उसकी गौरवगाथा की पुष्टि गिजा के महान स्फिक्स के समीप मिले एक शिलालेख से होती है।

1898 ई. में इस सम्राट की ममी के पास उसका धनुष भी प्राप्त हुआ था, जिस पर अंकित शब्द इस प्रकार थे—"गुफाओं के निवासियों पर प्रहार करने वाला, कुश पर विजय प्राप्त करने वाला, उनके नगरों को कष्ट पहुँचाने वाला, उनके नगरों को नष्ट करने वाला-मिस्र का महान प्राचीर (रक्षक) और उसके (राजा के) सैनिकों का संरक्षक।"

उसके पुत्र थुटमोस चतुर्थ ने अमेनहोटेप द्वितीय की मृत्यु के पश्चात् राज्यभार संभाला। वह भी एक सुयोग्य सम्राट था। उसने बेबीलोन के राजा से मैत्रीपूर्ण संबंध स्थापित किए तथा मिटानी के राजा से वैवाहिक संबंध कायम किए। नूबिया के विद्रोह को दबाने में उसने महत्त्वपूर्ण भूमिका निभायी। 1411 ई. पूर्व में थुटमोस चतुर्थ की मृत्यु हो गई।

(9) अमेनहेटोप तृतीय (1411 ई. पूर्व से 1375 ई. पूर्व)—थुटमोस चतुर्थ की मृत्यु के बाद उसके पुत्र अमेनहेटोप तृतीय को राजगद्दी सौंपी गयी। वह एक प्रतापी, महान और शानदार फराओ था। उसका शासनकाल 1411 ई. पूर्व से 1375 ई. पूर्व तक रहा था। वह शांतिप्रिय शासक था उसे कला एवं सौंदर्य का अच्छा ज्ञान था।

अमेनहेटोप तृतीय ने अपने शासनकाल के आरंभ में टाई नामक एक असाधारण महिला से विवाह किया। टाई ने शादी के बाद उसे अपने वश में कर लिया था। इस प्रभाव का अनुमान हम इस बात से लगाते हैं कि राज्य के समस्त दस्तावेजों पर राजा के साथ रानी टाई का नाम भी अंकित किया जाता था। राजकीय मामलों तथा सार्वजनिक उत्सवों में इस रानी ने काफी सहयोग किया था।

अमेनहोटेप तृतीय में सम्राट के संपूर्ण गुण विद्यमान थे। उसे महान की पदवी से विभूषित किया गया था। उसके शासनकाल में व्यापार व वाणिज्य का सर्वांगीण विकास हुआ था। उसको सुचारु रूप से चलाने के लिये कुछ नियम बनाये गये। फराओ ने पुलिस का प्रबंध किया, जो चुंगी वसूल करती थी। चुंगी फराओ की राज्य की आय का मुख्य साधन था। अमेनहेटोप तृतीय के काल में मिस्र की सभ्यता अपने चरम शिखर पर जा पहुँची।

अमेनहेटोप तृतीय को कला से काफी लगाव था, अतः उसके शासनकाल में कला-कौशल के क्षेत्र में बहुत अधिक विकास हुआ। उस काल में स्थापत्य कला का काफी विकास हुआ था। उसने थीब्स नगर में मंदिरों और इमारतों के निर्माण करवाया। उन सभी को मिस्री कला के सर्वोत्कृष्ट नमूनों में शामिल किया जा सकता है। इस काल में ही कला के क्षेत्र में काफी विकास हुआ था।

अमेनहोटेप के शासनकाल में ही मूर्तिकला काफी विकसित हो सकी थी। उस युग में बनी हुई मूर्तियाँ सुंदरता और सूक्ष्मता की दृष्टि से अत्यंत उत्कृष्ट हैं। इसमें जीवन की महत्त्वपूर्ण मनोदशा को सुंदर तरीके से दर्शाया गया है। अमेनहेटोप तृतीय के काल को मिस्र के प्राचीन इतिहास में स्वर्णयुग की संज्ञा दी जाती है। बिल ड्यूरेन्ट के कथनानुसार, "मिस्र का फराओ संसार का प्रथम पुरुष था। थीब्स में उपहारों की सरिता बहती थी। मंदिरों में भारी मात्रा में हीरे जवाहरात पाये जाते थे। समस्त संसार अमेनहेटोप की मित्रता के लिए आतुर था।"

(10) अखनाटन (1375 ई. पूर्व से 1358 ई. पूर्व)—अमेनहेटोप तृतीय की मृत्यु के बाद उसका पुत्र अमेनहोटेप को उसका उत्तराधिकारी बनाया गया था, उस समय उसकी आयु मात्र 12 वर्ष की थी जो आगे चलकर 'अखनाटन' नाम

से प्रसिद्ध हुआ। उसका शासनकाल 1375 ई. पूर्व से लेकर 1358 ई. पूर्व तक था। वह सूर्य देवता 'एटन' का परम भक्त था, अतः उसने अपना नाम अखनाटन रख लिया। अखनाटन का शाब्दिक अर्थ होता है—'जो एटन को प्रिय हो।' अखनाटन ने अखनाटन नामक एक नये शहर की स्थापना की थी तथा उसे मिस्र की राजधानी बना दिया था। पहले मिस्र की राजधानी थीब्स थी। अखनाटन को एटन देवता का पवित्र नगर घोषित किया गया। अखनाटन का शाब्दिक अर्थ होता है—'एटन का क्षितिज'। इस शहर को आधुनिक युग में 'टेल-एल-अमरना' की संज्ञा दी जाती है। अखनाटन एक शांतिप्रिय, महान दार्शनिक, विचारक, आदर्शवादी और महान कलाकार था। अपने धार्मिक और दार्शनिक विचारों के कारण उसे प्राचीन विश्व के इतिहास में 'पहला धार्मिक व्यक्ति' पुकारा जाता है। मानव इतिहास में अखनाटन को मानवतावादी एवं सिद्धांतवादी विचारों के कारण सदा स्मरण किया जायेगा।

एटन को अखनाटन के राजा बनने से पूर्व मिस्र के देवता की संज्ञा दी जाती थी। मिस्र के अतिरिक्त रा, ओसिरिस, इसिस तथा होरस आदि देवी-देवताओं की भी पूजा की जाती थी। मिस्र में लगभग दो हजार देवी देवताओं की पूजा की जाती थी। अखनाटन ने बहुदेववाद का विरोध करते हुए एकेश्वरवाद के सिद्धांत को प्रचलित किया। एकेश्वरवाद का प्रचार करने वाला पहला सम्राट अखनाटन था। मिस्र के पुराने पुजारी एवं सैनिक इस विद्वान दार्शनिक को पागल मानते थे और इसका कड़ा विरोध करते थे। एटन देवता को अखनाटन द्वारा साम्राज्य का सर्वश्रेष्ठ देवता घोषित कर दिया गया। यहीं से मिस्र के धर्म में क्रांति का भी उदय हुआ।

उसने मूर्तिपूजा का खण्डन किया। उसने एटन देवता को निराकार घोषित कर दिया। निःसंदेह इसके धार्मिक विचार, धार्मिक चिंतन के क्षेत्र में विशिष्ट स्थान रखते हैं। अखनाटन ने एटन को मिस्री साम्राज्य का राजकीय देवता भी घोषित कर दिया और शासन की सारी शक्ति इस देवता की पूजा के प्रचार में लगा दी।

अखनाटन के सारे कर्मचारी इस देवता की पूजा करने लगे। इस प्रकार उसने अपने व्यक्तिगत धर्म को सारी प्रजा का धर्म बना दिया जिससे प्रजा को मजबूरीवश धर्म को स्वीकार करना पड़ा।

अखनाटन ने एटन देवता की अराधना हेतु सुंदर प्रार्थनाओं की रचना की। इनमें उसके नये धर्म के सिद्धांतों की झलक मिलती है। उसने अपनी कब्र तथा स्मारकों पर इन धार्मिक प्रार्थनाओं को अंकित करवाया।

उसकी प्रार्थनाओं के कुछ अंश यहाँ दिये जा रहे हैं—

'हे एटन देवता! जब तुम पश्चिमी क्षितिज में डूब जाते हो, तब सारा विश्व मृतवत् अंधकार में लीन हो जाता है। तुम ही अंधकार के निर्माता हो, जो रात्रि के रूप में प्रकट होता है और इस रात्रिकाल में जंगली जानवर बाहर निकलते हैं। इसका कारण यह है कि विश्व का निर्माता ही जब क्षितिज में आराम करने चला जाता है, तब सारा संसार भी शांत हो जाता है।"

"हे एटन देवता! तुम्हीं ने स्त्रियों से मनुष्य को पैदा किया है। तुम ही बच्चों की माँ के शरीर में जीवन-दान करते हो। तुम्ही माँ के गर्भ में बच्चे को सांत्वना देते हो। इस प्रकार तुम गर्भ में भी धाय माँ का काम करते हो।"

अखनाटन की प्रार्थना सभाओं में धार्मिक चिंतन के साथ विश्व-बंधुत्व की भावना थी, जो एक आदर्श है। उसका मानना था कि एटन देवता सभी प्राणियों का माता-पिता है और वह सभी के प्रति एक जैसा पितृवत् प्रेम प्रदर्शित करता है। इस प्रकार अखनाटन पहला व्यक्ति था, जिसने विश्व-बंधुत्व के सिद्धांत का प्रचार किया। इस आधार पर अखनाटन को मानव-इतिहास के पहले पैगम्बर की संज्ञा भी दी जा सकती है।

अखनाटन के समय में एटन की पूजा का भार मित्रों एवं दरबारियों पर था, मिस्र की जनता का उनके प्रति कोई लगाव नहीं था। उसकी प्रजा उसके धार्मिक सिद्धांतों को समझने में असमर्थ थी। परिणामस्वरूप अकबर के दीन-ए-इलाही की भाँति अखनाटन का धर्म भी उसकी मृत्यु के साथ ही समाप्त हो गया। फिर भी यह स्वीकार करना पड़ेगा कि धार्मिक पैगम्बरों के आने के पूर्व अखनाटन विश्व का प्रथम व्यक्ति था, जिसने धर्म एवं चिंतन के क्षेत्र में सिद्धांत प्रतिपादित किए थे।

राजा बनने के पश्चात् अखनाटन को आंतरिक तथा बाह्य समस्याओं से गुजरना पड़ा था तथा किस तरह शासन करना है इसकी उसे जानकारी नहीं थी। वह शांतिप्रिय था और युद्धों में कोई रुचि नहीं रखता था। अतः उसके साम्राज्य में अराजकता फैलने लगी जिससे साम्राज्य टुकड़ों में विभक्त होना प्रारंभ हुआ।

(11) अखनाटन युग के बाद का इतिहास—अखनाटन के दामाद साक्रेन को उसके पश्चात् राजा बनाया गया था। अयोग्य होने के कारण कुछ समय बाद उसे पदच्युत कर दिया गया। इसके बाद अखनाटन का दूसरा दामाद तूतेनखाटन मिस्र की गद्दी पर बैठा। तुतेनखाटन को अखनाटन का नया धर्म तथा उसका शहर दोनों ही पसंद नहीं थे। एटन देवता के पुरोहितों के दबाव में आकर उसे अपनी राजधानी थीब्स में स्थानांतरित करनी पड़ी। इतना ही नहीं, उसने तुतेनखाटन के स्थान पर

अपने को 'तुतेनखामन' कहना आरंभ कर दिया। वह एटन देवता की पूजा करने लगा। 1234 ई. पूर्व में उसकी मौत हो गयी।

(12) उन्नीसवाँ राजवंश—तुतेनखामन के मरने के बाद शासन व्यवस्था सुदृढ़ नहीं रह सकी। लेकिन कुछ समय बाद पुरोहित वर्ग तथा सेना की सहायता से हरमहाब गद्दी पर बैठा। उसने उन्नीसवें राजवंश की स्थापना की। हरमहाब ने एटन देवता की अराधना के लिए मंदिर के द्वार खोल दिये उसने शासन व्यवस्था को पुनर्गठित किया और साम्राज्य में शांति तथा व्यवस्था कायम की।

हरमहाब के मृत्यु के बाद उसका कोई उत्तराधिकारी नहीं था इस कारण उसके एक सेनापति का बेटा रैमसेस प्रथम गद्दी पर बैठा। उसने 1315 ई. पूर्व से लेकर 1313 ई. पूर्व तक शासन किया।

(i) *सेटी प्रथम (1313 ई. पूर्व से 1292 ई. पूर्व)*—सेटी प्रथम में विजेता के सभी गुण विद्यमान थे, जिसके पिता का नाम रैमसेस प्रथम था जिसने अपने पिता की मृत्यु के बाद शासन का कार्य ग्रहण किया। उसने फिलिस्तीन, सीरिया, पेकेनान, रेतेनू और कादेश में हुए विद्रोहों का दमन किया। सम्राट की वापसी का उल्लेख एक लेख में मिलता है। उसमें कहा गया है कि "महामहिम देशों से लौट आये हैं—उन्होंने रेतेनू को पराजित कर दिया और उसके सरदारों को मार डाला" तब एशियावासी कह उठे, "यह देखो, वह उस अग्निशिखा की भाँति है, जो उठती ही जाती है और जिसे पानी भी नहीं बुझा सकता।" सेटी को कला से काफी लगाव था। उसने कई मंदिरों का निर्माण भी करवाया।

(ii) *रैमसेस द्वितीय (1292 ई. पूर्व से 1225 ई. पूर्व)*—रैमसेस द्वितीय को सेटी प्रथम के पश्चात् गद्दी सौंपी गयी। उसने 1292 ई. पूर्व से लेकर 1225 ई. पूर्व तक शासन किया। उसे एक महत्त्वाकांक्षी शासक भी कहा था। उसने 1288 ई. पूर्व में हिट्टाइटों के राजा को पराजित कर सीरिया पर विजय प्राप्त की। रैमसेस द्वितीय का हिट्टाइटों से संघर्ष आगे भी जारी रहा। 1272 ई. पूर्व में उसने हिट्टाइटों के राजा के साथ शांति और बंधुत्व का प्रसार किया। यह संधि प्राचीन विश्व के इतिहास की एक महत्त्वपूर्ण संधि है। इससे अंतर्राष्ट्रीय संबंधों के बारे में जानकारी प्राप्त होती है। इस संधि में राजनीतिक झगड़ों और प्रवासियों के विषय में भी शर्तें हैं, इसलिए भी इस संधि को बहुत अधिक महत्त्व दिया जाता है। इस संधि को मजबूती प्रदान करने के लिए हिट्टाइट राजवंश की राजकुमारी का विवाह रैमसेस द्वितीय के साथ कर दिया गया।

रैमसेस द्वितीय का कला से काफी लगाव था। उसने बहुत से मंदिरों, इमारतों तथा सड़कों का निर्माण करवाया। उसके समय में वीर रस की कविताओं की रचना की गई थी। इस काल के कहानियाँ लिखी गईं, जिसमें धनी वर्ग के जीवन का चित्रण किया गया है।

रैमसेस द्वितीय के काल में एटन देवता के पुरोहितों के प्रभाव में असाधारण रूप से वृद्धि हुई जिसके कारण डेढ़ सौ साल बाद फराओ को ही स्वयं एटन का प्रधान पुरोहित बनना पड़ा। रैमसेस का परिवार बहुत बड़ा था जिसमें लड़कों की संख्या 150 और लड़कियों की संख्या 50 थी जिन पर उसको गर्व था। 1225 ई. पूर्व में उसकी मृत्यु हो गई।

(iii) *रैमसेस द्वितीय के बाद के युग का इतिहास*—रैमसेस द्वितीय की मृत्यु के बाद उसके तेरहवें लड़के ने राज्य-भार संभाला। उसने 1224 ई. पूर्व से 1213 ई. पूर्व तक शासन किया। उसने एशियाई विद्रोहों का दमन किया और शांति तथा सुव्यवस्था की स्थापना की।

(13) बीसवाँ राजवंश : रैमसेस तृतीय—रैमसेस तृतीय 1198 ई. पूर्व में मिस्र की गद्दी पर बैठा और उसने बीसवें राजवंश की नींव डाली। वह एक प्रतापी राजा के रूप में प्रसिद्ध था। उसने तनख्वाह और भाड़े के सैनिकों की एक बहुत बड़ी स्थायी सेना का गठन किया। भूमध्यसागर के दक्षिणी तट पर बसी हुई हिब्रू जाति के विद्रोह का दमन किया। रैमसेस तृतीय ने सीरिया में एटन देवता के एक मंदिर का निर्माण कराया था। उसने प्रजा की सहायता के लिए सड़क के दोनों ओर वृक्षारोपण कराया तथा वह राज्य में शांति की स्थापना करना चाहता था।

रैमसेस तृतीय को कला में काफी रुचि थी। उसने कई नये मंदिरों का निर्माण करवाया और पुराने मंदिरों की मरम्मत करवाई। थीब्स नगर के पश्चिमी मैदान में उसने एटन देवता के एक सुंदर और भव्य मंदिर का निर्माण करवाया। इस मंदिर को देखने से यह अंदाजा लगाया जा सकता है उस दौरान भवन निर्माण कला काफी समृद्ध थी। रैमसेस तृतीय के समय में मिस्री कला को खूब प्रोत्साहन दिया गया। इस दृष्टि से वह मिस्र का अंतिम महान शासक था।

रैमसेस तृतीय के काल में मंदिरों का काफी विकास हुआ था, जिससे पुरोहित वर्ग का भी विकास हुआ और उनकी शक्तियों में बढ़ोत्तरी हुयी जो आगे चलकर मिस्री फराओ के लिए खतरनाक सिद्ध हुई। रैमसेस तृतीय की 1167 ई. पूर्व में मृत्यु हुई। उसके शासनकाल में मिस्र का साम्राज्य काफी विकसित नहीं हो सका था।

रैमसेस तृतीय की मृत्यु के पश्चात् उसके उत्तराधिकारी अत्यंत कमजोर एवं अयोग्य सिद्ध हुए। इन सभी शासकों को रैमसेस की संज्ञा दी जाती थी। इन शासकों के शासनकाल में मिस्र के पतन और विघटन की प्रक्रिया और जोरों से शुरू हुई। रैमसेस तृतीय के उत्तराधिकारी एटन देवता के पुरोहितों के हाथ की कठपुतली मात्र थे। उसके वंश का आखिरी शासक रैमसेस बारहवाँ था, जो एटन देवता के प्रधान पुरोहित के हाथ की कठपुतली मात्र था। उसकी मृत्यु 1090 ई. में हो जाने पर 'एटन' देवता के मुख्य पुरोहित हीरहारे ने मिस्र की गद्दी पर अपना अधिकार कर लिया। उसके द्वारा मिस्र के 21वें राजवंश की शुरुआत की गई थी।

मिस्र में 31 राजवंशों की स्थापना की गई थी साथ ही साथ 332 ई. पूर्व में यूनान के शासक सिकंदर महान ने मिस्र पर अपना आधिपत्य जमा लिया था। सिकंदर की मृत्यु के बाद मिस्र पर टोलमी वंश का शासन रहा। टोलमी वंश के बाद मिस्र पर ईरानी, यूनानी, रोमन, अरब और अंग्रेजों का शासन रहा। इस प्रकार मिस्र 332 ई. पूर्व से 1822 ई. तक लगभग 2254 वर्ष तक मिस्र में दासता कायम रही।

मिस्र की राजनीतिक स्थिति

मिस्र के राजा को 'फराओ' की संज्ञा दी जाती थी। इसका शाब्दिक अर्थ है–'बड़ा घर'। फराओ को असीम अधिकार प्राप्त थे। उसे निरंकुश या स्वेच्छाचारी शासक के रूप में भी जाना जाता था। वह जो कुछ आदेश देता था उसे ही कानून कहा जाता था और शासन की समस्त शक्तियाँ उसके हाथ में निहित थीं। दुनिया के इतिहास में मिस्र में ही सबसे पहले राजा को देवता मानने का रिवाज था। मिस्री लोग फराओ को ईश्वरतुल्य मानते थे। उनका ऐसा विश्वास था कि यह समस्त जमीन उसकी है। उसकी आज्ञा का पालन करना हमारा धर्म है उसको सब दंडवत् प्रणाम करते थे तथा उसकी कदमबोसी के लिए तरसते थे।

स्त्रियों को मिस्र में उत्तराधिकार प्राप्त होने लगा था। अतः राजकुमार अपनी सगी बहन के साथ विवाह करता था, जिससे उसका हक दृढ़ हो जाता था। फराओ देवता के समान थे जिनको सजाने के लिए 20 लोगों की नियुक्ति की जाती थी। जिनके ऊपर एक अधिकारी जिसे (ओवरसियर) कहा जाता था। उसके बाल बनाने वाला, मुकुट बाँधने वाला, काजल डालने वाला, नाखून काटने व रंगने वाला, गालों व होंठों पर लाली लगाने वाला, जूते उठाने व पहनाने वाले सेवक अलग-अलग होते थे। जब फराओ अपने सेवकों से ऊबकर नौका विहार को जाता था, तब खूबसूरत

युवतियाँ उसका मन बहलाने का कार्य करती थीं। ये युवतियाँ जाली की एक बारीक चादर के सिवाय कुछ भी नहीं पहनती थीं।

वजीर राजा को शासन संबंधी सलाह देता था। उसका मुख्य कार्य लगान वसूल करना, आय-व्यय का हिसाब रखना, मुकदमों पर फैसला देना तथा राजा के आदेशों का पालन करवाना था। राजा के नीचे वजीर ही सर्वोच्च न्यायाधीश था। सारू उन लोगों का समूह था जिनमें वृद्ध लोग आते थे जो फराओ के दरबारी थे। वे अपनी सलाह राजा को देते थे लेकिन उनकी सलाह मानना या न मानना फराओ के मन के ऊपर था।

फराओ ने शासन की सुविधा की दृष्टि से राज्य को कई भागों में विभाजित कर दिया था। प्रत्येक भाग को **नोम** तथा उसके शासक को **नोमार्क** कहा जाता था। नोमार्क को फराओ द्वारा नियुक्त किया जाता था। उसका मुख्य कार्य राजा की आज्ञा का पालन करवाना था। गाँवों का शासन-प्रबंध सामन्तों के हाथ में था, जिन्हें पुलिस तथा न्याय संबंधी अधिकार प्राप्त थे। प्रत्येक नगर में एक अधिकारी की नियुक्ति की जाती थी, जिसका मुख्य कार्य राजस्व कर वसूल करना और सरकारी कानूनों का पालन करवाना था।

फराओ के पास प्रारंभ में कोई स्थायी सेना नहीं थी इसके लिए वे सामन्तों पर आश्रित थे। आवश्यकता पड़ने पर फराओ द्वारा अपने सामन्तों से सैनिकों की सहायता ली जाती थी। बाद में 12वें राजवंश के समय से स्थायी सेना की व्यवस्था की। हिक्सास के आक्रमण के परिणामस्वरूप मिस्र वालों ने घोड़ों और रथों का प्रयोग सीखा, जिसके बल पर उन्होंने मिस्र के साम्राज्य का विस्तार किया।

भूमि कर ही राज्य का आमदनी का प्रमुख श्रोत था, जिसमें किसानों द्वारा उपजाये गये फसल का जो किसानों से उपज का 1/10 से लेकर 1/20 हिस्सा मौजूद होता था। सार्वजनिक निर्माण कार्य हेतु फराओ द्वारा जनता से बेगार लेने का भी प्रावधान था। कर जिन्स के रूप में लिया जाता था। सूडान की खानों से सोना आयात किया जाता था। अपनी आय में बढ़ोत्तरी करने हेतु राजा खुद ही व्यापार भी करता था। एशियाई प्रातों से अन्न तथा पशुधन और लूट का माल भी प्राप्त होता था। फराओ को अन्य राज्यों से नजराने के रूप में यह सब दिया जाता था। जो सामन्त उसके अधीन थे उसे ढेर सारे उपहार दिया करते थे। एक शिलालेख पर अंकित है कि "एक सामन्त ने अमेनहोटेप को सोने-चाँदी के रथ, हाथी दाँत और कीमती लकड़ी की मूर्तियाँ, जवाहरात, काँसे की 680 ढालें, 140 तलवारें और कीमती धातु के बने घड़े भेंट किये।" फराओ उपहार के बदले सामन्तों के लड़कों को दरबार में नौकरी दे दिया करता था।

न्याय देने का काम फराओ द्वारा किया जाता था। मुकदमा लिखित रूप में चलाया जाता था। जिस व्यक्ति का गवाह झूठा होता था उसे मार दिया जाता था। फराओ को मुकदमे का फैसला करने में तीन दिन का वक्त लगता था। अपराधी को कठोर सजा दी जाती थी, जैसे–डण्डे से पीटना, अंग-भंग करना, देश निकाला देना और जीवित मनुष्य की ममी बना देना आदि। न्याय देने का काम फराओ पैरों नामक भवन से दिया करता था।

सामाजिक जीवन

मिस्र के समाज का वर्गीकरण तीन भागों में किया जा सकता है–उच्च, मध्यम और निम्न वर्ग। उच्च वर्ग में राजा, सामन्त, पुरोहित, दरबारी, अमीर एवं उच्च पदाधिकारियों को शामिल किया जाता था; जो समृद्धि एवं विलासितापूर्ण जीवन बिताते थे। देश की सारी सम्पत्ति इन्हीं के हाथों में थी। इनके द्वारा भड़कीले वस्त्र काफी पसंद किये जाते थे तथा भोजन करने में सोने चांदी के बर्तनों का प्रयोग करते थे तथा ये लोग काफी विलासपूर्ण जीवन व्यतीत करते थे। पुजारियों या पुरोहितों का समाज पर पूरा नियंत्रण व प्रभाव था। ये लोग जादू-टोना, तंत्र-मंत्र तथा ताबीजें बेचकर धनसम्पत्ति एकत्रित करते थे। फराओ मंदिर में अपार धन दान देता था, वह भी पुरोहित को ही मिलता था, जिससे पुरोहित भी भोग विलास का जीवन व्यतीत करने लगे। जिन लोगों का संबंध उच्च वर्ग से था वे किसी प्रकार का कर नहीं देते थे तथा किसी प्रकार का सहयोग उनके द्वारा नहीं किया जाता था। मध्यम वर्ग में व्यापारी, शिल्पकार, बुद्धिजीवी और लिपिकों को शामिल किया जाता था। मिस्र की लिपि को समझने वाले को 'लिपिक' कहा जाता था। उन्हें समाज में आदर की दृष्टि से देखा जाता था। सरकारी नौकरियाँ ऐसे लोगों को ही दी जाती थीं।

मिस्र के लोग शाकाहारी तथा मांसाहारी दोनों भोजन पसंद करते थे। शाकाहारी लोग गेहूँ, जौ, चावल, दूध तथा दही खाते थे और मांसाहारी लोग सुअर, घड़ियाल तथा मछली का मांस खाते थे एवं शराब भी पीते थे। मिस्रवासियों का सामाजिक रहन-सहन काफी अच्छा था। पुरुष धोती धारण करते थे। स्त्रियाँ कमर के ऊपर का भाग खुला रखती थीं और कमर पर मिट्टी की गोलियों की मालाएं पहनती थीं। अमीर लोग सुंदर वस्त्र और आभूषणों का इस्तेमाल करते थे। अंगूठी और कर्णफूल आदि गहने स्त्री-पुरुष दोनों पहनते थे। स्त्रियां जंजीर, बाजूबंद, गले का हार और कंगन पहनती थीं। इस समय पुरुष और स्त्रियाँ दोनों ही अपने सिर के बाल मुंडवा लेते थे और फिर बालों को विभिन्न रंगों में रंगकर अपने सिर पर चिपका लेते थे।

मिस्र के लोग सौंदर्य प्रसाधनों का खूब प्रयोग करते थे। स्त्रियाँ होंठों पर लाली लगाती थीं और नाखून रंगती थीं। काजल और उबटन का प्रयोग होता था। यहाँ की स्त्रियाँ बालों में तेल लगाकर विभिन्न प्रकार के केश-विन्यास करती थीं। शृंगार के लिए दर्पण, कंघी, पाउडर का प्रयोग होता था। घरों में मेज, कुरसी, प्याले, चम्मच, तश्तरी आदि का इस्तेमाल किया जाता था। इस प्रकार उनका सामाजिक जीवन समृद्ध और रंगीन था।

मिस्र में स्त्रियों को राजनीति में भी स्थान प्राप्त था। उनकी दशा अच्छी थी। मैक्समूलर का मानना है, "किसी भी प्राचीन समाज में नारी को इतना ऊँचा स्तर प्रदान नहीं किया गया था, जितना मिस्र में। मिस्र में मातृसत्तात्मक परिवार व्यवस्था थी। पुरुषों पर स्त्रियों द्वारा शासन किया जाता था। मिस्र में नारी सम्पत्ति की स्वामी होती थी और सम्पत्ति माता से कन्या को प्राप्त होती थी। जिसके कारण राजकुमार को उत्तराधिकार प्राप्त करने के लिए अपनी सगी बहन से विवाह करना पड़ता था इसका अनुसरण जनता भी करती थी। इस बात के प्रमाण मिले हैं कि दूसरी शताब्दी तक मिस्र की दो-तिहाई जनता भाई-बहनों में ही विवाह करती थी। स्त्रियाँ विवाह के संबंध में काफी स्वतंत्रता प्राप्त थीं। प्राचीन मिस्र पर हातशेपतुस तथा क्लियोपेट्रा जैसी प्रतिभासम्पन्न रानियों ने राज्य किया। अतः इतिहासकार स्वेन ने ठीक ही लिखा है, "समाज में स्त्रियों को जो स्थान मिस्र में प्राप्त था, वह तत्कालीन किसी सभ्य देश में नहीं था।"

मिस्रवासी वाद्ययंत्रों तथा नृत्यकला द्वारा अपना मनोरंजन किया करते थे। इस समय पशु-युद्ध, जुआ, नाच-गाना, नटबाजी, साँड़ों का युद्ध, कुश्ती, घूँसेबाजी, चिड़ियों को लड़ाना और शराब—मनोरंजन के मुख्य साधन थे। मिस्रवासियों को मछली पकड़ने में काफी रुचि थी। मिस्रवासी युद्ध में पराजित अपने शत्रु का दाहिना हाथ काटकर उसे रिकार्ड के लिए सुरक्षित रखते थे।

इसी कारण से आधुनिक लोग मिस्र के लोगों से काफी सौहाद्रपूर्ण व्यवहार करते थे। मिस्र के एक कवि ने नागरिकों को संबोधित करते हुए इस प्रकार लिखा है "जिसके पास खेती नहीं है, उसे रोटी दो और सदा के लिए सुयश प्राप्त करो।" बूढ़े लोग बच्चों को शिक्षा दिलवाकर योग्य बना देते थे, ताकि वे संकट का सामना भली प्रकार कर सकें। कुछ शिक्षाएँ इस प्रकार थीं—"किसी विधवा की जमीन मत हड़पना। जबरदस्ती प्राप्त किये मन भर अनाज से ईश्वर द्वारा दिया गया एक सेर अनाज बेहतर है।" मिस्र के लोग लगभग 40 वर्ष तक समान आचरण करते रहे। मिस्र की महिलाओं को फूल-मालाओं से काफी लगाव था। पुरुष और स्त्रियाँ दोनों

ही फैशन प्रिय थे। इतिहासकार मैकनेल बर्न्स ने लिखा है "आभूषणों तथा सौन्दर्य प्रसाधनों की दृष्टि से प्राचीन मिस्र की महिलाओं को हमारी आधुनिकताओं से कुछ भी नहीं सीखना है।"

हिक्सास जाति के आक्रमण के बाद में बहु-विवाह को काफी बल मिल गया था, जिससे स्त्रियों का जीवन दुःखमय होने लगा। फराओ में अनेक रानियों को रखने का रिवाज था। मिस्र में भाई तथा बहन आपस में विवाह करते थे क्योंकि उनका मानना था इससे रक्त के शुद्धता बनी रहेगी। मिस्र में लड़कियों पर पति चुनाव करने के लिये किसी प्रकार का दबाव नहीं डाला जाता था। विवाह से पूर्व लड़के-लड़की का मिलना बुरा नहीं माना जाता था। शादी के समय पति यह प्रतिज्ञा करता था कि मैं जीवनभर अपनी पत्नी की आज्ञा का पालन करूँगा। जो स्त्री व्याभिचारिणी होती थी उसे छोड़ दिया जाता था। लड़कियां ही उस काल में प्यार की शुरुआत करती थीं। वे अपने प्रेमी को पत्र लिखना गौरव की बात समझती थीं। उस समय के एक प्रेम पत्र की कुछ पंक्तियाँ इस प्रकार हैं–"ओ मेरे सुंदर मित्र, मेरी इच्छा है कि मैं तुम्हारी पत्नी बनूँ, तुम्हारे धन की स्वामिनी बनूँ।"

मिस्र में माताओं को काफी सम्मान की दृष्टि से देखा जाता था इसकी व्याख्या करते हुए भोज पर लिखा गया है– "तू अपनी माँ को कभी मत भुलाना, उसने तेरा भार सहन किया, तुझे जन्म दिया, तीन साल तक तुझे कंधे पर लादे रही और दूध पिलाती थी और जब तू मदरसे में भरती हुआ और लिखने-पढ़ने लगा, तो वह रोज तेरे लिए घर से रोटी और शराब लेकर आती थी।" मिस्र में माँ के अतिरिक्त अन्य अपरिचित स्त्री को शंका और संदेह की दृष्टि से देखा जाता था। माँ स्वयं अपने लड़के को समझाती थी, "अनजान स्त्री से होशियार रहना। रास्ते में अगर वह मिल जाए, तो उसकी तरफ मत देखना और उससे जान-पहचान मत करना। यह गहरे पानी के एक भँवर की तरह है, जिसके चरित्र का अंदाजा लगाना कठिन है।" दूसरे स्थान पर माँ फिर अपने लड़के को शिक्षा देती है, "वह औरत, जिसका पति कहीं दूर गया हो, तुझे रोज चिट्ठी लिखेगी। लोगों की नजर बचाकर वह अपना जाल फैलायेगी।" मिस्र में महिलाओं को विशिष्ट स्थान प्राप्त था इसको समृद्धि का आधार माना जाता था।

मिस्र में सबसे सुंदर नारी को प्रतिवर्ष बड़ी धूम-धाम से बाढ़ भरी नील नदी में फेंक देने की प्रथा थी जिससे नील देवता प्रसन्न हो जाएँ और अन्य लोगों को न मारें। इस समय विषाद व झगड़े उत्पन्न करने वाली कन्याओं में से जो सबसे सुंदर होती थी, उसे अमीन देवता को अर्पण कर दिया जाता था। किसी बालक की मृत्यु

होने पर उसके माता-पिता को तीन दिन तक उसकी लाश को गोद में लेकर बैठे रहना पड़ता था। परिवार के सदस्यों की संख्या काफी अधिक होती थी और कई परिवारों में पिता के लिए बच्चों की गिनती व उनके नाम याद रखना भी मुश्किल हो जाता था। समाज में नर्तकियाँ होती थीं, जिनका प्रमुख कार्य अमीरों का मनोरंजन करना व उनको शारीरिक सुख देना था। यदि किसी लड़की पर दो भाई मोहित हो जाते और लड़की छोटे भाई से शादी करना चाहती, तब भी उसकी शादी बड़े भाई से ही की जाती थी। **सेवाइन** के अनुसार "महिलाओं का स्थान गरिमामय था, मिस्र में नारी का जो स्थान था, उसकी समानता प्राचीन सभ्यताओं में कोई दूसरी सभ्यता नहीं कर सकती थी और आधुनिक समय में भी कोई उसे पीछे नहीं छोड़ सका है।"

धार्मिक जीवन

मिस्र के लोग प्राकृतिक शक्तियों की देवता की भाँति पूजा करते थे। यहाँ तक कि मनुष्यों, देवताओं और पशु-पक्षियों तथा विविध वनस्पतियों की भी पूजा करने का विधान था। गौ, हंस, मगरमच्छ, बकरी, भेड़, बिल्ली, कुत्ता और सर्प आदि जानवरों को वे देवता मानते हैं। उनके प्रत्येक जिले, नगर, दिन और घंटे के लिए अलग-अलग देवता थे। प्रारंभ में इस प्रकार मिस्र में कुल मिलाकर तीन हजार देवता थे। रोम व भारत के अलावा इतने अधिक देवताओं वाला देश मिस्र ही है। मिस्र में सूर्य को काफी शक्तिशाली माना जाता था। इसे रे, रा, होरस एवं एटन आदि कई नामों से पुकारा जाता था। उसे ही सभी शक्तियों का केन्द्र माना जाता है। सूर्य के बाद नील नदी के देवता ओसिरिस का प्राधान्य था। इनके अतिरिक्त मिस्रवासी नूत (आकाश का देवता) तथा सिन (चन्द्रमा) की पूजा करने का विधान था। मिस्रवासियों का विश्वास था कि ओसिरिस ने अपनी बहन इसिस से विवाह किया है। ओसिरिस तथा इसिस के दाम्पत्य जीवन से मिस्रवासी काफी सीख लेते थे क्योंकि राजकुमार अपनी सगी बहन से विवाह करने का विधान मानता था। ओसिरिस के पुत्र होरस को एक आदर्श पुत्र की संज्ञा दी जाती थी। इसिस की पूजा पृथ्वी के प्रतिनिधि के रूप में की जाती थी।

मिस्र की सभ्यता में ओसिरिस नामक देवता को काफी शक्तिशाली माना जाता था। यह बाढ़ से उत्पन्न विनाश के बाद सारे देश को नवजीवन प्रदान करने का कार्य करता था। यह आशा और अमरत्व देने वाला तथा सत्य की विजय का प्रतीक था। ओसिरिस मृतक की आत्मा को उसके पाप-पुण्य के आधार पर नर्क और स्वर्ग प्रदान करता था। ओसिरिस के दरबार में निर्दोष सिद्ध करने के लिए पुरोहित लोग तंत्र,

मंत्र, जादू-टोना और ताबीज आदि बेचा करते थे। मृत्यु से पूर्व मिस्र के लोग पुरोहित से सदाचार का प्रमाण-पत्र ग्रहण करते थे। देवताओं को पूजा करने के लिय मिस्र में मंदिरों की स्थापना की जाती थी तथा पुजारियों को पूजा करने के लिये नियुक्त किया जाता था। **डॉ. राधाकृष्णन** ने मिस्र के देवालयों के बारे में लिखा है, "मिस्र के देवालय आज भी इस बात के प्रमाण हैं कि नील नदी की घाटी में बसे लोग परमात्मा में विश्वास करते थे। लक्जर के मंदिरों में पूजा कराने का कार्य कराया जाता था। उपासना की यही भावना आज भी विद्यमान है और वह स्थान आज भी उतना ही पवित्र है, जितना कि 1500 वर्ष पूर्व था।"

मिस्र के फराओ ने मरणोत्तर व्यक्ति को किसी प्रकार का कष्ट न हो इसलिए मृत शरीर को जीवित रखने के लिए ऊँचे-ऊँचे मकबरों का निर्माण करवाया, जिसे पिरामिड कहा जाता है। पिरामिड के निचले कमरे में खाने-पीने तथा मनोरंजन की सब वस्तुएँ रखी जाती थीं। मिस्रवासियों का मानना था कि मृत्यु के बाद भी इस शरीर को बचाना आवश्यक है। अतः वे लोग मृतक के शव को रासायनिक लेप लगाकर कब्र में सुला देते थे जिससे मृत शरीर को किसी प्रकार नुकसान नहीं होता था। मिस्र में आज भी हजारों साल पुराने मृत शरीर रखे हैं, जो 'ममी' कहलाते हैं।

मिस्र में परलोक को विशेष महत्त्व दिया जाता था। उनका यह मानना था कि मृत्यु के पश्चात् भी शरीर से आत्मा का सम्बन्ध बना रहता है, इसलिए वे प्रत्येक मृतक के साथ कब्र में भोजन, हथियार और सुख-सुविधा की अनेक वस्तुएँ रख देते थे, ताकि भोजन के अभाव में आत्मा मल का भक्षण न कर सके। इसके अतिरिक्त पिरामिडों की दीवारों पर अच्छे-अच्छे चित्रों का निर्माण किया जाता था, ताकि परलोक में मृतक के सुख में बाधा न आए। फराओ अपने परलोक को सुखी बनाने के लिए बहुत अधिक सम्पत्ति दान में देते थे। मृत्यु के बाद आत्मा सूर्य की तरह नाव में बैठकर परलोक के सत्य भवन में जाती थी, जहां अच्छे कार्यों के लिए स्वर्ग तथा बुरे कार्यों के लिए नर्क में भेजा जाता था।

इस संदर्भ में **डॉ. गोयल** ने लिखा है—"इतिहास में यह पहला उदाहरण है, जब किसी जाति ने पारलौकिक सुख-दुख को जीवन के ऐहिक कार्यों पर निर्भर माना।" पुण्य-कार्यों द्वारा स्वर्ग प्राप्त किया जा सकता था। वे **सत्यमेव जयते** के सिद्धांत में विश्वास करते थे। **प्लेटो व जीन ड्रमण्ड** ने लिखा—"यह समझा जाता था कि परलोक का प्रवेश-द्वार केवल उन लोगों के लिए खुला है, जो यह सिद्ध कर सकें कि उन्होंने इस पृथ्वी पर भला जीवन बिताया है।" इसलिए धर्माधिकारी मृतक की यात्रा को सुखमय बनाने के लिए कई प्रकार की

धार्मिक क्रियाएँ किया करते थे। कभी-कभी अंतिम संस्कार करते-करते सत्तर दिन व्यतीत हो जाते थे।

फराओ अमेनहोटेप चतुर्थ को अखनाटन नाम से जाना जाता है। इन्होंने बहुदेववाद के स्थान पर एकेश्वरवाद की उपासना का सिद्धान्त प्रचलित किया। उसने एटन (सूर्य) नामक देवता को संसार का सृष्टा, शासक और नियंता कहा तथा उसकी आराधना करने पर जोर दिया। यह निराकार देवता था, जिसकी मूर्ति-पूजा नहीं होती थी। इस देवता की उपासना का समय सूर्योदय और सूर्यास्त था। सूर्य के संदर्भ में अखनाटन का विचार था कि एटन दयालु एवं शांति का प्रतिनिधि था, जिसकी उपासना कोई व्यक्ति बिना पुरोहित की सहायता के भी कर सकता था। अखनाटन का कहना था कि दयालु पिता सूर्य किसी को नरक में नहीं भेजता।

अखनाटन के इस दृष्टिकोण का मिस्र की जनता पर कोई प्रभाव नहीं पड़ा। पुजारियों ने इसे अपराधी की संज्ञा दी है। अतः 1358 ई.पू. में अखनाटन की मृत्यु के साथ ही उसके धार्मिक विचार भी समाप्त हो गए। **बर्न्स** के शब्दों में "उसका धर्म उसके साथ समाप्त हो गया। इतने पर भी मिस्र के लोग महान् धार्मिक लोग थे।" पुजारियों ने अखनाटन की मृत्यु के बाद अपनी जादुई शक्ति के माध्यम से उसकी आत्मा को कष्ट पहुँचाने का भरसक प्रयास किया था, ताकि वह स्वर्ग में प्रवेश न कर सके और इधर-उधर भटकती रहे। वह सर्वप्रथम एकेश्वरवाद का प्रसार करना चाहता था। उसने एटन नामक देवता की आराधना प्रारंभ की, जो निराकार, दयालु एवं शान्ति का देवता था। उसने पुरोहितों की शक्ति का भी विरोध किया।

आर्थर वीगाल का मानना था–"अन्धविश्वासों के युग में तथा एक ऐसे देश में जहाँ बहु-ईश्वरवाद की मान्यता थी अखनाटन ने एकेश्वरवादी धर्म का विकास किया।......उस व्यक्ति का जन्म सबसे पहले धरती पर हुआ था। जिसने देवत्व के महत्त्व को भलीभांति समझा था। जिस समय विश्व युद्ध में ग्रस्त था, उसने मानव जाति के ज्ञात इतिहास में पहली बार शान्ति का पाठ पढ़ाया।.....वह पहला व्यक्ति था, जिसने सादगी, ईमानदारी, सत्यवादिता और हार्दिकता का उपदेश दिया और सबसे बड़ी बात तो यह है कि उसने यह उपदेश सिंहासन पर से दिया। फराओ में मानवतावादी के सभी गुण विद्यमान थे जो काफी सुहृदयी व्यक्ति था। उसने तीन हजार वर्ष पूर्व एक ऐसा उदाहरण प्रस्तुत किया, जो आज भी अनुसरण करने योग्य है। उसने एक ऐसा उदाहरण रखा कि एक आदर्श पति अथवा पिता कैसा होना चाहिए, एक ईमानदार मनुष्य को कैसा होना चाहिए, कवि की संवेदना कैसी होनी चाहिए, वैज्ञानिक की क्या आस्था होनी चाहिए और दार्शनिक को किस प्रकार सोचना

चाहिए। अपने सिद्धांतों के प्रसार हेतु उसने अपना सब कुछ समर्पित कर दिया था तथा अन्ततः उसका जीवन केवल यही सिद्ध कर पाया कि 'खेद है कि उसके सिद्धांत अव्यावहारिक थे।' ''तथापि इस बात से इन्कार नहीं किया जा सकता है कि उसके आदर्श तब तक सच्चे माने जाते रहेंगे, जब तक बत्तख काली नहीं हो जाती, कौआ सफेद नहीं हो जाता, पहाड़ियाँ यात्रा पर नहीं निकल पड़तीं और धरती का गर्भ नदियों में मिलकर दौड़ने नहीं लगता।''

फराओ (राजा) को मिस्र के सबसे बड़े पुजारी की संज्ञा दी जाती थी। वह धर्म पर अनुशासन तथा नियंत्रण रखता था। फराओ को देवता माना जाता था। वह सूर्य का पुत्र था, जिसे शासन करने के लिए दैवी अधिकार प्राप्त थे। धार्मिक उत्सवों की अध्यक्षता फराओ द्वारा की जाती थी। वह मन्दिरों की पूजा नहीं कर सकता था। अतः उसके अधीन सैकड़ों पुजारी होते थे। पुजारियों का चयन कुल के अनुसार किया जाता था तथा किसी प्रकार का कर लेने का विधान नहीं था। मिस्र के धार्मिक जीवन में ये भ्रष्टता लाने के लिए उत्तरदायी थे। पुरोहित या पुजारी, जादू-टोना और तंत्र-मंत्र के आधार पर ताबीज बनाकर लोगों को देते थे। उस समय पुरोहित व्यक्ति को ओसिरिस देवता के समक्ष यह शपथ दिलाता था, मैंने हत्या नहीं की ! मैंने चोरी नहीं की !! मैंने झूठ नहीं बोला !!! इस शपथ के बाद पुरोहित उस व्यक्ति को सदाचार का प्रमाण-पत्र देता था, जिसे मृत्यु के बाद उस व्यक्ति के शव के साथ कब्र में रख दिया जाता था। ऐसा करने के पीछे लोगों की धारणा थी कि मृतक को स्वर्ग में स्थान मिलता है। पुजारियों का यह खाने कमाने का तरीका था।

विज्ञान के क्षेत्र में प्रगति

मिस्र में विज्ञान का भी काफी विकास हुआ है। जमीन की पैमाइश, नहरों तथा पिरामिडों के निर्माण के सिलसिले में मिस्री लोगों ने रेखागणित का विकास किया। बाँध बनाना, नौकादार मीनार बनाना आदि वैज्ञानिक एवं इंजीनियरिंग की प्रगति के प्रमाण हैं। मिस्रवासी को गणित के बारे में काफी जानकारी प्राप्त थी। उन्हें 1 से 9 तक गिनती आती थी और इसके लिए उन्होंने चिह्न बना रखे थे। यदि उन्हें 3/7 लिखना होता, तो वे तीन बार 1/7, 1/7, 1/7 लिखते। यदि उन्हें एक हजार लिखना होता, तो वे एक कमल का फूल बना देते थे। इसी प्रकार सौ, हजार और लाख तक की संख्याओं के लिए उन्होंने चिह्न बना रखे थे। उनको जोड़, गुणा और भाग आदि आता था, परन्तु दशमलव का विकास करने में वे सफलता प्राप्त नहीं कर सके थे। नील नदी में बाढ़ आने के कारण प्रतिवर्ष सरकारी अधिकारियों द्वारा खेतों को नापा

जाता था। इस प्रथा से मिस्र में ज्यामिति (रेखागणित) का विकास हुआ। मिस्र में विश्व का पहला पंचांग बनाया गया। उन्होंने नक्षत्रों के आधार पर 365 दिन का साल बना लिया था। इनके एक वर्ष में बारह महीने होते थे और एक महीना 30 दिन का होता था। साल के अन्त में पाँच दिनों को जोड़ दिया जाता था। उनको चन्द्रग्रहण और सूर्य ग्रहण के बारे में भी ज्ञान था। आगे चलकर रोमवासियों ने इसी पंचांग से आधुनिक वर्ष बनाया।

बिल ड्यूरेन्ट के अनुसार–"मिस्र के लोग अनेक औषधियों का प्रयोग जानते थे। वे इस बात को जानते थे कि भोजन से ही बीमारी होती है और हृदय शरीर का सम्राट् है।" वे चेचक, लकवा, तपेदिक, पथरी, खून की कमी आदि बीमारियों से परिचित थे। मिस्र में एक सूची प्राप्त हुई है जिसमें बीमारियों से संबंधित 600 दवाइयों का उल्लेख किया गया है। यहाँ के चिकित्सक चीर-फाड़ में निपुण थे। वे ऑपरेशन करके शरीर से हृदय, फेफड़े, दिमाग, आँख निकाल लेते थे और उनको स्वर्ण कलशों में रखा जाता था। इन्हें गंजापन मिटाने की दवा ज्ञात थी और बीमारी का पता लगाने के लिए तापक्रम और नाड़ी देख लेते थे। उस दौरान चिकित्सक सफलतापूर्वक आंत की बीमारियों का इलाज करते थे।

रसायन उपयोग मिस्रवासियों द्वारा लेप आदि तैयार करने के लिये किया जाता था, जिनसे लाश को कई शताब्दियों तक यथावत् सुरक्षित रखा जा सकता था। यह रासायनिक चमत्कार नहीं तो क्या था ? मिस्र के वासियों द्वारा पाश्चात्य संस्कृति के अंतर्गत असभ्य व्यक्ति को सभ्य बनाया गया था। **प्रो. हर्नशा** के शब्दों में–"सभ्य जीवन का प्रत्येक विभाग इस प्रकार उन्नत हुआ, जितना इससे पहले किसी अन्य जाति अथवा और किसी काल में नहीं हुआ था।"

कला

विकसित कला की शुरुआत मिस्र में सर्वप्रथम की गई थी। मिस्री सभ्यता ने मानव कला के इतिहास को गौरवान्वित किया। **ब्रेस्टेड** के अनुसार, "प्राचीन मिस्री कला किसी भी आधुनिक काल की कला से श्रेष्ठ है तथा केवल यूनान की कला ही इसकी बराबरी कर सकती है।" मिस्र की कलाओं में तीन प्रकार की मुख्य विशेषताएं पायी जाती थीं जिसमें प्रमुख हैं–वह शक्तिशाली है, विशाल है और गौरवमयी है। मिस्र में विकसित विभिन्न प्रकार की कलाओं के बारे में निम्न जानकारी दी गई है–

(1) स्थापत्य कला—स्थापत्य कला की शुरुआत सर्वप्रथम मिस्र में की गयी थी। वहाँ के फराओ ने अपनी समाधियों के ऊपर विशाल पिरामिडों का निर्माण करवाया, जो विश्व की स्थापत्य कला के इतिहास में भवन-निर्माण कला के सुन्दर नमूने हैं। ये पिरामिड गगनचुम्बी भवन हैं, "जो अपनी भव्यता और विशालता की दृष्टि से विश्व इतिहास में बेजोड़ सिद्ध हुए हैं और दुनिया के आश्चर्यों में इनको शामिल किया गया है। फराओ को मरने के पश्चात् किसी प्रकार के कष्टों का सामना न करना पड़े, इस हेतु पिरामिडों का निर्माण कराया जाता था। पिरामिड शैली मिस्री स्थापत्य कला की सबसे बड़ी देन है। इसी की वजह से विश्व की स्थापत्य कला के इतिहास में मिस्र को अद्वितीय स्थान प्राप्त है।

पिरामिडों के संबंध में यह धारणा व्याप्त है कि, "समस्त संसार काल से पीड़ित है, परन्तु काल पिरामिडों से पीड़ित है।" गिजा का पिरामिड फराओ खूफ्रू अथवा खीओप्स ने बनवाया है, इसके निर्माण में 20 वर्ष का समय लगा और एक लाख बीस हजार व्यक्तियों ने काम किया। इस पिरामिड का प्रसार 13 एकड़ जमीन पर था, जिसमें ढाई-ढाई टन के 23 लाख पाषाण खण्डों का प्रयोग किया गया है। यह पिरामिड 480 फीट ऊँचा तथा 755 फीट लम्बा है। इसमें पत्थरों के टुकड़ों को इस प्रकार जोड़ा गया है कि कहीं कोई सुराख या छेद देखने तक को नहीं मिलता। पिरामिडों को संसार के महान आश्चर्यों में शामिल किया गया है। इसके अतिरिक्त कारनाक, थीब्स तथा लक्सौर के देवालय भी बहुत सुन्दर बने हुए हैं। ये तत्कालीन स्थापत्य कला का बोध कराते हैं।

(2) मूर्तिकला—मूर्तिकला की दिशा में भी मिस्र को विशिष्ट स्थान प्राप्त है। पत्थर की मूर्तियों में विशाल स्फिंक्स की मूर्ति बहुत प्रसिद्ध है। संसार में इतनी बड़ी मूर्ति कभी नहीं बनी। इस मूर्ति का शरीर सिंह का तथा सिर फराओ (राजा) का है। गीजे के पिरामिड के पास यह विशाल मूर्ति स्थापित है। यह मूर्ति प्राचीन मिस्रीकला की उत्कृष्टता का बोध कराती है। प्राचीन काल के दौरान मिस्र में धातु की मूर्तियाँ भी बनायी जाती थीं। इनमें पेपी प्रथम की लकड़ी पर ताँबा चढ़ाकर बनायी गयी मूर्ति विश्वप्रसिद्ध है। इसके अतिरिक्त कारनाक के मन्दिरों में 80 या 90 फीट तक ऊँची अनेक देवताओं की मूर्तियों का निर्माण किया गया था। इनका निर्माण पत्थर के विशाल टुकड़े को काटकर किया जाता है। मिस्री मूर्तिकार पशु-पक्षियों की मूर्तियाँ भी बनाते थे। मिस्र की मूर्तिकला के सम्बन्ध में **चार्ल्स पैरी** ने लिखा है, "यह मानना होगा कि मिस्री कलाकारों ने ऐसी कृतियाँ दी हैं, जिनकी तुलना यूरोप की कलाकृतियों से की जा सकती है।"

(3) चित्रकला—मिस्र की चित्रकला भी काफी विकसित हुई। मिस्र के कलाकार अपने चित्रों को रंगों से सजीव बना देते थे। चित्रों का निर्माण, दीवारों, मकानों, पिरामिडों के कमरों में कराया जाता है। थीब्स मन्दिर की दीवारों पर बने हुए चित्र उस समय की चित्रकला के सुन्दर नमूने हैं। उस समय चित्रकार फराओ का दरबार, शिकार, पशुओं, पक्षियों, मछलियों, नाव की यात्रा, पौधों, हरे-भरे खेतों के सुन्दर चित्र बनाते थे। कुछ ऐसे चित्र प्राप्त हुए हैं जो तत्कालीन पारिवारिक जीवन का बोध कराते हैं। रानी हातशेपसुत ने एक मन्दिर की दीवार पर तीन बड़ी नावों का चित्र बनवाया था, जिसमें नावों के पाल तथा नाविकों को डाँड चलाते हुए दिखाया गया है। मानो उसमें प्राण डाल दिये गये हों। आगे चलकर समुद्र यात्रा के चित्र भी बनने लगे थे। मिट्टी के सुन्दर बर्तनों को चित्रों से सजाया जाता था। इन चित्रों को देखने से यह स्पष्ट हो जाता है कि इनमें वास्तविकता पर अधिक ध्यान दिया जाता था।

(4) संगीत एवं नृत्य कला—मिस्र में बर्तनों पर नृत्य की अनेक मुद्राएँ प्राप्त हुई हैं जिससे इस बात का बोध स्पष्ट होता है कि देवालयों का संगीत आध्यात्मिक प्रकृति का था। यहां के लोगों को झांझ तथा बिगुल से निकला संगीत काफी पसंद था। इन लोगों को हार्प का संगीत काफी पसंद था। इस काल के प्रसिद्ध संगीतज्ञों में अमेनहोटेप, स्नेफेरू, नोफर तथा रेमरीप्रा आदि प्रमुख थे। प्रसिद्ध संगीताचार्य अमेनहोटेप की तानसेन से तुलना की गई है।

(5) मिस्र की गौण कलाएँ—मिस्र में मिट्टी के बर्तन, कुर्सी, आभूषण, ताबीज तथा घरेलू बर्तन का निर्माण भारी मात्रा में किया जाता था। बहुमूल्य पत्थरों से विभिन्न प्रकार के गहनों का निर्माण किया जाता था। कुर्सियों पर सोने-चाँदी से नक्काशी की जाती थी। वहां के कलाकार पत्थरों, हाथीदाँत तथा मूल्यवान धातुओं के सुन्दर आभूषण बनाने में दक्ष थे।

यहां लकड़ी से निर्मित वस्तुओं का निर्माण भारी मात्रा में किया जाता था। मेज, कुर्सी, तख्त के अलावा शव को रखने के लिए ताबूत भी बनाये जाते थे। मिस्र में लकड़ी के मकानों की छतें, दीवारें आर्कषक बनाई जाती थीं। सुंदर-सुंदर खिलौनों को निर्माण करने के लिए लकड़ियों का प्रयोग किया जाता था। लकड़ी पर आखेट के चित्र अंकित किये जाते थे, जिनका प्रयोग सजावट के लिए किया जाता था।

शिक्षा एवं साहित्य

ऐसा माना जाता है कि शिक्षा की शुरुआत सर्वप्रथम मिस्र में की गई थी। पहले बच्चे पुरोहितों के पास अपने मुहल्लों में ही पढ़ते थे। उसके बाद सरकारी स्कूलों में

शिक्षा प्राप्त करते थे। सरकार की ओर से मुख्य पुरोहित सारे देश में शिक्षा की व्यवस्था करता था। सरकारी अधिकारियों द्वारा विद्यालयों का समय-समय निरीक्षण किया जाता था। उस काल में मंदिरों में ही शिक्षा दी जाती थी। अतः इसे विद्यालय का भी दर्जा प्राप्त था। सेस और हैलियापोलिस उस समय के प्रसिद्ध केन्द्र थे। शिक्षा का मूल उद्देश्य राजकीय कार्य चलाने के लिए लिपिक तैयार करना था। विद्यार्थियों को वाणिज्य, नैतिक और अनुशासन आदि विषयों की शिक्षा दी जाती थी। महिलाओं को शिक्षा से संबंधित किसी प्रकार की रोक नहीं थी। बालकों को माँ की तरह योग्य बनने के लिए प्रेरित किया जाता था।

एक भोजपत्र पर लिखा है–"खूब मन लगाकर पढ़ो और अपनी माँ की तरह शिक्षा से प्यार करो।" एक अन्य भोजपत्र पर इस प्रकार लिखा है–"सैनिक होना दुर्भाग्य है, जमीन जोतना बड़े परिश्रम का काम है। दिन-भर और रात में भी पुस्तकें पढ़ने में ही आनन्द है।" अध्यापक बालकों को पट्टी पर लिखना सिखाते थे। इस समय भी शैतान छात्र होते थे, जिसका अंदाजा एक शिक्षक द्वारा दिए गये इस विचार से लगाया जा सकता है–"मेरे भूतपूर्व छात्र किताबों की बजाए शराब ज्यादा पसन्द करते हैं।"

साहित्य के क्षेत्र में देखा जाए तो मिस्र के साहित्य में कहानी और काव्य को ही शामिल किया जाता था। काव्य में दर्शन, धर्म और प्रेम की बातों का उल्लेख होता था। गीतों में उदाहरण से हर बात समझाई जाती थी। प्रेम के गीतों द्वारा नैतिकता की शिक्षा दी जाती थी। इस समय लड़कियों द्वारा गीतों की रचना की जाती थी, जिनमें सामाजिक बुराइयों पर विशेष बल दिया जाता था। यहाँ के गीतों से उस समय के समाज और साहित्य के बारे में जानकारी प्राप्त होती है। एक गीत की कुछ पंक्तियाँ इस प्रकार हैं–"मैं किससे बात करूँ ? भाई बुरे हैं, दोस्तों में प्यार नहीं है, सबके दिलों में बेईमानी भरी है, लोग पड़ोसी का धन हजम कर जाते हैं, औरतें चालाक व आदमी मतलबी हैं, ऐसे में मैं किससे बात करूँ ?"

साहित्य के क्षेत्र में महिलाओं का व्यापक प्रभाव था। उनके द्वारा उपमा तथा अलंकारों का इस्तेमाल किया जाता था। बन्दर को पेड़ों पर देखकर यहां के साहित्यकारों ने लिखा है–"प्रकृति की गोद में परमेश्वर निवास कर रहे हैं।" इस समय लोग 40 पृष्ठों की लम्बी कहानियाँ लिखते थे। इटकू-बिटकू की कहानियाँ सामाजिक शोषण पर प्रभाव डालती हैं। मिस्र का थीब्स नगर उन दिनों साहित्य का प्रसिद्ध केन्द्र था। हेरोडोटस का कहना है–"संसार के प्राचीन साहित्य और शिक्षा के क्षेत्र में कोई ऐसा देश नहीं, जिसकी तुलना मिस्र से की जा सके।"

मिस्र के ऐतिहासिक साहित्य में एक 'मृतकों की पुस्तक' का उल्लेख किया गया है, जिसमें मिस्र के शासकों के बारे में जानकारी दी गई। इस काल के धार्मिक प्रकार में दो प्रकार का साहित्य आता है–"मृतकों का साहित्य एवं शव रखे जाने वाले सन्दूकों का साहित्य। ये साहित्य कब्रों में प्राप्त हुआ था। इसमें मृत राजाओं के कार्यकलापों का उल्लेख है। इस समय की 'पिरामिड टेन्टस' नामक पुस्तक मिली है। इसमें देवताओं की प्रशंसा तथा मृतक की आत्मा की परलोक यात्रा के बारे में वर्णन किया गया है। इसके अतिरिक्त अमेनहोटेप के उपदेश भी उल्लेखनीय हैं।

मिस्र के धर्म-निरपेक्ष साहित्य में प्रणय-गीतों, धार्मिक प्रार्थनाओं, कहानियों तथा शिक्षाओं का समावेश था। कहानियों में एक अभागे राजकुमार की कहानी विशेष रूप से उल्लेखनीय है। इसके अतिरिक्त 'इयुवेर की भविष्यवाणी' महत्त्वपूर्ण साहित्य है। उस काल का साहित्य बोलचाल की भाषा में नहीं होने के कारण जनता में लोकप्रिय नहीं हो सका। लेखन कला का प्रादुर्भाव सर्वप्रथम मिस्र में ही हुआ था। शुरू में ही उनकी लिपि चित्रात्मक थी, परन्तु धीरे-धीरे उनमें शब्द-संकेत और वर्णमाला का समावेश होता गया। मिस्र की वर्णमाला में 2800 सांकेतिक चिह्नों का प्रयोग किया जाता था। साम्राज्यवादी युग में इन चिह्नों की संख्या घटकर 500 हो गई। ये लोग घर को 'पर' और सर्प को 'स' कहते थे। मिस्र में कागज का निर्माण पेपिरस घास से किया जाता था तथा सरकंडे की लकड़ी से कलम का निर्माण किया जाता था जिससे लिखा जाता था। स्याही के निर्माण के लिए राख और गोंद का इस्तेमाल किया जाता था, जो इतनी पक्की होती थी कि आज तक वैसी की वैसी है। **सरदेसाई** का मानना है कि, "लेखन-कला के आविष्कार ने मानव-समाज में सबसे बड़ी क्रान्ति उत्पन्न की है और इसके लिए संसार को मिस्र का कृतज्ञ होना चाहिए।" इतिहासकार **एच. ए. डेविस** के अनुसार "लेखन कला का आविष्कार तथा विकास मिस्र में ही हुआ और यहीं से यह अन्य भूमध्यसागरीय देशों में फैला।"

आर्थिक जीवन

मिस्र में कृषि पर काफी ध्यान दिया जाता था क्योंकि यहाँ की लगभग 80% जनता कृषि का कार्य करती थी। यहाँ की मुख्य उपज गेहूँ, जौ, कपास, सन और फलों में अंगूर, अंजीर एवं खजूर आदि थे। मिस्रवासी मछली पकड़ने के लिये जाल का प्रयोग करते थे। फराओ कृषि की ओर काफी ध्यान देते थे। सरकारी कर्मचारी कृषि का निरीक्षण करने का कार्य करते थे। उस दौरान सिंचाई की समुचित व्यवस्था

करते थे। सिंचाई के लिए नहरों का निर्माण किया जाता था और फसल बोने एवं काटने का समय निश्चित करते थे। किसानों से लगान 10 से 20 प्रतिशत तक ली जाती थी। किसानों को लगान वसूलने हेतु काफी प्रताड़ित किया जाता था। वे अपने साथ एक हब्शी गुलाम रखते थे, जो लगान न देने वाले व्यक्तियों को बांधकर नील नदी में उल्टा लटका देते थे, जहाँ मगरमच्छ उन्हें खा जाते थे।

मिस्र में गधा, बैल, बकरी, गाय, बछड़ा, बंदर और मुर्गी आदि जानवरों को पाला जाता था। सामान ढोने के लिए बैल और गधे का इस्तेमाल किया जाता था। फल तोड़ने के लिए बंदरों से काम लिया जाता था। मिस्रवासियों को ऊंटों के संबंध में विशेष ज्ञान नहीं था।

वाणिज्य और व्यापार के क्षेत्र में भी मिस्र काफी आगे था। उस दौरान उस क्षेत्र में काफी विकास हुआ था। वहाँ आंतरिक व्यापार करने हेतु नील नदी का प्रयोग किया जाता था। विदेशी व्यापार में मिस्र अधिक उन्नति नहीं कर सका, क्योंकि यहाँ पैदावार अधिक नहीं होती थी। मिस्र, भारत और अरब से मसाले, रंग, तेल, पाउडर और चंदन मंगवाता था। सिक्कों का प्रचलन नहीं होने से विनिमय का माध्यम सोने और चाँदी की अँगूठियाँ थीं। सूडान से सोना, हाथी-दाँत और गुलाम मँगवाए जाते थे। उस समय मिस्र का सीरिया, क्रीट और अन्य पड़ोसी देशों के साथ व्यापारिक संबंध स्थापित था।

मिस्र में विभिन्न प्रकार के उद्योग धंधे भी स्थापित थे। मिस्रवासी पत्थर काटने, गहने एवं बर्तन बनाने, ताँबे तथा काँसे के हथियार बनाने एवं लकड़ी का फर्नीचर बनाने में कुशल थे। मिस्र के लोग नाव एवं जहाज के निर्माण में भी निपुण थे। बाद की शताब्दियों में जहाज बनाना, मिट्टी के बर्तन बनाना तथा कपड़े बुनना महत्त्वपूर्ण उद्योग बन गये। कागज बनाने की कला का आविष्कार मिस्र में हुआ। वहाँ पेपिरस नामक घास के पौधे से कागज बनाया जाता था।

बिल ड्यूरेन्ट ने लिखा है—"यदि हम प्राचीन मिस्रवासियों के आविष्कारों की तुलना अपने आविष्कारों से करें, तो ऐसा लगता है कि वाष्प शक्ति से चलने वाले यंत्रों के आविष्कार से पूर्व हम किसी भी दृष्टि से उनसे आगे बढ़े हुए नहीं थे।" मिस्र की कब्रों से चमकते हुए मिट्टी के बर्तन, शीशे का सामान, सोने-चाँदी के बर्तन और गहने तथा सुंदर आराम-कुर्सियाँ प्राप्त हुई हैं। टुटुनखामन की कब्र में कुछ संदूक मिले हैं जिनमें प्राप्त राजकीय वस्त्रों पर सोने का काम किया गया है। इन नमूनों के आधार पर यह कहा जा सकता है कि प्राचीनकाल के दौरान कला की दृष्टि से मिस्र के कारीगर बहुत ही कुशल थे।

मिस्री सभ्यता का पतन

मिस्र पर 31 राजवंशों ने शासन किया। 332 ई. पू. में यूनान के शासक सिकन्दर महान ने मिस्र पर अधिकार कर लिया। सिकन्दर न यहाँ अलैक्जेंड्रिया नामक नगर की स्थापना की, जो शताब्दियों तक व्यापार, विद्या एवं संस्कृति का केन्द्र बना रहा। यूनान का प्रभाव समाप्त होने के बाद रोम ने मिस्र पर अधिकार कर लिया। इस सभ्यता के पतन पर **पं. जवाहरलाल नेहरू** ने लिखा है—''कई हजार वर्षों के गौरवमय इतिहास के उपरान्त मिस्र की प्राचीन सभ्यता लुप्त हो गई और सिवाय महान पिरामिड, स्फिंक्स व मेम्फिस के नगरों के पीछे कुछ भी निशान नहीं छोड़ गई।''

पतन के कारण—मिस्र की सभ्यता के पतन होने के कई कारण बतलाए गये हैं। कुछ प्रमुख कारणों को निम्न प्रकार स्पष्ट किया गया है—

1. पिरामिडों व मन्दिरों में धन का अपव्यय भी मिस्र के पतन के लिए उत्तरदायी था।
2. मिस्र पर निरन्तर विदेशी आक्रमण होते रहे और एक के बाद दूसरे देश का मिस्र पर अधिकार रहा, परन्तु वहां पर संगठित सैनिक व्यवस्था का अभाव था। सामन्त आपस में लड़ रहे थे। फराओ विलासी जीवन व्यतीत कर रहा था। इसका परिणाम यह हुआ कि मिस्र पर विदेशियों का अधिकार हो गया।
3. मिस्र के फराओ की साम्राज्यवादी भावना और पराजितों के विद्रोह ने उसका पतन अवश्यम्भावी कर दिया।
4. फराओ द्वारा मिस्र में नये-नये धर्मों को शुरुआत की थी। अतः जनता में फराओ के प्रति असन्तोष था।
5. मिस्र के सामन्तों और शासकों द्वारा किसानों, मजदूरों और दासों का शोषण किया गया। अतः इस वर्ग से संकट के समय शासक वर्ग को समर्थन प्राप्त नहीं हुआ।

मिस्र की देन

विश्व की विभिन्न सभ्यताओं में मिस्र की सभ्यता को काफी महत्त्वपूर्ण स्थान प्राप्त है। इस सभ्यता ने विश्व के उत्थान के लिए काफी कुछ किया है। प्राचीन सभ्यताओं की जननी मिस्र में माता एवं शिक्षकों को अत्यधिक आदर की दृष्टि से देखा जाता था। मिस्र में एक प्राचीन कहावत प्रचलित है कि "ज्ञान को माता के

समान प्यार करो।" इस सभ्यता को बुद्धि देने वाली सभ्यता की भी संज्ञा दी जाती है। यह विद्वानों को आश्चर्य में डाल देती है तथा वीरों को प्रेरणा की अनुभूति प्रदान कराती है। मिस्र की सभ्यता विद्वानों को असीम जिज्ञासा देती है। सेवाइन के अनुसार "प्राकृतिक परिस्थितियों ने ही नील नदी की घाटी को सभ्यताओं का पोषक होने में सहयोग प्रदान किया।" जे. एच ब्रेस्टेड ने पिरामिडों की चर्चा करते हुए कहा है कि, "यदि सौन्दर्यमयी नील अपनी विस्तृत उर्वर छाती में मिस्र को नहीं छिपाती, तो यह देश विशाल मरुभूमि बन गया होता।" तो दूसरी तरफ बीच का मानना है कि "महान नदी बंजर चट्टानों में से सकरी उपजाऊ मिट्टी लाती है, जो इसके किनारों को उपजाऊ बना देती है और अंत में अपनी सालाना बाढ़ से सिंचाई के निपुण साधन जुटाकर बाशिन्दों का जीवन सफल व सुखी बना देती है।" इसी प्रकार **बर्न्स** ने लिखा है, "आधुनिक संसार में मिस्र के महत्त्व को पीछे छोड़ने वाली बहुत कम प्राचीन सभ्यताएँ हैं।" प्लेट व जीन ड्रमण्ड ने लिखा है, "प्राचीन मिस्र ने यह सिद्ध कर दिया कि मनुष्य क्या कुछ नहीं कर सकता।" **प्रो. विलड्यूरेण्ट** का मानना है–"मिस्र की सभ्यता की प्रमुख देन कृषि, काँच, सन के वस्त्र, कागज, स्याही, घड़ी, ज्यामिति, जनगणना, प्रारंभिक व माध्यमिक शिक्षा का विकास, वर्णमाला, गृह को सजाने की वस्तुएँ और एकेश्वरवाद की भावना है। मिस्र की सभ्यता के कई प्रमुख तत्वों को सीरिया, क्रीट, यूनान व रोम के निवासियों ने अपनाया। परिणामस्वरूप यूरोप की प्राचीन सभ्यताएँ मिस्र की ऋणी हो गईं।" इन विचारों के आलोक में हम प्राचीन मिस्र की उपलब्धियों को निम्नलिखित बिन्दुओं के तहत स्पष्ट कर सकते हैं–

1. साहित्य में कथा व काव्य का प्रयोग शुरू किया।
2. समाज का गठन तथा उसकी मातृ प्रधानता मिस्र की देन है।
3. मिस्र ने ही सूर्य घड़ी तथा जल घड़ी का आविष्कार किया।
4. एकेश्वरवाद के सिद्धांत का प्रचलन, आत्मा की अमरता और परलोक के बारे में विचार दिए।
5. शव पर रासायनिक पदार्थों द्वारा निर्मित मसाले लगाकर वे मम्मी को कई वर्षों तक सुरक्षित रख सकते थे।
6. देवालयों को विद्यालय बनाकर उनमें शिक्षा का सर्वप्रथम प्रयोग यहीं हुआ।
7. एक से नौ तक की गिनती, जोड़, बाकी, गुणा एवं भाग का आविष्कार किया तथा 365 दिन तक का एक वर्ष और कैलेण्डर प्रदान किया।
8. मिस्र के चिकित्सक ऊंचे दर्जे के थे उन्होंने चिकित्सा जगत में औषधि विज्ञान का विस्तृत क्षेत्र खोल दिया।

9. धातुओं का प्रयोग व उनका मिश्रण करना सिखाया।
10. कागज व स्याही का प्रयोग तथा वर्णमाला एवं लेखन कला का आविष्कार किया।
11. मिस्र ने विश्वप्रसिद्ध पिरामिड दिये।
12. मिस्र ने विश्व को सिंचाई के तरीके—बाँध व नहर का निर्माण करना सिखाया।
13. लकड़ी का सुन्दर फर्नीचर, विलासिता की सामग्री और शृंगार के अनेक साधन दिये।
14. कृषकों से कर वसूल करना, बेगार लेना तथा सामन्तों द्वारा किसानों और मजदूरों का शोषण करना मिस्र ने विश्व को सिखाया।

3

मैसोपोटामिया की सभ्यता

विश्व की प्रमुख सभ्यताओं में मैसोपोटामिया की सभ्यता को प्रमुख स्थान प्राप्त है। प्राचीन काल में इराक को मैसोपोटामिया के नाम से जाना जाता था। मैसोपोटामिया को यूनानी भाषा से लिया गया था। यह दो शब्दों 'मेसो' और 'पोटामिया' से मिलकर बना है। मेसो का अर्थ 'मध्य' और पोटम का अर्थ 'नदी' होता है। इस प्रकार दो नदियों के बीच के स्थान को मैसोपोटामिया की संज्ञा दी जाती है। इन नदियों के नाम हैं—दजला और फरात। अतः जो प्रदेश दजला और फरात नदियों के बीच स्थित था, उसे ही मैसोपोटामिया कहा जाता था। इन नदियों के मुहाने पर सुमेरिया, मध्य में बेबीलोन एवं उत्तर में असीरियन सभ्यता का विकास हुआ था।

रौलिन्सन नामक अंग्रेज द्वारा सन् 1850 ई. में ईरान में बिहिस्तून के निकट एक ऊँचे पर्वत पर प्राचीन फारसी राजा देरियस द्वारा लिखित एक शिलालेख की खोज की गई। इसमें फारसी और बेबीलोनियन भाषा का प्रयोग किया गया था। रौलिन्सन ने इस लेख को पढ़ लिया। इसके पश्चात् दूसरे साहित्य को पढ़ने एवं समझने में आसानी हो गई।

सन् 1901 में एक अन्य शिलालेख सूसा में प्राप्त हुआ जो काले पत्थर पर था। इसमें बेबीलोनियन भाषा में 'कानूनी संहिता' को लिपिबद्ध किया गया था। बिहिस्तून शिलालेख का वह महत्त्व है, जो मिस्र में रोसेटा पत्थर का। प्रसिद्ध इतिहासकार **हेरोडोटस** द्वारा इस प्रदेश को 'अदन का बाग' कहा जाता है। इस संदर्भ में उन्होंने लिखा है—''जब मैंने लोगों को बताया कि इस सुरम्य भूमि में अन्न की कितनी लम्बी बालियाँ उगती हैं, तो उन्हें मुझ पर विश्वास नहीं हुआ।''

दजला और फरात नदियों ने मैसोपोटामिया सभ्यता को आगे बढ़ाने में महत्त्वपूर्ण भूमिका निभायी। ये नदियां सदा बाढ़ग्रस्त रहती थीं इस कारण कृषकों का जीवन अनिश्चित बना रहता था। **बिल ड्यूरेण्ट** का मानना है कि–"आज दजला नदी के किनारे फैले भग्नावशेषों को देखकर यह अन्दाजा लगाना कठिन है कि यहाँ कभी प्राचीन बेबीलोन की सभ्यता ने बड़ी-बड़ी ऊँचाइयाँ पार की थीं। इस प्रकार के अवशेष प्राचीन काल की राजधानियों से प्राप्त हुए हैं जिनका संबंध बेबीलोन से था। आज शान्ति से बहती हुई दजला और फरात नदियों को देखकर यह विश्वास कर पाना कठिन है कि यह वे नदियाँ हैं, जिन्होंने सुमेरिया और अक्काद को जीवनदान दिया था और बेबीलोन के प्रसिद्ध झूलेदार बगीचों को सींचा था।

मैसोपोटामिया में नई सभ्यताओं का विकास उत्तर दिशा से निरंतर खानाबदोशों के आक्रमण के पश्चात् हुआ था। प्रत्येक सभ्यता को अपने अस्तित्व को बनाये रखने के लिए कड़े संघर्षों से गुजरना पड़ा। इस संदर्भ में भारतीय इतिहासकार **सरदेसाई** ने लिखा है–"मैसोपोटामिया एक शक्ति से दूसरी शक्ति के अधीन जाता रहा; नवीन संस्कृति द्वारा प्राचीन संस्कृति अपने अन्दर मिला ली जाती थी। देश संस्कृतियों के विलुप्त होने का भाजन बन गया।"

जैसा कि पहले उल्लेख किया जा चुका है, मैसोपोटामिया दजला और फरात नदी के बीच स्थित है। ढेर सारी सभ्यता का विकास घाटियों में भी हुआ है। अतः वे सभ्यताओं को पालने व कब्रिस्तान के रूप में प्रसिद्ध हुई हैं। **प्लेट व जीन** ने लिखा है–"प्राचीन मैसोपोटामिया ने सिद्ध कर दिया कि प्रगति केवल मिस्र की बपौती नहीं थी।" **मैकनेल बर्न्स** ने भी लिखा है–"मैसोपोटामिया की सभ्यता मिस्र से भिन्न अपने ही ढंग की थी। इसका राजनीतिक इतिहास तीखे हस्तक्षेपों से चिह्नित था। इसका जातीय मिश्रण भी एक-सा नहीं था और इसका सामाजिक व आर्थिक ढाँचा व्यक्ति को नेतृत्व व प्रगति का विस्तृत अवसर प्रदान करता था।"

सुमेरियन, बेबीलोनियन, असीरियन और कैल्डियन आदि को मैसोपोटामिया की प्रमुख सभ्यताओं में शामिल किया जाता है। इन सभ्यताओं की चर्चा करते हुए कहा जाता है–"सुमेरिया ने सभ्यता को जन्म दिया, बेबीलोन ने उसे चरम सीमा पर पहुँचाया और असीरिया ने उसे ग्रहण किया।" **सेवाइन** के शब्दों में–"राजनीतिक व सांस्कृतिक क्षेत्र में बेबीलोन व असीरिया निवासियों ने महानतम प्रगति की।" **विल ड्यूरेण्ट** ने लिखा है–"यह सभ्यता इतिहास में अद्वितीय और सबसे अधिक रचनात्मक रही है।"

सुमेरिया की सभ्यता

इसे विश्व की एक प्राचीन सभ्यता माना जाता है जैसा कि डॉ. गोयल के विचार से स्पष्ट होता है–''सुमेरियन सभ्यता को विश्व की प्राचीनतम सभ्यताओं के इतिहास में अत्यन्त गौरवपूर्ण स्थान प्राप्त है। पश्चिमी एशिया के इतिहास की दृष्टि से सुमेरियनों को सभ्यता का जनक कहने में किसी की कोई आपत्ति नहीं हो सकती है।''

ऐतिहासिक तथ्यों से पता चलता है कि फारस की सुमेरियन जाति के लोगों ने ईसा से पाँच हजार वर्ष पूर्व मैसोपोटामिया पर आक्रमण किया और यहाँ की अक्काद, बेबीलोन, एलम एवं मूसा आदि अर्द्धसभ्य जातियों को युद्ध में पराजित कर मैसोपोटामिया पर अधिकार कर लिया। तत्पश्चात् मैसोपोटामिया में छोटे-छोटे नगर राज्यों की स्थापना हो गई। इंग्लैण्ड और फ्रांसीसी पुरातत्त्ववेताओं ने 16वीं शताब्दी में इस सभ्यता की खोज की। इस सभ्यता का विकास 4500 ई.पू. में हुआ था। इतिहासकार **रेविल** के अनुसार–'इरेक सुमेरियन जाति का पहला शासक था। 2358 ई. पू. में सेमेटिक जाति ने सुमेरिया पर अधिकार कर दिया। फिर भी सुमेरियन सभ्यता बनी रही।''

सुमेरिया में अकादियन वंश का प्रथम सम्राट सारगन प्रथम हुआ। यह शाही वंश से संबंधित नहीं था। उसके पिता के बारे में कोई विवरण प्राप्त नहीं होता। इतिहासकार **वीच** ने लिखा है–''यह एक बागवान का पुत्र था। अतः इसकी माता ने इसे छोटी-सी नाव में बिठाकर छोड़ दिया था।'' बड़ा होने पर उसने शासक के यहां एक साधारण सेवक की हैसियत से कृषि का कार्य किया। यह अपने जन्म को एक सराय के चौकीदार से बताया करता था। **नेल** का मानना है–''सारगन का जीवन कीश के शासक के प्याले उठाने वाले से प्रारम्भ होता है।''

उपरोक्त कथनों के आधार पर यह कहा जा सकता है कि सारगन प्रथम का जन्म एक साधारण परिवार में हुआ था। धीरे-धीरे वह उन्नति करता हुआ कीश का शासक बन गया। तत्पश्चात् उसने साम्राज्य का विस्तार किया। सारगन ने युद्ध में सुमेरियन जाति को पराजित किया और उसके साम्राज्य पर अधिकार कर लिया। इतिहासकार **वीच** ने लिखा है–''सारगन प्रथम के विवरण से ज्ञात होता है कि उसका साम्राज्य भूमध्यसागर तक पहुँच गया था और उसने साइप्रस पर भी अधिकार कर लिया था।''

सारगन प्रथम के शासनकाल के अन्तिम वर्षों में हुए विद्रोहों के परिणामस्वरूप राज्य में अशान्ति एवं अव्यवस्था का काफी प्रसार हो चुका था। उसके उत्तराधिकारी अयोग्य एवं दुर्बल सिद्ध हुए। **बिल ड्यूरेन्ट** का मानना है कि–"अकादियन साम्राज्य की वह शान शीघ्र ही विलुप्त हो गई और पूर्व की लड़ाकू एलमाइट जाति ने ऊर पर अधिकार कर लिया।" उसी प्रकार **जे. सी. रेविल** के अनुसार–"पहाड़ी लोगों के आक्रमण के परिणामस्वरूप वह साम्राज्य समाप्त हो गया।"

चूँकि अकादियन जाति के लोगों ने बाहर से आकर सुमेरिया पर अपना आधिपत्य जमा लिया था। अतः उन्होंने सुमेरियन सभ्यता को स्वीकार कर लिया था। अकादियन साम्राज्य में पुरोहितों का प्रभाव काफी कम हो गया था। 2000 ई. पू. तक अकादियन जाति की सभ्यता का भी काफी विकास हो चुका था।

शासन-व्यवस्था

सुमेरियन सभ्यता से यह जानकारी प्राप्त होती है कि उस दौरान सुमेरिया में ऊर, निपुर, लगाश, ऊरूक आदि नगर राज्य थे, जो एक दूसरे से स्वतंत्र थे। प्रत्येक नगर राज्य के स्वतन्त्र शासक को कहा जाता था। पटेसी के मुख्य कार्य थे–भूमि कर वसूल करना, बाहरी आक्रमणों से नगर की रक्षा करना, जनता के मुकदमों पर निर्णय देना आदि। सुमेरियन पटेसी ने कई अपराधों के दण्ड का निर्धारण किया था। अतः हम्मूराबी ने उनके बहुत से कानूनों को अपनी विधि संहिता में स्थान दिया। सुमेरियनवासी ज्यादातर सैनिक ही हुआ करते थे। उस समय बहादुर योद्धाओं की सूची देवालय या मन्दिरों में लगायी जाती थी। युद्ध के दौरान उन्हें पटेसी के नेतृत्व में युद्ध लड़ना पड़ता था। पैदल सैनिकों के मुख्य शस्त्र–भाला तथा लोहे की छड़ थीं। वे अपनी सुरक्षा करने हेतु ढ़ाल का प्रयोग करते थे। युद्ध में पराजित सैनिकों को गुलाम बना लिया जाता था। कभी-कभी देवताओं को प्रसन्न करने के लिए उनकी बलि चढ़ा देते थे।

सामाजिक जीवन

सुमेरिया के समाज का वर्गीकरण तीन भागों में किया गया था। उनमें प्रमुख हैं–उच्च वर्ग, मध्यम वर्ग और निम्न वर्ग। ये तीनों वर्ग अलग-अलग तरह के कार्य करते थे। **उच्च वर्ग** के अंतर्गत राजा, उच्च पदाधिकारी तथा पुरोहित को शामिल किया गया था। पुरोहितों का समाज में विशेष प्रभाव था। **मध्यम वर्ग** में सामन्त तथा व्यापारी आदि आते थे। **निम्न वर्ग** में दासों तथा किसानों को शामिल किया जाता

था। समाज में स्त्रियों की दशा काफी अच्छी थी। उस समय पुरुष घुटने तक कपड़े पहनते थे जबकि स्त्रियाँ कन्धे से शरीर को ढकने के लिए कपड़ा लटका लेती थीं। घर में काम करने वाली सेविकाएँ तथा सेवक कमर के ऊपर वस्त्र नहीं पहनते थे। कंगन, कण्ठहार, अँगूठी और बालियाँ आदि स्त्रियों के मुख्य आभूषण थे। इस संदर्भ में इतिहासकार **चाइल्ड** ने लिखा है–"सुमेरिया की तत्कालीन स्त्रियाँ आभूषणों में आज की अमेरिकन औरतों की भाँति लगती थीं।"

धार्मिक जीवन

पहले सुमेरिया के लोग एकेश्वरवाद में विश्वास करते थे, परन्तु ईसा से 3500 वर्ष पूर्व बहुदेववाद में विश्वास करने लगे। प्रत्येक नगर में एक नगर देवता होता था। ऊर नगर का देवता सिन (चन्द्रमा), लारसा नगर का शमाश (सूर्य), ऊरूक नगर का अनु (आकाश का देवता) निपुर नगर का एनलिल (तूफानों का देवता) एवं अरक नगर की देवी ईश्तर (रक्षा करने वाली) थी। इसके अतिरिक्त समुद्र का देवता 'आ' एवं वनस्पति का देवता 'तम्मुज' आदि की भी उपासना की जाती थी। देवताओं को प्रसन्न करने के लिए युद्धबन्दियों की सामूहिक रूप से बलि भी दी जाती थी। यहाँ के लोग अन्धविश्वासी होने के कारण शकुन एवं स्वप्न में भी विश्वास करते थे। मिस्र की तरह सुमेरिया में भी मृतक के शव के साथ उसकी प्रिय वस्तु को दफन कर दिया जाता था।

ज्ञान विज्ञान

सुमेरिया में विज्ञान का काफी विकास हुआ था। उन्होंने दस के अंक को गणना का आधार बनाया और 10 को 6 से गुणा किया और 60 को दूसरी इकाई माना। उन लोगों को रेखागणित की अधिक जानकारी नहीं थी, परन्तु बीजगणित के क्षेत्र में कुछ आरम्भिक आविष्कार किये थे। सुमेरियन लोगों ने 365 दिनों का एक वर्ष और एक वर्ष में बारह महीने माने। उन्होंने वीनस, जुपिटर, मार्स तथा सेटर्न आदि नक्षत्रों की खोज करके यह स्पष्ट किया कि नक्षत्र नियमानुसार परिक्रमा करते हैं।

सुमेरिया में कीलाक्षर लिपि नाम से पहली बार लिपि का आविष्कार किया गया। **स्वेन** का मानना है–"सुमेरिया सभ्यता की सबसे बड़ी देन उसकी लिपि ही है।" प्रारम्भ में यह लिपि चित्रात्मक थी, परन्तु कुछ समय पश्चात् अक्षर लिखे जाने लगे। यह लिपि मिट्टी की तख्तियों पर अथवा पट्टिकाओं पर दायीं से बायीं ओर लिखी जाती थी। इस तरह की मिट्टी की कई तख्तियाँ ऊर नगर की खुदाई में प्राप्त हुई

हैं। सुमेरिया में शिक्षा देने का कार्य देवालयों में किया जाता था, जहाँ विद्यार्थियों को कानूनी एवं व्यापारिक शिक्षा प्रदान की जाती थी। इतिहासकार **जेकाइस पिरेनी** का मानना है—"शिक्षा के कारण ही यह सभ्यता विकसित एवं स्थायी बन सकी थी।"

संगीत व कला

सुमेरिया संगीत व कला के क्षेत्र में भी काफी विकास हुआ था। उस समय देवालयों में संगीत का आयोजन होता था। उस काल के प्रसिद्ध वाद्ययन्त्रों में **वीन** प्रमुख थी। उस काल में देवताओं की मूर्तियों का निर्माण भी किया गया था, जिसके कारण मूर्तिकला का भी विकास हुआ। युद्ध के दृश्यों को चित्रकारों द्वारा चित्रित किया जाता था। इसके अतिरिक्त स्थापत्य कला के क्षेत्र में भी बहुत विकास हुए थे। उस समय घर के निर्माण में ईंटों का प्रयोग किया जाता था। धनी लोग ऊँचे-ऊँचे टीलों पर अपने मकान का निर्माण करवाते थे। उनके मकानों में जाने का केवल एक ही रास्ता होता था। कई नगरों की सड़कें तथा गलियाँ मोहनजोदड़ो के समान ही थीं। प्रत्येक नगर में विशाल मीनारों वाले एक देवालयों का निर्माण कराया जाता था, जिसके स्तम्भ, गुम्बद और मेहराबें बहुत सुन्दर होती थीं। ऊर नगर में निर्मित नानार का देवालय तत्कालीन कला का उत्कृष्ट नमूना है।

आर्थिक जीवन

सुमेरिया में कृषि पर काफी ध्यान दिया जाता था तथा गेहूँ, जौ, दाल और खजूर की खेती मुख्य रूप से की जाती थी। वे उत्पादन में वृद्धि हेतु अच्छी खाद का प्रयोग भी करते थे। दजला तथा फरात नदियों की बाढ़ से रक्षा करने के लिए बाँधों का निर्माण किया जाता था और सिंचाई के लिए नहरें भी निकाली जाती थीं।

व्यापार के क्षेत्र में भी सुमेरिया में काफी कार्य किये गये थे। वे भारत, मिस्र और फारस की खाड़ी के देशों से व्यापार करते थे। वे फारस की खाड़ी के देशों को सूती-ऊनी कपड़ा, चमड़े की वस्तुएँ तथा खाद्यान्न निर्यात करते थे और इसके बदले में सोने-चाँदी और लोहे आदि धातुओं का आयात करते थे। सुमेरिया में मुख्य रूप से व्यापार नगर में किया जाता था। व्यापार में लेन-देन के लिए चाँदी की छड़ों का प्रयोग होता था। ऋण देने की प्रथा सुमेरिया से ही शुरू हुई है।

सुमेरियन सभ्यता का पतन

सुमेरिया में बहादुर सैनिकों की कमी नहीं थी, उनके शासक भी योग्य थे, परन्तु फिर भी खानाबदोश अकादियन जाति ने सुमेरिया पर अपना आधिपत्य जमा लिया

था। इस प्रकार सुमेरियन सभ्यता का पतन हो गया। सारगन अकादियन जाति का प्रथम सम्राट था।

विश्व को देन

सुमेरिया की सभ्यता से कई महत्त्वपूर्ण बातें सामने आई हैं। यहाँ के निवासियों ने कृषि, व्यवसाय, व्यापार, लिपि, विज्ञान, ज्योतिष आदि अच्छी बातों को प्रारम्भ किया। अनेक दृष्टिकोणों से देखने से यह स्पष्ट हो जाता है कि यह सभ्यता मानव सभ्यता के विकास की अग्रदूत थी। सुमेरियन सभ्यता से बेबीलोन एवं फारस की सभ्यता ने बहुत-सी अच्छी बातें ग्रहण कीं। **बिल ड्यूरेन्ट** के अनुसार–"सिंचाई की सर्वप्रथम प्राचीन व्यवस्था, ऋण प्रणाली, लेखन कला, न्याय विधान, पुस्तकालय, विद्यालय, प्राचीन मंदिर व मूर्तियाँ और मेहराब व गुम्बद सुमेरिया की अभूतपूर्व देन हैं।"

बेबीलोनिया की सभ्यता

बेबीलोनिया सभ्यता का विकास मैसोपोटामिया के दक्षिणी भाग में हुआ। यह एक प्रकार से शहरी या नागरिक सभ्यता है। 2200 ई. पू. में सेमेटिक लोगों की एक शाखा एमराइट जाति ने सुमेर पर अपना अधिकार कर लिया। इसके पश्चात् अकादियन साम्राज्य पर अधिकार कर लिया और बेबीलोन को अपनी राजधानी बनाया। संभवतः इसी वजह से इस सभ्यता को बेबीलोनिया की सभ्यता कहते हैं। **एच. जी. वेल्स** का मत है–"सबसे पहले यह एमराइट नदी के किनारे एक छोटे नगर में बस गये और लगभग सौ वर्ष के निरन्तर संघर्ष व युद्धों के बाद महान् राजा हम्मूराबी की अधीनता में सम्पूर्ण मैसोपोटामिया के स्वामी हो गये।"

बेबोलोनिया पर ग्यारह राजवंशों ने शासन किया। इनके शासनकाल को निम्न प्रकार स्पष्ट किया गया है–

1. पहले राजवंश को एमराइट या हम्मूराबी युग भी कहा जाता है। इसका शासनकाल 2225 ई. पू. से 1926 ई. पू. तक था।
2. दूसरे राजवंश के शासकों ने 1926 ई. पू. से 1761 ई. पू. तक शासन किया।
3. तीसरे राजवंश को केस्साइट युग कहा जाता है। इस वंश के शासकों ने 1760 ई. पू. से 1185 ई. पू. तक शासन किया।
4. चौथे राजवंश का समय 1184 ई. पू. से 1053 ई. पू. तक था।
5. पाँचवें राजवंश के शासकों ने 1052 ई. पू. से 1032 ई. पू. तक शासन किया।

6. छठे राजवंश का समय 1031 ई. पू. से 1012 ई. पू. तक था।
7. सातवें राजवंश के युग को एलमाइट युग की संज्ञा दी जाती है। इस वंश के शासकों ने 1011 ई. पू. से 1006 ई. पू. तक शासन किया।
8. आठवें राजवंश का समय 1005 ई. पू. से 762 ई. पू. तक रहा।
9. नौवें राजवंश का समय 761 ई. पू. से 732 ई. पू. तक रहा।
10. दसवें राजवंश के युग को असीरियन युग भी कहा जाता है। इसका शासनकाल 732 ई. पू. से 625 ई. पू. तक रहा।
11. ग्यारहवें राजवंश के युग को नये साम्राज्य का युग कहा जाता है, जिसका समय 625 ई. पू. से 536 ई. पू. तक रहा।

हम्मूराबी (2124 ई. पू. से 2081 ई. पू.)

हम्मूराबी में योग्य शासक के सभी गुण विद्यमान थे। उसका संबंध एमराइट जाति से था। इसका शासनकाल 2124 ई. पू. से 2081 ई. पू. तक माना जाता है। यह बेबीलोनिया के नेता सिनुमुबालित का पुत्र था। जिस समय वह शासक बना, उस समय मैसोपोटामिया अनेक छोटे-छोटे राज्यों में बंटा हुआ था, जिनमें सदा लड़ाइयां होती रहती थीं। उसने अपनी योग्यता से निपुर, इरेक, लारसा एवं कीश आदि राज्यों को मिलाकर एक विशाल साम्राज्य की स्थापना की। हम्मूराबी ने बेबीलोन में विशाल राजधानी की स्थापना की थी। इसके पश्चात् उसने कठोर कानून की मदद से सारे देश में शान्ति-व्यवस्था स्थापित कर दी। हम्मूराबी ने बेबीलोनिया में राजनीतिक एकता की भी स्थापना की। बेबीलोन में काफी विकास भी हुआ था। उसकी विधि-संहिता का इतिहास में महत्त्वपूर्ण स्थान है, जिसके कारण अपनी मृत्यु के हजारों साल बाद तक वह न्याय का अवतार कहा जाता रहा। **बिल ड्यूरेन्ट** के अनुसार—"राज्य निर्माता के रूप में इसे पूजा जाता था। प्राप्त मोहरों और सीलों के आधार पर हम कह सकते हैं कि वह एक प्रतिभाशाली, अत्यन्त उत्साही और शक्तिशाली राजा था। युद्ध में वह बिजली की तरह नाचता था और अपने शत्रुओं को गाजर-मूली की तरह काटता चलता था। दुर्गम पर्वत भी उसकी सेना का रास्ता नहीं रोक सकते थे।"

जनोपयोगी कार्य

हम्मूराबी प्रजा के हित पर पूर्ण ध्यान देता था उसने प्रजा की भलाई के लिए कई प्रमुख कार्य किए जो निम्नलिखित हैं—

1. प्रजा की भलाई के लिए बाँधों का निर्माण करवाया।
2. उसने कानूनों का संकलन किया और संगठित शासन-व्यवस्था स्थापित की।
3. शासन संचालन की सुविधा की दृष्टि से साम्राज्य को प्रान्तों और जिलों में विभक्त किया और वहाँ योग्य अधिकारियों को नियुक्त किया।
4. कृषि का विकास करने के लिए कीश से फारस की खाड़ी तक नहर का निर्माण करवाया।
5. हम्मूराबी ने देवालयों को बाध्य किया कि वे अपने पास जमा धनराशि को गरीबों को ऋण के रूप में उधार दें।
6. हम्मूराबी न्यायप्रिय शासक था। उसने अपने समस्त साम्राज्य में निष्पक्ष न्याय की व्यवस्था की।
7. कर्जदारों को सुविधा देने के लिए रेहन रखने की प्रथा शुरू की गई।

प्लेट व जीन ने लिखा है–''बेबीलोन का राजा हम्मूराबी प्राचीन संसार के उन थोड़े से राजाओं में से एक था, जिन्होंने विधवाओं, अनाथों व गरीबों के प्रति सहानुभूति दिखाई। किसान और मजदूर शोषक महाजनों, बेईमान व धन-लोलुप अधिकारियों, क्रूर सामन्तों और पाशविक सैनिक अफसरों से रक्षा पाने के लिए उसका मुँह जोहते थे।''

इतिहासकार **स्वेन** के अनुसार–''हम्मूराबी निस्सन्देह एक महान् विजेता था ही, पर इतिहास के एक सुप्रशासक के रूप में अधिक विख्यात है।''

हम्मूराबी ने एनालिल के स्थान पर बेबीलोन के देवता मारदुक की उपासना पर सर्वाधिक बल दिया। कला और विज्ञान की दृष्टि से उसका शासनकाल अच्छा माना जा सकता है। उसके समय में कला-कौशल और विज्ञान के क्षेत्र में बहुत प्रगति हुई। वह अपने जीवन में एक भी युद्ध में पराजित नहीं हुआ। उसकी विधि संहिता ने उसे विश्व इतिहास में अमरता प्रदान की।

हम्मूराबी की विधि संहिता

विधि संहिता का आशय हम्मूराबी द्वारा प्रतिपादित कानून संग्रह से है। 1902 ई. में फ्रांस के एक पुरातत्त्ववेत्ता को ईरान में सूसा की खुदाई में हम्मूराबी की विधि संहिता प्राप्त हुई थी, जो बेबीलोनिया के प्रसिद्ध मन्दिर मारदुक के आठ फीट ऊँचे गोल बेलनाकार पत्थर पर खुदी हुई थी। इसमें सम्राट को सूर्य देवता शमास से कानून ग्रहण करते हुए दिखाया गया था। इसके माध्यम से हम्मूराबी यह दिखाने का प्रयास कर रहा है कि कानून दैविक शक्ति की देन है। उसकी यह विधि संहिता आज भी लन्दन के संग्रहालय में सुरक्षित रखी हुई है।

हम्मूराबी ने जिन कानून का निर्माण किया था उनमें उस काल के रीति-रिवाजों का आधार माना गया था। उसने पुराने राजाओं के निर्णयों तथा सुमेरिया के कानूनों को अपनी विधि संहिता में स्थान दिया था। उसने बेबीलोनिया के प्रसिद्ध मन्दिर मारदुक के सामने एक गोल बेलनाकार पत्थर पर अपनी विधि संहिता को खुदवा दिया था, जिससे साधारण जनता को भी कानून को जानकारी प्राप्त हो सके और वह उसके अनुसार आचरण कर सके। उसकी यह विधि संहिता न्याय सम्बन्धी विश्व की पहली पुस्तक कही जा सकती है।

हम्मूराबी ने स्वयं विधि संहिता की भूमिका के विषय में–"जब स्वर्ग और पृथ्वी के देवता अनु ने मानव जाति के कल्याण के लिए बेबीलोन नामक एक महान् देश की रचना की घोषणा की और संसार के कोने-कोने में सदा के लिए प्रसिद्ध कर दिया, तो उन्होंने मुझे, हम्मूराबी को, जो देवताओं का भक्त है और एक महान् नरेश है, इस देश में न्याय की स्थापना के लिए, दुष्टता और पाप के उन्मूलन के लिए, शक्तिहीन को शक्तिशाली के अन्याय से बचाने के लिए और मानव समाज के कल्याण के लिए बुलाया....।" इस संहिता में उच्च आदर्श एवं क्रूर दण्ड दिये जाते थे का प्रावधान रखा गया था। **बिल ड्यूरेन्ट** ने इसकी प्रशंसा करते हुए लिखा है–"कई मायनों में तो यह किसी आधुनिक यूरोपीय राज्य के कानूनों की बराबरी कर सकती है।"

इस संहिता के समापन में हम्मूराबी ने यह मत व्यक्त किया है कि–"इस प्रकार बुद्धिमान हम्मूराबी ने न्यायपूर्ण नियमों को लागू किया और देश में एक स्थायी सरकार की स्थापना की....मैं इस देश का शासक हूँ....सुमेर और अक्काद के क्षेत्र में रहने वाली प्रिय प्रजा का मैं हमेशा ध्यान रखता हूँ। मैंने उनको संयम और धैर्य की शिक्षा दी है, ताकि शक्तिहीनों को शक्तिशाली न दबा सकें और विधवाओं तथा अनाथों को पूर्ण न्याय प्राप्त हो सके। उत्पीड़ित व्यक्ति, जो किसी विशेष उद्देश्य से कष्ट सहन कर रहे हैं, इस न्यायप्रिय राजा की मूर्ति के सामने आएँ और इस लेख को पढ़ें। मेरे स्थायी महत्त्व के शब्द उन्हें प्रोत्साहन प्रदान करेंगे और उनकी सहायता से वे अपने उद्देश्य को और भी अच्छी तरह समझ सकेंगे। भविष्य में आने वाले दिनों में इस देश के राजा मेरी न्यायपूर्ण शिक्षाओं पर ध्यान दें–जिन्हें मैंने इस स्मारक पर स्थायी रूप से खुदवा दिया है।"

हम्मूराबी एक कुशल प्रशासक के साथ-साथ एक न्यायाप्रेय शासक भी था। **सेवाइन** ने लिखा है–"हम्मूराबी लौह हाथों से शासन करता था। उसकी सत्ता दैविक सिद्धान्तों पर आधारित थी, क्योंकि वह निरंकुश था। अतः देश और जनता का भाग्य

उसकी दया पर निर्भर करता था।" हम्मूराबी अपनी विधि संहिता के कारण विश्व इतिहास में अमर हो गया।

विधि संहिता की मुख्य धाराएँ

विधि संहिता में 12 अध्याय तथा 285 धाराएँ थीं जिसमें कुल मिलाकर 3600 पंक्तियाँ थीं। इसकी प्रमुख धाराओं का उल्लेख नीचे की पंक्तियों में किया जा रहा है–

1. समस्त ठेकों के सम्बन्ध में नियम बना दिये गये।
2. कर्जदारों को सुविधा देने हेतु रेहन रखने की प्रथा आरम्भ की गई।
3. नौकरों एवं मालिकों के लिए कानून बनाये गये, जिसमें उसके कर्त्तव्यों का भी उल्लेख कर दिया।
4. मुआवजा देने की व्यवस्था शुरू की गई।
5. डॉक्टरों की फीस एवं मजदूरों की मजदूरी निश्चित कर दी गई।
6. ब्याज की दरें ठेकेदारों के लिए 35% तथा व्यापारिक कार्य हेतु 20% निश्चित की गई।
7. देवालयों में बहुत धन जमा था। अतः उनको कर्जदारों को दान देने के लिए बाध्य किया गया, ताकि वे दासता से मुक्ति प्राप्त कर सकें।

विधि संहिता की विशेषताएँ

विधि संहिता में सेमेटिक भाषा का प्रयोग किया गया है। इसकी प्रमुख विशेषताओं पर निम्न बिन्दुओं पर प्रकाश डाला जा रहा है–

1. हम्मूराबी के कानूनों से पता चलता है कि तत्कालीन समाज तीन भागों में विभाजित किया गया था–उच्च वर्ग, मध्यम वर्ग एवं निम्न वर्ग। उच्च वर्ग को आमेलू एवं मध्यम वर्ग को मशकीनू कहा जाता था। दासों को तीसरे वर्ग में रखा गया था। उच्च वर्ग में कुलीन वर्ग, धर्माधिकारी, राजा, दरबारी और बड़े-बड़े अधिकारी आते थे। मध्यम वर्ग में व्यापारी, कारीगर और मजदूर आदि आते थे। निम्न वर्ग में दास आते थे।
2. इस विधि संहिता में विवाह और तलाक के संबंध में विशेष रूप से चर्चा की गई थी। स्त्रियों को भी तलाक का अधिकार दिया गया। इससे पूर्व सुमेरियन कानूनों में उन्हें ये अधिकार प्राप्त नहीं थे यदि कोई व्यक्ति अपनी पत्नी को तलाक देता था, तो उसे दहेज में प्राप्त सारा सामान पत्नी को वापस करना

पड़ता था। पत्नी का चरित्र दोषपूर्ण होने पर उसे पानी में डुबा देने प्रथा थी। इस प्रकार हम्मूराबी ने स्त्रियों के अधिकारों की रक्षा की। यदि पति, पत्नी को स्वेच्छा से तलाक देता था, तो उसे अपनी पत्नी तथा बच्चों का खर्चा देने का प्रावधान था, परन्तु पत्नी की गलती से तलाक होने पर पति को उसे खर्चा नहीं देना पड़ता था। पत्नी की बेवफाई सिद्ध होने पर पति द्वारा उसे गुलाम बना लिया जाता था।

हम्मूराबी के कानूनों से स्त्री को सम्पत्ति में पूरा अधिकार प्राप्त होने पर बल दिया गया। अब इसके लिए वह किसी भी अदालत की शरण के लिए स्वतंत्र थी। स्त्री से सतीत्व की अपेक्षा की जाती थी और सतीत्व भंग होने पर उसे कठोर सजा दी जाती थी। विवाहिता स्त्री परपुरुषगमन का अपराध सिद्ध होने पर उसे पानी में डुबोकर मार देने का प्रावधान था। यदि परपुरुषगमन का दोषारोपण स्त्री पर पति द्वारा लगाया जाता, तो स्त्री को अदालत में अपनी पवित्रता सिद्ध करनी पड़ती थी, लेकिन यदि दोषारोपण अन्य व्यक्तियों द्वारा लगाया जाता, जो स्त्री पानी पर चलने की परीक्षा (जल-परीक्षा) देकर अपने को निर्दोष सिद्ध कर सकती थी। पति द्वारा तलाक दिये जाने पर पत्नी को भी दूसरी शादी करने का अधिकार था। इस प्रकार हम्मूराबी के कानूनों को स्त्रियों के अधिकारों की रक्षा करना प्रमुख उद्देश्य था।

3. इस विधि संहिता में कठोर दण्ड देने का प्रावधान था हम्मूराबी का कठोर कानून इस कहावत को आधार माना गया था—"आँख के बदले आँख और दाँत के बदले दाँत।" उदाहरणस्वरूप, यदि मकान गिरने से मकान मालिक के लड़के की मृत्यु हो जाए, तो मकान बनाने वाले के लड़के को मृत्यु-दण्ड की सजा देने का विधान था। इस विधि संहिता में बहुत से अपराधों के लिए मृत्यु-दण्ड की सजा दी जाती थी। चोरी, व्यभिचार, हत्या, डकैती, कायरता, बलात्कार एवं झूठा दोष लगाने पर मृत्यु-दण्ड की सजा दी जाती थी। व्यभिचार में मृत्युदंड की सजा दोनों व्यक्तियों को देने का प्रावधान था। यदि किसी व्यक्ति ने मुकदमा दायर किया और वह अपने विपक्षी पर लगाये गये आरोप अगर गलत साबित हो गये, तो मुकदमा दायर करने वाले व्यक्ति को झूठा दोष लगाने के अपराध में मौत की सजा सुनायी जाती थी। अगर किसी व्यक्ति पर जादू टोने का अपराध सिद्ध हो जाता है, तो उसे नदी में फेंक दिया जाता था। अगर वह डूब ज़ाता, तो उसे अपराधी माना जाता था और उसकी सम्पत्ति दोष लगाने वाले को प्राप्त हो जाती थी, परन्तु यदि वह व्यक्ति नदी से जीवित

बाहर निकलकर आ जाता था, तो उसे निर्दोष करार दिया जाता था। पुजारियों के मदिरालय में जाने पर तथा विश्वासघात करने पर उन्हें भी मृत्यु-दण्ड की सजा दी जाती थी।

4. इस विधि संहिता में गोद लेने की प्रथा, विधवाओं के अधिकार और सम्पत्ति के उत्तराधिकार के बारे में भी विस्तृत नियम बनाये गये थे। घरेलू कार्यों में स्त्रियों को विस्तृत अधिकार प्राप्त थे।

5. एक ही जैसा अपराध करने पर उच्च, मध्यम व निम्न वर्ग के लिए अलग-अलग दण्ड देने का विधान था। उच्च वर्ग के व्यक्तियों को पशु चुराने पर पशु की तीस गुनी एवं निम्न वर्ग के व्यक्ति को दस गुनी कीमत हरजाने के रूप में अदा करनी पड़ती थी। जानबूझकर अपराध करने वाले व्यक्ति को कठोर दण्ड दिया जाता था। अगर किसी व्यक्ति से अनजाने में अपराध हो जाता है तो उसे कम सजा दी जाती थी। यदि डॉक्टर की लापरवाही से किसी रोगी को क्षति पहुँचती थी, तो डॉक्टर को कड़ी सजा दी जाती थी।

6. इस संहिता में न्याय देने की व्यवस्था का विकास हो चुका था। कानून की दृष्टि से सभी को समान नजरों से देखा जाता था किसी के साथ पक्षपात नहीं किया जाता था। सम्राट समय-समय पर न्यायाधीशों की नियुक्ति करता था। उस दौरान मंदिरों में ही न्याय किया जाता था, जिनमें न्यायाधीश न्याय करते थे। इनके निर्णयों के विरुद्ध अपील राजा के दरबार में की जा सकती थी, जो सबसे बड़ा न्यायालय था। नगर के वयोवृद्ध व्यक्ति भी न्यायाधीश के साथ बैठते थे। आधुनिक युग में इस प्रथा को जूरी कहा जाता है।

   हम्मूराबी ने न्याय विभाग से भ्रष्टाचार दूर करने के लिये काफी प्रयास किये थे। राजा के नीचे दो तरह के न्यायालय थे–दीवानी न्यायालय एवं धार्मिक न्यायालय। न्याय देने का काम न्यायाधीशों द्वारा किया जाता था। वकालत स्वयं करने का विधान था। मुकदमों के निर्णय में गवाहों का बहुत महत्त्व था। मुकदमों के निर्णयों का लिखित होना आवश्यक था।

   इसके अतिरिक्त अंग-भंग और कोड़ों से पीटने सजा दी जाती थी। जुर्माना देने का भी प्रावधान था। भागे हुए गुलाम को शरण देने पर जुर्माना होता था। दण्डित दास के कान काट लिए जाते थे। इसी कारण हम्मूराबी को संसार का प्राचीनतम कानूनदाता भी कहा जाता है।

7. हम्मूराबी ने कर्जदारों को काफी सहानुभूति की दृष्टि से देखा है। कानून से पहले कर्जदारों को गुलाम बना लिया जाता था। उनकी पत्नियों को दास

बनाकर उन्हें काफी प्रताड़ित किया जाता था। हम्मूराबी ने इस बुराई को समाप्त कर दिया। उसने देवालयों को बाध्य किया कि वे कर्जदारों को दान दें, ताकि कर्जदारों को कर्ज से मुक्ति मिल जाये।

8. इस विधि संहिता के द्वारा समाज के भिन्न-भिन्न वर्गों के आपसी सम्बन्धों पर प्रकाश डाला गया है। पिता-पुत्र, पति-पत्नी, महाजन-कर्जदार, जमींदार-कृषक, व्यापारी-ग्राहक एवं मालिक-मजदूर आदि के सम्बन्धों को स्पष्ट किया गया था।

9. गरीबों को प्रताड़ना से बचाना उस काल के कानून का प्रमुख उद्देश्य था। इस कानून का उद्देश्य समाज में सामाजिक समानता स्थापित करना और गरीबों की रक्षा करना था।

10. हम्मूराबी ने दासों के अधिकारों की चर्चा करते हुए कुछ नियम बनाये। इन नियमों द्वारा दासों का काफी उत्थान हुआ। उदाहरण के लिए वे सम्पत्ति रख सकते थे, व्यापार कर सकते थे, अपने विक्रय के विरुद्ध विरोध प्रकट कर सकते थे। दास रुपया देकर स्वतन्त्र हो सकते थे।

    हम्मूराबी के कानूनों द्वारा दासों पर अमानुषिक अत्याचारों और कठोर दण्डों को समाप्त कर दिया था। इस प्रकार उसके कानूनों के द्वारा दासों की दशा में काफी सुधार हुआ। दासों की स्थिति में सुधार बताते हुए **मैकनेल बर्न्स** ने लिखा है, "कर्ज के लिए बेचे गये गुलाम बच्चों व औरतों को चार वर्ष से अधिक गुलाम नहीं बनाया जा सकता था और जिस गुलाम स्त्री से मालिक की सन्तान जन्म ले ले, उसे फिर बेचा नहीं जायेगा।"

11. दीवानी कानूनों की व्यवस्था का भी उल्लेख इस विधि संहिता में किया गया था। इसमें पारिवारिक जीवन के सम्बन्ध में भी काफी कानून बनाये गये थे। लड़की का पिता दहेज में जो कुछ भी देता था, उस पर लड़की का अधिकार होता था। लड़की की मृत्यु हो जाने पर उसकी संतान को उसकी संपत्ति का हकदार बना दिया जाता था। स्त्री की निःसन्तान मृत्यु होने पर वह सम्पत्ति पुनः उसके पिता को दे दी जाती थी। पति, पत्नी की इच्छा से उप-पत्नी भी रख सकता था। पति को स्वेच्छा से धोखा देने वाली या वैवाहिक सम्बन्ध तोड़ने वाली स्त्री को पानी में डुबोकर मार दिया जाता था।

प्रत्येक विषय पर लिखित कानून का गठन हम्मूराबी की विधि संहिता में किया गया था। उसके अधिकारी उन कानूनों का पालन जनता से करवाते थे। उसके कानूनों से बेबीलोनिया के राजनीतिक, सामाजिक, धार्मिक एवं सांस्कृतिक विकास

के बारे में जानकारी प्राप्त होती है। स्पष्ट है कि हम्मूराबी ने अपनी विधि संहिता के माध्यम से ही समस्त साम्राज्य में सुव्यवस्थित शासन-प्रबन्ध की स्थापना की थी। अपने कानूनों से उसने कमजोर वर्ग और कर्जदारों को काफी सहयोग किया था हम्मूराबी के अनुसार, ''उसकी संहिता असहायों की शक्तिशाली व्यक्तियों से सुरक्षा तथा सर्वसाधारण की भलाई करने वाली है।''

हम्मूराबी की उपलब्धियाँ

हम्मूराबी एक कुशल शासक तथा प्रबंधक के साथ-साथ एक महान विजेता भी था। उसने अक्काद, एलम, सुमेर तथा असीरिया को पराजित कर दिया था। उसने अपने विशाल साम्राज्य में सुदृढ़ शासन-प्रबन्ध की स्थापना की। वह एक महान् विधान निर्माता था। उसकी विधि संहिता ने उसे अमर बना दिया। उसे गरीबों तथा कर्जदारों का मसीहा भी कहा जाता था। उसके द्वारा स्थापित सुदृढ़ शासन व न्याय व्यवस्था सैकड़ों वर्षों तक राजाओं का मार्गदर्शन करती रही।

सामुद्रिक देश के राजाओं का शासन

जब हम्मूराबी की मृत्यु हो गयी तब उसके पुत्र शम्सुइलुना ने उसके उत्तराधिकारी के रूप में राजगद्दी संभाली। उसने 2080 ई. पू. से 2043 ई. पू. तक शासन किया। उसने अपने पिता की भाँति न्याय और प्रशासन पर कड़ा नियन्त्रण रखा। उस दौरान केस्साइट जाति की शक्ति में वृद्धि होती रही।

शम्सुइलुना को प्रथम राजवंश का अंतिम महान् राजा कहा जाता था। उसी के द्वारा दो नहरों का निर्माण कराया गया तथा बेबीलोनिया एवं सिप्पर के मन्दिरों को सुसज्जित किया। उसके समय में उद्योग एवं व्यापार के क्षेत्र में विकास हुआ और जनता सुखी तथा समृद्ध थी।

शम्सुइलुना के पुत्र निसि-अमी जादुगा को उसकी मृत्यु के पश्चात् राजगद्दी सौंपी गई। इसके जमाने में बेबीलोनिया का महत्त्व बढ़ा। तत्पश्चात् उसका पुत्र सम्सुदिताना गद्दी पर बैठा, जो इस वंश का अन्तिम शासक था। उसके शासनकाल में अनातोलिया की हिट्टाइट जाति के लोगों ने फरात नदी से होकर बेबीलोनिया के उत्तर पश्चिमी भाग पर हमला कर दिया। हिट्टाइट के द्वारा काफी लूटपाट की गई थी। उन्होंने बेबीलोन शहर का अस्तित्व समाप्त कर दिया और वहाँ से बहुत से देवी-देवताओं की मूर्तियाँ चुरा लीं। सम्भवतः बेबीलोन के राजा सम्सुदिताना की मृत्यु राजधानी की रक्षा करते हुए हो गई। हिट्टाहट अपने देश लूट का माल लेकर वापस लौट गये थे।

बेबीलोनिया में हिट्टाइट के आक्रमण के पश्चात् चारों तरफ अराजकता फैल गयी थी। इसका लाभ उठाकर केस्साइट लोगों ने 1763 ई. पू. में बेबीलोनिया पर कब्जा कर लिया।

उत्तर दिशा में फारस की खाड़ी में दलदल की अधिकता होने का कारण इलाके को बेबीलोनिया के इतिहास में 'सामुद्रिक प्रदेश' की संज्ञा दी जाती है। सामुद्रिक प्रदेश के राजा का दक्षिणी बेबीलोनिया पर अधिकार था। इलुमा-इलुम नामक सरदार ने दक्षिणी बेबीलोनिया में फारस की खाड़ी के किनारे अपना राज्य स्थापित किया। यह प्रदेश दक्षिण दिशा में बसा हुआ है, जिसे सामुद्रिक राज्य भी कहा जाता था, लगभग 1710 ई. पू. तक स्थापित रहा। इया गामिल के राज्यकाल में इस राज्य का अस्तित्व लगभग समाप्त हो चुका था। केस्साइट लोगों ने ही सामुद्रिक प्रदेश के राज्य के विकास में महत्त्वपूर्ण योगदान दिया था।

केस्साइट लोगों का शासन (1760 ई. पू. से 1185 ई. पू.)

सम्पूर्ण बेबीलोनिया पर केस्साइटों का आधिपत्य था। इनका संबंध आर्यजाति से था। उन्होंने बेबीलोनिया की संस्कृति को स्व।कार कर लिया था। दूसरे शब्दों में हम यह कह सकते हैं कि केस्साइट लोगों ने बेबीलोनिया को पराजित कर दिया था, परन्तु सांस्कृतिक दृष्टि से बेबीलोनिया के लोगों ने उन लोगों पर विजय प्राप्त की थी। बेबीलोनिया ने केस्साइटों के रीति-रिवाजों, धर्म एवं लिपि को स्वीकार कर लिया था।

बेबीलोनिया पर केस्साइट लोगों का अधिकार और उनका शासन प्राचीन बेबीलोनिया के इतिहास में विशिष्ट स्थान रखता है। केस्साइट लोगों ने वर्षों की गणना राजाओं के राज्यकाल से आरम्भ की। उनका प्रधान देवता 'सूर्यांश' था, जो आर्य लोगों के देवता सूर्य से मिलता-जुलता था। इन लोगों ने 600 वर्ष तक बेबीलोनिया पर शासन किया।

केस्साइट लोगों के संस्थापक को गंदाश कहा जाता था। उसके बाद उसका लड़के अगुम को गद्दी सौंपी गयी, जिसने 22 वर्ष तक शासन किया। सत्रहवीं शताब्दी ई. पू. से लेकर पन्द्रहवीं शताब्दी ई. पू. के बीच केस्साइट वंश के तेरह राजाओं ने शासन किया। इन राजाओं के मिस्र तथा पश्चिमी एशिया के देशों के शासकों से मैत्रीपूर्ण सम्बन्ध थे। मिस्र के फराओं से मित्रता करने के लिये बेबीलोन के राजा अपनी लड़की की शादी उसके साथ करते थे, परन्तु मिस्र का राजा अपनी लड़की की शादी असीरिया, बेबीलोन के राजाओं के साथ करना अपनी प्रतिष्ठा के विरुद्ध समझता था।

बेबीलोनिया की भाषा, लिपि, कानून और न्याय-प्रणाली का पश्चिमी एशिया में केस्साइटों द्वारा काफी प्रचार किया गया था। एलम के लोगों के आक्रमण के कारण केस्साइट वंश के राजाओं का पतन हुआ। बेबीलोन की संस्कृति का केस्साइट लोगों के संपर्क में आने से काफी विकास हुआ था। उनके समय में व्यापार एवं वाणिज्य के क्षेत्र में प्रगति हुई। अन्तर्राष्ट्रीय क्षेत्र में इन्होंने बेबीलोनिया का सम्बन्ध हिट्टाइट, एलम, मिस्र और मित्तानी के राजाओं से किया। इस प्रकार केस्साइट लोगों के सम्पर्क के कारण बेबीलोन के सांस्कृतिक क्षेत्र में काफी बदलाव हुए।

केस्साइट शासन के बाद का इतिहास

नेबुचडरेज्जर को केस्साइट लोगों के पतन के पश्चात् राजगद्दी सौंपी गयी। यह चतुर्थ राजवंश का तीसरा शासक था। उसने अपने देश की प्रतिष्ठा को फिर से स्थापित किया और एलम के आक्रमण के खतरे को बहुत कम कर दिया। उसके द्वारा बेबीलोन को एक शक्तिशाली राज्य की संज्ञा दी गयी थी।

असीरिया के राजा को नेबुचडरेज्जर द्वारा मुंह की खानी पड़ी थी। उसने 1010 ई. पू. में असीरिया के राजा तिगलथ पिलेसर प्रथम के साथ दो लड़ाइयाँ लड़ीं। पहली लड़ाई में बेबीलोनिया जीत गया था। असीरिया का राजा दूसरी लड़ाई में विजय हुआ था तथा बेबीलोन नगर और अन्य प्रमुख शहरों पर अपना कब्जा जमा लिया था। बेबीलोनिया पुनः स्वतंत्र हो गया।

लगभग तीन शताब्दियों तक असीरिया तथा बेबीलोनिया के मध्य युद्ध लगातार होता रहा था। इस समय सेमेटिक जाति के लोग भी निरन्तर बेबीलोनिया पर आक्रमण करते रहे। इन लगातार आक्रमणों से बेबीलोनिया में अराजकता, अशान्ति एवं अव्यवस्था को काफी प्रसार हो चुका था। बेबीलोनिया में छठे राजवंश का शासनकाल 1031 ई. पू. से 1012 ई. पू. तक था। तत्पश्चात् एलम के एक शासक ने बेबीलोनिया पर अधिकार कर सातवें राजवंश की स्थापना की। यह सातवाँ राजवंश 1006 ई. पू. तक कायम रहा।

इसके पश्चात् आठवें राजवंश शासन की स्थापना की गई थी। इस वंश का शासन-काल 1005 ई. पू. से 762 ई. पू. तक था। कुछ समय बाद असीरिया ने बेबीलोनिया पर अधिकार कर लिया। इसके बाद असीरिया के शासक अशुर बनीपाल ने साम्राज्य विस्तार की नीति को अपनाया, लेकिन कुछ ही समय बाद बेबीलोनिया फिर स्वतंत्र हो गया।

शंशी अदाद चतुर्थ ने बेबीलोनिया पर शलमनेसर तथा उत्तराधिकारी के रूप में पुनः अपना अधिकार जमा लिया था। आठवें राजवंश का अंत तथा नौवें राजवंश का उदय कब हुआ था, इस सबन्ध में कोई जानकारी प्राप्त नहीं होती।

तिगलथ पिलेसर तृतीय ने 745 ई.पू. में असीरिया की गद्दी ग्रहण की। उसने साम्राज्यवाद की नीति अपनाई। वह प्राचीन विश्व इतिहास में आज भी काफी चर्चित है। तिगलथ पिलेसर तृतीय ने बेबीलोनिया के राजा नेबोनास्सर को हराकर संधि का न्यौता दिया। इस समय बेबीलोनिया में नौवां राजवंश समाप्त हो चुका था और दसवाँ राजवंश स्थापित हुआ।

दसवें राजवंश में विभिन्न वंशों के उन्नीस राजाओं का शासनकाल 732 ई. पू. से 625 ई. पू. तक था। इस काल में बेबीलोनिया पतन की ओर अग्रसर होता जा रहा था।

पुलु के उपनाम से तिगलथ पिलेसर चतुर्थ ने बेबीलोनिया पर राज किया। तत्पश्चात् उसके पुत्र शल्मानेसर पंचम ने उलु-लाई के नाम से 727 ई. पू. 722 ई. पू. तक बेबीलोनिया पर शासन किया।

सारगन द्वितीय

असीरिया की गद्दी सारगन द्वितीय को 722 ई. पू. में सौंपी गई थी। उसके समय में मेरोडाक बालादान नामक चाल्डिया के एक राजकुमार के नेतृत्व में बेबीलोनिया में विद्रोह हुआ। मेरोडाक ने एलम के शासक की सेना की सहायता से सारगन द्वितीय युद्ध में विजयी हुआ। परिणामस्वरूप मेरोडाक बेबीलोनिया की गद्दी पर बैठा और सारगन द्वितीय को असीरिया जाने के लिए विवश होना पड़ा।

कुछ समय के पश्चात् सारगन द्वितीय ने मेरोडाक पर आक्रमण किया। इस बार मेरोडाक को एलम के राजा ने सहायता नहीं दी। फलतः मेरोडाक पराजित होकर चाल्डिया भाग गया और सारगन द्वितीय 706 ई. पू. में पुनः बेबीलोनिया का राजा बना। इसके बाद अपने शासन के अन्तिम दिनों तक उसने बेबीलोनिया के शासक के रूप में राज्य किया।

सेन्नाचेरिब (705 ई. पू. से 681 ई. पू.)

705 ई.पू. में सेन्नाचेरिब को सारगन द्वितीय के पश्चात् राजगद्दी सौंपी गयी। उस दौरान एलम के राजा की सहायता से बेबीलोनिया में मेरोडाक द्वारा विद्रोह छिड़ गया। सेन्नाचेरिब ने मेरोडाक को पराजित करके अपने एक प्रतिनिधि बेल इबनी

को बेबीलोनिया की गद्दी सौंप दिया। दो वर्ष बाद जब सेन्नाचेरिब अपने साम्राज्य के पश्चिमी हिस्सों में विद्रोह दबाने के लिए गया, तो मेरोडाक ने बेबीलोनिया पर फिर आक्रमण कर दिया। मेरोडाक को बेल गुप्त रूप से सहायता पहुँचा रहा था। सेन्नाचेरिब ने इस विश्वासघात के कारण उसे बेबीलोनिया की गद्दी से हटा दिया और उसके स्थान पर अपने पुत्र अशुर-नादिन-शुम को बेबीलोनिया की गद्दी सौंप दी।

असीरिया की अधीनता से बेबीलोनियावासी छुटकारा चाहते थे। अतः उन्होंने एलम की सहायता से पुनः विद्रोह किया। सेन्नाचेरिब ने 686 ई. पू. में बेबीलोनिया और एलम की संयुक्त सेना को युद्ध में पराजित किया। एलम के राजा की इस युद्ध में मृत्यु हो गई। बेबीलोन पर असीरिया के शासन की पुनः स्थापना की गयी। बेबीलोनिया के लगातार विद्रोहों से क्रुद्ध होकर सेन्नाचेरिब ने बेबीलोन शहर की सुरक्षात्मक चारदीवारी को नष्ट कर दिया। मन्दिरों, महलों और घरों को नष्ट कर दिया गया था, बेबीलोनिया के प्रमुख देवता मारदुक की प्रतिमा को असीरिया ले जाया गया। बेबीलोनिया के निवासियों के घरों को छीन लिया गया और उन्हें खण्डहरों में बदल दिया गया।

उसके छोटे पुत्र एसरहादेन को 681 ई.पू. में सेन्नाचेरिब के पश्चात् राजगद्दी सौंपी दी गई। उसका शासनकाल 681 ई. पू. से 669 ई. पू. तक था। उसने बेबीलोन के प्रति प्रेम और सद्भाव की नीति अपनाई। बेबीलोन नगर की तीन वर्षों में पुनः नये सिरे से स्थापना की गई थी। मारदुक देवता की मूर्ति को बेबीलोन के मन्दिर में फिर से स्थापित किया गया था। एसरहादेन के बाद उसके पुत्र शमाश-शुम-उकिन को बेबीलोन की गद्दी सौंप दी गयी थी।

अशुर बनिपाल

अशुर बनिपाल को एसरहादेन के पश्चात् असीरिया का राजा बनाया गया था। वह असीरिया का अन्तिम महान शासक था। उसने साम्राज्यवादी नीति को अपनाया। 667 ई. पू. में एलम ने बेबीलोन पर हमला कर दिया था। एलम के शासक को अशुर बनिपाल ने हरा दिया। इस विजय के पश्चात् अशुर बनिपाल ने अपने एक प्रतिनिधि को एलम की राजगद्दी सौंप दी थी। 625 ई. पू. में अशुर बनिपाल के भाई शमाश-शुम-उकिन ने एलम और फीनिशियन नगरों के शासकों की सहायता से असीरिया के राजा के विरुद्ध बेबीलोनिया में विद्रोह किया। इस विद्रोह को समाप्त करने में बनिपाल ने महत्त्वपूर्ण भूमिका निभाई थी। इसमें शमाश-शुम-उकिन की मृत्यु हो गई। अशुर बनिपाल ने अब कंदालानु नामक व्यक्ति को बेबीलोन की गद्दी पर

बैठाया। उसने एलम को नीर्जन बना दिया था। उसने मुर्दों को भी नहीं छोड़ा उन्हें भी घसीटकर असीरिया भेज दिया गया।

अशुर बनिपाल आजीवन असीरिया और बेबीलोन पर राज्य करता रहा। उसके शासनकाल के उत्तरार्द्ध में सीथियन, मीडीज और परशियन के द्वारा काफी हमले किए गये, जिससे असीरिया की सैन्य शक्ति काफी कमजोर हो गयी और उसका पतन प्रारम्भ हुआ। इसी दौरान बेबीलोनिया के नबोपोलासर नामक व्यक्ति ने एक नया राजवंश स्थापित किया, जिसे ग्यारहवाँ राजवंश भी कहा जाता है लेकिन बेबीलोन के इतिहास में एक नये राजवंश के नाम से प्रचलित था।

बेबीलोनिया का नया राजवंश (625 ई. पू. से 539 ई. पू. तक)

बेबीलोनिया के नेता नबोपोलासर को असीरिया की कठिनाई से काफी फायदा हुआ उसने बेबीलोनिया में एक नये राजवंश की स्थापना की। इस वंश को प्राचीन बेबीलोनिया के इतिहास में एक विशिष्ट स्थान प्राप्त है। नबोपोलासर के समय में बेबीलोन का सर्वांगीण विकास हुआ। उसने एक शक्तिशाली सेना की स्थापना की। नबोपोलासर ने मिस्री प्रभाव को रोकने का निश्चय किया। उसने अपने लड़के नेबुचडरेज्जर की अध्यक्षता में एक सेना भेजी। मिस्र और बेबीलोनिया की सेना में 604 ई. पू. कारकेमिश नामक स्थान पर युद्ध हुआ, जिसमें मिस्री सेना को हार का सामना करना पड़ा और उसे भगाना पड़ा। शीघ्र ही सीरिया और पेलेस्टाइन के बहुत बड़े भाग पर बेबीलोन का एकछत्र राज हो गया। नबोपोलासर एक बहुत बड़ा निर्माता भी था।

नबोपोलासर के पुत्र नेबुचडरेज्जर को उसकी मृत्यु के पश्चात् गद्दी सौंपी गई थी। उसने साम्राज्यवादी नीति पर चलते हुए यरुशलम और फिनीशिया पर अधिकार कर लिया। उसने अपने शासन के 37वें वर्ष में मिस्र के राजा आमासिस को पराजित किया और मिस्त्र को अपने साम्राज्य का एक प्रान्त बना दिया।

नेबुचडरेज्जर को महान निर्माता भी कहा जाता था। उसने बारसिप्पा नगर में एजिदा नाम के प्रधान मन्दिर का निर्माण करवाया और अपने पिता के राजमहल के छज्जे और चबूतरे को शहर से इतना ऊँचा बनवाया, जो आज 'हैगिंग गार्डन' के नाम से विश्व के सात आश्चर्यों में से एक है। उसने बेबीलोनिया में एसागिला नाम के मन्दिर का पुनर्निर्माण करवाया और राजमहल तथा निन्मार मन्दिर के बीच ईश्तर देवी के नाम से एक बहुत बड़ा फाटक बनवाया, जिसका नाम 'ईश्तर फाटक' रखा। व्यापार वाणिज्य में नेबुचडरेज्जर के काल में महत्त्वपूर्ण विकास कार्य हुए थे। टेरेडन

नामक शहर की स्थापना उसी के द्वारा की गई थी। इस प्रकार नेबुचडरेज्जर ने बेबीलोनियानी की संस्कृति और आर्थिक समृद्धि में भी काफी चिलचस्पी ली थी।

अमेल मारदुक

बेबीलोनिया की गद्दी नेबुचडरेज्जर की मृत्यु के पश्चात् उसके पुत्र को सौंपी गयी। वह शासक के रूप में सफल सिद्ध नहीं हो सका। अतः तीन वर्ष में ही पुरोहित वर्ग ने उसकी हत्या कर दी। इसके बाद नेबुचडरेज्जर का बहनोई नेरिगलिस्सर गद्दी पर बैठा। वह बेबीलोनिया का प्रसिद्ध सेनापति था, जिसे नरगल-शर-अतसर के नाम से जाना जाता था। उसने सेना का पुनर्गठन किया, परन्तु चार वर्ष बाद ही उसकी मृत्यु हो गई। तत्पश्चात् उसके पुत्र मारदुक को वहां का राजा बनाया गया, जिसे नौ महीने बाद बेबीलोनिया के पुरोहित वर्ग ने गद्दी से पदच्युत कर दिया था।

पुरोहित वर्गों ने मारदुक के बाद नेबोनिडास को वहां का राजा बनाया था। उसका संबंध पुरोहित वर्ग से था। अतः उसे इतिहास और पुरातत्त्व से काफी लगाव था। इसके समय में फारस के राजा साइरस ने बेबीलोनिया पर हमला कर अपना आधिपत्य जमा लिया था। इस तरह बेबीलोनिया का प्रदेश फारसी साम्राज्य का एक हिस्सा बन गया।

सामाजिक जीवन

बेबीलोनिया की सभ्यता को शहरी सभ्यता की संज्ञा दी जाती है वहाँ का समाज तीन वर्गों में बांटा गया था–पहला उच्च वर्ग था जिसे 'आमेलू' भी पुकारा जाता था। इस वर्ग में मन्त्री, पदाधिकारी, सामन्त, राजवंश, पुजारी आदि आते थे दूसरा मध्यमवर्ग था, जिसे 'मशकीनू' की संज्ञा दी जाती थी। इस वर्ग में व्यापारी, छोटे-छोटे व्यवसायी और किसानों को शामिल किया जाता था। तीसरा निम्न वर्ग था, जिसे 'अरद' कहा जाता था। इस वर्ग में दासों को शामिल किया जाता था। दास वर्ग पर स्वामी का शासन चलता था। दास चार प्रकार के होते थे–जो दास के यहाँ पैदा होते थे, कर्ज चुकाने में असमर्थ रहने पर व्यक्ति को दास बना लिया जाता था और वह दास, अपने स्वामी की सेवा करके मुक्ति पा सकता था, खरीदकर बनाये गये दास एवं युद्धबन्दी के रूप में बनाये गये दास। बेबीलोनिया के दासों को कुछ अधिकार भी दिये गये थे।

संयुक्त परिवार प्रणाली बेबीलोनिया में काफी पसंद की जाती थी और पुत्र अपने पिता के ही व्यवसाय को आगे बढ़ाता था। वहाँ परिवार का कानूनी आधार

एक विवाह की प्रथा था, परन्तु कोई भी पुरुष एक या एक से अधिक उप-पत्नियाँ रखने को स्वतंत्र था। लड़की को विवाह के दौरान दहेज दिया जाता था, जिसे 'शेरिक्ट' कहा जाता था। दहेज पर आजीवन लड़की का अधिकार रहता था। उसके मरने के पश्चात् उसकी सम्पत्ति पर बच्चों का ही अधिकार हो जाता था। लड़की की निःसन्तान मृत्यु होने पर उसकी सम्पत्ति पर पिता का अधिकार हो जाता था। हम्मूराबी ने विवाह, तलाक, गोद लेने की प्रथा, बच्चों का पालन-पोषण, विधवाओं के अधिकार और उत्तराधिकार के सम्बन्ध में नियम बनाये थे।

अपना मनपसंद लड़का चुनने के लिये विवाह योग्य स्त्रियां स्वतंत्र थीं। विवाह की इच्छुक लड़कियाँ देवालय में हरे कपड़े पहनकर बैठ जाती थीं। वहाँ पर विवाह के इच्छुक युवक उन्हें देखने आते थे। यदि किसी लड़के को कोई लड़की पसन्द आ जाती, तो यह प्रस्तावस्वरूप एक सिक्का लड़की की गोद में डाल देता था। यदि उस लड़की को भी वह लड़का पसन्द आ जाता, तो वह सिक्का उठा लेती थी अन्यथा सिक्के को झोली से लुढ़का देती थी। तत्पश्चात् दोनों कुछ दिन तक एक साथ वक्त बिताते थे। यदि दोनों के स्वभाव में समानता होती है, तो दोनों विवाह के बंधन में बंध जाते थे अन्यथा लड़का व लड़की फिर अपने नये साथी को चुनने के लिए स्वतन्त्र थे। विवाह से पहले यह लड़के-लड़की का अधिकार रहता था। यदि कोई व्यक्ति दूसरी शादी करता, तो उसे अपनी पहली पत्नी का दहेज लौटाना पड़ता था।

स्त्रियों की दशा में हम्मूराबी द्वारा काफी बदलाव किये गये थे। इस समय एक पुरुष दो स्त्रियों को पत्नी के रूप में नहीं रख सकता था। यदि वह दूसरी स्त्री रखता, तो उसे उप-पत्नी के रूप में रख सकता था। दूसरे शब्दों में, एक पुरुष को सिर्फ एक ही पत्नी रखने का अधिकार था, परन्तु दूसरी स्त्री उसकी उप-पत्नी के रूप में ही रह सकती थी। कोई भी पुरुष अपनी आर्थिक दशा के अनुरूप एक से अधिक उप-पत्नियाँ रख सकता था।

पत्नी से सतीत्व की अपेक्षा की जाती थी। हम्मूराबी के अनुसार सतीत्व भंग होने पर कठोर दण्ड देने का विधान था। साथ ही, पति से भी अपनी पत्नी के प्रति वफादार रहने एवं उसके भरण-पोषण की अपेक्षा की जाती थी। यदि कोई पति जानबूझकर, बिना किसी गलती के, पत्नी का परित्याग कर देता है, तो पत्नी को पुनर्विवाह करने का अधिकार था। पति के युद्ध बन्दी बनाये जाने पर भी पत्नी को दूसरी शादी करने की स्वतन्त्रता थी।

विवाहित स्त्रियों को उस दौरान कुछ न्याय सम्बन्धी अधिकार भी प्राप्त थे। वे अदालतों में गवाही दे सकती थीं और अपने दासों को बेच सकती थीं। तलाक

के लिए न्यायालय में अपील करनी पड़ती थी। पति के प्रति पत्नी यदि पूर्ण वफादार एवं कर्त्तव्यपरायण नहीं रहती थी, तो उसे बिना किसी क्षतिपूर्ति के तलाक देने के लिए वह स्वतंत्र था, परन्तु पति के दोषी होने पर तलाक की अवस्था में पत्नी को भरण-पोषण का खर्चा वहन करना पड़ता था।

कानूनी स्तर पर पति को भी अपनी पत्नी पर कुछ अधिकार प्राप्त थे। वह अपनी इच्छानुसार अपनी पत्नी को दास बना सकता था। अगर वह चाहे तो उसे तीन महीने के लिए गिरवी भी रख सकता था। पत्नी द्वारा बेवफाई करने पर पति उसे बेच भी सकता था। अगर उसकी पत्नी को कोई संतान न हो तो पति उप-पत्नी रखने के लिये भी स्वतंत्र था। ऐसी स्थिति में वह अपनी पत्नी को किसी भी वक्त तलाक देने के लिये स्वतंत्र था, परन्तु दहेज में प्राप्त सारा सामान उसे पत्नी को सौंप देना पड़ता था। अगर पत्नी से कोई सन्तान उत्पन्न नहीं होने के बावजूद भी पति अपनी पत्नी से प्यार करता और तलाक नहीं देना चाहता, तो ऐसी दशा में वह एक उप-पत्नी भी रख सकता था। कई बार ऐसा भी होता है कि पत्नियाँ ही अपने पति के लिए उप-पत्नी खोज दिया करती थीं। पत्नी को उप-पत्नी की प्रतिद्वंदिता करने पर उसे गुलाम बनाने के लिये स्वतंत्र थी। ऐसी स्थिति में पत्नी, उप-पत्नी को बेच भी सकती थी। उप-पत्नी से यदि संतान प्राप्त हो जाती थी तो पतियों को दूसरी शादी करने का अधिकार नहीं था।

पत्नी को यदि किसी प्रकार रोगग्रस्त हो जाती है तो भी उसका पति उसे तलाक नहीं दे सकता था। वह केवल उप-पत्नी रख सकता था। पति से बेवफाई करने वाली पत्नी को पानी में डुबो कर मार दिया जाता था। बेबीलोनिया में बहु-विवाह वर्जित था। इस प्रकार कुल मिलाकर स्त्रियों की दशा सन्तोषजनक थी।

बेबीलोनिया में दास प्रथा को समाज में काफी बढ़ावा दिया जाता था। कर्ज न चुकाने वाले को भी दास बना लिया जाता था और वह अपने स्वामी की सेवा करके कर्ज से छुटकारा पा सकता था। कुछ इतिहासकारों का मानना था कि उस दौरान दासों की दशा काफी खराब थी। दासों के स्वामी उनको काफी प्रताड़ित करते थे। यदि कोई दास अपराधी सिद्ध होता, तो बाजार में उसको कोड़े लगाये जाते थे। प्रत्येक मालिक अपने दास के हाथ पर अपना चिह्न अंकित करता था। युद्ध के समय प्राप्त दासों को मंदिरों के निर्माण में लगा दिया जाता था। शैतान व भगोड़े दासों के कान काट दिये जाते थे इसके विपरीत कुछ स्वामी अपने दासों को अधिकार भी देते थे। दास मेहनत करके अपनी व्यक्तिगत सम्पत्ति एकत्रित कर सकता था और अपना कर्जा

चुकाकर दासता से मुक्ति पा सकता था। यही नहीं, वह अपनी इच्छानुसार लड़की से विवाह करने के लिये स्वतंत्र था।

अपनी विधि संहिता में हम्मूराबी ने दासों को काफी अधिकार प्रदान किये थे—जैसे वे अपनी बिक्री के विरुद्ध विरोध प्रकट कर सकते थे, जिसकी सुनवाई कानूनी अदालतों में होती थी। हम्मूराबी के कानूनों में दासों एवं उप-पत्नियों की दशा में काफी परिवर्तन किये गये थे। यदि किसी व्यक्ति की अपनी उप-पत्नी से सन्तान हो जाती थी, तो वह अपनी उप-पत्नी को बेच नहीं सकता था, परन्तु कुछ दिनों के लिए उसे ऋण के बदले में किसी को सौंप अवश्य सकता था।

मालिक की स्त्री को उसके गुलाम से पुत्र उत्पन्न हो जाता है, तो उसकी दासता समाप्त कर दी जाती थी। इसी प्रकार यदि दासी के स्वामी से पुत्र पैदा हो जाता था, तो वह उसकी पत्नी बन जाती थी। **मैकनेल बर्न्स** के शब्दों में—"कर्ज के लिये बेचे गये गुलाम बच्चों व औरतों को चार वर्ष से अधिक गुलाम रखने का प्रावधान नहीं था और जिस गुलाम स्त्री से मालिक की सन्तान जन्म ले ले, उसे फिर बेचा नहीं जा सकता था।"

पैसों के बल पर बेबीलोनिया के दास दासता से मुक्त हो सकते थे। बेबीलोनिया का प्रसिद्ध मारदुक देवता का मन्दिर दासों को कर्ज देता था, ताकि वे उस धन की सहायता से स्वतन्त्र हो सकें। भागे हुए दास को अगर किसी व्यक्ति द्वारा शरण दी जाती थी तो, शरण देने वाले व्यक्ति को मृत्युदण्ड की सजा दी जाती थी। कोई व्यक्ति भागे हुए दास को पकड़कर उसके स्वामी को लौटा देता था, तो तत्कालीन कानूनों के अनुसार उसे पुरस्कार देकर सम्मानित किया जाता था। इस प्रकार हम्मूराबी के कानूनों से दासों की दशा में सुधार हुआ था। कर्मठ और सुयोग्य दासों को उनके स्वामी द्वारा सम्मान दिया जाता था।

बेबीलोनिया में स्त्रियों की दशा को सुनिश्चित नहीं किया गया था। उनका विशेष सम्मान भी था और उन्हें नैतिकता से गिरने के लिए भी मजबूर किया जाता था। समयकालीन सभ्यता की तुलना में वेश्यावृत्ति का काफी प्रसार था। यूनानी इतिहासकार हेरोडोटस के अनुसार इस काल में नारी का स्थान गिरा हुआ था। इसके विपरीत सेवाइन, बर्न्स, विल ड्यूरेण्ट तथा एच. जी. वेल्स आदि इतिहासकारों का मत है कि नारी का काफी सम्मान था। वे शिक्षा प्राप्त करती थीं और सामाजिक उत्सवों में भाग लेती थीं। वे पुरुषों के समान शिक्षा प्राप्त करने को स्वतंत्र थीं। इतना ही नहीं, वे स्वतन्त्रतापूर्वक व्यापार भी कर सकती थीं। वे प्रशासकीय सेवाओं में भर्ती हो सकती थीं। इस युग में नारी को समाज में उच्च तथा प्रतिष्ठित स्थान प्राप्त था।

डॉ. एस. आर. गोयल ने लिखा है, "बेबीलोनियन समाज में स्त्रियों को जितनी स्वतंत्रता तथा प्रतिष्ठा प्राप्त थी, उतनी उन्हें वैदिक भारत और सम्भवतः मिस्र को छोड़कर अन्य किसी प्राचीन सभ्य देश में प्राप्त नहीं थी।"

यहाँ के निवासी तरह-तरह के आभूषण, शृंगार-प्रसाधन तथा विलासिता की वस्तुओं का इस्तेमाल करते थे। उस दौरान पुरुषों द्वारा जूता पहनने को प्रचलन नहीं था। यहाँ के लोग गले में दुपट्टा और तहमद पहनते थे। स्त्रियों द्वारा चमड़े की मुलायम जूतियों का प्रयोग किया जाता था। उच्च वर्ग की महिलाएँ चेहरे पर लाली और सोने की बालपिनों का प्रयोग खुद को सजाने के लिये करती थीं। वे नाक, कान, आँख, गला, कलाई और उँगलियों पर सोने के आभूषण पहनना अधिक पंसद करती थीं। उस दौरान स्त्रियां चुस्त कपड़े पहनना पसंद करती थीं और पुरुष हाथ में धनुष लेकर घूमते थे। इस प्रकार बेबीलोनिया में उच्च वर्ग की महिलाएँ सुखी तथा विलासी जीवन व्यतीत करती थीं। मध्यम वर्ग की स्त्रियाँ सोने व चाँदी के आभूषण तथा निम्न वर्ग की स्त्रियाँ मिट्टी के रंगीन आभूषण धारण करती थीं। **विल ड्यूरेण्ट** के अनुसार–"स्त्रियों के साज व शृंगार की दृष्टि से सचमुच ही तब से लेकर अब तक कोई विशेष परिवर्तन नहीं हुआ है।"

उस काल के लोग मांसाहारी तथा शाकाहारी भोजन का अधिक सेवन करते थे। शाकाहारी दूध, फल एवं अन्न आदि खाते थे, जबकि मांसाहारी मछली का सेवन करते थे। प्रत्येक व्यक्ति शराब का सेवना करता था और सैनिक भी शराब पीकर युद्ध लड़ते थे। जो लड़कियां अपनी इच्छा से देवदासी बन जाती थीं उन्हें भी अपने पिता की सम्पत्ति में अधिकार प्राप्त होता था। देवदासियों को भी विवाह करने अधिकार था, परन्तु उन्हें विवाह के बाद भी शारीरिक सम्बन्धों से दूर रहना पड़ता था। विवाहित स्त्रियाँ भी देवदासियाँ बन सकती थीं, परन्तु उनमें संतान उत्पन्न करने की क्षमता नहीं होती थी। यदि पत्नियां फिजूल खर्च करती हैं, तो उसे पति के घर में दासी बनाकर रखा जाता था। **सेवाइन** का कहना है–"जुलाहे, बढ़ई, रंगरेज, ईंट बनाने वाले, सुनार, जौहरी, मूर्तिकार, कुम्हार, दर्जी, ठठेरे और शराब बनाने वाले अपना स्तर बनाये रखते थे और उनके अधिकारों की रक्षा की जाती थी। कारीगर अपने हुनर का स्तर कठोरता से बनाये रखते थे। सड़कों और नहरों का निर्माण कार्य बेगारों द्वारा कराया जाता था।" इस कथन से स्पष्ट होता है कि समाज कार्य के आधार पर विभिन्न समूहों में विभक्त हो चुका था।

संगीत तथा नृत्य आदि को काफी पसंद किया जाता था। बाँसुरी, ढोल आदि वाद्य यन्त्र भी थे। वेश्याओं के नृत्य और जलसों में नाच-गाने आदि होते रहते थे।

उत्सव आदि मंदिरों में ही बनाये जाते थे। इनमें संगीत पर वेश्याएँ नृत्य करती थीं। परिवार में पिता को उच्च स्थान प्राप्त था और पुत्र आज्ञाकारी होते थे। **प्लेट व जीन** के अनुसार–'यदि कोई पुत्र अपने पिता को पीटे, तो उसकी उँगलियाँ काट दी जाती थीं।' इस प्रकार बेबीलोन का समाज संगठित और सुखी था।

आर्थिक दशा

कृषि ही बेबीलोनियावासियों का एक मात्र व्यवसाय हुआ करता था। अधिकांश भूमि सम्राट, सामन्तों, धनी व्यापारियों और पुरोहितों की सम्पत्ति थी। गुलाम मुख्य रूप से कृषि का कार्य किया करते थे। भूमि उपजाऊ थी और अनाज की बहुत बड़ी-बड़ी बालियाँ आती थीं। वहाँ की मुख्य पैदावार अन्न, खजूर, जैतून व अंगूर आदि थे। **हेरोडोटस** के अनुसार 'बेबीलोन अन्न उत्पन्न करने में सबसे अधिक समृद्ध था।' लगान कृषि योग्य भूमि पर ही लगाया जाता था जब कभी बाढ़, तूफान या सूखे से फसल को नुकसान पहुँचता, तो किसान को अपनी बीबी या बच्चे बेचकर लगान चुकाना पड़ता था। सामान को पहिएदार गाड़ियों द्वारा शहरों की मण्डियों में लाया जाता था।

कृषि से संबंधित सभी प्रकार की व्यवस्थाएं बेबीलोनिया में की गईं थीं। वहाँ के शासकों ने कृषि के विकास के लिए कई नहरों का निर्माण करवाया था। बेबीलोनिया के प्रथम राजवंश के करीब-करीब सभी राजाओं ने नई नहरें बनवायीं और पुरानी नहरों की मरम्मत करवायी। हम्मूराबी ने भी कई बड़ी नहरों का निर्माण करवाया था, जिनमें से सबसे प्रसिद्ध नहर का नाम हम्मूराबी था। **हेरोडोटस** के शब्दों में–"उन सब देशों में, जिनकी हमें जानकारी है, कोई ऐसा देश नहीं है, जो अन्न उत्पन्न करने में इतना समृद्ध है। यह इतना समृद्ध है कि यह दो सौ गुना उत्पादन करता है।" कृषि के अतिरिक्त बेबीलोनिया में बागवानी और पशु-पालन की समुचित व्यवस्था थी वहाँ के लोग गाय, भेड़, बकरी, सुअर, गधा एवं ऊँट पालते थे।

व्यापार के क्षेत्र में भी बेबीलोनिया काफी आगे बढ़ चुका था। वह आर्मीनिया से ताँबा, सीरिया और ईरान से टिन, एलम से चाँदी, सीरिया से देवदार, मिस्र से सोना, अरब से मसाले तथा भारत से सागवान की लकड़ी तथा बहुमूल्य रत्नों का आयात करता था। बेबीलोनिया से मिट्टी के सुन्दर बर्तन, विभिन्न प्रकार के हथियार, सूती कपड़े, औजार, सुगन्धित द्रव्य, चमड़े का सामान और खाद्यान्न आदि वस्तुएँ विदेशों को निर्यात की जाती थीं।

प्राचीन काल में वस्तु-विनिमय ही व्यापार का माध्यम हुआ करता था, लेकिन कुछ समय बाद सोना और चाँदी विनिमय का साधन बन गए। हम्मूराबी के कानून द्वारा व्यापारिक बाधाओं को दूर कर दिया। पैसे की कमी होने पर व्यापारी हुण्डी लिखकर वस्तुओं का क्रय कर सकता था। उधार में धन देने का कार्य पुरोहितों द्वारा किया जाता था वे ब्याज पर ही धन दिया करते थे। उस दौरान मंदिरों में धन संग्रह किया जाता था अतः उनका इस्तेमाल बैंकों के रूप में किया जाता था। बैंक व्यवस्था का सर्वप्रथम विकास बेबीलोन में ही हुआ। हर चीज का शुल्क पर कानून का पूर्ण नियंत्रण था। डॉक्टरों द्वारा उस काल में किसी प्रकार की फीस लेने का विधान नहीं था। उस समय राज्य की तरफ से नाप-तोल के बाट निर्धारित थे, जिन्हें शेकल, मीना और टेलेन्ट की संज्ञा दी जाती थी। वस्तुओं के आयात व निर्यात के नियमों को मूर्त्त रूप दिया गया था। इससे स्पष्ट होता है कि व्यापार पर सरकार का कठोर नियंत्रण था।

मैकनेल बर्न्स का मानना था ''बेबीलोनिया के शासक स्वतंत्र प्रतियोगिता में विश्वास नहीं रखते थे। फिर भी, व्यापार, बैंकिंग और उद्योग-धन्धे राज्य द्वारा संचालित थे।'' **सेवाइन** के अनुसार, ''व्यापार सरकारी देख-रेख में चलता था।'' बेबीलोनियावासी आधुनिक सुखी एवं विलासी जीवन जीते थे क्योंकि वे आर्थिक दृष्टि से काफी संपन्न हुआ करते थे। **एच. जी. वेल्स** का कहना है कि, ''ये लोग अत्यन्त सुन्दर पदार्थों से सुसज्जित सुन्दर गृहों में निवास कर नियमपूर्वक आडम्बरसहित अपनी जीवन-यात्रा पूरी किया करते थे। रत्नादि धारण करते थे और कामदार बहुमूल्य वस्त्र धारण करते थे।''

उद्योग एवं व्यापार के क्षेत्र में भी बेबीलोनिया में काफी बल दिया गया था। वहां के निवासी ऊनी व सूती वस्त्रों का अधिक प्रयोग करते थे। उस दौरान मिट्टी के बर्तन तथा लकड़ियों से ढ़ेर सारी वस्तुएं तैयार की जाती थीं। कुछ वस्तुओं का कारखानों में विशाल पैमाने पर उत्पादन किया जाता था। कारखानों में अपने संघों का निर्माण करने में मजदूर ही महत्त्वपूर्ण भूमिका निभाते हैं। यहाँ के लोग एक फुट में 12 इंच नापते थे। इस क्षेत्र में बेबीलोन ने काफी योगदान किया था। वहाँ माल तैयार करने, खरीदने और बेचने के भी नियम बने हुए थे। काफिलों द्वारा ही व्यापार किया जाता था, जिन्हें सरकार की सुरक्षा प्राप्त थी।

धार्मिक अवस्था

बेबीलोन में धर्म का उद्देश्य मुक्ति प्राप्ति सुधारना न होकर भौतिक लाभ की प्राप्ति तथा भय से छुटकारा पाने पर अधिक ध्यान दिया जाता था। यहाँ के लोग

उन्हीं देवताओं की आराधना करते थे, जिनसे उन्हें भौतिक लाभ प्राप्त होता था या जिनसे विनाश का डर रहता था। वे भूत-प्रेतों की पूजा भी करते थे, ताकि वे प्रसन्न हो जाएँ और विनाश न करें।

परलोक का उल्लेख 'गिलगमेश आख्यान' नामक महाकाव्य में किया गया है जिसमें बेबीलोन के लोगों के विचार अस्पष्ट थे। इस महाकाव्य के बारहवें खण्ड में यह उल्लेख किया गया है कि जब गिलगमेश अपनी वृद्धावथा में परलोक का रहस्य जानना चाहता है, तब अपने मित्र एनकीडू की मृत्यु के बाद एक बार पुनः उससे मिलने के लिए रोता और बिलखता है। देवता ने उसके मित्र एनकीडू की आत्मा को उसके पास ऐसी स्थिति उत्पन्न होने पर वापस दिया था। तब एनकीडू की आत्मा या प्रेत गिलगमेश से कहता है कि यदि मृत्यु के बाद कब्र में सामान और भोजन आदि नहीं रखा जाता है, तो उस आदमी के शरीर को कीड़े चाट जाते हैं। इसके बाद मृतक प्रेत बनकर सड़कों पर घूमते हैं, मल खाते हैं और गन्दी नाली का पानी पीते हैं यही कारण था कि बेबीलोन के लोगों का मानना था कि मृत्यु के बाद मनुष्य परलोक में जाता है। इसीलिए व्यक्ति के शव के साथ कब्र में भोजन और उसकी प्रिय वस्तुओं को रखा जाता था। ताकि वह व्यक्ति परलोक में शान्तिपूर्वक जीवन व्यतीत कर सके। ऐसा नहीं करने पर वे भूत-प्रेत बनकर दूसरों को कष्ट देते थे। उनकी आत्मा को शांति नहीं मिलती थी।

पुरोहित वर्ग को प्राचीन बेबीलोनिया में तीन भागों में विभाजित किया गया था—प्रथम वर्ग उन पुजारियों का था जो जादू के द्वारा दानवों को भगाकर लोगों की रक्षा करते थे। जो पुजारी भविष्यवाणी किया करते थे उन्हें दूसरे वर्ग में रखा गया था। तीसरा वर्ग उन पुजारियों का था, जो संगीत के माध्यम से मन्दिरों में देवताओं की प्रार्थना करते थे।

पुजारियों को इस युग में उच्च स्थान प्राप्त था। वे जादू-टोना करते, भूतों से लोगों की रक्षा करते थे। अतः लोग उनके कृपापात्र बनने का प्रयास करते थे, ताकि उनके भय से भूत-प्रेत दूर ही रहें। जादू-टोना असफल रहने पर उनको राजा की तरफ से कठोर दण्ड दिया जाता था। इस तरह जनता पुरोहितों तथा राजाओं से भयभीत रहती थी। समस्त धार्मिक कार्य पुजारियों के द्वारा किये जाते थे। ये देवता और आदमी के बीच मध्यस्थ का कार्य करते थे। पुजारियों के एक विशेष वर्ग को देवज्ञ कहते थे, जिनका प्रमुख कार्य अच्छे मुहूर्त और शकुन बताना था। देवज्ञ अच्छे और बुरे की भविष्यवाणी पहले से ही कर देते थे। ये देवज्ञ देवताओं को भेड़ की बलि चढ़ाते थे और भेड़ के जिगर के चिह्न को देखकर भविष्यवाणी करते थे। जिसे अपना

भविष्य जानना होता था, वह देवज्ञों को एक भेड़ बलि चढ़ाने के लिए देता था। बकरों का प्रयोग बलि चढ़ाने के लिये किया जाता था। यदि कोई व्यक्ति किसी देवता के क्रोध के कारण बीमार पड़ जाता था, तो उस देवता को प्रसन्न करने के लिए सुअर की बलि दी जाती थी।

ज्योतिषियों को पुरोहितों के दूसरे वर्ग में स्थान दिया गया था। ये नक्षत्रों का अध्ययन करके उनका राज्य पर शुभ-अशुभ प्रभाव बताते थे। इन लोगों के द्वारा पंचांग का निर्माण किया जाता था और नये वर्ष का नामकरण भी करते थे। हर साल का नामकरण किया जाता था, जो धार्मिक रूप से काफी महत्त्वपूर्ण होता था। यूरोपवासियों को ज्योतिष विद्या का ज्ञान बेबीलोनियावासियों से ही प्राप्त हुआ था। वहाँ एक अशिष्ट प्रथा यह थी कि जिन स्त्रियों को संतान उत्पन्न नहीं होती थी उन्हें हर पुरुष के साथ संबंध स्थापित करना होता था। इस वेश्यावृत्ति से प्राप्त धन का मन्दिर के लिए उपयोग किया जाता था।

पुजारियों का वर्गीकरण तीसर स्थल पर किया गया था, जिनका कार्य संगीत के माध्यम से मंदिरों में देवताओं की प्रार्थनाएँ करना और मंत्र अर्पित करना होता था। मंदिरों में पुजारी साँझ और सवेरे देवताओं की पूजा करते थे। इनके मंदिरों का निर्माण बीच चौराहे में किया जाता था। पशुओं की बलि देवताओं को खुश करने के लिये दी जाती थी। मंदिरों में तरह-तरह के चढ़ावे चढ़ाये जाते थे, जो पुजारियों के काम आते थे। पूजा में श्रद्धा तथा भक्ति का सर्वथा अभाव रहता था। पूजा करने के लिए धूप-दीप का प्रयोग किया जाता था तथा देवताओं की उपासना की जाती थी। एक भक्ति गीत में लिखा है—"जो पाप मैंने किया मैं नहीं जानता, मेरे देव ने मुझसे क्रोधित होकर दर्शन दिये, मैंने तो सहायता की प्रार्थना की, परन्तु किसी ने मेरा कर नहीं पकड़ा, मैं रोया, पर किसी ने न सुना, मैं अपने दयालु देवता की शरण में जाकर प्रार्थना करता हूँ। ए प्रभु! कब तक ए देव!! अपने इस दास को भूल मत जा, बल्कि मेरे पाप को एक वरदान में बदल दे।"

बेबीलोन के वासी ढेर सारे देवी-देवताओं की पूजा करते थे। प्रत्येक नगर, परिवार तथा व्यक्ति का अपना अलग-अलग देवता होता था। उस दौरान खेत-नदियां तथा पहाड़ों की पूजा-अर्चना करने का विधान था। विद्वानों के अनुसार इस युग में 65 हजार देवताओं की पूजा करने का विधान था। उनमें प्रमुख थे सूर्य (शमास, एटन या एनलिल) था। इसके अतिरिक्त अनु (आकाश का देवता), अन्नर (चन्द्रमा), तमुज (वनस्पति और उपज का देवता), ईश्तर (प्रेम की देवी) आदि देवी-देवताओं की यहाँ पूजा की जाती थी। देवताओं को प्रसन्न करने हेतु बलि देने का विधान था। बेबीलोन

के खास देवता सूर्य तथा मारदुक (सूर्य का पुत्र) को माना जाता था। यहाँ के लोगों के मतानुसार सूर्य तथा मारदुक ने राक्षसों या अशुरों को पराजित कर पृथ्वी पर शान्ति की स्थापना की थी। बेबीलोनिया में मारदुक का विशाल मन्दिर स्थित था, जिसमें हम्मूराबी ने अपनी विधि संहिता पत्थर पर अंकित करवाई थी। सूर्य का प्रसिद्ध मन्दिर लारसा नगर में बना हुआ था। बेबीलोनिया के लोग यहाँ के देवताओं को शरीरधारी मानते थे, जो खाना खाते थे, स्त्रियों को सन्तान दे सकते थे, मन्दिरों में रहते थे और पुजारियों से सेवा करवाते थे।

साहित्य एवं दर्शन

साहित्य के क्षेत्र में बेबीलोनिया ने काफी उन्नति की थी। सर्वप्रथम 'गिलगमेश' नामक महाकाव्य की रचना हुई। इस महाकाव्य में 12 अध्याय हैं जो 12 महीनों के प्रतीक हैं। मानव जीवन के संघर्षों के सजीव विवेचन की चर्चा इसमें मुख्य रूप से की गई है। इसमें मंत्र, गीत एवं प्रार्थनाएँ भी हैं। महाकाव्य में वर्णित धार्मिक शिक्षाओं का सार इस प्रकार है—"अपने माता-पिता का भरण-पोषण और आदर करो, बड़ों के हितों की रक्षा करो, अशिष्टता और घृणा से दूर रहो। बोलने में जल्दबाजी न करो आदि-आदि। वस्तुतः यह महाकाव्य विश्व सभ्यता को बेबीलोनिया की एक अमूल्य देन माना जाता है।"

इस महाकाव्य के अन्तर्गत गिलगमेश की अमर होने की भावना तथा पाताल के विषय में जानने की जिद्द आदि तथ्यों को बाद में समावेश किया गया है। इसमें युद्ध, साहसपूर्ण कार्य, मित्रता, स्त्री का प्रेम तथा घृणा आदि का उल्लेख है। पश्चिमी एशिया में इस महाकाव्य का विशेष रूप से प्रभाव रहा है। कुछ समय पश्चात् अन्य भाषाओं में भी इसका अनुवाद हुआ।

गिलगमेश नामक महाकाव्य में यह उल्लेख किया गया है कि उरूक राज्य का राजा गिलगमेश था जो अत्यधिक निरंकुश और शक्तिशाली था। वह अपनी प्रजा पर बहुत अत्याचार करता था। अतः जनता के आग्रह पर गिलगमेश की माँ ने मिट्टी के एक ढेले से एनकीडू नामक अत्यन्त शक्तिशाली व्यक्ति पैदा किया। एनकीडू को गिलमगेश की हत्या करने के लिए कहा गया किंतु वह सफल नहीं हुआ। ऐसी स्थिति में इन दोनों में मित्रता हो गई। दोनों ने मिलकर स्वर्ग के वृषभ तथा एलम के दैत्य हुबाबा का सर्वनाश किया। उनकी इस वीरता से प्यार की देवी ईश्तर एनकीडू पर मोहित हो गई, किन्तु इस वीर ने उसे अपमानित कर भगा दिया। इस पर ईश्तर ने श्राप दिया कि तेरी मृत्यु बहुत जल्दी और बीमारी की अवस्था में होगी। ईश्तर के

श्राप से एनकीडू काल का ग्रास बन गया था। उसकी मृत्यु गिलगमेश के लिये काफी कष्टकारी सिद्ध हुई थी। गिलगमेश यह जानना चाहता था कि पाताल का जीवन कैसा है? अतः देवता द्वारा तरस खाकर उसको कुछ समय के लिए फिर से जीवन दान दे दिया जाता था। तब एनकीडू परलोक यात्रा के बारे में गिलगमेश को जानकारी देता है। इस महाकाव्य में दर्शन, शौर्य, मित्रता, स्त्री का प्रेम और घृणा आदि प्रसंगों पर अधिक बल दिया गया है।

इस काल में गिलगमेश नामक महाकाव्य के अलावा कई कविताएं और कहानियाँ भी लिखी गई थीं। उस दौरान 'भाग्यलेख', 'एटन गड़रिए की कथा', 'मानव की आकाश में उड़ने की सबसे प्राचीन कहानी', 'अमद मछुए की कहानी' आदि प्रमुख कथाएं थीं। इन कथाओं के अतिरिक्त देवस्रोत और पूजा गीतों का भी साहित्य में महत्त्वपूर्ण स्थान है। इन गीतों के माध्यम से मनुष्य अपने पापों को स्वीकार करता था और उनके लिए देवताओं से माफी माँगता था।

दर्शन से बेबीलोनियावासियों को काफी लगाव था। न्यायप्रिय जीवन बिताने पर भी मृत्यु क्यों होती है? मृत्यु के बाद व्यक्ति कहाँ जाता है? मृत्युदण्ड क्यों दिया जाता है? सदाचारी व्यक्ति कष्ट क्यों पाते हैं? आदि अनेक प्रश्न उनके सामने थे। गिलगमेश काव्य में मृत्यु के रहस्य की पहेली को सुलझाने का काफी प्रयास किया गया है। सदाचारी को कष्ट पाते देखकर एक कवि ने कहा है—"अलु रोग ने मेरे शरीर को वस्त्र की तरह ढक लिया है। निद्रा ने अपने जाल में मुझे फँसा लिया है, मेरे नेत्र खुले हैं पर देख नहीं सकते, मेरे कान खुले हैं पर सुन नहीं सकते, निर्बलता ने मेरे शरीर को जकड़ा हुआ है।" इस प्रकार सदाचारी व्यक्ति कष्ट पाकर क्यों मरते हैं? इस प्रश्न का यह उत्तर था—"हमारी दृष्टि सीमित है तथा हम देवताओं का रहस्य नहीं समझ सकते।" बेबीलोनिया के निवासियों के अनुसार मनुष्य पर देवताओं की कृपा दृष्टि होती है और मृत्यु के पश्चात् उसको अपने कार्यों के अनुसार स्वर्ग तथा नर्क की प्राप्ति होती है। उस दौरान नैतिकता पर अधिक बल दिया जाता था। देवता के सामने सच बोलना, घमण्ड से बचना, अधिक खुशी में अपने होठों को बन्द रखना आदि उस काल के कुछ प्रमुख उपदेश थे।

कला

बेबीलोनिया शासकों के शासनकाल में कला के क्षेत्र में भी प्रगति हुई। यहाँ पर स्थापत्यकला, चित्रकला, मूर्तिकला तथा संगीत कला आदि का पर्याप्त विकास हुआ। बेबीलोन के लोग अन्य सभ्यताओं की अपेक्षा कला के क्षेत्र में काफी पीछे थे।

उस समय विशाल एवं ऊँचे देवालयों का निर्माण किया जाता था, जिनकी सबसे ऊपर की एक बुर्ज सोने से अलंकृत की जाती थी। मंदिरों के सामने पिरामिडों की भांति 'जिग्गुरात' का निर्माण करते थे जो उनकी कला के उत्कृष्ट नमूने हैं। बेबीलोन के लोग जिग्गुरात को 'सितारों का मंच' कहकर पुकारते थे। इनमें सबसे ऊपर सूर्य देवता का मंदिर होता था, इस मन्दिर का रंग सुनहरा होता था। सबसे नीचे की मंजिल काली होती थी, जिसमें शनि देवता का मंदिर होता था। जिग्गुरात ऊपर से पतले होते थे। भवन-निर्माण में मेहराब का भी निर्माण किया जाता था और इनके द्वारा बनाये गये भवन आकर्षक नहीं थे। **डॉ. गोयल** ने लिखा है कि, "कला के क्षेत्र में बेबीलोनियन जाति मिस्रवासियों से बहुत पीछे थी।"

कालान्तर में यूरोपियों ने बेबीलोन के लोगों से मेहराब तथा मीनार बनाने की कला सीखी। बेबीलोन के एक जिग्गुरात की ऊँचाई 600 फीट थी। डेल और बेबीलोन के जिग्गुरात उस समय की स्थापत्य-कला के शानदार नमूने हैं। इस संदर्भ में **बिल ड्यूरेन्ट** ने लिखा है कि "व्यापार, वाणिज्य, कामुकतापूर्ण मनोरंजन और इनको सन्तुलित करने के लिए बरती जाने वाली धार्मिकता से पूर्ण बेबीलोनिया के जीवन में थोड़ी-सी कलाप्रियता और रचनात्मकता भी शेष रह गयी थी।" राजदरबार में शाही मोहर के रूप में बनी हुई सीलें कला की शानदार नमूना थीं। इनमें संगीत और नृत्य की मुद्राएँ अंकित थीं। **सेवाइन** ने लिखा है कि "सीलें सुन्दर बनती थीं और हर आदमी की अपनी अलग सील होती थी, जिस पर विपरीत दिशाओं में मुँह किये सिर ऊपर की तरफ किये दो बैल देवता द्वारा गिराये गये पानी को पीते हैं। इनके ऊपर आदमी का नाम अंकित होता था। इससे पता चलता है कि वे पानी को ईश्वर की देन मानते थे।"

खिलौनों की दृष्टि से बेबीलोन काफी प्रसिद्ध था। यहाँ के बने खिलौने जैसे—बन्दर, गाड़ी, गाय, गधा, हिरण और शेर के खिलौने कला की दृष्टि से उत्कृष्ट कोटि के थे। बेबीलोन में सोने-चांदी पर नक्काशी का काम होता था। यहां के मुलायम कालीन और दरियाँ विश्व में प्रसिद्ध थीं। लकड़ी का बढ़िया फर्नीचर बनता था। इस प्रकार बेबीलोन के मंदिर, जिग्गुरात, खिलौने व सीलों की कला के प्रतीक हैं।

बेबीलोन के चित्रकार दीवारों की सजावट करने के लिये विभिन्न प्रकार के रंग-बिरंगें चित्रों का निर्माण करते थे। साधारण चित्रों में राजाओं, पशुओं एवं प्रकृति के चित्रों को शामिल किया जाता था। इन चित्रों में सात रंगों का प्रयोग किया जाता था। बेबीलोन के राजमहलों तथा देवालयों की दीवारों पर बहुत चित्र प्राप्त हुए हैं।

इनकी चित्रकला के कुछ नमूने आज भी जर्मनी के अजायबघरों में संभालकर रखे गये हैं।

बेबीलोनवासियों को संगीत से काफी लगाव था। देवालयों में धार्मिक उत्सवों के अवसर पर सामूहिक गानों में गायक लोग गाना गाते थे तथा महिलाओं द्वारा मंदिरों में नृत्य किया जाता था। उस समय के प्रमुख बाद्य-यन्त्र–बाँसुरी, बीन, सारंगी एवं ढोल आदि थे। बेबीलोन में विभिन्न प्रकार की मूर्तियों का निर्माण किया जाता था। यहाँ के कलाकार पत्थरों की विशालकाय मूर्तियाँ बनाते थे दासों तथा राजाओं की प्राप्त मूर्तियों से इस बात की पुष्टि होती है।

ज्ञान विज्ञान

शब्दकोश का आविष्कार बेबीलोन में ही हुआ था। उस दौरान अध्यापन का कार्य मंदिरों में किया जाता था। विद्यार्थियों को विद्यालयों में मिट्टी की तख्तियों पर शिक्षा दी जाती थी जिन्हें अभ्यास पुस्तक कहा जाता था। मिट्टियों से निर्मित ये तख्तियाँ जब गीली होती थीं, तब इन मिट्टी की तख्तियों पर शब्द लिखा जाता था और सूखने पर इन्हें पकाकर मिट्टी के चौकोर भाँडों में टाँड पर रख दिया जाता था। इस प्रकार की 30,000 तख्तियाँ बोर्शिया के एक पुस्तकालय में पाई गयी हैं।

हम्मूराबी काल के विद्यालय का अवशेष पाया गया है। यह विद्यालय एक मंजिल का 55 वर्गफुट के क्षेत्र में था और इसकी इमारत ईंटों की बनी हुई थी। इस विद्यालय में 4000 वर्ष पुरानी अभ्यास पुस्तकें पायी गई हैं। एक छात्र की तख्ती पर एक मुहावरा लिखा है–"जो सुन्दर लेख लिखने में निपुणता प्राप्त करेंगे, वे सूर्य के समान चमकेंगे।" यहाँ छात्रों को कानून, धर्म, दर्शन, ज्योतिष, इतिहास, भूगोल, गणित एवं विदेशी भाषा आदि विषयों का अध्यापन कराया जाता था। लड़कों को इसके अतिरिक्त धनुष चलाने तथा आखेट खेलने की भी शिक्षा प्रदान की जाती थी। लड़कियों को संगीत और नृत्य का ज्ञान दिया जाता था।

कीलक्षार लिपि को अपनाने से पूर्व बेबीलोनियावासियों ने काफी बदलाव किये थे। उनकी लिपि में 300 शब्द थे यहाँ पढ़े-लिखे आदमी को काम आसानी से मिल जाता था। बेबीलोन की भाषा सर्वप्रथम पढ़ने का श्रेय अंग्रेज राजदूत हेनरी रॉलिन्सन को जाता है, जिसने 12 वर्ष (1835-47) के कठोर परिश्रम के बाद मेडिया के पहाड़ों में बहिस्तान नामक स्थान पर 300 फुट ऊँची दुर्गम चट्टान पर खुदा हुआ लेख पढ़कर बेबीलोन की काँटेदार लिपि को स्पष्ट किया।

गणित के क्षेत्र में बेबीलोन ने काफी विकास किया था। उन्होंने गुणा करने की पद्धति तथा 1, 10 और 100 के तीन अंकों का सर्वप्रथम आविष्कार किया। इनको दशमलव प्रणाली का ज्ञान था तथा ये 1 से 9 तक की संख्याएँ भी लिख सकते थे। चार लिखने के लिए एक चिह्न को चार बार लिखते थे। इसी प्रकार दस, बीस, तीस तथा उसके बाद फिर साठ का एक चिह्न था, जिससे वे बड़ी-बड़ी संख्याएँ लिख सकते थे।

ज्योतिष के क्षेत्र में बेबीलोन के निवासियों ने काफी प्रगति की थी। यहाँ के पण्डित लोग जिग्गुरात की ऊपर की मंजिल में बैठकर नक्षत्रों का अध्ययन करते थे। उनकी धारणा थी कि आकाश के नक्षत्र मानव को सुख-दुःख देने वाले हैं। यहाँ के ज्योतिषी नक्षत्रों के ज्ञान के आधार पर सूर्य व चन्द्र ग्रहण की भविष्यवाणी करते थे। ये लोग कलैण्डर भी बनाते थे। ज्योतिषी धूप-घड़ी तथा जल-घड़ी द्वारा समय का पता लगा लेते थे, उनके अनुसार एक वर्ष में 12 महीने, एक दिन में 12 घण्टे तथा एक घण्टे में 60 मिनट होते थे। इस ज्ञान के कारण बेबीलोन ने **'खगोलविद्या को माता'** की उपाधि दी गयी है। बेबीलोन के लोग समुद्र में आने वाले तूफानों व हवाओं की भविष्यवाणी कर देते थे। **टॉयनबी** ने लिखा है कि "बेबीलोनिया के ज्योतिष अध्ययन ने ही ज्योतिष की नींव रखी है।"

हालांकि ये लोग अत्यधिक अंधविश्वासी थे। इसके अलावा भी बेबीलोनवासियों ने चिकित्सा विज्ञान जगत में काफी उन्नति की। यहाँ के लोग बीमारियों का इलाज करना जानते थे। इस सन्दर्भ में वूले ने लिखा है कि "औषधियाँ विकसित थीं और प्रत्येक रोग के लिए विशेष प्रकार की थीं, परन्तु यह माना जाता था कि रोग किसी भूत-पिशाच के प्रभाव के कारण हुआ है और उपचार भूत-प्रेत का झाड़ा दिये बिना नहीं हो सकता।" यहाँ के लोगों को यह विश्वास था कि रोग अथवा बीमारी होने का प्रमुख कारण भूत-प्रेत ही है।

अतः दवा के स्थान पर वे जादू-मंत्र, टोना एवं ताबीज का अधिक प्रयोग करते थे। रोगी के शरीर से प्रेत को भगाने के लिए दवाओं में साँप का मांस, धूल, सड़ा हुआ भोजन, चर्बी, तेल, कच्चा मांस, पिसी हुई हड्डी और मल-मूत्र पिलाते थे। ईलाज के दौरान जब किसी रोगी की मौत हो जाती थी तब सजा डॉक्टर को दी जाती थी उसके एक या दोनों हाथ काट दिये जाते थे।

सभ्यता का पतन

17वीं सदी ई.पू. विलासी जीवन व्यतीत करने के कारण केस्साइट बेबीलोन पर कब्जा नहीं कर सके थे। इतिहासकार **जेकाइस पिरेनी** के अनुसार, "केस्साइट

जाति के जंगली लोगों ने 17वीं शताब्दी ई. पू. में राजगद्दी ग्रहण की थी। सुमेरियन नगरों का पूर्ण पतन हो गया और बेबीलोन का सम्राट खानाबदोश लोगों से पराजित हो गया। केवल एक शहर बेबीलोन रहा, किन्तु वह भी राजधानी की सीमा क्षेत्र से बाहर था।

वास्तव में इस सभ्यता को एक जीवन्त सभ्यता की संज्ञा भी दी जाती है। इसने यूनान और रोम के माध्यम से यूरोपीय सभ्यता पर काफी गहरा असर छोड़ा था। यही नहीं, अरबों के माध्यम से मुस्लिम सभ्यता पर भी अपनी अमिट छाप छोड़ी। इन्हीं विशेषताओं के कारण प्राचीन बेबीलोनिया की सभ्यता विश्व की प्राचीन सभ्यताओं के अंतर्गत काफी उल्लेखनीय है। **सेवाइन** का मानना है कि, ''वास्तव में बेबीलोनिया ने ज्ञान के सागर के अज्ञात मार्गों को अंकित किया। उनके प्रबुद्ध लोग आने वाली कई शताब्दियों के विद्वानों के लिए मार्गदर्शक के संकेत बने रहे।'' **हर्नशा** ने लिखा है कि ''उनकी सभ्यता हमारे विधि-विधान, हमारे ज्योतिष ज्ञान, कलैण्डर, समय विभाजन आदि में आज भी जीवित है।''

विश्व को देन

प्राचीन बेबीलोनिया की सभ्यता विश्व की प्राचीन सभ्यताओं में एक मानी जाती है। दक्षिण पश्चिमी एशिया तथा यूनान की सभ्यता के विकास में बेबीलोनिया की सभ्यता ने महत्त्वपूर्ण भूमिका निभायी है। इसने मानव सभ्यता एवं संस्कृति पर गहरा असर छोड़ा है। बेबीलोन ने माप-प्रणाली का आविष्कार किया, जिससे लम्बाई, समय, तौल आदि नापा जा सकता था, गिना जा सकता था। **बिल ड्यूरेन्ट** के अनुसार ''एक मास का चार सप्ताहों में, घड़ी का 12 घण्टों में, घण्टे का 60 मिनट में और मिनट का 60 सेकण्डों में विभाजन बेबीलोन के अवशेष हैं।'' गणित, ज्योतिष, इतिहास, चिकित्सा, व्याकरण और दर्शन आदि की नींव बेबीलोन ने ही डाली है। बेबीलोनिया की सभ्यता में नगर राज्यों का उदय हुआ। **टॉयनबी** ने लिखा है कि ''ज्योतिष का प्रसार यहीं से हुआ। अतः भारत को इनका ऋणी होनी चाहिए।''

मानव सभ्यता के इतिहास में हम्मूराबी की विधि संहिता का अत्यधिक महत्त्व है। यहाँ के झूलते हुए बगीचे संसार के महान् आश्चर्यों में से एक हैं। बेबीलोन के लोगों ने महाकाव्य तथा लोकप्रिय कथाओं की रचना की। इन्होंने ही 12 राशियों, ग्रहों एवं नक्षत्रों के नाम रखे, सप्ताह के सात दिनों का नाम रखा। संसार ने इनसे ही मीनारें, मस्जिदें एवं गुम्बज बनाना सीखा। उन्होंने एक कलैण्डर भी तैयार किया। आज का कलैण्डर बेबीलोनिया के कलैण्डर पर आधारित है। इतिहासकार **हर्नशा** ने

बेबीलोन की विश्व को देन के सम्बन्ध में लिखा है, "उनकी सभ्यता हमारे विधि-विधान, हमारे ज्योतिष ज्ञान, पंचांग, समय विभाजन, तराजू-बाट, दर्जनों की गिनती में आज भी विद्यमान है। सम्भवतः गेहूँ की खेती, गिर्टी और पहिये का प्रयोग आदि बातें हमें उन्हीं से प्राप्त हुई हैं।" इस संदर्भ में **सेवाइन** का मानना है कि "बाद के विकास के लिए आधारभूमि के रूप में बेबीलोनियन सभ्यता के महत्त्व की अब पूरी तरह प्रशंसा की जा रही है।"

असीरिया की सभ्यता

असीरिया की सभ्यता का नाम अशुर नगर के नाम पर पड़ा जो सेमेटिक जाति के लोगों द्वारा दजला नदी के तट पर बसाया गया था। सेमेटिक जाति ने 700 वर्षों तक यहाँ राज्य किया। प्राचीनकाल में दजला नदी की ऊपरी घाटी के प्रदेश को असीरिया के नाम से पुकारा जाता था। चारों ओर पहाड़ियों से घिरा हुआ यह एक उपजाऊ प्रदेश था जो आजकल इराक का हिस्सा है।

तिगलथ पिलेसर प्रथम यहाँ का प्रथम शक्तिशाली राजा था, जिसने लगभग 1105 ई. पू. में शासन किया। वह बहुत ही बहादुर और प्रतापी शासक था। अपने शासनकाल में उसने सीरिया पर आक्रमण किया था और मिश्र से राजनयिक सम्बंध स्थापित किये थे। इस योद्धा ने बेबीलोन, आर्मीनिया और मिस्र तक अपना प्रभाव स्थापित किया। तिगलथ की मृत्यु के बाद 200 वर्षों तक यहाँ के इतिहास में अंधकार युग बना रहा। तिगलथ के बाद अशुर नासिरपाल द्वितीय ने पुनः असीरिया की सैन्य शक्ति का विस्तार किया। उसने 884 ई. पू. से 859 ई. पू. तक राज्य किया। वह विजित प्रदेशों में अपनी क्रूरता से आतंक फैला देता था। लूटपाट में इसे काफी सम्पत्ति और बहुत बड़ी संख्या में युद्ध बंदी मिले। अशुर नासिरपाल द्वितीय के बाद उसका पुत्र शाल मेनेसर तृतीय गद्दी पर बैठा। उसका शासन-काल 859 ई. से 824 ई.पू. तक था। अपने पिता के समान वह भी एक महान् विजेता था। उसने बेबीलोन को पराजित किया और वहाँ के शासक द्वारा वार्षिक कर देने पर शासन का भार उसे सौंप दिया। शाल मेनेसर तृतीय ने टौरस और सिलसिया को अपने कब्जे में कर लिया था। उसके बाद तिगलथ पिलेसर तृतीय ने शासन किया। उसके शासनकाल में असीरिया ने अपने खोये हुए वैभव को पुनः प्राप्त कर लिया। उसका शासनकाल 745 ई. पू. से 727 ई. पू. तक था। वह एक महान विजेता था। उसने एक अनुशासित सेना की स्थापना की। उसने बेबीलोनिया, दमिश्क तथा इजराइल पर विजय प्राप्त की। उसकी मृत्यु के उपरांत उसका सेनापति सारगन द्वितीय ने राजगद्दी ग्रहण की।

सारगन द्वितीय तिगलथ पिलेसर का सेनापति था। उसकी मृत्यु के पश्चात् सारगन ने राज्य पर अधिकार कर लिया व स्वयं शासक बन बैठा। उसमें योग्य शासक के सभी गुण विद्यमान थे जिसका शासनकाल 722 ई. पू. से 705 ई. पू. तक था। सारगन द्वितीय ने ही असीरियन साम्राज्य की नींव रखी। वह एक महत्त्वाकांक्षी शासक था, जिसने कई युद्धों में विजय प्राप्त की थी। सारगन द्वितीय ने इजराइल पर अधिकार कर उसे अपने साम्राज्य का एक प्रान्त बना दिया। उसने मिस्र के राजा की सेना को राफिया नामक स्थान पर पराजित किया। इसके बाद अरब प्रायद्वीप के दक्षिण में स्थित यीमेन तक अपने राज्य का प्रसार किया। मिस्र के बाद सारगन द्वितीय ने बेबीलोनिया और एलम के शासकों को युद्ध में हरा दिया गया। सारगन द्वितीय ने सुमेरियन एवं वान प्रदेश में रहने वाली बर्बर जातियों को पराजित कर अपने राज्य की उत्तरी सीमा में सुरक्षा के सभी प्रयास किये। सारगन द्वितीय के बाद उसका पुत्र सेन्नाचेरिब को राजगद्दी सौंपी गई। उसने अपने शासन के प्रारम्भिक वर्षों में अपनी राजधानी निन्वेह के सौन्दर्य एवं सजावट में वृद्धि की। उसने यहाँ के पुस्तकालय को भी समृद्ध बनाया। वह भी एक महान योद्धा तथा कुशल प्रशासक था। उसने अपने विशाल साम्राज्य में सभी विद्रोहों का अंत कर दिया तथा मिस्र तथा बेबीलोन के विद्रोहों को भी कुशलता से दबा दिया। उसने अपने साम्राज्य को प्रान्तों एवं जिलों में विभाजित कर दिया। व्यापार के विकास हेतु सड़कों का जाल बिछा दिया गया और डाक व्यवस्था का काफी विकास किया गया। सेन्नाचेरिब ने अपनी राजधानी निन्वेह नगर की रक्षा के लिए उसके चारों और दीवार का निर्माण करवाया। साथ ही एक नहर का निर्माण करवाया, ताकि जनता को पानी उपलब्ध हो सके। दुर्भाग्यवश सेन्नाचेरिब का उसके लड़के ने वध कर दिया। सेन्नाचेरिब की हत्या के बाद उसके पुत्रों में गृहयुद्ध आरम्भ हो गया, जिसमें पितृघाती पुत्र के छोटे भाई एसरहादेन को सफलता मिली और वह गद्दी पर बैठा। एसरहादेन ने 12 वर्ष तक शासन किया। वह बड़ा पराक्रमी एवं प्रजावत्सल सम्राट था। उसने अपने पिता द्वारा ध्वस्त बेबीलोन नगर का पुनर्निर्माण करवाया और वहाँ के निवासियों को पुनः वहाँ बसा दिया। उसने मिस्र तक अपने साम्राज्य का विस्तार किया और 'मिस्र के राजाओं का सम्राट' नामक उपाधि धारण की। वह एक कुशल प्रशासक था। उसने प्रांतों में गर्वनर नियुक्त किये। उसने 671 ई. पू. में मिस्र पर अधिकार कर लिया और नील की पश्चिमी घाटी में साई राज्य के अधीनस्थ राजा नेको को मिस्र में गवर्नर नियुक्त कर दिया। एसरहादेन के मिस्र से रवाना होते ही मिस्र में विद्रोह हो गया। इस विद्रोह का दमन करने के लिए वह रवाना हुआ, परन्तु मार्ग में ही उसकी मृत्यु हो गई। उसके

बाद अशुर बनिपाल 669 ई. पू. में असीरिया की गद्दी पर बैठा। वह असीरिया का अन्तिम प्रतापी और प्रसिद्ध शासक था। इसके राज्यकाल में असीरिया की शानशौकत और समृद्धि अपनी पराकाष्ठा पर पहुँच चुकी थी। अशुर बनिपाल का साम्राज्य बेबीलोन, मीडिया, फिनिशिया, सुमेरिया तथा एलम तक फैला था। उसने मिस्र को स्वतंत्र होने दिया तथा स्वाधीनता की प्राप्ति के बाद मिस्र के शासक सामेटिकस को अपना मित्र बना लिया। एलम के शिलालेख से पता चलता है कि अशुर बनिपाल के शासनकाल में सांस्कृतिक विकास अपनी चरम सीमा पर जा पहुँचा। उसकी मृत्यु के पश्चात् असीरिया का पतन हो गया।

प्रशासन व्यवस्था एवं कानून

पुरातात्विक साक्ष्यों से यह पता चलता है कि असीरिया के सम्राट युद्ध के समय क्रूर व अत्याचारी बनकर नगरों को जलाते थे और युद्धबंदियों का कत्ल कर देते थे। कई बार युद्ध बंदियों के अंग-भंग कर देते थे। युद्ध में शत्रु को आतंकित करने के लिए उनकी खाल खिंचवा देते थे। इन कार्यों को करने में उनको बहुत आनंद प्राप्त होता था। असीरिया में ऐसी धारण थी कि अशुर देवता राज्य की समस्त भूमि का स्वामी था तथा उसी के नाम पर राजधानी का नामकरण किया गया था। असीरिया का राजा उस देवता का प्रतिनिधि मात्र था। विजित प्रदेश पर उस देवता का अधिकार माना जाता था तथा असीरिया के शत्रु उस देवता के शत्रु माने जाते थे, इसलिए शत्रुओं को काफी सजा दी जाती थी। असीरिया के शासकों ने अपनी युद्ध नीति की सफलता तथा अपनी क्रूरता के द्वारा आसपास के प्रदेशों तथा विजित देशों को आतंकित कर रखा था। इस सभ्यता के उत्थान और पतन के लिए भी इस जाति की सैनिक प्रतिभा को जवाबदेह ठहराया जा सकता था।

असीरिया के सम्राट निरंकुश थे तथा शासन व्यवस्था काफी सुदृढ़ थी। वहां के सम्राट दैविक सिद्धांत के अनुसार प्रजा पर शासन करते थे। पुरोहितों के अपशकुन से यहां के राजा काफी भयभीत होते थे और परम्परागत नियमों को मानते थे। युद्ध के दौरान यहां के प्रमुख देवता 'अशुर' को प्रसन्न करने के लिए भयंकर अत्याचार किये जाते थे। उस दौरान सम्राट काफी शक्तिशाली हुआ करते थे।

असीरियाई सभ्यता अपने कुशल सैन्य संगठन के कारण प्राचीन विश्व के इतिहास में उसका काफी महत्त्व था। राजा सेना का सर्वोच्च नायक होता था। उसके पश्चात् लिम्मू नामक पदाधिकारी सेनाध्यक्ष होता था, जिसे 'तुर्तान' कहा जाता था। युद्ध नीति में विश्व की कोई भी प्राचीन सभ्यता उसकी बराबरी करने की क्षमता नहीं

रखती थी। असीरिया के सम्राटों ने अपने साम्राज्य में कुशल शासन-प्रबंध स्थापित किया। उन्होंने शासन संचालन की सुविधा की दृष्टि से अपने विशाल साम्राज्य को कई प्रांतों में विभक्त कर दिया और प्रांत में एक गर्वनर को नियुक्ति किया गया था, जिसका प्रमुख कार्य प्रांत में शान्ति एवं व्यवस्था बनाये रखना था। इसके साथ-साथ अतिरिक्त राजस्व कर वसूल करना एवं मुकदमों का फैसला करना भी उनका प्रमुख कार्य था। सम्राट प्रांतों तथा गवर्नरों पर सीधे नियंत्रण रखता था। कालांतर में प्रान्तों को जिलों और नगरों में विभक्त किया गया। नगरों के शासक को खजानू के नाम से पुकारा जाता था। जिले को परवटी तथा वहाँ के शासक को बेल परवटी अथवा शक्नू कहा जाता था। इन शासकों की मदद के लिए कई पदाधिकारियों की नियुक्ति की जाती थी।

असीरिया में लोगों को कठिन दंड देने का प्रावधान था। उस समय अंग-भंग करना, कोड़ों से पीटना, मृत्यु दण्ड देना, शारीरिक कष्ट पहुँचाना आदि सजाएँ अपराधियों को दी जाती थीं। असीरियन कानूनों से तत्कालीन सामाजिक एवं आर्थिक जीवन के बारे में काफी उल्लेख प्राप्त होता है।

असीरिया और बेबीलोनिया के दासों के क्रय-विक्रय सम्बंधी कानून एक जैसे ही थे। एक दास के विक्रय से उसका पूरा परिवार ही बिक जाता था। इस समय स्वामी अपने दास की पत्नी को अपनी उप-पत्नी बनाने के लिये स्वतंत्र थे। दास के नाम के साथ उसके पिता का नाम नहीं लगाया जाता था। दासों को भी अपनी सम्पत्ति के क्रय-विक्रय का अधिकार था तथा वे किसी भी मुकदमे में गवाही दे सकते थे। कुछ दास उन्नति करते हुए उच्च पदों पर भी नियुक्त हो जाते थे। 683 ई. पू. में एक रानी ने दास को नगर का निरीक्षक नियुक्त किया था।

असीरियन समाज में नैतिकता काफी आवश्यक होती थी। परिवार में पिता का परिवार के सदस्यों पर पूरा अधिकार था। पिता चाहे तो अपने पुत्र को बेच भी सकता था। कभी-कभी पिता अपनी पुत्री को ऋणदाता के पास जमानत के तौर पर रख सकता था। यही नहीं, पति अपनी पत्नी तथा पुत्रों को भी जमानत के रूप में रख सकता था। जमानत के रूप में दिये गये व्यक्ति को बेचना सही नहीं था और अपराधी को कठोर दंड दिया जाता था। यदि पिता अपनी पुत्री को जमानत से मुक्त न करा पाता, तो ऋण देने वाला व्यक्ति उस लड़की से विवाह कर सकता था। असीरिया में सामान्यतया एक-पत्नीवाद ही प्रचलित था, यद्यपि अभिजात्य वर्ग के लोग सुंदर दासियों को भी अपनी उप-पत्नी के रूप में रखते थे। असीरिया में स्त्रियां सम्मान की अधिकारी नहीं होती थी। यहाँ पुरुष दूसरी पत्नियों के साथ सम्भोग कर

सकते थे, परंतु स्त्रियों को पति के अतिरिक्त अन्य पुरुष के साथ सम्भोग का अधिकार प्राप्त नहीं था। समाज में वेश्यावृत्ति भयंकर रूप से प्रचलित थी और सरकार ने उसे संरक्षण दे रखा था। यहाँ स्त्री एवं पुरुष दोनों को जब चाहें एक दूसरे को तलाक दे सकते थे। यदि पति, पत्नी के भरण-पोषण का प्रबंध किये बिना पांच वर्ष तक लापता रहता, तो उसकी पत्नी को विवाह करने का अधिकार था।

समाज

असीरिया का समाज तीन वर्गों में विभाजित था—अभिजात्य वर्ग, शिल्पीवर्ग तथा श्रमिकवर्ग। अभिजात्य वर्ग में पुरोहित, सेनापति, राजा एवं सामंत आदि थे, जिन्हें राजपद भी दिया जाता था। कभी-कभी इस वर्ग की महिलाओं को भी गवर्नर के पद पर नियुक्त किया जाता था। प्राचीन विश्व की सभ्यताओं में इतने ऊँचे पदों पर महिलाओं को असीरिया ने ही सर्वप्रथम नियुक्त किया था।

शिल्पियों को दूसरे वर्गों में शामिल किया गया था। इस वर्ग में लिपिक, कुम्हार, बढ़ई तथा साहूकार आदि आते थे। साहूकारों को टमकारू, लिपिक को तुपशारू, कुम्हार को परवारू एवं बढ़ई को नग्नारू के नाम से पुकारा जाता था। यहाँ प्रत्येक शिल्प अपना निकाय या संघ का गठन करते थे। राजधानी में प्रत्येक पेशेवालों के लिए अलग-अलग मुहल्ले थे, जहाँ एक ही पेशे के लोग निवास करते थे। इस वर्ग के लोग राजकीय कर चुकाते थे।

दासों तथा श्रमिकों को समाज में तीसरा स्थान प्राप्त था उनकी दशा काफी दयनीय थी। बंदियों को काफी प्रताड़ित किया जाता था। उनकी खाल तक खींच ली जाती थी, जंगली जानवरों से लड़ने के लिए बाध्य किया जाता था, उनके सामने ही उनके बच्चों की आंखें निकाल दी जाती थीं।

धार्मिक दशा

धर्म से असीरिया के वासियों को विशेष रुचि नहीं थी। अशुर को यहां का शक्तिशाली देवता माना जाता था जिसके द्वारा सभी शक्तियों का नारा किया जाता था। जिसके द्वारा सम्पूर्ण विश्व तथा ब्रह्माण्ड का निर्माण किया गया है। उसका प्रतीक एक धनुष था, जिससे बाण छूटता हुआ दिखाया जाता था। ईश्तर नामक देवी को इस की पत्नी कहा जाता था। ईश्तर को बेलित के नाम से भी पुकारा जाता था।

असीरिया में युद्ध की देवी के रूप में ईश्तर की पूजा की जाती है। वहां के वासियों के अनुसार वह अशुर देवता के सभी शत्रुओं का अंत कर देती है। ईश्तर देवी के मन्दिर काला, निन्वेह तथा आरबेला नगरों में स्थित थे। अशुर तथा ईश्तर

के अतिरिक्त सिनु, शमश, मारदुक तथा नुस्कू आदि देवताओं को भी पूजते थे। अशुर देवता का प्रतीक असीरियाई झण्डों को लेकर जनता चलती थी। असीरियाई सैनिक जिन प्रदेशों में जाते थे, वहाँ के लोग इससे भयभीत हो जाते थे। इसके अलावा यहां के लोगों का यह भी विश्वास था कि मृत्यु के पश्चात् व्यक्ति की आत्मा को उसके कर्मों के अनुसार सजा दी जाती है। जो लोग बुरा काम करते हैं उनकी आत्मा को कष्टों का सामना करना पड़ता है। साथ ही साथ भूत-प्रेत से अपना बचाव करने के लिये जादू तथा मंत्रों द्वारा निर्मित ताबीज धारण करते हैं।

ज्ञान विज्ञान

बेबीलोनिया के इतिहास को असीरियाई वासियों द्वारा आज भी सुरक्षित रखा गया है तथा आने वाली सभ्यताओं को उस ज्ञान को विरासत के रूप में देकर मानव सभ्यता को समृद्ध बनाया। यहाँ के लोगों ने ग्रहों तथा तारों के अध्ययन के आधार पर फलित ज्योतिष का विकास किया। असीरियाई लोगों ने रोगों के लक्षणों का पता भी लगाया और उसका निर्धारण भी किया, जिनके आधार पर उनका निदान किया जाता था। यहाँ केन, केमल, चेरी, आदि के पौधों से दवाइयां तैयार की जाती थीं। उन्होंने जड़ी-बूटी और धातुओं के आधार पर रोगों के निवारण हेतु 500 प्रभावशाली औषधियों का निर्माण किया।

चित्रकला एवं साहित्य

असीरिया में चित्रकला के जगत में भी काफी उन्नति हुई तत्कालीन चीन में राजप्रासादों की दीवारों पर नक्काशी द्वारा मनुष्यों एक पशुओं के अत्यंत सजीव चित्र बनवाये जाते थे। इन नक्काशियों में अशुर बनीपाल के राजप्रासाद की दीवार पर अंकित शिकार में बाण से आहत सिंह का चित्रकला का एक उत्कृष्ट नमूना है। इसमें अशुर बनीपाल के बाण से आहत, मरते हुए सिंह की व्यथा का सजीव चित्रण हुआ है। असीरिया के चित्रकारों ने घोड़े, गधे, कुत्ते, हिरणों तथा पक्षियों आदि के चित्र भी सफलतापूर्वक चित्रित किये। अशुर बनीपाल के महल की दीवारों पर पेड़ की छाँव के नीचे अंगड़ाई लेते हुए एक सिंहनी का चित्र उस समय की कला का अद्वितीय नमूना है।

असीरिया का अशुर नगर चित्रकला का प्रमुख केन्द्र था। इस नगर की खुदाई में प्राप्त पत्थर की छोटी-छोटी मूर्तियाँ इस काल की कला का परिचय देती हैं। नवीं शताब्दी ई. पू. में असीरियाई मूर्तिकला अपने विकास की चरमसीमा पर पहुँच गई

थी। असीरियाई मूर्तिकला सजीव एवं जीवन के यथार्थ पक्ष पर आधारित थी। इस युग में मानव और पशुओं की मूर्तियां बनाने में पत्थरों का प्रयोग किया जाता था। पशुओं के चित्रण में असीरियाई मूर्तिकारों को महारथ हासिल थी। मानव शरीर के चित्रण में यहां के कलाकार मनुष्य के अंग विन्यास के चित्रण की अपेक्षा वस्त्र एवं आभूषण के चित्रण पर अधिक ध्यान देते थे। अशुर बनीपाल के शासनकाल में मूर्तिकला का विकास अपनी पराकाष्ठा पर पहुंच गया था। पत्थर की बनी हुई छोटी-छोटी मूर्तियों से उस काल की कला के बारे में जानकारी प्राप्त होती है। खोरसाबाद के नगर द्वार के पास बनी हुई बैलों की मूर्तियां तथा ब्रिटिश संग्रहालय में रखी अशुर बनीपाल द्वितीय की विशालकाय मूर्ति बहुत सुंदर एवं सजीव लगती है।

असीरिया के सम्राट ने स्थापत्य कला को विशेष रूप प्राथमिकता प्रदान की। अतः उन्होंने निन्वेह तथा अशुर में भव्य प्रासादों, मन्दिरों तथा पुस्तकालयों का निर्माण करवाया था। असीरिया का प्रत्येक राजा पुराने महल को त्यागकर अपने लिए नवीन महल बनवाता था। अपनी यश गाथा का वर्णन चित्रों तथा अभिलेखों द्वारा कराया गया था। असीरियन सम्राटों द्वारा बनाये गए राजप्रासादों में दर-शारूकिन नामक नगर में स्थित महल अत्यंत प्रसिद्ध है। सारगन द्वितीय ने आठवीं शताब्दी ई.पू. में इस महल का निर्माण करवाया था। इस महल में 200 कमरे थे और दर-शारूकिन नगर की रक्षा के लिए एक आयताकार चारदीवारी भी बनवाई गई थी। इस महल में आवास-गृह, स्वागत कक्ष एवं मन्दिर अलग-अलग बनाये गये थे। उसमें तीन सिंहद्वार तथा बुर्ज बने हुए थे। केन्द्र में स्थित सिंहद्वार पर गिलगमेश देवता की मूर्ति भी स्थापित की गई थी। महलों के सिंहद्वार से रथों का प्रवेश आसानी से हो सकता था।

युद्ध के दौरान प्राप्त धनों को एकत्रित करने हेतु भण्डारण कक्ष का निर्माण कराया जाता था। इस पर कड़ा पहरा लगाया जाता था। महल के अंदर ही परिचारकों, दासों तथा दासियों के निवास-स्थान बने हुए थे। राजप्रासादों का निर्माण कच्ची ईंटों से करवाया जाता था तथा उन पर गीली मिट्टी का प्लास्टर करवाया जाता था, ताकि चित्र आसानी से बनवाये जा सकें।

बड़े-बड़े भवनों का निर्माण असीरियाई सम्राटों द्वारा कराया गया जो देखने में काफी सुंदर नहीं होते थे। उन्होंने अपने महलों में मेहराबों पर स्तम्भों का प्रयोग अधिक मात्रा में किया। इतिहासकार बिल ड्यूरेन्ट ने अपनी पुस्तक 'सभ्यता की कहानी' में लिखा है—"ईरानियों ने स्तंभों का प्रयोग इन्हीं लोगों से सीखा।"

असीरिया के कलाकार आभूषण बनाने के लिये सोने, चांदी तथा तांबे के प्रयोग करते थे जिसमें हीरे-जवाहरात का भी प्रयोग किया जाता था। इस युग के हार, अंगूठी, बाजूबंद, कर्णफूल, नाक और कानों की बालियाँ देखते ही बनती हैं। हारों में बहुमूल्य पत्थर भी जड़े जाते थे। देवताओं की आकृतियों के छोटे प्रतीक भी गले में लटकाकर हार की तरह पहने जाते थे। असीरिया के कलाकारों को अनेकों प्रकार के आभूषण तथा गहनों की कला में महारथ हासिल थी।

उस दौरान साहित्य के क्षेत्र में काफी विकास हुआ था। वहां के साहित्यकारों ने बेबीलोनिया के साहित्यों को आज भी संजो कर रखा है। इस काल के पुरोहितों ने देवताओं की वाणी को लिपिबद्ध किया, ज्योतिषियों ने भविष्य विज्ञान को लेकर साहित्य तैयार किया तथा शकुन विचार पर भी काफी लिखा गया। वहाँ के लोग इतिहास भी लिखते थे, इस बात की पुष्टि खुदाई में प्राप्त मिट्टी तख्तियों से होती है। उन्होंने इतिहास में अपनी विजयों का बढ़ा-चढ़ाकर वर्णन किया है, परन्तु पराजयों का उल्लेख नहीं मिलता। अशुर बनीपाल ने साहित्य की सुरक्षा के लिए संग्रहालयों का निर्माण करवाया। उसकी राजधानी के पुस्तकालय से 30,000 अभ्यास पुस्तकों की तख्तियां प्राप्त हुई हैं, जिनसे उनके साहित्य के बारे में जानकारी मिलती है। सारगोनी वंश के शासनकाल में उत्कीर्ण शिलालेखों से प्रत्येक वर्ष की घटना के बारे में विस्तृत जानकारी प्राप्त होती है। अंत में असीरियाई विद्वानों ने बेबीलोनया के प्रमुख आख्यानों तथा महाकाव्यों को सुरक्षित रखकर विश्व सभ्यता को महान् देन दी है।

आर्थिक जीवन

सेन्नाचेरिब द्वारा कृषि में प्रगति लाने के लिये सिंचाई की समुचित व्यवस्था करने के लिये पक्की नहर को बनवाया था। असीरिया का प्रमुख धंधा कृषि था, जिसके द्वारा निन्वेह नगर से तीस मील दूर तक पानी पहुँचाया जाता था। असीरिया की मुख्य पैदावार गेहूँ, जौ, जैतून, कपास एवं अंगूर आदि थी। उस समय कई वस्तुओं का उत्पादन कारखानों में किया जाता था। प्रत्येक उद्योग के संघ या गिल्ड बने हुए थे। राजा ने उद्योगों को कई करों में छूट दे रखी थी। सेन्नाचेरिब संसार का पहला राजा था जिसने चाँदी के सिक्के चलाये थे।

वहाँ के सम्राट व्यापारिक मार्गों की सुरक्षा की व्यवस्था करते थे, जिसके कारण व्यापार के क्षेत्र में अधिक प्रगति हुयी। व्यापारियों के बड़े-बड़े काफिले (सुखारू) देश विदेश से व्यापार के लिए निकलते थे। ये साहूकारों से पूँजी उधार लेकर व्यापार करते

थे तथा 25% सूद के साथ मूलधन लौटाते थे। सूद की इतनी ऊँची दर से इस बात की पुष्टि होती है कि यहाँ व्यापार में मुनाफा होता था। विनिमय के साधन सोना, चांदी और ताँबे के टुकड़े थे। अधिकतर चाँदी के टुकड़ों से विनिमय होता था। व्यापारी को भी राज्य कर देने पड़ते थे।

साम्राज्य का पतन

असीरियन सम्राटों ने लगभग 150 वर्षों तक बिना कोई दबाव अथवा अंकुश के शासन किया। उनकी नीति के कारण राज्य में अशान्ति एवं अव्यवस्था बनी रही और व्यापार और कला के विकास का मार्ग भी अवरुद्ध हो गया। यहाँ का सामाजिक जीवन नष्ट हो गया। प्रसिद्ध इतिहासकार टायनबी ने अपनी पुस्तक 'स्टडी ऑफ हिस्ट्री' में इस सभ्यता के पतन के कारणों पर प्रकाश डालते हुए लिखा-"असीरियन सभ्यता के विनाश का कारण यह नहीं कि उसके शस्त्रों पर जंग लग गया था। सैनिक दृष्टि से वे निरंतर प्रगतिशील व योग्य रहे। आक्रांत नीति के परिणामस्वरूप ही उनका अस्तित्व समाप्त होने लगा था, जो पड़ौसियों को रास नहीं आया था।"

विश्व-सभ्यता को देन

असीरियावासियों की महान संस्कृति को आज भी संजो कर रखा है। साथ ही बेबीलोनिया की सांस्कृतिक धरोहर को सुरक्षा प्रदान की है। उन्होंने बेबीलोनिया की सांस्कृतिक धरोहर को सुरक्षित कर हम तक पहुँचाया है। डॉ. एस. आर. गोयल का मानना है कि "अगर असीरिया न होता, तो बेबीलोन का बहुत-सा ज्ञान विज्ञान पश्चिमी एशियाई जातियों की समान सम्पत्ति बने बिना विलुप्त हो जाता और आधुनिक इतिहासकार पश्चिमी एशिया के इतिहास का इतने विस्तार से पुनर्निर्माण न कर पाते।" यही उनकी सबसे बड़ी देन है। प्रांतीय शासन व्यवस्था की नींव असीरिया के द्वारा रखी गई तथा डाक व्यवस्था की शुरुआत सर्वप्रथम उन्हीं के द्वारा की गई।

असीरिया ने सुदृढ़ सैन्य तंत्र के आधार पर ही अपने साम्राज्य का प्रसार किया। इनके द्वारा स्थापित सैन्य व्यवस्था अपने समय में सफल सिद्ध हुई। डॉ. सुशील माधव पाठक ने लिखा है कि "वास्तव में असीरियाई सभ्यता अपनी सैन्य प्रणाली के लिए ही प्राचीन विश्व के इतिहास में अपना विशिष्ट स्थान रखती है। असीरियाई सैन्य विशेषज्ञ युद्ध लड़ना, लड़ाई के दॉव-पेंच को बहुत अच्छी तरह से समझते थे।" असीरिया के सैनिक युद्धकला में बहुत दक्ष थे और युद्ध अभियानों की

क्रूरता तथा निर्दयता के लिए विश्व में कुख्यात थे। इसके समाज का पतन सैन्य शक्ति के परिणामस्वरूप ही हुआ था।

उस काल की सभ्यता की जानकारी वहां से प्राप्त मिट्टी की तख्तियां से मिलती है। उनकी रक्तपात की नीति एवं हिंसावादी प्रवृत्ति से जनता असंतुष्ट थी। उनकी इसी नीति के कारण आगे चलकर साम्राज्य का पतन हो गया। फिर भी, बेबीलोनिया की सांस्कृतिक धरोहर की रक्षा एवं प्रसार के कारण मानव सभ्यता उनकी ऋणी रहेगी।

4

प्राचीन चीन की सभ्यता

विश्व की सभी सभ्यताओं में चीन की सभ्यता काफी पुरानी है। जब विश्व के कई देश सभ्यताओं का अन्वेषण कर रहे थे उस दौरान चीन की सभ्यता काफी प्रभावशाली थी। चीनी सभ्यता पर प्रकाश डालते हुए **वीच** महोदय ने लिखा है कि–''जिस समय रोम शब्द ही नहीं था, यूनान और ईरान का अस्तित्व ही नहीं था और जब अब्राहम ने अपनी महत्त्वपूर्ण यात्रा प्रारम्भ की थी, उसके बहुत पहले ही चीनी लोग अपने देश को सभ्य बना चुके थे। उपजाऊ भूमि ने उन्हें घुमक्कड़ नहीं बनने दिया। वहां के वासी मकानों में निवास करते थे, तम्बुओं में निवास नहीं करते थे। इन्हें इतिहास में 40 शताब्दियों का किसान कहा गया है।'' मैसोपोटामिया और सिंधु घाटी की सभ्यता से चीन की सभ्यता काफी प्राचीन है। आज जबकि मिस्र, मैसोपोटामिया, यूनान व रोमन आदि सभ्यताओं का अस्तित्व समाप्त हो चुका है, वहाँ चीन की सभ्यता आज भी जीवित है। **प्रो. तानयुनशान** ने चीनी सभ्यता पर निम्न प्रकार से प्रकाश डाला है–''पाश्चात्य विद्वान मिस्र और बेबीलोनिया की सभ्यता को काल के हिसाब से सबसे पुरानी मान लेने में गलती करते हैं। उनकी यह गलती इसलिए होती है कि लोगों को चीन के इतिहास का ज्ञान प्रायः नहीं के बराबर है एवं वे चीन की संस्कृति को हृदयांगम नहीं कर पाये हैं'' अन्य सभ्यताएं जन्मी और मर गयीं, लेकिन **प्लेट व जीन** के अनुसार-''प्राचीन चीन ने एक ऐसी सभ्यता को जन्म दिया जो कभी नहीं मरी।''

वाल्तेयर ने इस सभ्यता पर प्रकाश डालते हुए लिखा है कि–''चीनी साम्राज्य का शरीर बिना किसी परिवर्तन के चार हजार वर्षों से जीवित है, उसके

कानून, परम्पराएं, भाषा और फैशन आज भी वैसे ही हैं।'' चीन की विचित्रताओं पर प्रकाश डालते हुए **एलिस और जॉन** का मानना है–''चीन के नाम से रेशम के कीड़ों, दरियाई भैंसों, पंखों, कागज की लालटेनों और विशाल दीवार का, लकड़ी की तीलियों से चावल खाने वालों, खूबसूरत राजकुमारियों और लम्बे गाउन पहने अकड़कर बैठे सम्राटों का चित्रण आंखों के सामने नाचने लगता है। चीन अमेरिका की कल्पना को उत्तेजित करता है, क्योंकि वह इतना रंगीन और पश्चिमी देशों से भिन्न है।'' चीन की सभ्यता से विश्व को काफी लाभ पहुंचा है। **डिडरोट** महोदय ने इस सभ्यता के महत्त्व पर प्रकाश डालते हुए लिखा है कि ''चीन के लोग एशिया के अन्य लोगों से सभ्यता, बुद्धि, दर्शन और नीति में उच्च हैं, वे यूरोप के सभी लोगों से इस क्षेत्र में बाजी मार गये हैं।'' मिस्र, समुरिया तथा भारत में इस सभ्यता की नींव नदियों की उपजाऊ घाटियों में रखी गई थी।

चीन की भौगोलिक स्थिति

चीन की आबादी लगभग एक अरब है तथा इसका क्षेत्रफल सैंतीस लाख वर्गमील तक है। जनसंख्या और क्षेत्रफल की दृष्टि से विश्व में क्रमशः पहला और दूसरा स्थान है। चीन, एशिया के उत्तरी-पूर्वी भाग में स्थित है। इसके उत्तर में बर्फ जमी रहती है और दक्षिण में हिमालय पर्वत इसको अन्य देशों से अलग करता है। प्रशान्त महासागर इसकी पूर्वी सीमा पर स्थित है। पश्चिम में दो बड़े रेगिस्तान हैं–तुर्किस्तान का तकला मकान और मंगोलिया का गोबी। इस प्रकार प्रकृति ने चीन को विदेशी आक्रमण से एक प्रकार से सुरक्षित किया है। वहां तीन नदियाँ हैं–सिंक्यांग, दूसरी ह्वांग ह्वो और तीसरी वांग ह्वो। इन नदियों में बाढ़ आने के कारण चीनी लोग इन्हें 'चीन की विपत्ति' की संज्ञा देते थे। ये चीन की जीवनदायनी थीं।

प्राचीन काल में चीन को 'चुंग को' के नाम से जाना जाता है, जिसका अर्थ होता है–'स्वर्ग के नीचे का राज्य'। आगे चलकर जो विदेशी चुंग शब्द नहीं बोल सकते थे, वे इसे चीन कहने लगे। चीनियों का मानना था कि संसार का स्वर्ग यहीं पर था, लेकिन आदमी के कुकर्मों ने उसका अंत कर दिया है। चीनी लोग मंगोल जाति के थे। हम यहाँ पर उस सभ्यता का वर्णन करेंगे, जो चीन की सभ्यता का प्रतिनिधित्व करती है–वह थी ह्वांगह्वो नदी की घाटी में विकसित सभ्यता, जिसे मध्य या चीन का स्वर्ग का राज्य भी कहा जाता था।

इतिहास के स्रोत

तत्कालीन चीनी इतिहासकार अपने देश चीन की गौरव-गाथाओं पर प्रकाश डालते थे। इन पौराणिक कथाओं से चीन के तत्कालीन इतिहास के सन्दर्भ में बहुत कुछ जानकारी मिलती है। कन्फ्यूशियस द्वारा रचित 'शू-चिंग' (ऐतिहासिक कथाओं का संकलन) नामक पुस्तक में चीन के प्रारम्भिक इतिहास पर प्रकाश डाला गया है। इसके अतिरिक्त शी-चिंग अर्थात् 'काव्य-संग्रह' नामक पुस्तक से भी चीन के प्राचीन इतिहास के बारे में ज्ञान प्राप्त होता है। इन दोनों पुस्तकों में जिस सभ्यता का ज्ञान हमें मिलता है, वह आदिम सभ्यता नहीं, बल्कि एक विकसित सभ्यता थी।

चीन की राजधानी बीजिंग के 27 मील दक्षिण पश्चिम में चाउ-काऊ तियेन की गुफा में चीनी मानव के अवशेष प्राप्त हुए हैं। उन अवशेषों का अध्ययन करने से पता चलता है कि पूर्व पाषाणकाल में भी चीन में मानव सभ्यता का विकास हो चुका था। प्राचीन चीन में दो संस्कृतियों का विकास हुआ—चित्रित मृद्भाण्ड संस्कृति और कृष्णमृद्भाण्ड संस्कृति। ये दोनों संस्कृतियाँ 2000 ई. पू. तक रहीं। चीन में बहुत बड़ी संख्या में खुदाई में प्राप्त हड्डियों पर अंकित शिलालेखों से प्राचीन चीन के इतिहास के बारे में पता चलता है। इन हड्डियों पर भविष्य जानने के लिए खुदाई की जाती थी। अतः इन्हें 'आरेकल बोन' कहा जाता था। होनान प्रान्त के आन्यांग जिले में ऐसी हड्डियां काफी संख्या में पायी गयी हैं। इन हड्डियों पर उस समय के लोग प्रश्न खुदवाते थे और फिर उन्हें अपने पूर्वजों या देवताओं से पूछते थे। उन लोगों की मान्यता थी कि ऐसे प्रश्नों का उत्तर देवता स्वप्नों में आकर देते हैं। इसलिए इन हड्डियों पर खुदे हुए लेखों से प्रारम्भिक इतिहास के बारे में पता चलता है।

सृष्टि निर्माण के सम्बंध में चीनी कथाएँ

चीन की पौराणिक गाथाओं के अनुसार ईसा से लगभग 22 लाख 29 हजार वर्ष पूर्व पान कू नामक व्यक्ति ने सृष्टि का निर्माण किया। इसका शरीर अति विशाल था और यह दो रहस्यमय शक्तियों—यांग नाम के पुरुष एवं यिन नाम के स्त्री के संयोग से पैदा हुआ था। पान कू ने 18 हजार वर्ष तक शासन किया। ऐसी गाथाओं पर पूर्णरूप से विश्वास नहीं किया जा सकता है।

चीनी सभ्यता आज भी बिना किसी बाधा के प्राचीन काल से गतिमान है। चीन में बीजिंग के पास खुदाई में प्राप्त खोपड़ियों और पुराने औजारों से इस बात की पुष्टि होती है कि करीब पाँच लाख वर्ष पूर्व आदिम अवस्था में मनुष्य यहाँ रहता था। ऐसे मनुष्य को 'पेकिंग मैन' या पीकिंग का आदमी कहा गया है। मंगोल जाति

से उस मनुष्य का काफी समानता होती थी तथा उसका निवास स्थान उत्तरी चीन में था। पैकिंगमैन को आग के बारे में ज्ञान था और औजारों का प्रयोग जानता था। वह मनुष्यों को आहार के रूप में इस्तेमाल करते थे। पैकिंगमैन आदिम अवस्था से सभ्यतावस्था तक कैसे पहुँचा, इसके बारे में कोई सबूत नहीं मिलता है।

चीन का राजनीतिक इतिहास

उस दौरान मानव गुफाओं में रहता था इसकी जानकारी इतिहास के अध्ययन से मिलती है तथा वह शिकार करने के लिए औजारों का प्रयोग करते थे। वे जानवरों की खाल को वस्त्र के रूप में प्रयोग करते थे। उनमें नैतिकता का अभाव होने के कारण निकटतम सम्बन्धियों में विवाह कर लेते थे। संक्षेप में, अन्य आदिम जातियों के समान ही चीनी लोगों ने धीरे-धीरे सभ्यता के मार्ग को अपनाया। इस आदिम अवस्था के बाद पौराणिक शासकों का युग की शुरुआत हुई। इसका समय तीन हजार ई. पू. के आस-पास माना जा सकता है। चीनी मान्यताओं के अनुसार इस शासनकाल में चीनियों को घर बनाना, शिकार करना, जानवर पालना, संगीत, चित्रकला तथा रेशम के कीड़े पालना सीखा था। लेखन कला भविष्य दर्शन की शुरुआत भी उसी काल में हुई थी। उसने लोगों को आपस में सहयोग करना सिखलाया और चीनी सभ्यता की नींव डाली।

शेन-नुंग को चीन का दूसरा सम्राट कहा जाता था उसी के द्वारा कृषकों को खेती करने की शिक्षा दी गई थी। उसको कृषि के देवता के रूप में याद किया जाता है। इसके नेतृत्व में ही चीनी अपना घुमक्कड़ जीवन त्यागकर स्थायी रूप से कृषक जीवन गुजारने लगे। बाद में यह गांव छोटे-छोटे राज्य बन गये। इन राज्यों में आपस में लड़ाइयां होती रहती थीं। इनमें विजय प्राप्त करने वाले नेता को 'टी' की उपाधि दी जाती थी, जिसका अर्थ होता है—अधिराज। शेन नुंग ने दैनिक जीवन की आवश्यक वस्तुओं की नाप-तौल की विधि भी चालू की थी।

हुआंग टी को चीन का दूसरा सम्राट कहा जाता है। इस सम्राट को पीला सम्राट भी कहा जाता था। यह प्रथम व्यक्ति था, जिसने 'महासम्राट' की उपाधि धारण की थी। हुआंग टी ने छोटे-छोटे भू-भागों में विभाजित चीन को संयुक्त बनाया। उसके शासनकाल में यातायात के साधनों की काफी प्रगति हुई। नावों के निर्माण से उसने जलमार्ग से भी यातायात प्रारम्भ करवाया। उसने करीब 2700 ई. पू. में शासन किया। हुआंग टी ने चीनी राज्य के इर्द-गिर्द रहने वाली असभ्य जातियों को शांत किया और पैंतालीस नगरों का निर्माण करवाया।

हुआंग टी का पतन होने के उपरान्त याओ चीन का सम्राट बना। इसके शासनकाल में ह्वांग हो नदी में भयंकर बाढ़ आयी थी। उसके पुत्र यू ने बाढ़ को रोकने के लिए बड़ी-बड़ी नहरें बनवाकर पानी को इधर-उधर बाँट दिया। इस प्रकार उसने इस भयंकर बाढ़ पर नियंत्रण स्थापित कर लिया। याओ ने अपनी वृद्धावस्था में शासन का भार शुन को सौंप दिया। याओ और शुन का चीन के इतिहास में महत्त्वपूर्ण स्थान है। चीनी इतिहासकारों ने इन दोनों राजाओं को सर्वगुण सम्पन्न बतलाते हुए भावी शासकों के लिए आदर्श घोषित किया है। इन दोनों का शासन चीन के इतिहास में स्वर्ण युग माना जाता है। इस युग का काल हम 2456 ई. पू. से 2205 ई. पू. तक मान सकते हैं।

1. हासिया राजवंश

यू हासिया राजवंश का पहला शासक था, जिसने 2205 ई. पू. में इस वंश की स्थापना की। इस राजवंश ने 2205 ई. पू. से 1766 ई. पू. तक शासन किया। इस वंश के 18 राजाओं ने चीन पर शासन किया। इस राजवंश के शासकों ने योजनाबद्ध तरीके से भूमि का वितरण किया और शराब पीने पर प्रतिबंध लगाया था। इस युग के लोग शांग टी की पूजा करते थे। यह उनका सर्वोच्च देवता था। हासिया राजवंश का अठारहवाँ शासक 'की' था। यह एक अत्याचारी शासक था। की को हटाने के लिए शांग वंश के राजकुमार टांग ने एक विद्रोह का नेतृत्व किया, जो सफल रहा। टांग ने की को गद्दी से हटा दिया और वह स्वयं राजा बन गया। टांग ने ही शांग राजवंश की स्थापना की थी। इस राजवंश ने 1766 ई. पू. से 1122 ई. पू. तक शासन किया। टांग के काल से ही चीन की प्राचीन सभ्यता का स्वर्णकाल आरम्भ होता है।

2. शांग वंश

1466 ई. पू. से 1122 ई. पू. तक शांग वंश के राजाओं ने चीन पर शासन किया। उसके शासनकाल में चीन के प्रत्येक क्षेत्र में उन्नति हुई थी। चाऊ सिन को इस युग का अंतिम शासक कहा जाता था। वह एक योग्य शासक था, परन्तु उसने अपनी प्रेमिका ता-वी को प्रसन्न करने के लिए जनता पर भयंकर अत्याचार किये। इसका परिणाम यह हुआ कि उसके सेनापति चाऊ वूवांग ने चाऊ वंश की नींव डाली।

राजनीतिक दशा—चीन की शासन-व्यवस्था का शांग वंशकाल में काफी विकास हुआ था। राज्य कई प्रान्तों में बंटा हुआ था और उन पर पदाधिकारियों का

अधिकार होता था। इस काल की हड्डियों पर लिखे कुछ अभिलेख प्राप्त हुए हैं, जिनमें इस वंश के 30 राजाओं के नाम प्राप्त हुए हैं। इस वंश के पानकेंग नामक राजा ने हुआन नदी के किनारे पर स्थित आन्यांग नामक शहर को अपनी राजधानी बनाया था। आन्यांग की खुदाई से प्राप्त अवशेषों से शांग राजवंश के इतिहास के संबंध में काफी जानकारी प्राप्त होती है। सुरक्षा की दृष्टि से आन्यांग नगर की तीन दिशाओं में हुआंग नदी बहती थी। चौथी दिशा में एक मिट्टी की दीवार बनाकर सुरक्षा प्रबंध कर दिया गया था। शांग वंश के शासनकाल में रथ पर चढ़कर धनुष-बाण के द्वारा युद्ध करने की प्रथा प्रचलित थी। उस दौरान राजधानी में धनुर्विद्या प्रतियोगिता का भी आयोजन किया जाता था। धनुष-बाण के अतिरिक्त कुल्हाड़ी व बर्छे, धातुनिर्मित कवचों तथा टोपियों का भी युद्ध में इस्तेमाल किया जाता था। विजय प्राप्त करने के लिए प्रेतात्माओं से सहायता मांगी जाती थी। युद्ध में पराजित लोगों को या तो गुलाम बना लिया जाता था या बलिदान कर दिया जाता था।

सामाजिक अवस्था—शांग युग के शिलालेखों का अध्ययन करने से यह जानकारी मिलती है कि उस काल में पिता को ही परिवार का प्रमुख कहा जाता था। परिवार में पिता के बाद उसका छोटा भाई स्वामी होता था। इस युग में पूर्वजों और पितरों की पूजा की जाती थी और उनको समय-समय पर बलि चढ़ाई जाती थी, ताकि वे प्रसन्न होकर सुख सम्पत्ति प्रदान करें। इस युग में दासियाँ भी थीं, जिन्हें 'ची' कहा जाता था। ची का अर्थ होता है—रखैल या उप-पत्नी। स्वामी को दासियों से शारीरिक संबंध बनाने की पूर्ण स्वतंत्रता थी। इन उप-पत्नियों की संतानों को समाज में अधिकार भी दिये गए। उस दौरान स्त्रियों को सम्मान की दृष्टि से देखा जाता था।

आर्थिक दशा—उस काल में कृषि, पशुपालन तथा शिकार अर्थव्यवस्था के प्रमुख साधन हुआ करते थे। कृषि इस युग के लोगों का प्रमुख व्यवसाय था। पूर्वजों की पूजा के बाद ही फसलें बोई जाती थीं, ताकि उनके आशीर्वाद से प्रचुर मात्रा में उपज हो। यहाँ की प्रमुख पैदावार गेहूँ, जौ एवं बाजरा आदि थी। कृषि के अतिरिक्त उनका दूसरा व्यवसाय पशुपालन था। यहाँ के लोग कुत्ता, भेड़, सुअर, बकरी, हिरण, बैल, भैंस और बंदर पालते थे। इस युग में भोजन के लिए गाय, भैंस, बैल, सुअर, भेड़, कुत्ता और मुर्गियों का उपयोग होता था। इस वंश के लोग कुत्ते और सुअर का मांस बड़े चाव से खाते थे। बड़े-बड़े भोजों में कुत्ते के मांस को शौक से परोसा जाता था। आज भी चीन के कई भागों में कुत्ते के मांस को खाने के रूप में प्रयोग करते हैं। कुत्तों का शिकार में प्रयोग किया जाता था। भेड़ों, बकरियों, कुत्तों और सुअरों की बलि भी दी जाती थी।

शांग युग में कला-कौशल और उद्योग-धंधों की प्रगति भी कम नहीं हुई थी। पत्थरों, हड्डियों तथा धातुओं से बने सामान तथा मिट्टी के बर्तन प्राप्त हुए हैं। इस समय व्यवसाय के आधार पर समाज का वर्गीकरण हो चुका था। इस समय पत्थर के कंगन एवं अँगूठियां आदि गहने भी बनाये जाते थे। शांग युग के लोग पत्थरों को काटकर सुअरों, पक्षियों और मनुष्यों की आकृतियां बनाते थे। इस वंश के लोग बालों में खोंसने के लिए हड्डियों की पीन बनाते थे। इस समय लोग गाय, बैल और हिरण के सींग से हथियार और गहनों का निर्माण भी करते थे। उस समय लोग लकड़ी की कुल्हाड़ियां, धनुष-बाण, रथ और नाव बनाना भी जानते थे । इसके अलावा मिट्टी के सुंदर बर्तन बनाना भी जानते थे। शांग वंश के समय व्यापार, विनिमय के द्वारा ही होता था। घोड़ा, गाय-बैल तथा अनाज विनिमय के माध्यम माने जाते थे। चीन में नव-पाषाण युग में निर्मित कब्रों में कौड़ियाँ प्राप्त हुई हैं जिसे इस युग में सिक्कों के स्थान पर प्रयोग किया जाता था। इस युग में लिपि का विकास हो चुका था। इस युग में लकड़ी, बांस, कपड़ा या हाथीदांत पर लिखा जाता था। रेशमी वस्त्रों पर केवल ब्रश से लिखा जाता था। शांग वंश के लोग कलैंडर का प्रयोग करते थे और उन्हें ऋतुओं की भी जानकारी थी।

शांग युग में मूर्तिकला के क्षेत्र में काफी प्रगति हुई। इस समय पत्थर और कांसे से पक्षियों तथा जानवरों की मूर्तियां बनाई जाती थीं, जो कला की दृष्टि से परिष्कृत और काफी सुंदर होती थीं। इसके अलावा इस युग में कांसे की कला की काफी प्रगति हुई। इस समय धार्मिक अनुष्ठानों से सम्बद्ध बर्तन कांसे के बनाये जाते थे, जो देखने में काफी सुन्दर भी लगते थे। अन्यांग की खुदाई में कांसे के बने औजार, गहने तथा बर्तन प्राप्त हुए हैं। कांसे के बर्तनों पर परतदार सर्प, भैंस, भेड़, सांप, कीड़ों और पक्षियों के चित्र बनाये गये हैं।

धार्मिक स्थिति—प्राचीन काल में चीन में पूर्वजों का काफी आदर किया जाता था। लोगों का मानना था कि मृत्यु के बाद पूर्वजों के हाथ में असीम शक्ति आ जाती है। अतः चीनी लोग उनको शक्तिशाली देवता मानते थे और उनकी पूजा करते थे। चीनियों का मानना था कि शिकार, युद्ध, खेती तथा अन्य कार्य अच्छी तरह से तभी किये जा सकेंगे जब हमारे पूर्वज प्रसन्न रहेंगे। आन्यांग के पास तीन सौ कब्रों की खुदाई हुई है। इससे शव संस्कार की प्रक्रिया पर प्रकाश पड़ता है। यहां मुर्दों को कब्र में मुंह के बल लिटाया जाता था और कब्र में बर्तन तथा कुल्हाड़ी आदि रख दी जाती थी। जो व्यक्ति अमीर होते थे उनकी कब्रों में कांसे के आकर्षक बर्तन रखने का विधान था। राजाओं की कब्र में मिट्टी

के सुंदर बर्तन, संगमरमर की कलात्मक मूर्तियां, कांसे के बर्तन और हथियार आदि रखे जाते थे।

शांगकालीन व्यवस्था में धर्म का काफी महत्त्व था। यहां पूर्वजों और पितरों को प्रसन्न करने के लिए गाय, बैल, भेड़, सुअर, कुत्ता, मुर्गी और घोड़े की बलि देते समय शराब भी चढ़ायी जाती थी। यह विश्वास किया जाता था कि बलि देने से पूर्वजों और पितरों को भोजन प्राप्त होता है। चीन के वासियों के अनुसार बलि आदि देने से देवता तथा पितर खुश होकर विपत्तिकाल में उनकी सहायता करते हैं। इतिहासकारों का मानना है कि इस युग में नर बलि की प्रथा भी प्रचलित थी। नर बलि चढ़ाये जाने वालों में एक खास जाति का नाम शिलालेखों में बार-बार आता है—यह जाति है चियांग। कालांतर में युद्धबंदी तथा गुलाम के लिए चियांग शब्द का प्रयोग होने लगा। इस प्रकार शांग वंश के काल में कोई भी धार्मिक क्रिया-कलाप बिना बलि के सफल नहीं माने जाते थे।

3. चाऊ वंश (1122 ई. पू. से 225 ई. पू.)

1122 ई.पू. चाऊ व वांग द्वारा चाऊ वंश की स्थापना की गई थी। इस समय चीन ने सभ्यता एवं संस्कृति के क्षेत्र में आश्चर्यजनक उन्नति की। इस युग में कृषि का विकास हुआ। धातुओं के सुंदर बर्तन बनाये गये। मुद्रण कला तथा बारूद का आविष्कार हुआ। इस वंश के शासक स्वेच्छाचारी थे, परन्तु प्रजा की भलाई का कार्य करना अपना कर्तव्य मानते थे। जो कर्मचारी परीक्षा में सफल हो जाते थे, उन्हें ही नियुक्त किया जाता था।

प्रत्येक क्षेत्र पर समान रूप से ध्यान दिया गया था। दर्शन, राजनीति, धर्म सभी क्षेत्रों में सुधार किया गया। इस युग में 'काव्यसंग्रह' तथा 'ऐतिहासिक संग्रह' आदि की रचना हुई। चीनी दर्शन के महान आचार्य-कन्फ्यूशियस, लाओत्से जैसे दार्शनिक भी ईसा पूर्व छठवीं सदी में इसी युग में हुए। अतः चाऊ वंश का शासनकाल चीन के इतिहास में 'स्वर्णयुग' के नाम से जाना जाता है। इस बात की पुष्टि आधुनिक इतिहासकार तान यून शान के विचारों से भी होती है उन्होंने कहा है—"इस युग में संस्कृति तथा सभ्यता का सर्वतोन्मुखी विकास हुआ।"

चीन के इतिहास में चाऊ को 'सामन्तीयुग' भी कहा जाता है। इस वंश का साम्राज्य अत्यन्त विस्तृत होने के कारण, उन्होंने राज्य को प्रांतों में बांट दिया तथा उसका शासन प्रबन्ध अपने मित्रों को सौंप दिया। कमजोर सम्राटों के समय में इन सामंतों ने स्वतंत्र राज्य स्थापित करने का प्रयास किया, जिससे चाऊ वंश का पतन हो गया। अराजकता के इस काल में भी सांस्कृतिक विकास होता रहा।

4. चिन वंश (225 ई. पू. से 203 ई. पू. तक)

चीनी सामंतों में आपसी विद्रोह के चलते राज्य में अराजकता का माहौल था। चिन वंश के राजाओं ने वंश के अस्तित्व की रक्षा के लिए पहली बार केन्द्रीय शासन की स्थापना की। इस वंश के नाम पर ही पूरे देश का नाम 'चीन' पड़ा।

इस वंश का महान् योद्धा और प्रतापी सम्राट शी हुआंग टी था। इसके नाम का अर्थ है—प्रथम सम्राट। उसने 221 ई. पू. में अपने को चीन का सम्राट घोषित किया। वह एक महान् विजेता और कुशल प्रशासक था।

शी हुआंग टी ने चीन को राजनीतिक एकता के सूत्र में बांध दिया और प्रशासन को सुचारु रूप से चलाने के लिए राजकीय पदों पर योग्य व्यक्तियों की नियुक्ति की। बिल ड्यूरेन्ट ने उसे लौहपुरुष तथा भयानक व्यक्तित्व का सम्राट कहा है और इस क्षेत्र में उसकी तुलना बिस्मार्क से की है। शी हुआंग ने अपनी राजधानी सियेनयंग में एक शानदार महल का निर्माण करवाया था। यह महल 500 फीट चौड़ा तथा 2500 फीट लम्बा था। उसने अपने जीवनकाल में ही लिशन की पहाड़ी पर अपनी समाधि बनवा दी थी। विश्व के सात आश्चर्यों में से एक चीन की दीवार उसी के द्वारा बनवाई गई थी।

चीन की दीवार—चीन की दीवार जो सात आश्चर्य में से एक है, शी हुआंग टी द्वारा बनवाई गई थी। इसे बनवाने का उद्देश्य उत्तर पश्चिमी सीमा पर हूणों के आक्रमणों से रक्षा करना था। यह 1500 मील लम्बी, 20 फीट चौड़ी तथा 22 फीट ऊँची थी। इसमें 20 हजार गुम्बदें, 23 हजार स्तंभ और 10 हजार सुरक्षा चौकियां बनी हुई हैं। इस दीवार का निर्माण दस वर्षों में किया गया था। इस पर अंकित शब्द इस प्रकार हैं—"स्वर्ग के नीचे यह सबसे बड़ी सैनिक रोक है।" इसने चीन की हूणों और तुर्कों के आक्रमणों से रक्षा की।

5. हानवंश (202 ई.पू. से 220 ई.)

इस वंश के शासनकाल को सुधार के शासनकाल की संज्ञा दी जाती है। क्योंकि इस दौरान पूरे देश में व्यापक स्तर पर सुधार कार्य किये गए। लीयू-ची नामक व्यक्ति ने सफल क्रांति कर हानवंश की स्थापना की। राजा बूती को इस वंश का सबसे शक्तिशाली राजा माना जाता था। उसका शासनकाल पचास वर्षों का था तथा एक विशाल साम्राज्य की स्थापना की। बूती ने अनेक राष्ट्रों पर अपना अधिकार स्थापित कर अपने साम्राज्य का विस्तार किया। इस समय चीन में बौद्धधर्म का प्रचार हुआ।

आर्थिक सुधार—हानवंश के शासनकाल में चीन के आर्थिक क्षेत्र में महत्त्वपूर्ण सुधार हुए। इस सन्दर्भ में निम्न प्रकार जानकारी दी गई है—

1. राज्य की आमदनी में वृद्धि करने के लिए नमक पर एकाधिपत्य कायम कर लिया।
2. राज्य के कर्मचारियों को वेतन का आधा नकद व आधे वेतन का अनाज दिया जाता था।
3. भूमि-कर उपज का दसवां भाग लिया जाता था।
4. व्यापार के विकास के लिए 175 ई. पू. में सम्राट टीसिन ने तांबे के सिक्के चलाए और 130 ई. पू. में इन सिक्कों में सुधार किया गया।
5. राज्य की सुरक्षा के लिए एक विशाल सेना रखी गई, जिसका खर्चा जनता से टैक्स लेकर चलाया जाता था।
6. 15 से 56 वर्ष के पुरुषों से टैक्स लिया जाता था।

शासन-संबंधी सुधार—इस वंश के द्वारा समाज में फैली असमानता को समाप्त करने का काफी प्रयास किया गया। कानून पर हम्मूराबी के कानूनों का प्रभाव काफी था। न्यायालयों में अमीर-गरीब का भेद मिटा दिया गया। अपराधियों को कठोर दंड देने का प्रावधान किया गया। सैनिक अफसरों को हटाकर राज्यपालों को नियुक्त की गई। सरकारी कर्मचारियों का चयन परीक्षा लेने के पश्चात् ही किया जाता था।

केन्द्रीय शासन-प्रबंध—इस वंश के शासक दैवी को सही मानते थे। राज्य की वास्तविक शक्ति उनके हाथ में केन्द्रित रहती थी। इस युग के सम्राट निरंकुश और स्वेच्छाचारी थे। राजा की सहायता के लिए प्रधानमंत्री होता था। इस वंश के शासकों ने हर क्षेत्र में गुप्तचर लगा रखे थे जिससे प्रजा को किसी प्रकार की समस्या न हो।

व्यापार का विकास—हानवंश के शासकों ने व्यापार के विकास पर बल दिया। चीन के व्यापारी भारत, फारस, सीरिया और रोम आदि देशों के साथ व्यापार करते थे। चीन इन देशों को रेशम, चमड़ा, रबर, दाल और चीनी आदि वस्तुएँ निर्यात करता था।

विदेशी सम्पर्क का प्रभाव—चीन में व्यापार के विकास के कारण विदेशों से कला का आदान-प्रदान भी शुरू हो गया। उर्गा की खुदाई में प्राप्त उपकरणों से पता चलता है कि चीन पर मंगोलिया की कला का प्रभाव पड़ा था। चीन की मूर्तिकला को रोम ने प्रभावित किया। चीन की संगीत कला, गणित, ज्योतिष आदि को यूनान ने प्रभावित किया। इस प्रकार विदेशी सम्पर्क के कारण चीन का अन्य देशों से सांस्कृतिक आदान-प्रदान हुआ।

विज्ञान का विकास—धूप की घड़ी हानवंश के शासनकाल की ही देन है। सू-य-चियेन ने चीन में एक नया पंचांग बनाया। वंग-यूंग ने भूकम्प के कारणों का पता लगाया। लुंग-हेल नामक ग्रंथ से चंद्रग्रहण के बारे में पता लगाया गया। नी चिंग इस युग का प्रसिद्ध चिकित्सक था, जिसने 'केनन ऑफ मेडिसन' नामक पुस्तक लिखी। इस पुस्तक में उसने शल्यचिकित्सा पर प्रकाश डाला।

दर्शन—हानवंशीय शासक दार्शनिक क्षेत्र से भी विशेष लगाव रखते थे। लाओत्से तथा कन्फ्यूशियस जैसे दर्शन-वेताओं ने चीन के दर्शन को बहुत अधिक प्रभावित किया, परन्तु हानवंश के शासकों को ताओवाद ने अधिक प्रभावित किया।

संगीत कला का विकास—इस वंश के शासक संगीत प्रेमी थे, वे अपने दरबार में कई संगीतकारों को आश्रय देते थे। इस युग के वाद्ययंत्रों में पि-पा (वीणा), कुंगहाऊ तथा जिथर आदि प्रमुख थे। इस समय संगीत जनता के मनोरंजन का प्रमुख साधन था।

शिक्षा का विकास—शासकों ने विभिन्न क्षेत्रों में विद्यालयों की स्थापना कर शिक्षा के विकास को प्रोत्साहन दिया। चीन में हीनयांग को शिक्षा का एक प्रसिद्ध केन्द्र बनाया गया, जो आगे चलकर ज्ञान विज्ञान का एक प्रसिद्ध केन्द्र बन गया। शिक्षकों को विदेशी भाषा का काफी ज्ञान होता था। उस दौरान इतिहास, ज्योतिष व प्राकृतिक विज्ञान आदि विषयों की शिक्षा दी जाती थी। विश्वविद्यालयों में चंगन विश्वविद्यालय विशेष रूप से प्रसिद्ध था, जिसमें 30 हजार छात्र पढ़ते थे।

बौद्ध धर्म का प्रचार—उस दौरान चीनवासी बौद्ध धर्म के समर्थक थे, जिसने चीन के धार्मिक चिन्तन पर बहुत अधिक प्रभाव डाला। हानवंश के सम्राट मिंग टी ने बौद्ध धर्म स्वीकार कर लिया, तत्पश्चात् बौद्ध धर्म चीन का प्रमुख धर्म बन गया। आज भी वहाँ के लोग काफी संख्या में बौद्ध धर्म को मानने वाले हैं।

6. तांग वंश

लीयान द्वारा ही तांग वंश की स्थापना की गई थी। इससे पहले यहाँ 581-619 ई. तक सूई वंश का शासन रहा जिसका संस्थापक सूई नामक व्यक्ति था। 611-614 ई. तक इस वंश के शासकों का कोरिया के साथ युद्ध हुआ जिसमें उन्हें हार का सामना करना पड़ा तथा जन व धन की अपार हानि उठानी पड़ी। फलस्वरूप चीन में अराजकता एवं अव्यवस्था फैल गई। राज्यपालों पर किसी प्रकार का दबाव नहीं था। इसी बीच ली यान ने सूई वंश को समाप्त कर तांग वंश की

स्थापना की। इस वंश के शासक ताई सुंग ने अपनी नीति के परिणामस्वरूप ही चीनी साम्राज्य का प्रसार किया था।

तांग वंश का अंतिम प्रतापी सम्राट मोगहुआंग था, जो काफी विलासी प्रकृति का था। वह शासन के प्रति उदासीन हो गया था। अंत में उसने राज्य अपने पुत्र को सौंप दिया। **मोराडक** का मानना है–"इस समय चीन सभ्यता के मामले में सबसे आगे था। चाय इसी युग की देन है।"

इस वंश के शासनकाल में चीन का काफी उत्थान हुआ था, पूरे एशिया में उसे शक्तिशाली देश की संज्ञा दी जाने लगी। तांग वंश के शासकों ने साम्राज्य विस्तार की नीति पर चलते हुए मंगोलिया, तुर्किस्तान, अनाम एवं चम्पा आदि राज्यों पर अधिकार कर लिया जिसके कारण 631 ई. में जापान ने भी अपना बाजार चीनियों के लिए खोल दिया। इस प्रकार इस काल में चीन के आर्थिक क्षेत्र में काफी विकास हुआ था। तांग वंश के शासकों ने विभिन्न क्षेत्रों में सुधार किए। इस दौरान हुए सुधार कार्यों पर निम्न प्रकार प्रकाश डाला गया है–

केन्द्रीय शासन प्रबंध–उस काल में केन्द्रीय शासक काफी शक्तिशाली हो चुका था। इस समय चीन में एक सुदृढ़ केन्द्रीय शासन की स्थापना हुई। सम्राट् के अधीन तीन मंत्रियों का एक मंत्रिमंडल होता था। पहला प्रधानमंत्री था, जो आन्तरिक विषय, कृषि व न्याय-व्यवस्था की देखभाल करता था तथा राजा के आदेशों का पालन करवाता था। दूसरा मंत्री उद्योग, यातायात एवं जनहित के कार्यों की देखभाल करता था। तीसरा मंत्री सेनाध्यक्ष होता था। राज्य के समस्त महत्त्वपूर्ण विभाग इन मंत्रियों के ही अधीन होते थे। शिक्षा पर सरकार का नियंत्रण था। सरकार ने स्थान-स्थान पर स्कूल खुलवाकर जनता को शिक्षित करने का प्रयास किया। राज्यों में राज्यपाल के पद पर सैनिक अधिकारी नियुक्त किये जाने लगे। इस प्रकार तांग वंश के समय सुदृढ़ केन्द्रीय शासन की स्थापना होने से चीन में एक नये युग की शुरुआत हुई।

भूमि-सम्बंधी सुधार–राज्य में भूमि को अपनी सम्पदा घोषित कर भूमि का वितरण अपनी इच्छानुसार करना शुरू कर दिया जेकाइस पिरेनी के अनुसार "सन् 1917 की रूसी क्रांति के सिवाय चीन के भूमि सम्बंधी सुधारों में ऐसा कठोर सुधार किसी भी देश ने नहीं किया था।" किसानों का भूमि पर से अधिकार खत्म कर, उनसे वार्षिक किराया लिया जाने लगा। भूमि के बदले आवश्यकता पड़ने पर कृषकों से सैनिक सेवा भी ली जाती थी।

धार्मिक नीति—इस दौरान चीन में बौद्धधर्म का प्रचार होने लगा, परन्तु तांग वंश के शासकों ने धार्मिक असहिष्णुता की नीति पर चलते हुए बौद्धों के समस्त मठों को धराशायी करवा दिया। केवल तीन मठ रहने दिये।

न्याय व्यवस्था—इस वंश के शासकों ने 637 ई. में एक कानून संहिता तैयार करवाई। यह कानून संहिता मानवता व सामाजिक समानता पर आधारित थी। राजकीय पदों पर योग्य व्यक्तियों को नियुक्त किया जाने लगा। इस संहिता के बनने के बाद समाज में असमानता दूर हो गई। इस प्रकार स्पष्ट है कि तांग वंश के समय में चीनी साम्राज्य का विस्तार हुआ तथा जनता सुखी तथा समृद्ध थी। इसीलिए इस काल को चीन के इतिहास में द्वितीय स्वर्णकाल कहते हैं।

7. शुंग वंश

चीन में शुंग वंश की स्थापना चाओ क्वांग यीन शांग द्वारा की गई। इस वंश का शासनकाल 10वीं सदी से 13वीं सदी तक था। चाओ क्वांग यीन एक कुशल राजनीतिज्ञ सम्राट था। वह शक्ति के सहारे राज्य नहीं करना चाहता था। उसने प्रजा की भलाई के लिए कई सुधार किये, जिन्हें जनसाधारण ने स्वीकार किया। उन सुधार कार्यों पर निम्न बिन्दुओं में प्रकाश डाला जा रहा है—

1. राज्य में बेइमानी व छल-कपट को दूर करने के लिए माप-तौल सम्बन्धी नियम बनाए गये।
2. विदेशी आक्रमणों से राज्य की रक्षा के लिए उसने चीन में एक विशाल तथा शक्तिशाली सेना का गठन किया।
3. उसने कृषकों के हित के लिए ग्रीन शूट्स नियम बनाये। इसके अंतर्गत सरकार किसानों को बिना ब्याज के ऋण देती थी।

इन सुधारों के बावजूद भी शुंग वंश के अंतिम शासकों के शासनकाल में चीन में अराजकता एवं अव्यवस्था का काफी प्रसार हुआ था। ऐसी परिस्थितियों में 1279 ई. में मंगोल नेता कुबलाई खां ने अन्तिम शुंग सम्राट को मारकर चीन पर अधिकार कर लिया। इस प्रकार चीन पर मंगोलों का प्रभुत्व स्थापित हो गया। सेवाइन ने उस युग की विशेषता पर प्रकाश डालते हुए कहा है कि, "राज्य को व्यापार, उद्योग, कृषि आदि की व्यवस्था पूर्णरूप से अपने हाथ में ले लेनी चाहिए, ताकि गरीबों की रक्षा हो सके और अमीर उन्हें धूल में न मिला दें।" तथा चीन में युयान वंश की नींव पड़ी और प्राचीन युग का अंत हो गया। स्पष्ट है कि चीन पर विभिन वंशों ने राज किया तथा विदेशियों द्वारा काफी

हमले भी किये गये। फिर भी चीन की सभ्यता लगभग 4000 वर्ष तक निरंतर फलती-फूलती रही।

चीन की सभ्यता का विश्लेषण

चीन की शासन व्यवस्था, आर्थिक, सामाजिक स्थिति आदि को वृहद् रूप में निम्न प्रकार स्पष्ट किया गया है।

1. शासन व्यवस्था

चीन की शासन व्यवस्था पर इस प्रकार प्रकाश डाला गया है–

(1) राजा–चीन में राजा को 'वांग' कह कर पुकारा जाता था। वह सबसे बड़ा न्यायाधीश तथा पुरोहित था। राजा को ईश्वर का प्रतिनिधि माना जाता था। राजा द्वारा किये गये निर्णय को मान्य माना जाता था। सम्राट ईश्वर के प्रति उत्तरदायी होता था। चीन के सम्राट स्वेच्छाचारी होते हुए भी प्रजा की भलाई करना अपना प्रमुख कर्तव्य मानते थे। उनका प्रमुख कार्य वीजिंग में स्थित 'स्वर्ग की देवी' की पूजा करना था। चीन में सम्राट को 'स्वर्ग का पुत्र' कहा जाता था। फिर भी यहां राजनीतिक एकता का सदा अभाव रहता था। **एलिस** और **जॉन** ने इसके विपरीत विचार व्यक्त करते हुए लिखा है, "सम्राट को स्वर्ग पुत्र का खिताब मिला हुआ था और उसका बहुत सम्मान किया जाता था, लेकिन उसकी शक्ति बहुत कम थी। विभिन्न राज्यों में आपस में युद्ध चला करते थे। शक्तिशाली कमजोर को जीत लेता था और अंत में राज्यों की संख्या 1500 से घटकर 52 हो गई।"

(2) मंत्रिपरिषद्–मंत्रिपरिषद् का कार्य शासन व्यवस्था में राजा की मदद करना था। साथ ही सुझाव भी देती थी। उसके अधीन चार मंत्री होते थे, जो राजा को प्रशासनिक कार्यों में परामर्श देते थे। इसके अतिरिक्त छः सदस्यों की समिति, माल व वित्त समिति थी। राजा स्वेच्छाचारी एवं कुलागत होते थे। राजा जिले में एक कमिश्नर नियुक्त करता था, जिसे 'सेंसर' कहते थे। चीन की जनता का मुख्य नारा था–"भरपेट रोटी और बच्चों का लालन-पालन सरकार का काम है।" राजा का मन्त्रिपरिषद् पर पूरा नियंत्रण था। वह नीति निर्धारण व शासन सम्बन्धी विषयों पर मन्त्रिपरिषद् से विचार-विमर्श करता था, परन्तु अन्तिम निर्णय राजा का ही होता था।

(3) नियुक्ति का ढंग–किसी भी सरकारी पद पर नियुक्ति में योग्यता को प्राथमिकता दी जाती थी। सरकारी पदों के लिए कोई आरक्षण नहीं था। इस समय नियुक्तियां लोकसेवा आयोग के द्वारा की जाती थीं। परीक्षाओं में उत्तीर्ण व्यक्तियों

को प्रशिक्षण देने के बाद योग्यतानुसार पद पर नियुक्त कर दिया जाता था। अधिकारी के अपराधी सिद्ध होने पर कठोर दंड दिया जाता था। चीन में राजकीय पदों पर नियुक्ति चीन की संसार को एक महत्त्वपूर्ण देन है।

(4) प्रांतीय शासन-व्यवस्था—दो या तीन हीन गाँवों के समूह का एक फू बनता था, जो प्रांत के समान होता था। प्रांतों को सैंग भी कहा जाता था। सम्राट ने विशाल साम्राज्य को प्रांतों में विभक्त कर दिया था, ताकि शासन व्यवस्था को सुचारू रूप से चलाया जा सके, जिनका शासन प्रबंध एक न्यायाधीश और राज्यपाल द्वारा चलाया जाता था। इनकी नियुक्ति सम्राट स्वयं करता था। सामंतों द्वारा सम्राट को सैनिक सहायता और कर दिये जाते थे। यही नहीं, समय-समय पर दरबार में जाकर निष्ठा व्यक्त करनी पड़ती थी। इसके बदले में सम्राट उन्हें जागीर तथा उपाधियाँ प्रदान करता था।

समय के साथ प्रांत के सामन्त शक्तिशाली होने लगे। वे जनता पर अत्याचार करके बहुत-सा धन वसूल करते थे, परन्तु सम्राट को कुछ भी नहीं देते थे। इस प्रकार चीनी सम्राज्य के पतन में इन सामन्तों की महत्त्वपूर्ण भूमिका रही। उस दौरान भूमि कर ही आय का प्रमुख स्रोत हुआ करता था। **बेन फिगर** ने लिखा है, "हेनरी जार्ज ने जिस भूमि कर पर 19वीं शताब्दी में जोर दिया था, वह भूमिकर चीन में उस समय था।"

(5) ग्रामों का शासन-प्रबंध—चीन के ग्रामीण इलाकों व नगरों की शासन व्यवस्था एक-दूसरे से काफी भिन्न थी। प्रत्येक नगर या गाँव का एक मुखिया होता था, जो वहाँ के शासन-प्रबंध का संचालन करता था। कई गाँवों के समूह को 'हीन' कहा जाता था और दो या तीन हीन का एक फू बनता था, जो प्रांत के समान होता था। प्रत्येक हीन में एक मुख्यिा का चयन किया जाता था। उसकी सहायता के लिए एक न्यायाधीश, एक कोषाध्यक्ष और एक कर वसूल करने वाले अधिकारी की नियुक्ति की जाती थी। ये सभी मिलकर अपने गाँव का शासन चलाते थे। जो व्यक्ति काम नहीं करना चाहते थे वे चोर समझे जाते थे।

चीन में दण्ड-व्यवस्था काफी कठोर थी। अपराधियों को मृत्युदंड के साथ-साथ हाथ-पैर काटने, नाक काटने की सजा दी जाती थी। अपराधियों को जुर्माना भी देना पड़ता था। **डॉ. गोयल** ने लिखा है—"राजनीतिक दृष्टि से संघर्षमय होते हुए भी परवर्ती चाऊ यग सांस्कृतिक, व्यवस्थापन, प्रगति और प्रसार युग था।" इतिहासकार **विल ड्यूरेण्ट** ने चीन की शासन-व्यवस्था के बारे में लिखा है, "चीन का प्रशासन राजतंत्र और कुलीनतंत्र का एक सुंदर समन्वय था।"

2. आर्थिक दशा

चीन की आर्थिक दशा को निम्न प्रकार उजागर किया गया है–

(1) कृषि एवं पशुपालन–चीनी लोगों द्वारा कृषि तथा पशुपालन पर अधिक बल दिया जाता था। ये हल-बैल चलाते थे। बाजरा, चावल, गेहूँ तथा जौ और फलों की खेती होती थी। उपजाऊ भूमि पर नौ परिवार मिलकर सामूहिक रूप से खेती करते थे। मध्य भूमि में जो फसल पैदा होती थी, उसे सब बराबर बांट लेते थे और आस-पास के भाग पर वे परिवार अलग-अलग खेती करते थे। इस व्यवस्था को 'चिंगतियेन प्रणाली' कहा जाता था।

सैद्धान्तिक दृष्टि से समस्त भूमि पर राजा का अधिकार होता था। उपजाऊ भूमि पर सामूहिक रूप से खेती की जाती थी और कर भी सामूहिक रूप से चुकाया जाता था। हल लकड़ी, पत्थर व लोहे के बनते थे। यहाँ के लोग अच्छी किस्म के खाद का प्रयोग किया करते थे। राज्य द्वारा नहरों व बांधों का निर्माण करवाया जाता था, ताकि खेतों में पानी पहुंचाया जा सके। हान वंश के सम्राटों ने कृषि के विकास के लिए 56 नहरें खुदवाई थीं। कृषि के अतिरिक्त उनका दूसरा मुख्य व्यवसाय पशुपालन भी था। यहाँ के लोग भेड़, सुअर, बैल एवं कुत्ता आदि पशुओं को पालते थे। प्रसिद्ध चीनी विद्वान प्रो. क्रील के अनुसार चीनी लोग घोड़ों को भी पालते थे, जिनका उपयोग रथों को खींचने के लिए किया जाता था।''

(2) उद्योग धंधे-चीन में उद्योग धंधों का आश्चर्यजनक विकास हुआ था। चीनियों का मुख्य व्यवसाय रेशम के कीड़े पालकर रेशम तैयार करना था। रेशम का काम घर में होता था। यहां के व्यापारी रेशम बेचने विदेश जाते थे तथा वर्षों बाद वापस आते थे। यह काम बड़ा मेहनती होता था। वह रेशम की गाँठ पीठ पर लादकर विदेश चले जाते थे, जहाँ से वर्षों बाद लौटकर आते थे। चीन में स्त्रियाँ भी रेशम का व्यवसाय करती थीं। ये स्त्रियां रेशम के एक कीड़े को घास के गड्ढों में डालती थीं और वह कीड़ा 48 घंटे में 9500 कीड़ों को पैदा कर देता था। इससे यहाँ के लोग रेशम के उच्चकोटि के वस्त्र बनाकर पश्चिमी देशों को निर्यात करते थे।

चीन में बढ़ई उद्योग का भी काफी विकास हो चुका था। यहाँ के बढ़ई लकड़ी के मकान और सुंदर फर्नीचर बनाते थे। यहाँ पर दीवारों को खोदकर मूतियाँ बनाई जाती थीं। चीन में आये दिन अकाल की स्थिति पैदा होती गयी जिससे वहां की गरीब जनता ने भूख से बचने के लिये अपने को ही बेचना प्रारम्भ कर दिया। चीन में आये दिन अकाल पड़ते रहते थे।

चीन का एक मुख्य व्यवसाय मछली पकड़ना भी था। यहां के घर शीशे के भी बनाये जाते थे। 200 ई. पू. में चीनियों ने सूत कातना सीखा और सूती कपड़ा भी बनने लगा। यहां की सरकार बेरोजगार को रोजगार देती थी। यहां वृद्धों तथा बेरोजगारों को सरकार की ओर से सहायता दी जाती थी। लगभग 50 प्रतिशत भूमि पर खेती होती थी। विल ड्यूरेंट के शब्दों में–"एक परिवार सालाना 83 हजार डालर कमाता था और औसतन एक आदमी पर दो सेंट प्रतिदिन का खर्च होता था।" चीन में नदियों की बाढ़ के प्रकोप के कारण लोग अपनी आवश्यकताओं को सीमित रखते थे जिससे उनको कम नुकसान उठाना पड़े। सेवाइन के अनुसार-"एक चीनी की आवश्यकता एक मुट्ठी दाना, एक लंगोटी और टोपी मात्र थी।" चीन में किसानों की दशा दयनीय थी। सेवाइन के अनुसार–"गुलामी और बेगार साधारण चीज थी। चीन का विचित्र किसान छोड़ा हुआ आवश्यक कीड़ा था, जिसकी रुचि पेट भर खाने से थोड़ी अधिक मात्र थी। वह प्रकृति का उतना ही महत्त्वपूर्ण अंग था, जितना वह जमीन जिसे वह जोतता और वे प्रकृति के जानवर जिन्हें वह पालता था।" इस प्रकार चीन में किसान को गुलाम की संज्ञा दी जाती थी।

चीनी द्वारा वंशानुगत व्यवसाय करने की प्रथा थी और उन्हें बदलना पाप समझते थे। यहां केवल त्यौहारों पर छुट्टी दी जाती थी। रविवार को अवकाश नहीं दिया जाता था। 1876 ई. में जब अंग्रेजों ने चीन में पहली बार 10 मील लम्बी रेल लाइन बिछाई तो उसका इतना जबरदस्त विरोध हुआ कि सम्राट को रेल की कीमत चुकाकर रेल का इंजन, गाड़ी तथा पटरी को समुद्र में फिकवाना पड़ा। चीन में मुख्य रूप से कागज का निर्माण किया जाता था। ये चिथड़े, वृक्ष की छाल एवं रेशम के छोटे-छोटे टुकड़ों से कागज बनाते थे। विश्व में सर्वप्रथम कागज का प्रयोग चीन में ही किया गया था।

(3) व्यापार–चीन में व्यापार के क्षेत्र में काफी विकास हुआ था। चीनी व्यापार को बढ़ावा देने के लिए उसके सम्राट शी हुआंग टी ने सड़कों का बहुत अधिक विकास किया। चीन में व्यापारियों के संघ बने हुए थे। मजदूरों की मजदूरी व कार्य के घंटे निर्धारित थे। यहाँ के लोग चाय, रेशम, चीनी मिट्टी के बर्तन, बारूद तथा ताश का निर्यात किया करते थे और विदेशों से अफीम, ऊन, तम्बाकू, शीशा और कीमती पत्थर का आयात किया करते थे। चीनी व्यापारियों के मलाया, तुर्किस्तान, भारत, ईरान, मैसोपोटामिया व रोम आदि देशों के साथ उनके व्यापारिक संबंध थे। यहाँ सोने के सिक्कों का प्रचलन होने से व्यापार में काफी सुविधा हो गई। यहां व्यापारिक बैंक भी थे, जहाँ लोगों को ऊँची दरों पर ब्याज दिया जाता था।

3. सामाजिक दशा

(1) सामाजिक वर्ग—चीनीवासियों का ऐसा मानना था कि संसार को बनाने वाले पानकू ने समाज का चार भागों विभाजित किया है—प्रथम वर्ग मन्दारिन का है जो सर्वश्रेष्ठ है। इसमें प्रबुद्ध व्यक्ति आते हैं जिनके द्वारा समाज को दिशा-निर्देश और परामर्श दिया जाता था। इसीलिए क्रेन ब्रिन्टन के अनुसार, "इस वर्ग ने चीन में बाहरी विचारों को आने से ही नहीं रोका, वरन् इसने चीन की सभ्यता को स्थायी बना दिया।" दूसरे वर्ग में कृषकों को शामिल किया गया था, जिनकी दशा काफी दयनीय थी। तीसरे वर्ग में कारीगरों एवं चौथे वर्ग में व्यापारियों को शामिल किया गया था किन्तु सामान्यतया समाज दो भागों में विभक्त था—अधिकारी और कर्मचारी। इन दोनों वर्गों में बड़ा भेदभाव था। समाज में पहला स्थान जनता का, दूसरा स्थान देवताओं का और तीसरा स्थान राजा का था। चीनी लोग शान्तिपूर्ण जीवन बिताते थे। इतिहासकार **डेविस** ने लिखा है—"चीनी सभ्यता सुनिश्चित रूप से शान्ति के लिए संगठित है और चीन ही केवल एक ऐसा देश है, जहां पर सैनिक होना अपमानजनक समझा जाता है।"

(2) संयुक्त परिवार प्रथा—भारतवर्ष की भाँति चीन में सामाजिक जीवन की आधारशिला संयुक्त प्रथा थी। यहां समाज पितृसत्तात्मक परिवार पर आधारित था। परिवार के सभी सदस्य मुखिया (पिता अथवा वरिष्ठ सदस्य) की आज्ञा का पालन करना अपना कर्तव्य मानते थे। प्रत्येक व्यक्ति की आय मुखिया के पास जमा होती थी। घर का सारा खर्चा वही व्यक्ति चलाता था। परिवार में पुत्री की अपेक्षा पुत्र को अधिक महत्त्व दिया जाता था। पुत्र और पुत्रियों की शादियाँ माता-पिता द्वारा की जाती थीं। संयुक्त परिवार में प्रत्येक सदस्य अपने पूर्वजों की पूजा करते थे। चीन में बड़े परिवार का होना बड़प्पन का चिह्न समझा जाता था। **प्लेट** और **जीन** के अनुसार—"जो व्यक्ति चीनी परिवार को नहीं समझता, वह चीन को नहीं समझ सकता। चीन में बड़े परिवार वाला होना बड़प्पन का चिह्न समझा जाता था।" परिवार में माता तथा पिता को अत्यंत सम्मानित स्थान प्राप्त था।

सामान्यतया पिता की मृत्यु के पश्चात् उसका ज्येष्ठ पुत्र उसका उत्तराधिकारी घोषित किया जाता था। उप-पत्नियाँ अपने पुत्रों को उत्तराधिकारी बनाने के लिए सदैव प्रयत्नशील रहती थीं। परिवार में पिता के बाद माता को अत्यंत सम्मानित स्थान प्राप्त था। मुखिया की मृत्यु के बाद उसकी विधवा पत्नी परिवार की शासिका बन जाती थी।

(अ) भ्रातृ-प्रेम—चीन में भ्रातृ-प्रेम बहुत अधिक था। एक भाई-दूसरे भाई के लिए जान देने को तैयार रहता था।

(ब) प्रतिशोध—परिवार की प्रतिष्ठा के लिए अपमान का बदला लेना ही पारिवारिक निष्ठा का एक रूप था। कहा गया कि पिता, भाई अथवा परिवार के अन्य सदस्यों की हत्या का बदला लेना व्यक्ति का धर्म है। इसके लिए अपराधी व्यक्ति का अथवा उसके परिवार के किसी भी व्यक्ति की हत्या करके बदला लेना चाहिए। ऐसे प्रतिशोध को नैतिक विचारकों ने उचित बतलाया।

(स) कन्फ्यूशियस के विचारों का प्रभाव—कन्फ्यूशियस ने परिवार के प्रति निष्ठा की भावना को सुदृढ़ कर दिया। उनके अनुसार पिता की गलती को छिपाना पुत्र का कर्तव्य है तथा पुत्र की गलती को छिपाना पिता का कर्तव्य है। एक बार राज्य के शासक कन्फ्यूशियस ने कहा कि—

"मेरे प्रदेश में ईमानदारी की परिभाषा भिन्न है। यदि पिता चोरी करे, तो उसे छिपाना पुत्र का कर्तव्य है तथा यदि पुत्र चोरी करे, तो पिता भी उसे छिपाता है।"

कन्फ्यूशियस ने परिवार की मर्यादा की रक्षा के लिए झूठ को सही बताया है। अतः उसे पारिवारिक परम्परा का सबसे बड़ा हिमायती और पोषक माना जाता है।

(3) दासों की दशा—चीन में दासों की नियुक्ति तीन साल के लिये की जाती थी। इससे अधिक समय तक उनको दास नहीं रखा जा सकता था।

(4) सामाजिक नैतिकता—चीनी समाज द्वारा विनम्रता और शिष्टाचार पर काफी ध्यान दिया जाता था। परिवार में छोटे लोग अपने बड़ों को सम्मान तथा आदर की दृष्टि से देखते थे। बड़े लोग भी अपने व्यवहार एवं आचरण से छोटों को प्रभावित करते थे। जो व्यक्ति अपने परिवार के प्रति निष्ठावान नहीं रहता था, समाज में उस पर कोई विश्वास नहीं करता था।

(5) खानपान—चीन के धनी लोग मुर्गियाँ, सुअर एवं मछली का सेवन करते थे। कुलीनवर्ग के लोगों को भोजन बाँस, कांसे, या मिट्टी की तश्तरियों में परोसा जाता था। वे लकड़ी या हाथीदांत की तीलियों का प्रयोग भोजन करने के दौरान करते थे। चीनी समाज में गरीब और अमीर में बड़ा अंतर होता था। चीन में चीना गरीब आदमियों का भोजन था।

(6) भवन—चीन में अधिकांश लोग ईंटों, सरकंडों, बांस और मिट्टी से बने मकानों में निवास करते थे। मकानों का फर्श कच्चा होता था, परन्तु अमीर लोग भव्य मकान बनवाते थे, जिसके चारों ओर बगीचे और सुंदर सरोवर होते थे।

(7) रहन-सहन—चीनी प्रारम्भ में सन (जूट) के वस्त्रों का प्रयोग करते थे। बाद में सूती वस्त्र पहनने लगे। ठंड से बचने के लिये मन्दारिन लोग कीमती वस्त्र पहनते थे और सिर पर टोपी धारण करते थे। उस समय स्त्रियां कंधे से एड़ी तक एक चोगा धारण करती थीं और फूलों तथा पंखों से अपने बाल सजाती थीं। इस समय स्त्रियाँ नाक, कान, हाथ और गले में जेवर धारण करती थीं।

(8) मनोरंजन एवं आमोद-प्रमोद—इस काल में कुलीन लोगों के मनोरंजन के लिए प्रमुख साधन संगीत, नृत्य, शराब, धार्मिक समारोह, शिकार एवं तीरंदाजी प्रतियोगिताएँ आदि का आयोजन किया जाता था। धार्मिक समारोहों में नर्तकों द्वारा नृत्य किया जाता था। इसके सम्बन्ध में **एलिस** और **जान** का ऐसा विचार है कि, ''कुलीनों के पास शतरंज खेलने, शिकार पर जाने, घोड़ों को प्रशिक्षण देने, जुआ खेलने व मुर्गों की लड़ाई देखने और मनमौजी खेलकूदों में भाग लेने के लिए पर्याप्त समय रहता था। दूसरी ओर गरीब लोगों को आजीविका उपार्जन के लिए अपनी जाग्रत अवस्था के सभी घंटे खर्च करने पड़ते थे।''

(9) महिलाओं की स्थिति- चीनी परिवारों में कन्फ्यूशियस से पहले महिलाओं का स्थान प्रधान था लेकिन छठी शताब्दी में पुरुष प्रधान हो गया। चीन में स्त्रियों की दशा दयनीय थी। परिवार में पुत्री की अपेक्षा पुत्र को अधिक महत्त्व दिया जाता था। यहां कुँवारी लड़की की सुन्दरता का प्रतीक उसके छोटे पैर होते थे जिसके कारण उन्हें बचपन से लोहे के जूते पहनाये जाते थे। चीनी समाज में स्त्रियों के चरित्र पर बहुत जोर दिया जाता था। अगर किसी अविवाहित कन्या को कोई पुरुष छू लेता, तो वह आत्महत्या कर लेती थी।

(अ) विवाह—चीन में विवाह प्रत्येक स्त्री के लिए आवश्यक एवं अनिवार्य था। विवाह की उम्र कन्या के लिए बीस वर्ष तथा पुरुष के लिए तीस वर्ष थी। सगाई बाल्यावस्था में हो जाती थी। विवाह पिता की इच्छा से होता था। चीन में सगोत्र विवाह दूर के सम्बन्धियों में भी वर्जित था। ऐसा विश्वास किया जाता था कि सगोत्र विवाह से नस्ल खराब होती है। वैज्ञानिक दृष्टि से यह बात बहुत सही भी है।

इस काल में बाल-विवाह की प्रथा नहीं थी। लड़की को परिवार का अस्थाई सदस्य समझा जाता था, क्योंकि वह शादी के बाद दूसरे घर की सदस्य बन जाती थी। शादी के बाद जो लड़की सबसे ज्यादा पुत्र पैदा करती थी, उसे समाज में सबसे ज्यादा सम्मान दिया जाता था। विवाह की निश्चित उम्र तक लड़की-लड़का का विवाह न करने वाले माता-पिता को राज्य दण्डित करता था। चीन में कभी-कभी बेमेल विवाह भी होते थे, जिनमें वृद्धा स्त्रियां जवान लड़कों से तथा वृद्ध व्यक्ति जवान

लड़की से विवाह कर लेते थे। पति की मृत्यु के कुछ समय बीतने के बाद विधवा पुनर्विवाह कर सकती थी। इस समय सती-प्रथा प्रचलित नहीं थी।

इस युग में पति अपनी पत्नी को तलाक भी दे सकता था। तलाक के बाद स्त्री दहेज के साथ अपने पिता के घर लौट जाती थी। अगर विवाह के बाद संतान न हो तो पुरुष अपनी स्त्री को तलाक देकर दूसरा विवाह कर सकता था। पत्नी के लिये तलाक के कुछ निश्चित नियम थे, परन्तु कुछ विशिष्ट अवस्थाओं में स्त्रियों को तलाक देने की प्रथा नहीं थी। यदि पति विवाह के समय गरीब हो और विवाह के बाद मालदार बन गये हों, अथवा पत्नी के रहने के लिए मायके का घर नहीं हो अथवा जिसने पति के माता अथवा पिता की मृत्यु होने पर उनके श्राद्ध में भाग लिया हो, तो इन तीन अवस्थाओं में स्त्री को तलाक देने का विधान नहीं था।

(ब) बहु-विवाह एवं उप-पत्नीवाद—उस समय चीन में राजवंश तथा कुलीन वर्ग के लोगों में एक से अधिक विवाह करने की प्रथा थी। इन वर्गों में विवाह के समय पत्नी के साथ उसकी छोटी बहनें अथवा रिश्ते की बहनें या अन्य राजपरिवारों की लड़कियां आती थीं, जिन्हें राजा अथवा सामंत दूसरी पत्नियां बनाकर रख लेते थे। साधारण राजकर्मचारी दो पत्नियां रखने के लिये स्वतंत्र था, बड़े अधिकारी तीन और राजा नौ।

इस उच्चकुल की उप-पत्नियों के साथ साधारण वर्ग की स्त्रियाँ भी उप-पत्नी के रूप में रखने के लिये स्वतंत्र थे। जिनको 'वी' के नाम से भी जाना जाता था। अभिजात्य वर्ग की उप-पत्नियों की अवस्था बहुत अच्छी थी। साधारण वर्ग की स्त्रियों को घरेलू काम करने के लिए रखा जाता था। उनके मालिकों को इस बात का अधिकार था कि वे चाहे जिस प्रकार का उनके साथ व्यवहार करें। यहीं से उप-पत्नीवाद प्रथा का जन्म हुआ। इस प्रकार की स्त्रियों का प्रयोग मनोरंजन करने के लिये किया जाता था। ऐसी उप-पत्नियाँ भी अपने गुणों और सुंदरता से अपने स्वामी को प्रभावित कर अपने पुत्रों को पिता का उत्तराधिकारी बनाने में सफल हो जाती थीं। फिर भी उनको सम्मान प्राप्त नहीं था। उदाहरण के लिए, लू राज्य के प्रधानमंत्री की प्रशंसा में ये शब्द कहे गये थे—"वह इतना ईमानदार तथा मितव्ययी था कि न तो उसकी उप-पत्नियाँ रेशमी कपड़े पहनतीं थीं और न उनके घोड़े बाजरा खाते थे।"

साधारण वर्ग की उप-पत्नियों को किसी प्रकार के अधिकार नहीं दिये गये थे। प्रमुख पत्नी पति से बिना पूछे उनकी हत्या करवा सकती थी। बहु-पत्नीवाद तथा

उप-पत्नीवाद की वजह से ही सुख शांति व्यवस्था में बाधा उत्पन्न होती थी साथ ही गृहयुद्धों का सामना करना पड़ता था।

राजपरिवारों में तथा कुलीन वर्ग के अंतःपुर की देखभाल करने में हिजड़े महत्त्वपूर्ण भूमिका निभाते थे। कभी-कभी ये हिजड़े शासक और स्वामियों के कृपापात्र भी बन जाते थे। सम्भवतः इन हिजड़ों का उपयोग इसी युग में प्रारम्भ हुआ।

जिस लड़की का परिवार (पिता का घर) मजबूत होता था उसको ससुराल में काफी सम्मान की दृष्टि से देखा जाता था। उसका विरोध करने में भय का अनुभव करते थे।

(स) पर्दा प्रथा—चीनियों में कुँवारी लड़कियों में भी पर्दे का प्रचलन था। राजपरिवार तथा अभिजात्य वर्ग के लोग अपने भोग-विलास के लिए कई रखैलें भी रखते थे। फिर भी उनकी पत्नियों को अपना चरित्र उज्ज्वल रखना पड़ता था। इस प्रकार से स्पष्ट है कि चीन में स्त्रियों की दशा बहुत दयनीय थी। चीन के कवि ने महिलाओं की स्थिति के बारे में लिखा है, "कन्या के जन्म से किसी को खुशी नहीं थी। युवा होने पर वह पुरुषों से छिपकर कमरे में रहती थी, पुरुषों से मिलने में डरती थी। वह नित्य झुकती थी, कहना मानती थी और छुप-छुप कर रोती थी। कितना दुःखी था नारी होना। संसार में इतनी सस्ती वस्तु न थी।"

विवाहित स्त्रियाँ घरेलू कामकाज देखती थीं। यदि कोई व्यक्ति पति के लिए उपहार लाता, तो पत्नी के लिए भी उपहार लाना अनिवार्य माना जाता था। प्रायः स्त्रियां अशिक्षित होतीं थीं, उनमें गहरी सूझ-बूझ तथा बुद्धिमत्ता के प्रमाण भी प्राप्त हुए हैं। इस समय स्त्रियां कविताएं भी लिखती थीं। लू राज्य की एक वृद्धा स्त्री के बारे में उल्लेख मिलता है। चीन की वृद्धा स्त्रियाँ राजनीति तथा प्रशासन के बारे में भी सलाह देतीं थीं तथा उनकी बात ध्यान और आदर के साथ सुनी जाती थी। संकट की घड़ी में पुरुष भी ऐसी स्त्रियों से सलाह लेते थे।

तत्कालीन धारणाओं के अनुसार स्त्रियों को सार्वजनिक जीवन से दूर रहने की सलाह दी जाती थी। विनम्र और आज्ञाकारी होना उनका गुण माना जाता था। काव्य-संग्रह के अनुसार निर्भीक तथा जबरदस्ती स्त्रियों से विवाह नहीं करना चाहिए। स्त्रियों के लिए विधान था कि उनकी गणना पुरखों में तभी हो सकती है, जब उनकी मृत्यु उस कमरे में हो जो उनके रहने के लिए निश्चित किया गया है।

इस समय नीतिशास्त्र राजाओं तथा शासकों को चेतावनी देते थे कि वे स्त्रियों के परामर्श से कार्य न करें, क्योंकि स्त्रियों के परामर्श को मानने के कारण ही बहुत से शासकों का विनाश हुआ है। स्त्रियों के बारे में यह धारणा प्रचलित थी कि वे

षड्यंत्र रचती हैं और रहस्यों को कभी गोपनीय नहीं रख सकतीं, इसलिए कोई भी रहस्यात्मक बात उनसे नहीं करनी चाहिए। स्त्रियों के विरुद्ध प्रचलित धारणाओं की झाँकी हमें 'प्रतिष्ठित काव्य संग्रह' के उद्धरणों से मिलती है–''बुद्धिमान पुरुष नगरों की दीवारों को सुदृढ़ करते हैं। पर बुद्धिमती स्त्रियां उनका विनाश करना जानती हैं। वास्तव में बुद्धिमती स्त्रियां भी, एक उल्लू की ही बुद्धि रखती हैं। स्त्रियों तथा हिजड़ों से किसी सदुपदेश की अपेक्षा करना मूर्खता है।''

इस प्रकार तत्कालीन धारणाओं के अनुसार स्त्रियों की सलाह पर काम करना पुरुषोचित नहीं माना जाता था, इस समय चीन के समाज में अनेक अंधविश्वास प्रचलित थे। वे मृतकों के श्राद्ध आदि भी बहुत करते थे।

4. कानून विकास

प्राचीन समय में चीन के निवासी सामाजिक परंपराओं में अधिक विश्वास रखते थे इसी आधार पर यहां कानून का विकास हुआ। चाऊ काल में सम्राटों को प्राचीन विवेकशील एवं प्रतापी राजाओं के पथ पर चलने एवं प्राचीन ऋषियों के ग्रंथों को पढ़ने के लिए कहा जाता था। यह बात इस काल के साहित्य में दिखायी देती है। इस काल में जो राजा सामाजिक मान्यताओं का अपमान करते थे उन्हें अपनी शक्ति गवाना पड़ता था।

इस समय सैनिक कानून एवं नागरिकों के लिये फौजदारी कानून का विकास चाऊकाल के 'प्रतिष्ठित प्रलेख' के स्थान से ज्ञात होता था। शायद ये अलिखित होते थे, किन्तु सर्वमान्य थे। सम्राट प्राचीन राजाओं के ग्रंथों तथा परम्पराओं के आधार पर न्याय करते थे एवं कुल के आधार पर सजा देते थे।

चाऊ काल में न्यायाधीशों की ईमानदारी पर बहुत बल दिया जाता था, किन्तु कभी-कभी उन्हें घूस या सुंदर स्त्रियों के द्वारा कर्त्तव्योविमुख करने का प्रयास भी किया जाता था। इस काल में सम्राटों ने अपने अधीनस्थ अधिकारियों को जनता के साथ निष्पक्ष न्याय करने का आदेश दे रखा था। न्याय में विभिन्न प्रकार के शारीरिक दंड जैसे अंग-भंग करना, उबलते पानी में डुबोकर मारना, बड़े लकड़ी के तख्ते को गले में लटकाना, आदि दंड दिये जाते थे परन्तु समृद्ध वर्ग को दण्ड देना बहुत कठिन था।

इस काल में कानून का पालन करना राजा के लिए अनिवार्य नहीं था। उन्हें दास तथा दासियों को और अपने विपक्षी शासकों तथा मंत्रियों को मृत्यु दण्ड देने का अधिकार था।

5. धार्मिक जीवन

(1) बलि तथा पूजा–चीनी जनता में दो मतों का प्रचलन था–विद्वान वर्ग एकेश्वरवाद तथा जनता बहुदेववादी थी। यहाँ के लोग प्रकृति की उपासना करते थे। पर्वत, वृक्ष, नदियां, आकाश (यंग), वायु तथा पृथ्वी (चिन) आदि इनके मुख्य देवता थे। उनके आकाश और पृथ्वी (चिन) आदि मुख्य देवता थे। वे आकाश और पृथ्वी को क्रमशः पुरुष और स्त्री के रूप में समझते थे। आकाश उनका सर्वशक्तिमान देवता था। चीनी लोग अपने पूर्वजों तथा पितरों की पूजा करते थे उनको प्रसन्न करने के लिए यज्ञ अथवा बलि भी दी जाती थी। बलि के लिए भेड़, कुत्ता, सुअर, मुर्गी तथा घोड़े का भी इस्तेमाल होता था। मदिरा भी चढ़ाई जाती थी। चाऊ युग में नरबलि की प्रथा थी लेकिन कन्फ्यूशियस के प्रभाव से धीरे-धीरे यह प्रथा समाप्त हो गई।

पितरों तथा पूर्वजों की पूजा के द्वारा इस युग के लोग मुख्यतः निम्न वस्तुओं की कामना करते थे–

अपने वंश को आगे बढ़ाने के लिये इस युग के लोग पुत्र की कामना करते थे। लम्बी आयु, वंश वृद्धि, समृद्धि और सुख की कामना की जाती थी तथा असंख्य संतानों की प्राप्ति के लिए भी प्रार्थना की जाती थी। युद्ध में विजय और राज्य का विस्तार उनका प्रमुख उद्देश्य होता था। चीनी लोगों का मानना था कि संकट के समय पूर्वज ही उनकी रक्षा और मनोकामना की पूर्ति करते हैं, इसलिए वे उनके सम्मान में कई उत्सव मनाते थे।

चीनी लोग अंधविश्वासी प्रकृति के थे। यहाँ के लोग देवता को प्रसन्न करने के लिए अनुष्ठान करते थे। देवता को प्रसन्न करने के लिए मांस मदिरा भी चढ़ाते थे और बलि भी देते थे। देवता की पूजा गांव के टीले या पहाड़ी पर होती थी। लगभग हर परिवार में पूर्वजों की पूजा की जाती थी। उनका यह मानना था कि हर रोज पूजा करने से उनके पूर्वजों को भोजन मिल जायेगा, तो वे भूत बनकर इधर-उधर नहीं भटकेंगे। इसके अतिरिक्त पूजा से प्रसन्न होकर पूर्वज उनकी मनोकामना पूर्ण करेंगे।

(2) पुरोहित तथा मन्दिर-चीन में पूर्वजों का मन्दिर परिवार के जीवन और उसकी प्रवृत्तियों का केन्द्र बिंदु माना जाता था। प्रत्येक परिवार के महत्त्वपूर्ण समारोह, विवाह, श्राद्ध तथा अनुष्ठान आदि इसी मन्दिर में सम्पन्न होते थे। राज्याभिषेक भी मन्दिर में ही हुआ करते थे। युद्ध के अभियान का प्रारंभ तथा विजय का समारोह, राजदूतों की नियुक्ति, सामंतों के बारे में निर्णय एवं भोजों का आयोजन भी यहीं सम्पन्न होता था। वर्ष में एक बार सम्राट देवता के रूप में वस्त्र धारण करता था।

पृथ्वी और आकाश को बलि भी मन्दिर में ही चढ़ाई जाती थी। वहां के लोगों के अनुसार यह मन्दिर ईश्वर के पुत्र का मंदिर था।

चीन में राजकीय कर्मचारी तथा पदाधिकारी ही धार्मिक अनुष्ठानों को पूरा कराते थे, जिन्हें वेतन दिया जाता था। धार्मिक मामलों में इन्हें कोई विशेष अधिकार प्राप्त नहीं थे। कभी-कभी दास भी इन धार्मिक कार्यों में भाग लिया करते थे।

(3) देवताओं से संवाद—चीन में देवताओं के साथ बात की जाती थी। चीन के धर्म की भारत के धर्म से तुलना करते हुए जान बाउल ने लिखा है -"भारतीय धर्म चाहे काल्पनिक हो, परंतु चीन का धर्म वास्तविक, धार्मिक कार्यों से सम्बन्धित ठीक आचरण वाला था।"

चीनी जनता पर कन्फ्यूशियस और लाओत्से का गहरा प्रभाव था। इतिहासकार क्रेन ब्रिन्टन का तो यह कहना है कि—"चीन में भारत, यूरोप व अरब की भांति विशेष धर्म नहीं था।" चीन के धर्म में भारतीयों जैसी धार्मिक भावना और यूनानियों का दार्शनिक दृष्टिकोण दोनों का समावेश था। चीन के धर्म का बहुत अधिक असर था। चीनी लोग भूत-प्रेत से डरते थे और भाग्य में विश्वास करते थे। चीनियों पर, कन्फ्यूशियस की विचारधारा तथा बौद्धधर्म का काफी प्रभाव था। प्लेट व जीन के अनुसार, "बहुत से चीनी बहुत समय से एक से अधिक धर्मों को मानते रहे हैं।"

6. दर्शन

विश्व का कोई भी देश दर्शन के क्षेत्र में चीन का मुकावला नहीं कर सकता था। 1250 ई. पू. में चीनी दार्शनिक यू तिज ने चीनी दर्शन को व्यक्त करते हुए लिखा है कि—"वह जो ख्याति को छोड़ देता है, उसे कोई दुःख नहीं होता।" चाऊ वंश में दार्शनिक नगर-नगर में घूमकर अपने विचारों का प्रचार किया करते थे। इस कार्य में उन्हें प्रांतीय शासकों और अमीर व्यापारियों की ओर से भी सहायता मिली।

प्राचीन चीन में छठी शताब्दी ईसा पूर्व में कन्फ्यूशियस की विचारधारा अधिक प्रभावशाली व लोकप्रिय थी। ईसा पूर्व छठी शताब्दी में चीन में धार्मिक विचारकों का जितना जोर था उतना पहले या बाद में कभी नहीं रहा।

मैन्सियस प्रजातंत्र का समर्थक था। अतः उसने युद्ध की निंदा की। चीन के दार्शनिक विश्वबंधुत्व के सिद्धांत में विश्वास करते थे। उनका मानना था कि ईश्वर भलाई करता है और बुराई से घृणा करता है । इतिहासकार बेन फिंगर के अनुसार—"चीनी दार्शनिक मनुष्यों को आपस में प्रेम करना, सहयोग देना व सहिष्णुता का पाठ पढ़ाते थे। ये लोग शत्रु से भी शिक्षा लेते थे।" चीनी कहावत थी,

"मेरे शत्रु में भी कुछ है, जिससे मैं कुछ सीख सकता हूँ।" इस समय के प्रमुख दार्शनिक कन्फ्यूशियस, लाओत्से, मैन्सियस एवं मोत्सू आदि बहुत लोकप्रिय थे।

कन्फ्यूशियस (551 से 479 ई. पू.)

ईसा से छठी शताब्दी पूर्व भारत में महावीर और गौतम बुद्ध तथा फारस में जरथुस्त्र की भांति चीन में भी दार्शनिक कन्फ्यूशियस ने सामाजिक और धार्मिक सुधार आंदोलन चलाया। निस्संदेह कन्फ्यूशियस, जिसे चीनी लोग 'कुंग-जु' के नाम से भी पुकारते हैं, इस युग का सबसे बड़ा दार्शनिक एवं विचारक था। उसका जन्म 551 ई. पू. में शान्तुंग प्रांत के लू नामक नगर में एक उच्च कुल में हुआ था। कन्फ्यूशियस के पिता ने 70 वर्ष की आयु में एक और विवाह किया था। उसी से कन्फ्यूशियस पैदा हुआ था। इस प्रकार वह अपने पिता के बुढ़ापे की औलाद था। कन्फ्यूशियस के पिता का नाम कुंगफू था। जब वह तीन वर्ष का हुआ, उसके पिता की मृत्यु हो गई। अतः इनका पालन-पोषण उसकी विधवा माँ ने किया। धन का अभाव होने के कारण उसकी शिक्षा पूरी नहीं हो सकी थी। उन्नीस वर्ष की अवस्था में उसने शादी की, जिससे एक लड़का पैदा हुआ। चार वर्ष बाद यानि 23 वर्ष की अवस्था में उसने अपनी पत्नी का परित्याग कर दिया।

एक शिक्षक के रूप में—कन्फ्यूशियस ने एक अध्यापक के रूप में अपना जीवन प्रारम्भ किया। इस समय उन्होंने अनेक विद्वानों के दार्शनिक ग्रंथों का अध्ययन किया, जिसके कारण उसके ज्ञान में अत्यधिक वृद्धि हुई। प्लेट व जीन के शब्दों में—"कन्फ्यूशियस ने आनंद की सक्रिय खोज का प्रचार किया। जब लाओत्से बूढ़ा हो गया था और उसके शरीर पर झुर्रियां पड़ गई थीं, तब एक युवक और उत्साही शिक्षक, जिसका नाम कन्फ्यूशियस था, उससे मिलने आया और उनसे बहुत लम्बा वार्तालाप हुआ, किन्तु वे इस विषय पर एकमत न हो सके कि आनंद तक पहुंचने का सही मार्ग कौन सा है?"

चीनी भाषा में शिष्टाचार को 'ली' कहते थे। चीन में धर्म समाज में बहुत से दोष थे जिन्हें दूर करने के लिए कन्फ्यूशियस ने स्कूल खोला। अपने स्कूलों में उसने शिष्टाचार के पालन पर अधिक बल दिया। उसका कहना था, "मनुष्य के चरित्र का निर्माण कविताओं द्वारा होता है और चरित्र की पूर्णता संगीत द्वारा प्राप्त होती है।"

कन्फ्यूशियस समानता में विश्वास रखते थे। इनका मुख्य उद्देश्य जनसामान्य को समृद्ध बनाना था। अतः दीन-दुखियों में वह चर्चित था। सेवाइन का मत है—"गौतम की तरह कन्फ्यूशियस ने पहले विलासी जीवन व्यतीत किया। उसके

अशांत मन और तीक्ष्ण मस्तिष्क ने उसे चुप नहीं बैठने दिया। सुकरात की तरह उसने स्कूल खोला और वह महान शिक्षक बना।''

कन्फ्यूशियस ऊंचे आदर्श को मानने वाला दार्शनिक था। सरकारी कर्मचारियों की शिक्षा पर वह अधिक बल देता था। उसके अनुसार मनुष्य ऐसे कर्म करे, जो दूसरों के लिए उदाहरण बनें। मनुष्य को अपना जीवन सुखी बनाने के लिए पूर्वजों के पद्चिह्नों पर चलना चाहिए। उन्होंने यह भी लिखा है कि एक अच्छे व्यक्ति में प्रतिभा, साहस और परोपकार आदि गुण निश्चित रूप से विद्यमान होने चाहिए।

कन्फ्यूशियस ने जनसामान्य को समृद्ध करने के लिए जीवन के सभी अंगों के नियम बनाये। वह पारिवारिक जीवन को सुखी बनाने की दृष्टि से स्त्री को पुरुष के अधीन रखने का पक्षधर था। उसके अनुसार मनुष्य अपने अच्छे आचरण से स्वयं का तथा परिवार का कल्याण कर सकता है। उसने पिता-पुत्र के सम्बंधों तथा उनके कर्त्तव्यों का विश्लेषण काफी अच्छे तरीके से किया।

कन्फ्यूशियस किस आदर्श को मानते थे इसकी झलक हमें निम्नलिखित वाक्यों से स्पष्ट देखने को मिल जाती है—''पुरातन युग के शासक अपने राज्य को सुशोभित करने के लिए पहले अपने परिवार को नियन्त्रित करते थे। परिवार के नियमन के उद्देश्य से पहले अपने आपको सुशिक्षित एवं सुनियंत्रित बनाते थे। उनके परिवार के सुनियंत्रित होने से उनके राज्य सुशासित होते थे, उनके राज्यों के सुशासित होने से उनका साम्राज्य सुव्यवस्थित तथा समृद्ध होता था।''

एक प्रशासक के रूप में-कन्फ्यूशियस अपने सिद्धांतों से प्रभावित होकर लू के सम्राट ने उनको चुंगतु नगर का मजिस्ट्रेट नियुक्त किया। उसने अपराधों का दमन करने में महत्त्वपूर्ण भूमिका निभायी और सुव्यवस्थित शासन प्रबंध स्थापित किया। कन्फ्यूशियस ने मानव जीवन का स्तर ऊँचा उठाने के लिए जीवन के प्रत्येक अंग के नियम बनाये। यहां तक कि नागरिक जीवन को भी समानता और एकता के सूत्र में पिरो दिया था। उसने लोगों का भोजन तथा वस्त्र निश्चित कर दिया। उसके नगर में सभी लोग एक जैसा भोजन करते थे और एक से वस्त्र पहनते थे। कन्फ्यूशियस जिस नगर का शासक था ''वहाँ वफादारी और अच्छी भावनाएं हर व्यक्ति में जाग्रत थीं और पवित्रता तथा नम्रता हर नारी की शोभा थी।''

कन्फ्यूशियस ने मजिस्ट्रेट के पद पर आसीन रहते हुए भी मानव की भलाई में अपार श्रद्धा रखी। उनके अनुसार सरकार मनुष्यों के बीच केवल प्राकृतिक सम्बंधों

को कायम रखती है। इससे शासक में शासकीय गुणों का विकास होता है। इसके अतिरिक्त उसकी राजनीतिक समझ पिता-पुत्र के सम्बंधों की तरह होती है। उसके अनुसार पुरातन आदर्शों तथा मूल्यों की स्थापना से सुशासन की स्थापना हो सकती है।

कन्फ्यूशियस ने प्रशासक के पद पर महत्त्वपूर्ण कार्य किये। अतः उसे लू राज्य के न्यायमंत्री के पद पर नियुक्त किया गया। उसने सामाजिक बुराइयों को दूर करने के लिए राज्य-शक्ति का प्रयोग किया। उसके सद्प्रयत्नों से राज्य में चोरी और अधिकारियों के अत्याचार का अंत हो गया। कन्फ्यूशियस के अनुसार शासन का उद्देश्य प्रजा का सुख एवं कल्याण होना चाहिए, वह मृत्युदंड का विरोधी था। राजा के पूछने पर उसने उत्तर दिया–"श्रीमान् राज्य में मृत्यु-दंड की आवश्यकता ही क्या है? यदि आप वास्तव में अच्छा होने की इच्छा करोगे, तो प्रजा भी आपकी भांति अच्छी हो जायेगी। शासक में हवा का गुण होना चाहिए और प्रजा में सांस का।" उसके द्वारा जो भी सुधार किये गये थे जनता उसकी कायल हो चुकी थी, परन्तु भोग-विलास में डूबे सामंत कन्फ्यूशियस के सिद्धांतों से परेशान थे। अतः उन्होंने लू के शासक के कान भरे। शासक ने कन्फ्यूशियस को उसके पद से हटा दिया। जो सुधार उनके द्वारा कराये गये थे उनका अस्तित्व समाप्त हो चुका था।

कन्फ्यूशियस ने जीवन भर चीनी लोगों को अधिक समृद्ध व शिक्षित करने का भरपूर प्रयत्न किया। उसे उच्चकोटि का साहित्यकार, कवि और आलोचक भी कहा जा सकता है। उसने अपने दार्शनिक विचारों को साहित्यिक रचनाओं के माध्यम से जनसाधारण तक पहुँचाने का प्रयास किया। उसने ली चिंग, शी चिंग, शू चिंग, आई चिंग एवं छुन-छिऊ चिंग नाम के पांच ग्रंथों की रचना की जिन्हें चिंग कहा जाता है।

उसकी रचनाओं का विवरण निम्न बिंदुओं में किया जा रहा है–

(1) कर्मकाण्ड एवं शिष्टाचार का ग्रन्थ–इसका चीनी नाम आई ली है। शिष्टाचार का अन्य ग्रंथ भी है, जिसका चीनी भाषा में नाम ली-चिंग है। इसमें सामाजिक परम्पराओं, उत्सव, सदाचार एवं कानून आदि का स्पष्ट विवरण किया गया है।

(2) परिवर्तन का ग्रंथ–इसका चीनी नाम 'आई चिंग' है। इसमें आध्यात्मिक विचारों का वर्णन किया गया है।

(3) काव्य-ग्रंथ–इस ग्रंथ का चीनी नाम शी-चिंग है। इसमें उसने गीतों और कविताओं का वर्णन किया है।

(4) इतिहास के प्रतिष्ठित प्रलेख—चीनी भाषा में इसके दो नाम मिलते हैं—शू-चिंग और शांग-शू। इसमें चीन के राजनीतिक इतिहास का उल्लेख किया गया है।

(5) वसंत और शरत् का इतिहास—इसमें उसने अपने राज्य लू का इतिहास लिखा।

इस प्रकार कन्फ्यूशियस ने साहित्य रचनाओं के द्वारा जनसामान्य की सेवा की। उसकी कलम में इतनी शक्ति थी कि तत्कालीन शासक उससे विचलित हो उठे और उन्होंने उसके समस्त साहित्य को अग्नि को भेंट चढ़ाने के आदेश दे दिए।

कन्फ्यूशियस का जब देहांत हो गया उसके बाद उसके प्रसिद्ध शिष्यों ने उसके उपदेशों का विवरण निम्न पाँच ग्रंथों में दिया, जिन्हें कन्फ्यूशियसवाद का शास्त्रीय एवं प्रतिष्ठित ग्रंथ माना जाता है। जिनके बारे में पांच बिन्दुओं के माध्यम से स्पष्ट विवरण किया जा रहा है—

(1) सर्वोच्च विद्या—इसमें कन्फ्यूशियस के मूल विचारों का वर्णन टिप्पणी के साथ किया गया है।

(2) मध्यममार्ग का सिद्धांत—इसकी रचना कन्फ्यूशियस के पोते ने की थी।

(3) पुत्रोचित भक्ति का शास्त्रीय ग्रंथ—इसमें कन्फ्यूशियस के उपदेशों का वर्णन किया गया है।

(4) सूक्ति-संग्रह—कन्फ्यूशियस के शिष्यों ने उसके विचारों एवं उक्तियों को सूक्तियों के रूप में संग्रहीत किया है।

(5) मैन्सियस के कथन—इसमें कन्फ्यूशियस के प्रसिद्ध शिष्य मैन्सियस के कथन संकलित किये गये हैं।

दार्शनिक के रूप में—कन्फ्यूशियस ईश्वर, मोक्ष एवं मृत्यु आदि विषयों को पसन्द नहीं करता था। उसका प्रथम उद्देश्य आदर्श नागरिक तैयार करना था। जे.ई. स्वेन के अनुसार—"कन्फ्यूशियस सामाजिक एवं राजनीतिक सुधारक था। उसकी शिक्षाओं में दार्शनिकता की अपेक्षा व्यावहारिकता अधिक थी।"

कन्फ्यूशियस धार्मिक विषयों के स्थान पर मानव विचारों पर अपने विचार व्यक्त करता था। जब एक शिष्य ने मृत्यु के बारे में प्रश्न किया तो उसने उत्तर दिया—"जब तुम जीवन को नहीं समझते, तब मृत्यु को कैसे समझ पाओगे?" वह संसार से पलायनवाद के विरुद्ध था। उसका कहना था कि ईश्वर की खोज में समय व्यतीत करने के स्थान पर मानव सेवा में अपने समय का सदुपयोग करना चाहिए। कन्फ्यूशियस सामान्यतया परिवर्तन को भी एक बुराई ही मानता था।

कन्फ्यूशियस का पतन

कन्फ्यूशियस ने चीन के प्रत्येक राज्य का भ्रमण किया, परन्तु किसी भी सम्राट ने उसके उपदेशों के प्रचार में सहायता नहीं की। वह अपने जीवन से निराश हो गया था। इसी समय उसके एक प्रिय शिष्य की मृत्यु हो जाने से उसे बहुत आघात पहुँचा। 479 ई. पू. में 72 वर्ष की आयु में लू राज्य में ही उसकी मृत्यु हो गई। अंत समय में उसने निराशापूर्ण शब्दों में कहा—"इस साम्राज्य में कोई ऐसा नहीं, जो मुझे अपना गुरु बनाये। सचमुच अब मेरे मरने का समय आ गया है।" यद्यपि कन्फ्यूशियस शिक्षा और शिक्षक को अपने सुधार और सिद्धांतों का आधार मानता था। उसके अनुसार प्रत्येक व्यक्ति को शिष्टाचारपूर्ण व्यवहार करना चाहिए। माता-पिता तीर्थ के समान होते हैं। गुरुजनों का आदर करना चाहिए। मनुष्य को सबके प्रति नम्र व्यवहार रखना चाहिए। मित्र के प्रति सच्चा और ईमानदार रहना चाहिए और अपने कर्तव्य का पालन करना चाहिए। कन्फ्यूशियस ने व्यक्ति के नैतिक विकास पर बहुत अधिक बल दिया। उसका कहना था कि मनुष्य को असत्य भाषण, क्रोध, ईर्ष्या और निंदा से दूर रहना चाहिए। ईमानदारीपूर्वक कानून अनुसार आचरण करना चाहिए। उसके उपदेशों को नैतिक नियमों का संग्रह कहा जा सकता है।

कन्फ्यूशियस राजतंत्र में आस्था रखता था। उसने प्रशासकों के कर्तव्यों का कोड बनाया था। उसके अनुसार राजा को अपने कर्तव्यों का पालन करना चाहिए ताकि जनता बिना आदेश दिये उसका अनुसरण करने लगे। राजा को अपनी शक्ति का उपयोग सही प्रकार से करना चाहिए। उसका मुख्य उद्देश्य प्रजा की भलाई करना होना चाहिए। कन्फ्यूशियस के अनुसार राज्य, प्रशासन एवं जनता में नैतिकता का प्रसार करना चाहिए। राजाओं को दयावान होना चाहिए, अपना चरित्र उज्ज्वल रखना चाहिए, जनकल्याण के कार्यों में सहयोग दो, राज्य की भलाई पर ध्यान दो, अच्छी बातों को प्रोत्साहन दो, विदेशियों के प्रति अच्छा व्यवहार करो, योग्य व्यक्तियों को सम्मान दो, जनसाधारण के साथ उचित आचरण एवं मंत्रियों का सम्मान करो।

कन्फ्यूशियस का मत था कि मानव का जीवन तभी सुखी रह सकता है जब उनमें—दया, ज्ञान, न्याय, सत्यता और सेवा भक्ति आदि पांच गुण विद्यमान रहेंगे। जीवन जितना सरल और सदाचारी होगा, उतना ही वह सुखी होगा। उसका मानना था कि निष्काम कर्म की भाँति मनुष्य को कर्म करना चाहिए, फल तो अपने-आप मिलेगा ही। मनुष्य को स्वार्थ त्यागकर अच्छे सामाजिक सम्बंध बनाने चाहिए।

कन्फ्यूशियस ने चीन की सामाजिक मान्यताओं में अंधविश्वास को खत्म करने का सुझाव दिया। उसने चीनी परम्पराओं और आदर्शों पर 305 शृंगार रस के

गीतों की रचना की, जिनके कारण वह यूनान में होमर की भांति चीन में विख्यात हो गया। वह बुद्ध की भाँति धर्म प्रचारक नहीं था, अपितु उपदेशक था। उसने धर्म में सुधार का प्रयास नहीं किया। परन्तु वह धर्म प्रचारक के रूप में विख्यात हुआ। इन्होंने अपने शिष्यों को अनुशासनपूर्ण जीवन व्यतीत करने तथा कुछ नियमों का पालन करने का आदेश दिया। कन्फ्यूशियस मानववाद के सिद्धांतों में विश्वास करता था। स्वार्थमय जीवन का उसकी नजर में कोई महत्त्व नहीं था। उसकी दृष्टि में सच्चा मानव वही था जो दूसरों के लिए जीता था। उसका मानववाद चार बातों पर आधारित था—रीति-रिवाज, सद्गुण, शुद्ध सामाजिक मापदंड और पंच-सम्बंधी रीति-रिवाज। नामकरण आदमी के कार्यों को निश्चित करता था। पंच-संबंधों में आदमी के राजा व मंत्री, पिता पुत्र, पति-पत्नी, वृद्ध-युवा और मित्रों में सम्बंध निश्चित किये गये थे। इस प्रकार आदमी का रीति-रिवाज और समाज के अन्य लोगों के प्रति व्यवहार ही मानववाद था।

उपदेश—कन्फ्यूशियस ने आम जनता को सुधारने के लिए विभिन्न उपदेश दिये—गुरुजनों का सम्मान करना, पूर्वजों की पूजा तथा सम्मान करना, विद्वान और योग्य व्यक्तियों का सदा आदर करना, व्यक्ति को अपना चरित्र अच्छा रखना, गरीब व दुखियों के प्रति दया का भाव रखना, निःस्वार्थ कर्तव्यों का पालन करना, राजा के आदेशों का पालन करना, शिष्टाचार के नियमों का पालन करना, विदेशियों के प्रति अच्छा व्यवहार करना, मित्र के प्रति सच्चा व ईमानदार बनना, सार्वजनिक जन कल्याण के कार्यों में हमेशा सहयोग देना, साधारण जनता के प्रति सहानुभूति एवं अच्छा व्यवहार करना, नैतिक जागृति के लिए अच्छे कार्यों को प्रोत्साहन देना और हर काम समाज व राज्य की भलाई के लिए करना आदि प्रमुख हैं।

विल ड्यूरेण्ट के अनुसार कन्फ्यूशियस अपने उपदेशों के माध्यम से चीन में सामूहिक सहयोग की भावना जगाना चाहता था। उसने लिखा है—"इस दर्शन की सहायता से चीन में सम्मिलित सामूहिक जीवन की विद्या और ज्ञान के प्रति प्रशंसा की, उत्साहमय भावना जाग्रत हुई।"

कन्फ्यूशियस का कथन

वर्तमान समय में भी कन्फ्यूशियस की निम्नलिखित कहावतें विख्यात हैं—जो तुम अपने साथ किया जाना पसंद नहीं करते, वह दूसरों के साथ मत करो। सही बात को समझना और उसके अनुसार आचरण न करना कायरता है। चोट का बदला न्याय से दो और दयालुता का बदला दयालुता से दो। बिना सोचे-समझे

अपना समय और श्रम नष्ट करना है। बिना पढ़े विचार करना खतरनाक है। ज्ञानी मनुष्य की पहचान यह है कि वह जानता है कि वह क्या चीज जानता है और क्या नहीं जानता? स्वर्ग में दो सूर्य नहीं हैं अतः जनता के दो शासक नहीं होने चाहिए। मानव अन्य मानव के साथ और दूसरों के लिए जीता है। सही आचरण ही शक्ति का आधार होता है। जब तुम जीवन को नहीं समझते तो तुम मृत्यु को क्या समझोगे? जो उत्सुक न हो, उसे ज्ञान मत दो और जो सहायता न माँगे, उसे सहायता मत दो। ज्ञान की बात बार-बार मत दोहराओ। जो व्यक्ति गलती कर रहा है और उसे सुधारता नहीं तो वह दूसरी गलती कर रहा है। जो व्यक्ति बेहया होकर शेखी मारता है उसे अपनी शेखी के अनुरूप कार्य करने में बहुत कठिनाई प्रतीत होगी।

कन्फ्यूशियस ने कहा कि महान वही व्यक्ति हो सकता है जिसमें निम्नलिखित गुण विद्यमान होगा जो इस तरह है—वह स्पष्ट देखता, दूसरों के प्रति आदर करता, वफादारी बरतता, व्यापार में सावधान रहता, प्रश्न पूछता, क्रोध में दूसरों की कठिनाइयों पर विचार करता, लालच के समय ईमानदारी की सोचता हो और शक्ल तथा भावभंगिमा से दयालु और भद्र स्वभाव का हो।

कन्फ्यूशियस का प्रभाव—चीन के जन जीवन पर कन्फ्यूशियस का बहुत प्रभाव था। उसके विचार भी सामंतों को बुरे लगते थे। लेकिन वह महापुरुषों की तरह अधिक प्रसिद्धि प्राप्त नहीं कर सका। कन्फ्यूशियस की मृत्यु के लगभग 100 वर्ष बाद मैन्सियस नामक दार्शनिक का जन्म हुआ जिसने कन्फ्यूशियस के विचारों का प्रसार किया और उसे लोकप्रिय व अमर बना दिया। 20वीं शताब्दी के मध्य तक चीन के लोगों पर कन्फ्यूशियस के विचारों का अत्यधिक असर था।

कन्फ्यूशियस की मौत के बाद उसकी मूर्ति की स्थापना कर लोग उसकी पूजा करने लगे। चीनी उसी के सिद्धांतों के लकीर के फकीर की तरह पालन करते रहे, जिसके कारण चीन का अधिक विकास नहीं हो सका। किन्तु उसका साहित्य विश्व को एक महान् देन है।

लाओत्से (604-517 ई. पू.)

कन्फ्यूशियस के समकालीन दार्शनिक लाओत्से ने भी चीन में काफी प्रसिद्धि हासिल की। जब वह पचास वर्ष का था, तब कन्फ्यूशियस का जन्म हुआ था। लाओत्से का जन्म 604 ई. पू. में होनान नामक प्रांत में हुआ था। उसका मूल नाम 'ली' था, जिसका अर्थ होता है 'बैर'। बाद में उसने 'लाओ' की उपाधि धारण की,

जिसका अर्थ है, 'पुराना आचार्य' (वृद्ध गुरु)। अतः प्रसिद्धि प्राप्त करने से उसे लाओत्से कहा जाने लगा।

लाओत्से ने अपनी वृद्धावस्था के दौरान 'ताओ-ते-चिंग' नामक एक पुस्तक की रचना की। ताओ का अर्थ 'मार्ग और ते का अर्थ 'सद्गुण'। अतः इस ग्रंथ का अर्थ 'मार्ग तथा सद्गुण का ग्रंथ' हुआ। इस ग्रंथ के आधार पर ही चीन में 'ताओवाद' नामक एक नये पंथ की स्थापना हुई। उसने मनुष्य और ईश्वर के बीच सम्बंध स्थापित करने का प्रयास किया। उसका मानना था कि गहन चिंतन एवं प्रार्थना के माध्यम से परमात्मा के विषय में जानकारी प्राप्त की जा सकती है। उसने लालच को दुःख का मूल कारण बताया। जीवन के उत्थान के लिए उसने नैतिकता को आवश्यक माना है। लाओत्से ने स्थान-स्थान पर भ्रमण कर अपने ताओवाद का प्रचार किया रूसो की भाँति वह यह भी मानता था कि प्रकृति ने मनुष्य के जीवन को सरल और शांतिपूर्ण बनाया परंतु मनुष्य ने ज्ञान प्राप्त करके इसे जटिल कर दिया। अगर मनुष्य प्रकृति के जाल को काटकर प्राकृतिक जीवन अपना ले तो फिर से सुखी हो सकता है। उसके अनुसार प्रकृति चुपचाप अपना कार्य सम्पन्न करती है। अतः मानव को भी अपनी प्रकृति के अनुकूल कार्य करते रहना चाहिए। लाओत्से के अनुसार मनुष्य को भोगविलास को छोड़कर पवित्र, सरल एवं शान्तिपूर्ण जीवन व्यतीत करना चाहिए। उसका कहना था कि "जो भले हैं, उनके लिए मैं भला हूँ और जो भले नहीं हैं उनके लिए भी मैं भला हूँ।" इस प्रकार यह स्पष्ट होता है कि लाओत्से के विचार कितने आदर्श थे।

ताओवाद के सिद्धांत

ताओवाद दर्शन की एक अवधारणा मानी जा सकती है जिसका जन्म लाओत्से की पुस्तक 'ताओ-ते-चिंग' से हुई है। ताओवाद संबंधी कुछ प्रमुख सिद्धांत इस प्रकार हैं—

(1) प्रेम व दयापूर्ण व्यवहार पर बल—लाओत्से ने लोगों को सद्भावपूर्ण रहने को कहा तथा उपदेश दिया कि—"यदि तुम किसी से झगड़ा न करो तो संसार में किसी को भी तुमसे झगड़ा करने का साहस न होगा। यदि तुम्हें कोई चोट पहुंचाए तो उसका उत्तर दयालुता से दो। संसार में सबसे कोमल वस्तु सबसे कठोर वस्तु से टकराकर उसे परास्त कर देती है।" लाओत्से का मानना था कि मनुष्य को आघात का बदला दयालुता से देना चाहिए।

(2) शिक्षा के प्रसार का विरोध—लाओत्से शिक्षित व्यक्ति को सामाजिक समस्या का कारण मानता था। इसलिए अशिक्षित मनुष्य ही सुखी जीवन व्यतीत कर

सकता है। उसका कहना था—"शिक्षा के प्रसार के साथ मूर्खों की संख्या बढ़ती है। बुद्धिमान जन राज्य के संकट का कारण बन जाते हैं।" चीन में उसका दर्शन 'अज्ञान' के नाम से प्रसिद्ध है। चीन में सैकड़ों अशिक्षित लोग उसके अनुयायी बन गये। कहा जाता है कि जब कन्फ्यूशियस कुछ सीखने की दृष्टि से लाओत्से के पास पहुँचा तो लाओत्से ने उससे कहा था, "जाओ, अपना अहंकार, वासनाएं, भोगवृत्ति और महत्त्वाकांक्षाओं को छोड़ दो ये नुकसानदायक हैं।"

(3) प्राकृतिक विचार—लाओत्से प्रकृति की पूजा करता था उसका मत था कि प्रकृति के नियमानुसार मानव को जीवन बिताना चाहिए ताकि उसे सुख एवं शान्ति प्राप्त हो सके। वह जीवन की सादगी के लिए शहरी जीवन को भी घृणास्पद समझता था। राज्य, समाज और कानून को महत्त्व नहीं देता था। लाओत्से नैतिक, राजनीतिक, आर्थिक और सामाजिक विचारों में कन्फ्यूशियस का विरोधी था। वह समाज को आदिम अवस्था में जीवन बसर करने के लिए प्रोत्साहित करता था।

(4) शान्तिपूर्ण जीवन में विश्वास—लाओत्से भाग्य में यकीन रखता था तथा शान्तिपूर्ण जीवन बसर का समर्थक था। उसकी इस विचारधारा के कारण चीन के विकास का मार्ग अवरुद्ध हो गया। वह शान्तिपूर्ण किसान जीवन का पक्षपाती था, जहाँ कम से कम आवश्यकताएं हों। उसका कहना था कि मनुष्य की बढ़ती हुई आवश्यकताएं उसके सुंदर जीवन का अंत कर देती हैं।

लाओत्से द्वारा प्रतिपादित ताओवाद का चीन में काफी प्रचार हुआ। इसमें पुरोहित, मंदिर और मूर्तियां भी थीं। लाओत्से युद्ध का विरोधी था। उसका मानना था कि युद्ध में निरपराध व्यक्ति अकारण ही मारे जाते हैं। लाओत्से की नजर में धन तथा सम्पत्ति कोई खास महत्त्व नहीं रखते थे। अतः चीन के तमाम दरिद्र और अशिक्षित लोग उसके अनुयायी बन गये। एक अंग्रेज सेनापति ने चीन में युद्ध के मैदान में बैठे-बैठे समस्त चीनी दर्शन पढ़ लिया था। उसने लिखा है "मैं चीनी दर्शन से इतना डूबा हुआ था कि मुझे तोपों की आवाज तक का पता नहीं चला।" लाओत्से की मृत्यु के बाद उसे एक देवता मान लिया गया और उसकी शिक्षाओं में जादू-टोने का समन्वय कर दिया गया। प्रो. टर्नर के अनुसार "लाओत्से की विचारधारा शहरी सभ्यता की अशान्ति के विरुद्ध किसान शिल्पकार प्रतिक्रिया की प्रतीक थी।"

मो-टी

चीन के इस महान दार्शनिक के जीवनकाल को लेकर कुछ अनिश्चितता है जिसके कारण यह स्पष्ट रूप से नहीं कहा जा सकता कि मो-टी कन्फ्यूशियस का

समकालीन था या नहीं, फिर भी यह माना जाता है कि मो-टी का अधिकांश जीवन पांचवीं सदी के पूर्वार्द्ध में व्यतीत हुआ था। इसका जन्म लू प्रान्त में हुआ। मो-टी तत्कालीन समाज को बदलना चाहता था जिसके लिए उसने अपना एक नया मार्ग अख्तियार किया। मो-टी ने शिष्टाचार पर या कर्मकाण्ड के स्थान पर ईश्वरीय इच्छा एवं तार्किक बुद्धि के अनुसार जीवन व्यतीत करने पर बल दिया। उसने तर्कशास्त्र की एक नयी शैली को जन्म दिया, जिसमें परिभाषाओं का विशेष महत्त्व था। मो-टी ने सर्वोच्च सुख प्राप्त करने के लिए ईश्वरीय इच्छा के पालन का उपदेश दिया। वह शांतिपूर्ण जीवन में विश्वास रखता था। इसलिये वह युद्ध का प्रबल विरोधी था। मो-टी ने प्रेम और नैतिकता पर बल दिया। मो-टी प्रेतात्माओं में विश्वास करता था। वह अधिक व्ययसाध्य श्राद्ध व कर्मकाण्डों को स्वीकार नहीं करता था। इनका मानना था कि मानव अपने प्रयासों द्वारा अपने भाग्य को भी सुधार सकता है। उनके द्वारा दिये गये उपदेशों का चीनी सभ्यता पर सदियों तक प्रभाव विद्यमान रहा। कई विद्वानों ने इन्हें स्वीकार किया।

कन्फ्यूशियस के अनुयायी मैन्सियस ने मो-टी के उपदेशों का घोर विरोध किया। उसका मानना था कि मो-टी ने पारिवारिक प्रेम के स्थान पर विश्वजनीन प्रेम तथा सहानुभूति पर बल दिया है, अतः उसके विचार समाज का विघटन कर देंगे।

मैन्सियस(372-288 ई.पू.)

मैन्सियस लू राज्य का रहने वाला था तथा कन्फ्यूशियस का शिष्य था। उसने अपने गुरु के विचारों को प्रचारित किया। उस पर उसकी मां का अत्यधिक प्रभाव था जिसे चीन में आदर्श मां कहकर पुकारा जाता है। इसके विचारों का प्रमाणिक संकलन "मैन्सियस के विचार" नामक ग्रंथ में पाया जाता है, जिसका चीनी नाम 'मेंग-त्सू-शू' है।

मैन्सियस का मत था कि मनुष्य जन्म से अच्छे आचारण का होता है परन्तु जीवनभर इसका पालन करेगा यह जरूरी नहीं है। वह लोगों को विनम्रता व नैतिकता की शिक्षा देता था। उसकी धारणा थी कि नैतिक जीवन से ही सफलता प्राप्त होती है। अतः मनुष्य को अपने माता-पिता के प्रति सम्मान का भाव रखना चाहिए। मैन्सियस के राजनीतिक विचार कन्फ्यूशियस से बहुत मिलते थे। उसका विचार था कि राज्य शस्त्र के बल पर नहीं, राजा के सुचरित्र पर निर्भर होता है। वह 'यथा राजा तथा प्रजा' नामक कहावत में विश्वास करता था एवं उसका मानना था कि राजा वही बन सकता है जो प्रजा की भलाई के लिए कार्य करे।'

मैन्सियस राजतंत्र में विश्वास रखता था उसके अनुसार–''जो कुछ राजकुमार में गलती है उसे ठीक कर दो। यदि राजकुमार सुधर गया तो, राज्य व्यवस्थित हो जाएगा।'' वह प्रजातंत्र का विरोधी था। उसके अनुसार इस व्यवस्था की सफलता के लिए जनता का शिक्षित होना आवश्यक था, जो बड़ा मुश्किल काम था। वह प्रशासन में व्याप्त भ्रष्टाचार का महान विरोधी था। उसकी मान्यता थी कि योद्धा अपराधी है सरकार का काम जनता की सेवा करना है शोषण नहीं। उसने कहा था–''कोई ऐसा युद्ध नहीं हुआ, जो अच्छा रहा हो।'' उसने मानवमात्र के भाईचारे पर बल दिया। उसने कहा परमात्मा की इच्छा है प्रेम, सबसे प्रेम और किसी प्रकार का भेदभाव किये बिना प्रेम।'' सेवाइन के अनुसार, "मैन्सियस की दार्शनिक पुस्तक चीन के दर्शन की सर्वोच्च कृति है।"

फाचिया सम्प्रदाय

चाऊकालीन विचारधाराओं में यह अन्तिम विचारधारा मानी जाती है। 'फाचिया' का अभिप्राय 'विधिवादी' या 'कानून का सर्मथक' होता है। इस सम्प्रदाय का जन्म चौथी सदी ई. पू. में अशांति और अराजकता के वातावरण में हुआ था। इस काल में कन्फ्यूशियस के आदर्श भी विफल सिद्ध हो रहे थे। अतः इस सम्प्रदाय के समर्थकों ने कहा कि समाज तथा शासन का नियमन कानूनों द्वारा ही नियंत्रित किया जा सकता है। कानून समाज की आवश्यकताओं तथा परिस्थितियों के अनुसार बनाये जाने चाहिए। कानून ही एक ऐसा माध्यम है जो मनुष्यों की आपराधिक प्रवृत्तियों पर नियंत्रण रखने में सहायक कहा जा सकता है। इस सम्प्रदाय में अभिजात्य वर्ग एवं राज्य को विशेष महत्त्व दिया गया था तथा कृषि और आत्मनिर्भरता पर बल दिया गया था। इस सम्प्रदाय की विचारधारा में साम्यवादी तत्व भी कुछ हद तक समाहित हैं।

कालांतर में जब कन्फ्यूशियस लोकप्रिय होने लगे तो फाचिया सम्प्रदाय का पतन होने लगा, तथापि इस बात से इंकार नहीं किया जा सकता कि इसने चीनी संस्कृति पर गहरा प्रभाव डाला। शांग एवं ली-स्सू नामक महान राजनीतिक नेता भी इस विचारधारा को मानते थे। ये दोनों नेता चाऊ काल के पतन के समय प्रसारवादी एवं सामन्ती राज्य चीन के मंत्री थे। इन दोनों नेताओं द्वारा विकसित आदर्शों के आधार पर चीन के नरेश शी-हुआंग-टी ने चाऊ वंश का अंत किया और चीन को राजनीतिक एकीकरण के सूत्र में बांध दिया।

कला

चीन में प्राचीन कला के नमूने आज भी देखे जा सकते हैं। चीन में स्थापत्य कला, चित्रकला, मूर्तिकला एवं संगीतकला के क्षेत्र में बहुत अधिक विकास हुआ। इनकी स्थिति को निम्न प्रकार स्पष्ट किया गया है–

(1) **स्थापत्य कला**–चीन में स्थापत्य कला का विकास बहुत अधिक हुआ है। विश्व के सातवें अजूबे में सम्मिलित चीन की दीवार स्थापत्य कला का नमूना है इसके मेहराब, दरवाजे तथा चौकोर बुर्ज दर्शन योग्य हैं। शी हुआंग टी का प्रासाद भी उस समय की भवन निर्माण कला का शानदार नमूना था। पैगोडा चीन की स्थापत्य कला का श्रेष्ठ नमूना है। ये 15 मंजिल तक के होते थे। बीजिंग के नजदीक बुद्ध का मंदिर स्थापत्य कला का शानदार उदाहरण है।

(2) **मूर्तिकला**–प्राचीनकाल के दौरान चीन में मूर्तिकला का काफी विकास हुआ। शुंग और चाऊ वंश के समय के कांसे के बर्तनों पर यह चित्रकला चित्रित है। चीन में बौद्ध धर्म के प्रसार के बाद तांग वंश के समय में महात्मा बुद्ध की सुंदर मूर्तियों का निर्माण हुआ।

(3) **चित्रकला**–चीनी चित्रकला में चित्र के भावों को महत्त्व देना एवं रेखाओं द्वारा दर्शन करना तथा प्राकृतिक दृश्यों के चित्र बनाना सबसे महत्त्वपूर्ण विशेषता चीनी चित्रकार प्रकृति के आश्चर्यजनक चित्र बनाते थे। यहां मिट्टी के बर्तनों पर सुंदर चित्र बनते थे। हानवंश के समय चित्रकला का विकास पराकाष्ठा पर जा पहुंचा। इस वंश का प्रसिद्ध चित्रकार कुनाई था, जिसने एक शृंगारदान के ढक्कन पर एक पक्षी का सुंदर चित्र बनाया था। उस समय चित्रकला में प्राचीन परम्पराओं का चित्र बनाया जाता है। फूलों के समूह बड़े सुंदर थे, जो आज भी चीन की विश्व को एक अमूल्य भेंट है। अन्य प्रसिद्ध चित्रकारों में सैगवी, लिन्सी एवं हुंगता ओजू आदि के नाम लिए जा सकते हैं। इन्होंने 40 हजार चित्र बनाए।

(4) **संगीत कला**–चीनी लोग संगीत को मानसिक तनाव दूर करने का साधन मानते थे। इससे यह पता चलता है कि चीन में संगीतकला का कितना महत्त्व है। कहा जाता है कि चीनियों ने पांच हजार वर्ष पूर्व संगीत का आविष्कार कर लिया था। उनका प्रारम्भिक संगीत दर्शन शास्त्र पर आधारित था। कुछ समय पश्चात् उन्होंने उच्चकोटि के संगीत की रचना की।

भाषा एवं साहित्य

चीन में 40 हजार चिह्न है जिनमें से लिखने के काम में 600 चिह्न उपयोग में आते हैं एक चिह्न से एक विचार व्यक्त होता था। उदाहरणस्वरूप, सुबह व्यक्त करने के लिए एक सीधी रेखा पर एक मोड़ चिह्न था। चीनी की लिपि चित्रात्मक थी। इस लिपि में 40 हजार चिह्न होने के कारण उसको याद रखना बहुत कठिन था जिसके कारण शिक्षा की उपेक्षा की गई, फलस्वरूप वहां के अधिकांश निवासी शिक्षा से वंचित रह गए।

चीन में शिक्षा राज्य का काम था। शिक्षा का प्रमुख उद्देश्य अच्छे नागरिक तैयार करना था। चीन में विद्यार्थियों को उदाहरणों तथा दृष्टांतों से शिक्षा दी जाती थी। वहाँ निःशुल्क शिक्षा नहीं होने से गरीब व्यक्तियों के बच्चे शिक्षा पाने में असफल रहते थे। प्रायः अमीर व्यक्तियों के बच्चे ही शिक्षा ग्रहण करते थे। अनुशासन के नियम कठोर थे। नियमित रूप से होने वाली परीक्षाओं में विद्यार्थियों की स्मृति और साहित्यिक योग्यता की परख की जाती थी। चीन के छात्र लकड़ी की तख्तियों व लिनन के वस्त्र पर लिखते थे। बच्चों को चित्रलिपि, कन्फ्यूशियस के गीत याद करने पड़ते थे।

प्राचीन काल के दौरान चीन में कविताओं का विशेष प्रचलन था फलस्वरूप वहां साहित्य पद्यात्मक था। उस दौरान चीन के लोग अपने विचारों की अभिव्यक्ति कविताओं में करते थे। यहां के कवि सुंदर कविताओं की रचना करते थे, लेकिन श्रेष्ठ कविता वही समझी जाती थी, जो कम-से-कम शब्दों में अधिक भावों को अभिव्यक्त करती हो।

इस प्रकार कन्फ्यूशियस चीन का एक महान साहित्यकार हुआ। पूर्व में वर्णित उसकी रचनाओं ने चीनी साहित्य को अमर बना दिया। उसकी निम्नलिखित रचनाएँ आज भी प्रसिद्ध हैं—

(1) आई-चिंग—इस पुस्तक का अनुवाद 'परिवर्तनों की पुस्तक' के नाम से किया गया है। इस पुस्तक में शांग राजवंश के पतन व चाऊ राजवंश के उदय पर प्रकाश डाला गया है। वस्तुतः इस पुस्तक की रचना जादू-टोने, शकुन विचार तथा भविष्यवाणी में मंत्रों के संग्रह के लिए की गई थी, अतः इसे तंत्र-मंत्र जानने वाले ही समझ सकते थे।

(2) शू-चिंग या शांग शू—इस पुस्तक में राजाओं तथा शासकों द्वारा दिए गए आदेश, भाषण, उपदेश, पत्र तथा घोषणाएं लिखित हैं। 'इतिहास के प्रतिष्ठित प्रलेख' के नाम से इस पुस्तक का अनुवाद किया गया है।

(3) शी-चिंग—यह कृति काव्य की दृष्टि से अनुपम है। इस पुस्तक का अनुवाद 'प्रतिष्ठित काव्य संग्रह' या 'काव्यसंग्रह' के नाम से किया गया है। इस पुस्तक में कन्फ्यूशियस की 311 कविताओं को संकलित किया गया है। शी-चिंग प्रेम, प्रकृति और उत्सवों की अद्वितीय पुस्तक है।

चीनी साहित्य की एक प्रसिद्ध कृति 'शिष्टाचारों का ग्रंथ' है। 'आई-ली-पी ने 30 ग्रंथ लिखे। उसने अपनी पुस्तक तू-फू में करुणा भरे गीत लिखे। वह दुःखी और असंतुष्ट था इसलिए उसके गीतों में दुःख और आंसुओं की कथा ही प्राप्त होती है।

चीन में मंगोल आक्रमण के वक्त गद्य साहित्य का अत्यधिक विकास हुआ। राजा शी हुआंग टी ने सारा साहित्य नष्ट करवा दिया था। एच. जी. वेल्स ने लिखा है—प्रथम चीन सम्राट ने सारा साहित्य नष्ट कर दिया, किन्तु ज्योंही वह चला गया, छिपी हुई पुस्तकें पुनः बाहर निकल आयीं।"

विज्ञान

चीन में गणित, ज्यामिति, ज्योतिष विद्या, दर्शनशास्त्र एवं चिकित्सा विज्ञान के क्षेत्र में बहुत उन्नति हुई थी। गणित-ज्योतिषि के क्षेत्र में महत्त्वपूर्ण अध्ययन किए गए। ज्योतिषियों ने वर्ष में 365 दिन निर्धारित किए तथा सूर्यग्रहण और चन्द्रग्रहण का अध्ययन किया। घड़ी का प्रयोग धूप की सहायता से होता था। बृहस्पति तथा शनि ग्रहों की गति का अध्ययन किया गया। चीन में बीजगणित एवं रेखागणित पर पुस्तकें लिखी गईं। चाऊ के सामंत ने कुतुबनुमा का आविष्कार किया था, जिसके कारण रात्रि के समय भी नाविक दिशा का पता लगा सकते थे। बारूद के आविष्कार का श्रेय भी चीन को ही प्राप्त है।

चीन कागज और छापेखाने के मामले में बहुत आगे था और यूरोपियों ने छपाई का काम चीन से सीखा। सुंदर बढ़िया रेशम के कपड़े भी सबसे पहले चीनियों ने ही बनाये थे। ये लोग नक्शा बना लेते थे। व्यक्तियों की पहचान के लिए अंगुलियों की छाप के महत्त्व को समझने वाले सर्वप्रथम चीनी ही थे। राख और चिपकने वाले रस को मिलाकर ये स्याही बना लेते थे और चावल के भूसे, चिथड़े तथा शहतूत की छाल को पीसकर कागज बनाते थे।

चीन में चिकित्सा विज्ञान का काफी विकास हुआ। चाऊ वंश के समय में 'चिकित्सा के सिद्धांत' नामक पुस्तक रचना की हुई जिसमें रोगों के नाम और उनको दूर करने वाली औषधियों का उल्लेख था। ये लोग दवा का प्रयोग भी करते थे। नाड़ी देखकर वे बीमारी का पता लगा लेते थे। चीर-फाड़ का प्रयोग भी चीन में प्रचलित

था। दूसरी शताब्दी में एक प्रसिद्ध चिकित्सक चांग चुंग-चिंग हुआ था, जिसे चीन में 'औषधि का अंत' के नाम से पुकारा जाता है, ने टायफायड बुखार की औषधि का आविष्कार किया था। इसी शताब्दी में हुवातो नामक एक प्रसिद्ध सर्जन भी हुआ था। इन सबके बाद भी अन्धविश्वास का प्रभाव होने के कारण जादू-टोने में लोगों का अधिक विश्वास था। यही नहीं बाद में अनेक चीनी विद्वानों ने बौद्ध ग्रन्थों, संस्कृत की कृतियों के चीनी अनुवाद किए और साहित्य की श्री वृद्धि की।

चीन की विश्व सभ्यता को देन

चीन की सभ्यता को विश्व की महान सभ्यताओं में शामिल किया जाता है। यहां के लोग विश्वबंधुत्व के सिद्धांत में विश्वास करते थे। इन लोगों ने सारे संसार को शांति का उपदेश दिया। चीनी लोग युद्ध से घृणा करते थे और सेनापति को अपराधी मानते थे। विश्व में चीन सम्भवतः पहला देश होगा, जहां सैनिक होना बुरा समझा जाता था और युद्ध को एक बुरा तथा अनैतिक कार्य माना जाता था। उनका कहना था कि आज तक कोई ऐसा युद्ध नहीं हुआ, जिसके अच्छे परिणाम रहे हों।

चीन में अध्यापक व विद्वतजन आदरणीय माने जाते थे। छोटे, बड़ों का आदर करते थे। **एच. जी. वेल्स** ने लिखा है–"यही कारण है कि आक्रमणकारी और राजवंश आये और चले गये, लेकिन चीनी सभ्यता का जीवन क्रम अभी भी अपरिवर्तित रूप से मौजूद है।" चीनी सम्राटों की एक महत्त्वपूर्ण विशेषता यह थी कि उन्होंने अन्य धर्मों के प्रति भी धार्मिक सहनशीलता की नीति अपनायी। चीन ने विश्व को आठ अमूल्य उपहार दिये, जिसके लिए संसार चीन का सदा ऋणी रहेगा। ये उपहार हैं–कागज, छापाखाना, चाय, ताश, रेशम, कुतुबनुमा, बारूद और प्रतियोगिता परीक्षा। यूरोप में नवजागरण जितना यूनानी विद्याओं के पुनरुत्थान के कारण हुआ, उतना ही चीन के दिशासूचक यंत्र, बारूद तथा मुद्रण के आविष्कार के कारण संभव हुआ।

5

प्राचीन यूनान की सभ्यता

विश्व में जितनी भी प्राचीन सभ्यताएं थीं उसमें यूनान की सभ्यता का विशेष स्थान था। विश्व की सभ्यता में यूनान का विज्ञान, कला एवं साहित्य जगत में अद्वितीय योगदान है प्राचीन यूनान में बड़े-बड़े कवि, लेखक, नाटककार एवं दार्शनिकों ने सर्वश्रेष्ठ रचनाएं लिखीं जो वर्तमान समय में बड़े चाव से पढ़ी जाती हैं यूनान ने पूर्वी सभ्यता को यूरोप में प्रसारित किया था। वर्तमान यूरोप के राजनीतिक सिद्धांत एवं आदर्श भी यूनान की देन है। यूनानी सभ्यता रोम के द्वारा पाश्चात्य देशों में फैली इसलिए इतिहासकार यूरोपीय सभ्यता का जनक प्राचीन यूनान को मानते हैं। इसलिए पश्चिमी देशों को सबसे अधिक यूनानी सभ्यता का कर्जदार माना जाता है। विश्व प्रसिद्ध कवि शैली महोदय ने लिखा है कि "हम सभी यूनानी हैं। हमारे कानून, हमारा साहित्य, हमारा धर्म, हमारी कलाएँ इन सबका मूल यूनान में है।"

विल ड्यूरेण्ट के अनुसार "मशीनों के अलावा हमारी सभ्यता का जन्म यूनान में ही हुआ। हमारी संस्कृति में ऐसी कोई वस्तु नहीं, जिसकी प्रेरणा यूनान से न मिली हो।" **एलिस व जौन** के अनुसार "विश्व ग्रीको का कर्जदार है।" रोमन सभ्यता के विकास के मार्ग पर प्रकाश डालते हुए **प्लेट व जीन** ने लिखा है कि, "सभ्यता यूनान के रास्ते यूरोप पहुँची।" **आंग्ल कवि बाइरन** के अनुसार, "यूनान के द्वीप जहाँ कलाकार और योद्धा समाधियों में सो रहे हैं, जहाँ कला, युद्ध व शान्ति का प्रादुर्भाव हुआ, जहाँ डिलास का उदय हुआ और फ्रूब्रूस चमका, किन्तु आज वहाँ सब कुछ मिट चुका है और डूबता हुआ सूर्य मात्र नजर आता है।" **टॉयनबी** ने यूनान को पाश्चात्य

सभ्यता की भूमि मानते हुए लिखा है कि "यूरोपीय सभ्यता का यूनान के समाज रूपी शरीर में इस प्रकार विकास हुआ, जिस प्रकार बच्चे का गर्भ में होता है।" यूनान ने पूर्व से सभ्यता ग्रहण कर उसे पश्चिम को सौंप दिया। मून का मानना है कि "यूनानी अतीत के उत्तराधिकारी थे और अच्छे प्रचारक भी। उन्होंने बहुत कुछ पाया और उससे अधिक दिया।"

सेवाइन ने यूनान के प्रबुद्ध लोगों की तारीफ करते हुए यह लिखा है कि, "यह सन्देहपूर्ण है कि अन्य किसी भी समय या स्थान पर ऐसे प्रबुद्ध मस्तिष्कों का समूह रहा हो, जैसा कि पेरिक्लीज के युग में एथेन्स में था। भारत के गुप्तकाल की भाँति पेरिक्लीज का काल भी यूनान के इतिहास का स्वर्णयुग कहलाता है। **डब्ल्यू.एन. वीच** के अनुसार, "पाँचवीं ई. पू. के मध्य में लगभग 30 वर्ष तक एथेन्स में एक ही व्यक्ति इतना श्रेष्ठ था कि यह यूनान के इतिहास का महानतम युग सदा उसका नाम लेता रहेगा। वह नाम पेरिक्लीज था।" पेरिक्लीज ने अपने साम्राज्य में शान्ति एवं व्यवस्था बनाये रखी और सभी क्षेत्रों में आश्चर्यजनक विकास हुआ। **मैकनेल बर्न्स** का मानना है कि, "कोई भी सावधान इतिहासकार इस बात से इन्कार नहीं कर सकता कि यूनानियों की उपलब्धियाँ विश्व के इतिहास में सबसे अधिक उल्लेखनीय हैं। ज्ञान की प्रत्येक शाखा पर यूनानी छाप स्पष्ट रूप से दृष्टिगोचर होती है। निःसन्देह यूनान को एक अत्यन्त उन्नत तथा समृद्ध संस्कृति का जनक कहा जा सकता है।"

यूनान तीन ओर से भूमध्यसागर से घिरा है तथा यूरोप के दक्षिणपूर्व में अवस्थित है। इसका समुद्री किनारा भी कटा-फटा है। इस देश का क्षेत्रफल 25 हजार वर्गमील है। यूनान के एथेन्स नगर के उत्तर में पिंड्स पहाड़ में सोने, चाँदी और संगमरमर की अत्यधिक खानें हैं। पर्वतीय भाग होने के कारण यहां कृषि योग्य भूमि नहीं है। प्राचीनकाल में यूनान का सम्पर्क मिस्र, मैसोपोटामिया, फारस और इटली आदि देशों से था। यूनानियों ने इन देशों से बहुत कुछ सीखा और यूरोपीय देशों में इसका प्रसार किया। इस प्रकार यूनान, यूरोप तथा एशिया दोनों को मिलाने में एक सेतु का काम किया।

यूनान में टापुओं की संख्या लगभग पांच सौ दो है जिनमें क्रीट, ट्राय, साइप्रस और स्पार्टा आदि मुख्य हैं। यूनानियों ने अपनी शक्तिशाली नौसेना के द्वारा अनेक उपनिवेशों की स्थापना की। पर्वत शृंखलाओं व पठारों के कारण ही यहाँ नगर राज्य आबाद हुए। इन छोटे-छोटे नगर राज्यों में प्रजातन्त्र का ही विकास हुआ, किसी विशाल साम्राज्य का नहीं। उनमें भी आपसी प्रतिद्वन्द्विता और ईर्ष्या विद्यमान थी।

पर्वत शृंखलाओं से प्राप्त उच्चकोटि के प्रस्तर के कारण ही यूनान स्थापत्यकला के क्षेत्र में अत्यधिक विकास कर सका। इस प्रकार यूनान की जलवायु तथा भौगोलिक स्थिति ने भी यूनानियों की महत्ता में सहयोग दिया।

एजियन सभ्यता

ऐतिहासिक दृष्टि से यूनान के विभिन्न द्वीपों में क्रीट द्वीप का अत्यधिक महत्त्व है। क्रीट की सभ्यता यूनान की प्राचीन सभ्यता मानी जाती है। यूनान में ग्रीक जाति के आने से पहले उनके पूर्वजों ने अपनी सभ्यता का विकास सर्वप्रथम यहीं किया। इस सभ्यता को एजियन सभ्यता या मिनोअन सभ्यता कहते हैं। नौसस एवं फीस्टस आदि सभ्यता के प्रधान केन्द्र थे। यह सभ्यता यूनान व एजियन सागर के आर-पार पूर्वोत्तर में ट्राय तक फैली हुई थी और मिस्र, बेलीलोन की सभ्यताओं के समकक्ष थी। क्रीट के राजवंशों का पतन लगभग 1400 ई. पू. में हुआ था।

माइसीनियन सभ्यता

यूनान में इस सभ्यता का विकास क्रीट सभ्यता के पतन के उपरांत हुआ था। माइसीन एवं टिरिंस इस सभ्यता के प्रधान केन्द्र थे। यह सभ्यता 1600 ई. पू. से 1200 ई. पू. तक जीवित रही। इसके पश्चात् इस सभ्यता का पतन हो गया।

यूनान में इमोनियम सभ्यता का उदय

यूनान में आर्य जाति का आगमन होने से नवीन सभ्यता का उदय हुआ। आर्य जाति की दो शाखाओं—एकियन एवं डोरियन ने यूनान में प्रवेश किया। एकियन जाति ने एथेन्स तथा डोरियन जाति ने स्पार्टा सभ्यता का विकास किया। इन दोनों के समन्वय से 'इयोनियन सभ्यता' का उदय हुआ। आर्यों ने यूनान का नाम सबसे ऊँचे पहाड़ हेलास के नाम पर 'हेलास' रखा। हेलास की ऊँचाई 9700 फुट है। पेरीक्लीज ने इसका नाम यूनान रखा और जब 145 ई. में रोमनों ने इस पर अधिकार कर लिया तो इसका नाम बदलकर ग्रीस रख दिया।

राजनीतिक स्थिति

अन्धकार युग—यह युग 1200 ईसा पूर्व से 800 ईसा पूर्व तक माना जाता है इस युग को 'होमर युग' भी कहा जाता है। होमर इमोनिया का निवासी था वह

अन्धा था होमर के महाकाव्यों से प्राचीन यूनानी सभ्यता एवं संस्कृति के बारे में जानकारी प्राप्त होती है। उसने इलियड नामक महाकाव्य में ट्राय के घेरे का वर्णन किया था और ओडेसी नामक महाकाव्य में यूनानी सेनापति ओडेसियस का ट्राय विजय से लौटने की यात्रा का वर्णन किया है। होमर के ये महाकाव्य उसी प्रकार महत्त्वपूर्ण हैं, जिस प्रकार भारत में रामायण और महाभारत। ट्राय युद्ध की कहानी कुछ हद तक रामायण की कहानी से मिलती-जुलती है। अन्धकार युग अर्थात् होमर युग को वीरों का युग भी कहा जाता है।

इलियड में ट्राय के घेरे का उल्लेख—होमर ने इस महाकाव्य में यूनानियों और ट्रायवासियों के बीच हुए युद्ध के बारे में लिखा है। ट्राय को प्राचीन यूनानी भाषा में 'इलियोस' या 'इलियोन' और लैटिन भाषा में 'इलियम' कहते थे। हेज का मानना है कि 'इलियड' का नाम 'इलियम' से लिया गया है, जबकि कुछ इतिहासकारों के अनुसार यह 'इलियोन' से लिया गया है। ट्राय यूनान का एक टापू था, जो टर्की के समुद्र तट पर बसा हुआ था।

ट्राय युद्ध का विवरण

स्पार्टा के राजा मैन्यूलस की पत्नी हेलन काफी सुंदर थी। ट्राय और स्पार्टा के राजा के बीच आये दिन झगड़े होते रहते थे। इस आपसी वैमनस्य को समाप्त करने के लिए ट्राय के राजा प्रायम के पुत्र पेरिस स्पार्टा के शासक मैन्यूलस के दरबार में आया। पेरिस ने मैन्यूलस के दरबार में जिस निर्भीकता और विधि से विचार व्यक्त किये, उसके कारण रानी हेलन उस पर मोहित हो गई। पेरिस भी रानी पर मोहित हो गया। रात्रि को पेरिस हेलन को लेकर ट्राय भाग गया। इससे यूनान की प्रतिष्ठा को आघात पहुँचा। मैन्यूलस को जब इस बात का पता चला तो उसे बहुत गुस्सा आया। स्पार्टा व ट्राय के बीच यह घटना युद्ध का कारण बन गई।

यूनान के सभी राजाओं ने इस अपमान का बदला लेने और पुनः रानी हेलन को प्राप्त करने के उद्देश्य से ट्राय के विरुद्ध युद्ध अभियान किया। ट्राय नगर एक ऊँची पहाड़ी पर स्थित था और वह चारों ओर से पाषाण-प्राचीर से घिरा हुआ था। यूनानियों का सबसे बड़ा योद्धा एकीलीज और ट्राय का सबसे बड़ा योद्धा हेक्टर था। यूनानियों ने दस वर्ष तक ट्राय को घेरे रखा, परंतु उन्हें कोई खास लाभ नहीं मिला। दसवें वर्ष की सबसे महत्त्वपूर्ण घटना यह थी कि इस संघर्ष में ट्राय का सेनापति हेक्टर मृत्यु को प्राप्त हुआ, परन्तु पेरिस ने हिम्मत नहीं हारी और ट्राय के द्वार नहीं खोले। इस पर ओडेसियस ने छल-कपट से ट्राय को जीतने के लिए एक नई योजना बनाई।

योजना के अनुसार लकड़ी का एक विशाल घोड़ा बनाया गया और दस चुने हुए यूनानी योद्धा उसमें छिपा दिए गए थे।

एक दिन रात में यूनानी सिपाहियों ने इस घोड़े को ट्राय नगर के बाहर रखकर लौट जाने का नाटक किया। यूनानी सैनिक वहाँ से रवाना होकर समीप के द्वीप के पीछे छिप गए। यूनानियों के जाने के पश्चात् ट्राय के लोगों ने द्वार खोल दिए और लकड़ी के घोड़ों का यूनानियों द्वारा दिया विजय का पुरस्कार समझकर उसे नगर के अन्दर ले आए। रात्रि को ट्राय के द्वार बन्द कर दिए गए। इसके बाद यूनानियों के भागने की खुशी में ट्राय के सैनिक शराब पीकर जश्न मनाते रहे और फिर सो गए। होमर के अनुसार रात्रि में जब ट्रायवासी सो रहे थे, तब घोड़े के पेट में छिपे हुए यूनानी सैनिकों ने ट्राय के द्वार खोल दिए। अब तक यूनानी सेना वापस लौटकर ट्राय आ गई थी। रात्रि के अन्धेरे में सोये हुए ट्रायवासियों पर यूनानियों ने एकाएक धावा बोल दिया जिसमें ट्रायवासियों को अत्यधिक जन-धन की हानि उठानी पड़ी। पेरिस और उसके आठ भाई युद्ध करते हुए मारे गए और यूनानी सैनिकों ने हेलन को अपने अधिकार में ले लिया। यूनानी सैनिकों ने बदले की भावना से प्रेरित होकर ट्राय को लूटा और जलाकर राख कर दिया। इस प्रकार यूनानियों ने ट्राय पर विजय प्राप्त की और आसपास के प्रदेश में अपने उपनिवेश स्थापित किये। इस प्रकार दस वर्ष बाद स्पार्टा की रानी हेलन को शक्ति के बल पर पुनः स्वराज्य लाया गया।

ओडेसी—ट्राय पर यूनानी सेनापति ओडेसियस अथवा यूलिसिस ने विजय प्राप्त की थी इसलिए होमर ने दूसरे महाकाव्य का 'ओडेसी' नाम रखा था। ट्राय को अग्नि की भेंट चढ़ाकर ओडेसियस इताका के योद्धाओं को लेकर स्वदेश रवाना हुआ। मार्ग में तूफान आया जिसके कारण ओडेसियस दो बार ऐसे द्वीपों पर पहुँच गया, जहाँ दैत्य निवास करते थे। दैत्यों ने 12 पोतों में से 11 को नष्ट कर दिया और यूनानियों को जान से मार डाला। ओडेसियस अपना पोत राक्षसों से बचाकर निकल गया। फिर मार्ग में जीयस (वर्षा एवं बिजली का देवता) ने नाराज होकर बिजली गिरा दी; जिससे उसका जहाज नष्ट हो गया तत्पश्चात् ओडेसियस तैरकर समुद्र के किनारे पहुंचा। इस घटना के पश्चात् ओडेसियस लगभग दस वर्षों तक इधर-उधर भटकता रहा। जब वह इताका पहुँचा तो उसे पता चला कि उसके मकान पर संभ्रांत लोगों ने अधिकार कर लिया है। उसने उन लोगों को वहाँ से मार भगाया और फिर इताका पर अधिकार कर राज्य करने लगा।

होमर ने इस महाकाव्य में लिखा है कि ओडेसियस की पत्नी का नाम पेनीलोप था जिसे प्राप्त करने के लिए वह ट्राय वापस आने पर भटकता रहा।

उसके प्रेमी ने उसे अपने जाल में फँसाने का प्रयास किया, परन्तु उसे असफलता हाथ लगी। पेनीलोप अन्त तक अपने पति के प्रति स्वामिभक्त बनी रही। अन्त में जब ओडेसियस (यूलिसिस) लौटकर आया, तो वह बहुत प्रसन्न हुई। भूमध्य सागर में यूलिसिस के भटकने का इतिहास भी यूरोप की अनेक भाषाओं में लिखा गया है।

ओडियस द्वारा ट्राय पर विजय को यूनान के निवासी अधिक महत्त्व देते थे इस बारे में **वीच** ने लिखा है कि, "युद्ध के लगभग तीन शताब्दी बाद होमर नामक असाधारण प्रतिभा के कवि ने इन गाथाओं से दो महाकाव्यों की रचना की, जो आज भी विश्व की श्रेष्ठ रचनाओं में गिने जाते हैं और सम्मान से पढ़े जाते हैं।" ये महाकाव्य यूनानियों के रहन-सहन एवं जन-जीवन पर प्रकाश डालते हैं। होमरकालीन यूनानी वैभव पर प्रकाश डालते हुए **मैकने बर्न्स** ने लिखा–"तभी यूनान राष्ट्र का जन्म हुआ था और अनेक सामाजिक व राजनीतिक संस्थाओं का जन्म हुआ, जो आने वाली शताब्दियों में विकसित हो सकीं।"

होमर युग को कुछ इतिहासकारों ने वीरगाथा का युग भी कहा है। ट्राय एशिया माइनर के पश्चिमी किनारे पर एजियन सागर के तट पर एक द्वीप है। इस महाकाव्य से यूनानी उपनिवेशों के बारे में जानकारी प्राप्त होती है। लगभग 800 ई. पू. तक यूनानियों ने भूमध्यसागर के सभी किनारों पर अपने उपनिवेश स्थापित कर लिए थे। अफ्रीका, एशिया माइनर, इटली, फ्रांस तथा स्पेन तक यूनानियों के उपनिवेश स्थापित हो चुके थे। इन सारे उपननिवेशों को 'वृहत्तर यूनान' का नाम दिया गया था।

राजनीतिक जीवन

होमरकालीन यूनानी शासक राजा होता था। राजा अपनी प्रजा का प्रमुख पुरोहित होता था। वह राज्य का सर्वोच्च न्यायाधीश था। उसका निर्णय अन्तिम माना जाता था। राजा युद्ध के समय सेना का नेतृत्व करता था। उसे प्रजा ईश्वर के समान पूजती थी। उसका पद वंशानुगत होता था। धार्मिक पूजा एवं उत्सवों में देवताओं को चढ़ाई गई खाद्य-सामग्री राजा को प्राप्त होती थी। राजा एक परिषद् या काउंसिल के परामर्श से शासन चलाता था। काउंसिल के परामर्श के बिना राजा कुछ भी नहीं कर सकता था। काउंसिल में उच्चवर्ग के सम्मानित व्यक्ति होते थे, जो राजा की शक्ति पर नियन्त्रण रखते थे। इस काउंसिल का नाम ब्यूल था। कभी-कभी राजा अपनी नीति का समर्थन प्राप्त करने हेतु जनसमुदाय की आम सभा का आयोजन करता था। इस सभा को 'एगोरा' कहते थे। इस आमसभा में समस्त स्वतन्त्र नागरिक भाग

लेते थे तथा राजा एवं काउंसिल द्वारा प्रस्तावित विषयों पर अपनी सहमति प्रकट करते थे। इसे विवाद करने एवं प्रस्तावित करने का अधिकार नहीं था।

आर्थिक जीवन

इस युग में यूनान की अर्थव्यवस्था का प्रमुख साधन कृषि एवं पशुपालन था। यहाँ की मुख्य पैदावार गेहूँ, जौ एवं बाजरा आदि थी। सम्पत्ति का मूल्यांकन पशुओं की संख्या से होता था। इस काल की स्त्रियाँ वस्त्र भी बुनती थीं। होमर युग में सिक्कों का प्रचलन नहीं था, इसलिए यहाँ के व्यापारी ताँबे, सोने या चाँदी के टुकड़ों या बैलों के द्वारा वस्तुओं का मूल्य निर्धारित करते थे विभिन्न प्रकार के कुटीर उद्योगों के द्वारा दैनिक जीवन की वस्तुएँ बना ली जाती थीं। गाँवों में तलवार बनाने वाले लुहार, कुम्हार आदि सम्मानित दृष्टि से देखे जाते थे। यहाँ के लोग गाय, भेड़, बैल, बकरी, सुअर, कुत्ता तथा घोड़ा आदि पशुओं को पालते थे।

धार्मिक जीवन

यूनान निवासी प्रकृति की पूजा करते थे तथा धर्म में अधिक विश्वास करते थे। यहाँ के मुख्य देवता थे—जीयस (बिजली तथा तूफान का देवता), पोसीडोन (समुद्र का), हेस्टिया (गृह का), हेड्स (मृतकों का), जियस का पुत्र एरिस (युद्ध का), अपोलो (प्रकाश का), हिप्पास्टस (अग्नि का), डायोनिसस (फल के बागों का), जियस की पुत्री एथेना (कला की देवी) एवं एफ्रोडाइट (प्रेम की देवी) आदि। ये लोग भूत-प्रेत में विश्वास रखते थे तथा निजी स्वार्थपूर्ति के लिए देवताओं की पूजा करते थे।

यूनान में ओलम्पिया में जियस देवता के मन्दिर के सामने प्रतिवर्ष एक बड़ा मेला लगता था। यहाँ आयोजित खेल-कूद प्रतियोगिताओं में एक-दूसरे के विरोधी राज्यों के नागरिक भी बड़े प्रेम से भाग लेते थे। इसी प्रकार डेल्फी में अपोलो देवता के मन्दिर के पुजारी यूनान के लोगों का भविष्य बताते थे।

सामाजिक जीवन

होमरकाल में यूनानी निवासी गाँवों में रहते थे। परिवार के सभी सदस्यों को मुखिया की आज्ञा का पालन करना पड़ता था। भूमि पर पूरे परिवार का अधिकार होता था किन्तु भूमि को बेचने का अधिकार परिवार के मुखिया को भी नहीं था। कई परिवारों के समूह को फ्रेट्रा या बिरादरी कहते थे। कई ग्रामों के समूह को फाइल या ट्राइब कहा जाता था।

तत्कालीन समाज चार भागों में विभाजित था। जिसमें प्रथम, कुलीन वर्ग था। यह वर्ग विशाल भू-सम्पत्ति का स्वामी था तथा इसके पास बहुत बड़ी संख्या में दास होते थे। यह वर्ग युद्ध के समय नेतृत्व करता था तथा अपनी वीरता एवं शौर्य के लिए प्रसिद्ध था। दूसरा वर्ग कृषकों का था जो अपनी भूमि पर कृषि करके जीवन निर्वाह करता था। तीसरा वर्ग स्वतन्त्र श्रमिकों को था, जिसे 'थीट्स' कहा जाता था। चौथा वर्ग दासों का था, जो या तो युद्धबन्दी होते थे या समुद्री नौकर होते थे या समुद्री लुटेरों से खरीदे जाते थे। इस युग में दासों को अधिक महत्त्व दिया जाता था।

होमरकालीन सभ्यता एवं संस्कृति प्रमुख रूप से एक ग्रामीण संस्कृति व सभ्यता थी यहाँ माता-पिता का बहुत आदर किया जाता था। स्त्रियों को समाज में सम्मानपूर्ण स्थान प्राप्त था, पर उनके कभी-कभी लड़ाइयाँ हो जाती थीं। ट्राय का युद्ध इसका सबसे बड़ा प्रमाण है। यहाँ मदिरापान की प्रथा भी थी।

होमर युग में कानून का अस्तित्व नहीं था। धार्मिक विश्वासों तथा सामाजिक प्रथाओं का समाज पर नियन्त्रण था। कुछ अपराधों की सजा देवताओं के द्वारा दी जाती थी। किसी व्यक्ति की हत्या के अपराधी को दण्ड देना मृत व्यक्ति के परिवार के सदस्यों का कर्त्तव्य माना जाता था। राजा का निर्णय अन्तिम समझा जाता था।

तत्कालीन यूनान में कुछ रीति-रिवाज भी विद्यमान थे जिन्हें समाज पूरी तरह से निभाता था। समुद्री यात्रियों और जहाजों को लूटना बुरा कार्य नहीं माना जाता था। एक अजनबी व्यक्ति को किसी नए स्थान पर कोई भी मार सकता था, पर यदि वह उस नए स्थान के किसी व्यक्ति का अतिथि बन जाए, तो उसे कोई नहीं मार सकता था।

इस तरह होमरकालीन यूनान में सभ्यता एवं संस्कृति की बुनियाद रखी गयी। यह युग यूनानी सभ्यता का ऊषाकाल था। बाद में विकसित होने वाली यूनानी सभ्यता की नींव इस युग में रख दी गई थी।

यूनान के प्रमुख नगर राज्य

लगभग छठीं सदी के आस-पास यूनान में नगर राज्यों का उदय हुआ। नगर राज्य को पोलिस भी कहा जाता था। प्रत्येक नगर की अपनी अलग सेना और सरकार थी। इनका अपना अलग-अलग देवता था, जिसका मन्दिर नगर के मुख्य द्वार के अन्दर बना हुआ होता था। नगरों में व्यापारिक प्रतिस्पर्द्धा होने के कारण प्रत्येक नगर विकास करता रहा। इन नगर राज्यों में स्पार्टा व एथेन्स के नगर राज्य प्रमुख थे।

सेवाइन ने लिखा है कि, "नगर राज्य प्राचीन सर्वोच्च यूनान की उत्कृष्ट राजनीतिक प्राप्ति है।" नीचे स्पार्टा राज्य पर संक्षिप्त प्रकाश डाला गया है।

स्पार्टा नगर राज्य

यूनान के दक्षिणी छोर पर स्थित स्पर्टा नगर कृषि के दृष्टिकोण से बहुत अच्छा था। आर्य जाति की डोरियन शाखा ने पेलोपेनेसस के दक्षिण पूर्व में स्थित लकोनिया पर अधिकार कर एक नगर बसाया, जो बाद में स्पार्टा के नाम से विख्यात हुआ। डोरियन जाति के लोगों ने यहाँ के लोगों को अपना गुलाम बना लिया। ये गुलाम लोग उनके लिए कृषि का कार्य करते थे। स्पार्टा नगर की सुरक्षा दीवार थी तथा सैनिक हमेशा हथियारों से लैस रहते थे।

तत्कालीन यूनान में शासन प्रणाली राजतन्त्रात्मक थी जिसकी पद्धति निरंकुश थी। यहाँ के सैनिक विश्व में वीरता एवं शौर्य के लिए प्रसिद्ध थे। स्पार्टा का संविधान लाइकर्गस नामक व्यक्ति ने तैयार किया थे। इसका उद्देश्य स्पार्टा को एक शक्तिशाली और सैनिक दृष्टिकोणवाला राज्य बनाना था,। अतः संविधान में अनुशासन, स्वास्थ्य और सैनिक शिक्षा पर अधिक बल दिया गया था। स्पार्टा में दो शासक होते थे। इनके पद वंशानुगत होते थे संविधान में दो शासकों की व्यवस्था के पीछे मुख्य उद्देश्य यह था कि एक राजा दूसरे राजा की निरंकुशता पर अंकुश रख सके। दोनों ही राजा शासन, न्याय और धर्म के अधिकारी थे। स्पार्टा के राजाओं के अधिकार कम होते हुए भी उनको अत्यधिक सम्मान की दृष्टि से देखा जाता था। स्पार्टा के राजा की जब मृत्यु हो जाती थी तो घुड़सवार पूरे राज्य में उसकी मृत्यु की सूचना दे देते थे। राजा की मृत्यु पर प्रत्येक परिवार के दो सदस्य शोक मनाने वाले वस्त्र धारण कर लेते थे जो परिवार ऐसा नहीं करता था, उसे दण्ड दिया जाता था। दस दिनों तक सभी सार्वजनिक काम बन्द रहते थे। राजा की अन्त्येष्टि क्रिया अत्यन्त सम्मान के साथ सम्पन्न की जाती थी। उसके पश्चात् वंशानुगत आधार पर राजा के ज्येष्ठ पुत्र को राजा बना दिया जाता था।

यूनान में दो राजा होते थे जो शासन काउंसिल की सहायता से चलाते थे काउंसिल को सीनेट भी कहा जाता है। सीनेट की अनुमति के बिना दोनों ही शासक किसी भी शक्ति से युद्ध या सन्धि नहीं कर सकते थे। स्पार्टा के संविधान में काउंसिल या सीनेट को 'जेरूसिया' कहा जाता था। इसके सदस्यों की संख्या 30 थी, जिनमें दोनों राजा भी शामिल थे। सीनेट के सदस्य 60 वर्ष की आयु से अधिक उम्र के अभिजात्य वर्ग के लोग ही बन सकते थे। इसके सदस्य आजीवन के लिए

होते थे। यह संस्था राजा को महत्त्वपूर्ण विषयों पर सलाह देती थी और फौजदारी मुकदमों का निर्णय करती थी। इसका सदस्य होना गौरव का प्रतीक समझा जाता था।

एसेम्बली स्पार्टा संविधान की एक प्रमुख अंग थी। अतः स्पार्टा के संविधान में यह जनता की सभा थी। इसे अपेला कहा जाता था। 30 वर्ष की अवस्था प्राप्त होने पर प्रत्येक नागरिक इसका सदस्य समझा जाता था। इसके सदस्य लगभग 8000 थे। सभी नागरिक इस सभा में आकर प्रशासन के कार्य पर अपना मत व्यक्त करते थे। एसेम्बली के सदस्य ही जेरूसिया, मजिस्ट्रेटों और एफोरेट के सदस्यों का चुनाव करते थे। युद्ध एवं सन्धि के प्रश्न, वैदेशिक नीति एवं उत्तराधिकार आदि एसेम्बली द्वारा ही निश्चित किये जाते थे। सैद्धान्तिक दृष्टि से यह सभा काफी शक्तिशाली थी, क्योंकि सभी महत्त्वपूर्ण प्रश्नों का निर्णय यही करती थी, पर व्यावहारिक रूप में एसेम्बली के निर्णयों को काउंसिल के सदस्य तथा मजिस्ट्रेट रद्द कर सकते थे, क्योंकि अन्तिम निर्णय उनके हाथ में था। अतः स्पार्टा का संविधान सैद्धान्तिक रूप से गणतन्त्रात्मक था।

स्पार्टा के संविधान में पाँच सदस्यों की एक संस्था थी, जिसे 'एफर' कहा जाता था। एसेम्बली द्वारा प्रतिवर्ष इसका चुनाव किया जाता था। ये एफर अपने कार्यों के लिए जनता की सभा के प्रति उत्तरदायी थे। इन एफरों के अधिकार राजाओं से भी अधिक थे। उनका प्रमुख कार्य जनता के अधिकारों की रक्षा करना था। वे राजा की निरंकुशता पर अंकुश रखते थे। दीवानी मुकदमों पर उनका निर्णय अन्तिम माना जाता था। इस प्रकार, एफर स्पार्टा के संविधान में सबसे अधिक समृद्धशाली थी।

स्पार्टा में तीस वर्ष की अवस्था से साठ वर्ष की अवस्था तक के प्रत्येक नागरिक को सैनिक जीवन व्यतीत करना अनिवार्य था। स्पार्टा का संविधान राजतन्त्र का, एफर गणतन्त्र का तथा काउंसिल उच्च कुल का प्रतिनिधित्व करती थी। अतः स्पार्टा के संविधान को एक मिश्रित संविधान कहा जा सकता है, जिसमें राजतन्त्र, गणतन्त्र और उच्च कुलतंत्र तीनों के तत्त्व शामिल किये थे।

सामाजिक अवस्था

स्पार्टा का समाज तीन वर्गों में विभाजित था। प्रथम वर्ग सैनिकों का था। समाज में सर्वाधिक सम्मान इसी वर्ग को प्राप्त था। दूसरा वर्ग स्वतन्त्र मनुष्यों का था, जिन्हें फ्रीमैन कहा जाता था। इनको स्वार्थ की सीमा सुरक्षा में मदद देनी पड़ती थी जिसके बदले इन्हें व्यापारिक सुविधाएं मिलती थी। गुलामों को तीसरे वर्ग में

शामिल किया गया था जिन्हें 'हेलौट' कहा जाता था। स्पार्टावासी युद्ध में पराजित लोगों को गुलाम बनाकर उनसे खेती करवाते थे। गुलामों को स्पार्टा से बाहर जाने का अधिकार नहीं था। इनके साथ क्रूर व निर्दयी व्यवहार किया जाता था। इनको नागरिक अधिकार प्राप्त नहीं था। गुलामों की दशा अच्छी नहीं थी। उन पर उनके स्वामी बहुत अत्याचार करते थे। स्पर्टा के नागरिक को कठोर सैनिक शिक्षा दी जाती थी जिससे गुलामों के विद्रोह करने पर उनका मुकाबला किया जा सके। **मैकनेल बर्न्स** ने लिखा है, "नागरिक वर्ग की निरंकुश सत्ता के लिए लौह अनुशासन और कठोर नियन्त्रण आवश्यक था और उनकी दूसरों के प्रति घृणा ने उन्हें युद्ध में व्यस्त रखकर मिटा दिया।"

स्पार्टा के प्रत्येक नागरिक को 30 से 60 वर्ष की उम्र तक सैनिक जीवन व्यतीत करना पड़ता था इसलिए स्पार्टा को सैनिक राज्य भी कहते हैं। यहाँ के समाज में वीर सैनिकों को आदर की दृष्टि से देखा जाता था। स्पार्टा के लोग युद्ध प्रेमी थे और सैनिकवाद में विश्वास करते थे। यहाँ बच्चों के स्वास्थ्य पर अधिक ध्यान दिया जाता था। **प्लेट व जीन ड्रमण्ड** के अनुसार "स्पार्टा के सैनिक परिवार पर निर्भर करते थे। सभी सदस्यों के लिए परिवार के मुखिया की आज्ञा का पालन करना स्पार्टा में आवश्यक था। स्पार्टा में अगर अस्वस्थ तथा निर्बल शिशु पैदा होता था तो उसे टेजिटस की पहाड़ी पर फेंक कर मार दिया जाता था। स्पार्टा की एक माँ अपने बच्चे को इस प्रकार उपदेश देती थी—"अपनी ढाल के साथ लौटना या उस पर लौटना।" इसका अर्थ यह है कि या तो युद्ध में विजय प्राप्त करके घर आना या फिर युद्ध के मैदान में ही शहीद हो जाना। जो व्यक्ति युद्ध में लड़ते हुए मारे जाते, उनकी माताओं को मालाएँ पहनाई जाती थीं, परन्तु जिस घर का व्यक्ति युद्ध में हारकर घर आता था, वहाँ मातम मनाया जाता था। जन्म से लेकर मृत्युपर्यन्त तक स्पार्टा के प्रत्येक नागरिक का जीवन कठोर अनुशासन से नियन्त्रित था।

स्पार्टा में प्रेम का कोई स्थान नहीं था यहां विवाह करने का मुख्य उद्देश्य पुत्र पैदा करना था। लड़के 30 वर्ष तथा लड़की की 20 वर्ष की आयु होने पर विवाह करने का प्रावधान था। समाज में कुँआरों को अच्छी दृष्टि से नहीं देखा जाता था। स्पार्टा में प्रत्येक युवक अपने साथियों के साथ सैनिक आवासों में रहता था और वहीं भोजन करता था। भोजन के लिए वह मासिक चन्दा देता था। स्पार्टा के लोगों को गृहस्थ जीवन व्यतीत करने की स्वतन्त्रता नहीं थी। अतः यहाँ का युवक कभी-कभी गुप्त रूप से रात्रि में थोड़े से समय के लिए अपनी पत्नी से मिल सकता था। स्पार्टा में

पति-पत्नी दिन में नहीं मिल सकते थे। प्लुटार्क ने लिखा है, 'पुरुष दिन के प्रकाश में अपनी पत्नी का चेहरा देखे बिना ही बाप बन जाते थे।'

स्पार्टा की कोई भी नारी अपने पति की स्वीकृति से बलिष्ठ पुत्र प्राप्त करने के लिए बलवान पुरुष से गर्भाधान कराने के लिए स्वतंत्र थी। यहाँ की स्त्रियाँ अपने भय को दूर करने के लिए विशेष अवसरों पर अर्द्धनग्न होकर सार्वजनिक सभाओं एवं व्यायामशालाओं में जाती थीं। यदि उन्हें वहाँ कोई भी व्यक्ति बुरी नजर से देखता तो उसे दण्ड दिया जाता था।

स्त्रियों की स्थिति स्पार्टा में काफी अच्छी थी। उन्हें पुरुषों की भाँति सामाजिक तथा राजनीतिक अधिकार प्राप्त थे। उन्हें निजी सम्पत्ति एकत्रित करने का अधिकार था। इतना ही नहीं, वे अपना उत्तराधिकारी भी नियुक्त कर सकती थीं। यहाँ स्त्रियां धार्मिक उत्सवों में भाग लेती थीं और सार्वजनिक समस्याओं पर अपने विचार व्यक्त करती थीं। अपने सतीत्व के लिए वे प्रसिद्ध थीं तथा राज्य की सेवा एवं भक्ति के लिए सदैव तत्पर रहती थीं। पुरुषों के समान ही नारियां साहसी होती थीं। यूनान के अन्य राज्यों की स्त्रियाँ पर्दे में रहती थीं, जबकि यहाँ की नारियाँ स्वतन्त्रता से जीवन गुजारती थीं।

साहित्य एवं कला

साहित्य तथा कला के क्षेत्र में भी स्पार्टा का विकास नहीं हुआ था। स्पार्टा का समाज सैनिकवाद में विश्वास करता था। युद्ध करना ही इनका प्रमुख उद्देश्य हुआ करता था। इसके अतिरिक्त वे अन्य कोई कार्य नहीं कर सकते थे। अतः उन्होंने युद्ध में तो नाम कमाया, लेकिन सांस्कृतिक क्षेत्र में कोई विशेष प्रगति नहीं कर सके। अतः उनकी सभ्यता की उन्नति का मार्ग अवरुद्ध हो गया। दूसरे शब्दों में साहित्य, विज्ञान एवं कला के क्षेत्र में स्पार्टा की देन शून्य थी।

यूनान की प्रतिष्ठा में वृद्धि स्पार्टा के शासक लियोनीदास के कारण हुई इन्होंने थनोपोली युद्ध में अद्वितीय वीरता का प्रदर्शन किया। तत्पश्चात् स्पार्टा ने दक्षिण के यूनानी राज्यों को मिलाकर 'पेलोपोनेशियन संघ' का निर्माण किया। एथेन्स की साम्राज्यवादी नीति पर अंकुश लगाना ही इस संघ का प्रमुख उद्देश्य था। स्पार्टा को अपने उद्देश्य में सफलता प्राप्त हुई। उसने इस संघ के माध्यम से एथेन्स की बढ़ती हुई शक्ति पर प्रतिबन्ध लगा दिया। छठी शताब्दी में एथेन्स की शक्ति के कारण स्पार्टा का गौरव खत्म हो गया।

शिक्षा

स्पार्टा में शिक्षा इसलिए दी जाती थी ताकि सभी नागरिकों को अनुशासनबद्ध सैनिक बनाया जा सके। वहाँ प्रत्येक बच्चे की 9 वर्ष की अवस्था होते ही राज्य द्वारा नियुक्त कर्मचारी उसे सैनिक स्कूल में ले जाकर प्रविष्ट करा देते थे। यहाँ उसे 12 वर्ष तक सैनिक शिक्षा दी जाती थी। इस प्रकार 19 वर्ष की आयु में वह सेना का अंग बन जाता था। उनको ऐसी शिक्षा दी जाती थी जिससे वह सभी मुसीबतों का मुकाबला सरलता से कर सके। उनकी शिक्षा के प्रमुख विषय कुश्ती, बाक्सिंग, जिम्नास्टिक, लम्बी दौड़ तथा अस्त्र-शस्त्र संचालन में निपुणता आदि थे। स्पार्टा की नारियों को भी लम्बी दौड़ तथा जिम्नास्टिक की शिक्षा दी जाती थी ताकि वे स्वस्थ एवं बलिष्ठ सन्तान को जन्म दे सकें। डब्ल्यू.एन. वीच के अनुसार यूनान की स्त्रियों को कठोर प्रशिक्षण दिया जाता था जिससे शक्तिशाली बच्चा पैदा हो।

आर्थिक दशा

स्पार्टा निवासी सैनिकवाद में यकीन रखते थे जिससे उनकी आर्थिक स्थिति बहुत खराब थी। स्पार्टा में उद्योग-धंधों का विकास भी नहीं हो पाया था। यहाँ के लोग विदेशी सम्पर्क को महत्त्व नहीं देते थे जिसके कारण यहाँ का व्यापार विकसित नहीं हो सका था। स्पार्टा में लोहे के सिक्के प्रचलित थे, जिनको ढोना असुविधाजनक था। इन सिक्कों का प्रचलन जानबूझकर किया गया था ताकि नागरिक सम्पत्ति एकत्र करने की ओर प्रभावित न हों।

एथेन्स का नगर राज्य

एथेन्स यूनान का दूसरा बड़ा एवं अत्यधिक महत्त्वपूर्ण देश माना जाता था। जैसे पेलोपोनेसस के प्रदेश में स्पार्टा का विकास हुआ, वैसे ही कोरिन्थ खाड़ी के उत्तर में एटिका प्रदेश में एथेन्स के नगर राज्य का विकास हुआ। एथेन्स में आर्यों की आयोनियन शाखा का प्रभुत्व था। यूनान के प्रत्येक नगर राज्य का एक इष्ट देवता होता था। एथेन्स के लोग एथिना देवी की पूजा करते थे, जिसका मन्दिर निवास नामक स्थान पर था। इस देवी के नाम पर ही इस नगर का नाम एथेन्स पड़ा। यह नगर एक्रोपोलिस नामक दुर्ग के चारों तरफ बस गया था। इस नगर की सुरक्षा के लिए इसके चारों तरफ लकड़ी की दीवार बनवाई गई थी। एथेन्स की सभ्यता का विकास आर्यों की आयोनियन शाखा द्वारा किया गया था। यहाँ कला, साहित्य, दर्शन एवं विज्ञान की अभूतपूर्व उन्नति हुई। एथेन्स ने अपूर्व कुशलता के साथ यूनानी

जगत का नेतृत्व किया। यूनान में होमर युग के बाद कुलीन राजतन्त्र की स्थापना हुई और स्वेच्छाचारी शासकों के युग की शुरुआत हुई।

होमर की मृत्यु के बाद कुलीन वर्ग ने राजसत्ता पर अधिकार कर लिया था। इस प्रकार यूनान में कुलीन राजतन्त्र की स्थापना हुई। इस काल में राज्य के उच्च पदों पर कुलीन वर्ग के व्यक्तियों को ही नियुक्त किया जाता था। आर्कन्स द्वारा ही राज्यों का शासन प्रबंध का संचालन किया जाता था। आर्कन्स कुलीन (सम्भ्रान्त) लोगों में से ही दस वर्ष के लिए निर्वाचित होते थे और हर निर्वाचित व्यक्ति दस वर्ष तक राज्य करता था। इसके बाद उच्च वर्ग के किसी अन्य व्यक्ति को आर्क के पद पर दस वर्ष के लिए नियुक्त किया जाता था। यह व्यवस्था लगभग सौ वर्ष तक यूनान में प्रचलित रही।

कुलीन तंत्र के लोगों के पास अच्छे सैनिक के गुण विद्यमान नहीं थे। ये किसानों और व्यापारियों का शोषण भी बहुत करते थे। अतः उनकी शासन-व्यवस्था अधिक दिनों तक नहीं चल सकी। ऐसी स्थिति में सेनापतियों ने राज्य का कार्य अपने हाथ में ले लिया और उनके शासनकाल को अत्याचारियों का काल कहा गया। निःसन्देह इस समय के शासकों ने अपनी प्रजा पर बहुत अत्याचार किये। उनकी तुलना आज के तानाशाहों से की जा सकती है। यूनान के इतिहास में अत्याचारी शासकों को टाइरेंट कहा जाता था।

इस युग के शासक निरंकुश होते हुए भी प्रजा की भलाई करना अपना दायित्व समझते थे। उनके शासनकाल में यूनान ने व्यापार, कला व धर्म के क्षेत्र में पर्याप्त उन्नति की। इतिहासकार **वीच** ने लिखा है, "वे योग्य एवं उत्साही व्यक्ति थे जिन्होंने व्यापार को प्रोत्साहन दिया और नगरों के सौन्दर्य व धन को बढ़ाया। उन्होंने प्रजा के कार्यों पर व्यय कर गरीबों को रोजी-रोटी दी।" **क्रेन ब्रिटन** ने लिखा है–"टाइरेन्ट आधुनिक अर्थ में निष्ठुर नहीं थे। कई नगर राज्यों में उन्होंने निरंकुश शासन की बुराइयों व निर्बलताओं को दूर करने के लिए कई सुधार किए। इसके परिणामस्वरूप उन्होंने असन्तुष्ट लोगों का तत्परता से सहयोग प्राप्त कर लिया।" इनके शासनकाल की तुलना आधुनिक यूरोप के शासकों से की जा सकती है। वे वर्तमान समय की तरह जनता का शोषण नहीं करते थे। शासन को कुशल बनाने की दृष्टि से उन्होंने कुछ सुधार भी किये, परन्तु जनता फिर भी उनसे सन्तुष्ट नहीं थी।

प्राचीन यूनान राज्य छोटे-छोटे नगर राज्यों के रूप में विभाजित था। सभी नगर राज्यों का अपना एक देवता होता था। हर नगर राज्य में अलग-अलग शासन-प्रणाली का प्रचलन था। ये सभी नगर एक दूसरे से युद्ध किया करते थे। परन्तु फारस के

आक्रमण के समय इन सभी राज्यों ने संयुक्त होकर एथेन्स के नेतृत्व में युद्ध का सामना किया था।

प्रसिद्ध विद्वान पाइथोगोरस का जन्म इसी युग में हुआ था। इस समय भवन निर्माण कला के क्षेत्र में विकास हुआ। यूनान में कई मन्दिरों का निर्माण हुआ। इस युग में काँसे व संगमरमर की अनेक मूर्तियाँ बनीं, जिसके कारण मूर्तिकला का भी विकास हुआ। इस युग में यूनानी सभ्यता को विशेष महत्त्व दिया गया एवं कला व विज्ञान के क्षेत्र में अधिक विकास हुआ।

एथेन्स में गणतन्त्र की स्थापना—अत्याचारियों के युग में कार्यपालिका की शक्ति राजा, आर्कन (न्यायाधीश) तथा पोलमार्क (सेनापति) का अधिकार था। आर्कन दीवानी मुकदमों का अन्तिम न्यायाधीश था। पोलमार्क प्रधान सेनापति था, जिसे न्याय-सम्बन्धी अधिकार भी प्राप्त थे। राजा का पद विशेष सम्मानित पद था। काउन्सिल के सभापति के रूप में उसी का चयन किया जाता था और इसी के प्रति उत्तरदायी होता था। इस समय शासन संचालन के सहायता देने के लिए काउन्सिल (ब्यूल) और एक्सलेशिया आदि संस्थाएँ थीं। काउन्सिल को ऐरियोपैगस की काउन्सिल की संज्ञा दी गई थी। इसके सदस्य पूर्व आर्कन होते थे। यह एक शक्तिशाली सभा होती थी और आर्कन के कार्यों पर पूर्ण नियन्त्रण रखती थी।

यह काउन्सिल हत्या, विष देने तथा आग लगाने के मुकदमों का निर्णय करती थी तथा अपराधियों को दण्ड भी देती थी। काउंसिल के निर्णय कुलीन वर्ग के लोगों के पक्ष में होते थे। यह आर्कन के निर्वाचन में महत्त्वपूर्ण भूमिका निभाती थी। इसके अतिरिक्त एक्सलेशिया नामक संस्था जनता की सभा थी। कुलीन वर्ग के उस प्रशासन में लिखित कानून नहीं थे, जिसके कारण मजिस्ट्रेट भी निष्पक्ष न्याय नहीं करते थे। अतः लिखित कानून बनाये गये। ड्रेको पहला आर्कन था, जिसने पुराने कानूनों में सुधार किया तथा नये कानून का निर्माण किया।

ड्रेको की विधि संहिता—ड्रेको का संबंध आर्कन से था। उसने 621 ई. पू. में कानूनों का प्रथम लिखित संग्रह निकाला। उनके कानून काफी कठोर हुआ करते थे। ड्रेको ने सामन्तों के अपराधों की जाँच के लिए एक विशेष न्यायालय की स्थापना की और सामन्तों के विशेष अधिकारों को समाप्त कर दिया। इसके परिणामस्वरूप सामन्त तथा ड्रेको के मध्य मतभेद हो गया था और उन्होंने विद्रोह कर दिया, जिसे बड़ी कठोरता से दबा दिया गया। अतः ड्रेको द्वारा संशोधित कानूनों से जनसाधारण को कोई लाभ नहीं हुआ और कानून पहले से अधिक कठोर हो गए। ड्रेको के कानूनों

से जनता को केवल यही लाभ हुआ कि वह कानूनों से परिचित हो गई किन्तु उसकी दयनीय दशा में कोई बदलाव नहीं आया।

सोलन के सुधार—594 ई. पू. में सोलन को आर्कन का पद सौंपा गया था। वह उच्चकोटि का विद्वान तथा एक अच्छा कवि भी था। वह एक व्यापारी तथा समाज में सर्वाधिक सम्पन्न वर्ग का सदस्य था। आर्कन बनने के बाद उसके द्वारा किये गये सुधार निम्नलिखित हैं—

सोलन ने अपने वैधानिक सुधारों द्वारा एथेन्स में गणतान्त्रिक शासन की नींव डाली। इसी कारण उसे एथेन्स में गणतन्त्र का संस्थापक भी कहा जाता है। सोलन ने निम्नतम वर्ग (थीट्स) को एसेम्बली (जनता की सभा एक्सलेशिया) की सदस्यता प्रदान की। न्यायालयों का निर्माण कराने में उसने महत्त्वपूर्ण भूमिका निभायी थी जिन्हें 'हीलिया' के नाम से पुकारा जाता था। कोई भी नागरिक , चाहे वह कितना भी गरीब क्यों न हो, इन न्यायालयों का जज चुना जा सकता है। इन न्यायालयों में किसी भी मजिस्ट्रेट के पद त्याग के बाद उसके विरुद्ध मुकदमा चलाया जा सकता था। सोलन ने एरियोपैगस नामक संस्था के अधिकार कम कर दिए। अब इस संस्था को शासन के समस्त विषयों पर विचार करने का अधिकार प्राप्त नहीं था। सोलन ने 400 सदस्यों की संख्या वाली काउंसिल 'ह्यूक' का निर्माण किया जिससे शासन का संचालन किया जा सके। इस काउन्सिल का प्रमुख कार्य एसेम्बली का कार्यक्रम निर्धारित करना था। इसका नाम 'बौल' भी था।

सोलन ने यूनान में अनेक दासों को दासता से मुक्त कर दिया। इसके साथ ही सोलन ने कानून में यह भी सुधार कर दिया कि कोई भी व्यक्ति ऋण नहीं चुका सकने के कारण गुलाम नहीं बनाया जा सकता। उसने गरीबों को भी ऋणमुक्त कर दिया। उसके ऋण-सम्बन्धी सुधारों को न केवल यूनान की वरन् प्राचीन विश्व की महान घटना मानते हैं। सोलन ने भूमि सम्बन्धी कानूनों में संशोधन करके भूमि की सीमा निश्चित कर दी, जिससे अधिक भूमि कोई भी व्यक्ति अपने पास नहीं रख सकता था। सोलन ने कानून बनाया कि वैसे लोगों को दण्ड दिया जाए जो राजनीतिक कामों में भाग नहीं लेते हैं।

उसने वेश्यावृत्ति को वैध घोषित कर दिया। एटिका में उत्पादित वस्तुओं का निर्यात बन्द कर दिया। इससे वस्तुएँ सस्ती हो गईं तथा जनता को लाभ पहुँचा। युद्ध में मृतक सैनिकों के बच्चों की व्यवस्था राज्य की ओर से की जाने लगी। व्यक्तियों के शारीरिक विकास के लिए राज्य की ओर से शारीरिक व्यायामशालाओं को स्थापित किया। उसने एथेन्स के सिक्कों में सुधार किया

तथा कुछ नये सिक्के भी प्रचलित किए, जिसके कारण व्यापार के क्षेत्र में उन्नति हुई।

सोलन को यूनान का एक महान सुधारक के रूप में जाना जाता था। उसने एथेन्स के नगर राज्य में समानता, स्वाधीनता और एकता लाने की कोशिश की। उसके सुधारों से समाज के सभी वर्ग पूर्णरूप से सन्तुष्ट थे। यूनान में प्रजातन्त्र की स्थापना में सोलन के सुधार एक महत्त्वपूर्ण कदम थे। अतः उसको एथेन्स के गणतन्त्र का संस्थापक माना जाता है।

क्लैस्थिनीज के सुधार—जनसाधारण के लिए सोलन द्वारा किये गये सुधार काफी लाभदायक सिद्ध हुए। अतः प्रजापीड़क फिसिस ट्रेटस ने उसके सुधारों को समाप्त कर दिया। फिसिस ट्रेटस ने 546 ई. पू. से लेकर 527 ई. पू. तक शासन किया। 527 ई. पू. में फिसिस ट्रेटस की मृत्यु हो गयी। उसकी मृत्यु के बाद उसके दोनों पुत्रों—हिप्पियस तथा हिपकर्स में गद्दी के लिए संघर्ष आरम्भ हो गया। हिप्पियस यूनान छोड़कर चला गया और हिपकर्स को मौत के घाट उतार दिया गया। इसके बाद सोलन का भतीजा क्लैस्थिनीज को 510 ई. पू. में राजगद्दी सौंपी गई।

क्लैस्थिनीज ने कुलीन वर्ग का होते हुए भी इस वर्ग के व्यक्तियों को शासन व्यवस्था में उच्च पदों पर नियुक्त नहीं किया। उसको एथेन्स गणतन्त्र के दूसरे संस्थापक की संज्ञा दी गई थी। उसने गणतन्त्र शासन प्रणाली को सुदृढ़ करने के लिए निम्न सुधार किये—

1. एसेम्बली के अधिकारों में वृद्धि कर दी गई। काउन्सिल द्वारा रखे गये किसी भी विधेयक में यह संशोधन कर सकती थी। युद्ध की घोषणा करने का अधिकार भी एसेम्बली को ही था।
2. प्रत्येक जाति अपने सेनापति नियुक्त करती थी। ये सेनापति क्रम से नियुक्त किए जाते थे।
3. क्लैस्थिनीज ने यूनान के समाज को चार वर्गों के स्थान पर दस वर्गों या श्रेणियों में विभाजित कर दिया गया।
4. सीनेट (ब्यूल) के सदस्यों की संख्या बढ़ाकर 500 कर दी गई और प्रत्येक श्रेणी को 50 प्रतिनिधि भेजने का अधिकार दिया गया।
5. एटिका के दासों को दासता से मुक्त कर दिया गया।
6. सदस्यों की नियुक्तियाँ निर्वाचन के माध्यम से होने लगीं।
7. उसके समय में साधारण सभा का अधिवेशन दस दिन में एक बार बुलाया जाने लगा।

यूनान और फारस का युद्ध

यूनान और फारस के मध्य युद्ध 490 ईसा पूर्व से 479 ईसा पूर्व तक हुआ। फारस की गद्दी पर सबसे पहले दारा या दारियस 521 ईसा पूर्व आसीन हुआ। वह फारस के एक महान शासक के रूप में प्रसिद्ध हुआ। उसने मिस्र, लीडिया, असीरिया, बेबीलोन के विद्रोह का दमन करने के पश्चात् साम्राज्यवादी नीति अपनाई। उधर एथेन्स के शासक भी विस्तारवादी नीति पर चल रहे थे। अतः फारस और यूनान में प्रतिद्वन्द्विता आरम्भ हो गई। हालांकि युद्ध की शुरुआत फारस द्वारा की गई थी लेकिन इसका परिणाम फारस के लिए फायदेमंद साबित नहीं हुआ था। दारा की मृत्यु के पश्चात् भी फारस का यूनान के साथ संघर्ष चलता रहा। फारस और यूनान के मध्य हुए पहले युद्ध को मैराथन युद्ध कहा जाता है।

इतिहासकार **एच. जी. वेल्स** ने लिखा है, "यूनान की मुख्य भूमि पर पहला आक्रमण 490 ई. पू. में हुआ था। इस आक्रमण को समुद्री आक्रमण भी कहा जा सकता था जो एथेन्स नगर पर किया गया था। फारस और यूनान के बीच यह युद्ध 12 वर्ष तक चलता रहा। इस युद्ध को मैराथन युद्ध भी कहा जाता था। एशिया और यूरोप में हुए इस युद्ध के बहुत भयानक परिणाम हुए।

मैराथन का युद्ध

यह युद्ध 490 ईसा पूर्व हुआ था। डेरियस सम्पूर्ण ईरान पर शासन करता था। उसका शासन न केवल विश्व क्षेत्र तक सीमित था अपितु ईजियन सागर जो कि पश्चिम में है और पूर्व में सिन्धु नदी तक तथा उत्तर और दक्षिण दिशा में भी फैला हुआ था। उसका राज्य कुल 20 प्रांतों में बँटा हुआ था तथा प्रत्येक प्रांत का प्रमुख अधिकारी था। इसलिए उसने ग्रीक जनता को खुश रखने के लिए इस प्रांत का अधिकारी (सत्रप) भी ग्रीक नागरिक को बनाया। ग्रीक डेरियस के घोर विरोधी थे। ग्रीक आरिस्टागोरास ने एथेंस को सहायता देने से इन्कार कर दिया। अब ग्रीक आरिस्टागोरास ने एथेंस की सहायता माँगी और एथेंस के साथ मिलकर डेरियस का मुकाबला किया। अंततः सैन्य-शक्ति एवं संगठन कमजोर होने के कारण ग्रीक की सेनाएं पराजित हो गईं जिससे ग्रीक फिर से बिखर गया।

राजा डेरियस का साम्राज्यवाद अर्थात् शासन निरन्तर बढ़ता ही जा रहा था। एक दिन डेरियस ने सब ग्रीक लोगों को संदेशा भेजा कि "इस बात को जतलाने के लिए कि तुमको हमारी अधीनता स्वीकार है, तुम इस जासूस के द्वारा मिट्टी और

पानी भेज दो।'' थीब्स तथा ईजीना ने तो दासता स्वीकार कर ली, परंतु एथेंस और स्पार्टा ने इसका विरोध किया तथा ईजीना को भी लड़कर अपने अधीन कर लिया। ईरानी शासक डेरियस ने बदला लेने के लिए भारी जहाजी सेना के साथ ग्रीस पर चढ़ाई कर दी और इस युद्ध का शुभारंभ हो गया।

ग्रीस पर अधिकार जमाने के उद्देश्य से ईरान से अपनी बहुत बड़ी सेना तैयार की और ईरान पर आक्रमण भी किया और उन्होंने अंततः सफलता प्राप्त की इस युद्ध में उन्होंने विभिन्न टापुओं को जो कि मार्ग में आए और डरिट्रिया को भी बन्दी बना लिया और जलाकर नष्ट कर दिया। मैराथन के मैदान में अपनी सेना का पड़ाव लगा दिया। ईरानी सेना का मुकाबला करने के लिए प्लेटिका के ग्रीक लोगों को स्पार्टा का सहयोग लेना आवश्यक समझा, इसलिए अपने धावकों को भेजा। जिन्होंने 150 मील की दूरी 48 घंटे में तय की। स्पार्टा के सहयोग से तथा प्रतिभाशाली एवं साहसी मिल्टियाड्स के कुशल नेतृत्व में 11,000 ग्रीक सैनिकों ने ईरानी डेरियस के नेतृत्ववाली 20,000 सैनिकों की सेना को पूर्णतया पराजित कर दिया।

ग्रीस की सेना में अधिकतर जो लोग थे वह राजा के गुलाम थे और उन्हें किसी प्रकार की शिक्षा आदि नहीं दी जाती थी। शिक्षा के अभाव में भी वह अत्यन्त कुशल दिखाई पड़ते थे। इसका रहस्य यह था कि ग्रीक सेनापति ने उन्हें वचन दिया था कि यदि इस युद्ध में विजय मिली तो उन्हें स्वतंत्र कर दिया जाएगा। इस सफलता से मिल्टियाड्स की प्रतिष्ठा बहुत बढ़ गई। इस युद्ध में पराजय से डेरियस (ईरानी) को बड़ा आघात पहुंचा और पुनः बदला लेने के लिए जोरदार सैनिक तैयारी की, परंतु इतने में ही उसका देहांत हो गया।

युद्ध के कारण—फारस में राजतन्त्रात्मक शासन व्यवस्था थी। यहां का शासक निरंकुशतापूर्वक अपने विशाल राज्य पर शासन करता था, जबकि यूनान में छोटे-छोटे स्वतन्त्र नगर राज्यों में विभाजित थे। इन नगर राज्यों में प्रजातन्त्र शासन प्रणाली प्रचलित थी। अतः फारस के महत्त्वाकांक्षी निरंकुश शासकों ने इन छोटे-छोटे स्वतन्त्र नगर राज्यों की आपसी फूट का लाभ उठाने का अच्छा अवसर समझा और यूनान पर आक्रमण कर दिया। इसके अलावा फारस के सम्राट डेरियस को यह चिन्ता थी कि एथेन्स तथा अन्य यूनानी नगर राज्यों में प्रचलित प्रजातंत्र की भावना का प्रसार फारस में न हो जाए। अतः वह यूनान के नगर राज्यों के अस्तित्व को समाप्त करना चाहता था।

यूनान निवासी विभिन्न देवताओं की पूजा करते थे और फारसी एकेश्वरवादी थे। धर्म के क्षेत्र में यह विभिन्नता भी युद्ध का कारण बनी, क्योंकि दोनों एक दूसरे पर धार्मिक प्रभुत्व स्थापित करना चाहते थे।

यूनान और फारस के शासक अपने साम्राज्य को अधिक-से-अधिक फैलाना चाहते थे। दोनों ही सभ्यताओं की राज्य विस्तार के लिए सीरिया, फिनीशिया और पेलेस्टाइन में सीधी टक्कर हो गई। जब फारस ने फिनीशिया पर कब्जा कर लिया, तो दोनों के बीच युद्ध आवश्यक हो गया।

यूनान के लोग भूमध्यसागर के सभी राज्यों से व्यापार करते थे। यहां तक कि फारस का व्यापार भी विदेशों से यूनानी जहाजों के माध्यम से ही होता था। फारस ने अपने व्यापारिक पिछड़ेपन को दूर करने एवं विश्व व्यापार को हस्तगत करने हेतु यूनान पर अधिकार करना आवश्यक समझा। युद्ध का प्रमुख कारण व्यापारिक प्रतिस्पर्द्धा ही था।

साइरस एवं दारा 521 ईसा पूर्व जब सम्राट बना तो वह और अधिक महत्वाकांक्षी हो गया। उसके पूर्वज साइरस ने मिस्र पर विजय प्राप्त की थी, इसलिए वह भी साइरस के समान एक विशाल साम्राज्य की स्थापना करना चाहता था। कहा जाता है कि दारा के दरबार में एक यूनानी हकीम रहता था। वह यूनान (अपने घर) जाना चाहता था। अतः उसने दारा को यूनान पर आक्रमण करने के लिए उकसाया। उसी के प्रभाव में आकर दारा ने यूनान पर अधिकार करने का निश्चय किया और अपने दूत यूनान भेजे। **एच.जी. वेल्स** का मत है, "दारा के आक्रमण ने बाल्कन प्रदेशों पर से परदा हटा दिया, जिनके बारे में अब तक हमने कुछ नहीं कहा है।" दारा की साम्राज्यवादी भूख के कारण मैराथन युद्ध हुआ।

दारा के सत्ता संभालते ही सिथिमनों ने विद्रोह आरम्भ कर दिया जिसका उसने दमन कर दिया और काला सागर के प्रमुख द्वार बासफोरस पर कब्जा कर लिया। इसके पश्चात् दूसरा विद्रोह एशिया माइनर के यूनानी जाति के लोगों द्वारा किया गया। लगभग छठी शताब्दी ई. पू. से ही ये लोग फारस के अधीन थे। दारा अपनी सेना लेकर विद्रोह का दमन करने के लिए समुद्र के किनारे तक आया। इस समय एथेन्स ने 20 पानी के जहाज भेज कर इन विद्रोह करने वाले बस्तियों की सहायता की। इस पर यूनानियों ने सार्डिस पर अधिकार कर लिया। इसके बाद यूनानियों ने सार्डिस को बुरी तरह लूटा और जलाकर नष्ट कर दिया। दारा को दो वर्ष लग गये। विद्रोह का दमन करने के पश्चात् दारा एथेन्स को सजा देने के लिए 490 ई. पू. में यूनान पर आक्रमण कर दिया।

यूनान के शासक फिसिस ट्रेटस की मृत्यु के पश्चात् उसका पुत्र हिप्पियन यूनान की गद्दी पर बैठा। यह यूनान का अन्तिम प्रजापीड़क था। जब उसे गद्दी छोड़ने को बाध्य कर दिया गया, तो वह भागकर फारस के सम्राट

दारा की शरण में चला गया। उसी ने दारा को यूनान पर आक्रमण करने के लिए प्रेरित किया।

युद्ध के परिणाम—मैराथन का युद्ध विश्व इतिहास में अपना एक प्रमुख स्थान रखता है। इतिहासकार हैज ने मैराथन युद्ध को इतिहास का एक महान निर्णायक युद्ध माना है। मैराथन के युद्ध से पूर्व दारा एक प्रभावशाली व अविजित शासक समझा जाता था और उसकी सेना का पड़ोसी देशों पर आतंक बना हुआ था, परन्तु जब यूनानियों के हाथों वह मैराथन के युद्ध में पराजित हो गया तो उसकी सैन्य दुर्बलता प्रकट हो गई। यह युद्ध फारस की प्रतिष्ठा के लिए घातक सिद्ध हुआ और ईरानी साम्राज्य का विस्तार रुक गया।

इस युद्ध में यूनान की विजय होने के कारण यूनानी सभ्यता के विकास में आने वाली बाधा समाप्त हो गई। यदि इस युद्ध में यूनानी पराजित हो जाते, तो फारस के सैनिक उनकी संस्कृति को हमेशा के लिए नष्ट कर देते। मैराथन के युद्ध में यूनानियों की विजय हुई जिसके चलते वे अपनी स्वतन्त्रता बनाए रखने में समर्थ हुए और उनकी संस्कृति भी नष्ट होने से बच गई। इस युद्ध ने यूनान के उत्कर्ष का मार्ग खोल दिया और फारस पतन की ओर अग्रसर हो गया। यूनान के नगर राज्यों में व्यापार एवं कला का असाधारण विकास हुआ। अब यूनान साम्राज्यवादी नीति पर चलने लगा। फारस को पराजित करने पश्चात् एथेन्स के प्रयत्नों के परिणामस्वरूप नगर राज्यों की सुरक्षा हेतु डेलियन संघ की नींव रखी गयी। डेलियन संघ अत्यधिक प्रसिद्ध हुआ और अत्यधिक सीमा तक सफल भी हुआ।

एथेन्स और स्पार्टा के मध्य संघर्ष का प्रमुख कारण मैराथन का युद्ध था। चूंकि इस युद्ध के पूर्व से ही इन दोनों के मध्य मतभेद चले आ रहे थे, तथापि मैराथन के युद्ध में इन दोनों ने एकजुट होकर फारस को परास्त किया था। इस युद्ध के पश्चात् एथेन्स एक शक्तिशाली राज्य यूनानी सभ्यता के प्रमुख केन्द्र के रूप में उभरकर सामने आया। एथेन्स ने अपने नगर राज्यों की सुरक्षा हेतु डेलियन संघ की स्थापना की जिससे भयभीत होकर स्पार्टा ने भी डेलियन संघ के विरुद्ध अपना संघ बनाया। इस तरह एथेन्स और स्पार्टा के मध्य युद्ध की शुरुआत हो गई।

थर्मोपोली का युद्ध

दारा की 485 ईसा पूर्व मृत्यु के बाद उसका पुत्र जेरेक्सीज फ्रांस की गद्दी पर आसीन हुआ। यह अपने पिता की भांति वीर तथा महत्त्वाकांक्षी सम्राट था। उसने अपने पिता की पराजय का बदला लेने एवं साम्राज्य विस्तार के लिए 480 ई. पू.

में एक विशाल सेना के साथ यूनान पर आक्रमण कर दिया। यूनान ने स्पार्टा के शासक लियोनिदास के नेतृत्व में उसका मुकाबला किया।

पहाड़ियों के बीच अवस्थित थर्मोपोली में यूनान और फारस के मध्य युद्ध हुआ। युद्ध से पूर्व थर्मोपोली पहुंचने के बाद जेरेक्सीज ने लियोनिदास को आत्मसमर्पण करने के लिए कहा। इस पर लियोनिदास ने निर्भीकता के उत्तर दिया, "जाओ और ले जाओ"। इसके बाद जेरेक्सीज ने अपना एक दूत यूनानी सेनापति के पास भेजा। फारसी दूत ने यूनानी सेनापति से कहा, "कोई बात नहीं, हम अंधेरे में लड़ने को तैयार हैं।" इस पर युद्ध आरम्भ हो गया। युद्ध दो दिन तक चलता रहा। यूनान की सेना लियोनिदास की मृत्यु के कारण पराजित हो गई।

स्पार्टा के राजा लियोनिदास ने इस युद्ध में बड़ी वीरता व साहस से अपने प्रतिद्वन्द्वियों का मुकाबला किया था। इससे स्पार्टा की प्रतिष्ठा में चार चांद लग गये और लियोनिदास विश्व इतिहास में अपना नाम सदा के लिए अमर कर गया। कुछ वर्षों बाद युद्ध स्थल पर एक शिलालेख स्थापित किया गया, जिससे लियोनिदास तथा उसके तीन सौ स्पार्टा के सैनिकों के बलिदान को अभूतपूर्व श्रद्धांजलि अर्पित की गई थी।

युद्ध के परिणाम—थर्मोपोली के युद्ध में फारस को सफलता मिली और यूनानियों को पराजय का मुख देखना पड़ा। फारस के शासक ने एथेन्स पर अधिकार कर लिया। इस पर यूनानी पहाड़ों में भाग गये। फारस के सैनिकों ने सारा एथेन्स अग्नि देवता को भेंट चढ़ा दिया। एथेन्स में कई दिनों तक धुएँ का बादल छाया रहा।

सेलामिस का युद्ध

जेरेक्लीज ने थर्मोपोली के युद्ध में सफलता प्राप्त करने के बाद यूनान पर आक्रमण कर दिया। इस समय यूनानियों का नेतृत्व थेमीस्टोक्लीज कर रहा था। फारस और यूनान के बीच सेलामिस नामक टापू पर युद्ध हुआ। इस युद्ध में यूनानी सेनापति थेमीस्टोक्लीज ने फारस के जहाजी बेड़े को हराया। इस बेड़े के 200 पोत जल में डूब गये बाकी सुरक्षित वापस आ गये और शेष जहाज वहां से भाग गए। जेरेक्सीज प्राण बचाकर भाग गया। इस प्रकार 23 सितम्बर, 480 ई. पू. के सेलामिस के युद्ध में फारस की पराजय हुई और यूनान को शानदार विजय प्राप्त हुई। सेलामिस युद्ध को विश्व इतिहास के निर्णायक युद्धों में से एक माना जाता है। इसने समूचे युद्ध का पासा ही पलट दिया था।

प्लेटिया का युद्ध

479 ई. पू. में फारस ने पुनः यूनान पर आक्रमण कर दिया। यह युद्ध प्लेटिया के मैदान में हुआ था जहाँ फारस की पराजय हुई और उसका सेनापति मारडोनियस वीरगति को प्राप्त हुआ। यूनानी सैनिकों ने फारस के अधिकांश सैनिकों को जान से मार डाला। यह एक निर्णायक युद्ध हुआ, जिसमें फारसी जहाजरानी एक बार फिर पराजित हो गई और फारस का यूनान पर अधिकार करने का स्वप्न पूरा नहीं हो सका। फारस की असफलता के संदर्भ में **एच. जी. वेल्स** महोदय ने लिखा है कि, "479 ई. पू. के बाद मीडिया और फारस की सरकार के शरीर से आत्मा और उत्साह चला गया। उस महान् साम्राज्य का क्षय आरम्भ हो गया।" प्लेटिया के युद्ध में यूनान की शानदार विजय हुई और फारस की सेना ने फिर कभी यूनान पर आक्रमण करने का साहस नहीं किया। इस युद्ध के बाद फारस कभी नहीं पनपा और एक एक करके उसके सभी राज्य उससे अलग हो गये।

युद्ध के परिणाम—फारस और यूनान के मध्य हुए युद्ध में फारस के सम्राट की साम्राज्यवादी नीति को आघात पहुंचा। यूनान ने विस्तारवादी नीति अपनाई। यूनान के नगर राज्यों में कला एवं व्यापार के क्षेत्र में असाधारण विकास हुआ। एथेन्स यूनान के नगर राज्यों में प्रमुख हो गया। एथेन्स यूनानी सभ्यता व संस्कृति का प्रमुख केन्द्र बन गया। एथेन्स का बढ़ता हुआ प्रभाव एथेन्स और स्पार्टा के बीच शत्रुता का कारण बना। एथेन्स फारस को पराजित कर अपने नागरिकों में लोकतंत्र की भावना को और अधिक बढ़ाने में सफल हो गया।

पराजय का कारण—फारस के सम्राट सामन्तों की सेना पर निर्भर रहता था। सामन्तों की सेना उनके प्रति ही उत्तरदायी होती थी, फारस के राजाओं के प्रति नहीं। यह सेना अनुशासित नहीं थी और कभी-कभी सम्राट के खिलाफ विद्रोह कर देती थी। इन सैनिकों की बदौलत विजय प्राप्त करना असंभव थी।

फारस की पराजय का एक प्रमुख कारण सैनिकों में धनलोलुपता भी था। अतः फारस के सैनिक धन के लालची थे और उनका उद्देश्य धन कमाना था, न कि देश के लिए लड़ना, जबकि यूनानियों में देशभक्ति की प्रबल भावना विद्यमान थी। अतः ऐसी स्थिति में फारस के लिए विजय प्राप्त कर पाना एक चुनौती थी।

फारस के सेनापति की तुलना में यूनान का सेनानायक अधिक कुशल था। अतः फारस को पराजय का स्वाद चखना पड़ा। यूनानी सैनिक गुरिल्ला युद्ध पद्धति में निपुण थे, जबकि फारस के सैनिक खुले मैदानों में युद्ध करना जानते थे। अतः

फारस के सैनिकों को यूनान की तंग घाटियों और पहाड़ों में युद्ध करने में कठिनाई हो रही थी जिसका लाभ यूनान को मिला। भौगोलिक दृष्टि से फारस और यूनान में बहुत दूरी थी, जिससे फारस अपनी सेना को समय पर मदद नहीं भेज पाता था जिसके कारण हार हुई।

यूनानियों का जहाजी बेड़ा फारस के जहाजी बेड़े से अत्यधिक मजबूत व समृद्धशाली था। अतः सेलामिस, माइकेल तथा प्लेटिया के युद्धों में फारस को मुंह की खानी पड़ी और उसकी शक्ति क्षीण हो गयी। फारस की सेना में राष्ट्रीयता की भावना नहीं होने के कारण यूनान को सफलता मिली।

युद्ध के बाद यूनान की स्थिति

यूनानियों को फारस की सेना का मुकाबला करने में अत्यधिक चुनौतियों को झेलना पड़ा था लेकिन इन युद्धों के परिणाम यूनान की समृद्धि में वृद्धिकारक सिद्ध हुए। यूनान ने प्लेटिया के युद्ध में फारस की सेना को पराजित करने के बाद एशियाई कोचक पर अधिकार कर लिया। एथेन्स, यूनान का पथ प्रदर्शक बन गया और थेमीस्टोक्लीज यूनान का नेता बन गया। वह महत्त्वाकांक्षी था। अतः उसने साम्राज्यवादी नीति अपनाई। थेमीस्टोक्लीज ने एथेन्स की रक्षा तथा साम्राज्य विस्तार करने के लिए डेलियन संघ की स्थापना की। इस संघ के माध्यम से थेमीस्टोक्लीज स्पार्टा को पराजित कर एथेन्स के साम्राज्य का विस्तार करना चाहता था।

डेलौस का संघ अथवा डेलियन संघ

फारस को युद्ध में हराने के उपरांत भी एथेन्स व स्पार्टा को अपनी सुरक्षा की चिन्ता बनी रही। इस कारण दोनों राज्यों ने 478-477 ई. पू. एजियन समुद्र के आयोनिया के द्वीप और एशिया माइनर के तटों के पास यूनानी द्वीपों को मिलाकर एक संघ का निर्माण किया, जिसे डेलौस द्वीप कहा जाता था। इसमें 200 से भी अधिक नगर राज्य सदस्य थे। इस संघ का अध्यक्ष एथेन्स नगर राज्य था। संघ की नौसेना व थल सेना संयुक्त थी। प्रत्येक सदस्य को नगर राज्य की नौसेना के लिए कुछ निश्चित धनराशि देनी पड़ती थी।

चूँकि डेलौस संघ का मुख्यालय डेलौस द्वीप में था, अतः इसका नाम डेलौस का संघ रखा गया। इस संघ का कोष अपोलो मन्दिर में रखा गया तथा इसकी बैठकें डेलौस द्वीप में बुलाई जाती थीं। थेमीस्टोक्लीज डेलौस संघ का निर्माता था, अतः एथेन्स यूनान का नेता बन गया। उसने विस्तारवादी नीति का पालन किया। इस

संघ के प्रमुख उद्देश्य थे—अपने सदस्य राज्य की फारस के आक्रमण से रक्षा करना, समुद्री डाकुओं का दमन करना और अपने सदस्य राज्यों के वाद-विवादों का निपटारा करना इत्यादि। इस प्रकार डेलियन संघ की तुलना वर्तमान के संयुक्त राष्ट्र संघ से की जा सकती है।

इसकी स्थापना के पश्चात् कुछ समय तक डेलौस संघ काफी प्रभावशाली रहा। फारस यूनान पर आक्रमण करने का साहस नहीं कर सका, जिसके कारण यूनान में प्रजातन्त्र का निरन्तर विकास होता चला गया। इस संघ ने समुद्री डाकुओं का सफाया कर दिया। इस कारण यूनान के व्यापार का विकास हुआ। परन्तु ज्यों-ज्यों एथेन्स का प्रभाव संघ पर बढ़ता गया, यह संघ विवाद का कारण बनता गया। एथेन्स संघ के सदस्य राज्यों से अवैध तरीके से धन लेने लगा। यही नहीं, संघ के धन को एथेन्स अपने विकास और अपने उपनिवेशों की स्थापना पर खर्च करने लगा। इस प्रकार लगभग 20 वर्षों की अवधि में एथेन्स ने इस संघ को अपना साम्राज्य बना डाला था। प्रसिद्ध इतिहासकार **ग्रोट** ने ठीक ही लिखा है, "इस संघ के सदस्य राज्य, अनजाने तौर पर एथेंस के अधीनस्थ राज्य बन गए एथेंस बिना किसी पूर्व निर्धारित योजना के संघ के नेता से निरकुंश शासक के रूप में परिवर्तित हो गया।" जिससे संघ के सदस्य राज्यों में असन्तोष बढ़ गया।

संघ के माध्यम से एथेन्स का शासक स्पार्टा को युद्ध में हराकर अपने राज्य में मिलाना चाहता था। इस कोष से थेमीस्टोक्लीज ने अपनी नौ सेना का विस्तार किया तथा उसे सुदृढ़ किया। साइमन स्पार्टा से दुश्मनी नहीं चाहता था इसलिए उसने थेमीस्टोक्लीज का विरोध किया। एथेन्स की सभा ने साइमन की नीति का समर्थन किया और थेमीस्टोक्लीज को उसके पद से हटा दिया। अब एथेन्स की गद्दी पर साइमन विराजमान हुआ और उसने स्पार्टा के साथ मित्रतापूर्ण सम्बन्ध बनाए रखा, परन्तु 461 ई. में स्पार्टा के नागरिकों ने विद्रोह कर दिया। साइमन इस विद्रोह का दमन करने में असफल रहा। एथेन्सवासी स्पार्टा को विद्रोह के लिए सजा देना चाहते थे। अतः एथेन्स एसेम्बली ने पेरिक्लीज को एथेन्स का शासक बना दिया जो जनतान्त्रिक दल का होता था।

पेरिक्लीज

एथेन्स का शासक बनने पर पेरिक्लीज में पूरे यूनान को अपनी ओर प्रभावित कर लिया। उसके समय में यूनान में साहित्य, कला एवं दर्शन के क्षेत्र में आश्चर्यजनक विकास हुआ। इस युग में एथेन्स गणतन्त्र का सर्वांगीण विकास हुआ

और वह समस्त यूनान का बौद्धिक केन्द्र बन गया, जहां लोग शिक्षा प्राप्त करने आते थे। पेरिक्लीज का शासनकाल इतना अच्छा रहा कि इतिहास में यह 'पेरिक्लीज युग' के नाम से प्रसिद्ध हुआ। पेरिक्लीज के शासनकाल में एथेन्स ने प्रत्येक क्षेत्र में आश्चर्यजनक विकास किया, अतः उसके शासनकाल को यूनान का 'स्वर्णयुग' माना गया।

पेरिक्लीज का जन्म 493 ई. पू. में एक संभ्रान्त एवं सम्पन्न परिवार में हुआ था। इसके पिता का नाम जैन्थिप्पस था, जो एथेन्स का भूतपूर्व जल सेनापति था। इसकी माता विख्यात सुधारक क्लैस्थिनीज की भतीजी थी। पेरिक्लीज युवावस्था में ही एथेन्स की राजनीति में प्रसिद्ध हो गया था। उसने अच्छी सैनिक शिक्षा प्राप्त की थी। तत्कालीन प्रसिद्ध संगीतकार डेमन ने उसे संगीतशास्त्र की तथा प्रसिद्ध दार्शनिक एनेक्सागोरस ने उसे दर्शनशास्त्र की शिक्षा प्रदान की। **डॉ. गोयल** के मतानुसार, "उसके व्यक्तित्व में कुलीनता, शौर्य तथा तत्कालीन यूनानी संस्कृति के सर्वोत्तम तत्वों का अद्भुत समन्वय हो गया था। वह अत्यन्त गम्भीर और अल्पभाषी था।" वह एक कुशल वक्ता तथा जनकल्याणकारी शासक था। **डब्ल्यू एन.** के शब्दों में, "एथेन्स के निवासी, जो अपने नेताओं के लिए तीव्र प्यार या घृणा का भाव अनुभव करते थे, किन्तु कदाचित ही किसी को सम्मान देते थे और जनता ने उसे 'सर्वशक्तिमान' का उपनाम दे दिया था।"

पेरिक्लीज एथेन्स की गद्दी पर 461 ई. पू. में बैठा था। उसने 32 वर्ष तक अर्थात् 429 ई. पू. तक शासन किया। पेरिक्लीज ने यूनान को एक समृद्ध तथा सुन्दर नगर के रूप में बदल दिया। उसके शासनकाल में कला, साहित्य, संगीत तथा दर्शन में असाधारण उन्नति हुई। इसलिए उसके शासनकाल को प्राचीन यूनान का स्वर्णकाल कहा गया है। **जे.सी. रेविल** के अनुसार, "पेरिक्लीज का शासनकाल एथेन्स के इतिहास में सर्वाधिक गौरव का काल है।"

पेरिक्लीज ने एथेंस की यूनानी सभ्यता को केन्द्र बिन्दु में रखते हुये पुनः निर्माण करवाया। पेरिक्लीज ने विस्तारवादी नीति को अपनाया। उसने विदेशों में कई बस्तियों की स्थापना की, ताकि मुसीबत के समय इनसे मदद ली जा सके। वह इन बस्तियों में एथेन्स की सभ्यता एवं संस्कृति के प्रसार हेतु प्रयत्न भी करना चाहता था। किन्तु दुर्भाग्यवश वह इसमें सफल न हो सका। पेरिक्लीज की विस्तारवादी नीति ने उसके साम्राज्य के लिए पतन का मार्ग प्रशस्त किया, तथापि इस बात से इन्कार नहीं किया जा सकता कि उसका शासनकाल यूनानी इतिहास का गौरवपूर्ण स्वर्णकाल था।

पेरिक्लीज एथेन्स का विस्तार करना चाहता था अतः उसने विस्तारवादी नीति को अपनाया। फारस के विरुद्ध युद्धों के दौरान थेमीस्टोक्लीज ने यूनान के कई राज्यों को मिलाकर डेलियन संघ की नींव रखी, जिसका नेता एथेन्स था। फारस को पराजित करने के बाद संघ के कई सदस्य अलग हो जाना चाहते थे, किन्तु पेरिक्लीज ने उन्हें ऐसा नहीं करने दिया। इतना ही नहीं, उसने कुछ अन्य राज्यों को भी संघ का सदस्य बनने हेतु विवश किया। अब डेलियन संघ का कोष एथेन्स द्वारा संग्रहीत किया जाने लगा और एथेन्स के राजकोष में रखा जाने लगा।

डेलियन संघ पर इस समय एथेन्स का आधिपत्य था। डेलियन संघ ऐटिका, थैसली, अर्कोलिस, अकेट्या आदि द्वीपों से कर एकत्र करता था। इन द्वीपों की विदेशी नीति का निर्धारक भी पेरिक्लीज ही था। इसके अतिरिक्त वह संघ के सदस्य राज्यों के आन्तरिक मामलों में भी दखल देता था। पेरिक्लीज के इस बढ़ते प्रभुत्व से तंग आकर कुछ सदस्य राज्यों ने विद्रोह कर दिया जिसका पेरिक्लीज ने दमन कर दिया। पेरिक्लीज ने अपने समुद्री बेड़े को और सुदृढ़ बनाया। उसने थैसली, अर्गोस आदि राज्यों से मैत्रीपूर्ण सम्बन्ध स्थापित किए। डेलियन संघ ने एथेंस की सुरक्षा सुनिश्चित करने के लिये दोनों तरफ दीवारों का निर्माण करवाया पेरिक्लीज ने संघ को समृद्धि का साधन बनाया।

एथेन्स संघ की गद्दी पर जब पेरिक्लीज आसीन हुआ तो उसने स्पार्टा के एगिना उपनिवेश पर अधिकार कर लिया। पेरिक्लीज के शासनकाल में ही 459 ई. पू. में स्पार्टा तथा एथेन्स के बीच संघर्ष आरम्भ हो गया। यह युद्ध 'पेलोपोनोशियन युद्ध' के नाम से प्रसिद्ध है, जो 459 ई. पू. से 446 ई. पू. तक चला। यह युद्ध अनिर्णीत रहा और दोनों राज्यों में 446 ई. पू. में सन्धि हो गई। कुछ समय पश्चात् 431 ई. पू. में दोनों में फिर युद्ध शुरू हो गया। इस युद्ध के समय राज्य में 'प्लेग' नामक महाभारी फैलने एवं अन्य राज्यों की मदद नहीं मिलने से एथेन्स पराजित हो गया। पेरिक्लीज ने अपने शासनकाल के अन्तिम वर्षों के दौरान कई नगर राज्यों के सहयोग से स्पार्टा पर विजय प्राप्त की। इन संघर्षों के बावजूद पेरिक्लीज की छत्रछाया में एथेन्स की संस्कृति विकास के मार्ग पर अग्रसर रही।

यूनान के प्रसिद्ध इतिहासकार थ्यूसीडाइडीज ने पेरिक्लीज के आदर्शों का वर्णन किया है। पेरिक्लीज ने एथेन्स में सुदृढ़ शासन व्यवस्था कर शान्ति व्यवस्था बनाये रखी। वह निहायत ईमानदार था। पेरिक्लीज सहिष्णु था और उसने जनता को भी व्यक्तिगत जीवन में तथा सामाजिक जीवन में सहिष्णुता अपनाने का उपदेश दिया। वह एक महान् योद्धा होने के साथ-साथ कला व साहित्य का महान् संरक्षक भी था।

उसने कला, दर्शन, साहित्य, कविता, नाटक आदि के विकास हेतु व्यापक प्रयास किया। अतः पेरिक्लीज यूनानी इतिहास का महान् सम्राट तथा उसका शासनकाल यूनानी इतिहास का स्वर्णकाल कहलाता था। **एच.जी. वेल्स** ने लिखा है, ''वह गरीब ही रहा और गरीब ही मर गया, कदाचित् वह प्रजातन्त्रियों में सबसे ईमानदार आदमी था।''

एथेन्स की शासन प्रणाली लोकतन्त्रात्मक थी। यहां पर एक एसेम्बली होती थी, जिसका सदस्य बनने का प्रत्येक नागरिक को अधिकार था। इसकी बैठक सप्ताह में कम से कम एक दिन होती थी, जिसमें निर्णय बहुमत प्रणाली पर आधारित था। दासों, स्त्रियों और विदेशियों को शासन कार्यों में भाग लेने का अधिकार प्राप्त नहीं था। इस काल में एक कौन्सिल भी थी, जिसका मुख्य कार्य केवल एसेम्बली द्वारा पारित कानूनों पर अपनी स्वीकृति की मुहर लगाना था। इसके अतिरिक्त 'स्ट्रेटोगोई' नामक संस्था भी होती थी, जिसमें दस जनरल होते थे, जो एथेन्स की सेना एवं विदेशी नीति का निर्धारण करते थे।

पेरिक्लीज के शासनकाल में नागरिकों को भाषण, अभिव्यक्ति एवं विचार की स्वतन्त्रता थी। किसी भी सभा में 6,000 व्यक्तियों द्वारा एकमत होकर किसी भी नागरिक से उसके मौलिक अधिकारों को छीन लिया जाता था। पेरिक्लीज द्वारा हीलिया नामक एक नये न्यायालय की नींव रखी गई। उसने एथेन्स में छः हजार ज्यूररों (जजों) को नियुक्त किया। इन जजों का चुनाव जनता करती थी। प्रत्येक नागरिक को जीवन में एक बार जूरी का सदस्य बनने का अवसर मिलता था। जूरी के सदस्य वैतनिक होते थे। ताकि उनका नैतिक स्तर ऊँचा रह सके। **डॉ. एस. आर. गोयल** ने लिखा है, ''सम्भवतः विश्व में इससे अधिक जनवादी न्याय व्यवस्था कभी कहीं स्थपित नहीं हुई।'' इस काल में चलित न्यायालय भी स्थापित किए गए। इस काल में दण्ड विधान कठोर था। अपराधी जूरी के सामने अपना पक्ष प्रस्तुत कर सकता था। इस सम्बन्ध में **डॉ. सुशील माधव** ने लिखा है, ''इन सुधारों के द्वारा पेरिक्लीज ने एथेन्स के गणतांत्रिक संविधान को पूर्ण किया। पेरिक्लीज के युग में जनता के हाथों में पूर्णरूपेण शासन का अधिकार आ गया। उसके नेतृत्व में गणतंत्र के विकास में जो बाधाएं थीं, वे दूर की गईं तथा एथेन्स एक पूर्ण गणतंत्र बन गया। इस प्रकार एथेन्स की शासन प्रणाली ने वर्तमान प्रजातन्त्रों के लिए पथ प्रदर्शक का काम किया है।

इस काल में नारियों को शासन एवं सामाजिक उत्सवों में भाग लेने का अधिकार नहीं था। दासों की स्थिति बहुत शोचनीय थी। वे शासन कार्यों में भाग

नहीं ले सकते थे। यहां के लोग नाटक देखने के बहुत शौकीन थे। शासन पूर्णतः लोकतांत्रिक था। नागरिकों को भाषण, अभिव्यक्ति व विचारों की स्वतंत्रता प्राप्त थी। पेरिक्लीज के शासक पद पर किसी भी व्यक्ति को आसीन करने की व्यवस्था से सभी वर्गों को लाभ हुआ। दास, स्त्रियाँ तथा विदेशी शासन कार्यों में भाग नहीं ले सकते थे। एथेन्स में नागरिक प्रत्यक्ष रूप से शासन में भाग लेते थे, इसे ''प्रत्यक्ष प्रजातन्त्र' कहते हैं। पेरिक्लीज स्वयं कहता था कि, ''उस व्यक्ति का जीवन निरर्थक है, जो नागरिक सेवा में भाग नहीं लेता।''

अपराधियों को अधिकार दिया गया था कि वे जूरी के सामने अपना पक्ष रख सकें। पेरिक्लीज ने जूरी के सदस्यों के उच्च नैतिक स्तर को बनाये रखने हेतु उनके लिए वेतन की व्यवस्था की। जन सभा के सदस्य नागरिकों द्वारा निर्वाचित किए जाते थे। यदि किसी सभा में छः हजार नागरिक किसी नागरिक के विरोध में मत देते थे, तो उस व्यक्ति को मौलिक अधिकारों से वंचित कर दिया जाता था। इसके अतिरिक्त 500 सदस्यों वाली एक कौन्सिल भी होती थी। एथेन्स के प्रजातंत्र को पेरिक्लीज ने स्थायित्व प्रदान किया। **प्लैट व जीन ड्रमण्ड** ने लिखा है, ''एथेन्स के लोकतंत्र की शानदार सफलताओं को आंखों से ओझल नहीं करना चाहिए। आज मेरे विश्व में एक भी लोकतंत्र ऐसा नहीं है, जो एथेन्स का ऋणी न हो।" **मैकनेल बर्न्स** ने लिखा है, ''पेरिक्लीज के शासनकाल में एथेन्स का प्रजातन्त्र अपनी पूर्ण निपुणता को प्राप्त कर चुका था।''

पेरिक्लीज के समय एथेन्स में प्रत्येक नगर के लिए अलग-अलग देवता होता था। देवताओं की पूजा का कार्य पुरोहितों द्वारा किया जाता था। बलि देने का भी प्रचलन था। प्रत्येक व्यक्ति अपने चार इष्ट देवताओं को भोजन के समय शराब और भोजन चढ़ाता था। यूनानी धर्म में आध्यात्मिक विचारधारा की काफी कमी थी।

पेरिक्लीज की शासन व्यवस्था बहुत ही अच्छी थी। उसने सुव्यवस्थित एवं सुदृढ़ शासन प्रबन्ध की स्थापना की। उसका शासन प्रबन्ध प्रत्यक्ष प्रजातन्त्रात्मक था। सभी नागरिक शासन कार्यों में प्रत्यक्ष रूप से भाग लेते थे। नागरिकों को भाषण, अभिव्यक्ति और विचार की स्वतन्त्रता थी। पेरिक्लीज के शासनकाल में जनता सुखी और समृद्ध थी। सरकारी पदों पर नियुक्ति योग्यता के आधार पर की जाती थी। इस सुदृढ़ शासन व्यवस्था के कारण राज्य में शांति और समृद्धि विद्यमान थी तथा एथेन्स का निरन्तर विकास हो रहा था।

आर्थिक जीवन

पेरिक्लीज का युग आर्थिक दृष्टि से समृद्धि का युग था। उसने अपने शासनकाल में रोजगार के विभिन्न अवसर उपलब्ध कराये जिससे सबको रोजगार मिल सके। पेरिक्लीज ने कृषकों के प्रति सहानुभूति की नीति अपनाई जिसके कारण उनकी दशा में निरन्तर सुधार हो रहा था। उसने करों में वृद्धि की, फिर भी जनता उससे सन्तुष्ट थी। उसके समय में जनता आर्थिक कठिनाइयों से मुक्त थी। इस प्रकार इस समय जनसाधारण की आर्थिक दशा बहुत अच्छी थी। पेरिक्लीज ने विदेशी विस्तार नीति को अपनाकर जनसाधारण की आर्थिक स्थिति सुधारने का प्रयास किया। उस समय यूनान के मिस्र तथा एशिया के देशों से व्यापारिक सम्बन्ध थे। उसके समय में यूनान ने व्यापारिक क्षेत्र में असाधारण उन्नति की। एथेन्स डेन्यूब से दास एवं पशु, मिस्र तथा मैसोपोटामिया से गलीचे, रेशम, मसाले, बहुमुल्य धातुएं तथा भूमध्यसागर के निकटवर्ती प्रदेशों से अनाज, लकड़ी, चांदी और सोने का आयात करता था। इनके बदले में यूनान से इन देशों को मिट्टी के बर्तन, शराब तथा आभूषण आदि वस्तुएं निर्यात की जाती थीं। इससे यह पता चलता है कि उस समय व्यापार का चौतरफा विकास हुआ। **प्रो. ब्रेस्टेड** के अनुसार, "देश का व्यापार विकसित था। उद्योग धन्धे सुविकसित थे और उत्पादन में 30 प्रतिशत तक लाभ होना तो एक सामान्य बात थी। काले सागर तक व्यापार करने पर एथेन्सवासियों को अपना व्यय निकालकर शत प्रतिशत लाभ होता था। राज्य द्वारा विदेशी व्यापार को बहुत प्रोत्साहन दिया जाता था।"

साहित्य

पेरिक्लीज के शासनकाल में साहित्यिक उन्नति अपनी चरम सीमा पर जा पहुंची। इस दौरान अत्यन्त प्रसिद्ध कवि, नाटककार तथा इतिहासकार हुए, जिन्होंने उच्चकोटि के ग्रन्थों की रचना की। उनकी रचनाएं आज भी आदर्श मानी जाती हैं। पेरिक्लीज की शासनावधि में प्रणय गीत, शोक गीत, विलाप गीत और वीर गीत आदि की रचना की गई। आरचीलोकस, अलकेअस, सेफो, एनाक्रियन एवं पिण्डार आदि इस दौरान के प्रसिद्ध कवि थे। समाज की वास्तविक स्थिति का वर्णन आरचीलोकस ने गीतों के द्वारा किया। प्रकृति की सुन्दरता का वर्णन सेफो ने किया। पिण्डार (522 ई. पू. से 448 ई. पू.) पेरिक्लीज के काल का सबसे प्रसिद्ध कवि था। उसका जन्म थीब्स में हुआ था। उसकी रचनाओं में राष्ट्रप्रेम झलकता था उनके लिखे कई गीत बहुत लोकप्रिय हुए।

एच. जी. वेल्स ने लिखा है, ''गद्य साहित्य का जन्म सबसे पहले इतिहास के रूप में हुआ था, जिसका जनक हेरोडोटस है। उसने पेरिक्लीज के समय में एथेन्स का भ्रमण किया था।'' उसके दरबार में हेरोडोटस एवं थ्यूसीडाइडीज नामक दो प्रसिद्ध इतिहासकार थे। **हेरोडोटस (484 ई. पू. से 425 ई.पू.)** ने सर्वप्रथम इतिहास लिखने का काम शुरू किया। इसीलिए उसे 'इतिहास का पिता' कहा जाता है। उसने अपनी पुस्तक **'यूनानी पारसीक युद्धों का इतिहास'** में मुख्य रूप से यूनान एवं फ्रांस के युद्धों में सामाजिक संरचना तथा राजनीति का वर्णन मिलता है। इसके बारे में **सेवाइन** ने लिखा है, ''तीक्ष्ण बुद्धि वाले यूनानियों ने जिस साहित्य की रचना की, उस साहित्य का पिता हेरोडोटस था। वह स्वयं के लिखे पर विश्ववास नहीं करता था।'' **थ्यूसीडाइडीज (460 ई. पू. से 400 ई. पू)** इस युग का दूसरा प्रसिद्ध इतिहासकार था। एथेन्स और स्पार्टा के मध्य हुए पेलोपोनेशियन युद्ध का इतिहास थ्यूसीडाइडीज ने लिखा यह पहला इतिहासकार था जिसने वैज्ञानिक ढंग से इतिहास लिखा था। इसने विश्व वैज्ञानिक इतिहास लिखने की कला को जन्म दिया। इसने एथेन्स के साम्राज्य के पतन का इतिहास भी पूरी छानबीन के बाद वैज्ञानिक ढंग से लिखा था। पेरिक्लीज के युग में यूनान में नाटकों का असाधारण विकास हुआ। वह स्वयं नाटकों से बहुत प्रेम करता था। उसने अपने दरबार में नाटककारों को सरंक्षण प्रदान किया, जिन्होंने अत्यंत उच्चकोटि के दुःखान्त एवं सुखान्त नाटक लिखे। इन नाटकों के द्वारा वे नाटकयुग के रूप में प्रसिद्ध हुये।

एस्काइलूस (525 ई. पू. से 456 ई. पू.) दुःखान्त नाटकों के क्षेत्र में सबसे प्रसिद्ध नैतिकतावादी नाटककार थे। इन्हें दुःखान्त नाटकों का जन्मदाता माना जाता है। इनका जन्म एथेन्स में हुआ था। इन्होंने अपना जीवन एक सैनिक के रूप में आरम्भ किया था। उसने धार्मिक और पौराणिक विषयों पर 8 नाटक लिखे। यह देवताओं के न्याय को ही सर्वोपरि मानता था। यूनानी लोग सुखान्त नाटकों की अपेक्षा दुःखान्त नाटकों के प्रेमी थे। अतः एस्काइलूस को अपने दुःखान्त नाटकों पर तेरह बार पुरस्कार मिला।

सोफोक्लीज (496 ई. पू. से 406 ई. पू.) इस युग का दूसरा प्रसिद्ध दुःखान्त नाटककार था। इनके समय में यूनानी नाटक का चरम उत्कर्ष हुआ। इन्होंने अपने नाटकों में निराशा एवं दुख का मिश्रित एवं भावपूर्ण वर्णन किया इन्हें दुःखद नाटक पर पुरस्कार प्रदान किया गया। सोफोक्लीज ने लगभग 100 नाटकों की रचनी की, जिनमें आज 7 ही उपलब्ध हुए हैं। प्रसिद्ध नाटकों में 'एण्टीगोण' और 'इलेक्ट्रा' आदि विशेष रूप से उल्लेखनीय हैं। यह एक आदर्शवादी नाटककार थे।

यूरीपीडीज (480 ई. पू. से 406 ई. पू.) इस युग का तीसरे प्रसिद्ध दुःखान्त नाटककार थे। इन्होंने अपने नाटकों में विशेष रूप से दलितों एवं पीड़ित वर्ग के प्रति संवेदना व्यक्त की। इन्होंने अपने नाटकों में एथेन्स की साम्राज्यवादी नीति की भी आलोचना की। इसने लगभग 75 नाटक लिखे थे, जिनमें 'द ट्रोजन वीमेन' (ट्राय की नारियाँ) एवं 'मीडिया' विशेष रूप से उल्लेखनीय हैं। यूरीपीडीज 'द ट्रोजन वीमेन' नामक नाटक में ट्राय की नारियों के युद्धकालीन कष्टों का वर्णन किया गया है।

सुखान्त नाटक लिखने वालों में एरिस्टोफेनीज का नाम विशेष रूप से उल्लेखनीय है। इन्होंने कई हास्य रस के नाटकों की रचना की, जिनमें तत्कालीन नेताओं पर तीखा व्यंग किया गया था। इसके राजनैतिक व्यंग बहुत लोकप्रिय एवं प्रसिद्ध हुए। इन्होंने अपने जीवनकाल में 42 नाटक लिखे। 'नाइट्स', 'वास्पूस', 'बर्ड्स', 'पार्लियामेन्ट ऑफ विमेन' इत्यादि महत्वपूर्ण नाटक हैं। एरिस्टोफनीज ने 'पार्लियामेन्ट ऑफ विमेन' प्रसिद्ध नाटक था। इस नाटक में तर्क के आधार पर स्त्रियों को दिये गए अधिकारों का मजाक उड़ाया है।

एथेन्स निवासी दुःखी नाटकों को देखना अधिक पसन्द करते थे। नाटककार को राष्ट्रीय पुरस्कार देकर सम्मानित किया जाता था। यूनान के प्रसिद्ध थियेटर डायोनिसस में वर्ष में दो बार नाटक आयोजित किये जाते थे। इसकी सीटें पत्थर की बनी हुई थीं। इस थियेटर में हजारों लोग प्रत्येक रात्रि को नाटक देखने के लिए आते थे।

ज्ञान विज्ञान

पेरिक्लीज के शासनकाल में अरस्तु, हिपोक्रेटीज, डेमाक्रेटीज, एनेक्सागोरस आदि प्रमुख वैज्ञानिक थे। अरस्तु भौतिक विज्ञान का जन्मदाता था, जिसने पशुओं का वर्गीकरण कर जीव विज्ञान की नींव रखी। हिपोक्रेटीज को यूनान में चिकित्सा विज्ञान का पिता माना जाता था। उसने सिद्ध किया कि प्रत्येक बीमारी शारीरिक कारणों से होती है। वह प्रेत आत्माओं में विश्वास नहीं करता था। उसने बीमारियों और औषधियों पर प्रकाश डाला है। डेमोक्रेटीज ने रेखागणित में शोधकार्य को आगे बढ़ाया। उसने बताया कि विश्व का निर्माण अणुओं से हुआ है। इसके अतिरिक्त एनेक्सागोरस नामक ज्योतिषी ने सूर्यगहण, चन्द्रग्रहण और नक्षत्रों का अध्ययन किया। उसका विश्वास था कि मानव का विकास जानवरों से हुआ है तथा पृथ्वी के अतिरिक्त अन्य ग्रहों पर भी मानव का बसेरा है।

ज्ञान एवं दर्शन—दर्शन के क्षेत्र में भी इस युग में बहुत विकास हुअ। यहां पर दर्शन का विषय जीव, आत्मा एवं ईश्वर आदि नहीं था, अपितु यहां के दार्शनिक ने प्रकृति के रहस्यों का पता लगाने का प्रयास किया। **थेलीस** का मानना है कि जल नामक पदार्थ से ही इस सृष्टि की उत्पत्ति हुई है। उसका यह सिद्धांत पूर्णरूप से सत्य नहीं है। परन्तु इसका सुपरिणाम यह हुआ कि दार्शनिकों का सृष्टि की उत्पत्ति के सम्बन्ध में लिपिबद्ध धार्मिक कहानियों से विश्वास हट गया।

एनेक्जामेंडर का मत था कि मछली से मानव का विकास हुआ है।

पाइथागोरस (582 ई. पू. - 507 ई. पू.) के अनुसार, धार्मिक तथा नैतिक शुद्धिकरण से आत्मा को मुक्ति प्राप्त हो सकती है। उसने रेखागणित को जन्म दिया। इसके अतिरिक्त वह संगीतशास्त्र का भी प्रेमी एवं ज्ञाता था।

जेनोफनीज ने बहुदेववाद की आलोचना करते हुए एकेश्वरवाद के सिद्धांत का समर्थन किया।

इम्पेडोक्लीज (490 ई. पू. - 430 ई. पू.) के अनुसार, सृष्टि की संरचना चार तत्वों द्वारा हुई है—वायु, भूमि, अग्नि एवं जल। उसने यह भी सिद्ध किया कि संसार के जीवन संघर्ष में योग्यतम व्यक्तियों को ही विजय प्राप्त होती है।

डेमोक्रिटस (460 ई. पू. - 370 ई. पू.) नामक दार्शनिक ने अणु सिद्धांत का प्रवर्तन किया। इसके अनुसार, विश्व की उत्पत्ति अणुओं से हुई है, जो अजर और अमर हैं, गतिशील हैं तथा इनके विलय के कारण ही किसी वस्तु का उदय और विघटन होता है।

एनेक्सागोरस पेरिक्लीज के युग का सबसे प्रसिद्ध दार्शनिक था। वह पेरिक्लीज का गुरु भी था। वह ईश्वर के अस्तित्व में विश्वास नहीं करता था। उसने बताया कि विश्व की उत्पत्ति में किसी दैवी शक्ति का हाथ नहीं है, अपितु इसकी उत्पत्ति भौतिक तत्वों के कारण हुई है।

सोफिस्टों ने भी अपने दार्शनिक विचारों में तर्क एवं स्वतंत्र चिन्तन पर अधिक जोर दिया। इनमें से उच्च कोटि के विद्वान, विचारक एवं दार्शनिक हुए, जिन्होंने विश्व साहित्य को अमूल्य देन दी। पेरिक्लीज के समय में निम्न सोफिस्ट हुए, जिन्होंने अपने विचारों से इस युग को समृद्ध बनाया।

प्रोडिकस एक निराशावादी विचारक था। उसने बताया कि संसार में सुख की अपेक्षा दुःख की मात्रा कहीं अधिक है।

प्रोटोगोरस ने यूरोप में व्याकरणशास्त्र को जन्म दिया। उसका देवताओं के अस्तित्व में विश्वास नहीं था, जिसके कारण उसे एथेन्सवासियों के कोप का भाजन

बनना पड़ा। उसने एक पुस्तक में देवताओं के अस्तित्व में सन्देह प्रकट किया। इस पुस्तक के कारण उसे एथेन्स छोड़कर सिसली भागना पड़ा। इसी यात्रा के दौरान समुद्र में उसकी मृत्यु हो गई।

जौर्जियस एक प्रसिद्ध दार्शनिक एवं वक्ता था। इसकी रचनायें भावुकतापूर्ण होने के कारण सीधी हृदय को छूने वाली होती थीं। इन सोफिस्टों का पेरिक्लीज के युग के सांस्कृतिक वैभव की वृद्धि में बहुत बड़ा हाथ था। सुकरात नामक दार्शनिक ने इस युग के बौद्धिक आन्दोलन को चरम सीमा पर पहुंचा दिया था।

सुकरात (469 ई. पू. - 399 ई. पू.) यूनान का प्रसिद्ध दार्शनिक था। उसकी गिनती विश्व के महानतम दार्शनिकों में की जाती है। वह सत्य को जानने के लिए तर्क पर सर्वाधिक बल देता था। उसने कहा कि प्रत्येक मनुष्य को आत्मनिरीक्षण करना चाहिए और सभी के साथ अच्छा व्यवहार करना चाहिए। इस प्रकार सुकरात ने दर्शन के क्षेत्र में एक नई परम्परा का विकास किया। युवकों को भ्रष्ट बनाने का आरोप सुकरात पर लगा दिया गया तथा इस बहाने से उसे मौत के घाट उतार दिया गया। उस समय सुकरात ने कहा, "अपने ही ढंग से किसी बात को कहकर मृत्यु का आलिंगन अधिक श्रेष्ठ है, इसकी अपेक्षा कि मैं तुम्हारी कही बात को कहकर जीवित रहूँ।" एथेन्स के इतिहास में यह घटना सबसे कलंकित है।

प्लेटो (427 ई. पू. - 347 ई. पू.)—प्लेटो सुकरात का शिष्य था और उसके विचारों पर सुकरात का प्रभाव दृष्टिगत होता है। वह एक प्रसिद्ध दार्शनिक ही नहीं, वरन् एक अच्छा लेखक भी था। उसने 'रिपब्लिक' एवं 'लॉज' आदि ग्रन्थों की रचना की। इन ग्रन्थों में उसने एक आदर्श राज्य एवं एक आदर्श समाज का स्वरूप प्रस्तुत किया।

अरस्तु (384 ई. पू. - 322 ई. पू.)—अरस्तु का गुरु प्लेटो था तथा शिष्य सिकन्दर महान था वह भी महान दार्शनिक था एवं तर्कशास्त्र का प्रकाण्ड पण्डित था। उसने दर्शन के क्षेत्र में अपूर्व प्रतिभा का परिचय दिया। उसको तर्कशास्त्र में अच्छा ज्ञान था, जो आज भी आदर्श है। उसने **"पोलिटिक्स"** नामक पुस्तक लिखी, इसमें तत्कालीन नगर राज्यों की सरकारों की अच्छाइयों एवं बुराइयों पर प्रकाश डाला गया है। **लिविंगस्टन** ने लिखा है, "अरस्तु का क्षेत्र आधुनिक लेखकों की अपेक्षा अधिक विस्तृत है। उसे मानव बुद्धि की उस दुर्लभ तथा सर्वोत्तम श्रेणी में रखा जा सकता है, जहां मानववाद व तर्कशास्त्र दोनों मिलते हैं।"

दर्शन के क्षेत्र में पेरिक्लीज के शासनकाल के समय अद्वितीय विकास हुआ। **सेवाइन** ने इस सम्बन्ध में लिखा है, "सम्भवतः किसी भी युग या स्थान पर ऐसे

प्रबुद्ध मस्तिष्कों का समूह नहीं रहा, जैसा कि पेरिक्लीज के युग में एथेन्स में था।'' **बिल ड्यूरेन्ट** ने लिखा है, ''यूरोप के पुनर्जागरण के पूर्व किसी भी काल में दर्शन और तर्क का इतना विकास नहीं हुआ, जितना पेरिक्लीज के युग में एथेन्स में हुआ था।''

कला—इस युग में कला क्षेत्र के विकास पर अत्यधिक ध्यान दिया गया। पेरिक्लीज ने एथेन्स को एक बहुत ही सुन्दर नगर बना दिया। उसके समय में स्थापत्यकला, चित्रकला, मूर्तिकला एवं संगीत कला के क्षेत्र में आश्चर्यजनक विकास हुआ। पेरिक्लीज ने स्थापत्य कला के विकास में बहुत योगदान दिया। शासक बनने के बाद सर्वप्रथम उसने उन मन्दिरों का पुनर्निर्माण करवाया, जो ईरानी (फारस) आक्रमण के समय शत्रु द्वारा तोड़ दिये गये थे। उसने एथेन्स में लम्बी-चौड़ी सड़कों, सुन्दर मन्दिरों एवं भव्य भवनों का निर्माण करवाया। उसने एथेन्स की सुरक्षा के लिए उसके चारों ओर दीवार का निर्माण भी करवाया था। एथेन्स के मन्दिरों के निर्माण में यूनान के कलाकारों ने डोरिक, आयोनिक एवं कोरिथियन आदि तीनों शैलियों का सम्मिश्रण किया है। डोरिक शैली के मन्दिर में स्तम्भ कम भारी और सादे बने हुए हैं। आयोनिक शैली के मन्दिर के स्तम्भ कम भारी और सुन्दर बने हुए हैं। कोरिथियन शैली के मन्दिर के स्तम्भ बहुत लम्बे और अलंकृत हैं।

पाथेनान का मन्दिर—पेरिक्लीज के शासनकाल में अनेक सुन्दर मन्दिरों का निर्माण हुआ। उसके द्वारा बनवाए गये मन्दिरों में सबसे सुन्दर एवं प्रसिद्ध मन्दिर पाथेनान का था। यह एथेन्स की देवी का मन्दिर एक्रोपोलियस पहाड़ी पर प्रसिद्ध वास्तुकार इक्टिनस के द्वारा बनाया गया था। यह मन्दिर डोरियन शैली का उत्कृष्ट नमूना है। यह पूरा मन्दिर सफेद संगमरमर का बना हुआ है। **बी.वी. राव** ने लिखा है, ''पाथेनान का देवालय रंगीन संगमरमर में निर्मित सर्वाधिक सुन्दर था।'' इस मन्दिर में एथेना देवी की विशाल कांस्य मूर्ति स्थापित की गई है। मन्दिर चारों ओर मण्डपों से घिरा हुआ था। इस मन्दिर की लम्बाई 228 फीट, चौड़ाई 101 फीट एवं ऊँचाई 65 फीट थी। इस मन्दिर में 34-34 फुट के 46 स्तंभ लगे थे। इन स्तम्भों की चौड़ाई ऊपर कम होती जाती थी। यह मन्दिर 432 ई. पू. में बनकर तैयार हो गया था। यह देवालय पेरिक्लीज के समय की वास्तुकला का अनुपम नमूना है। **एलिस व जौन** ने लिखा है, ''पाथेनान का मन्दिर उस समय की स्थापत्य कला का शानदार नमूना है और विश्व की सबसे प्रसिद्ध इमारत है''। इसके अतिरिक्त फीडियस नामक कलाकार ने डायोनिसस नामक देवता के मन्दिर का निर्माण करवाया। इस युग में अनेक दुर्गों एवं सुन्दर भवनों का निर्माण भी हुआ। बाउल ने

लिखा है, ''उस समय यूनान में मिस्र के नमूने के देवालय अवश्य बनते थे, किन्तु वे मिस्र के देवालयों की भांति विशालकाय नहीं होते थे।''

इस समय डायोनिसस नामक एक थियेटर बनवाया गया। यह थियेटर एक्रोपोलिस की पहाड़ी पर बना हुआ था। यह उस काल की स्थापत्य कला का एक उत्कृष्ट नमूना है। इस थियेटर में लोगों के बैठने के लिए पत्थर की सीटें बनी हुई थीं। इसमें वर्ष में कई बार नाटक खेले जाते थे, जिन्हें देखने के लिये हजारों लोगों में उत्साह होता था।

पेरिक्लीज ने अपने कठिन प्रयत्नों से एथेन्स को सुन्दर नगर बना दिया, जिस पर यूनानी गर्व करते थे। एक प्राचीन लेखक ने एथेन्सों के बारे में कहा है–''यदि तुमने एथेन्स नहीं देखा, तो तुम मूर्ख हो। यदि देखकर उस पर मोहित नहीं हुए, तो गधे हो और यदि स्वेच्छा से वहां से चले आये तो निरे ऊँट हो।'' **प्लैट व जीन ड्रमण्ड** ने लिखा है, ''देशभक्त एथेन्सवासी पेरिक्लीज का समर्थन इसलिए करते थे, क्योंकि उसने एथेन्स को एक बहुत ही सुन्दर नगर बना दिया था।''

पेरिक्लीज के शासनकाल में मूर्तियों के निर्माण पर अधिक ध्यान दिया गया। इस युग में मूर्ति बनाने में पाषाण, संगमरमर, हाथी दांत, सोने एवं कांसे का प्रचुरता से प्रयोग किया गया था। इस काल में देवी देवताओं, खिलाड़ियों तथा पशु पक्षियों की मूर्तियाँ अधिक बनाई जाती थीं। इस युग की मूर्तिकला की मुख्य विशेषता यह थी कि मूर्तियों में शरीर के अंगों का सुन्दर चित्रण किया जाता था। इस युग में फीडियस, माइरन और पोलीक्लेटस प्रसिद्ध मूर्तिकार थे।

पेरिक्लीज शासनकाल में फीडियस ने आकर्षक नग्नमूर्ति बनाई। पाथेनान के मन्दिर में एथेना देवी की एक विशाल एवं अत्यंत सुन्दर मूर्ति का निर्माण भी फीडियस ने किया था। यह मूर्ति कांसे की बनी हुई थी, इसकी ऊँचाई 38 फीट थी। एथेना देवी की मूर्ति मन्दिर के बीच में मुस्कराती मुद्रा में तथा सुनहरे वस्त्रों में सजाकर रखी हुई थी। देवी के सिर पर शिरस्त्राण था। उस युग में यह मूर्तिकला का सर्वोत्तम उदाहरण था।

इसके अलावा फीडियस ने हाथी दांत से 60 फीट ऊंची मूर्ति बनाई जो ओलम्पिया के मन्दिर में 'जियस' के रूप में स्थित है। फीडियस की मूर्तियों में सौन्दर्य तथा कोमलता के भाव दृष्टिगोचर होते हैं। **मैकनेल बर्न्स** ने लिखा है–''शहर में फैली शोहरत के अनुसार यूनानी मूर्तिकला ने फीडियस के युग में सर्वोच्चता प्राप्त कर ली थी।'' माइरन इस युग का दूसरा शिल्पी था। वह खिलाड़ियों की मूर्तियां बनाने में प्रवीण था। उसने 'डिस्कस थ्रोअर' की अनेक मूर्तियां बनाईं। यह मूर्तिकला की

दृष्टि से अनुपम है। इस काल का तीसरा प्रसिद्ध शिल्पकार पोलीक्लेट्स ने मानवों की विभिन्न मूर्तियों का निर्माण किया।

पेरिक्लीज के युग में चित्रकला के क्षेत्र में भी अत्यधिक प्रगति हुई। टेम्पेरा शैली में चित्रकारों द्वारा अण्डे को सफेदी में मिलाकर चित्रकारी के चित्र में रंगों का प्रयोग इस तरह से किया जाता था कि वे सजीव लगते थे इस काल में प्रसिद्ध चित्रकारों में पोलिग्नोट्स, ज्यूक्सिज और परसियस आदि के नाम विशेषरूप से उल्लेखनीय हैं। पोलिग्नोट्स ने 'ट्राय का ध्वंस' और 'ओडेसियस' के सुन्दर चित्र बनाये। डेल्फी के मन्दिर में भी उसने सुन्दर चित्र बनाये थे। ज्यूक्सिज ने 'धावक' का बड़ा ही सजीव चित्र बनाया था। इस चित्र में उसने पसीने की बूंदों इस प्रकार दर्शाया है जैसे अभी नीचे गिरने वाली हैं। इसने पांच रमणियों के नग्न चित्र भी बनाये थे। इसके पीछे उसका उद्देश्य उनके सौष्ठव का अध्ययन करना था। इसके अतिरिक्त ज्यूक्सिज ने 'हेलन' का सुन्दर चित्र बनाया था, जो नारी सौन्दर्य का आदर्श नमूना है। यहां के चित्रों के सम्बन्ध में **रॉबिन्सन** ने तो यहां तक लिखा है, ''विश्व में इतनी कलात्मक चित्रकारी न देखी गई और न देखी जायेगी।''

पेरिक्लीज के युग में संगीतकला के माध्यम से नाटकों को अधिक ख्याति प्राप्ति हुयी जिसके कारण संगीतकला के क्षेत्र में बहुत अधिक उन्नति हुई। हर नाटक के आरम्भ तथा अन्त में गीतों की धुनें बजाई जाती थीं। इस समय वाद्य तथा शास्त्रीय संगीत का बहुत प्रसार हुआ।

निष्कर्ष–उपर्युक्त विवेचन से स्पष्ट है कि पेरिक्लीज ने एथेन्स में सुन्दर मन्दिरों एवं भव्य भवनों का निर्माण करवाया। उसने एथेन्स को विश्व का एक सुन्दरतम नगर बना दिया। पेरिक्लीज ने एथेन्स के साम्राज्य का विस्तार कर उसे कई नगर राज्यों का शासक बना दिया। इस प्रकार एथेन्स नगर राज्य से साम्राज्य में परिवर्तित हुआ। इस समय एथेन्स में कई महान व्यक्तियों का जन्म हुआ। पेरिक्लीज ने एथेन्स में सुदृढ़ लोकतन्त्र की स्थापना कर उसे राजनीति का भी केन्द्र बना दिया।

इस प्रकार हम देखते हैं कि पेरिक्लीज का युग विश्व इतिहास में बौद्धिक विकास एवं सांस्कृतिक वैभव के लिए प्रसिद्ध है। इस युग में कला, साहित्य, विज्ञान एवं दर्शन का विकास अपनी चरमसीमा पर जा पहुंचा तथा एथेन्स नगर यूनान की सांस्कृतिक गतिविधियों का केन्द्र बन गया जिसने पेरिक्लीज के 'स्वर्णयुग' की उपाधि को सिद्ध कर दिया।

बिल ड्यूरेन्ट ने लिखा है, "इतिहास में शायद ही कोई ऐसा युग हो, जिसमें इतनी अधिक मात्रा में सांस्कृतिक व आर्थिक उन्नति हुई हो।"

डॉ. आर.पी. त्रिपाठी का इस बारे में मानना है कि पेरिक्लीज युग यूनान का स्वर्णयुग था। उसके युग में एथेन्स ने कला कौशल, साहित्य ज्ञान विज्ञान में ऐसी अद्भुत उन्नति एवं चमत्कार दिखाया कि उसका नाम संसार के इतिहास में अमर तथा यूरोप के इतिहास में सर्वोपरि हो गया।" **डॉ. सुशील माधव पाठक** का मानना है कि "पेरिक्लीज युग में एथेन्स में समस्त यूनान से लोग ज्ञान प्राप्ति के लिए आते थे इस युग में कला साहित्य एवं दर्शन तथा गणतंत्र का सबसे अधिक विकास हुआ। भव्य भवनों तथा कलात्मक वस्तुओं से एथेन्स का सौन्दर्य सौ गुना बढ़ गया। एथेन्सवासी स्वतंत्र एवं उन्मुक्त जीवन व्यतीत करते थे। इन्हीं कारणों से इस युग को स्वर्णयुग की संज्ञा दी गई है।"

मूल्यांकन

एथेन्स के महान शासक पेरिक्लीज का 429 ईसा पूर्व देहांत हो गया। उसके समय में जनता अधिक खुशहाल थी। **रेविल** के अनुसार, "पेरिक्लीज के शासनकाल में प्रत्येक क्षेत्र में प्रगति हुई और वह प्रगति अपना अनुपम प्रभाव छोड़ गई।" प्रसिद्ध राजनीतिज्ञ शूमाँ ने लिखा है, "पेरिक्लीज के मरते ही एथेन्स का गौरव दीप टिमटिमाने लगा और कालान्तर में बुझ गया।" पेरिक्लीज ने अपने शासनकाल के समय यूनान में सर्वोच्च सभ्यता को जन्म दिया। इस समय एथेन्स में साहित्य, विज्ञान, दर्शन एवं कला के क्षेत्र में आश्चर्यजनक उन्नति हुई और वह यूनानी सभ्यता तथा संस्कृति का प्रमुख केन्द्र बन गया।

पेरिक्लीज की जब मृत्यु हो गई उसके बाद यूनान का पतन होने लगा। क्योंकि उसने डेलौस संघ का धन एथेन्स के विकास में लगा दिया था जिसके कारण संघ के सदस्य पहले से ही नाराज थे। इसके अतिरिक्त पेरिक्लीज की साम्राज्यवादी नीति से स्पार्टा के लोग आशंकित हो गए, जिसके कारण एथेन्स और स्पार्टा में युद्ध हुआ और यूनान पराजित हो गया।

पेलोपोनेशियन युद्ध

एथेन्स और स्पार्टा दोनों ने मिलकर अपने शत्रु फारस को युद्ध में पराजित कर दिया लेकिन कुछ समय बाद दोनों में आपसी सामंजस्य न होने के कारण स्वयं लड़ने लगे। स्पार्टा एक सैनिक राज्य था, जहां प्रत्येक नागरिक को अनिवार्य रूप से सैनिक

शिक्षा दी जाती थी। यहां के लोग खेलकूद के प्रेमी थे। अतः प्रतिवर्ष यहां ओलम्पिक खेलों की प्रतियोगिता आयोजित की जाती थी। आज की ओलम्पिक प्रतियोगिता स्पार्टा की मुख्य देन है। दूसरा राज्य एथेन्स था, जिसने पेरिक्लीज के काल में सभी क्षेत्रों में आश्चर्यजनक उन्नति की। पेरिक्लीज ने डेलौस संघ के धन को एथेन्स के निर्माण कार्यों पर लगा दिया, जिससे स्पार्टा नाराज हो गया। इसके अतिरिक्त पेरिक्लीज की साम्राज्यवादी नीति से भी स्पार्टा के लोग भयभीत हो गए अतः आगे चलकर एथेन्स और स्पार्टा दोनों के बीच युद्ध प्रारम्भ हो गया। यही युद्ध इतिहास में पेलोपोनेशियन युद्ध के नाम से जाना जाता है।

पेलोपोनेशियन युद्ध के कारण—फारस यूनान संघर्ष के दौरान यूनान में दो गुटों का निर्माण हो गया। प्रथम, डेलियन संघ एवं द्वितीय, पेलोपोनेशियन संघ। डेलियन संघ का निर्माण एथेन्स ने किया था। इस संघ के सदस्य आयोनियन जाति के थे। इसका नेतृत्व एथेन्स के हाथ में था। एथेन्स ने धीरे धीरे अपने प्रभाव में वृद्धि करके इस संघ के सदस्य राज्यों पर अधिकार कर वहां अपना साम्राज्य स्थापित कर लिया। इससे स्पार्टा नाराज हो गया। दूसरा संघ पेलोपोनिशियन था, जिसका निर्माण स्पार्टा ने किया था। इस संघ के सदस्य डोरियन जाति के स्वतन्त्र राज्य थे। यह संघ दक्षिण यूनान के राज्यों की आक्रमणकारियों से रक्षा करने हेतु बनाया गया था। इसका नेतृत्व स्पार्टा के हाथ में था। डेलियन संघ के विरोध में ही स्पार्टा ने पेलोपोनेशियम संघ का निर्माण किया था। इस कारण एथेन्स व स्पार्टा दोनों के आपसी सम्बंध बिगड़ गये।

इन दोनों नगर राज्यों में अलग-अलग व्यवस्था विद्यमान थी। स्पार्टा में कुलीन राजतंत्र था, जबकि एथेन्स में प्रजातंत्र। एथेन्स ने व्यापार के क्षेत्र में अत्यधिक उन्नति कर ली थी। स्पार्टा भी अपने व्यापार का विकास करना चाहता था। इससे दोनों में टकराव की स्थिति उत्पन्न हो गयी।

एथेन्स में ज्ञान, दर्शन, साहित्य एवं कला पर अत्यधिक ध्यान दिया जाता था जबकि स्पार्टा में सादगी और अनुशासन पर अधिक बल दिया जाता था। इस प्रकार यह स्पष्ट है कि दोनों नगर राज्य एक दूसरे के विपरीत अवस्था में थे। अतः उनमें युद्ध अनिवार्य था। डेलियन संघ के सदस्यों ने एथेन्स की अधीनता से मुक्त होने के लिए स्पार्टा से गुप्त सहायता प्राप्त करने का प्रयास किया। एथेन्स और स्पार्टा दोनों ही महत्त्वाकांक्षी राज्य थे। पेरिक्लीज युग में एथेन्स यूनानी सभ्यता और संस्कृति का प्रमुख केन्द्र बन गया जिससे स्पार्टा उसका विरोधी बन गया। एथेन्स ने डेलियन संघ के कोष पर अपना अधिकार जमा लिया और उस धन को वह एथेन्स के विकास

पर खर्च करने लगा, तो इस संघ के सदस्य राज्य एथेन्स से बहुत नाराज हुए स्पार्टा भी एथेन्स की सुन्दरता से ईर्ष्या करने लगा। इस प्रकार स्पार्टा और एथेन्स एक दूसरे के दुश्मन हो गए जिसका प्रमुख कारण संघ था।

पेरिक्लीज साम्राज्यवादी नीति का समर्थक था। उसने एक विशाल साम्राज्य का निर्माण किया, जिससे एथेन्स नगर राज्यों से शक्तिशाली साम्राज्य के रूप में परिवर्तित हो गया। इससे स्पार्टा को भय उत्पन्न हो गया और यही आगे चलकर दोनों के बीच संघर्ष का कारण बन गया। एथेन्स ने स्पार्टा के प्रभाव क्षेत्र कोरिन्थ के कोर्सिका नामक प्रदेशों को अपना उपनिवेश बना लिया। स्पार्टा कोरिन्स को मदद देकर अवसर का भरपूर लाभ लेना चाहता था। एथेन्स और स्पार्टा के बीच (459 ई. से 446 ई. पू.) अनिर्णीत युद्ध भी आगे चलकर संघर्ष का कारण बना। पेरिक्लीज ने 433-432 ई. पू. में डेलियन संघ के सदस्यों पर मेगारा से व्यापार करने पर प्रतिबन्ध लगा दिया जिसके कारण दोनों के बीच युद्ध प्रारम्भ हो गया। एथेन्स के मित्र देश प्लेरिया पर थीबिया ने हमला कर दिया इस युद्ध में स्पार्टा ने थीबिया की मदद की जो युद्ध का प्रमुख कारण बनी।

युद्ध की घटनाएँ—एथेन्स जलशक्ति और स्पार्टा थल शक्ति था 431 ईसा पूर्व से 404 ईसा पूर्व तक दोनों एक दूसरे से लड़ते रहे। इस समय प्रकृति ने स्पार्टा का साथ दिया। युद्ध के आरम्भ होते ही एथेन्स में 'प्लेग' नामक संक्रमण रोग फैल गया फलस्वरूप लगभग 60-70% आबादी इसका शिकार हो गयी। यहाँ तक कि खुद पेरिक्लीज भी इसके प्रकोप में आ गया जिससे उसकी शक्ति क्षीण हो गयी। इसी समय स्पार्टा की सेना ने प्लेरिया पर अधिकार कर लिया। 425 ई. पू. में एथेन्स का मेसीडोनिया में पाइलोस पर अधिकार हो गया। इसके पश्चात् यूनान का प्रसिद्ध इतिहासकार थ्यूसीडाइडीज स्पार्टा की सेना के हाथों पराजित हुआ। तत्पश्चात् स्पार्टा की सेना ने एम्फीपोलिस नगर पर अधिकार कर लिया। अभी तक दोनों में से किसी को भी निर्णायक विजय प्राप्त नहीं हुई थी। अन्तः में 421 ई. पू. में दोनों (एथेन्स व स्पाटा) ने एक शांति सन्धि पर हस्ताक्षर कर दिए। यह सन्धि निकीयस नामक स्थान पर पचास वर्ष के लिए हुई थी। इस सन्धि के अनुसार दोनों ने यथास्थिति को स्वीकार कर लिया।

इस सन्धि के पांच वर्ष पश्चात् ही एथेन्स और स्पार्टा के बीच पुनः युद्ध शुरू हो गया। 417 ई. पू. में एथेन्स ने मेलोस पर बलपूर्वक अधिकार कर उसे अपना उपनिवेश बना लिया और मेलोस को डेलियन संघ का सदस्य भी बना दिया। इसी समय सेगेस्टा और सीरेक्यूज के बीच भी युद्ध आरम्भ हो गया। सेगेस्टा की प्रार्थना

पर एथेन्स ने अपने चार सेनापति उसकी सहायता के लिए भेजे, परन्तु सफलता नहीं मिल सकी। इससे एथेन्स की प्रतिष्ठा को आघात पहुंचा। अब एथेन्स के अधीन उपनिवेशों में विद्रोह होने लगे। फारस के राजा ने स्पार्टा को सहायता देना स्वीकार कर लिया जिसका परिणाम यह हुआ कि 404 ई. पू. में हलेस्पौण्टेक के पास एगोसपोटामी नामक स्थान पर स्पार्टा और एथेन्स के बीच भीषण युद्ध छिड़ गया। इस युद्ध में स्पार्टा के सेनापति ने एथेन्स को आत्मसमर्पण करने के लिये मजबूर कर दिया।

स्पार्टा ने युद्ध में विजय प्राप्त करने के बाद एथेन्स पर अधिकार कर लिया, एथेन्स पर 404 ई. पू. से 307 ई. पू. तक स्पार्टा का अधिकार बना रहा। इसके बाद स्पार्टा के शासक ने भी साम्राज्यवादी नीति पर चलते हुए आसपास के प्रदेशों पर बलपूर्व अधिकार करना शुरू कर दिया। परिणामस्वरूप एथेन्स ने थीबिया से सहायता प्राप्त की और स्पार्टा को परास्त कर दिया।

युद्ध के परिणाम—युद्ध में एथेन्स की पराजय होने से उसकी प्रतिष्ठा को आघात पहुंचा। दोनों नगर राज्यों के आपसी संघर्ष के कारण यूनान निर्बल हो गया और अन्त में तीसरी शक्ति सिकन्दर का यूनान पर अधिकार हो गया। युद्ध में स्पार्टा की विजय होने से अन्तर्राष्ट्रीय स्तर पर उसकी प्रतिष्ठा में वृद्धि हुई। स्पार्टा यूनान का सबसे शक्तिशाली राष्ट्र हो गया। इस युद्ध में स्पार्टा की विजय होने से उसने एथेन्स पर अधिकार कर लिया और उसकी सुरक्षा दीवारों को खत्म कर दिया, जहाज पर कब्जा कर लिया जिससे एथेन्स को मजबूर होकर स्पार्टा का अधीनता स्वीकार करनी पड़ी। स्पार्टा ने तीस सदस्यों की एक परिषद् बनाई, जिसका कार्य एथेन्स की शासन व्यवस्था का संचालन करना था। यह परिषद् एथेन्सवासियों पर अत्याचार करती थी।

एथेन्स की पराजय के बाद भी स्पार्टा ने लगातार युद्ध किया। फारस में गृहयुद्ध चल रहा था। अतः वहां के शासक ने स्पार्टा से सहायता मांगी। इस पर स्पार्टा की ओर से दस हजार सैनिक जेनोफेन के नेतृत्व में भेजे गए, परन्तु अचानक ही साइरस की मृत्यु हो गई। परिणामस्वरूप स्पार्टा की सेना एशिया माइनर में फंस गई। फारस ने स्पार्टा की मदद से उस पर अपना अधिकार जमा लिया।

स्पार्टा और फारस के युद्ध का फायदा उठाकर एथेन्स ने थीब्स की सहायता से 371 ई. पू. में स्पार्टा को युद्ध में पराजित कर दिया। इसके बाद एक सम्मेलन बुलाया गया, ताकि स्पार्टा और थीब्स के बीच सन्धि हो सके। सम्मेलन में थीब्स ने भाग नहीं लिया। इस कारण स्पार्टा ने फिर युद्ध प्रारम्भ कर दिया। इसी बीच एथेन्स

और स्पार्टा ने आपस में सन्धि कर ली और साथ मिलकर थीब्स पर हमला कर दिया परन्तु पराजित हो गया। इसका लाभ मकदूनिया ने उठाया।

मकदूनिया राज्य यूनान के उत्तरपूर्व में अवस्थित तथा 359 ईसा पूर्व फिलिप ने यहां का शासन सम्भाला। 354 ई. पू. में डेलौस संघ का पतन हो चुका था। यूनान के एथेन्स और स्पार्टा के बीच गृहयुद्ध प्रारम्भ हुआ जिसका पूरा लाभ, मकदूनिया के शासक फिलिप ने इन पर अपना साम्राज्य स्थापित कर उठाया। इसके बाद वह 346 ई. पू. में एम्पीकार्ट ओनिक संघ का अध्यक्ष बन गया। जब एथेन्स और थीब्स की सेना ने संयुक्त रूप से फिलिप के विरुद्ध युद्ध घोषित किया, तो फिलिप ने केरोनिया के मैदान में इन दोनों की संयुक्त सेना को बुरी तरह परास्त किया। इसके बाद 338 ईसा पूर्व यूनान पर फिलिप ने अपना विजयी पताका फहरा दिया परन्तु 336 ईसा पूर्व उसके पुत्र सिकन्दर ने हत्या करके खुद शासक बन गया।

विश्व विजेता सिकन्दर मेसीडोनिया के राजा फिलिप का पुत्र था। सिकन्दर का समय विश्व इतिहास में 'हेलोनिस्टिक युग' के नाम से प्रसिद्ध है। सिकन्दर ने 336 ई. पू. में अपने पिता फिलिप का वध कर दिया और मकदूनिया (मेसोडोनिया) का शासक बना। वह अपने पिता से भी अधिक साम्राज्यवादी था। उसने यूनान में हुए विद्रोहों को कुचल दिया और स्पार्टा राज्य को अपने साम्राज्य में मिला लिया। इस प्रकार सिकन्दर का समस्त यूनान पर अधिकार हो गया।

यूनान के पश्चात् सिकंदर ने फारस की तरफ रुख किया और उस पर विजय प्राप्त करने के लिए 30 हजार पैदल और 50 हजार घुड़सवारों के साथ प्रस्थान किया। उसने फारस के शासक दारा तृतीय को ईसस के मैदान में बुरी तरह परास्त किया और फारस पर अधिकार कर लिया। सिकन्दर ने 331 ई. पू. में मिस्र पर विजय प्राप्त की और वहां अपने नाम पर सिकन्दरिया नामक नगर बसाया। तत्पश्चात् उसने अफगानिस्तान और ऑक्सन नदी के प्रदेशों पर विजय प्राप्त की। इसी समय उसे तक्षशिला के शासक ने भारत आने का निमन्त्रण भेजा जिसको उसने स्वीकार कर लिया।

सिकन्दर तक्षशिला के शासक के निमन्त्रण पर भारत आया। यहां झेलम और चिनाव के बीच के प्रदेशों का शासक पुरु था। वह एक वीर तथा शक्तिशाली शासक था। सिकन्दर और पुरु के बीच 326 ई. पू. में युद्ध हुआ, जिसमें पुरु परास्त हुआ तथा सिकन्दर को शानदार विजय प्राप्त हुई। युद्ध में विजय प्राप्त करने के पश्चात् सिकन्दर पुरु की वीरता और निर्भीकता से बहुत प्रभावित हुआ और उसने पुरु को उसका राज्य वापस लौटा दिया। सिकन्दर व्यास नदी से आगे बढ़ना चाहता था,

परन्तु जब उसे पता चला कि महापद्मनन्द एक विशाल सेना का स्वामी है तो उसने भयभीत होकर वापस यूनान की ओर प्रस्थान किया। वापस लौटते समय सूसा (बेबीलोन के पास) के स्थान पर 323 ई. पू. में उसकी मृत्यु हो गई। इस समय उसकी आयु मात्र 32 वर्ष थी। उसकी मृत्यु के पश्चात् उसके राज्य का पतन होना प्रारम्भ हो गया परन्तु उसके जीते हुये प्रदेशों में यूनानी सभ्यता एवं पूर्वी सभ्यताओं का मिला-जुला विकास हुआ।

कोई उत्तराधिकारी न होने के कारण सिंकदर की मृत्यु के पश्चात् उत्तराधिकार के लिए गृह युद्ध प्रारम्भ हो गया। इस समय टोलमी ने यूनान पर अधिकार कर लिया। आश्चर्य की बात यह है कि निरन्तर आक्रमणों के बावजूद यूनान की सभ्यता लगातार प्रगति पर बनी रही।

हेलेनिस्टिक युग

हेलेनिस्टिक वंश की स्थापना फिलिप ने की। इसने मकदूनिया की गद्दी पर बैठने के पश्चात् सम्पूर्ण यूनान पर कब्जा कर लिया। इस वंश के शासकों का शासन 400 ई. पू. 200 ई. तक यूनान पर रहा। इस समय एशिया माइनर, सीरिया, मिस्र तथा बेबीलोन में यूनानी सभ्यता एवं संस्कृति का प्रसार हुआ। मकदूनिया के शासक ने फारस को हराकर उस पर अपना अधिकार स्थापित कर लिया। उसके बाद 336 ई. पू. में अपने पिता का वध कर सिकन्दर मेसीडोनिया का शासक बना। सिकन्दर ने शक्तिशाली सैनिक की मदद से मिस्र, फारस, सीरिया और भारत के आम्भी, पोरस और कठों के प्रदेशों पर अधिकार कर लिया। सिकन्दर जब भारत से यूनान लौट रहा था, तब सूसा नगर में 232 ई. पू. में उसकी मृत्यु हो गई। उसने सिर्फ 13 वर्षों की शासन अवधि में सबसे बड़े सम्राज्य की स्थापना कर ली परन्तु उसकी मौत के बाद यूनान का पतन होने लगा।

हेलेनिस्टिक सभ्यता सिकन्दर के समय से लेकर रोमन विजयों तक विकसित होती रही। इस युग में यूनानी सभ्यता का पूर्वी देशों में प्रचार हुआ। इस प्रकार एशियाई संस्कृतियों के सम्पर्क से यूनानी संस्कृति में भी परिवर्तन हुए। पूर्वी पश्चिमी सभ्यता की मिली-जुली संस्कृति को इतिहास में 'हेलेनिस्टिक संस्कृति' की संज्ञा दी गई जो 'हेलेनिस्टिक युग' के नाम से प्रसिद्ध हुई। इस युग में यूनानी सभ्यता अपने विकास की चरमसीमा पर जा पहुंची थी। **प्रो. टर्नर** का मानना है, "हेलेनिस्टिक युग में पूर्व और पश्चिम एक दूसरे के पास आ गये और किसी ने एक दूसरे पर सांस्कृतिक राज्य की स्थापना नहीं की।" **प्रो. अलबर्ट** के मतानुसार, "पाश्चात्य सभ्यता के

इतिहास में यह सम्पूर्ण युग प्रमुख महत्त्व का है, क्योंकि पेरिक्लीयन संस्कृति ने नहीं, वरन् हेलेनिस्टिक संस्कृति ने रोमन सभ्यता के लिए पृष्ठभूमि प्रस्तुत की और ईसाई धर्म के विकास के लिए भूमि तथा वातावरण प्रदान किया।''

हेलेनिस्टिक युग में यूनान का साम्राज्य काफी समृद्ध था इसलिए व्यापार के क्षेत्र में बहुत विकास हुआ। अलेक्जेण्ड्रिया इस समय की प्रसिद्ध बन्दरगाह थी, जिस पर यूनान का अधिकार था। सिकन्दर ने यूनान में कई बैंकों की स्थापना की और सिक्के प्रचलित किये। इससे व्यापार में सुविधा हो गई। बैंकों द्वारा ऋण लेकर व्यापारी एवं कृषकों ने भरपूर लाभ उठाया। इस युग में नाटक एवं कविता के क्षेत्र में बहुत अधिक विकास हुआ। मिनांडर इस युग का प्रसिद्ध सुखान्त नाटककार था। इस काल के प्रसिद्ध कवि थियोक्रेटिस ने अपनी कविताओं में प्रकृति के दृश्यों का सुन्दर चित्रण किया। इस युग का दूसरा प्रसिद्ध कवि पोलीबियस था। उसने अपनी कविताओं में रोम की कार्थेज व पूर्वी देशों पर विजय का बहुत सुन्दर वर्णन किया है। इस युग में स्थापत्य कला के क्षेत्र में बहुत उन्नति हुई। इस काल में विशेष रूप से महलों एवं पुस्तकालयों तथा मूर्तियों को देखकर स्थापत्य कला का ज्ञान होता है। इस समय के प्रसिद्ध मूर्तिकार लिसपस ने अनेक मूर्तियों का निर्माण किया। इस काल की मूर्तियों में वेदना व सुख के भावों के साथ सौन्दर्यता आदि का प्रदर्शन भी किया जाता था। इस समय यूनानी लोग एकेश्वरवाद में विश्वास करते थे। पूर्वी देशों के धार्मिक विचारों का यूनान पर काफी प्रभाव पड़ा। अब यूनानी लोग रहस्यवादी विचारधारा, पाप और मोक्ष आदि बातों पर भी विश्वास करने लगे। इस युग में यूनान का साम्राज्य बहुत विस्तृत था। सिकन्दर ने एक विशाल साम्राज्य की स्थापना की, जिसकी सीमा एजियन सागर से सिन्धु नदी तक विस्तृत थी। सिकन्दर की मृत्यु के पश्चात् यूनान साम्राज्य का विघटन तीन रूपों में हो गया जिसमें रोम अधिक प्रभावशाली हो गया। इस युग में दर्शन के क्षेत्र में भी अत्यधिक विकास हुआ। भारतीय दर्शन का प्रभाव यूनानी दर्शन में देखने को मिलता है। अब यूनानियों ने आत्मा के आनन्द पर विचार करना शुरू कर दिया। इस युग के प्रसिद्ध दार्शनिकों में स्टोइक, इफिक्यूरस तथा सिनिक्स आदि प्रमुख थे। इन्होंने दर्शन के क्षेत्र में महत्त्वपूर्ण रचनाएं रचीं। स्टोइक के अनुसार, मनुष्य को बुराई पर विजय प्राप्त करनी चाहिए और दूसरों के साथ भाइचारे का व्यवहार करना चाहिए। इफिक्यूरस के अनुसार, मनुष्य को सच्चा सुख प्राप्त करने के लिए इन्द्रियों पर नियन्त्रण स्थापित करना चाहिए। सच्चे सुख की प्राप्ति के बाद मनुष्य के हृदय में ग्लानि उत्पन्न नहीं होती। सुख

ही जीवन का आदि व अन्त है। सिनिक्स नामक दार्शनिक ने उस युग के शासकों तथा अमीर लोगों का मजाक उड़ाया। इस युग में विज्ञान का समुचित विकास हुआ। इस काल के प्रसिद्ध गणितज्ञों में यूक्लिड, एपोलोनियस, हिपाकारस तथा हेरन आदि प्रमुख थे। यूक्लिड ने ज्यामिति शास्त्र पर खोज की। हिपाकरस ने ट्रिगनोमेट्र के नवीन सिद्धांत प्रतिपादित किए। हेरन ने बीजगणित के साधारण नियमों की खोज की जिससे गणित एक रोचक विषय बन गया। इस समय प्रसिद्ध भौतिकशास्त्री आर्कमीडिया ने घनत्व के सिद्धांत का आविष्कार किया।

हेलिनिस्निक युग में प्रसिद्ध चिकित्सक हेराफिलस ने शरीर विज्ञान में खोजकर चिकित्सा क्षेत्र के विकास में प्रमुख योगदान दिया। हेरोक्लिटीज ने सर्वप्रथम यह बताया कि पृथ्वी अपनी धुरी पर घूमती है तथा अन्य ग्रह इसके चारों ओर चक्कर लगाते हैं। ऐरिस्टार्कस ने बताया कि पृथ्वी के साथ अन्य ग्रह भी सूर्य के चारों ओर चक्कर लगाते हैं। इस युग में वनस्पति विज्ञान का असाधारण विकास हुआ। अरस्तु के शिष्य थियोफ्रेस्टस ने पौधों का इतिहास लिखा। आर्कमिडिकल ने वाष्प चक्की का आविष्कार किया। टेसीवियस ने जल घड़ी तथा अग्नि इंजन का आविष्कार किया। इस काल में भूगोल तथा विद्या की अद्वितीय प्रगति हुई। डाकेरेक्स ने विश्व का प्रथम मानचित्र बनाया जिसमें संसार को दर्शाया। पाइथियस ने सर्वप्रथम यह बताया कि चन्द्रमा के कारण ही समुद्र में ज्वार भाटा आता है।

शासन व्यवस्था—यूनान में उस समय प्रत्येक नगर में स्वतंत्र नागरिक, विदेशी नागरिक एवं गुलाम या दास थे यहां नगर राज्यों की संख्या 150 थी। स्वतन्त्र नागरिकों को मौलिक अधिकार प्राप्त थे और वे शासन में भाग ले सकते थे। उस समय प्रत्येक नगर राज्य में अलग-अलग शासन व्यवस्था थी। एथेन्स में प्रत्यक्ष प्रजातन्त्रामक शासन व्यवस्था थी, जबकि स्पार्टा में राजतन्त्रात्मक, व्यवस्था विद्यमान थी।

एथेन्स—एथेन्स में प्रजातंत्र होते हुए भी दासों, विदेशी नागरिकों और महिलाओं को राजनीति में भाग लेने का अधिकार नहीं था। एथेन्स का प्रत्येक नागरिक वहां के राजनीतिक कार्यों में भाग लेता था। वहां वर्ग के आधार पर तीन दलों का निर्माण किया गया था। प्रथम दल श्रमिकों एवं कारीगरों का था, जिसे 'तट' कहते थे। द्वितीय दल कुलीन वर्ग के व्यक्तियों का था, जिसे 'मैदान' कहते थे। तृतीय दल किसानों का था, जिसे 'पहाड़' कहते थे। वहां के नागरिकों को अपनी अभिव्यक्ति प्रकट करने की पूर्ण आजादी थी। पेरिक्लीज ने आर्कन पद पर कुलीन

वर्ग के व्यक्ति की नियुक्ति संबंधी नियम में बदलाव कर दिया। इसके बाद जनसाधारण भी आर्कन पद पर नियुक्त हो सकता था। एथेन्स में प्रत्यक्ष प्रजातन्त्र था। वहां के समस्त नागरिक शासन के कार्यों में भाग लेते थे।

एथेन्स में 'एक्सलेशिया' सदस्यों का चुनाव करते थे। यहां का प्रत्येक नागरिक जनसभा का सदस्य बन सकता था। इसकी बैठक सप्ताह में एक बार होती थी। बैठक में समस्याओं पर बहुमत के आधार पर निर्णय लिये जाते थे। एसेम्बली द्वारा पारित कानूनों पर काउंसिल स्वीकृति देने के लिए विवश थी। एथेन्स के समस्त नागरिक सभा में भाग लेते थे और शासन सम्बन्धी मामलों पर अपना मत देते थे। जनसभा के अलावा दूसरी संस्था बौल थी। इसके सदस्यों की संख्या 500 थी जिसमें दो तरह के विभागों का गठन था, उसमें एक ज्यूरी शासन कार्य को देखता था तथा दूसरा विभाग सेना तथा विदेशी विभाग का संचालन करता था। एसेम्बली एक वर्ष के लिए जनरलों का चुनाव करती थी। **एच. जी. वेल्स** ने लिखा है, "वहां की समस्याओं का अन्तिम निर्णय न तो राजा करता था और न ही पुरोहित। उसका निर्णय मुख्य पुरुषों की परिषद् अथवा जनसभाएं करती थीं।"

स्पार्टा—स्पार्टा में निरंकुश राजतन्त्रात्मक शासन व्यवस्था विद्यमान थी। लाइकर्गस नामक व्यक्ति स्पार्टा का संविधान निर्माता था। इन नगर में दो राजा शासन करते थे जिनको सीनेट के संरक्षण में कार्य का संचालन करना पड़ता था। इसके 28 सदस्य होते थे। सीनेट के सदस्य वही व्यक्ति बन सकते थे, जिनकी आयु 60 वर्ष से अधिक होती थी। सीनेट की अनुमति के बिना दोनों ही शासक किसी भी प्रकार का युद्ध या सन्धि नहीं कर सकते थे। एक अन्य संस्था एफोरेट थी। इसके सदस्यों की संख्या पांच थी। यह संस्था शासकों को शासन संचालन में सहायता देती थी इसके अतिरिक्त 800 सदस्यों की एक संस्था अपोलो थी जिसका सदस्य 30 वर्ष से अधिक की आयु वाला व्यक्ति ही बन सकता था।

सामाजिक जीवन—यूनान का समाज चार वर्गों में विभक्त था, जिसमें नागरिकों को विशेष अधिकार प्राप्त थे। राज्य की दृष्टि में समस्त नागरिक, एक समान थे। फिर भी, समाज में कुलीन वर्ग के व्यक्तियों का प्रभाव अधिक था। दूसरा वर्ग किसानों का था जिसे राजनीतिक अधिकार प्राप्त थे, परन्तु उनका प्रशासन पर कोई विशेष प्रभाव नहीं था। तीसरा वर्ग दासों का था जिनको राजनीतिक तथा मौलिक अधिकार प्राप्त नहीं थे। समृद्ध घरों में प्रत्येक सदस्य के लिए एक दास होता था। **विल ड्यूरेण्ट** ने लिखा है, "एक तगड़े गुलाम जवान की कीमत एक सफेद रीछ की खाल के बराबर थी।"

यूनान में गरीब रोटी सब्जी तथा अमीर मांस-मछली व शराब का सेवन करते थे। शहद को सभी बड़े चाव से खाते थे। वे विभिन्न प्रकार के कपड़ों का प्रयोग नहीं जानते थे और चौकोर कपड़े को शरीर के चारों तरफ लपेट लेते थे। अमीर पुरुष तथा स्त्रियां रेशमी वस्त्र पहनते थे। स्त्रियां अपने चेहरे पर जुल्फों की लटें निकालती थीं और बालों का जूड़ा बनाती थीं।

यूनान का मनोरंजन का प्रमुख साधन कुश्ती, नाटक, मलयुद्ध, बाक्सिंग, नृत्य, संगीत था। नाटककार को राज्य और अमीर लोग पुरस्कार देते थे। यूनान में धार्मिक उत्सवों पर कई प्रकार की प्रतियोगिताएं आयोजित की जाती थीं। स्पार्टा में प्रति चौथे वर्ष ओलम्पिक प्रतियोगिता आयोजित की जाती थी। ओलम्पिक खेल की शुरुआत सबसे पहले स्पार्टा ने 1776 ई. में की। इसके अतिरिक्त एथेन्स में यूनान का सबसे बड़ा आकर्षक और कलात्मक थियेटर (रंगमंच) बनाया गया, जो आज भी विश्व में डायोनिसस के नाम से विख्यात है। इस थियेटर की गिनती विश्व के सर्वोत्तम भवनों के रूप में की जाती है।

यूनानी लोग दासों के साथ बहुत अत्याचार करते थे। अन्य नगर राज्यों की तुलना में एथेन्स में दासों के साथ अच्छा व्यवहार किया जाता था। **मैकनेल बर्न्स** का मत है, "कुल मिलाकर उनके साथ अच्छा व्यवहार किया जाता था और वफादारी एवं पूर्ण सेवा पर उन्हें पुरस्कारस्वरूप स्वतन्त्र कर दिया जाता था। वे वेतन पर काम करते थे और सम्पत्ति रख सकते थे। उनमें से कुछ महत्त्वपूर्ण जन अधिकारी के पद पर भी काम करते थे, जैसे बैंक के मैनेजर।" दासता से मुक्ति तभी मिल सकती थी जब वो धन देते या कुश्ती में पुरस्कार जीतते। चौथा वर्ग विदेशियों का था, जिनकी संख्या बहुत कम थी। इस वर्ग के लोगों को राजनीतिक अधिकार प्रदान नहीं किये गये थे।

यूनानी समाज में पितृसत्तात्मक परिवारों का उल्लेख मिलता है, जिससे स्पष्ट होता है कि महिलाओं की स्थिति अच्छी नहीं थी। केवल उनको औपचारिकता के रूप में स्वतन्त्रता प्राप्त थी। उनको केवल गृहकार्य और पुरुष के अधीन रहना पड़ता था। **वीच** ने लिखा है, "नारी के लिए विवाह के सिवाय कोई विकल्प नहीं था। उसे कानूनी स्वतन्त्रता कभी नहीं दी गयी। शादी का दिन उसके जीवन का महानतम दिवस था। अपने नये घर में वह गुलामों की देखरेख करती थी। कातने और बुनने में अपना समय लगाती और अपने वस्त्र व जेवरों का प्रयोग अपने स्वामी को मोहित करने में करती थी।"

पांचवीं शताब्दी में यूनान में स्त्रियों के असन्तोष में वृद्धि होने लगी थी और उन्होंने अपने नीरस जीवन में परिवर्तन की मांग की। इस बात की पुष्टि समकालीन साहित्य से भी होती है। वैसे यूनानी महिला अपरिचित ही मर जाती थी। **पेरिक्लीज** ने कहा था, "नारी की ख्याति इसी में है कि अच्छे या बुरे के लिए उसका नाम आदमी के होठों पर कम से कम आए।"

इस समय आदमी एक ही विवाह करता था। स्वयं पेरिक्लीज भी अपनी प्रेमिका असुपासिया से सामाजिक बन्धनों के कारण विवाह नहीं कर सका था। स्त्रियों के लिए उसका पति ही सर्वसर्वा होता था और वे एक वीर बालक को जन्म देना अपना सौभाग्य मानती थीं माता-पिता ही लड़के-लड़की का विवाह निश्चित करते थे। विवाह से पहले लड़का-लड़की से निसंकोच मिल सकता था। उनके यहाँ विशेष प्रकार की रीति थी जिसके अन्तर्गत लड़का-लड़की के घर रात्रि में जाकर उसका अपहरण करता था, जिसमें सफल होने पर ही विवाह उत्सव मनाया जाता था। शादी के बाद जब तक एक संतान नहीं हो जाती, तब तक पति पत्नी साथ नहीं घूम सकते थे। जन्म के बाद बालक को शराब से स्नान करवाकर तीन दिन के लिए गुफा में छोड़ दिया जाता था। यदि वह बालक तीन दिन बाद जीवित मिलता, तो उसे वीर संतान समझा जाता था। उस समय स्पार्टा की लड़कियां कुश्ती व मल्लयुद्ध के लिए विख्यात थीं और हर मुहल्ले में अखाड़े बने हुए थे। दूसरे राज्यों में स्त्रियों का क्षेत्रफल केवल घर था। विवाह के बाद स्त्रियाँ घर से बाहर नहीं जाती थीं। वे सिर्फ सामाजिक उत्सवों में आ जा सकती थीं।

यूनान के प्रसिद्ध नाटककार सोफोक्लीन ने स्त्री की दशा का वर्णन करते हुए अपने एक नाटक में नायिका से कहलवाया है, "हम औरतें कुछ भी नहीं, हमारा बचपन सुखमय था, परन्तु जब हमने यौवन की सीढ़ी पर कदम रखा, तो हमें वस्तु की तरह बेच दिया गया और हमें कहना पड़ा कि हम खुश हैं।" **विल डयूरेण्ट** ने लिखा है, "औरतों का प्रशिक्षण अत्यन्त चतुराई से होता था। उन्हें कम देखने, कम बोलने और कम सुनने की शिक्षा दी जाती थी।"

एथेन्स के नागरिकों के मध्य कोई भेदभाव नहीं था सबको समान भाव दिया जाता था। **मैकनेल बर्न्स** ने लिखा है, "नागरिक, विशेषज्ञ और गुलाम कन्धे से कन्धा मिलाकर काम करते थे और सबको समान वेतन मिलता था। एक जहाज में तो फोरमैन एक दास था।"

आर्थिक स्थिति—यूनान में जहाजरानी सुदृढ़ होने एवं उपनिवेश के कारण व्यापार का बहुत विकास हुआ। एथेन्स से अपनी सुरक्षा प्रदान करने के लिये उन्हें

कुछ कर के रूप में भेंट करते थे। इसके द्वारा उसको अधिक धन प्राप्त होने लगा साथ ही उनसे कच्चा माल लेकर उसे तैयार कराते थे जिससे उनका औद्योगिक विकास हुआ। विदेशी व्यापार से यूनान की बन्दरगाहों का विकास हुआ।

यूनान मिस्र एवं मैसोपोटामिया से खाद्य सामग्री, कपड़ा एवं रेशम तथा पूर्वी देशों से बढ़िया वस्त्र, मिर्च, मसाले और सौन्दर्य प्रसाधन की सामग्री खरीदता था। इसके बदले में यूनान मिट्टी के बर्तन, शराब, जैतून का तेल एवं लकड़ी का फर्नीचर आदि वस्तुओं का निर्यात करता था। यूनान का अधिकांश व्यापार विदेशी नागरिक ही करते थे।

यूनान के प्रत्येक नगर राज्य की राजधानी में व्यापारिक मण्डी होती थी जिससे व्यापार को बढ़ावा मिलता था। यूनान में मुद्रा प्रणाली के आविष्कार तथा बैंक प्रथा के प्रचलन से व्यापार को और प्रोत्साहन मिला। डेलफी में स्थित अपोलो का मन्दिर यूनान का एक प्रसिद्ध अन्तर्राष्ट्रीय बैंक था। उस समय व्यापारी इस मन्दिर से ऊंची दर पर व्याज लेकर व्यापार करता था। यूनानवासी सब प्रकार से सम्पन्न थे उनकी किसी प्रकार की समस्या नहीं थी। वे खुशहाल जीवन व्यतीत करते थे। जिस कारण वहाँ सांस्कृतिक सभ्यता का विकास तेजी से हुआ।

सिकन्दर की विजयों के बाद एक विश्व बाजार की स्थापना हुई, जिसका क्षेत्र, भारत, मध्य एशिया से पश्चिमी अफ्रीका तक फैला हुआ था। विश्व व्यापार के केन्द्रों में मिस्र के सिकन्दरिया तथा सीरिया के एनटोव का नाम विशेष रूप से उल्लेखनीय है। नई सड़कें बनीं और बन्दरगाह विकसित हुए। सेवाइन का मत है, "उच्च सामाजिक वर्ग अपनी विलासिता का भारी प्रदर्शन करने लगा। विशाल सजे हुए भवन, तड़क-भड़कदार वेशभूषा और महंगे त्यौहार स्पष्ट नजर आते थे। समाज के दूसरे सिरे पर यातना और व्यक्तिगत शोषण व्याप्त था। हर मजदूर के सिर पर कर्ज और गुलाम बनाये जाने का आतंक लटक रहा था।" कर्जदार को उसका मालिक गुलाम बना लेता था। एथेन्स के पास पाईरियस नामक बन्दरगाह थी, जो विश्व की प्रसिद्ध बन्दरगाहों में से एक थी। एलिस व जौन ने लिखा है, "पाईरियस की गलियां बहुत व्यस्त रहती थीं। यहां लगभग हर देश के व्यापारी अपना माल लाते थे और यहां से एथेन्स अपने व्यापारियों को भूमध्य सागरीय जगत के चारों तरफ भेजता था। पेरिक्लीज चाहता था कि एथेन्स एक मालदार नगर के अलावा भी कुछ बने।

यहाँ के लोगों ने अपना ध्यान उद्योग-धन्धों पर केन्द्रित किया जिससे इस क्षेत्र में प्रगति हुयी। यहां के लोग मिट्टी के बर्तन, अस्त्र-शस्त्र और फर्नीचर आदि बनाते थे। लकड़ी की नावें भी बनती थीं। यूनान में कांस्य पात्र, मृद्‌ भाण्ड तथा ऊनी कपड़े

बनाने में कोरिन्थ ने सबसे अधिक प्रसिद्धि प्राप्त की थी। यूनान के पहाड़ों से सोना, चांदी, जस्ता और लोहा निकलता था। खानों में गुलाम कार्य करते थे। कारखानों में दैनिक प्रयोग की चीजें बनती थीं।

यूनानियों का मुख्य व्यवसाय कृषि नहीं था। पठारी प्रदेश होने के कारण खाद्य सामग्री बाहर से मंगवाई जाती थी। यहां की मुख्य पैदावार गेहूं, जौ, अंजीर, अंगूर तथा जैतून आदि थी। यहां के लोग भेड़, बकरी, गाय और घोड़ा आदि जानवरों को पालते थे। मछली पकड़ना भी इनका प्रमुख व्यवसाय था।

भाषा एवं दर्शन—यूनान में भाषा का भी विकास हुआ। यूनानियों ने सेमोटिकों की लिपि का विकास किया। होमर ने अपने महाकाव्यों की रचना प्राचीन यूनानी भाषा में की, परन्तु अरस्तु के समय भाषा का बहुत अधिक विकास हुआ। इस समय विद्वानों ने गद्य, नाटक आदि सरल और भावात्मक भाषा में लिखे।

यूरोप में दार्शनिक विचारों का अभ्युदय सर्वप्रथम यूनान में हुआ। यहां बहुत उच्च कोटि के दार्शनिक हुए, जिनकी रचनाएं आज भी दर्शन साहित्य की अमूल्य निधि हैं।

पांचवीं शताब्दी ई. पू. में यूनान में सोफिस्ट विचारधारा का उदय हुआ। सोफिस्ट का अर्थ है—बुद्धिमान। सोफिस्ट शिक्षक नास्तिक थे तथा तर्क के द्वारा शिक्षा का प्रचार करते थे। सोफिस्टों का उद्देश्य ज्ञान का प्रचार करके धन अर्जित करना था। उनके विचारों से जनता भ्रमित होने लगी। सुकरात ने सोकिस्टों को पाखण्डी बताया व इनकी विद्वता पर विराम लगा दिया।

सुकरात (469 ई. पू.—399 ई. पू.)—सुकरात का जन्म 469 ईसा पूर्व एथेन्स में हुआ। उसका पिता मूर्तिकार तथा माता दाई थीं। उसने अपना जीवन एक सैनिक के रूप में प्रारम्भ किया और दार्शनिक के रूप में उसे व्यतीत किया और एक शहीद के रूप में अपनी जीवनलीला को समाप्त किया। उसने तीन बार एथेंस की तरफ से युद्ध में भाग लिया तथा वीरता का भी परिचय दिया लेकिन युद्ध की विभीषिका को देखकर सुकरात दार्शनिक हो गया। उसका मुख्य उपदेश था—"लोग-बाग यह जानते हुए भी यह समझते हैं कि वे सब कुछ जानते हैं और मैं यह जानता हूँ कि मैं (स्वयं) कुछ नहीं जानता।"

सुकरात हमेशा आम आदमी से सवाल करता था कि सत्य क्या है? सुन्दरता क्या है? सुकरात अपने शिष्यों के साथ बाजारों में भ्रमण करता था और शराब का सेवन करता था। वीच ने लिखा है, " वह कहता था कि मैं अज्ञानी हूँ, किन्तु यूनान के आगामी सभी दार्शनिक उसी के शिष्य थे।"

सुकरात का सबसे बड़ा शत्रु एक जूरी एनीटस था, जिसका लड़का सुकरात का प्रखर शिष्य था, पर वह शराबी बन गया था। अतः एनीटस ने सुकरात पर युवकों को पथ भ्रष्ट करने का आरोप लगाया और 399 ई. पू. में उसे विषपान द्वारा मृत्युदण्ड दिया। तब उसने कहा, ''मैंने लोगों को सिखाया कि कैसे जीवित रहना चाहिए। और अब मैं उन्हें सिखा रहा हूँ कि कैसे मरा जाए।'' सुकरात ने अपनी मृत्यु से पूर्व कुछ कविताओं की रचना की, जिनमें रोते हुए लोगों से कहा गया था, ''चूंकि हम सबमें से अभी तक कोई मरा नहीं है, इसलिए किसी को मालूम नहीं कि मृत्यु जीवन की अपेक्षा अधिक बुरी है।''

399 ई. पू. में सुकरात ने विष पीकर अपना जीवन समाप्त कर लिया। उसका विषपान एथेन्स के गौरव पर सबसे बड़ा कलंक है। **डेविस** ने लिखा है, ''एथेन्स के प्रजातन्त्र ने सबसे बड़ा घृणित कार्य जो किया, वह सुकरात को प्राणदण्ड देना ही था। यदि इस कार्य का उद्देश्य सुकरात की शिक्षाओं को नष्ट करना था, तो अपने उद्देश्य की प्राप्ति में यह कार्य बुरी तरह असफल रहा।'' सुकरात ने कोई पुस्तक नहीं लिखी थी। अब उसके विषय में हमें जानकारी प्लेटो की रचनाओं से ही मिलती है।

प्लेटो (427 ई. पू. - 347 ई. पू.)—यूनान के एक महान दार्शनिक के रूप में प्रसिद्ध प्लेटो ने अपने गुरु सुकरात से काफी कुछ सीखा था। उसका वास्तविक नाम एरिस्टोक्लीज था। उसे अफलातून भी कहा जाता है। उसका विशालकाय शरीर था, इसलिए उसके एक शिक्षक ने उसे प्लेटो का उपनाम दे दिया था। इसे पाश्चात्य दर्शन का प्रवर्तक माना जाता है। सुकरात की मृत्यु के पश्चात् प्लेटो ने उसके विचारों को लिपिबद्ध किया और उनका प्रचार भी किया। उसका जन्म 427 ई. पू. में एक कुलीन परिवार में हुआ था। वह एक अच्छा कवि होने के साथ-साथ कला के प्रति भी विशेष लगाव रखता था।

सुकरात का प्रभाव उसके शिष्य प्लेटो पर पड़ा। उसकी मृत्यु के पश्चात् प्लेटो का प्रजातन्त्र पर से विश्वास टूट गया। इसके बाद उसने दस वर्ष तक मिस्र व इटली आदि देशों का भ्रमण किया और वहां से लौटकर 387 ई. पू. में एक अकादमी नामक स्कूल की स्थापना की। इस स्कूल में उसके शिष्य उसके विचारों को सुनने के लिए आते थे। प्लेटो ने अपनी पुस्तकों में सुकरात के विचारों का समावेश किया है। वह अपने गुरु से बहुत प्रभावित था। उसका मानना था, ''सच्चा ज्ञान विचारों का ज्ञान है, जो बुद्धि से ही प्राप्त किया जा सकता है।'' **डॉ. गोयल** के अनुसार, "राजनीतिक दार्शनिक के रूप में उसने एक ऐसे आदर्श समाज की कल्पना की, जो वैयक्तिक स्वार्थ और वर्ग संघर्ष से मुक्त हो।"

प्लेटो के अनुसार अधिकतर लोग मूर्ख होते हैं। उसने सुझाव दिया कि शासक की सम्पत्ति नियत कर दी जाए। वह सामान्य व्यक्ति के लिए भी न्याय की पूर्ण व्यवस्था चाहता था। **सेवाइन** का मत है, ''यह नहीं भूल जाना चाहिए कि यूनानियों ने ही सामाजिक सम्बन्धों पर प्रथम प्रेरणा प्रदान की थी। '' प्लेटो ने कहा, ''प्रजातंत्र सीमित लोगों के शासन के विरुद्ध प्रतिक्रिया से आता है, जिसमें अराजकता को स्वाधीनता, फिजूलखर्ची को शान-शौकत और अशिष्टता या निर्लज्जता का साहस कहा जाता है। सुकरात जो प्लेटो का गुरु था उसे प्रजातंत्र ने मौत की सजा दी थी इसलिए उसे प्रजातंत्र से नफरत हो गई थी। **एच. जी वेल्स** ने लिखा है, "प्लेटो में अभी बहुत कुछ है, जिसकी तरफ हम एक नजर भी नहीं डाल सकते, लेकिन यह इतिहास में एक सीमा चिह्न व महत्त्वपूर्ण घटना है, मानव के विकास में यह एक नई चीज है।"

प्लेटो में तीन ग्रंथों की रचना की– प्रथम यूरोपिया, द्वितीय रिपब्लिक एवं तृतीय लॉज। उसने अपनी पुस्तकें प्रश्नोत्तर शैली में संवाद के रूप में लिखी हैं। उसकी इन पुस्तकों में शासन, संगीत, विज्ञान साहित्य, न्याय और पुण्य आदि विषयों पर संवाद थे। 'यूरोपिया' नामक पुस्तक में प्लेटो ने एक आदर्श समाज के बारे में कल्पना की है। उसकी मान्यता थी व्यक्तिगत सम्पत्ति खत्म होने पर ही समाज से बुराइयां मिट सकती हैं। इससे स्पष्ट है कि वह समाजवादी विचारधारा का प्रथम प्रणेता था। **डॉ. गोयल** के अनुसार–''प्लेटो का मानना था कि सामाजिक बुराइयों को दूर करने के लिए व्यक्तिगत पूंजी को खत्म करने से ही आदर्श समाज का गठन होगा।''

'रिपब्लिक' पुस्तक की रचना प्लेटो ने की जो बहुत प्रसिद्ध हुई। इसमें उसने आदर्श राज्य की कल्पना की है। उसने राजा को दार्शनिक होना अनिवार्य बताया। इसीलिए प्लेटो को 'राजनीति का जनक' तथा 'नवीन विचारधारा का प्रणेता' कहा जाता है। प्लेटो ने अपनी तीसरी पुस्तक **'लॉज'** में कानून और विधान के बारे में वर्णन किया है। प्लेटो ने एक आदर्श राज्य व समाज के निर्माण पर जोर दिया था। वह स्त्रियों को समानता का अधिकार दिये जाने के पक्ष में था। इतिहासकार वीच ने लिखा है, ''वह पाश्चात्य संसार के दार्शनिकों में सबसे ऊँचा है। आने वाली शताब्दियों के विचारक उसकी अवहेलना नहीं कर सके। वे उसके उपदेशों के सदा ऋणी रहेंगे। वह ज्ञान रूपी झरने का वह उद्गम स्थान है, जिससे आदर्शवादी सदा प्रेरणा लेते रहे हैं। मनुष्य का परेशान मस्तिष्क जब भौतिक संसार से हारकर ईश्वर की वास्तविकता जानने को उत्सुक होता है, तो प्लेटो उसका मार्गदर्शन करता है।''

प्लेटो की मृत्यु 347 ई. में हो गयी, तब तक वह 'लॉज' नामक पुस्तक को पूरा नहीं कर पाया था।

अरस्तु (348 ई. पू. - 322 ई. पू.)—सिकन्दर का गुरु महान दार्शनिक अरस्तु था। वह विचारक, गम्भीर, विद्वान, उच्चकोटि का वैज्ञानिक एवं तार्किक तथा बहुमुखी प्रतिभा सम्पन्न दार्शनिक था। अरिस्टोटल (अरस्तु) का जन्म 384 ई. पू. में मेसीडोनिया के राजा के वैद्य के घर में हुआ था। उसने तीस वर्ष तक प्लेटो से शिक्षा प्राप्त की। मेसीडोनिया के राजा फिलिप के आदेशानुसार अरस्तु ने सात वर्ष तक उसके लड़के सिकन्दर महान को शिक्षा दी। इसके पश्चात् 326 ई. पू. में वह एथेन्स लौट आया और लाइसियस में उसने एक स्कूल खोला, जिसमें छात्रों को दर्शन, राजनीति, काव्य, ज्योतिष, विद्या, तर्कशास्त्र और भौतिकशास्त्र आदि विषयों की शिक्षा दी जाती थी। उस समय का प्रसिद्ध शिक्षण केन्द्र लाइसियस था जिसमें लोग शिक्षा ग्रहण करते थे।

अरस्तु बहुत व्यवहारकुशल था। उसने राजनीतिशास्त्र एवं आचारशास्त्र आदि विषयों पर कई पुस्तकें लिखीं। उसके जीवन का प्रमुख उद्देश्य था—लोगों के लिए सुख की खोज करना। अरस्तु ने अपने प्रसिद्ध ग्रंथ 'पोलिटिक्स' में अपने समय के नगर राज्यों की सरकारों की अच्छाइयों और बुराइयों पर प्रकाश डाला है। एक अन्य पुस्तक 'एथिक्स' में यह चेतावनी दी है कि किसी भी विषय में चरम सीमा तक जाना उचित नहीं है। उसने कहा, मनुष्य एक सामाजिक प्राणी है और समाज में ही वह अपना पूर्ण विकास करता है। इसके अतिरिक्त राज्य का मुख्य उद्देश्य आदर्श नागरिकों का निर्माण करना है।

अरस्तु को तर्कशास्त्र का अच्छा ज्ञान था। उसके राजनीतिक विचार सदियों तक राजनीतिक विचारकों के लिए आधार बने रहे। आज भी तर्कशास्त्र एवं दर्शनशास्त्र में उसके सिद्धांत अत्यन्त महत्त्वपूर्ण माने जाते हैं। **लिविंगस्टन** ने कहा है कि, "अरस्तु का क्षेत्र आधुनिक लेखकों की अपेक्षा अधिक विस्तृत है। उसे मानव बुद्धि की उस दुर्लभ तथा सर्वोत्तम श्रेणी में रखा जा सकता है, जहां मानववाद व तर्कशास्त्र दोनों मिलते हैं।" अरस्तु ने चिकित्सा विज्ञान में कई प्रयोग किये। उसका मानना था कि सूर्य पृथ्वी के चारों तरफ चक्कर लगाता है, किन्तु यह सिद्धांत असत्य है। इसके बाद भी उसकी रचनाओं के महत्त्व से इन्कार नहीं किया जा सकता।

शिक्षा एवं साहित्य—स्पार्टा के स्कूलों में विद्यार्थियों को जिमनास्टिक, दौड़, मल्ल युद्ध और सैन्य प्रशिक्षण दिया जाता था ताकि वे बलिष्ठ एवं स्वस्थ सन्तान पैदा कर सकें। एथेन्स में वहां की शिक्षा का प्रमुख उद्देश्य आदर्श नागरिकों का निर्माण

करना था। वहां सिर्फ लड़कों को शिक्षा ग्रहण करने का अधिकार था। लड़कियां घर के कामों में कुशल होती थीं। यहां के स्कूलों में संगीत, गणित, ज्योतिष, व्याकरण, दर्शनशास्त्र, इतिहास और साहित्य आदि विषयों की शिक्षा दी जाती थी। यूनान में शिक्षकों को 'सोफिस्ट' कहा जाता था। ये वाद-विवाद में विजय पाने की शिक्षा देते थे। एथेन्स में सुकरात, प्लेटो व अरस्तु आदि दार्शनिकों ने स्कूल खोल रखे थे। इनमें विद्यार्थी दार्शनिक विषयों के बारे में शिक्षा प्राप्त करते थे।

यूनान के प्राचीन रचनाओं से वर्तमान समय में भी कवि एवं नाटककार प्रेरणा लेते हैं। यूनानी साहित्य के बारे में **एच. जी. वेल्स** ने लिखा है, "यह संसार का पहला महान् साहित्य था।" **प्लेट व जीन** ने लिखा है, "प्राचीन यूनानी साहित्य बहुत आधुनिक है। यह एक ताजे झरने के समान था, जिसमें से अनेक शाखाओं वाली विशाल नदी निकली थी।" इन विचारों से स्पष्ट हो जाता है कि यूनान का साहित्य कितना विकसित था।

प्राचीन यूनान में होमर ने 'इलियड' और 'ओडेसी' नामक दो महाकाव्यों की रचना की, जिनका अनुवाद विश्व की लगभग समस्त भाषाओं में हो चुका है। ये दोनों महाकाव्य विश्व सभ्यता को यूनान की अनुपम देन हैं।

हिसियड—यूनान में होमर के बाद हिसियड नामक एक महान कवि हुआ। उसने 'कार्य तथा काल' नामक पुस्तक की रचना की। इस पुस्तक में हिसियड ने किसानों की दयनीय दशा का उल्लेख किया है। वह उन्हें बगावत करने हेतु उकसाता है। उसने 'थियोमोनी' नामक एक पुस्तक और लिखी। यह कृति देश भक्ति पर आधारित है। हिसियड का समय आठवीं शाताब्दी ई. पू. के आस-पास था।

होमर—होमर यूनान का सबसे पुराना कवि था। उसने 'इलियड' तथा 'ओडेसी' नामक दो महाकाव्यों की रचना की। 'इलियड' नामक महाकाव्य में यूनानियों और ट्राय के बीच हुए दस वर्षीय युद्ध पर प्रकाश डाला गया है। इन महाकाव्यों की तुलना रामायण और महाभारत से की जा सकती है। इन दोनों महाकाव्यों से यूनानी लोग प्रेरणा ग्रहण करते हैं। इलियड में वर्णित कहानी रामायण की कहानी सीताहरण से बहुत मिलती है। ये महाकाव्य विश्व साहित्य की अमूल्य निधि हैं। इतिहासकार **वीच** ने लिखा है, "होमर ने गाथाओं को महाकाव्य में परिणित कर दिया, जो आज भी संसार के महान् काव्यों में अपना स्थान सुरिक्षत रखते हैं और बड़े चाव से पढ़े जाते हैं।"

आरचीलोकस, सेफो, एनाक्रियन और पिण्डार आदि प्रमुख कवि हुए जिन्होंने यूनान में गीत काव्य का विकास किया।

सेफो—इस प्रसिद्ध कवयित्री का जन्म छठी शताब्दी ई. पू. में हुआ। उसने भी अपनी रचनाओं के लिए प्राचीन यूनान में होमर की भांति प्रसिद्धि प्राप्त की। उसने अपने गीतों में प्रकृति के सुन्दर तथ्यों पर प्रकाश डाला है।

एनाक्रियन—एनाक्रियन गीति काव्य का एक अन्य प्रसिद्ध कवि था। इसका समय 560 ई. पू. से 475 ई. पू. था। उसने प्रेम तथा वियोग के गीत लिखे। वह सुरा सुन्दरी का उपासक था और इन्द्रियों के सुख का उपयोग गीतों में करता था।

आरचीलोकस—इस समय के प्रसिद्ध कवि आरचीलोकस ने अपने गीतों में सामाजिक बुराइयों पर प्रकाश डाला है।

पिण्डार—पिण्डार के समय में गीति काव्य अपनी चरमसीमा पर पहुंचा। उसका समय पांचवीं शताब्दी ई. पू. माना जाता है। उसके गीतों में देश प्रेम का भाव मिलता है। उसने अपने गीतों में एथेन्स की विजयों और हेलेनिस्टिक सम्यता की महानता का वर्णन किया। उसके गीत प्राचीन यूनान में बहुत प्रसिद्ध हुए।

नाटक कला का जन्म यूनान में हुआ। इसके अलावा उनके अभिनय के लिए नाट्यशालाओं का निर्माण भी यहीं हुआ। यूनान में प्राचीन समय में अनेक प्रसिद्ध दुःखान्त नाटककार हुए, जिनमें एस्काइल्स, यूरीपिडीज एवं सोफोक्लीज आदि के नाम विशेष रूप से चर्चित है।

यूरीपीडिज—इसका समय 480 ईसा पूर्व से 406 ईसा पूर्व माना जाता है। यह भी एक दुःखान्त नाटककार था। उसने अपने नाटकों में एथेंस की साम्राज्यवादी नीति की आलोचना करते हुए पीड़ितों तथा दलितों के प्रति सहानुभूति व्यक्त की। उसने 7 नाटक लिखे, जिनमें से 'मीडिया', 'हिपोलिटस' तथा 'ट्राय की नारियां' आदि काफी चर्चित रहे।

सोफोक्लीज—अपनी सम्पूर्ण जीवन अवधि में सोफोक्लीज ने 113 नाटक लिखे थे। इसका समय 496 ईसा पूर्व से 406 ईसा पूर्व था। उसे 18 बार पुरस्कृत किया गया था। वह निराशावादी, संसार में अरुचि रखने वाला और जीवन की क्षणभंगुरता में विश्वास रखता था। उसके प्रसिद्ध नाटकों में 'एण्टीगोन', 'इलेक्ट्रा', 'ओडियस रेक्स' आदि विशेष रूप से उल्लेखनीय हैं। बर्न्स का मत है, "उसका बर्ताव समानता और शान्ति के प्यार में झलकता है। वह प्रजातंत्र के प्रति सम्मान रखता था और मानव की दुर्बलताओं के प्रति सहानुभूति।"

एस्काइल्स (525 ई.पू. से 456 ई.पू.)—दुःखान्त नाटककार के रूप में प्रसिद्ध एस्काइल्स ने अपने जीवन काल में 80 नाटक लिखे जिनमें से सात नाटक

उपलब्ध हैं। उसके प्रसिद्ध नाटकों में 'प्रोमोथियस बाउण्ड द पर्शियन', 'ओरेस्टिया' तथा 'सेवेन अगेन्सट थीब्स' आदि विशेष रूप से चर्चित हैं।

एरिस्टोफेनीज (448 ई. पू. से 385 ई. पू.)–पेरिक्लीज युग में यह दुःखान्त नाटककार के रूप में प्रसिद्ध हुआ। इसने 42 नाटक लिखे, जिनमें तत्कालीन समाज का चित्रण किया गया है। उसने अपने रहस्य रस के नाटकों में तीखे व्यंग किये। उसने प्रसिद्ध नाटकों में 'नाइटस', 'बर्ड्स' 'पार्लियामेन्ट ऑफ वीमेन' आदि प्रमुख थे। यूनान में दुःखान्त नाटककार को पुरस्कार मिलता था क्योंकि इसकी मांग अधिक थी। **मैकनेल बर्न्स** ने लिखा है, "यूनानियों की श्रेष्ठ साहित्य प्राप्ति दुखान्त नाटक थी।"

इतिहास–संभवतः इतिहास की रचना यूनान में ही शुरू हुई थी क्योंकि इस युग का प्रसिद्ध इतिहासकार हेरोडोटस (484 ई. पू. से 400 ई. पू.) था। उसे इतिहास का जन्मदाता और विश्व का प्रथम इतिहासकार माना जाता है। उसने फारस और यूनान के बीच हुए युद्धों का वर्णन अत्यन्त रोचक ढंग से किया है। उसे इतिहास लेखन की कला का भी जन्मदाता माना जाता है। एथेन्स का भ्रमण उसने पेरिक्लीज के समय में किया था। दूसरा प्रसिद्ध इतिहासकार थ्यूसीडाइडीज (460 ई. पू. से 400 ई. पू.) था। वह वैज्ञानिक इतिहास का जन्मदाता था। सेनापति होते हुए भी उसने विधिवत इतिहास की रचना की। मैकाले ने उसे संसार का महानतम इतिहासकार बतलाया है। उसने एथेन्स और स्पार्टा के बीच हुए पेलोपोनेशियन युद्ध का इतिहास लिखा।

ज्ञान विज्ञान

यूनान ने विज्ञान के क्षेत्र में काफी प्रगति की। उस समय वहां गणित, ज्योतिष और चिकित्सा आदि क्षेत्रों में असाधारण विकास हुआ। प्राचीन यूनान में निम्नलिखित वैज्ञानिक हुए हैं–

अरस्तु (384 ई. पू.–322 ई. पू.)–प्राकृतिक विज्ञान की शुरुआत प्रसिद्ध दार्शनिक अरस्तु ने की जिसने मछली की उत्पत्ति के बारे में सर्वप्रथम लिखा। उसने वनस्पति विज्ञान एवं जन्तु विज्ञान के विकास के क्षेत्र में भी सराहनीय योगदान दिया।

थियोफ्रेस्टस–अरस्तु के शिष्य थियोफ्रेस्टस ने वनस्पति विज्ञान को सर्वप्रथम शास्त्रीय रूप दिया।

एनेक्जीमैण्डर (611 ई.पू.–547 ई. पू.)–एनेक्जीमैण्डर के अनुसार मनुष्य प्रारम्भ में मछली के रूप में था, धीरे धीरे उसने विकास किया।

एम्पीडोक्लीज (490 ई.पू.—430 ई.पू)—एम्पीडोक्लीज नामक वैज्ञानिक के अनुसार वायु, भूमि, अग्नि व जल इन चार तत्वों से सृष्टि का निर्माण हुआ है। इसने विकासवादी सिद्धांत का विकास किया। इसके अनुसार अनुकूल परिवर्तनों से विकास की प्रक्रिया निश्चित होती है।

थेलिस—विज्ञान का पिता प्रसिद्ध दार्शनिक थेलिस को कहा जाता है। उसने बताया कि 'जल नामक पदार्थ से सृष्टि की उत्पत्ति हुई है।

डायोस्कोरइडीज—इसे दर्शन का पिता माना जाता है। इसने विज्ञान के क्षेत्र में भी महान कार्य किए। उसके अनुसार 'जल' नामक तत्व से विश्व का विकास हुआ। उसने इस सिद्धांत का प्रतिपादन इसलिए किया था, ताकि विश्व में अनेकता में एकता की व्याख्या की जा सके।

एरिस्टार्कस—यह 320 ईसा पूर्व से 310 ईसा पूर्व के समय में यूनान के प्रसिद्ध वैज्ञानिक के रूप में विख्यात हुआ। उसने बताया कि पृथ्वी सूर्य के चारों तरफ घूमती है। इसने पृथ्वी से चन्द्रमा तक की दूरी का भी लगभग ठीक अनुमान लगाया।

एनेक्सागोरस—एनेक्सागोरस, पेरिक्लीज के समय का प्रमुख वैज्ञानिक था। जिसने संसार की उत्पत्ति में देवी शक्ति का खण्डन करते हुये बताया इसकी उत्पत्ति भौतिक तत्वों द्वारा हुई।

गणित—गणित के क्षेत्र में यूनान का बहुत योगदान है। यूनान में रेखागणित का विशेष रूप से अध्ययन हुआ। प्राचीन यूनान में निम्नलिखित गणितज्ञ हुए।

थेलिस—थेलिस यूनानी दर्शन एवं विज्ञान का पिता था। उसे गणितशास्त्र का जन्मदाता भी माना जाता है। उसने बिन्दु एवं रेखा की कल्पना की थी।

यूक्लिड—300 ईसा पूर्व इसने रेखागणित के ज्ञान को विकसित किया। उसने 'ज्यामिति' नामक पुस्तक लिखी, जो आज भी स्कूलों में पढ़ाई जाती है। उसे आधुनिक रेखागणित का जनक माना गया है।

आर्किमिडीज—287 ईसा पूर्व से 212 ईसा पूर्व के समय में यह गणितशास्त्र का प्रमुख विद्वान था। उसके सिद्धांत आज भी विश्वविख्यात हैं।

पाइथागोरस—582 ईसा पूर्व से 507 ईसा पूर्व के काल में उसने रेखागणित के विभिन्न नये सिद्धांतों के महत्त्व को स्पष्ट किया। उसने गणित के आधार पर यह सिद्ध किया कि पृथ्वी गोल है। इसलिये उसके सिद्धांत आज भी रेखागणित में प्रयोग किये जाते हैं।

चिकित्साशास्त्र—यूनान में चिकित्साशास्त्र का भी काफी विकास हुआ। यहाँ के अनेक चिकित्साशास्त्री हुए जिन्होंने इस दिशा में यूनान का नाम रोशन किया। कुछ प्रमुख प्राचीन चिकित्साशास्त्री निम्न प्रकार हैं—

हिप्पोक्रेटिज—460 ईसा पूर्व से 377 ईसा पूर्व के समय में यूनान के हिप्पोक्रेटिज ने चिकित्सा शास्त्र को जन्म दिया, इसमें भूत आत्माओं का खण्डन किया गया, बीमारी का प्राकृतिक कारण होने की पुष्टि की। हिप्पोक्रेटिस नब्ज को देखकर बीमारी का पता लगा लेता था। उसने बीमारियों और औषधियों पर प्रकाश डाला। उसने बीमारी दूर करने के लिए सफाई, रक्त निष्कासन तथा पसीना आने पर जोर दिया। उसने वैद्यों के लिए शपथ लेने की प्रथा शुरु की। आजकल के चिकित्सा विद्यालयों के स्नातक हिप्पोक्रेटिज की शपथ ग्रहण करते हैं।

ज्योतिषशास्त्र—इस समय यूनानियों ने यह खोज कर ली थी कि इस सृष्टि का निर्माण पृथ्वी, जल, वायु और अग्नि से हुआ है।

हिपाकरस—उसने सूर्य और तारों का मानचित्र बनाया था।

एनेक्सागोरस—यह प्राचीन यूनान का प्रसिद्ध ज्योतिषी था। उसने सूर्य ग्रहण, चन्द्र ग्रहण एवं नक्षत्रों का अध्ययन किया। इस प्रकार, प्राचीन यूनान में विज्ञान, चिकित्सा, गणित, भूगोल एवं ज्योतिष के क्षेत्र में अत्यधिक उन्नति हुई।

डायोजिनीज (500 ई. पू. - 470 ई. पू.)—यह प्रसिद्ध चिकित्सक था। उसने 'एनाटोमी' नामक पुस्तक लिखी। यह पहली पुस्तक थी, जिसमें प्रथम बार शरीर विज्ञान तथा शरीर के चीर-फाड़ एवं विश्लेषण पर प्रकाश डाला गया है।

अल्कमेपन—प्रसिद्ध चिकित्सक अल्कमेपन ने 'ऑन नेचर' नामक पुस्तक लिखी। इस पुस्तक में उसने बताया कि तन्त्र मन्त्र कुछ नहीं है। बीमारी शारीरिक कारणों से होती है। अल्कमेपन ने सर्वप्रथम पशुओं की शल्य चिकित्सा आरम्भ की।

हेरोफिलस (300 ई. पू.)—इसे सर्जरी का पिता कहा जाता है। इसने मानव शरीर की चीर-फाड़ की और मांसपेशियों का अध्ययन किया।

यूराईफ्रेन—यूनान के प्रसिद्ध चिकित्सक यूराईफ्रोन ने फेफड़ों की बीमारी की खोज की और कब्ज की बीमारी उत्पन्न होने के कारणों को स्पष्ट किया।

कला—यूनानी कला में प्रमुख रूप से सौन्दर्य बोध, क्रीड़ा प्रेम, अलंकरण और देवताओं का मानवीकरण के साथ-साथ राष्ट्रीय गुणों को दर्शाया जाता था। यूनानी कला में यथार्थवाद और आदर्शवाद स्पष्ट रूप से दृष्टिगोचर होता है। प्राचीनकाल के दौरान यूनान में मूर्तिकार मुख्य रूप से सोने, कांसे तथा पत्थर का प्रयोग करते थे। जिनमें वे स्त्री सौन्दर्य का प्रदर्शन, पुरुष के गठीले शरीर की मांसपेशियों के प्रदर्शन

पर बहुत ध्यान देते थे। प्राचीन यूनान के प्रसिद्ध मूर्तिकारों में फीडियस (500 ई. पू. से 435 ई. पू.), माइरन और पोलिक्लीटस (480 ई. पू. - 420 ई. पू.) थे। **फीडियस** प्राचीन यूनान के मूर्तिकारों में सबसे प्रसिद्ध था। बर्न्स ने लिखा है–"शहरों में फैली शोहरत के अनुसार यूनानी मूर्तिकला ने फीडियस के युग में सर्वोच्चता प्राप्त कर ली थी।" फीडियस ने एथेना देवी की मूर्ति बनाई थी, जो अत्यन्त सुन्दर एवं सजीव थी। वह पांचवीं शताब्दी ई. पू. का मूर्तिकार था। पोलिक्लीटस को पहलवानों की कांसे की मूर्तियां बनाने में कुशलता प्राप्त थी।

स्थापत्य कला के समय यूनान में सड़कें, आकर्षक इमारतें और भव्य मंदिरों का निर्माण किया गया। एथेन्स में एक्रोपोलिस की पहाड़ी पर बना हुआ पार्थेनान का मंदिर डोरिक शैली का उत्कृष्ट नमूना है। यह पूरा मंदिर संगमरमर का बना हुआ है। इसमें एथेना देवी की सुन्दर मूर्ति स्थापित की गई है। पार्थेनान का मंदिर अपनी विशालता, नक्काशी और भव्यता की दृष्टि से स्थापत्य कला का एक शानदार नमूना है। **एलिस और जौन** का मानना है कि, "एथेन्स के एक्रोपोलिस में भव्यतम ग्रीक इमारतें थीं, जो सभी एथेना देवी की स्मृति में निर्मित हैं। इनमें से एक पार्थेनान संभवतः विश्व की सबसे प्रसिद्ध इमारत है।" आयोनिक शैली का शानदार नमूना इरेकथियस मंदिर है। एथेन्स में स्थित थीसियस का मंदिर भी उस समय काफी प्रसिद्ध था। एक्रोपोलिस की पहाड़ी पर डायोनिसस का थियेटर बनाया गया था, जो उस समय की स्थापत्यकला का शानदार नमूना है।

यूनान के लोग संगीत के बहुत शौकीन थे इसलिए संगीत कला का भी अत्यधिक विकास हुआ। ये लोग सितार और बांसुरी का प्रयोग करते थे। आपोलो के वार्षिकोत्सव पर संगीत प्रतियोगिताओं का आयोजन होता था, जिन्हें सुनने के लिए एथेन्स के घरों में ताले लग जाते थे। यूनानी लोग सामूहिक रूप से देशभक्ति तथा शौर्य के गीत गाते थे। यूनान में नाटकों की शुरुआत और अन्त में संगीत का प्रयोग निश्चित रूप से किया जाता था।

चित्रकला के विकास में यूनान अग्रणी रहा। इस समय के चित्रकार अधिकतर चित्र सुराहियों, घड़ों, मिट्टी के प्यालों, शराब की प्यालियों, फूलदानों तथा बर्तनों पर बनाते थे। जिन पर धार्मिक कथाओं, शृंगार, आमोद-प्रमोद, खेलकूद व आखेट का चित्र बनाया जाता था उन पर लाल और काले रंग का प्रयोग किया जाता था। ईसा से 500 वर्ष पूर्व यूनानी चित्रकला अपने विकास की चरमसीमा पर जा पहुंची थी। रोम के अजायबघर में ईसा की 300 वर्ष पूर्व महत्त्वपूर्ण 'तश्तरी' जिसमें मानव की 250 से अधिक आकृतियां अंकित हैं, उसको सुरक्षित रखा है।

पोलिग्नोटस, ज्यूक्सिज, अपोलोडोरस और परसियस आदि यूनान के प्रमुख चित्रकार हुए। प्रसिद्ध चित्रकार पोलिग्नोटस ने बहुत से समूह चित्रों को तैयार किया। पोलिग्नोटस ने 'ट्राय का विनाश' नामक चित्र बनाया था। डेल्फी के मंदिर में भी उसने सुन्दर चित्र बनाए। दूसरा प्रसिद्ध चित्रकार अपोलोडोरस था, जिसने लकड़ी के तख्तों पर सुन्दर चित्र बनाए। यह चौथी शताब्दी ई. पू. में हुआ था। ज्यूक्सिज ने धावक का चित्र बड़ा ही सजीव बनाया था।

धार्मिक जीवन

यूनान में मूर्तिपूजा एवं बहुदेववादी प्रथा थी। वे लोग प्रकृति एवं जानवरों की पूजा करते थे। उनका भूत-प्रेत में भी विश्वास था। अपने देवता को मनुष्य के रूप में मानते थे, जिसमें मानव की भांति गुण एवं दोष भी होते थे। यहां के देवता कामुक, अनैतिक, झगड़ालू और स्वार्थी थे। इन देवताओं में आध्यात्मिकता का पूर्ण अभाव था। आदमी और देवता में सिर्फ यही अन्तर था कि देवता अमर होते थे। यूनानियों का मानना था कि उनके देवता उत्तरी यूनान में ओलम्पस पर्वत पर निवास करते थे। उनका प्रमुख देवता 'जियस' था, जो बिजलियां गिराता था। यहां बहुत से देवताओं को पशुबलि भी दी जाती थी। यहां के लोग परियों तथा अप्सराओं में भी विश्वास करते थे।

यूनान में जियस (आकाश देवता), अपोलो (सूर्य), हेरा (जियस की पत्नी एवं विवाह की देवी), एथेना (जियस की पुत्री तथा नगर रक्षक देवी), अफ्रोडाइट (प्रेम और सुन्दरता की देवी), हर्मस (व्यापार व वाणिज्य का देवता), पोसीडॉन (समुद्र का देवता), डेमीटर (अन्न की देवी), मार्स (युद्ध का देवता), डायोनिसस (शराब का देवता), एरोस (जियस का पुत्र एवं कामदेव) आदि की प्रमुख देवता के रूप में पूजा की जाती थी। यहां के लोग अपने देवताओं को प्रसन्न रखते थे, ताकि आपत्तिकाल में वे उनकी मदद करें। यहां देवताओं और परम्पराओं को चुनौती देने वाले व्यक्ति को मृत्यु दण्ड दिया जाता था। यूनान के धर्म में पूजा विधि अत्यन्त सरल थी। यहां पुरोहित या पुजारी वर्ग नहीं था। राजा और प्रजा मिलकर पूजा कर लेते थे।

यूनान में प्रमुख देवताओं के सम्मान में राष्ट्रीय स्तर पर धार्मिक उत्सव मनाये जाते थे तथा अवकाश भी घोषित किया जाता था, जिसमें 'बसन्त' महत्त्वपूर्ण त्यौहार होता था। देवताओं को खुश करने के लिये नाटकों का आयोजन किया जाता था। एथेन्स में नाटक और कला धर्म पर आधारित होते थे। स्वयं पेरिक्लीज ने कहा था "हम सुन्दरता के प्रेमी हैं" जियस देवता को खुश करने के लिए प्रति चौथे वर्ष

ओलम्पिक खेल आयोजित किये जाते थे। अपोलो देवता को खुश करने के लिए पीथियन उत्सव मनाया जाता था। ओलम्पिक खेल प्रतियोगिता के समय यूनान के आन्तरिक युद्ध स्थगित कर दिये जाते थे। ओलम्पिक खेलों में प्रथम स्थान प्राप्त करने वाले व्यक्तियों का अपने नगर में भारी सम्मान होता था। यूनान में उत्सव और शौर्य को धर्म का अभिन्न अंग माना जाता था।

यूनान के लोग बहुत अंधविश्वासी था। 'ओरेकल' नामक जगह देवताओं की भविष्यवाणी सुनने का स्थान था। यूनानियों का परलोक में भी विश्वास था। उनका मानना था कि धार्मिक जीवन व्यतीत करने वालों को स्वर्ग एवं बुरे कार्य करने वालों को नर्क में भेजा जाता था। इस कारण लोगों के जीवन में पाप और पुण्य की भावना भी जाग्रत थी। मृत्यु के पश्चात् वे भी आर्यो की भांति दाह-संस्कार करके समाधियां बनाते थे।

यूनानी संस्कृति की विश्व को देन

यूनानी सभ्यता संस्कृति ने दुनिया को अनुपम देन दी है। यूनानी संस्कृति के कई विचारों को रोम ने अपनाया और उनका पाश्चात्य देशों में प्रसार किया। यूरोपवासियों ने मशीनों, थियेटर, पोलिटिक्स, डेमोक्रेसी आदि कई शब्द यूनानी भाषा से ही सीखे हैं। प्रसिद्ध अंग्रेजी कवि मिल्टन की रचनाओं पर भी यूनान का प्रभाव दृष्टिगत होता है।

राजनीति में प्रजातन्त्र को प्रत्यक्ष बढ़ावा यूनान ने दिया जो आज भी विश्व के लिये गौरव है। यहां किसी भी समस्या का समाधान अथवा कोई भी निर्णय बहुमत के आधार पर लिया जाता था। यूनान में हर नागरिक शासन के कार्यों में रुचि रखता था। प्लेटो ने 'रिपब्लिक' नामक पुस्तक लिखी, जिसमें उसने राज्य के कर्तव्यों और विभिन्न शासन प्रणालियों का मूल्यांकन किया है। **प्रो. जिमरन** के अनुसार, "राजनीतिक अध्ययन के लिए यूनानियों की प्रथम देन इस बात में है कि उन्होंने शासन विधान का आविष्कार किया।"

विज्ञान के क्षेत्र में भी यूनानियों की देन उल्लेखनीय रही है। यूनानियों ने चिकित्सा शास्त्र, गणित, ज्योतिष, भूगोल विद्या आदि क्षेत्रों में कई महत्त्वपूर्ण सिद्धांतों का प्रतिपादन किया। यूनानी विद्वानों ने एकता पर बल दिया। इसके परिणामस्वरूप पश्चिमी और पूर्वी क्षेत्रों में सांस्कृतिक और व्यापारिक क्षेत्रों में काफी आदान-प्रदान हुआ।

यूनान ने मनोरंजन के क्षेत्र में भी महत्त्वपूर्ण देन दी है। नाटकों का सर्वप्रथम विकास करने का श्रेय यूनान को ही है। यूनानी दुःखांत नाटकों को अधिक महत्त्व देते थे। इससे समझा जा सकता है, कि वे जीवन में स्थायित्व नहीं मानते थे।

कला के क्षेत्र में भी यूनान की देन बहुमूल्य रही है। यूनानियों ने कई भव्य मन्दिरों, आकर्षक तथा विशाल मूर्तियों का निर्माण करवाया। एलिस और जॉन ने लिखा है कि, 'यूनानी विशेषकर एथेन्सवासी विश्व के लिए भवन-निर्माण और मूर्ति कला के ऐसे नमूने छोड़ गये हैं, जिन्हें विश्व ने पहले कभी नहीं देखा।'' रॉबिन्सन के शब्दों में "यूनानी, रोमवासियों की तरह भौतिकवादी नहीं थे, परन्तु वे जीने की कला समझते थे।" यूरोप के दार्शनिकों ने यूनान के दार्शनिकों से बहुत कुछ सीखा। सुकरात, अरस्तु, प्लेटो आदि यूनानी दार्शनिक अपने सिद्धांतों के लिए चिरस्मरणीय रहेंगे। यूनानी सभ्यता की विशेषता थी कि उन्होंने दूसरी सभ्यताओं का सम्मान किया और उनसे भी सीख ली। **प्लेटो** के अनुसार, ''दूसरी जातियों से हम कुछ भी ले सकते हैं और अन्त में उसे बदलकर अच्छा बना सकते हैं।'' **सेवाइन** ने लिखा है, "इसमें शंका नहीं कि अन्य किसी भी देश में, किसी भी समय, विद्वानों का ऐसा चमत्कारिक समूह नहीं हुआ, जैसा पेरिक्लीज के समय यूनान में।'' **मून** ने लिखा है, ''यूनानी अतीत के उत्तराधिकारी थे और अच्छे प्रचारक भी। उन्होंने बहुत कुछ पाया और उससे अधिक दिया।'' **मैकनेल बर्न्स** ने लिखा है, ''कोई भी सावधान इतिहासकार इस बात से मना नहीं कर सकता कि यूनानियों की उपलब्धियां विश्व के इतिहास में सबसे अधिक उल्लेखनीय हैं।'' **हेनरीमेन** के अनुसार, ''प्रकृति की शक्तियों को छोड़कर इस विश्व में कोई भी चेतन पदार्थ ऐसा नहीं है, जिसका उद्भव यूनान में न हुआ हो।'' **टॉयनबी** ने अपने विचार इस प्रकार व्यक्त किए हैं, ''संक्षेप में यूनानी सभ्यता का आधार व्यक्तिगत स्वतंत्रता, आशावादिता, धर्म निरपेक्षता एवं मानवता के आदर्शों में निहित है।''

स्पार्टा में बालकों को कई तरह के शारीरिक प्रशिक्षण देकर उनको अच्छा सैनिक बनाया जाता था। इसके अतिरिक्त ओलम्पिया में खेल-कूद प्रतियोगिताएं भी आयोजित की जाती थीं। इस प्रकार अन्त में निष्कर्ष के रूप में यदि कहा जाए कि यूनानी सभ्यता ने विश्व को चिरस्मरणीय देन दी है, तो कोई अतिश्योक्ति नहीं होगी और यूनान का नाम तब तक आदर के साथ लिया जाएगा। जब तक मानव सभ्यता मौजूद रहेगी।

6

प्राचीन रोम की सभ्यता

प्राचीन एवं आधुनिक सभ्यताओं के मध्य रोम ने एक सीढ़ी का काम किया है। यूनानी सभ्यता की तरह ही रोम की सभ्यता संस्कृति भी बहुत पुरानी है। पाश्चात्य देशों में यूनानी संस्कृति का अत्यधिक प्रसार रोम के कारण हुआ। एलिस व जौन के अनुसार रोमनों ने शासन की क्षमता से दुनिया को प्रभावित किया वही गीक्रों ने कला व साहित्य से विश्व पर अपनी छाप छोड़ी। सड़कों के द्वारा रोम ने अपने विशाल साम्राज्य को एक सूत्र में बांध दिया था क्योंकि यहां की सड़कें पूरे विश्व से जुड़ी थीं।

प्लेटो व जीन का मत है कि, ''रूमानिया में गड़रिये रोमन भाषा में बातचीत करते थे, मैसोपोटामिया में लैटिन व्यापारी रोमन मुद्रा में सामान की कीमत चुकाते थे। रोमन न्यायाधीशों द्वारा सुदूर इंग्लैण्ड में अपराधियों को सजा दी जाती थी।'' **एच. जी. वेल्स** ने लिखा है, ''यह नया रोमन साम्राज्य अपने पूर्व के सभी साम्राज्यों की तरह किसी महान विजेता की देन नहीं था, न सारगोन, न थुतमोस, न साइरस, न सिकन्दर ही इसका निर्माता नेता था। इसका निर्माण एक गणतंत्र द्वारा किया गया था, जिसका विकास मानवीय सम्बन्धों की क्रमिक संगठन शक्ति से आवश्यक विचारों की एकाग्रता से हुआ था।'' **बर्न्स** के अनुसार, "यह बहुत ही आकर्षक सत्य है कि संसार रोम का विस्तृत कर्जदार है।" इतिहासकार **नेवई** के शब्दों में, ''जैसे नदियां समुद्र में गिरती हैं, वैसे ही भूमध्यसागरीय प्रदेशों का इतिहास रोम के इतिहास में विलीन हो जाता है।''

रोम में न्याय और कानून का राज था। कृषि, शासन व्यवस्था, व्यापार, वाणिज्य, सैन्य संगठन आदि क्षेत्रों में रोम की देन सदा स्मरणीय रहेगी। रोमन संस्कृति ही यूरोप की सामाजिक व्यवस्था, भाषा एवं संगठन शक्ति का मूल स्रोत है। रोमन लोगों ने यूनानी सभ्यता एवं संस्कृति को अपनी जरूरत के अनुरूप बदलकर अपने समाज के प्रसार में उपयोग किया। **सेवाइन** के अनुसार, ''रोमन योग्यता और श्रम आवश्यक रूप से कृषि, कानून सरकार और युद्ध की ओर निर्देशित थी। रोमन सभ्यता निर्णायक रूप से पश्चिमी यूरोप की सर्वश्रेष्ठ सभ्यता का प्रतिनिधित्व करती है।''

रोम को सात पहाड़ी कहा जाता था क्योंकि करीब एक हजार ईसा पूर्व यह पहाड़ियों के बीच एक छोटा-सा गांव था और ये धीरे-धीरे एक देश बन गया साथ ही इसका साम्राज्य भी विशाल हो गया। जो आज इटली की राजधानी है।

इटली के तीन तरफ समुद्र है और उत्तर में यूरोप का सबसे ऊंचा पर्वत आल्पस है जो अन्य देशों से पृथक करता है। इटली की दो नदियां—पो एवं टाइबर आल्पस पर्वत के समीप से निकलती हैं। यहां अच्छे और उपजाऊ मैदान भी हैं और खनिज पदार्थों से भरपूर पहाड़ियां भी हैं। उस समय टाइबर नदी के मुहाने से 25 किलोमीटर ऊपर नदी के बायें तट पर रोम नाम का एक छोटा सा नगर बसा हुआ था। प्राचीन समय में भूमध्यसागर पर रोम का पूरा नियंत्रण था।

कतिपय विद्वानों ने इटली का स्वरूप एक टांग जैसा बतलाया है, जो भूमध्यसागर में फैली हुई है। **बर्न्स** का मत है,''आल्पस मध्य यूरोप के लोगों के प्रभाव के विरुद्ध कोई प्रभावशाली रुकावट नहीं डालता था और उनके स्थानों के नीचे किनारे सागर से आक्रमणकारियों को निमंत्रण देते थे। परिणामस्वरूप विदेशी आधिपत्य और रक्त का सम्मिश्रण स्वाभाविक हो गया। इसी वजह से इटली के लोग शुरू से ही सैनिक प्राप्तियों में लग गये क्योंकि उन्हें विदेशी आक्रमणों से अपनी रक्षा करना आवश्यक था। इटली के लोगों को एक कुशल सैनिक बनाने में वहाँ की भौगोलिक दशा भी सहायक रही। **सेवाइन** का मत है, ''हल्का तापमान अधिकांश स्थानों में वर्षा की बहुतायत और पर्याप्त धूप इसमें रहने की लालसा पैदा करता है और भूमध्यसागर के बीच में होने से अन्य देशों पर आधिपत्य स्थापित कर सका।''

रोम की स्थापना

ऐसा अनुमान लगाया जाता है कि आर्य जाति नामक शाखा ने 2000 ई.पू. इस पर अपना अधिकार कर लिया था। लेकिन नौवीं शताब्दी में मध्य एशिया की

एट्रस्कन नामक जाति शाखा ने आर्यों को हराकर उनसे रोम का राज्य छीन लिया। यह आर्यों की पहली पराजय थी। एट्रस्कन जाति ने रोम की सभ्यता के विकास और प्रसार में महत्त्वपूर्ण योग दिया। 800 ई. पू. के आसपास यूनानियों ने इटली में अपने उपनिवेशों की स्थापना की। यूनान ने इटली के सिसली द्वीप और सम्पूर्ण दक्षिणी इटली के तट पर अपना अधिकार जमा लिया। उस समय वह क्षेत्र 'वृहत्तर यूनान' के नाम से प्रसिद्ध हो गया और रोम का कोई विशेष महत्त्व नहीं था। 753 ई. पू. में रोम एक सैनिक चौकी और व्यापारिक केन्द्र मात्र था। रोम की स्थापना 753 ई. पू. में लैटिन लोगों ने की थी। कहा जाता है कि रोमुलस ने टाइबर नदी के किनारे पर रोम नामक नगर राज्य की स्थापना की थी।

रोम की स्थापना से कई जनश्रुतियां जुड़ी हुई हैं। पहली जनश्रुति में ऐसा वर्णन मिलता है कि लगभग 753 ई.पू. ताइबर नामक नदी में दो बच्चे (रोमुलस और रीमस) बहकर आ रहे थे। उनके रोने की आवाज को सुनकर मादा भेड़िया ने उन्हें बचा लिया फिर उनको किसान ने संरक्षण प्रदान किया। उन्हीं बालकों ने रोम नगर की नींव रखी। द्वितीय जनश्रुति, में ऐसा वर्णन है कि ये दोनों बालक युद्ध के देवता मार्स और प्रेम की देवी वीनस की संतान थे। इनका जन्म लैटिन कबीले के राजा के घर में पुत्र के रूप में हुआ था। इनके चाचा ने गद्दी हथियाने की नियत से उन्हें टाइबर नदी में बहा दिया। एक किसान ने उन्हें बचाया और पाला। युवा होने के बाद बालकों ने अपने चाचा की हत्या कर राज्य पर अधिकार कर लिया। रोम नगर के चारों तरफ दीवार बनवाते समय रोमुलस और रीमस में विवाद हो गया रोमुलस ने रीमस की हत्या कर खुद रोम का शासक बन गया। ऐसा माना जाता है कि रोमुलस ने अपने नाम पर रोम नगर की स्थापना की। इस नगर में कई पुल, सड़कें व भवन थे, जो सात छोटे पहाड़ों पर बसा था।

प्राचीनकाल में रोम पर एट्रस्कन जाति ने आधिपत्य स्थापित कर लिया जिसके बाद विशाल भवनों का निर्माण करवाया और अनेक नगरों की स्थापना की। इटलीवासियों को अस्त्र-शस्त्र से लेकर वर्णमाला युद्ध की कला एट्रस्कन जाति की देन थी। इस जाति के शासकों के अधीन रोम ने बहुत विकास किया। 500 ई. पू. में रोम के लैटिन आर्यों ने एट्रस्कन जाति को परास्त किया और रोम पर अपना अधिकार जमा लिया। इसके बाद विकास मार्ग पर रोम अग्रसर हो गया।

राजनीतिक स्थिति

यूनानियों ने इस देश का नाम इटली रखा। वे व्यापार के लिए यहां आए थे। इसका अर्थ है—वहां जाकर रहना। रोम इटली की राजधानी है। उसके राजनीतिक

इतिहास का अध्ययन सुविधा की दृष्टि से चार भागों में विभाजित किया जा सकता है जो निम्नलिखित हैं–

राजतंत्र काल (753 ई. पू.–509 ई. पू.)

जनश्रुतियों के शब्दों में रोम का पहला राजतंत्र शासक रोमुलस था इसके बाद छः और शासकों ने शासन किया। सातवां शासक या अन्तिम सम्राट टार्क्विन था। इस राजतंत्र काल में रोम में अनेक सड़कें, नहरें और पुल बने। रोमुलस ने 753 ई. पू. तक लगभग 37 वर्ष तक शासन किया। उसने पड़ौसी नगरों के दासों और अपराधियों को आश्रय दिया, जिसके कारण रोम की जनसंख्या में वृद्धि हुई। उसने रोमन लोगों को दो भागों में विभक्त कर दिया–पैट्रिशियन वर्ग एवं प्लेबियन वर्ग।

टार्क्विन एट्रस्कन जाति का पहला राजा था जिसने रोम को विकास की गति प्रदान की। इसके बाद सर्वियस टुलियस शासक बना जिसने रोम नगर की चारदीवारी बनवाई तथा कई मंदिरों का निर्माण करवाया। इस काल का अन्तिम राजा टार्क्विन था। वह बड़ा घमण्डी और अत्याचारी था। उसने जनता पर बहुत अत्याचार किए। इस पर रोमन जनता ने उसके विरुद्ध क्रान्ति की और 509 ई. पू. में उसे हटाकर गणतंत्र की स्थापना की। इस प्रकार रोम में राजतंत्र के स्थान पर गणतंत्र स्थापित हुआ। **स्वेन** का कहना है, इसके उपरान्त रोम में लगभग 500 वर्षों तक गणतंत्र बना रहा। इतिहासकार **वीच** ने लिखा है, "परम्परा इस बात का प्रमाण है कि असन्तुष्ट जनता क्रान्ति कर अपने राजा को निकाल देती थी। इस प्रकार स्पष्ट है कि रोम की जनता अयोग्य राजा को सिंहासन से हटाकर स्वस्थ परम्पराओं का पालन करती थी।"

राजतंत्रकाल में राजा राज्य का अध्यक्ष होता था। उसके अधिकारों की कोई सीमा नहीं थी। युद्ध के समय राजा सेना का नेतृत्व करता था। उसका पद वंशानुगत नहीं होता था। सीनेट सदस्यों के माध्यम से राजा जनता का नेतृत्व करता था राजा की मौत हो जाने के बाद सीनेट के सदस्य जिनकी संख्या 300 होती थी, वे अगले राजा का चुनाव करते थे। इस प्रकार प्राचीनतम रोमन सरकार का राजा जनता का प्रतिनिधि होता था। राजतंत्रकालीन समाज के दो वर्ग थे–पैट्रिशियन वर्ग एवं प्लेबियन वर्ग। पैट्रिशियन वर्ग में लैटिन लोग थे, जो रोम के ही वास्तविक निवासी थे। इस वर्ग में रोम के उच्च एवं कुलीन परिवार के व्यक्ति आते थे। इनको राज्य में उच्च पद दिया जाता था। इस वर्ग के लोगों को राजनीतिक अधिकार प्राप्त थे। दूसरा वर्ग प्लेबियनों का था, जिसमें स्वतंत्र दास, भूमिहीन और गरीब व्यक्ति आते थे, जिनको राजनीतिक अधिकार प्राप्त नहीं थे। अतः प्लेबियन वर्ग के संघर्ष को

देखते हुये 'कमीटिया सेचुरियेटा' नामक सभा का गठन किया गया जिसमें दोनों वर्ग शामिल थे।

इस दौरान रोम में सड़कों, नहरों व पुलों का बड़े पैमाने पर निर्माण किया गया। रोम के चारों तरफ एक दीवार का निर्माण करवाया गया। रोम में सुन्दर भवन और मंदिर बने। इन लोगों ने भवन निर्माणकला, मूर्तिकला, चित्रकला और भाषा आदि यूनानियों से सीखी थी। इस काल में रोम ने व्यापार के क्षेत्र में भी काफी उन्नति की। इसके फोनिशिया कार्थेज और मिस्र आदि देशों के साथ व्यापारिक सम्बन्ध थे। यूनान को लोहा और तांबा भेजा जाता था और यूनान से मिट्टी के बर्तन, कपड़ा और हथियार आदि रोम आते थे। इस युग में सम्पूर्ण लैटिन प्रदेश पर रोम ने अधिकार कर लिया था।

गणतंत्र काल (500 ई. पू.-133 ई. पू.)

स्वेन के अनुसार राजतंत्र की समाप्ति के पश्चात् रोम में 500 वर्षों तक गणतांत्रिक व्यवस्था रही। गणतंत्र की स्थापना के बाद रोम प्रगति की ओर अग्रसर होता रहा। **एम.आर. रे** ने लिखा है, "इसी समय से रोम का वास्तविक इतिहास आरम्भ होता है और यह बिना किसी अनुच्छेद के अपने स्वाभाविक मार्ग पर सदियों तक चलता रहा।"

पैट्रिशियन और प्लेबियन वर्ग में संघर्ष गणतंत्र शासन में वर्चस्व के लिए हुआ। सेवाइन ने लिखा है, "अपने राजनीतिक अस्तित्व के लगभग 500 वर्ष तक रोम एक प्रकार की गणतांत्रिक सरकार के अधीन था। यह सरकार प्लेबियन और पैट्रिशियन वर्ग के आधिपत्य के लिए संघर्ष का मन्द परिणाम थी।"

पैट्रिशियन और प्लेबियन का वर्ग संघर्ष

पैट्रिशियन और प्लेबियन के बीच संघर्ष के दो प्रमुख कारण थे—पहला कारण यह था कि पैट्रिशियन वर्ग के व्यक्ति ही राज्य में उच्च पदों पर नियुक्त हो सकते थे। उनको राजनीतिक अधिकार प्राप्त थे, परन्तु वे प्लेबियन वर्ग के लोगों पर अत्याचार करते थे। दूसरा कारण यह था कि प्लेबियन वर्ग के लोग साधारण वर्ग के थे। उनको राजनीतिक अधिकार प्राप्त नहीं थे साथ ही उन्हें राज्य में उच्च पद से वंचित रखा जाता था तथा उन्हें कर्ज देकर दास बना लिया जाता था। उनको किसी भी प्रकार की सामाजिक स्वतन्त्रता प्राप्त नहीं थी। पैट्रिशियन वर्ग पूर्णरूप से प्लेबियन लोगों पर आधारित था। रोम का व्यापार, कृषि, दस्तकारी और सैनिक शक्ति

सभी प्लेबियन वर्ग के लोगों के हाथ में थी। इस प्रकार प्लेबियन वर्ग के व्यक्ति ही पैट्रिशियन वर्ग का सारा काम करते थे।

पैट्रिशियन वर्ग के अत्याचारों से तंग होकर प्लेबियन वर्ग के लोगों ने अधिकारों की प्राप्ति के लिए संघर्ष प्रारम्भ कर दिया। प्लेबियनों ने बिना शस्त्र युद्ध के उनको धमकी द्वारा डराकर अपने अधिकारों को किश्तों पर प्राप्त कर लिया क्योंकि पैट्रिशियन वर्ग पूरी तरह से प्लेबियन वर्ग पर आधारित था। वे ही मेहनत करके रोम को मजबूती प्रदान करते थे। उनके चले जाने से रोम की स्थिति खराब हो जाती।

संघर्ष का प्रथम चरण (494 ई. पू.)—494 ई. पू. में प्लेबियन वर्ग ने रोम छोड़कर चले जाने की धमकी दी, जिसके फलस्वरूप उन्हें चार रियायतें प्राप्त हुईं।

1. उनके कर्जों को माफ कर दिया गया।
2. कर्जदार गुलामों को स्वतंत्र कर दिया गया।
3. एक ट्रिब्यून नामक संस्था स्थापित की गई जिसमें दो प्लेबियन अधिकारी नियुक्त किये गये। इन अधिकारियों को मजिस्ट्रेट और सीनेट के निर्णयों को रद्द करने का अधिकार था। कुछ समय बाद इनकी संख्या दो से बढ़कर दस कर दी गयी।
4. प्लेबियन के मुकदमों की सुनवाई के लिए ईडाइल नामक दो अधिकारी और नियुक्त किये गये।

इस प्रकार संघर्ष के प्रथम चरण में प्लेबियनों ने दासता से मुक्ति प्राप्त कर ली। उन्हें पैट्रिशियनों के किसी भी निर्णय को रद्द करने का अधिकार मिल गया था। उनके मुकदमों की सुनवाई के लिए अलग न्यायाधीश नियुक्त किये गये। ट्रिब्यून की नियुक्ति के बाद पैट्रिशियनों की निरंकुशता पर पूरा अंकुश लग गया। इतिहासकार वीच ने लिखा है, "ज्यों-ज्यों समय गुजरता गया, ट्रिब्यूनों ने वीटों का खुलकर प्रयोग किया और नगर के सम्पूर्ण जीवन पर आधिपत्य स्थापित कर लिया।"

द्वितीय चरण (471 ई. पू.)—इन दोनों वर्गों के बीच दूसरा संघर्ष 471 ई. पू. में शुरू हुआ जो 21 वर्ष तक चला। अंततः 449 ई. पू. में प्लेबियन वर्ग को दूसरी बार विजय प्राप्त हुई। प्लेबियनों की मांग पर 471 ई. पू. में एक काउंसिल को समस्त नागरिकों के लिए कानून बनाने का अधिकार था। इसकी स्वीकृति के बिना कोई भी नया विधेयक पारित नहीं हो सकता था। इस प्रकार प्लेबियनों ने रोम छोड़ने की धमकी देकर कानून जानने, कानून बनाने और मजिस्ट्रटों के विरुद्ध अपील करने का अधिकार प्राप्त कर लिया।

तृतीय चरण–प्लेबियन वर्ग व पैट्रिशियन वर्ग के बीच संघर्ष का तीसरा चरण लगभग 170 वर्ष तक चला, जिसके फलस्वरूप प्लेबियनों को निम्न पांच रियायतें प्राप्त हुईं–

445 ई.पू. में प्लेबियन और पैट्रिशियन वर्ग के आपसी विवाहों को कानूनी मान्यता प्रदान कर दी गई। 421 ई. पू. में उन्हें कोषाध्यक्ष चुनने का अधिकार प्राप्त हो गया। 376 ई. पू. में उनका एक सदस्य कौन्सिल के रूप में चुना जाने लगा। 355 ई. पू. में प्लेबियनों को मजिस्ट्रेट और अन्य पदों पर भी नियुक्त किया जाने लगा, जिससे उन्हें कानून के समक्ष समानता का अधिकार मिल गया। 289 ई. पू. में प्लेबियनों की सभा को राज्य की सर्वोच्च विधानसभा के रूप में मान्यता दे दी गयी, जिसके बनाये गये कानून सीनेट के विरोध करने पर भी देश के कानून बन जाते थे।

प्लेबियनों ने अपने अधिकार के लिए पैट्रिशियन वर्ग से संघर्ष किया। **वीच** ने लिखा है, "रोमन आरम्भ से अन्त तक कभी भी इस सिद्धांत से दूर नहीं जा सके कि जनता शासक नहीं, शासन करने के लिए होती है।"

गाल जातियों का आक्रमण–पैट्रिशियन वर्ग व प्लेबियन वर्ग के बीच संघर्ष का लाभ उठाकर गाल जाति ने रोम पर अधिकार कर लिया। ऐसे समय में रोमनों ने धन देकर गाल जाति को फ्रांस लौटने के लिए विवश कर दिया। इस घटना से रोम की प्रतिष्ठा को आघात पहुंचा। रोम ने अपनी खोई हुई प्रतिष्ठा को पुनः प्राप्त करने का प्रयास किया। इस उद्देश्य की पूर्ति के लिए एक सुदृढ़ सेना गठित की गयी और रोम की रक्षा के लिए चारों ओर एक मजबूत दीवार बनवाई गई। परिणामस्वरूप जब 348 ई. पू. में गाल जाति ने पुनः रोम पर आक्रमण किया, तो उसकी अपमानजनक हार हुई।

गणतंत्र की साम्राज्यवादी नीति–रोम में गणतंत्र की स्थापना के बाद यहां के शासकों में सम्राज्यवादी नीति अपनाकर सार्डीनिया और कोर्सिका पर आधिपत्य स्थापित कर लिया। रोम और इटली के दक्षिण में स्थित इपरिस नगर के बीच भी युद्ध हुआ। इस युद्ध में रोम ने काथेत की सहायता से इपरिस नगर के नेता परिहुस को युद्ध में हरा दिया। इस विजय के परिणामस्वरूप इटली के दक्षिण में न केवल यूनानी राज्य समाप्त हुए, वरन् दूर-दूर तक रोमन साम्राज्य फैल गया। उसके बाद रोम और कार्थेज के बीच 100 वर्षों तक युद्ध रुक-रुककर चलता रहा जो इतिहास में प्यूनिक युद्ध के नाम से जाना जाता है।

प्यूनिक युद्ध—कार्थेज का राज्य अफ्रीका के उत्तरी पूर्वी किनारे पर स्थित था। इस उपनिवेश को फोनेशिया के व्यापारियों ने बसाया था और इसे प्यूनिक उपनिवेश भी कहते थे। रोम के उत्कर्ष से सैकड़ों वर्ष पूर्व ही कार्थेज ने भू-मध्यसागर के तटों पर अपना व्यापारिक एकाधिकार स्थापित कर लिया था। आगे चलकर कार्थेज और रोम के बीच युद्ध प्रारम्भ हो गया। यह युद्ध प्यूनिक युद्ध के नाम से इतिहास में विख्यात है।

कारण—रोम और कार्थेज दोनों ही साम्राज्यवादी नीति पर थे इसलिये दोनों एक-दूसरे से युद्ध की आशंका करते थे क्योंकि रोम ने अपना साम्राज्य कार्थेज की सीमाओं तक विस्तृत कर लिया था। इसलिए कार्थेज, रोम के प्रति आशंकित हो गया। इसके अतिरिक्त रोम की साम्राज्यवादी नीति में कार्थेज जैसे स्वतंत्र राज्य के लिए कोई स्थान नहीं था। इस प्रकार साम्राज्य विस्तार की भावना के कारण युद्ध अवश्यम्भावी हो गया। इतिहासकार **वीच** ने लिखा है,"शक्ति विस्तार की भावना ने नये सम्पर्क जगाये। युवा सैनिक राज्य को अपने से पुराने सभ्य देशों से टक्कर लेनी पड़ी। दक्षिण इटली में यूनानी, सिसली और यूनान तथा समुद्र पार कार्थेज निवासियों से टक्कर लेनी अनिवार्य हो गई।"

कार्थेज व रोम दोनों के बीच व्यापार के प्रति होड़ लगी थी। दोनों ही देश पश्चिमी भूमध्यसागर पर आधिपत्य स्थापित करना चाहते थे। **सेवाइन** ने लिखा है, "रोम और कार्थेज के बीच एक भयंकर युद्ध अनिवार्य हो गया था। वे दोनों प्रतिद्वन्द्वी सभ्यताएं थीं, जिनमें से प्रत्येक की महत्त्वाकांक्षा थी कि पाश्चात्य भूमध्यसागर पर अपना आधिपत्य स्थापित करें।" रोम के उत्थान से पूर्व कार्थेज का सारे भूमध्यसागर पर व्यापारिक एकाधिकार था। यहां के निवासी भूमध्यसागर के माध्यम से स्पेन के सिसली, जिब्राल्टर, फ्रांस तथा अफ्रीका आदि देशों से व्यापार करते थे। कार्थेज के जहाज लाल ध्वज फहराते हुए हाथी दांत, सोना, टीन, ऊनी कपड़े, गर्म मसाले और श्रृंगार की वस्तुएं लेकर जिब्राल्टर तक जाते थे और वहां से आवश्यक सामान लेकर कार्थेज वापस आ जाते थे। इस समय कार्थेज ने स्पेन में अपना उपनिवेश राज्य बना लिया था, जो 'न्यू कार्थेज' कहलाता था।

सम्पूर्ण भू-मध्य सागर पर कार्थेज ने अधिकार कर लिया इसलिए उसे 'कार्थेज की झील' कहा जाता था। इस क्षेत्र में बिना उसकी अनुमति के कोई भी प्रवेश नहीं कर सकता था। उस समय कार्थेजवासी बड़े गर्व से कहा करते थे, "कोई भी रोमन बिना हमारी आज्ञा लिए भू-मध्यसागर में हाथ नहीं धो सकता था।" उधर रोम अपने व्यापारिक विकास के लिए भू-मध्यसागर पर अधिकार करना चाहता था, ताकि

कार्थेज के व्यापारिक एकाधिपत्य को समाप्त किया जा सके। रोम ने इस व्यापारिक अधिकार को समाप्त करने के लिए भू-मध्यसागर पर अधिकार करने का प्रयास किया, तो कार्थेज से उसका युद्ध अनिवार्य हो गया।

कार्थेज अपने समय का समृद्धिशाली और बहुत सम्पन्न नगर था। इसलिए कार्थेज व रोम एक दूसरे के प्रति ईर्ष्या की भावना रखते थे। यही कारण था कि इनका परस्पर संबंध अच्छा नहीं था। **एलिस व जौन** ने लिखा है, "शक्तिशाली और धनी कार्थेज और टाइबर नदी के तट पर बसे गरीब लेकिन महत्त्वाकांक्षी नगर के बीच ईर्ष्या थी।" इस समय तक कार्थेज की सभ्यता बहुत विकसित हो चुकी थी। सारे भूमध्यसागर पर उसका व्यापारिक एकाधिकार था। सैन्य दृष्टि से भी वह काफी सशक्त था। उसके पास एक प्रशिक्षित सेना तथा सुदृढ़ सामुद्रिक बेड़ा था। कार्थेज का साम्राज्य बड़ा और आर्थिक स्थिति से भी मजबूत था जिसको देखकर रोम ईर्ष्या करता था। इस प्रकार रोम कार्थेज की सम्पत्ति, व्यापार और उपनिवेशों से जलता था, तो दूसरी तरफ कार्थेजवासी रोम की गरीबी का मजाक उड़ाते थे और उसे हीन दृष्टि से देखते थे। इसके अलावा कार्थेज के सेनापति हैनीबाल की रोम के प्रति घृणा भी दोनों के बीच युद्ध की एक बड़ी कारण बनी।

रोम व कार्थेज दोनों सिसली पर अधिकार करना चाहते थे। यह दोनों देशों के बीच में स्थिति था इसलिए भी दोनों इस क्षेत्र पर अपना-अपना हक जताते थे। इस क्षेत्र पर इसलिए भी दोनों की नजर थी क्योंकि यहां की भूमि बहुत उपजाऊ थी। प्लेट व जीन ने लिखा है, "रोम और कार्थेज दोनों ही सिसली के उपजाऊ द्वीप पर जो इन दोनों के बीच में पड़ता था, अधिकार करना चाहते थे।" रोमन शासक ने अपने साम्राज्य के विस्तार के लिए टारेन्टुम नगर पर आक्रमण किया, तो सिसली के शासक परिहुस ने टारेन्टुम की सहायता के लिए रोम पर आक्रमण कर दिया। इस पर रोम ने कार्थेज की सहायता से परिहुस को युद्ध में निर्णायक रूप से पराजित किया और उसे इटली छोड़ने के लिये मजबूर कर दिया। इस युद्ध के बाद रोम ने दक्षिणी इटली में यूनानी प्रदेशों पर अधिकार कर लिया और कार्थेज ने सिसली के अधिकांश भाग पर अपना अधिकार जमा लिया। तब सिसली के राजा द्वारा भविष्यवाणी की गई कि आगे आने वाले समय में कार्थेज और रोम में युद्ध होगा उसका पूर्वानुमान सही निकला। जब कार्थेज ने सिसली पर अधिकार कर लिया, तो रोम को भावी आशंकाओं का भय सताने लगा। **एच.जी. वेल्स** ने लिखा है, "रोम आक्रमणकारी रक्षात्मक युद्ध में कूद पड़ा।"

रोम इस बात को लेकर आशंकित हो गया कि कार्थेज सिसली पर अधिकार करके उसके विकास मार्ग को रोक देगा साथ ही उसकी स्वतन्त्रता को नष्ट कर देगा। इस भय को समाप्त करने के लिए रोम युद्ध में कूद पड़ा। **एच. जी. वेल्स** ने लिखा है, "इस प्रकार अत्यधिक व्यर्थ और विनाशकारी युद्ध शृंखला का प्रारम्भ हुआ, जिसने मानव इतिहास को कलंकित एवं अंधकारपूर्ण बनाया।" जब कार्थेज ने सिसली पर अधिकार कर लिया तो उसके बाद रोम ने उसकी प्रगति को रोकने के लिए 264 ई. पू. में सिसली के मेसेना नामक नगर पर अधिकार कर लिया। इस घटना से कार्थेज और रोम के बीच युद्ध शुरु हो गया। यह युद्ध प्यूनिक युद्ध के नाम से जाना गया है।

युद्ध के चरण–264 ई. पू. से 146 ई. पू. तक रोम और कार्थेज के बीच तीन बार युद्ध हुआ। यह युद्ध रुक-रुककर 119 वर्ष तक चलता रहा, जिसमें धन और जन की अपार क्षति हुई। युद्ध के तीन चरण इस प्रकार हैं–

पहला चरण (264 ई. पू.–241 ई. पू.)–प्रथम प्यूनिक युद्ध 264 ई. पू. से 241 ई. पू. तक चला। कार्थेज एक नाविक शक्ति था। अतः उसके पास एक शक्तिशाली जहाजी बेड़ा था। रोम एक स्थल शक्ति था और उसके पास एक विशाल संगठित सेना थी। दोनों के बीच समुद्र था। अतः रोम ने एक शक्तिशाली जहाजी बेड़ा तैयार किया और 260 ई. पू. में माइली के जल युद्ध में कार्थेज को बुरी तरह पराजित किया। इस युद्ध में रोम कार्थेज के पचास युद्धपोत या तो बन्दी बना लिए या नष्ट कर दिए। रोम ने एकनोमस के जलयुद्ध में कार्थेज को दुबारा पराजित किया।

रोम द्वारा स्थल मार्ग से दो सेनाओं से आक्रमण करवाया गया। कार्थेज के सेनापति हेमिलकर ने इन सेनाओं से युद्ध किया। इस युद्ध में भी रोम की विजय हुई और उसने नगर में दस मील दूर स्थित प्यूनिक नगर पर अधिकार कर लिया। इससे कार्थेजवासी घबरा गये और अन्त में 241 ई. पू. में उन्होंने रोम से सन्धि कर ली। इस सन्धि में निम्नलिखित बातें निर्धारित की गईं।

1. कार्थेज ने युद्ध कर क्षतिपूर्ति के रूप में 3200 टेलेन्ट, जो 788,000 पौंड के बराबर थे, रोम को देना स्वीकार कर लिया।
2. कार्थेज ने सिसली का देश रोम को दे दिया। इसके अलावा सार्डीनिया तथा कोर्सिका पर भी रोम का अधिकार हो गया।

प्यूनिक के युद्ध में कार्थेज को पराजित कर रोम ने एक नया इतिहास रचा। इसके बाद उसने अपने साम्राज्य को बढ़ाया। सिसली पर अधिकार से उसका

इतिहास बदल गया। उसका अन्तर्राष्ट्रीय स्तर पर सम्मान भी बढ़ा। **जेकॉइस पिरोनी** का मत है, "इससे रोम की आर्थिक दशा दिनोंदिन सुधरती गई और यूनान के नगर राज्यों के कारण रोम अंतर्राष्ट्रीय व्यापार में अगुआ होने लगा। इसके अलावा रोम के लोगों को अपनी शक्ति पर आत्मविश्वास तथा जल सेना पर अभिमान बढ़ गया।" इस सन्धि का प्रभाव लम्बे अर्से तक रहा। दोनों देशों के बीच 20 वर्ष तक शान्ति रही। लेकिन कार्थेज को अपनी पराजय का मलाल था। वह अन्दर ही अन्दर इस अपमानजनक हार का बदला लेने की ताक में लगा था।

दूसरा चरण (218 ई. पू.-205 ई. पू)–प्रथम युद्ध में रोम को सफलता मिली उसने कार्थेज के तीन प्रदेश सिसली, सार्डीनिया और कोर्सिका पर अधिकार कर लिए थे। फिर भी कार्थेज की शक्ति लगातार बढ़ती गई। कार्थेज ने स्पेन में अपने नये साम्राज्य की स्थापना की। 229 ई. पू. में कार्थेज के सेनापति हेमिलकर की मृत्यु हो गई। इसके पश्चात् उसका पुत्र हैनीबाल कार्थेज का सेनानायक नियुक्त हुआ। उसे विश्व के योग्य सेनापतियों में स्थान प्राप्त है। हैनीबाल के नेतृत्व में ही कार्थेज ने दूसरा प्यूनिक युद्ध लड़ा था। उसने 218 ई. पू. में रोम के मित्र राज्य सुगुनटुम पर अधिकार कर लिया। इस पर रोम ने कार्थेज के विरुद्ध युद्ध घोषित कर दिया, जिससे द्वितीय प्यूनिक युद्ध आरम्भ हो गया। इस युद्ध के सन्दर्भ में **प्लेट व जीन** ने लिखा है, "दूसरे प्यूनिक युद्ध की कहानी हैनीबाल के जीवन चरित्र-सी है।"

हैनीबाल में राष्ट्रीयता की भावना कूट-कूट कर भरी थी। वह अपने पिता की पराजय का प्रतिशोध लेने पर आमादा था। अतः उसने बीस हजार सैनिकों और छः हजार घुड़सवारों के साथ इटली पर आक्रमण किया। 216 ई. पू. में कैनी नामक स्थान पर उसने रोम के सेनानायक सीपियो को बुरी तरह परास्त किया। रोग के लिए यह युद्ध बहुत ही हानिकारक साबित हुआ क्योंकि इसमें 70 हजार रोमन सैनिक मारे गये। तत्पश्चात् वह रोम नगर के सामने जा पहुंचा। हैनीबाल 15 वर्ष तक इटली में कत्लेआम मचाता रहा और उस पर अधिकार जमाये रहा। इस समय उसने रोमन सेनापतियों को पराजित किया था। हैनीबाल ने दो बार रोमनों को पराजित कर समस्त यूरोप को स्तंभित कर दिया। **एच. जी. वेल्स** ने लिखा है, "अगले 15 वर्ष का इतिहास प्रखर और विनाशकारी आक्रमणों का इतिहास है। हैनीबाल ने 15 वर्ष तक इटली को अपनी मुट्ठी में दबाए रखा। वह विजयी और अपराजित था। रोम के सेनापति उसके आगे न टिक सके और जहाँ कहीं भी उसके सामने आते, पराजित हो जाते।"

'न्यू कार्थेज' पर रोमन सेनापति कार्नेलियस ने अधिकार कर लिया और हैनीबाल की रसद का मार्ग काट दिया। उसका भाई हस्ड्रबाल सहायता लेकर आ रहा था कि रोमन सेना ने उसे मार डाला और हैनीबाल के शिविर में उसके भाई का कटा हुआ सिर भेज दिया। हैनीबाल को बड़ा क्रोध आया। उसने इटली में फिर मार-काट मचाई और रोम के अतिरिक्त सारी इटली को अपने अधीन कर लिया। तब 'स्पेन' पर रोमन सेनापति सीपियो अपने अधीन कर चुका था और उसने कार्थेज पर हमला कर दिया। कार्थेज के राजा ने हैनीबाल को वापस बुला लिया और 202 ई.पू. में कार्थेज के पास जामा नामक स्थान पर युद्ध हुआ। इस युद्ध में रोमन सेनापति सीपियो ने हैनीबाल को निर्णायक रूप से पराजित कर दिया। रोमन सैनिकों ने हैनीबाल का पीछा किया, परन्तु उसने अपनी अँगूठी में रखा जहर खा लिया जिससे उसकी मृत्यु हो गई।

इसके पश्चात् कार्थेज के शासक ने रोम के साथ एक अपमानजनक सन्धि पर हस्ताक्षर कर दिये। यह सन्धि 201 ई. पू. में हुई थी, जिसकी प्रमुख शर्तें निम्न थीं–

1. कार्थेज के जहाजों की संख्या घटाकर दस कर दी गई।
2. स्पेन रोम को दे दिया गया।
3. कार्थेज ने 50 वर्ष तक रोम को कर देने का वचन दिया।
4. कार्थेज ने युद्ध की क्षतिपूर्ति के लिए 10,000 टेलेन्ट (40,00,000 पौण्ड) रोम को देना स्वीकार कर लिया।
5. कार्थेज ने भविष्य में रोम की पूर्व स्वीकृति के बिना किसी भी देश से युद्ध न करना स्वीकार कर लिया।
6. कार्थेज ने रोम को भू-मध्यसागर का स्वामी स्वीकार किया।

इस प्रकार, इस सन्धि के द्वारा कार्थेज को पूर्णरूप से शक्तिहीन बना दिया गया। परन्तु कुछ समय पश्चात् कार्थेज फिर पनप गया और समृद्ध हो गया तो रोमनवासी कहने लगे, कार्थेज को नष्ट कर डालना चाहिए।

तृतीय चरण (149 ई. पू.–146 ई. पू.)–कार्थेज को दो बार रोम से पराजित होना पड़ा। रोम अब इस प्रयास में लगा था कि किसी तरह कार्थेज की शक्ति को पूर्णरूपेण नष्ट कर दिया जाए लेकिन उसने धीरे-धीरे पुनः अपनी स्थिति मजबूत कर ली। सन् 149 ई. पू. में कार्थेज ने अपने पड़ोसी न्यूमिडिया पर बिना रोम की स्वीकृति के आक्रमण कर दिया। इस पर रोम को बहाना मिल गया। उसने कार्थेज पर सन्धि की शर्तों के उल्लंघन का आरोप लगाते हुए उस पर आक्रमण कर दिया। लेकिन

कार्थेज किसी भी प्रकार का युद्ध नहीं चाहता था। वहां अकाल पड़ा हुआ था। अतः कार्थेज सन्धि करना चाहता था, परन्तु रोमन सेनापति सीपियो कार्थेज को मिटा देने पर तुला हुआ था। अतः कार्थेज ने वार्ता को भंग कर युद्ध की तैयारी प्रारम्भ कर दी। इस युद्ध में वहाँ की लड़कियों ने अच्छा सहयोग दिया। **एम. आर. रे** ने लिखा है, "इस समय कार्थेज के लोगों ने समस्त गुलामों को मुक्त कर दिया और प्रत्येक मनुष्य व बच्चे को सुरक्षा निर्मित शस्त्र में लगा दिया। रात-दिन काम चलता रहा और ऐसा कहा जाता है कि स्त्रियों ने इंजन के लिए रस्सियाँ बँटवाने के लिए अपने बाल कटवा दिए।" युद्ध फिर से प्रारम्भ हो गया तथा कार्थेज के लोगों ने देश की सुरक्षा के लिए सब कुछ बलिदान कर तीन वर्ष तक युद्ध किया। इस दौरान बड़े पैमाने पर जनसंहार हुआ। 5 लाख आबादी बाले कार्थेज में सिर्फ 50 हजार लोग ही जीवित बचे। उन्हें भी दास के रूप में जीवन व्यतीत करना पड़ा।

रोम की इस विजय का श्रेय सेनापति सीपियो को जाता है। उसने हत्या और लूटपाट के साथ-साथ सारे कार्थेज को रोमनों ने आग लगा दी और वहाँ एक भी मकान नहीं रहने दिया। इस प्रकार रोमनों ने कार्थेज का नामोनिशान मिटा दिया। **एच. जी. वेल्स** ने लिखा है, "सारे नगर को जला दिया गया और खण्डहरों के निशान मिटाने के लिए उन पर हल चला दिया गया और बड़ी गम्भीरता से श्राप खुदवा दिया गया कि जो कोई उसे पुनः बसाने की चेष्टा करेगा, उसका सर्वनाश होगा।

पराजय के कारण—कार्थेज व रोम के बीच प्यूनिक में हुए तीनों युद्ध कार्थेज के लिए बहुत ही घातक सिद्ध हुए। इनमें उसे हार के साथ-साथ अपार धन-जन की हानि झेलनी पड़ी। युद्धों में कार्थेज की पराजय इसलिए हुई क्योंकि कार्थेज की सरकार ने अपने विजित प्रदेशों में सुदृढ़ शासन प्रबन्ध स्थापित नहीं की। कार्थेज के सैनिक धन के लोभी थे और आक्रमण के समय धन लूटना अपना परम धर्म समझते थे। उनमें राष्ट्रीय भावना का पूर्ण रूप से अभाव था। कार्थेज की सरकार अपने सेनानायकों को उनकी सफलता पर इनाम और पदोन्नति देकर उत्साहित नहीं करती थी, इसके विपरीत असफलता प्राप्त होने पर सेनानायकों को मृत्युदण्ड देती थी। कार्थेज के व्यापारियों ने अपने सेनानायकों को किसी प्रकार का सहयोग नहीं दिया, क्योंकि वे सेनानायकों से द्वेषभाव रखते थे। शनैः-शनैः जनसाधारण में राष्ट्रीय भावना का लोप हो रहा था। कार्थेज के उपनिवेशों ने युद्ध में कार्थेज के प्रति सच्ची स्वामिभक्ति प्रदर्शित नहीं की।

प्यूनिक युद्धों के परिणाम—रोम ने कार्थेज को हराकर पूर्वी देशों में अपना विस्तार किया। इस संदर्भ में **मैकनेल बर्न्स** ने लिखा है, "कार्थेज युद्ध के तत्काल

प्रभाव स्पष्ट हो गये।" सर्वप्रथम इससे रोम का भू-मध्यसागर की सभी शक्तियों से संघर्ष शुरू हो गया और इस प्रकार विश्व आधिपत्य का मार्ग प्रशस्त हो गया। रोम ने पूर्वी देशों को विजय करने के लिए सेना भेजी। इसने यूनान, एशिया माइनर और मिस्र पर अधिकार कर लिया। अब रोम, इटली और यूरोप की ही नहीं, अपितु संसार की एक महानतम शक्ति बन गया। **वीच** ने लिखा है, रोम का आदेश भूमध्यसागर के एक सिरे से दूसरे सिरे तक हवा की तरह फैल जाता था। यह प्रश्न हल हो चुका था कि आने वाले युग में कौन भू-मध्यसागर का स्वामी होगा।

द्वितीय प्यूनिक युद्ध के समय रोम ने पश्चिम में स्पेन पर अधिकार कर लिया था। जूलियस सीजर द्वारा 58 ई.पू. फ्रांस और ब्रिटेन पर अपना अधिकार कर लिया। इस प्रकार ईस्वी सन् के प्रारम्भ में रोम एक विशाल साम्राज्य का स्वामी बन गया। **पं. जवाहरलाल नेहरू** ने लिखा है, "कार्थेज की अन्तिम पराजय व उसके विनाश के उपरान्त रोम पश्चिमी दुनिया में बिना किसी प्रतिद्वन्द्वी के सर्वोच्च हो गया।" **सेवाइन** ने लिखा है, "तीसरे प्यूनिक युद्ध में कार्थेज को नष्ट कर दिया गया और रोम पश्चिम की सबसे महान शक्ति हो गया। रोमन साम्राज्य ने विस्तार की पराकाष्ठा इसी युग में प्राप्त की और 113 ई. में वह सबसे बड़ा राज्य था।"

प्यूनिक युद्धों से रोम की सीमा बढ़ गई। इसका साम्राज्य यूरोप में भी फैल गया। रोम ने सिसली, कोर्सिका, स्पेन, सार्डीनिया और उत्तरी अफ्रीका पर विजय प्राप्त की, जिसके कारण वह एक विशाल साम्राज्य का स्वामी बन गया। इसके बाद रोम एक साम्राज्यवादी देश बन गया। इस युद्ध ने अफ्रीका के सबसे बड़े साम्राज्य कार्थेज का अस्तित्व मिटा दिया। कार्थेज पर रोम का अधिकार हो गया। अब भू-मध्यसागर को कार्थेज के स्थान पर 'रोमन झील' कहा जाने लगा।

कार्थेज को नष्ट करने के पश्चात् रोम का संपर्क यूनान की सभ्यता से हुआ। उसने यूनानी सभ्यता की कई विशेषताएँ ग्रहण कीं। प्रथम प्यूनिक युद्ध के बाद रोमनों ने सिसली में संगमरमर से निर्मित यूनानी मन्दिर व मूर्तियाँ देखीं, तो वे यूनानियों की कला से प्रभावित हुए बिना नहीं रह सके। द्वितीय प्यूनिक युद्ध के बाद रोमन यूनानी मूर्तियों को रोम ले आए। फिर उनकी रुचि यूनानी साहित्य के प्रति बढ़ी जिसके कारण उन्होंने उसकी संस्कृति को खुद अपनाया साथ ही यूरोपीय देशों में इसका प्रचार-प्रसार किया।

व्यापार की दृष्टि से प्यूनिक युद्ध लाभकारी साबित हुआ क्योंकि इससे व्यापार के विकास में काफी सहायता मिली। रोम के वैभव में दिन-प्रतिदिन वृद्धि होती गई। अब रोम एक सम्पन्न तथा समृद्धिशाली विशाल साम्राज्य के रूप में परिणित हो

गया। रोमन साम्राज्य का अत्यधिक विस्तार हो गया था, जिसका नतीजा यह हुआ कि दूरस्थ प्रदेश के सदस्यों को एसेम्बली में शामिल होना बन्द हो गया। अतः सीनेट में रिश्वतखोरी और भ्रष्टाचार में निरन्तर वृद्धि होती रही। फलस्वरूप सीनेट सदस्य बड़ी-बड़ी जागीरों के स्वामी बन गये। इसके साथ गणतन्त्रीय शासन प्रणाली भंग होने लगी। इस समय सीनेट व रोम में गृहयुद्ध आरम्भ हो गया, जिसमें जनता को सैनिकों का सहयोग प्राप्त हो गया। रोमन जनता ने 82 ई. पू. में सुल्ला को रोम का शासक बना दिया। अब शासक जनता पर निरंकुश रूप से शासन करने लगे। इसका परिणाम यह हुआ कि रोम प्रजातन्त्र के स्थान पर एकतन्त्रात्मक शासन-व्यवस्था की ओर अग्रसर होने लगा।

युद्ध के चलते किसानों की हालत इतनी दयनीय हो गई कि उन्हें रोजी रोटी के लाले पड़ गए। वे सेना में भर्ती होकर युद्ध करने के लिए विवश हो गए। परन्तु उन्हें सीनेटर लूट का माल नहीं देते थे। इसके अतिरिक्त कृषक सैनिक की अनुपस्थिति में लगान न देने के कारण जमींदार उनकी भूमि पर अधिकार कर लेते थे। इससे कृषक वर्ग शासकों से पूर्णरूप से असन्तुष्ट हो गया था। रोमन शासक युद्ध में बन्दी बनाये गये लोगों को दास बना लेते थे। यहाँ के सामाजिक जीवन का आधार दास-प्रथा थी। रोम में दासों का जीवन बड़ा दयनीय और कठोर था। उन्हें एक-दूसरे के साथ जंजीरों में बाँधकर खेतों में काम करवाया जाता था। दासों को गरम लोहे से दागा जाता था जिससे कि उनकी पहचान की जा सके। रात्रि को उन्हें तहखानों में ठूँस दिया जाता था। यदि कोई दास अपने स्वामी की आज्ञा नहीं मानता था, तो उसे रोमन दर्शकों के मनोरंजन के लिए भूखे शेर से लड़ने के लिए विवश किया जाता था। दासों को सिर्फ इतना भोजन दिया जाता था कि वे जीवित रह सकें। दासों की संख्या बढ़ जाने से नौकरी की समस्या हो गई। एक छोटी-सी नौकरी के लिए लोगों की लाइन लग जाती थी।

सिसली सरकार ने अपनी दासता से मुक्ति पाने के लिये 100 ई.पू. विद्रोह कर दिया लेकिन जब इस विद्रोह का दमन कर दिया गया तो दासों ने अपनी तलवारें आपस में एक-दूसरे को भोंक दीं ताकि उन्हें भूखे शेरों से लड़ने के लिए बाध्य नहीं होना पड़े। दास विद्रोह तो समाप्त हो गया, किन्तु गृहयुद्ध के लिए रंगमंच सज गया। ऐसी स्थिति में दासों की दशा में सुधार के लिए प्रयास किये गये। प्लेट व जीन ने लिखा है, "दासत्व-प्रथा ने गणराज्य को निर्बल कर दिया।"

गृहयुद्ध के दौरान टाइबेरियस ने प्लेबियनों की मदद की। वह कहता था, वन्य

लड़ते-मरते हैं, उनके उपभोग के लिए केवल वायु और प्रकाश ही है। तुमको विश्व का स्वामी कहा जाता है, पर तुम्हारे पास एक फुट जमीन भी ऐसी नहीं, जिसे तुम अपनी कह सको। टाइबेरियस ने दासों को उनके अधिकारों के प्रति सचेत किया जिसके कारण रोम में गृहयुद्ध प्रारम्भ हो गया। टाइबेरियस और उसके साथियों को मौत के घाट उतार दिया और उन्हें टाइबर नदी में फेंक दिया गया। अब रोम की सत्ता दो अधिनायकों के हाथों में आ गयी, जिनमें पहला एक धनी प्लेबियन मारियस था और दूसरा कुलीन वर्ग का सुल्ला था।

प्रशासन व्यवस्था

रोम में गणतन्त्रात्मक शासन व्यवस्था का प्रसार था। सीनेट के हाथों में ही केंद्रित राज्य की वास्तविक शक्ति का चुनाव जनता द्वारा किया जाता था। सीनेट के सदस्यों की संख्या 300 थी, परन्तु ये सब सदस्य पैट्रिशियन वर्ग के होते थे। कोई भी कानून सीनेट की स्वीकृति के बिना पारित नहीं किया जा सकता था। वही उच्च अधिकारियों की नियुक्ति करती थी। सीनेट की अनुमति के बिना युद्ध और शान्ति समझौते नहीं किए जा सकते थे। सीनेट के सदस्य पैट्रिशियन वर्ग के होने के कारण प्लेबियन वर्ग के लोगों की ओर कोई ध्यान नहीं देते थे जिसके कारण दोनों में संघर्ष चलता रहता था।

इसमें राजा की जगह दो न्यायाधीश नियुक्त किए जाते थे जिन्हें काउंसिल कहते थे। इनकी नियुक्ति एक वर्ष के लिए की जाती थी। वे मुख्य न्यायाधीश, सेनापति तथा प्रशासक थे। सीनेट के द्वारा ही इनका चुनाव किया जाता था। दो की नियुक्ति इसलिए की जाती थी, ताकि वे एक-दूसरे पर अंकुश रखें और निरंकुश न बन सकें। संकट के समय काउंसिल को हटाकर छः महीने के लिए एक अधिनायक नियुक्त किया जा सकता था। वह स्वतंत्र रूप से अपने अधिकारों का पालन करता था।

क्वेस्टर्स नामक वित्त अधिकारी काउंसिल की सहायता करता था। इसके अतिरिक्त प्रशासन में सहायता देने के लिए तीन पदाधिकारी और होते थे—सेन्सर्स (कर वसूल करने वाला अधिकारी), एल्डीज (शान्ति व्यवस्था बनाए रखने वाला) और प्रोटोर (न्यायाधीश)। ये एक वर्ष के लिए नियुक्त लिए जाते थे। प्रान्तों के शासन-प्रबन्ध का संचालन करने के लिए गवर्नर नियुक्त किए जाते थे। ये भी एक वर्ष के लिए नियुक्त किए जाते थे। गवर्नरों को वेतन न मिलने के कारण वे जनता से मनमाना धन वसूल करते थे। कानून का गठन सीनेट तथा एसेम्बली नामक दो

संस्थाओं द्वारा किया जाता था। सीनेट के सभी सदस्य पैट्रिशियन वर्ग के व्यक्ति होते थे। दूसरा सदन असेम्बली था, जिसके सदस्य प्लेबियन होते थे। असेम्बली को यह अधिकार नहीं था कि वह सीनेट द्वारा पारित कानून को अस्वीकार कर सके।

आर्थिक दशा

रोम में उद्योगों का सन्तोषजनक विकास नहीं हो सका था इसलिए वहां की अर्थव्यवस्था प्रमुख रूप से कृषि व पशुपालन पर ही आधारित थी। गेहूँ, जौ, बाजरा, अंगूर, जैतून, सेव आदि मुख्य फसलें थीं।

सामाजिक दशा

रोम में सामाजिक जीवन का मूल आधार परिवार ही था। परिवार संयुक्त होते थे। परिवार के सदस्यों को मुखिया की आज्ञा का पालन करना पड़ता था। समाज में स्त्रियों की स्थिति सम्मानपूर्ण थी। वे सार्वजनिक उत्सवों में भाग लेती थीं। उपेक्षित होने के कारण दासों की हालत बहुत ही चिन्ताजनक थी।

साहित्य

रोम में साहित्य के क्षेत्र में यूनानियों की परम्परा को आगे बढ़ाया गया। वहां व्यक्तिगत रूप से इस दिशा में कोई उल्लेखनीय कार्य नहीं किया गया। प्रसिद्ध यूनानी कवि होमर की रचनाएँ इलियड तथा ओडेसी का लैटिन भाषा में अनुवाद किया गया। प्रसिद्ध रोमन कवि कैटुलस ने यूनानी कवियों की शैली को आधार बनाकर कई कविताएँ लिखीं। यथार्थवादी एवं सुंदर कविताओं की रचना ल्यूक्रैशियस द्वारा की गई थी। उसने अपनी कविताओं में मानव सभ्यता के क्रमिक विकास की विवेचना की है। विख्यात रोमन नाटककार टिरेन्स तथा प्लोट्स ने सुखान्त नाटक लिखे जो यूनानी नाटकों पर आधारित थे, किन्तु इन नाटकों को अनुपम नहीं माना जा सकता। रोम के प्रसिद्ध गद्य लेखक सिसरो ने कई निबन्धों की रचना की।

धार्मिक जीवन

प्रो. डेविस के अनुसार, "रोम के निवासी प्रकृति के देवताओं की अपेक्षा आत्माओं की उपासना में अधिक विश्वास करते थे।" आत्माओं की उपासना में रोमनों की विशेष आस्था थी। यूनानी संस्कृति के प्रभाव के परिणामस्वरूप रोमन जूपिटर (देवाधिदेव), मार्स (युद्ध का देवता) और वीनस (प्रेम की देवी) आदि देवी-देवताओं में भी आस्था रखने लगे। धार्मिक विचारधारा ही रोम की शासन व्यवस्था की प्रमुख

आधार थी। रोम में धार्मिक त्यौहारों पर सार्वजनिक अवकाश रहता था। धार्मिक कार्य पुरोहितों द्वारा करवाये जाते थे। रोमन लोगों ने मिस्र की प्रमुख देवी 'आइसिस' की भी उपासना आरंभ कर दी थी। रोमन लोग अन्धविश्वासी भी थे।

दर्शन

रोम के दर्शन में कई त्रुटियाँ पायीं जाती हैं। उदाहरणस्वरूप; यूनानी दार्शनिक इपिक्यूरस ने जीवन का प्रमुख उद्देश्य सुख प्राप्ति बताया था। यह सिद्धांत रोमनों के समझ के बाहर था और उन्होंने सुख का अर्थ सांसारिक सुखों से लगाया और वे भोग-विलास में डूब गये। तर्कों पर भी रोमनों द्वारा अधिक बल दिया जाता था।

कला

रोमनों में कला के क्षेत्र में विशेष योगदान किया था जिसके लिये उसे याद किया जा सके। स्थापत्यकला में उन्होंने यूनानी शैली को तथा चित्रकला के क्षेत्र में मिस्र की शैली को आधार बनाया। मूर्तिकला के क्षेत्र में उनकी देन कुछ उल्लेखनीय रही है। रोमन मूर्तियाँ सजीव लगती हैं तथा उनमें यथार्थता भी दृष्टिगोचर होती है।

सैनिक अधिनायकों का युग (133 ई.पू.-27 ई. पू.)

रोम में 133 ई. पू. में दासों की हालत इतनी चिन्ताजनक हो गई थी कि सैन्य अधिनायकों को शासन व्यवस्था अपने हाथ में लेनी पड़ी। इन्होंने अत्याचारियों को टाइबर नदी में फेंक दिया। रोम में 133 ई. पू. से लेकर 27 ई. पू. तक पाँच अधिनायकों ने शासन किया। इन पांचों अधिनायकों के बारे में संक्षिप्त जानकारी निम्न प्रकार दी गई है–

टाइबेरियस–133 ई.पू. में टाइबेरियस पहला ट्रिब्यून चुना गया। उसने भूमि की अधिकतम सीमा 500 जोगेरा (666 एकड़) रखी और जिन अमीरों के पास इससे अधिक भूमि थी, वह छीन ली गई और भूमिहीन किसानों में बाँट दी गई। टाइबेरियस के इस निर्णय का सीनेटरों ने विरोध किया और उन्होंने 130 ई. पू. में टाइबेरियस की हत्या करवा दी। टाइबेरियस की मृत्यु के बाद उसका छोटा भाई कायस ग्रेकस रोम का अधिनायक चुना गया। वह भी अपने भ्राता की भाँति सुधारवादी था। उसने सत्ता संभालने के बाद सुधार कार्य के प्रति विशेष ध्यान दिया। उसने गरीबों को अनुदान और बाजार में सस्ता अनाज दिलवाने का प्रबन्ध किया। इस कमी की पूर्ति के लिए उसने एशियाई भागों के करों में वृद्धि की। सीनेटरों ने अगले चुनाव में कायस

ग्रेकस को हरा दिया। जब जनता ने उसे दुबारा अधिनायक बनाने के लिए आन्दोलन शुरू किया, तो 121 ई. पू. में सीनेटरों ने उसके 3000 साथियों सहित उसकी हत्या करवा दी। टाइबेरियस और कायस ग्रेकस के सुधारकों को संयुक्त रूप से ग्रेकस सुधारों की संज्ञा दी गई है। हालाँकि दोनों भाइयों का अन्त दुःखान्त रहा, परन्तु मजदूर व कृषकों के लिए सुधार कार्यों ने रोम के इतिहास में उन्हें अमर बना दिया।

मारियस–इसके अन्दर एक खास बात यह थी कि यह एक कुशल सेनापति था। इसकी वीरता का उदाहरण प्यूनिक युद्ध हैं। उसने छः वर्ष तक कौन्सिल का काम किया। इसके समय में दासों ने विद्रोह किया और रोम में गृहयुद्ध प्रारम्भ हो गया। इसने दोनों विद्रोहों का दमन कर सम्पूर्ण इटली के नागरिकों को रोम की नागरिकता प्रदान की। मारियस ने एक ऐसी सेना बनाई, जो रोम के प्रति निष्ठावान न होकर सिर्फ उसके प्रति निष्ठावान थी।

सुल्ला–सुल्ला को सीनेट का तथा मारियस को असेम्बली का समर्थन प्राप्त था। इसी समय एशिया माइनर में एक विद्रोह हो गया, तो सीनेट ने इस विद्रोह को दबाने के लिए सुल्ला को और एसेम्बली ने मारियस को नियुक्त किया। इसी प्रश्न पर दोनों में घमासान लड़ाई छिड़ गई, जिसमें सुल्ला को सफलता मिली। इसके बाद सुल्ला विद्रोह को दबाने एशिया माइनर चला गया। सुल्ला की अनुपस्थिति में मारियस ने उसके कई समर्थकों को मार डाला। सुल्ला चार वर्ष बाद वापस लौटा। तब उसने मारियस समर्थकों की हजारों की संख्या में हत्या करवा दी और उनकी सम्पत्ति को अपने अधिकार में कर लिया। इस प्रकार मारियस को हटाकर भ्रष्ट सुल्ला सीनेट की मदद से अधिनायक बन गया।

सीनेट–सीनेट मारियस विरोधी होने के कारण उसे कौंसिल के पद से हटाना चाहती थी। ऐसे समय में 82 ई. पू. में सुल्ला ने सीनेट व पोम्पी के सहयोग से मारियस को हटा दिया और रोम का अधिनायक बन गया। सुल्ला ने 82 ई. पू. से 78 तक रोम पर शासन किया। उसने सीनेट के अधिकारों में वृद्धि की। इतिहासकार **सरदेसाई** ने इस संदर्भ में लिखा है कि, "निरंकुश सीनेट ने धीरे-धीरे प्रजातंत्रीय रूप छोड़ दिया।" सुल्ला की मृत्यु लगभग 70 ई. पू. में हो गयी।

पोम्पी–सुल्ला के बाद पोम्पी रोम का अधिनायक बन गया। पोम्पी, सुल्ला का सेनापति था। उसने 40 दिन में भूमध्यसागर में डाकुओं का दमन कर शान्ति व्यवस्था स्थापित की थी। उसने 70 ई. पू. से 48 ई. पू. तक रोम पर शासन किया। उसने 63 ई. पू. में यरुसलम को एक प्रान्त बनाया तथा बिथिनिया, सिलसिआ और सीरिया आदि प्रदेशों को जीत लिया।

सीनेट द्वारा पोम्पी पर 62 ई.पू. रोम वापस लौटने पर उस पर आरोप लगाए, तो उसने जूलियस सीजर से सहायता ली। आगे चलकर पोम्पी और सीजर में आंतरिक मनमुटाव पैदा हो गए। अतः 48 ई. पू. में सीजर ने थैसले के युद्ध में पोम्पी को हरा दिया। वह मिस्र भाग गया, जहाँ मिस्र के सैनिकों ने उसकी हत्या कर दी।

जूलियस सीजर—इसका जन्म 90 ई. पू. में एक कुलीन परिवार में हुआ था। वह एक अच्छा योद्धा व महत्त्वाकांक्षी युवक था। मारियस की पत्नी उसकी मौसी थी और उसने जनतांत्रिक नेता की पुत्री से विवाह कर लिया था। उसने पोम्पी से अपनी पुत्री का विवाह कर दिया था। जिसका लाभ उसने राजनीति को सुरक्षित बनाने में उठाया साथ ही साथ उसने अपने को लोकप्रिय बनाने के लिये वह कर्ज लेकर बड़ी-बड़ी दावतें दिया करता था। वह बचपन से ही बड़ा महत्त्वाकांक्षी था। एक दिन युवक जूलियस सीजर सिकन्दर महान की जीवनी पढ़ते-पढ़ते रोने लग गया। जब मित्रों ने इसका कारण पूछा, तो उसने उत्तर दिया, "क्या यह मेरे लिए आँसू बहाने की बात नहीं है? मेरी आयु में सिकन्दर महान ने कितने ही राष्ट्रों को जीत लिया था। मैंने अब तक क्या किया है?" **एच. जी. वेल्स** ने लिखा है, "व्यक्तिगत रूप से जूलियस सीजर एक चकाचौंध करनेवाला सितारा था, ऐसा मानव जाति के इतिहास में कभी नहीं हुआ।"

ई. पू. 59 में रोम की शासन व्यवस्था चलाने के लिये 'त्रिगुट' बना जिसके सदस्य पोम्पी, क्रेसस, जूलियस सीजर थे। पोम्पी में एक कुशल सेनानायक के सभी गुण विद्यमान थे, क्रेसस पूँजीपति था और सीजर कुशल राजनीतिज्ञ, विद्वान, लेखक, कुशल शासक तथा योग्य वक्ता था। इन तीनों राजनीतिज्ञों ने शासन का विभाजन कर लिया। पोम्पी को रोम का शासक बनाया गया। सीजर को गाल पर और क्रेसस को फारस पर अधिकार करने के लिए भेजा गया। 53 ई. पू. में फारस में ही क्रेसस की इहलीला समाप्त हो गई।

58 ई. पू. में सीजर गाल का गवर्नर बना और आठ वर्ष तक वहाँ युद्ध करके समस्त गाल (फ्रान्स) पर अधिकार कर उसे रोमन साम्राज्य में मिला लिया। इसके पश्चात् सीजर ने जर्मनी, फ्रान्स और स्पेन पर अधिकार कर लिया। चार वर्ष बाद उसने इंग्लैण्ड को जीतकर रोम का एक प्रान्त बना दिया। गाल लोगों ने स्वतन्त्रता प्राप्ति के लिए विद्रोह किया परन्तु सीजर ने इस आन्दोलन को सफल नहीं होने दिया। गाल विजय से सीजर को बहुत धन-सम्पत्ति प्राप्त हुई। गाल प्रदेश में रहकर उसने अपनी एक निजी सेना बनाई सीजर ने फ्रांस अथवा गाल प्रदेश में 'गाल युद्धों' पर टिप्पणी नामक पुस्तक में अपनी सैन्यशक्ति की सफलता के बारे में लिखा जिसमें

रोम निवासियों को बताया गया कि जूलियस सीजर ही इस समस्त संसार का महान सेनापति क्यों है। यह पुस्तक ने सीजर की लोकप्रियता बढ़ाने में सहायक साबित हुई। परन्तु पोम्पी और सीनेट दोनों ही उससे नाराज हो गए, क्योंकि पोम्पी तो रोम का वास्तविक शासक बनना चाहता था और सीनेट यह नहीं चाहती थी कि कोई सेनापति अधिक लोकप्रिय बने।

पोम्पी ने सीनेट की राय से सीजर को आदेश दिया कि वह अपनी विशाल सेना को भंग करके अकेला रोम लौट आए। सीजर आदेश की अवहेलना करते हुए सेनासहित रोम लौटा और उसने कहा—"पासा फेंका जा चुका है।" (दी डाई इज कास्ट) सीजर ने रोम पर आक्रमण कर दिया और 48 ई. पू. में थैसले के युद्ध में पोम्पी को पराजित कर रोम का अधिनायक बन गया। पोम्पी मिस्र की ओर भाग गया। वहाँ उसने रानी क्लियोपेट्रा से शादी कर ली, परन्तु सीजर के समर्थकों ने उसकी हत्या कर दी। यही नहीं, सीजर के सैनिकों ने मिस्र पर भी अधिकार कर लिया। उसी दौरान मिस्र की रानी क्लियोपेट्रा के प्यार में सीजर फंस चुका था। अतः वे दोनों एक वर्ष तक मिस्र में एक साथ रहे थे। इस समय एशिया माइनर में विद्रोह हुआ। उसको सीजर ने बिना किसी कठिनाई के दबा दिया। इसके बाद उसने सीनेट को अपनी रिपोर्ट भेजी, जिसमें लिखा था "मैं आया, मैंने देखा और मैंने जीत लिया।" इसके बाद सीजर ने स्पेन के विद्रोह को दबाने में सफलता प्राप्त की।

सीजर ने रोम की सारी सत्ता का अधिनायक बन जाने के बाद पूरे रोम पर कब्जा कर लिया और जीवन पर्यन्त उस पर राज्य किया। बाउल के अनुसार "जूलियस सीजर की सादगी अन्य सेनानायकों को युद्ध करके राजनीतिक सत्ता हथियाने का आदर्श बन गयी।" सीजर ने सीनेट में अपने समर्थकों को भरकर उसे एक शक्तिहीन संस्था बना दिया। उसने अपने समर्थकों को उप-कौंसिल नियुक्त किया और ट्रिब्यून के अधिकारों में कमी कर दी। अब सीजर के लिए किसी भी देश के साथ युद्ध और शांति समझौता करने के लिए सीनेट की अनुमति लेना आवश्यक नहीं था। वह चाहे तो आजीवन काउंसिल के पद पर बना रह सकता था। सीजर को 'देश का पिता' की उपाधि से सुशोभित किया गया। उसने अपने नाम के सिक्के भी जारी किया।

सीजर एक योद्धा और सुधारक था। वह अपने गंजे सिर पर लौरेल के पत्तों की माला धारण करता था। **प्लेट व जीन** के अनुसार, "सीजर से प्राचीन यूनान के निरंकुश शासकों की याद आती है। उन्हीं की तरह अवैध तरीके से उसने सत्ता प्राप्त की और उन्हीं की तरह स्थिति को सुधारने का भी यत्न किया। सीजर रोम का

पुनर्निर्माण करना चाहता था जो शान्ति, समृद्धि तथा सुरक्षा का जगत होगा और उस एक रोमन जगत की बागडोर थामे उसका संचालक होगा जूलियस सीजर।

सीजर के सुधार—सीजर ने अनेक सुधार भी किए, जिनका उल्लेख नीचे की पंक्तियों में किया गया है—

1. उसने रोम को सुन्दर और आकर्षक बनवाने के लिए एक योजना तैयार की।
2. उसने सरकार द्वारा दिए जाने वाले ऋण की राशि पर ब्याज की दर घटा दी।
3. राजकीय कोष में वृद्धि करने के लिए अधीन राजाओं को भेंट देने के लिए मजबूर किया।
4. उसने देश का व्यापार बढ़ाने के लिए भी कई प्रयास किए। विदेशों से आने वाले माल पर आयात कर लगा दिया। उसने रोम में एक नवीन बन्दरगाह बनवाई।
5. उसने बेरोजगार और भूमिहीन लोगों को अन्य प्रान्तों में भूमि दे दी।
6. वह अपने शत्रुओं के प्रति उदार व्यवहार करते हुए उन्हें क्षमा कर देता था और उन्हें अपने दरबार में सरकारी पदों पर नियुक्त कर वफादार सेवकों में परिणित कर लेता था।
7. प्रान्तीय लोगों को पराजय भुलाने के लिए उन्हें रोम की नागरिकता प्रदान कर देता था।
8. सीजर ने रोम की बढ़ती हुई जनसंख्या को बसाने के लिए टाइबर नदी की धारा को बदल दिया। इससे रोमवासियों को बसने के लिए भूमि उपलब्ध हो गई।
9. उसने राज्य की जनगणना करवाई तथा रोम के आसपास कई बस्तियाँ बसाईं।
10. देश की बेरोजगारी को दूर करने तथा मध्यम वर्ग को रोजगार दिलाने के लिए गुलामों की संख्या निर्धारित की।
11. उसने धार्मिक सहिष्णुता की नीति अपनायी ताकि सभी देश उसे अपना शासक मान सकें।
12. नगरों में म्युनिसिपल से कर वसूली का अधिकार छीन लिया गया।
13. सरकारी अधिकारियों को एशिया के रोमन प्रान्तों से कर वसूली का अधिकार दिया गया।
14. उसने अपनी सेना में सभी क्षेत्रों के व्यक्ति भर्ती किए।
15. रोम के अधीन प्रान्तों को नागरिकता के अधिकार प्रदान किए और उन्हें मताधिकार भी दिया गया।

16. उसने जूलियस सीजर पंचांग प्रारंभ किया।
17. उसने कई स्थानों पर रोमन उपनिवेश स्थापित किए।
18. सीजर भ्रष्ट कर्मचारियों और अधिकारियों को कठोर दण्ड देता था।
19. प्रान्तों में अनेक स्थानों पर विद्यालय स्थापित किए गये।
20. उसने न्यायालयों में निष्पक्ष तथा ईमानदार जजों की नियुक्तियाँ कीं।

उपरोक्त सुधार कार्यों के अध्ययन से पता चलता है कि जूलियस सीजर एक महान सुधारवादी था। उसमें एक कुशल प्रबंधक के भी सभी गुण विद्यमान थे। इस सन्दर्भ में **एलिस व जौन** ने लिखा है, "इन सब सुधारों से प्रकट होता है कि वह सिर्फ तीक्ष्ण बुद्धिवाला राजनीतिज्ञ ही नहीं, अपितु एक दूरदर्शी राष्ट्रनिर्माता के रूप में भी प्रसिद्ध था। **डॉ. आर. पी. त्रिपाठी** ने सीजर के सुधारों की चर्चा करते हुए लिखा है कि, सीजर के सुधार उसकी आश्चर्यजनक कर्मठ, प्रेरक तथा प्रबन्ध शक्ति का दीप्यमान प्रमाण है।"

मूल्यांकन—सीजर दिन-प्रतिदिन सफलता अर्जित करता जा रहा था। फलस्वरूप सीनेटर व विरोधी सेनापति उससे ईष्या करने लगे थे। उसने जब अपने आपको देवताओं का वंशज बताया तो रोमन जनता भी उसका विरोध करने लगी। इस समय सीजर अपनी प्रेयसी क्लियोपेट्रा के वशीभूत होता जा रहा था जो रोमन जनता के बर्दाश्त के बाहर थी। उसके विरोधियों ने उस पर यह दोषारोपण किया कि यह प्रजातंत्र को समाप्त कर राजतन्त्रात्मक शासन-व्यवस्था स्थापित करना चाहता है। इस समय उसके एक ईर्ष्यालु मित्र ब्रूटस ने 15 मार्च, 44 ई. पू. को सीनेट हाल में ही सीजर को छुरा भोंककर उसकी हत्या कर दी।

सीजर ने रोम पर कुल पांच वर्ष तक शासन किया इस दौरान उसने वहां शान्ति व्यवस्था स्थापित कर रोमन साम्राज्य को सशक्त बना दिया। उसके द्वारा कई महत्त्वपूर्ण सुधार किए गये। वह परास्त एवं शरणागत शत्रुओं के साथ भी उदारता का व्यवहार करता था। इस प्रकार सीजर न केवल एक महान विजेता था बल्कि एक कुशल शासन-प्रबन्धक भी था। **रोबिन्सन** के शब्दों में "सीजर की मृत्यु के पश्चात् कुछ समय के लिए रोम में अशान्ति उत्पन्न हो गई।" **मोनसन** के अनुसार, "उसकी संगठन शक्ति अद्‌भुत थी। वह एक राजा बना, परन्तु राजाओं जैसा व्यवहार उसने कभी नहीं किया।" **डॉ. आर. पी. त्रिपाठी** ने सीजर का मूल्यांकन करते हुए लिखा है, "वह (सीजर) केवल योद्धा और चतुर, साहसी, धैर्यवान और निर्भीक सेनापति ही नहीं था, वरन् बहुमत तथा विचारशील वक्ता और लेखक भी था। उसमें उत्साह, उद्योग, शौर्य, तेज और प्रतिभा आदि गुण पाये जाते हैं। उसके विचार और योजनाएँ

बहुमुखी और स्वअर्जित थीं। यदि वह अधिक काल तक जीवित रहता, तो बहुत कुछ कर जाता और यश प्राप्त करता।" ट्रेवर ने लिखा है, "विश्व के इतिहास में कतिपय महान पुरुष ही सीजर के राजनीतिक एवं सैन्य गुणों की क्षमता का मूल्यांकन कर सकते हैं।"

साम्राज्यवादी रोम (27 ई. पू.–476 ई.)

जूलियस सीजर की मृत्यु के बाद शासक बनने के लिए रोम में तीन उम्मीदवारों का चुनाव किया गया। मार्क एण्टोनी को प्रथम उम्मीदवार के रूप में चुना गया। वह विशालकाय, शक्तिशाली और अनुभवी योद्धा था। इसके अतिरिक्त कूटनीतिज्ञ भी था। वह सीजर का घनिष्ठ मित्र और ऑक्टेवियन का बहनोई था। ऑक्टेवियन को दूसरे उम्मीदवार के रूप में चुना गया। वह सीजर की बहन का पौत्र और सीजर का दत्तक पुत्र था। सीजर ने अपनी सम्पत्ति उसी के नाम वसीयत की थी। उसने ऑक्टेवियन को अपना उत्तराधिकारी भी घोषित कर दिया था। लेपिडस को तीसरे उम्मीदवार के रूप में चुना गया था जो सीजर का विश्वसनीय सेनापति था।

द्वितीय ट्राटमविरेट–रोम का काउंसिल बनने के लिए मार्क एण्टोनी ने व्यापक प्रयास किए। अन्ततः उसे सफलता भी मिली और उसे रोम का काउंसिल नियुक्त कर लिया गया। सैनिकों के बल पर ही लेपिडस सीजर का काउंसिल पद ग्रहण कर लिया। ऑक्टेवियन, लेपिडस के सहयोग से रोम का काउंसिल बन गया। इस प्रकार रोम में द्वितीय ट्राइमविरेट (शासकत्रयी) का निर्माण हुआ। इस त्रिगुट में एण्टोनी, ऑक्टेवियन एवं लेपिडस आदि थे, जिनके हाथों में राज्य की समस्त शक्ति निहित थी। इस त्रिगुट का मुख्य उद्देश्य सीजर के हत्यारों को दण्डित करना था।

फिलिप का युद्ध–सिसरो जो कि गणतंत्र का प्रबल प्रवक्ता था, उसकी संदेह के आधार पर एण्टोनी ने हत्या करवा दी। इसके उपरान्त ऑक्टेवियन, लेपीडस और एण्टोनी की संयुक्त सेना ने सीजर के हत्यारे ब्रूटस और कैसियस पर आक्रमण कर दिया। दोनों के बीच फिलिप (मेसीडोनिया के समीप) नामक स्थान पर भयंकर युद्ध हुआ, इसमें रोम को विजय मिली। कैसियस और ब्रूटस ने मैदान से भागकर आत्महत्या कर ली। सीजर की हत्या में जिन त्रिगुट सदस्यों का हाथ था, उन सिनेटरों को प्राण दंड की सजा दी गयी। इसके बाद तीनों ने रोमन राज्य को आपस में बाँट लिया। मार्क एण्टोनी मिस्र, यरुसलम, एशिया माइनर आदि पूर्वी देशों पर राज करने लगा। उसने पूर्वी प्रान्त की राजधानी सिकन्दरिया को बनाया और मिस्र की रानी

क्लियोपेट्रा के साथ विलासितापूर्वक जीवन व्यतीत करने लगा। यद्यपि क्लियोपेट्रा ने उम्र में एण्टोनी से बड़ी होने के बावजूद भी उससे विवाह कर लिया था। स्पेन तथा पश्चिमी भाग पर लेपिडस ने राज्य कायम किया। कुछ समय बाद उसने त्याग-पत्र दे दिया फलस्वरूप पश्चिम पुनः रोम के अधीन हो गया। ऑक्टेवियन को रोम सहित पश्चिमी देशों का शासक बनाया गया।

जिस प्रकार सीजर रोम का एक निरंकुश शासक था उसी प्रकार ऑक्टेवियन भी निरंकुश शासक बनना चाहता था। अतः उसने रोम में लोकप्रियता प्राप्त करने के लिए हर संभव प्रयास किये। ऑक्टेवियन की बहन से मार्क एण्टोनी ने विवाह रचाया था फिर भी, वह मिस्र की रानी क्लियोपेट्रा के प्यार में इतना फँस गया था कि उसने उससे विवाह कर लिया। इसके बाद एण्टोनी ने ऑक्टेवियन की बहन को तलाक दे दिया। दोनों ही सम्पूर्ण रोमन साम्राज्य पर सत्ता कायम करना चाहते थे। रोम में उस समय यह खबर फैली कि एण्टोनी और क्लियोपेट्रा रोम पर अधिकार करना चाहते हैं।

एक्टियम का युद्ध (31 ई.पू.)—एण्टोनी और ऑक्टेवियन के मध्य अच्छे संबंध नहीं रह गये थे। एण्टोनी ने फ्रांस विजय के लिए ऑक्टेवियन से सहायता माँगी और जब उसने सहायता देने से इन्कार कर दिया तो एण्टोनी ने क्रुद्ध होकर 31 ई.पू. में रोम पर आक्रमण कर दिया। दोनों के बीच यूनान में एक्टियम अन्तरीप के समीप युद्ध हुआ; जिसमें ऑक्टेवियन की विजय हुई। एण्टोनी परास्त होकर क्लियोपेट्रा के शरण में चला गया था। ऑक्टेवियन ने 30 ई.पू. में सिकन्दरिया पर आक्रमण कर दिया। एण्टोनी और क्लियोपेट्रा काल के ग्रास में समा गये। इसके बाद मिस्र को रोम साम्राज्य में मिला लिया गया। अब रोमन साम्राज्य का शासक ऑक्टेवियन बन गया जिसका भूमध्यसागर पर भी आधिपत्य था।

आगस्टस सीजर (31 ई.पू.–14 ई.पू.)—एण्टोनी एक्टियम से हार गया था जिसके परिणामस्वरूप ऑक्टेवियन (आगस्टस) रोमन साम्राज्य का अकेला शासक बन गया था। रोमन जनता ने उसे 'प्रिन्सेप' और 'इम्परेटर' की उपाधि से विभूषित किया। प्रिन्सेप का अर्थ होता है—प्रथम नागरिक तथा इम्परेटर विजयी सेनापति का सूचक है। सीनेट ने उसे 'आगस्टस की उपाधि से अलंकृत किया, जिसका अर्थ था—'सौभाग्यशाली'। महान व्यक्तियों को आगस्टस की उपाधि दी जाती थी। सीजर शब्द राजा के लिए प्रसिद्ध था। इसके बाद ऑक्टेवियन आगस्टस सीजर के नाम से चर्चित हो गया। उसने शासन का बाहरी स्वरूप प्रजातंत्रीय रहने दिया और सीनेट, ट्रिब्यून तथा काउंसिल आदि भी बनाये रखे, लेकिन आन्तरिक रूप से राज्य की

समस्त शक्तियाँ अपने हाथ में केन्द्रित कर रोम का सम्राट बन गया। तत्पश्चात् रोम में अप्रत्यक्ष रूप से राजतंत्र का प्रसार हो गया था। आगस्टस ने 31 ई. पू. से लेकर 14 ई. पू. तक रोम पर शासन किया। यहीं से रोमन साम्राज्य का इतिहास प्रारम्भ होता है। उसका काल रोम के इतिहास में अति उल्लेखनीय रहा और उसे रोमन इतिहास में 'स्वर्णकाल' की संज्ञा दी गई है।

शासन प्रबन्ध—इस दौरान दोहरी शासन व्यवस्था प्रचलित थी। आगस्टस के शासनकाल में शासन की शक्तियाँ सम्राट तथा सीनेट के मध्य विभक्त थीं। अतः शासन व्यवस्था को ये दोनों संयुक्त रूप से देखते थे। रोम के आस-पास के प्रदेशों का शासन संचालन सीनेट द्वारा किया जाता था जबकि दूर के प्रदेशों का शासन सम्राट द्वारा संचालित किया जाता था। युद्ध के दौरान सम्राट द्वारा ही सेना का नेतृत्व किया जाता था। शनैः-शनैः शासन की समस्त शक्ति का राजा के हाथों में केन्द्रीयकरण होता चला गया अन्ततः सीनेट एक परामर्शदात्री समिति बनकर रह गई और सम्पूर्ण शासन व्यवस्था पर राजा का एकाधिकार हो गया। सीनेट के सदस्यों का चयन सम्राट करता था। अब सीनेट के सदस्यों की संख्या में भी काफी कमी कर दी गई। इसके परिणामस्वरूप सम्राट का सीनेट पर नियंत्रण स्थापित हो गया। दूसरे सदन एसेम्बली में सम्राट ने अपने विरोधियों को हटाकर अपने विश्वासपात्रों को सदस्य नियुक्त किया और एसेम्बली पर भी नियंत्रण स्थापित कर लिया।

साम्राज्य के विभिन्न प्रान्त बनाए गए जिनकी शासन व्यवस्था देखने के लिए प्रान्तपतियों की नियुक्ति की गई। इनकी नियुक्ति सम्राट द्वारा की जाती थी और वे उसके प्रति ही उत्तरदायी होते थे। इनका प्रमुख कार्य प्रान्त में शान्ति व व्यवस्था बनाये रखना, कर वसूलना तथा युद्ध के समय प्रान्तीय सेना का नेतृत्व करना था। प्रान्तों से वसूला गया कर वहाँ के सार्वजनिक कार्यों पर खर्च किया जाता था। मिस्र से प्राप्त धन का प्रयोग सम्राट अपने निजी कार्यों पर व्यय करता था। मिस्र से जो धन मिलता था उस पर राजा का एकाधिकार था। अर्थात् उस धन को वह अपने व्यक्तिगत कार्यों के लिए उपयोग में लाता था।

विदेशी प्रान्तों में शासन का संचालन सम्राट द्वारा नियुक्त विश्वासपात्र प्रतिनिधि करते थे। सम्राट द्वारा ही सभी उच्च पदाधिकारियों की नियुक्ति की जाती थी। इस प्रकार सम्राट शासन का सर्वेसर्वा था। उसे रोम का प्रथम नागरिक भी माना जाता था। लैटिन भाषा में सम्राट को 'प्रिंसेप' कहा जाता था।

साम्राज्य की सुरक्षा हेतु कार्य—आगस्टस ने अपने साम्राज्य की सुरक्षा हेतु महत्त्वपूर्ण कदम उठाये। कुछ प्रमुख कार्यों को निम्न प्रकार स्पष्ट किया गया है—

1. आगस्टस ने उपद्रवी तत्त्वों का दमन कर साम्राज्य में शान्ति-व्यवस्था की स्थापना की।
2. सम्राट ने अपने साम्राज्य की सुरक्षा के लिए एक स्थायी सेना गठित की।
3. उसने कई सैनिक चौकियाँ स्थापित कीं तथा वहाँ सैनिक टुकड़ियाँ रखीं।
4. उसने यहूदियों से मैत्रीपूर्ण सम्बन्ध स्थापित किये।
5. आगस्टस ने जर्मनी से मैत्रीपूर्ण सम्बन्ध स्थापित करने हेतु जर्मनों को भी अपनी सेना में भर्ती किया।
6. सामुद्रिक आक्रमणों से सुरक्षा हेतु उसने एक शक्तिशाली जहाजी बेड़े का गठन किया।

सैन्य प्रबन्ध—अपनी सेना में आगस्टस ने काफी बदलाव किये थे। उसने दो लाख पच्चीस हजार सैनिकों वाली एक स्थायी सेना का गठन किया। सैनिकों तथा सेनापतियों की नियुक्ति स्वयं सम्राट द्वारा की जाती थी। आगस्टस ने अपनी सैनिक शक्ति का प्रयोग अपने साम्राज्य की सुरक्षा हेतु ही किया। एक अलग कोष का निर्माण सेना हेतु ही किया गया था। सेना के भर्ती, सेवाकाल, वेतन, अनुशासन आदि के सम्बन्ध में नियम बने हुए थे। इससे सेना में आगस्टस की लोकप्रियता बहुत बढ़ गयी। सम्राट द्वारा एक सैनिक दल 'प्रेयटरी गार्ड' भी स्थापित किया गया, जिसका कार्य सम्राट की सुरक्षा करना था।

सामाजिक दशा—इस काल में रोमन समाज तीन वर्गों में बँटा हुआ था। पहला वर्ग, पैट्रिशियन लोगों का था। पैट्रिशियन वर्ग के लोग ही सीनेट के सदस्य होते थे तथा प्रान्तपति भी इसी वर्ग में से नियुक्त किये जाते थे। सामन्तों को दूसरे वर्ग में शामिल किया गया था। ये सेना में उच्च पदों पर नियुक्त किये जाते थे। प्लेबियनों को तीसरे वर्ग में रखा गया था। इसमें जनता तथा निर्धन व्यक्ति सम्मिलित थे। इस वर्ग की स्थिति अच्छी नहीं थी। इन्हें शासन-कार्यों में भाग लेने का अधिकार नहीं था। पैट्रिशियन लोग प्लेबियनों पर अत्याचार करते थे, अतः प्लेबियनों में असंतोष था। उच्चवर्ग के व्यक्ति भोगविलास में डूबे रहते थे और उनका नैतिक पतन हो रहा था।

आगस्टस ने गाँवों के विकास के लिए बहुत प्रयत्न किये। उसने शिक्षा के प्रचार के लिए गाँवों में अनेक स्कूलों की स्थापना की। स्त्रियों की स्थिति उस दौरान काफी अच्छी नहीं थी। सम्राट ने कानून द्वारा यह निश्चित कर दिया कि एक व्यक्ति अपनी श्रेणी में ही विवाह करेगा। जो व्यक्ति दूसरी श्रेणी से वैवाहिक सम्बन्ध स्थापित करता था, उसे दण्डित किया जाता था।

आगस्टस ने ढेर सारे मंदिरों का निर्माण कराया था तथा देवताओं की उपासना के लिए पुरोहितों को नियुक्त किया। आगस्टस के प्रयत्नों से रोम में सम्राट की पूजा की प्रथा की शुरुआत हुई। पहली सदी में रोम में यहूदी तथा फारसी धर्म का बहुत प्रसार हुआ। इस काल में जब रोमन लोग यहूदी धर्म को अपना रहे थे, तब सरकार द्वारा इस पर प्रतिबन्ध लगा दिया गया। दूसरी सदी में रोमन पशु-बलि, अपशकुन, स्वप्न आदि में विश्वास करने लगे। इस समय रोमन लोग धार्मिक उत्सवों के दौरान बकरे के खून से स्वयं को रंगते थे और सड़कों पर नृत्य करते थे।

यही वह समय था जब रोम में शानवाद का प्रसार हुआ। इसके समर्थकों ने ईसाई धर्म का विरोध किया तथा इस बात पर बल दिया कि व्यक्ति जादू-टोने तथा धार्मिक क्रियाओं से ही ज्ञान प्राप्त कर सकता है। ज्ञान प्राप्ति के पश्चात् ही व्यक्ति को मुक्ति मिल सकती थी। चूँकि यहूदी एवं ईसाई धर्म ने सम्राट पूजा का विरोध किया, इस लिए सम्राट ने विभिन्न प्रकार के प्रतिबंध लगाकर इन धर्मों के विकास के मार्ग को अवरुद्ध कर दिया।

आगस्टस युग की विशेषता—आगस्टस की शासन व्यवस्था बहुत ही उच्च कोटि की थी। इतिहासकारों ने उसके शासनकाल को स्वर्णयुग की संज्ञा दी है। उसका युग शान्ति और समृद्धि का युग था। उसके अधीन रोम ने जो प्रगति की, वह उल्लेखनीय है। इस युग में भौतिक तथा सांस्कृतिक विकास अपनी चरमसीमा पर जा पहुँचा। इस दौरान रोम का वैभव काफी बढ़ चुका था। उसके अधीन व्यापार में वृद्धि, कानून का गठन, साहित्य में प्रगति, कला का विकास तथा प्रत्येक क्षेत्र में रोम ने अभूतपूर्व उन्नति की। आगस्टस ने अपने विशाल साम्राज्य में सुदृढ़ शासन-प्रबन्ध की स्थापना की। उसके शासनकाल में जनता सुखी तथा समृद्ध थी। इस युग में रोम की भौतिक समृद्धि भी अपनी चरमसीमा पर पहुँच गयी। रोम का सर्वांगीण विकास इसी दौरान हुआ। अतः यदि हम आगस्टस के शासनकाल को रोम का स्वर्णकाल कहें, तो कोई अतिश्योक्ति नहीं होगी। इतिहासकार **ट्रेवर** के शब्दों में "आगस्टस का युग पेरिक्लीज एवं एलिजाबेथ के युग के समान था।" **डॉ. आर.पी. त्रिपाठी** ने इस सम्बन्ध में लिखा है, "शान्ति, सुव्यवस्था, राजकोष की सम्पन्नता, प्रान्तों के बढ़ते हुए सम्पर्क तथा ग्रीस, पश्चिमी एशिया और मिस्र की सभ्यता तथा संस्कृति के संसर्ग से रोम में कला, साहित्य, नयी भावनाओं और उदार विचारों का काफी प्रसार हुआ था।"

राष्ट्रीय चरित्र के उत्थान के सन्दर्भ में आगस्टस द्वारा किए गए कार्य उल्लेखनीय हैं। उसने कानून द्वारा नैतिक जीवन को सुधारने का प्रयास किया

तथा दुराचार पर रोक लगाने के लिए कठोर दण्ड की घोषणा की उसने स्त्रियों के व्यायाम सम्बन्धी खेलों के देखने पर प्रतिबन्ध लगा दिया और कुछ ऐसे कठोर कानून बनाए जिनसे तलाक की प्रथा पर नियंत्रण पाया जा सके। निःसंतान विवाहित लोगों को अधिक उत्तराधिकार कर देने का आगस्टस काफी पक्षधर था। उसके द्वारा बनाये गये कानून के अनुसार अविवाहित लोगों को सम्पत्ति का उत्तराधिकारी नहीं बनाया जा सकता था। जिन लोगों की तीन से अधिक सन्तानें थी, उन्हें कुछ करों में छूट दी गई तथा कुछ पदों पर नियुक्ति में विशेष रियायतें दी गईं। इस प्रकार, आगस्टस ने राष्ट्रीय चरित्र के उत्थान के लिए भरसक प्रयास किया।

उद्योग धंधों के क्षेत्र में भी आगस्टस के काल में काफी विकास हुआ था। उसके समय में मिट्टी के सुन्दर तथा चमकीले बर्तन बनते थे, जो विदेशों को निर्यात किये जाते थे। इस युग में लोहे के हर तरह के औजार केम्पेनिया प्रदेश में बनते थे। यहाँ से निर्मित कांसे के बर्तन विश्व में प्रसिद्ध थे।

आगस्टस ने राजकीय कोष की दशा में सुधार करने के लिए कर-प्रणाली में भी काफी बदलाव किया था। उसने कर वसूल करने के लिए सरकारी अधिकारी की नियुक्ति की थी। उन्हें कृषकों को परेशान न करने का आदेश दिया गया। कृषकों से उपज कर दस प्रतिशत कर के रूप में लिया जाता था। आगस्टस की कर-सुधार प्रणाली के फलस्वरूप दूरस्थ प्रान्तों से कर के रूप में अपार धन रोम आने लगा, जिससे रोम के राजकीय कोष में धन की काफी बढ़ोत्तरी हो गयी। इस प्रकार, आगस्टस ने रोम की आर्थिक अवस्था में सुधार किया।

आगस्टस ने बंजर भूमि को कृषि-योग्य भूमि में परिवर्तित कर दिया था। उसने इटली, ब्रिटेन, जर्मनी और यूनान आदि देशों में बड़े-बड़े दलदलों को साफ कर भूमि को कृषि-योग्य बनाया। नहरों तथा कुओं का निर्माण सिंचाई हेतु कराया गया था। इतना होने पर भी अधिकांश भूमि पर पूँजीपतियों का अधिकार होने से कृषकों की दशा शोचनीय थी।

आगस्टस ने सत्ता सँभालते ही पूँजीपतियों को समाप्त करने का प्रयास किया। उसने बैंकों व खानों का राष्ट्रीयकरण कर दिया तथा प्राइवेट कम्पनी व अन्य व्यापारियों द्वारा कर वसूल करने की प्रथा को समाप्त कर दिया। रोम में जलापूर्ति हेतु उसने एक नहर का निर्माण करवाया। इसके अतिरिक्त आगस्टस ने बेरोजगार व्यक्तियों को रोजगार दिया व दीन मनुष्यों के लिए सस्ते अनाज की व्यवस्था की। आगस्टस के शासनकाल में जीविकोपार्जन के संपूर्ण साधन मौजूद थे। इस प्रकार,

उसके आर्थिक सुधारों से जनसाधारण का कल्याण हुआ और रोम में आर्थिक समृद्धि के युग का सूत्रपात हुआ। **डॉ. सुशील माधव पाठक** ने लिखा है, ''इस युग की वास्तविक महत्ता इस युग की भौतिक समृद्धि है। आगस्टस का युग, पेरिक्लीज के युग की भांति अपने बौद्धिक और कलात्मक वैभव के लिए उतना प्रसिद्ध नहीं है, जितना अपनी भौतिक समृद्धि के लिए। आगस्टस युग में रोम की भौतिक समृद्धि अपनी पराकाष्ठा पर पहुंच गई थी।''

आगस्टस ने शान्ति-व्यवस्था एवं सुदृढ़ शासन-प्रबन्ध को प्राथमिकता दी। इस दिशा में उसने महत्त्वपूर्ण कदम उठाए। उसने अपनी कुशाग्र बुद्धि तथा शक्ति के सहारे विशाल रोमन साम्राज्य को सुरक्षित कर दिया। पूर्व में यहूदी लोग रोम के लिए संकट उत्पन्न करते रहते थे, परन्तु सम्राट आगस्टस ने कूटनीति से उनको अपना मित्र बना लिया। पश्चिम में जर्मनों की ओर से रोम को कुछ संकट रहता था, पर आगस्टस ने जर्मनों को अपनी सेना में भर्ती करके उनको अपना मित्र बना लिया। क्रांतिकारी तथा उपद्रवी तत्वों का आगस्टस द्वारा दमन कर दिया गया। यही नहीं, उसने साम्राज्य की सुरक्षा के लिए स्थायी सेना की व्यवस्था की और राज्य के सीमान्त प्रदेशों में सैनिक चौकियों की स्थापना की। आगस्टस ने समुद्री किनारे की रक्षा के लिए एक सुदृढ़ जहाजी बेड़े की भी स्थापना की थी। **डॉ. सुशील माधव पाठक** ने लिखा है, ''आगस्टस के युग की यह विशेषता थी कि प्रथम बार पूरे भूमध्यसागरीय प्रदेश में पूर्ण शांति थी।''

प्रजा के हित की दृष्टि से आगस्टस का शासनकाल बहुत ही अच्छा रहा। इस दौरान जनता के सुख व समृद्धि में अपार वृद्धि हुई। साम्राज्य विशाल एवं सुरक्षित था। उसके शासन-सम्बन्धी सुधारों से जनता अधिकारियों के अत्याचारों से मुक्त हो गयी। इस प्रकार आगस्टस के अधीन कृषि, वाणिज्य-व्यापार एवं उद्योग-धन्धों के क्षेत्र में सर्वांगीण विकास किया था। पेरिक्लीज के युग में जहाँ एथेन्स इतिहास में अपने सांस्कृतिक वैभव तथा बौद्धिक उत्थान के लिए प्रसिद्ध है, वहाँ आगस्टस का युग भौतिक ऐश्वर्य के कारण भी बहुत प्रसिद्ध है।

आगस्टस के शासनकाल में भूमध्यसागर रोम के लिए सुरक्षित व्यापारिक मार्ग बन गया था। उसने एक स्थायी जहाजी बेड़े का निर्माण कर भूमध्यसागर में समुद्री डाकुओं को समाप्त कर दिया था। इस प्रकार, भूमध्यसागर पर रोम का अधिकार होने से उसके व्यापार का अभूतपूर्व विकास हुआ; क्योंकि समस्त व्यापार भूमध्यसागर के माध्यम से ही किया जाता था। इस प्रकार स्पष्ट है कि आगस्टस ने व्यापार के विकास हेतु उल्लेखनीय कार्य किए।

इस काल में रोम पूर्वी देशों से तैयार माल तथा पश्चिमी देशों से कच्चा माल लाया जाता था। रोम मिस्र से पेपीरस मँगवाता था। एशिया के देशों से शराब, तेल, हीरे व जवाहरात आदि वस्तुएँ रोम में आयात की जाती थीं। भारत से विलासिता की सामग्री, पूर्वी देशों से मसाले, चीन से रेशम का आयात होता था। सिडान से शीशा, एशिया माइनर से कालीन तथा सुदूरपूर्व से सिल्क का आयात होता था। रोम नमक, धातु, मछली और मकान बनाने का सामान आदि वस्तुएँ विदेशों को निर्यात करता था। आगस्टस ने व्यापार को उन्नत करने के लिए अनेक नवीन बन्दरगाह बनवाईं और पुरानी बन्दरगाहों का जीर्णोद्धार करवाया। इस प्रकार, आगस्टस के शासनकाल में व्यापार के क्षेत्र में असाधारण विकास परिलक्षित होते हैं।

आगस्टस के शासनकाल में रोम ने साहित्य के क्षेत्र में काफी विकास किया था। उसने अपने दरबार में कवियों, लेखकों तथा इतिहासकारों को उदारतापूर्वक संरक्षण प्रदान किया, जिन्होंने अपनी रचनाओं से इस युग के साहित्य को समृद्ध किया और विश्व साहित्य में काफी योगदान किया था। आगस्टस के शासनकाल में गद्य एवं पद्य साहित्य दोनों ही क्षेत्रों में बहुत अधिक विकास हुआ। **ट्रेवर** ने तो साहित्य सृजन की दृष्टि से आगस्टस युग की तुलना पेरिक्लीज एवं एलिजाबेथ के युग तक से कर डाली है।

वर्जिल, होरेस और प्रोपर्टियस आदि इस युग के महत्त्वपूर्ण कवि थे, जिन्होंने अपनी कृतियों से इस युग को समृद्ध किया। वर्जिल न केवल आगस्टस के समय का सबसे महान कवि माना जाता, अपितु प्राचीन विश्व के महान कवियों में से एक था। उसका जन्म मण्टुआ ग्राम में हुआ था। उसने तीन ग्रन्थों की रचना की—'ईनिड', 'जौर्जिक्स' एवं 'एक्लोग्ज'। उसने यूनान की शैली पर लैटिन भाषा में अपनी कविताओं को लिखा था। इसकी तुलना होमर तथा दांते जैसे महान कवियों से की जाती है। **ईनिड** उसका सुन्दरतम ग्रन्थ माना जाता है। यह एक महाकाव्य है। इसकी रचना उसने होमर के इलियड तथा ओडेसी महाकाव्यों के अनुकरण पर की है। ईनिड नामक महाकाव्य की तुलना होमर-रचित 'इलियड' तथा मिल्टन-रचित 'पेराडाइज लास्ट' से की जाती है। ईनिड को विश्व साहित्य की अनुपम में शामिल किया गया है। इसमें ट्राय के योद्धा ईनियस के साहसिक कार्यों का वर्णन है। ईनिड अपनी सुन्दर कथावस्तु, संगीतमय शैली तथा कारुणिक भावों के लिए अत्यन्त प्रसिद्ध है। वर्जिल ने 'जौर्जिक्स' नामक महाकाव्य की भी रचना की, जिसमें ग्रामीण किसानों के जीवन पर प्रकाश डाला गया है।

कवि होरेस को इस युग का दूसरा प्रसिद्ध कहा जाता था, जिसने काफी संख्या में गीति-काव्यों की रचना की। इसने ग्रीक छन्दों में भी अपनी रचनाएँ रचीं। यह उस युग का मुक्तक काव्य का सम्राट था। होरेस ने अपनी रचनाओं में धार्मिक उत्सवों, समारोहों तथा रोम के पतन के कारणों पर प्रकाश डाला है एवं सामाजिक बुराइयों पर कड़ा प्रहार किया है। होरेस कम शब्दों में गूढ़ भावनाओं को व्यक्त करने में पारंगत था। इनकी रचनाओं का अनुवाद अन्य कवियों की तुलना में सर्वाधिक हुआ था। इसकी रचनाएँ तत्कालीन ग्रामीण जीवन को उजागर करती हैं।

प्रोपर्टियस ऐसा पहला कवि था जिसने प्रेम-काव्य पर आधारित गीत लिखे। उसने अपनी कविताओं में अपने हृदय को उड़ेल दिया। आगस्टस के काल में प्रणय-गीतों का भी अच्छा प्रचलन था। ओविड अपने प्रणय-गीतों के लिए विख्यात था। अन्य कवियों की प्रणय सम्बन्धी कविताओं के आडम्बर में भाव अधिक दिखाई देते हैं। **विलडूरां** ने लिखा है, "इस युग की काव्यधारा कामुकता का विद्रोह था।"

टाइटस, लिवी, टैसीटस और प्लूटार्क आदि गद्य लेखकों ने अपनी रचनाओं से विशेष प्रसिद्धि प्राप्त की। लिवी रोम का सबसे बड़ा इतिहासकार माना जाता था। उसने पर्याप्त अध्ययन के उपरान्त 142 खण्डों में रोम का इतिहास लिखा, जिसका अब केवल एक-चौथाई अंश उपलब्ध होता है। उसने 753 ई. पू. से आगस्टस के युग तक का इतिहास बड़े स्पष्ट ढंग से लिखा था, परन्तु इसमें एक कमी यह थी यह एक-पक्षीय था। इस काल का दूसरा प्रसिद्ध इतिहासकार टैसीटस था। उसने दो ग्रंथों की रचना की--जर्मेनिया तथा एनल्स। टैसीटस ने इस ग्रन्थों में रोमन सम्राटों की आलोचना की है और रोम के पतन के कारणों पर प्रकाश डाला है। उसके ग्रन्थ ऐतिहासिक दृष्टि से खरे नहीं उतरते, परन्तु गद्य साहित्य की दृष्टि से वे महत्त्वपूर्ण हैं। प्लूटार्क को गद्य साहित्य का तीसरा रचियता माना जाता था जिसने रोम के प्रसिद्ध 46 व्यक्तियों की जीवनियाँ लिखकर काफी ख्याति अर्जित की।

आगस्टस ने स्थापत्य कला, चित्रकला और मूर्तिकला आदि के विकास पर काफी ध्यान दिया। आगस्टस को जब रोम का शासक बनाया गया था, उस दौरान रोम ईंटों का बना हुआ था, पर आगस्टस ने उसे संगमरमर के भवनों से सुशोभित किया। उसने रोम तथा अन्य कई स्थानों पर शानदार भवनों तथा मन्दिरों का निर्माण करवाया, जो पूर्ववर्ती भवनों से कहीं अधिक भिन्न तथा सुन्दर हैं। आगस्टस ने कहा था, "मैंने ईंटों के नगर रोम को संगमरमर के नगर में परिणत कर दिया।" उसने भवनों को उद्यानों से सुसज्जित किया और अनेक विजय सूचक तोरण द्वार भी बनवाये।

जूलियस सीजर की भाँति आगस्टस ने अपने नाम से एक फोरम का निर्माण कराया था। फोरम में ही मंगल देवता (मार्स) के लिए एक नया मन्दिर बनवाया। उसने कई मन्दिरों का पुनरुद्धार किया। इस प्रकार, आगस्टस के समय में रोम में भव्य-भवन, जलाशय, सुन्दर स्नानगृहों का निर्माण कराया था। आगस्टस ने मैक्सिमस नामक विशाल इमारत का निर्माण करवाया, जिसमें दो लाख पच्चीस हजार व्यक्ति एक साथ बैठे सकते थे। उसने रोम के विशाल थियेटर या नाट्यशाला तथा सार्वजनिक स्नानागार का निर्माण भी करवाया।

आगस्टस ने पेलेटाइन की पहाड़ी पर एक सुन्दर मन्दिर का निर्माण भी कराया था। देव अपोलो के देवालय का निर्माण भी आगस्टस के समय हुआ था। इतिहासकार **लिवि** ने उसके इन कार्यों की प्रशंसा करते हुए लिखा है, ''आगस्टस रोम के समस्त देवालयों का संस्थापक तथा उद्धारकर्ता था।'' रोम के देवालयों में पैन्थियन का मन्दिर काफी प्रचलित है। इस मन्दिर का निर्माण भी आगस्टस के शासनकाल में हुआ था। इस मन्दिर की गुम्बद का व्यास 104 फीट था। यह रोमन स्थापत्यकला के भव्य नमूनों में शामिल किया जा सकता है। आगस्टस का प्रासाद भी तत्कालीन स्थापत्यकला का अच्छा नमूना है। उसने साम्राज्य की सुरक्षा के लिए पुलों और सड़कों का निर्माण करवाया। उसने जूलियस सीजर की यादगार में एक नये सीनेट भवन का निर्माण करवाया। इस प्रकार, आगस्टस के समय का रोम सैलानियों के आकर्षण का केन्द्र बन गया था। आगस्टस के समय की भवन-निर्माणकला पर यूनानी शैली का बहुत प्रभाव था।

मूर्तिकला का भी इस युग में काफी विकास हुआ था। इस काल की मूर्तिकला पर यूनानी प्रभाव स्पष्ट रूप से दृष्टिगोचर होता है। इस समय में रोम सैनिक वेशभूषा में आगस्टस की एक मूर्ति का निर्माण किया गया, जिसमें शरीर की सुडौलता दर्शनीय है। आगस्टस की शान्ति वेदी भी स्थापत्यकला की एक अच्छी कृति मानी जाती है। **जान बाउल** ने लिखा है, "घुड़सवारों की मूर्तियों के धड़, जो रोम के अजायबघर में रखे हुए हैं व जानवरों की मूर्तियाँ उस समय की मूर्तिकला की अनुपम कृतियाँ हैं, और उनके अवलोकन से रोम की उस समय की सभ्यता का आभास हो सकता है।" रोम में मूर्तिकार केवल सम्राट और शक्तिशाली व्यक्तियों की मूर्तियाँ बना सकते थे, क्योंकि उन पर राज्य का बहुत अधिक नियन्त्रण था। यही कारण था कि यहाँ के मूर्तिकार स्वतंत्रापूर्वक कार्य नहीं कर सकते थे, जिसके कारण मूर्तिकला अधिक विकसित नहीं हो सकती थी।

इस समय चित्रकला के क्षेत्र में भी पर्याप्त विकास हुआ था। आगस्टस के काल के चित्रों पर यूनानी प्रभाव स्पष्ट रूप से दृष्टिगोचर होता है। इस समय ऐतिहासिक और प्रकृति प्रमुख विषय थे। पोम्पी के अध्वंसावशेषों से जो चित्र प्राप्त हुए हैं वे उस समय की चित्रकला के सुन्दर नमूने हैं। रोमन चित्रकारों ने प्रकृति चित्रण में यूनानियों से भी अधिक उन्नति कर ली थी।

उपरोक्त विवरणों के आधार पर यह कहा जा सकता है कि आगस्टस के काल में रोम नगर तथा रोमन साम्राज्य ने काफी विकास किया। रोम की भौतिक समृद्धि और प्रतिष्ठा अपनी चरमसीमा पर जा पहुँची। रोम का साहित्यिक तथा सांस्कृतिक उत्थान भी हुआ। आगस्टस ने अपने साम्राज्य की पिछड़ी हुई जनता को सभ्य बनाया और स्पेन से बेबीलोन तक तथा जर्मनी से सहारा तक रोमन संस्कृति का प्रसार किया। संक्षेप में, आगस्टस के अधीन रोम ने प्रत्येक क्षेत्र में असाधारण उन्नति की और साम्राज्य अपने गौरव की चरमसीमा पर पहुँच गया। इन सब दृष्टिकोण से यदि उसके शासनकाल को रोमन सभ्यता का 'स्वर्णयुग' कहा जाए तो कोई अतिश्योक्ति नहीं होगी।

सीजर वंश के अन्य राजा

सीजर वंश का आगस्टस ही अन्तिम प्रभावशाली शासक रहा। इसके शासनकाल में राज्य का चहुंमुखी विकास हुआ। आगस्टस के बाद इस वंश के चार सम्राटों ने 68 ई. तक शासन किया। नीरो इस युग का अंतिम शासक था। उसका साहित्य व कला से विशेष लगाव था। आरम्भ में वह जनता में लोकप्रिय था, लेकिन कालान्तर में जनता उससे घृणा करने लगी। उसने अपने शासनकाल में कई लोगों को मार गिराया था। यहाँ तक कि उसने अपनी माता, दो पत्नियों और गुरु सेनेका को भी नहीं बख्शा। बहुत बदनामी होने के कारण नीरो ने 69 ई. में आत्महत्या कर अपनी जीवनलीला समाप्त कर दी। इतिहास में नीरो को निर्दयता के लिए याद किया जाता रहेगा।

चार सम्राटों का शासन—नीरो की मृत्यु के पश्चात् सेना के अधिकारियों ने चार सम्राटों को राजसिंहासन सौंप दिया था। उन्होंने 69 ई. से 96 ई. तक रोम पर शासन किया। इस वंश का अन्तिम सम्राट टाइटस यहूदियों का घोर शत्रु था। अतः उसने यरुसलम नगर को नष्ट कर दिया। उसके शासनकाल में ज्वालामुखी का विस्फोट होने के कारण इटली का प्रसिद्ध नगर पोम्पी नष्ट हो गया।

पाँच सद्व्यवहारी सम्राट (96 ई.–180 ई.)—प्लेबियन वर्ग के शासकों के पश्चात् रोम की सत्ता पाँच सद्व्यवहारी सम्राटों के हाथ आ गई। उन्होंने 96 ई. से

लेकर 180 ई. तक शासन किया। उन्होंने जनहित के बहुत से कार्य किये। जनता की आर्थिक दशा में सुधार करने के लिए करों में कमी कर दी गई। इनमें से एक सम्राट ट्रेजन था, जिसने पार्थियन जाति को परास्त कर पश्चिमी फारस पर कब्जा कर लिया था। ट्रेजन के समय में रोम में प्लेग की महामारी फैल जाने से सुन्दर रोम वीरान हो गया। ऐसे समय पर जर्मनी ने इटली पर आक्रमण कर दिया।

रोमन साम्राज्य का पतन

लगभग 500 वर्षों तक रोमन साम्राज्य कायम रहा। 180 ई. के उपरान्त इसका पतन आरम्भ चुका था। चौथी शताब्दी में रोम के गृहयुद्ध में सफलता प्राप्त कर कान्सटेन्टाइन रोम की गद्दी पर बैठा। उसका शासनकाल 323 ई. से 333 ई. तक था। कान्सटेन्टाइन ने पूर्वी साम्राज्य के शासन के लिए कान्सटेन्टीनोपल (कुस्तुन्तुनिया) नाम का शहर बसाया और रोम के स्थान पर कुस्तुन्तुनिया को रोमन साम्राज्य की राजधानी बनाया गया। कान्स्टेन्टाइन ने ईसाई धर्म स्वीकार कर लिया। उसने ईसाइयों को धार्मिक स्वतंत्रता प्रदान की और उन पर लगे हुए प्रतिबन्धों को हटा दिया। विश्व के महान सम्राटों में उसे शामिल किया गया था। **बिल ड्यूरेन्ट** ने लिखा है, "कान्सटेन्टाइन एक महान सेनापति, प्रशंसनीय प्रशासक और उच्चकोटि का राजनीतिज्ञ था। उसने डिओक्लिशियन के कार्य को पूर्ण किया।"

थियोगेसियस कान्सटेन्टाइन के मृत्यु के पश्चात् रोम पर शासन करने लगा। उसने समस्त रोमन साम्राज्य को पूर्वी और पश्चिमी दो भागों में विभक्त कर दिया। उसने पूर्वी भाग का शासक अपने पुत्र आर्केडियस को बनाया और इसकी राजधानी कान्सटेन्टीनोपल बनाई गई। पश्चिमी भाग का शासक अपने दूसरे पुत्र होनारियस को बनाया और इस भाग की राजधानी रोम ही रखी गई। साम्राज्य के इस विभाजन से रोम की शक्ति को गहरा आघात पहुँचा। रोम का वैभव दिन-पर-दिन कम होने लगा।

विदेशियों ने रोम पर आक्रमण करना शुरू कर दिया था। पाँचवीं शताब्दी में एशिया की हूण जाति ने इटली साम्राज्य का बल क्षीण कर दिया। अन्त में 476 ई. में जर्मनी की जंगली जातियों के आक्रमण ने पश्चिमी साम्राज्य को समाप्त कर दिया।

रोम की शासन-व्यवस्था एवं कानून

रोम की जनता ने देश की शासन व्यवस्था व कानून के संचालन में बहुत योगदान दिया है। रोम के प्रजातंत्र में राजतंत्र और कुलीनतंत्र का समन्वय देखने को मिलता है। वर्तमान प्रजातंत्रीय देशों ने अपनी शासन-व्यवस्था का संचालन करने के

लिए अधिकांश सिद्धांत रोम से ग्रहण किये हैं। सीनेट के सदस्य पैट्रिशियन वर्ग के होते थे और एसेम्बली के सदस्य प्लेबियन वर्ग के। काउंसिल व मजिस्ट्रेट सम्राट की भाँति शासन का संचालन करते थे। आज संयुक्त राज्य अमेरिका के संविधान पर रोम के संविधान का प्रभाव स्पष्ट रूप से दृष्टिगोचर होता है। जिस प्रकार आगस्टस ने सीजर की उपाधि ग्रहण की थी उसी प्रकार जर्मनी के सम्राट ने कैसर व रूस के सम्राट ने जार की उपाधि ग्रहण की थी।

रोम में कार्यपालिका को व्यवस्थापिका से अलग रखा गया था। यही व्यवस्था वर्तमान प्रजातांत्रिक देशों में भी देखने को मिलती है। निर्वाचन प्रणाली रोम की देन है जिसमें अधिकारियों की नियुक्ति, धारासभाओं और सीनेट द्वारा शासक का चयन होता था उसका चयन आजीवन होता था। जूलियस सीजर के 600 वर्ष बाद जस्टिनियन ने एक विधान-ग्रन्थ तैयार किया था, जिसे 'जस्टिनियन कोड' के नाम से पुकारते हैं। अधिकांश यूरोपीय देशों ने इस पुस्तक की मदद से ही अपने संविधान बनाए हैं।

विश्व को 'कानून' देने का श्रेय रोमन सभ्यता को ही प्राप्त है। रोमन लोग कानून-निर्माण में कुशल थे। रोमन कानून बौद्धिक क्षेत्र में विश्व को रोम की एक अमिट देन है। संसार का आधुनिक कानून रोमन कानून पर आधारित है। **बी. वी. राव** के अनुसार संसार का आधुनिक कानून रोमन कानून पर आधारित है। उन्होंने आगे लिखा है कि, "रोमन्स कानूनों ने विश्व के लगभग समस्त सभ्य देशों पर गहरा प्रभाव डाला है।"

रोम का कानून सामाजिक प्रथाओं, तर्क तथा औचित्य आदि पर आधारित था जो कि रोमन कानून की एक महत्त्वपूर्ण विशेषता थी। रोमन कानून का मुख्य सिद्धान्त यह था, "किसी भी निर्दोष व्यक्ति को अनुचित रूप से दण्ड नहीं दिया जाना चाहिए, भले ही कोई दोषी व्यक्ति दण्ड पाने से बच जाए।" इस सन्दर्भ में **प्लैट व जीन** ने लिखा है, "रोमन कानून आधुनिक संसार को एक महान उपहार है। सम्भवतः कानून ही एक ऐसा विषय है, जिसमें रोमनों ने सबसे बड़ा योगदान दिया। **लार्ड ब्राइस** के अनुसार, "यदि रोमन कानून नहीं होते तो लोग रोमन साम्राज्य को भी भूल जाते। **बी. वी. राव** के अनुसार, "इस कथन में कोई अतिश्योक्ति नहीं है कि उनके (रोमन्स) कानूनों ने विश्व के लगभग समस्त सभ्य देशों पर गहरा प्रभाव डाला है।

रोम के कानून का रूप क्रमिक है, जिसमें पहले न्याय प्राचीन परम्पराओं के आधार पर होता था क्योंकि वहां कोई लिखित कानून नहीं था। अतः कुलीन वर्ग के

लोग या शासक अपनी इच्छानुसार इन परम्पराओं का अर्थ लगा देते थे। रोम ने यूनानी कानूनों को ग्रहण किया और इनका विकास किया। जब रोम नगर राज्य था, तब वहाँ कूनन बहुत कठोर थे। 450 ई. में प्लेबियनों द्वारा स्वतन्त्रता एवं अधिकारों के लिए आन्दोलन चलाया गया, तब पहली बार रोम में इन कानूनों का 12 काँसे की पट्टियों पर संग्रह किया गया। इन बारह भागों में से 10 भाग रोमन नागरिकों के लिए और शेष दो भाग पराजित देशों के लिए थे। इनमें परिवार, उत्तराधिकार, विवाह, धर्म, तलाक, नागरिकता, व्यापार, उद्योग, धार्मिक रीति-रिवाज और राष्ट्रीयता आदि विषयों पर कानून बने हुए थे। इस संग्रह के तीन प्रमुख सिद्धान्त निम्न हैं :

1. कानूनी रूप से सभी व्यक्तियों को समान समझा गया।
2. व्यापारिक लेन-देन और व्यवहार को वैधानिक घोषित किया गया।
3. किसी झगड़े में घायल हुए व्यक्ति के लिये प्रतिशोध के स्थान पर जुर्माना निश्चित किया गया।

रोमन ने कानून की शुरुआत संग्रह से की। तत्पश्चात् न्यायाधीशों की व्याख्या और निर्णयों से रोमन कानून विकास की सीढ़ियाँ चढ़ता गया। न्यायाधीश प्रेटर कहलाते थे। वह पद-भार सम्भालते समय उन सिद्धान्तों की घोषणा करता था, जिनके अनुसार वह न्याय करता था। वह कभी-कभी नये कानून भी बना देता था। रोमन नागरिकों एवं विदेशियों के मुकदमों का निर्णय अलग-अलग प्रेटर करते थे। रोम में धीरे-धीरे समयानुकूल कानून में भी परिवर्तन हुआ। इस समय समझौते का कानून और सम्पत्ति से सम्बन्धित कानून का भी विकास हुआ। इसके द्वारा व्यक्तियों के पारस्परिक सहयोग को कानून द्वारा निश्चित कर दिया गया। रोमन कानून की मुख्य विशेषता यह थी जो भी कानून बनाया जाये उसमें जनता के हितों का ध्यान रखना जरूरी था साथ ही समान रूप से लागू भी किया जाये।

रोमन अधिनियम—रोम में इस अधिनियम का अत्यधिक महत्त्व था। इनका यूरोप पर बहुत प्रभाव पड़ा। इसने पश्चिम की सांस्कृतिक परम्परा के आधार का रूप ग्रहण कर लिया। इस दीवानी कानून में निम्नलिखित विशेषताएं विद्यमान थीं—

1. रोमन कानून में पहली बार कारपोरेशन अथवा निगम की कल्पना की गयी। किसी विशिष्ट उद्देश्य की पूर्ति के लिये एक व्यक्ति की तरह काम करने वाले व्यक्तियों के किसी दल को कानून द्वारा एक इकाई माना गया।
2. रोमन कानूनों द्वारा सम्पत्ति को तीन भागों में बांटा गया था जो निम्नवत हैं— धार्मिक सम्पत्ति, सार्वजनिक सम्पत्ति और व्यक्तिगत सम्पत्ति। पहले प्रकार की सम्पत्ति में देवभूमि, देवमन्दिर एवं देवपात्र को शामिल किया गया। इन्हें पवित्र

माना गया। दूसरी तरह की सम्पत्ति को दो भागों में बाँटा गया—पहले भाग में वायु, समुद्र, बहते हुए जल को रखा गया, जबकि दूसरे भाग में दीवार, फाटक, गली, सड़कें, जलमार्ग आदि को शामिल किया गया।

सम्पत्ति पर अधिकार के सम्बन्ध में तीन तरीके निर्धारित किये गये जो निम्नलिखित हैं—

1. गवाह की उपस्थिति में नियमों के अनुसार विक्रय से सम्पत्ति पर अधिकार किया जा सकता था।
2. यदि न्यायाधीश के आदेश से सम्पत्ति एक व्यक्ति से दूसरे व्यक्ति के पास आ जाये तो उस सम्पत्ति पर दूसरे व्यक्ति का अधिकार माना जाता था।
3. अचल सम्पत्ति पर दो वर्ष तक और चल सम्पत्ति पर एक वर्ष तक व्यवहार करने से सम्पत्ति पर स्वामित्व प्राप्त किया जा सकता था।

रोम के कुछ कानून आज भी महत्त्वपूर्ण स्थान प्राप्त किए हुए हैं जैसे—इकरारनामा सम्बन्धी कानून, नागरिक या सिविल कानून आदि। सम्पत्ति के लेन-देन के लिये रोमन ने कान्ट्रेक्ट लॉ लागू किया जिसके अन्तर्गत प्रथम देन का प्रस्ताव, द्वितीय प्रस्ताव की स्वीकृति की पूर्ति। यह कानून आज भी उसी रूप में विद्यमान है।

रोमन कानून के विकास के चरण—रोम में विदेशियों के लिये 176 ई.पू. में कानून बनाया गया। ये कानून 'जुसजेनिशयम' कहलाते हैं। ये कानून औचित्य और मानवता के आधार पर बनाये गये थे। आगे चलकर इन कानूनों का विलय दीवानी कानून में कर दिया गया।

थियोडोसियन कोड—रोम में 438 ई. पू. में थियोडोसियस ने विभिन्न कानूनों को एक पुस्तक के रूप में संग्रहीत किया, जिसे थियोडोसियन कोड की संज्ञा प्रदान की गयी। इस कोड में ईसाई धर्म के आदर्शों को और प्राकृतिक कानून से भी कई बातें ग्रहण की गई हैं।

जस्टीनियन कोड—सम्राट जस्टीनियन के शासनकाल में कानून जगत में क्रान्तिकारी परिवर्तन हुआ। उसने 534 ई. में दस व्यक्तियों की एक समिति कानून में सुधार करने के लिए बनाई, जिसका अध्यक्ष ट्रीबोनियन को बनाया गया था। इस समिति ने विभिन्न कानूनों में सुधार कर एक पुस्तक के रूप में उसका संकलन किया, जिसे 'जस्टीनियन कोड' का नाम दिया गया। इसमें रोम के प्रसिद्ध कानून विशेषज्ञों के मतों तथा विभिन्न सम्राटों के आदेशों को संग्रहीत किया गया है। इस विशाल कोड में दीवानी, फौजदारी, धार्मिक और सामाजिक आदि विषयों पर कानून बने हुए हैं। यह कोड चार भागों में विभाजित है जो निम्नलिखित हैं—

पहला भाग कोड कहलाया। यह कानून के विकास में सहायक राजकीय आदेशों और शासनों का संग्रह था।

संग्रह का दूसरा भाग डाइजेस्ट कहलाया। यह कानून के पंडितों और न्यायाधीशों के विचारों का संकलन था।

तीसरा भाग इंस्टीच्यूट्स कहलाया। यह एक पाठ्य-पुस्तक थी, जो कानून के विद्यार्थियों के लिये थी। इसमें कानून का आलोचनात्मक विश्लेषण किया गया था।

चौथा भाग नावेल्स कहलाया जो कानून की नवीनताओं के संग्रह के उद्देश्य से लिखा गया था। यह कानून में हुए संशोधनों तथा परिवर्तनों का संग्रह था।

सम्राट जस्टीनियन को एक महान् कानूनदाता की उपाधि दी गयी। उसके कोड को रोमन कानून का सबसे महत्त्वपूर्ण ग्रन्थ अथवा उसका सार माना जा सकता है। इसने कालान्तर में यूरोपीय कानूनों के लिए एक आदर्श कानून का काम किया। इंग्लैंड, फ्रान्स व अमेरिका आदि देशों के आधुनिक कानून इसी रोमन कानून पर आधारित हैं। **सेवाइन** के अनुसार, "रोमन लोगों का सबसे विलक्षण बौद्धिक योगदान कानून का निर्माण था, जो न्याय का यन्त्र बन गया। यह केवल परम्पराओं पर ही नहीं, वरन् तर्क पर भी आधारित था।

रोमन अधिनियम की विशेषता—रोमन कानून ने यूरोप के कानूनों के लिये एक आदर्श का काम किया था। मध्यकालीन यूरोपीय कानून मूलरूप से रोमन कानूनों पर ही आधारित थे। इसके अतिरिक्त रोमन कैथोलिक चर्च के धार्मिक कानूनों के मूल आधार रोमन कानून ही थे। वर्तमान समय में भी यूरोपीय कानून रोमन कानूनों पर ही आधारित हैं। विश्व में व्यक्तिगत सम्पत्ति के अधिकार की घोषणा रोमन कानून की देन थी। रोमन कानून में हमें जनता की प्रभुता की भी झलक दिखायी देती है। अतः रोमन कानून ने लोकतन्त्र के विकास में एक प्रेरक का काम किया।

कानून की कमियाँ—रोमन कानून में कुछ कमियां विद्यमान थीं जिन्हें निम्न प्रकार स्पष्ट किया गया है—

1. इनके कानून में संकीर्णता थी, वे केवल विशेष वर्ग के लिये ही बनाये गये थे।
2. इनमें विदेशियों और गुलामों के लिये कोई स्थान नहीं था। केवल रोमन नागरिक ही कानूनी अधिकारों का उपयोग कर सकते थे और कानून भी उनके हितों के अनुकूल थे।
3. रोमन अधिनियम या कानून का सबसे बड़ा दोष यह था कि इसमें समृद्ध तथा उच्चवर्ग को मृत्युदण्ड एवं शारीरिक दण्ड नहीं दिया जाता था, जबकि निम्न वर्ग के व्यक्ति सभी तरह के दण्ड भुगतते थे।

4. गुलामों को साधारण अपराधों के लिये भी मृत्युदण्ड दे दिया जाता था। यह रोमन कानून की उज्ज्वलता पर एक कलंक की भांति था।

हालांकि यह सही है कि रोमन कानून में उपरोक्त कमियां थीं लेकिन इनकी अपेक्षा गुण अधिक थे इसलिए इस बात से इन्कार नहीं कर सकते कि रोमन कानून विश्व को रोम की मौलिक, स्थायी एवं महान् देन है। मध्यकालीन तथा आधुनिक यूरोप के कानूनों तथा रोमन कैथोलिक चर्च के धार्मिक कानूनों की जड़ें भी रोमन कानून में ही निहित हैं। इन कानूनों के लिये रोम चिरस्मरणीय रहेगा और विश्व रोम का सदैव ऋणी रहेगा। इस सम्बन्ध में **वेब्स्टर** ने लिखा है कि, "इंग्लैण्ड का सार्वजनिक कानून, जिसे अमेरिका ने भी स्वीकार किया है कुछ अंशों तक जस्टीनियन की विधि संहिता से प्रभावित हुआ है। रोम का कानून अपने विस्तृत प्रभाव के कारण उनकी महान देन है।"

रोम की सामाजिक स्थिति

रोम की यदि सामाजिक स्थिति पर नजर डालें तो पला चलता है कि वहां का समाज तीन वर्गों में बंटा हुआ था। प्रथम वर्ग **पैट्रिशियन** कहलाता था, इन तीनों में पैट्रिशियन वर्ग को समाज में सम्मान के साथ देखा जाता था क्योंकि इनके पास समाज एवं प्रशासन में विशेष अधिकार प्राप्त थे तथा शासन पर भी बहुत अधिक प्रभाव था। दूसरा वर्ग **प्लेबियनों** का था। इस वर्ग में कृषक, मजदूर और गरीब लोग आते थे। प्रारम्भ में इस वर्ग के लोगों को किसी प्रकार के अधिकार प्राप्त नहीं थे। धीरे-धीरे इस वर्ग ने भी संघर्ष करके राजनीतिक, सामाजिक और आर्थिक अधिकार प्राप्त कर लिए थे। तीसरा वर्ग दासों का था जिनकी दशा बहुत दयनीय थी। रोम का सामाजिक और आर्थिक ढाँचा गुलामों पर ही आधारित था। उनके साथ पशुओं की भाँति व्यवहार किया जाता था। उन्हें सिर्फ इतना भोजन दिया जाता था कि वे जीवित रह सकें। 'डेलोस दीप' को दासों के क्रय-विक्रय के नाम से जाना जाता था।

दासों की पहचान के लिये उनको दाग का निशान लगाया जाता था और उनको जजारों में एक-दूसरे को बांधकर कृषि कार्य करवाया जाता था। यदि वे आज्ञा का पालन नहीं करते तो उन्हें भूखे शेर से लड़ना पड़ता था। दासों की दयनीय अवस्था का वर्णन करते हुए **एच. जी. वेल्स** ने लिखा है, "यदि कोई दास अपने स्वामी का वध कर डालता, तो उस घर के सब दास सूली पर चढ़ा दिये जाते थे। स्वामी अपने दासों पर बलात्कार कर सकते थे। उनका अंग-भंग कर सकते थे।" परन्तु यत्र-तत्र दासों को शिक्षित भी किया जाता था। शिक्षित दासों के साथ कुछ अच्छा व्यवहार

किया जाता था। धीरे-धीरे उन्हें सम्पत्ति में भी अधिकार दिया जाने लगा और भूखे शेरों के आगे डालना बन्द कर दिया गया। फिर भी दास वर्ग की दशा अत्यधिक दयनीय थी।

रोमन में संयुक्त परिवार प्रथा का चलन था। यहाँ का समाज पितृसत्तात्मक था। परिवार का मुखिया पिता होता था, जिसकी आज्ञा का पालन परिवार के सभी सदस्य करते थे। मुखिया अपनी इच्छानुसार घर के किसी भी सदस्य को निर्दयतापूर्ण सजा दे सकता था और बेचकर गुलाम भी बना सकता था। घर में बहुत कठोर अनुशासन होता था, परन्तु माता-पिता अपने बच्चों से बहुत प्यार करते थे।

यूनान की अपेक्षा रोमन समाज में महिलाओं की स्थिति अच्छी थी। वहाँ पर्दा-प्रथा नहीं थी और स्त्रियाँ सामाजिक कार्यों में भाग ले सकती थीं। वे उच्चशिक्षा भी प्राप्त कर सकती थीं। **एलिस व जौन** के अनुसार, ''प्राचीन जगत में कहीं भी स्त्रियों की वह उच्चस्थिति नहीं थी, जो रोमन स्त्रियों की थी।'' वह घर की मालकिन होती थी। घरेलू मामलों में उसके परामर्श को उचित महत्त्व दिया जाता था। तलाक की प्रथा उस समय बहुत कठोर थी। रोमन समाज में निर्बल एवं अंगहीन बच्चों को कलंक समझा जाता था उनको जन्म के समय या बाल्यकाल में मौत की नींद में सुला दिया जाता था। यदि पिता अंगहीन बच्चे को गोदी में उठा ले तो उसे जीवित रखा जाता था अन्यथा उस शिशु को मार दिया जाता था। पिता द्वारा स्वीकार किये गये बच्चे का नामकरण किया जाता था। उस समय बालक के गले में एक छोटा-सा ताबीज या लॉकेट डाल दिया जाता था, जो बालक की दुष्ट आत्माओं से रक्षा करता था।

रोम में बाल विवाह व बहु विवाह का व्यापक प्रचलन था। लड़कियों का विवाह चौदह वर्ष में कर दिया जाता था। आर्थिक रूप से सम्पन्न पुरुष एक से ज्यादा (6 या 7) विवाह करते थे। व्यभिचारिणी स्त्री को तलाक दिया जा सकता था। यदि कोई पुरुष अपराधी हो, उसे छूत की बीमारी हो, गुलाम या देशद्रोही हो गया हो तो स्त्री उसे तलाक दे सकती थी। रोम में चापलूसों की संख्या भी बहुत थी। इस सम्बन्ध में **बर्न्स** ने लिखा है, ''जो लोग परिस्थितियों और व्यापारिक संघर्ष के कारण निकम्मे हो जाते थे, वे अमीरों के चारों तरफ झुंड बनाकर मीठे-मीठे शब्दों में उनकी चापलूसी कर रोटी प्राप्त कर लेते थे। रोम में चापलूसों की कमी नहीं थी।'' रोमन समाज में पुनर्विवाह और विधवा-विवाह भी प्रचलित थी। साम्राज्यवादी युग में स्त्रियों की दशा काफी दयनीय हो गई थी। जननी की अपेक्षा वे एक कामनी के रूप में देखी जाने लगीं।

रोम के लोग नृत्य व सकेस के बहुत शौकीन थे। मनोरंजन के लिए यहाँ के लोग दो शक्तिशाली गुलामों को आपस में लड़ा भी देते थे। इसके अतिरिक्त कोलोसियम के स्टेडियम में एक-साथ कई गुलाम छोड़ दिए जाते थे, जो जिन्दा रहने के लिए भूखे शेरों से युद्ध करते थे। इन कोलोसियम में हजारों व्यक्तियों के बैठने की व्यवस्था होती थी। आगस्टस के दौरान वर्ष में लगभग 66 दिन तक इन स्टेडियमों (कोलोसियम) में रोमन जनता का मनोरंजन करवाया जाता था। नीरो के शासनकाल में रोम में अकाल पड़ गया जिसके कारण लाखों लोगों की मृत्यु हो गयी थी, इसके बाद भी सम्राट जहाजों में विदेश से अखाड़ों के लिये बालू मंगवाता था। रानी के नहाने के लिये गुलाब और 500 गायों का दूध रोज मंगवाता था। इसीलिए यह कहा जाता है, ''जब रोम जल रहा था, तब नीरो अपनी बाँसुरी बजा रहा था।'' यह परिस्थिति रोमन साम्राज्य के पतन में सहायक साबित हुई।

एच. जी. वेल्स का मानना है कि, ''यह निर्माण का नहीं, अपव्यय का युग था। स्थापत्य और व्यापार का एक ऐसा युग था, जिसमें अमीर अधिक अमीर हो गए और गरीब बिल्कुल धनहीन हो गये व्यक्ति की आत्मा और भावनाएँ लुप्त हो गईं।

रोम की आर्थिक स्थिति

रोम की आर्थिक व्यवस्था में मुख्य रूप से कृषि, बागवानी एवं पशुपालन का अधिक योगदान था। यहाँ की मुख्य पैदावार गेहूँ, जौ, जैतून, अंगूर व नारंगी आदि थी। पशुओं में ये गाय, बैल, घोड़ा, गधे और बकरी पालते थे। रोम में भूमि पर धनी पुरुषों का अधिकार था। इस वर्ग के लोग दासों से खेतों और कारखानों में काम करवाते थे। इसलिए कृषि के प्रति कृषकों की अधिक रुचि नहीं थी। यही कारण था कि रोम कृषि के क्षेत्र में अधिक उन्नति नहीं कर सका। **प्लैट व जीन** के अनुसार, "धन मुख्यतया लूट, करों और साहूकारों से प्राप्त होता था।" इस प्रकार कुछ थोड़े लोग धनी बन गए। रोमनों ने कभी भी पर्याप्त वाणिज्य का अथवा बड़े पैमाने पर उद्योग का विकास नहीं किया। श्रमिकों की आय कम थी, क्योंकि उनकी प्रतियोगिता दासों के श्रम के साथ थी। इसी प्रकार बहुत कम रोमन ऐसे थे, जो अच्छे खरीददार हो सकते थे। इसका परिणाम यह हुआ कि बहुत-से व्यवसाय घाटे के कारण बन्द हो गए।

रोम ने अपने साम्राज्य विस्तार के साथ व्यापार, वाणिज्य एवं उद्योग धन्धों का भी समुचित विकास किया। रोम अफ्रीका से कीमती धातु, भारत से मलमल, चीन से रेशम, फारस से इत्र तथा यूनान से लोहा मँगवाता था। राज्य की आय के मुख्य

साधन लगान, कर और भेंट आदि थे। रोम विदेशों से भोग-विलास की चीजें अधिक मँगवाता था। **सेवाइन** ने लिखा है, "मालिक और नौकर दोनों के लिए तन ढकने और पेट भरने का साधन सुलभ नहीं था। सरकार इस दशा से परिचित थी। अतः हाथ खोलकर दान देती थी। आगस्टस के समय ऐसे 20,000 लोग मुफ्त खाना खाते थे। यही रोमन साम्राज्य के पतन का एक मूल कारण था। रोम में वस्त्र, बर्तन, काँच का समान एवं सोने-चाँदी के आभूषण की कारीगरी की जाती थी। राज्य को खानों, मछलियों का व्यापार तथा नमक उत्पादन से काफी आमदनी होती थी। इसके अतिरिक्त राज्य की आय के मुख्य साधन भूमि-कर, आय-कर, चुंगी-कर आदि थे।

338 ई. पू. में रोम में ताँबे के सिक्के प्रचलित किए गए। धीरे-धीरे यहाँ बैंक भी स्थापित किए गये और चारों तरफ सड़कों का जाल बिछा दिया गया। विदेशी व्यापार के लिए सरकार जहाज भी बनाती थी। जहाजों के मार्ग-दर्शन के लिए समुद्र के तटों पर प्रकाश स्तम्भ स्थापित किये गये। यातायात के साधनों का विकास होने के कारण रोम के व्यापार में वृद्धि हुई। इस प्रकार व्यापार, वाणिज्य एवं उद्योग-धन्धों का विकास होने के कारण रोम सम्पूर्ण विश्व का एक व्यापारिक केन्द्र बन गया।

धार्मिक स्थिति

रोम में धर्म को विशेष महत्त्व दिया जाता था। वहां के लोग मूर्ति पूजा करते थे। उनके प्रमुख देवताओं में जूपीटर देवाधिदेव (शान्ति का देवता), मार्स (युद्ध का देवता), अपोलो (संगीत व कला का देवता), वीनस (प्रेम और सुन्दरता की देवी), वैस्टा (अग्नि देवी) और लारेस (खेतों का देवता), आदि प्रसिद्ध थे, शुरू से ही ये प्रकृति की पूजा करते थे। रोम में प्रत्येक कार्य के लिए अलग देवता था। रोमवासी चमत्कार और अन्धविश्वासों में विश्वास रखते थे। यूनानियों की भाँति उनके देवताओं का स्वरूप भी मानव स्वरूप से मिलता था। रोमवासी देवताओं को प्रसन्न करने के लिये उनके व्रत एवं उपवास रखते थे, साथ ही बलि का भी विधान था। कठिन समय में मानव बलि भी दिया करते थे। रोमवासी अपनी सम्पन्नता का श्रेय अपने देवताओं को देते थे। इसलिए उनकी उपासना बहुत ही श्रद्धापूर्वक की जाती थी।

रोम में सम्राज के पूजन का भी प्रचलन था। आगस्टस सम्राट के मंदिर कई प्रांतों में बनवाये गये तथा उनमें विधि-विधान की पूजा अर्चना की जाती थी। धार्मिक उत्सवों को बहुत महत्त्व दिया जाता था। कभी-कभी तो धार्मिक उत्सवों के लिए सीनेट की बैठक भी स्थगित कर दी जाती थी, परन्तु फिर भी रोमवासियों में धार्मिक सहिष्णुता थी। धार्मिक मामलों में रोमनवासी दूसरों का अनुकरण तेजी से करते थे।

उन्होंने यूनानियों से जूपीटर, मार्स तथा वीनस आदि देवताओं की अराधना करना सीखा रोमनों ने मिस्रवासियों की देवी आइसिस को भी अपना लिया था। इसके अतिरिक्त उन्होंने यूट्रास्कन लोगों से शकुन व भविष्यवाणी पर विश्वास करना सीखा। यहूदियों से एकेश्वरवाद के विचार को ग्रहण किया। **प्लैट व जीन** के अनुसार, "समय आने पर करोड़ों रोमन ईसाई धर्म में दीक्षित हो गए। कुल मिलाकर रोमन लोग सहिष्णु थे।"

रोम में रोमन देवताओं के प्रति आदर व्यक्त करने के बाद व्यक्ति किसी अन्य देवता की पूजा भी कर सकता था, परन्तु आगस्टस के बाद धार्मिक सहिष्णुता की नीति समाप्त हो गई थी। पहले तो यहूदी धर्म के प्रचार पर प्रतिबन्ध लगा दिया गया, इसके बाद ईसाई धर्म पर। रोम में ईसाइयों को कोलोसियम में भूखे शेरों के सामने फेंक दिया जाता था। उन्हें जिन्दा अग्नि देव की भेंट चढ़ा दिया जाता था। रोमन सम्राटों ने ईसाइयों पर बहुत अत्याचार किये, लेकिन उनके बलिदान को देखते हुये दासों और मजदूरों ने ईसाई धर्म को अपना लिया। रोमन सम्राट कान्स्टेन्टाइन ने ईसाई धर्म को राजधर्म घोषित कर दिया। रोम की अधिकांश प्रजा ईसाई हो गई। आगे चलकर यही ईसाई धर्म रोमन साम्राज्य के पतन का एक कारण बन गया।

शिक्षा एवं साहित्य

राज्य के सर्वांगीण विकास हेतु शिक्षा का विकास आवश्यक माना जाता था इसलिए रोम शासकों ने शिक्षा के विकास को प्राथमिकता थी। छात्रों को स्कूल में कानून और साहित्य आदि विषयों की शिक्षा दी जाती थी। रोम ने शिक्षा के क्षेत्र में यूनान का अनुसरण किया। वहाँ निर्धन छात्रों को मुफ्त शिक्षा दी जाती थी। 17 वर्ष का बालक शिक्षा प्राप्त करने के पश्चात् रोम का नागरिक बन जाता था। जल्दी विवाह होने के कारण लड़कियों को घर पर ही शिक्षा दी जाती थी। **बेन फिंगर** ने लिखा है कि रोम आधुनिक सामान्य शिक्षा का निर्देशक था।

रोम ने साहित्य के क्षेत्र में प्रगति की। रोमन साहित्य की सबसे बड़ी देन लैटिन भाषा है, जो आगे चलकर यूरोप की बहुत-सी आधुनिक भाषाओं—फ्रांसीसी, इतालवी, स्पेनी, रूमानियन आदि की जननी बन गई। रोम लोगों ने लैटिन भाषा को अन्तर्राष्ट्रीय स्तर तक ले जाने में अहम् भूमिका निभाई। आज विश्व की प्रसिद्ध अन्तर्राष्ट्रीय भाषा अंग्रेजी है, वह भी लैटिन भाषा से ही निकली है। रोम विद्वानों ने प्रारम्भ में यूनानी शैली को आधार बनाकर अपने ग्रन्थों की रचना की, परन्तु कालान्तर में उन्होंने मौलिक ग्रन्थों की रचना कर लैटिन भाषा के साहित्य को समृद्ध बनाया।

वेब्स्टर का कहना है कि ''रोम की भाषा तथा कानून ने मानवजाति के बौद्धिक जीवन को अधिक धनी बनाया है।

महाकाव्य—वर्जिल तथा होरेस दो महाकवियों ने महाकाव्यों की रचना करके लैटिन साहित्य को समृद्धशाली बनाया।

वर्जिल (70 ई. पू. से 19 ई. पू.)—वर्जिल आगस्टस का दरबारी कवि था, जो आज भी संसार के श्रेष्ठ कवियों में अपना स्थान रखता है। उसकी तुलना होमर से की जाती है। उसने 'ईनिड' नामक महाकाव्य लिखा, जिसके कारण वह अमर हो गया। वर्जिल ने ईनिड में ट्राय के योद्धा ईनियस के चरित्र का वर्णन किया है। ईनिड की तुलना होमर के महाकाव्य इलियड और ओडेसी से की जाती है। वाल्तेकर ने ईनिड को विश्व का सर्वोत्तम ग्रंथ बताया है। कीट्स ने इसका अंग्रेजी में अनुवाद किया है। इसके अलावा वर्जिल, जोर्जिक्स ने ग्रामीण परिवारों की जीवन शैली और कृषि कार्य में लगे कृषकों का सरल एवं मार्मिक चित्रण किया। वर्जिल अपने समय में व्याप्त विलासिता एवं दुराचार को रोकना चाहता था। वह लोगों को प्राचीन काल के सद्गुणों की ओर आकृष्ट करना चाहता था।

होरेस—अपनी कविताओं की वजह से होरेस पूरे रोम में प्रसिद्ध है। टेनिसन ने होरेस को कोमलतम कवि बताया है। इनकी रचनाओं में तत्कालीन ग्राम्य जीवन पर बहुत ही सुन्दर ढंग से प्रकाश डाला गया है। इसने ग्रीक छन्दों में रचनाएँ कीं और काफी संख्या में गीतिकाव्य लिखे। उसने दो ग्रन्थों की रचना की—ओड्स तथा सेटायर्स। लैटिन भाषा के कवियों में इनकी रचनाओं का सबसे अधिक अनुवाद हुआ है। होरेस ने यद्यपि कई काव्य संग्रहों की रचना की लेकिन कविता 'पायरा को' बहुत प्रसिद्ध हुई।

गीतिकाव्य—इस प्रकार के कवियों में ल्यूक्रेशियस, कैटुलस, ओविड, प्रोपर्टियस आदि के नाम विशेष रूप से उल्लेखनीय हैं। इन्होंने अपनी रचनाओं में बहुत हृदयस्पर्शी तथा मार्मिक चित्रण लैटिन भाषा में किया है। अतः इन चारों कवियों के विषय में संक्षिप्त विवरण आगे दिया गया है—

ल्युक्रेशियस—यह लैटिन भाषा का उच्चकोटि का कवि था। इसने यूनानी दर्शन के आनन्दवाद को आधार बनाकर उच्चकोटि की कविताओं को लिखा है।

कैटुलस—यह लैटिन भाषा का प्रसिद्ध कवि था। इसकी प्रेमपूर्ण कविताएं पूरे विश्व में प्रसिद्ध हैं। इसने अपनी कविता में अपनी प्रेयसी लेस्बिया को सम्बोधित करते हुए कहा था, ''मैं घृणा और प्यार करता हूँ : तुम पूछो यह कैसे, कौन जाने? मैं अनुभव करता हूँ, यह सत्य और वेदना है।''

ओविड—यह भी लैटिन भाषा का अत्यन्न उच्चकोटि का कवि था। दांते ने उसे विश्व का महान कवि बताया है। उसने अपने ग्रन्थ 'प्रेम की कला' में समकालीन प्यार का सजीव चित्रण किया है। इस ग्रन्थ के कारण ओविड को दस वर्ष का देश-निकाला दे दिया गया था। इसने काव्य के माध्यम से कहानियाँ लिखीं। 'मेटामौफोसेस' उसकी प्रसिद्ध रचना है।

प्रोपर्टियस—ये मूलतः रोम के कवि हैं। इनकी प्रेम पूर्ण कविताएं विश्व प्रसिद्ध हैं।

नाटक—रोम के प्रसिद्ध नाटककारों में प्लौटस तथा टिरेन्स आदि प्रमुख थे, जिन्होंने अपनी रचनाओं से लैटिन साहित्य को समृद्ध बनाया। प्लौटस के सुखान्त नाटकों में यूनानी शैली का वर्णन मिलता है। **सेवाइन** ने लिखा है—"रोम के निवासी नाटक रचना में यूनानियों से सबसे अधिक प्रभावित हुए। उनका सबसे बड़ा नाटककार प्लौटस था। प्रसिद्ध नाटककार टिरेन्स ने दार्शनिक नाटकों की रचना की।

इतिहास—रोमन इतिहासकारों ने इतिहास लिखने की आधुनिक प्रणाली को जन्म दिया। निम्न रोमन इतिहासकार प्रसिद्ध हैं—

पोलिबियस—पोलिबियस ने रोम के न्यूनिक युद्धों का प्रथम इतिहास लिखा।

टैसिटस—यह रोम का दूसरा बड़ा इतिहासकार था। उसने 'ऐनल्स', हिस्ट्रीज' तथा 'जर्मानिया' आदि ग्रन्थों का प्रणयन किया। उसने 'जर्मानिया' नामक ग्रन्थ में जर्मन जाति का प्रारम्भिक इतिहास लिखा है और रोम के पतन के कारणों पर भी प्रकाश डाला है।

लिवी—रोमन इतिहासकार लिवी आगस्टस का समकालीन था। उसने अपने ग्रंथ 'रोम का इतिहास' में 753 ई. पू. से लेकर आगस्टस के युग (30 ई.) तक के इतिहास का वर्णन किया है जिसकी गणना विश्व के सफलतम इतिहास में की जाती है। उसने ऐतिहासिक स्रोतों की छानबीन के बाद अपने ग्रन्थ की रचना की थी। लिवी ने अपने ग्रन्थ में आगस्टस की आवश्यकता से अधिक प्रशंसा की है। अतः यह ग्रन्थ एकपक्षीय था।

जूलियस सीजर—यह एक महान सेनानायक, राजनीतिज्ञ, निबन्धकार और कुशल इतिहास लेखक था। उसने दो ग्रन्थ लिखे—'गाल के युद्ध' तथा 'गृहयुद्ध'। गृहयुद्ध नामक पुस्तक में सीजर ने तत्कालीन रोम के गृहयुद्ध का सजीव चित्र उपस्थित किया है। उसकी रचनाओं से यूरोपीय साहित्य का गौरव और बढ़ गया।

प्लूटार्क—प्रसिद्ध रोमन इतिहासकार प्लूटार्क ने 'पेरलल लाइब्ज' नामक ग्रन्थ का प्रणयन किया। उसने अपनी इस कृति में यूनानी और रोमन राजनीतिज्ञों तथा

योद्धाओं का तुलनात्मक वर्णन किया है। इसके अतिरिक्त प्लूटार्क ने रोम के 46 प्रसिद्ध व्यक्तियों की जीवनियाँ लिखीं।

गद्य साहित्य—सिसरो गद्य कला का महान लेखक और निबन्धकार था। उसकी रचनाएँ आज भी आदर्श मानी जाती हैं। यह लैटिन साहित्य का निर्माता था। उसे आधुनिक यूरोपीय गद्य का जनक कहा जाता है। उसने 'ओरेशन्स' नामक ग्रन्थ लिखा। उसके निबन्धों में 'ओल्ड ऐज' और 'फ्रेंडशिप' विशेष रूप से उल्लेखनीय हैं। उच्चकोटि के गद्य लेखक उसकी रचनाओं से आज भी प्रेरणा ग्रहण करते हैं। सिसरो ने रोमन साहित्य के विषय में इस प्रकार लिखा है—"ऐसा अध्ययन युवकों को लाभदायक तथा वृद्धावस्था में प्रसन्नता प्रदान करता है। ऐसे अध्ययन से सौभाग्यशाली अवस्था में हमारी प्रसन्नता बढ़ती है और आपातकाल में वे सांत्वना तथा रक्षा प्रदान करते हैं।.....रात्रिकाल में वे हमारे समीप रहते हैं और ग्रामीण जगह की भी सैर करते हैं।"

दर्शन

रोम में कुछ दार्शनिक भी हुए जिन्होंने दर्शन के क्षेत्र में अपनी अमिट छाप छोड़ी। कुछ प्रमुख दार्शनिकों के बारे में संक्षिप्त जानकारी निम्न प्रकार दी गई है—

गैलने—यह रोम के एक प्रसिद्ध दार्शनिक थे। इन्होंने तर्कशास्त्र पर कई पुस्तकें लिखीं।

सेनेका—स्पेन निवासी यह दार्शनिक रोमन सम्राट नीरो का गुरु था। उसने नीरो के व्यवहार से परेशान होकर आत्महत्या कर ली। सेनेका ने ग्रीक दर्शन के स्टोइक मत का प्रचार किया। उसके अनुसार मनुष्य को प्राकृतिक नियमों के अनुसार अपना जीवन व्यतीत करना चाहिए और सुख तथा दुःख का एक जैसा सामना करना चाहिए। वह सदाचार, नैतिकता तथा मानव सेवा का पोषक था।

सिसरो—प्रसिद्ध दार्शनिक सिसरो गद्य लेखक के साथ-साथ ओजस्वी वक्ता भी था। उसने दर्शनशास्त्र पर एक पुस्तक लिखी। इसने समस्त यूरोप में स्टोइक विचारधारा का प्रचार किया।

ल्यूक्रेशियस—रोम में स्टोइक मत के साथ-साथ यूनान के आनन्दवाद अथवा एपिक्यूरियन मत का भी प्रचार हुआ। रोम में एपिक्यूरियन नामक मत का प्रसार ल्यूक्रेशियस ने किया। इस मत के अनुयायी सामाजिक तथा राजनीति कार्यों में रुचि नहीं रखते थे। जब रोमन साम्राज्य पतन के मार्ग पर अग्रसर हुआ तब इस मत की लोकप्रियता काफी बढ़ी।

मार्क्स आरेलियस–आरेलियस रोम का सम्राट अपनी साधुता और दार्शनिक विचारों के लिये आज भी इतिहास में प्रसिद्ध है। उसने अपनी पुस्तक 'मेडिटेशन्स' में अपने दार्शनिक विचारों को व्यक्त किया तथा स्टोइक मत की व्याख्या की।

कला

रोम में विभिन्न कलाओं के क्षेत्र में भी काफी विकास हुआ। रोम ने स्थापत्य कला को अधिक प्रोत्साहन दिया। इसलिए रोमनों को 'विश्व में महान निर्माता' कहा जाता है। रोमन स्थापत्य कला यूनानी शैली से प्रभावित थी। इस समय रोम तथा अन्य स्थानों पर संगमरमर के शानदार भवन बने। इसके अतिरिक्त विजयी नेताओं के सम्मान में अनेक तोरण बने। रोमन लोगों ने अनेक सड़कों का निर्माण करवाया। सड़कों को समकोण पर मिलाने वाली व्यवस्था रोम से ही शुरू हुयी। रोम में अनेक पुलों का भी निर्माण हुआ। इसके अतिरिक्त रोमवासियों ने स्नानागारों, नहरों तथा थियेटरों का भी निर्माण करवायां। आगस्टस के युग में रोम नगर संगमरमर के भव्य भवनों, मन्दिरों तथा सार्वजनिक स्नानागरों से सजकर रमणीक नगर बन गया। रोम की स्थापत्य कला पर टिप्पणी करते हुए **रशफोर्थ** ने कहा है कि, "इस कथन में कोई अतिश्योक्ति नहीं कि रोम विश्व में प्रथम नगर था, जिसकी अपनी महान लौकिक वास्तुकला थी।"

रोम में स्टेडियम के निर्माण में यूनान की तीनों शैलियों को उपयोग में लाया गया। इसकी पहली मंजिल में डोरिक, दूसरी मंजिल में आयोनिक तथा तीसरी मंजिल में कोरिन्थियन शैली के स्तम्भ लगाये थे। इस स्टेडियम में 50,000 दर्शक एक साथ बैठकर खेल देख सकते थे। रोम ने तोरण बनाना यूट्रास्कनों से तथा गुम्बद बनाना मैसोपोटामिया से सीखा। डॉ. आर. पी. त्रिपाठी का मानना है कि, "गुम्बद बनाने की कला में रोमनों ने अभूतपूर्व सफलता ही प्राप्त नहीं की, वरन् उसको पराकाष्ठा पर पहुँचा दिया। सैकड़ों वर्षों तक उस कला में कोई वैसी उन्नति नहीं कर सका।" **विल ड्यूरेन्ट** के अनुसार, "रोम प्राचीन मिस्र, बेबीलोन और यूनानी कलाओं का संग्रहालय था, जिसके बड़े-बड़े भवन, ऊँचे विशाल खम्भे, दैत्याकार आकृति के महल, गोल विशाल गुम्बद और खुले चौड़े दालान, प्रायः सभी विभिन्न कलाओं के प्रतीक हैं।"

आगस्टस ने अपने शासनकाल में स्टेडियम का निर्माण कराया जो रोम की सबसे बड़ी इमारत थी। इसमें दो लाख पच्चीस हजार दर्शक एक साथ बैठ सकते थे। यह इमारत अंग्रेजी शब्द 'यू' आकृति जैसी थी। रोम में पैन्थियन का मन्दिर रोम

की आदर्शभूत इमारत है। आगस्टस ने अपोलो का देवालय तथा जूलियस सीजर की स्मृति में सीनेट का संगमरमर का नया भवन बनवाया, जो भवन निर्माण कला के सुन्दर नमूने हैं। 79 ई. में पोम्पी नामक नगर भूकम्प के कारण ध्वस्त हो गया था। यह उस समय स्थापत्यकला का एक प्रसिद्ध केन्द्र था। खुदाई में प्राप्त इस नगर की दीवारें, जल-व्यवस्था, गलियाँ, गृह, कुएं, बाजार, मन्दिर, थियेटर और स्टेडियम आदि से रोमन कला का सही अन्दाज लगाया जा सकता है। इसके अलावा हेड्रियन ने वीनस का मन्दिर तथा कान्स्टेन्टाइन ने वाजिल्का में गिरिजाघर का निर्माण करवाया था। ये दोनों भवन उस समय की स्थापत्य कला के ज्वलन्त उदाहरण हैं।

यूनान की मूर्तिकला का रोम की मूर्तिकला पर स्पष्ट प्रभाव देखा जा सकता है। यहाँ सम्राट, सरदारों व देवताओं की मूर्तियाँ बनाई जाती थीं। मूर्तियाँ, काँसे, मिट्टी और पत्थर की बनती थीं। सम्राट आगस्टस, मार्क्स ओरेलियस तथा एण्टोनी की मूर्तियाँ उस समय की कलापूर्ण कृतियाँ हैं।

रोमवासियों ने चित्रकला के क्षेत्र में यूनानियों का अनुकरण किया था। रोमन चित्रकारों ने प्रकृति के चित्रों का निर्माण करने में यूनानियों से अधिक उन्नति कर ली थी। वे मकान के अन्दर दीवारों पर पेड़ों की कतारें इस प्रकार बनाते थे, मानो पेड़ों के बीच बैठे हों। लकड़ी और मिट्टी के सजावट के सामानों पर चित्र बनाते थे। यहाँ के चित्रकार युद्धों (ऐतिहासिक विषयों) तथा जलूसों के सामूहिक चित्रों का निर्माण करते थे। इसके अलावा उस समय पलंग के दोनों तरफ उत्तेजक कामुक चित्र बनाये जाते थे। कोलोसियम की मेहराब पर अंकित जलूस का चित्र तत्कालीन चित्रकला की उत्कृष्टता को उजागर करता है। रोम के चित्र सबसे पहले टर्की के राजमहलों में प्राप्त हुए। पोम्पी और इरीट्रिया नगरों के भग्नावशेषों से प्राप्त चित्र उस समय की चित्रकला के सुन्दर नमूने हैं। **मैकनेल बर्न्स** के अनुसार, "रोमन चरित्र का सही चित्रण स्थापत्य और मूर्तिकला में मिलता है।

रोम ने यूनानियों की संगीतकला का अनुसरण किया। इस समय प्रचलित वाद्य यन्त्रों में बाँसुरी एवं लयर आदि प्रमुख थे। नाटकों और खेल-तमाशों के समय संगीत का आयोजन किया जाता था।

रोम में विभिन्न विषयों का विकास

ज्ञान विज्ञान—रोम में विज्ञान के सम्बन्ध में यह उक्ति प्रचलित है कि, "रोमनों ने विज्ञान का उपयोग किया, उसका अध्ययन नहीं।" **प्लैट व जीन ड्रमण्ड** के अनुसार, "रोमन विज्ञान प्राचीन ज्ञान का संग्रह था। रोमन वैज्ञानिकों ने नवीन

आविष्कार बहुत कम किये, किन्तु पुराने आविष्कारों का संग्रह काफी किया।'' रोम वैज्ञानिकों में प्लिनी का नाम विशेष रूप से उल्लेखनीय है।

प्रसिद्ध रोमन वैज्ञानिक प्लिनी ने 'प्राकृतिक इतिहास' नामक ग्रन्थ की रचना की, जिसमें उसने सृष्टि का निर्माण, भूगोल, मानव विज्ञान, जन्तु विज्ञान, वनस्पति विज्ञान, चिकित्सा विज्ञान और धातु विज्ञान के बारे में वर्णन किया है। प्लिनी ने अपने ग्रन्थ की रचना में 2000 ग्रन्थों की सहायता ली थी। उसका यह ग्रन्थ लैटिन भाषा में विज्ञान पर सबसे प्रसिद्ध ग्रन्थ है जिसमें उसने कहा कि प्रकृति मानव के लिये सभी आवश्यक वस्तुओं का सृजन करती है। प्लिनी के अनुसार, "यदि कोई मनुष्य बहुत समय तक निराहार रहे तो उसकी श्वांस इतनी विषैली हो जाती है कि उससे साँप भी मर सकता है।"

भूगोल—भूगोल के क्षेत्र में भी रोम ने काफी उन्नति की। स्ट्रेबो ने 'भूगोल' नामक पुस्तक का प्रणयन किया, जिसमें प्राचीन विश्व की भौगोलिक स्थिति का वर्णन किया है। सेनेका ने भी प्राकृतिक भूगोल पर पुस्तक लिखी। अलैक्जैंड्रिया निवासी टोलेमी भूगोल के पण्डित के रूप में विश्व-इतिहास में विख्यात है। उसने मानचित्र बनाने की कला का आविष्कार किया तथा मानचित्र में अक्षांश और देशान्तर के आधार पर कई स्थानों की स्थिति को निश्चित किया। टोलेमी ने बताया कि पृथ्वी के चारों ओर सात ग्रह चक्कर लगाते हैं।

कैलेण्डर सुधार—सर्वप्रथम रोम के शासक जूलियस सीजर ने अपने नाम के कैलेण्डर का आविष्कार किया यह कैलेण्डर सूर्य पर आधारित था। इसके अनुसार एक वर्ष में 365 दिन माने गये और हर चार साल में एक दिन जोड़ दिया जाता था। यूनानी लोग 10 दिन का एक सप्ताह मानते थे, रोमनों ने 7 दिन का एक सप्ताह माना। यह कैलेण्डर 1 जनवरी, 45 ई. पू. से लागू हुआ। जूलियस सीजर के नाम पर सातवें महीने का नाम 'जुलाई' रखा गया। रोमन ज्योतिष में राशि चक्र के आधार पर बीमारी दूर करने का उपाय बताया जाता था और भविष्यवाणियाँ भी की जाती थीं।

चिकित्सा शास्त्र—इस क्षेत्र में भी रोम में पर्याप्त प्रोत्साहन दिया गया। आधुनिक अस्पतालों के संगठन की कल्पना रोमन सभ्यता की देन है। प्रत्येक नगर में चिकित्सालय खोले गये, जिनमें सरकार चिकित्सक नियुक्त करती थी, जो बीमारियों का इलाज करते थे। इन चिकित्सकों को सरकार की ओर से वेतन दिया जाता था। रोम में गरीबों की निःशुल्क चिकित्सा होती थी। इसके बावजूद रोमवासियों में अंधविश्वासों की कमी नहीं थी। वे चिकित्सा से जादू-टोने को अधिक महत्त्व देते थे।

प्रसिद्ध रोमन चिकित्सक गैलेन ने चिकित्सा विज्ञान पर 150 पुस्तकें लिखीं, जिनमें उसने श्वांस प्रणाली, रीढ़, हृदय तथा माँसपेसियों के बारे में वर्णन किया था। शरीर के इन अंगों की व्याख्या चिकित्सा शास्त्र में गैलेन की बहुमूल्य देन थी। सेल्सुस ने अपनी पुस्तक में शरीर की चीरफाड़ के बारे में वर्णन किया था।

रोमन सभ्यता की विश्व को देन

विश्व के इतिहास में रोमन सभ्यता का महत्त्वपूर्ण स्थान है। **प्रो. ल्यूकस** के अनुसार "रोमन सभ्यता ने मानव सभ्यता को दो देन दी हैं—प्रथम, रोम ने यूनानी सभ्यता और संस्कृति को अपनाया और उसे जीवित रखा व इस सभ्यता को विकसित कर उसका अपने विशाल साम्राज्य में प्रसार किया।" यूरोप में पुनर्जागरण लैटिन भाषा की देन थी। आधुनिक प्रजातन्त्र प्रणाली रोमन प्रजातन्त्रीय व्यवस्था पर आधारित है। **प्रो. ल्यूकस** के अनुसार, "जहाँ रोम ने संसार के अधिकांश भाग को लूटा, वहाँ उसने सभ्यता भी प्रदान की। साम्राज्य के एक छोर से दूसरे छोर तक रोमन शासनकाल में विशाल नगरों का निर्माण किया गया। इस सन्दर्भ में **बिल ड्यूरेन्ट** ने लिखा है, "यदि यूनान ने एक सुविकसित संस्कृति को जन्म दिया तो रोम ने उसकी रक्षा की और उसे दूर-दूर तक फैलाया। यूनानियों के आदर्शवाद को उन्होंने व्यावहारिक रूप प्रदान किया।"

रोमन संस्कृति में यूनानी संस्कृति के तत्वों को मिलाकर एक नवीन संस्कृति का उदाहरण पेश किया। उन्होंने इस समन्वित संस्कृति का पूरे यूरोप में प्रसार किया। रोमन साम्राज्य ने लगभग 200 वर्षों तक शांति एवं व्यवस्था कामय रखी एवं उसके बाद के 200 वर्षों तक उसकी रक्षा का हर सम्भव प्रयास किया। शांति एवं व्यवस्था के क्षेत्र में रोमन साम्राज्य की यह एक महत्त्वपूर्ण देन थी। रोमनों ने लिखित विधान की आवश्यकता को अनुभव करते हुए विश्व को एक विकसित विधि संहिता प्रदान की। रोम ने सम्पूर्ण देश में एक समान कानून का निर्माण किया और उसका अनुसरण भी किया।

रोमन सभ्यता ने ही लैटिन भाषा को जन्म दिया। ऐसा माना जाता है कि फ्रांसीसी, इतालवी, स्पेनी, रूमानियन और अंग्रेजी आदि भाषाएँ इसी भाषा से उत्पन्न हुई हैं। ट्रेवर के शब्दों, "अंग्रेजी भाषा एवं साहित्य का जो स्वरूप आज देखने को मिल रहा है, वह लैटिन भाषा की ही देन है।" रोमन साहित्यकारों की रचनाओं ने यूरोपीय साहित्य के विकास पर गहरा प्रभाव डाला है। सिसरो की पात्र-लेखन कला ने यूरोप के गद्य साहित्य के लेखकों पर विशेष रूप से प्रभाव डाला है। आधुनिक

पंचांग जूलियस सीजर के जूलियन पंचांग पर आश्रित है। विश्व के सबसे बड़े ईसाई धर्म का विकास एवं प्रसार रोमन साम्राज्य की देन है। संसार का वर्तमान कानून रोमन कानूनों पर ही आधारित है।

रोमन साम्राज्य के नष्ट हो जाने के बाद भी उसकी प्राचीन सभ्यता परम्पराओं के रूप में आज तक जीवित है। **सैण्डर्सन** ने ठीक ही लिखा है, "रोम के आधिपत्य की स्थापना के साथ सारा प्राचीन इतिहास उसमें विलीन हो गया और रोम के स्रोत से आधुनिक इतिहास का सूत्रपात होता है।" **जे. ई. स्वेन** के शब्दों में "रोमन सभ्यता, जो विश्व सभ्यता के विकास में बहुत महत्त्वपूर्ण स्थान रखती है, वह मध्यकालीन राजनीति, कानून, धर्म और आर्थिक जीवन में आधारभूत बन गई।" इसी प्रकार **बिल ड्यूरेन्ट** ने लिखा है, "यदि यूनान ने एक सुव्यवस्थित संस्कृति को जन्म दिया, तो रोम ने उसकी रक्षा की और अन्य क्षेत्रों में उसका प्रसार किया। यूनानियों के आदर्शवाद को उन्होंने व्यावहारिक रूप प्रदान किया।" **एस्क्विथ** का मानना है कि, "साहित्य, कला और धर्म के क्षेत्र में रोम ने ऐसा पुल बनाया, जिससे होकर प्राचीनकालीन सर्वोत्तम विचार और आदर्श मध्य युग में आये, तत्पश्चात् वर्तमान जगत में।" आधुनिक यूरोपीय-सभ्यता का जन्म रोमन-सभ्यता के गर्भ से हुआ है। रोम प्रथम विश्व राज्य था। अतः इसकी सभ्यता एवं संस्कृति का प्रभाव यूरोप तक ही सीमित न रहकर विश्वव्यापी सिद्ध हुआ है।

7

भारत में नदी-घाटी सभ्यता

भारत की प्राचीन नदी-घाटी सभ्यता को सिंधु घाटी सभ्यता तथा हड़प्पा सभ्यता के नाम से भी जाना जाता है। यह एशिया महाद्वीप के सबसे प्राचीनतम ज्ञात नगरीय संस्कृतियों में महत्त्वपूर्ण स्थान रखती है, इस सभ्यता की प्रथम जानकारी पंजाब में हड़प्पा नामक जगह पर 1921 में और फिर सिन्धु नदी के समीप 1922 में मोहनजोदड़ो में की गई थी। अब ये दोनों स्थान पाकिस्तान में हैं। बाद में सभ्यता के प्रमाण कराची से 480 कि.मी. पश्चिम में अरब सागर तट के समीप सुतकागंडोर दौर और पूर्वोत्तर में 1600 कि.मी. दूर शिवालिक पहाड़ियों की तराई में स्थित रोपड़ तक मिले हैं। बाद में हुई खोज से दक्षिण की ओर पश्चिम तट पर खंभात की खाड़ी तक, कराची के दक्षिण-पूर्व में 800 कि.मी. और पूर्व की ओर दिल्ली के उत्तर में 50 कि.मी., यमुना नदी के बेसिन तक इस सभ्यता का अस्तित्व स्थापित हुआ है। यही कारण है कि यह तीन शुरुआती सभ्यताएं निर्णायक तौर पर सबसे बड़ी हैं। यह एक महत्त्वपूर्ण तथ्य है कि मैसोपोटामिया और मिस्र की सभ्यताएं इससे पहले की हैं।

ज्ञात है कि, इस सभ्यता में पांच विशाल नगरः हड़प्पा, मोहनजोदड़ो, कच्छ में धोलावीरा, पाकिस्तान में अब सूख चुकी हकरा नदी की निम्नभूमि के पास गनवेरीवल, और सतलुज-जमुना विभाजन क्षेत्र में द्रष्डवती नदी के समीप राखी गढ़ी शामिल थे। इनमें से हड़प्पा व मोहनजोदड़ो, दोनों की परिधि 5-5 कि.मी. से ऊपर थी, इसके अलावा तीन नगर इनकी अपेक्षा काफी छोटे थे और इन तीनों नगरों की परिधि 1.5 कि.मी. और 2.5 कि.मी. के मध्य थी। इसके अतिरिक्त नगर व गांवों की संख्या 100 से भी अधिक थी, जो अपेक्षाकृत छोटे आकार के थे, ऐसा लगता है कि यह

एक विशाल साम्राज्य था, जिसका राजनीतिक केंद्र मोहनजोदड़ो था। इस सभ्यता में साक्षरता थी और इसकी लिपि की, जिसमें लगभग 350 मूल वर्ण थे, पहचान आंशिक तौर पर फ़िलहाल द्रविड़ मानी गई है। इसकी तिथियां लगभग 2600-1800 ई.पू. की मालूम होती हैं।

मैसोपोटामिया के साथ व्यापार करने से हड़प्पा की अर्थव्यवस्था को मजबूती मिलती थी। तांबा, सोना, इमारती लकड़ी, हाथी दांत, मोती, सेलखड़ी, लाजवर्द (नीलमणि) और नक्काशीदार गोमेद मैसोपोटामिया को भेजी जाने वाली प्रमुख वस्तुएं थीं। इनमें कई वस्तुएं दूरदराज़ के इलाकों से प्राप्त की जाती थीं। उत्तरी राजस्थान, ओमान और शायद बलूचिस्तान से तांबा, दक्षिण भारत व अफ़गानिस्तान से सोना तथा अफ़ग़ानिस्तान से ही नीलमणि लाए जाते थे।

यद्यपि हड़प्पा के स्थलों और उसके बहुत पहले की आरंभिक सिंधु सभ्यता के स्थलों की सांस्कृतिक परंपराओं में निश्चित समानताएं हैं, फिर भी इन बस्तियों के इतिहास के बदलाव इन्हें अतीत रूप से जुड़े रहने का संकेत नहीं देते। जिस प्रकार से सिंधु सभ्यता की प्रगति हुई थी, उसे देखकर ऐसा प्रतीत होता है कि यहाँ पर पूर्णतया सामाजिक, राजनीतिक तथा आर्थिक संगठनों की प्रगति हो चुकी थी। इस सभ्यता में आजीविका का मुख्य साधन कृषि और पशुपालन था तथा मछली एवं पशुओं का शिकार इसमें पूरक भूमिका निभाते थे। गेहूँ और छह क्यारियों वाली जौ की खेती की जाती थी; गोल मटर, सरसों, तिल और खजूर की कुछ गुठलियां एवं कपास के कुछ पुरातन अवशेष भी मिले हैं। कूबड़धारी मवेशी, भेड़ और बकरियां पालतू पशुओं में शामिल थीं।

कई उत्तरवर्ती ताम्रपाषाण संस्कृतियां हडप्पा सभ्यता के उपरान्त आई, जो किसी तरह की सांस्कृतिक तारतम्यता प्रदर्शित नहीं करतीं। ये ताम्र-पाषाण संस्कृतियां ग्रामीण प्रकृति की थीं और छोटे पैमाने पर थीं। मिट्टी के बर्तनों के आकार और उन पर रोग़न की कला में समरूपता को सिंधु घाटी सभ्यता या हड़प्पा परंपरा का जीवित रहना नहीं माना जाना चाहिए।

इस सभ्यता के अंत के कोई निश्चित प्रमाण अब तक नहीं मिले हैं, परन्तु इसके लिए प्राकृतिक आपदाओं के बजाय हड़प्पा राज्य व्यवस्था के 'संरचनात्मक दबावों' को ज़िम्मेदार ठहराया जा सकता है। मोहनजोदड़ो के उत्तरकालीन स्तरों से यह पूरी तरह स्पष्ट हो जाता है। न सिर्फ़ निर्माण की दृष्टि से मकान घटिया होते गए, बल्कि लगता है कि उनमें विभाजन भी होते गए। जो शायद सामाजिक उथल-पुथल का परिचायक है। राजनीतिक अस्थिरता के कई अन्य सूचक भी हैं।

खंडित संरचनाएं और बहुमूल्य वस्तुओं के भंडार उस काल की असुरक्षा को दर्शाते हैं। मोहनजोदड़ो में तोड़ी गई पाषाण प्रतिमाएं और भीतरी क़ब्रों से आंतरिक संघर्ष और आक्रमणों का पता चलता है। ऐसा मालूम होता है कि आखिरी आघाट अचानक लगा, लेकिन नगर सामाजिक और आर्थिक पतन के कगार पर पहले ही पहुंच चुका था।

सिंधुघाटी सभ्यता के विशेष नमूने सिंधु घाटी सभ्यता से सम्बन्धित पाई गई छोटी मुहरें हैं जो कि सेलखड़ी से बनी हैं। विशिष्ट प्रकार तथा अद्‌भुत गुणवत्ता वाली इन मुहरों पर कई तरह के पशु अंकित हैं, जिनमें वास्तविक—जैसे हाथी, बाघ, गैंडा और हिरन तथा काल्पनिक, अक्सर मिश्रित भी, दोनों तरह के पशु शामिल हैं। कभी-कभी मानव आकृतियों को भी सम्मिलित किया जाता था। सिंधु पाषाणशिल्प के कुछ उदाहरण मिले हैं, जो सामान्यतः छोटे आकार के हैं और मानव मूर्तियां हैं। यहां पर मिट्टी से बनी मानवों और पशुओं की छोटी-छोटी मूर्तियां भी अधिक मात्रा में मिली हैं।

सिन्धु घाटी की सभ्यता का काल

सिंधु घाटी सभ्यता का कालक्रम अब तक निर्धारित नहीं किया जा सका है। इसकी भाषा को अभी तक पढ़ा नहीं जा सका है। इस कारण निश्चित तिथि का ज्ञान नहीं है। कार्बन तिथि निर्धारण पद्धति से यह काल ई. पू. 2300 से 1750 प्राप्त होता है। इसकी तिथि निश्चित करने के लिए हमें दूसरे देशों में पायी जाने वाली सभ्यताओं पर निर्भर रहना पड़ता है। कुछ बर्तन और मोहरें मैसोपोटामिया और बेबीलोन में मिले हैं, जो सिन्धु घाटी के बर्तनों और मोहरों से समानता रखते हैं। इन देशों की सभ्यता का काल लगभग 3000 वर्ष पहले का माना जाता है। इसी कारण यह सभ्यता आज 5000 वर्ष पहले की मानी जाती है।

नगर निर्माण योजना के आधार पर इस सभ्यता के कालक्रम का निर्धारण किया जाता है। मोहनजोदड़ो की खुदाई में सात स्तर प्राप्त हुए हैं। ऐसा डॉ बी.टी. पुलस्कर का मानना है। इसके आधार पर इस सभ्यता को 3250 से 2750 और 2200 ई. पू. के मध्य माना जाता है। इन स्तरों में तीन स्तर उत्तर काल के, तीन मध्य काल के और एक प्राचीन काल का है। सम्भवतः यहाँ और भी प्राचीन स्तर रहे होंगे परन्तु वे पाताल अथवा जल के गर्त में विलीन हो गये हैं। प्रत्येक के लिए 500 वर्ष की अवधि ज्ञात स्तरों में निर्धारित की गई है। इस आधार पर सभ्यता का जीवन काल निर्धारित करने का प्रयत्न किया गया है। इन विभिन्न आचारों पर कहा

जा सकता है कि इस सभ्यता का विकास 2800 ई. पू. से 2200 ई. पू. तक हुआ होगा। कहा जाता है कि सिंधु घाटी सभ्यता का प्रारम्भ पूर्व में भी रहा होगा। हड़प्पा और मोहनजोदड़ो का विकसित नागरिक जीवन निश्चित रूप से शताब्दियों के प्रयत्न का फल रहा होगा। 5000-6000 वर्ष तक इस सभ्यता का काल माना जाता है।

सिन्धु सभ्यता के निर्माता

इस बात को लेकर इतिहासकारों में पर्याप्त मतभेद है कि सिंधु सभ्यता के निर्माता कौन थे। कुछ इतिहासकारों का मानना है कि इसका सम्बन्ध सुमेरियन जाति अथवा क्रीट निवासियों से था। कुछ लोग इस संस्कृति के जन्मदाता को द्रविड़ मानते हैं। यहां पर कोई ऐसी जाति नहीं रहती थी ऐसा सर जान मार्शल का मानना है, अपितु अनेक वर्गों के लोग व्यापार एवं जीविकोपार्जन के लिए यहां आकर रहने लगे थे।

नगर निर्माण योजना

खुदाई द्वारा प्राप्त हुए स्थलों से मालूम होता है कि उस समय अधिकांश लोग शहरों में निवास करते थे। इस सन्दर्भ में डॉ. पुलस्कर महोदय का मानना है कि मोहनजोदड़ो में जाने वाले व्यक्ति उन लोगों के नगर निर्माण को देखकर चकित रह जाते होंगे। इन खण्डहरों में आकर ऐसा प्रतीत होता है कि हम लंकाशायर के नगर में खड़े हैं। नगर का निर्माण एक विस्तृत योजना के अनुरूप किया गया है। इस सम्बन्ध में डॉ. मैके (Dr. Mackay) का एक कथन उल्लेखनीय है–"It is interesting to note that these ancient sites of the Indus are the earliest yet discovered where a scheme to town planning existed."

जो नगर इस सभ्यता में मिले उनके चारों ओर बड़ी-बड़ी सड़कें बनीं थीं। ये सड़कें एक दूसरे से मिलकर आधुनिक सड़कों के समान चौराहे बनाती थीं। मैके के विचार में ये सड़कें और गलियाँ इस तरह बनी हुई थीं कि एक दिशा में चलने वाली वायु दूसरी दिशा में शहर को स्वयं ही साफ कर देती थी। यह कहना कठिन है कि सफाई का कार्य एक व्यक्ति द्वारा किया जाता था अथवा किसी संगठन के द्वारा। फिर भी नागरिकों को कोई कष्ट न हो इसके लिए पर्याप्त व्यवस्था थी। ऐसी व्यवस्था किसी अन्य सभ्यता से नहीं प्राप्त होती है। यात्रियों के ठहरने के लिए सरायों की स्थापना की गई थी। गलियों में प्रकाश की उचित व्यवस्था थी। यात्रियों की रक्षा के लिये पूरी व्यवस्था की गई थी।

यह एक विशेष तथ्य है कि आधुनिक नगरों की तरह कूड़े-करकट और गन्दे पानी को निकालने हेतु एक खास व्यवस्था थी नगर निर्माण योजना के बारे में यह एक विशिष्ट तथ्य माना जाता है। गन्दे पानी को निकालने के लिए पक्की नालियाँ बनी हुई थीं। इन नालियों का निर्माण वैज्ञानिक ढंग से किया गया था। नालियों का निर्माण मिट्टी, चूने, खड़िया और एक तरफ के सीमेन्ट से किया गया था। नालियां खुली और ढकी दोनों प्रकार की होती थीं। छोटी नालियां बड़ी नालियों से जुड़ी हुई थीं। बड़ी नालियाँ नाले से जुड़ी थीं। नाले नगर के बाहर निकाले जाते थे। कई जगह पर टैंकों का निर्माण कूड़ा-करकट एकत्र करने के लिए किया गया था। थोड़े-थोड़े समय पर इसकी सफाई की जाती थी। इस प्रकार उन्नति की व्यवस्था वैज्ञानिक व्यवस्था थी।

भवन निर्माण कला

उतवनन के अवशेषों के विश्लेषण से ज्ञात होता है कि वास्तुकला ने आश्चर्यजनक उन्नति की थी। इस युग के भवन अथवा प्रायः मकान पक्की ईंटों के सड़कों और गलियों के किनारे बनाये गये थे। मकान एक कमरे से लेकर बड़े-बड़े भवन तक बनाये जाते थे। ये भवन तीन प्रकार के होते थे—(i) आवासीय घर (ii) पूजागृह अथवा सार्वजनिक हाल (iii) सार्वजनिक स्नानागार। आवासीय मकान कई प्रकार के होते थे जो प्रायः पक्की ईंटों और मिट्टी के बने होते थे। प्राप्त सीढ़ी के अवशेष से पता चलता है कि मकान एक मंजिल से अधिक के होते थे। भवनों में धूप और हवा आने-जाने के लिए रोशनदान एवं दरवाजे बने थे। प्रत्येक मकान में चारों ओर कमरे और उनके सामने बरामदे बने हुए थे और बरामदे के सामने आंगन बने हुए थे। एक ओर रसोई घर और स्नानगृह बना होता था। दूसरे प्रकार के भवन-पूजागृह और सार्वजनिक हाल होते थे जो राज्य-कार्य चलाने के लिए इस्तेमाल किये जाते थे। तीसरे प्रकार के भवन सार्वजनिक स्नानागार थे। मोहनजोदड़ो का स्नानागार सम्भवतः इन सबसे बड़ा था। प्राचीन काल में यह सरोवर अत्यधिक प्रसिद्ध था एवं कमरे एवं बरामदों की इसके चारों तरफ उचित व्यवस्था थी। इसमें नीचे उतरने एवं चढ़ने के लिए सीढ़ियों की व्यवस्था थी। गंदा पानी निकालने के लिए अलग कुएं का प्रबन्ध था। इस तालाब की मजबूती का इस बात से पता चलता है कि हजारों वर्षों से बिना नष्ट हुआ यह तालाब लगभग उसी रूप में पाया गया है। इस सम्बन्ध में डॉ. मुकर्जी ने लिखा है—"The construction of such a swimming both reflicts great credit on engineering of those days."

अन्य कलायें

मकानों की निर्माण कला के अतिरिक्त नक्काशी की कला, मूर्तिकला, चित्रकला एवं मिट्टी के बर्तन बनाने की कला में सिन्धु घाटी के लोगों ने खास उन्नति की थी। मूर्ति कला में मनुष्यों एवं पशुओं की मूर्तियां प्राप्त हुई हैं। इन मूर्तियों से ज्ञात होता है कि सिन्धु घाटी के लोग मूर्तिकला में बड़े चतुर थे। इन मूर्तियों में एक सांड, कुत्ता एवं शाहधारण किये हुए योगी की मूर्तियां मिली हैं। सिन्धु घाटी के लोग नक्काशी की कला में भी बड़े चतुर थे। अनेक स्थानों पर सुन्दर ढंग से कई तरह के चित्र बने हुए हैं। ये चित्र सांड, बैल, बारहसिंगा एवं हाथी आदि के हैं। इन पर आधुनिक रोगन एवं पॉलिश मिलती है। पॉलिश किये हुए बर्तन विश्व में अपने प्रकार का प्रथम नमूना है।

लेखन कला

सुमेरिया और मिश्र की तरह सिन्धु घाटी सभ्यता के लोग लेखन कला से भी विदित थे। उनकी मुद्राओं में जहाँ मनुष्य और विभिन्न पशुओं के चित्र थे, उनके साथ कुछ लेख भी अंकित हैं। ऐसे चित्र संकेत लगभग 400 से अधिक प्राप्त हुए हैं। 50 वर्षों से इस लिपि को पढ़ने का प्रयत्न किया जा रहा है, परन्तु कोई भी इसको पढ़ने में सफल नहीं हो सका है। मिश्र और सुमेरिया की ऐसी चित्र लिपि पढ़ी जा चुकी है। यह अनुमान लगाया जाता है कि शीघ्र ही इस लिपि को पढ़ा जा सकेगा जिससे संभावना व्यक्त की जा सकती है कि सिन्धु घाटी सभ्यता में अनेक नये आयाम होते हैं।

राजनैतिक जीवन

यद्यपि इस सभ्यता के राजनैतिक संगठन के बारे में कुछ भी निश्चित नहीं कहा जा सकता है, परन्तु सच तो यह है कि किसी भी सभ्यता की उन्नति के पीछे राज्य की विशेष भूमिका रहती है। खुदाई के उपरान्त मिले विशाल मकानों के अवशेषों से ज्ञात होता है कि किसी खास मौके के लिए अथवा शासन आदि के लिए इस्तेमाल किये जाते रहे होंगे। वास्तव में उन दिनों कौन-सी राजनैतिक प्रणाली थी, इस विषय में कोई भी लिखित जानकारी नहीं प्राप्त होती है। यही कारण है कि उनका राजनैतिक जीवन अन्धकार से घिरा हुआ है।

सामाजिक जीवन

सिंधु घाटी की सभ्यता के सामाजिक संगठन के बारे में अब तक पर्याप्त प्रमाण नहीं मिले हैं। फिर भी हड़प्पा एवं मोहनजोदड़ो की खुदाई से ज्ञात होता है कि इनके समाज को निम्न चार वर्गों में विभाजित किया जाता था—योद्धा, विद्वान, श्रमजीवी और व्यवसायी। अन्य सामान्य विशेषतायें निम्नलिखित थीं—

(i) **भोजन**—प्रायः भोजन में अनेक प्रकार के अनाज—गेहूँ, जौ, चावल और दालें एवं सब्जियों और फलों आदि का इस्तेमाल करते थे। कुछ लोग शराब और मांस का प्रयोग करते थे।

(ii) **वस्त्र**—खुदाई द्वारा प्राप्त तकलियां के अवशेष से ज्ञात होता है कि ये लोग सूती, ऊनी कपड़ा बनाना जानते थे और उनका प्रयोग करते थे। चित्रों से ज्ञात होता है कि ये लोग आधे भाग में धोती और ऊपर शाल अथवा चादर का प्रयोग करते थे।

(iii) **साज-सज्जा**—सिन्धु घाटी सभ्यता के लोग सुन्दरता के प्रेमी थे। वे भिन्न-भिन्न प्रकार से शृंगार करते थे। वे कई प्रकार के पाउडर, सुगन्धित तेल एवं लिपिस्टक का इस्तेमाल करते थे। अपने केशों को कंघे के द्वारा कई प्रकार से सजाते थे।

(iv) **आभूषण**—इस सभ्यता में कई तरह के आभूषणों का भी प्रयोग इन लोगों द्वारा किया जाता था। इन आभूषणों में अंगूठी, हार, करधनी, कुंडल आदि का इस्तेमाल करते थे। आभूषण बनाने के लिए सोना, चाँदी, कीमती पत्थर, हाथी दांत एवं हड्डियों आदि को प्रयोग में लाया जाता था।

(v) **मनोरंजन**—इस सभ्यता के लोग कई प्रकार से अपना मनोरंजन करते थे। मिले अवशेषों से विदित होता है कि घरों में शतंरज खेलने की व्यवस्था थी। ये मछली पकड़कर, सांड़ों की लड़ाई देखकर, शिकार करके और पक्षी पकड़कर भी लोग अपना मनोरंजन करते थे।

आर्थिक जीवन

सिंधु घाटी सभ्यता में लोगों के आर्थिक जीवन का अध्ययन निम्नलिखित बिन्दुओं के अंतर्गत किया जा सकता है—

(क) पशुपालन—सिन्धु घाटी सभ्यता के लोग अपने जीविकोपार्जन तथा भरण-पोषण हेतु पशु पालन करते थे। वे पालतू पशुओं में बैल, बकरी, सुअर, भैंस, ऊँट

आदि और जंगली जानवरों में बन्दर, रीछ, खरगोश, चीता और गैंडा आदि पालते थे।

(ख) **कृषि**–इन सभ्यता के लोगों का प्रधान व्यवसाय कृषि था। अनेक प्रकार के अनाजों और सब्जियों की खेती कृषि द्वारा की जाती थी। अच्छा उत्पादन प्राप्त करने के लिए लोग खेती में अनेक प्रकार के यन्त्रों का प्रयोग करते थे और सिंचाई की जाती थी।

(ग) **धातु एवं अन्य उद्योग**–यह युग धातुओं के प्रयोग का युग था। धातुओं में सर्वप्रथम ताँबा और काँसे का प्रयोग आरम्भ हुआ। उपरांत में अन्य धातुओं जैसे सोने चांदी आदि का भी प्रयोग करने लगे। कीमती धातुओं से आभूषण और सस्ती धातुओं से बर्तन एवं हथियार बनाये जाते थे। इनका प्रमुख उद्योग कपड़े का निर्माण करना भी था। कीमती पत्थरों, हड्डियों और हाथी दांत से आभूषण बनाने का कार्य किया जाता था।

(घ) **व्यापार तथा वाणिज्य**–खुदाई से प्राप्त स्रोतों से ज्ञात होता है कि वाणिज्य एवं व्यापार इस युग में भी किया जाता था। चिह्नों से अंकित एक छड़ से ज्ञात होता है कि लोग लम्बाई मापने के पैमाने से परिचित थे। यहाँ बाटों के कई अवशेष मिले हैं जो 1, 2, 4, 8, 16, 32, 64 आदि के अनुपात में हैं। ऐसा लगता है लोग व्यापार करने के लिए दूसरे देशों में भी जाते थे। सिन्धु घाटी की सभ्यता की मुद्राएँ मैसोपोटामिया से प्राप्त हुई हैं। स्पष्ट है यहां के लोगों का व्यापार मैसोपोटामिया से चलता था। व्यापार करने के लिए जल मार्ग एवं स्थल मार्ग दोनों का ही प्रयोग किया जाता था।

(ङ) **कुम्हार**–इस सभ्यता के लोग मिट्टी के बर्तन बनाने की कला में निपुण थे। विभिन्न प्रकार के वर्तनों को चाक की सहायता से बनाया जाता था एवं पकाने के लिए आंच का प्रयोग किया जाता था।

अनेक प्रमाण ऐसे प्राप्त हुए हैं जिनसे ज्ञात होता है कि ये लोग मूर्तिपूजा भी किया करते थे। यद्यपि मन्दिर आदि के अवशेष नहीं प्राप्त हुए हैं। हड़प्पा और मोहनजोदड़ो की गोल चकरियों पर स्त्री आकृतियाँ प्राप्त हुई हैं। उनकी कमर में एक करधनी बंधी है और सिर के ऊपर वह कुछ पहने हुए हैं। ऐसा अनुमान लगाया जाता है कि ये सभी पृथ्वी माता के चित्र रहे होंगे। उसकी आराधना संसार के विशाल क्षेत्र में की जाती थी। यह भी माना जाता है कि ये काली देवी का आरण्विक स्वरूप है। इसके अलावा एक देवता की आकृति प्राप्त हुई है। इसके तीन मुख हैं और वह योगासन में बैठा है। उसके सिर पर दो सींग हैं। देवता के दोनों ओर चार पशु–हाथी,

बारहसिंगा, वृषभ और भैंस हैं। यह शिव (पशुपति) की मूर्ति है ऐसा विद्वानों का मानना है। इन देवी-देवताओं के अलावा वृक्षों में पीपल, पक्षियों में फख्ता, पशुओं में चीता, गैंडा, मगरमच्छ, बकरी और सर्प आदि की पूजा की जाती थी। ये लोग पूर्व जन्म में विश्वास करते थे कि नहीं इसके बारे में उचित जानकारी प्राप्त नहीं हुई है।

सिन्धु घाटी की सभ्यता के पतन के कारण

ऐसा माना जाता है कि इस सभ्यता का अंत 1750 ई.पू. के आस-पास शुरू हो चुका था। यह एक विकसित और विश्व प्रसिद्ध सभ्यता थी। इसका विनाश किस प्रकार हुआ, यह एक आश्चर्य की बात है। विद्वानों में इसके अंत के कारण को लेकर मतभेद है। इस सम्बन्ध में निम्नलिखित विचारधारायें दी गई हैं–

(1) सिन्धु नदी में भीषण बाढ़–कुछ इतिहासकारों का मानना है कि सिन्धु नदी में भयंकर बाढ़ आ जाने के कारण जान-माल दोनों की भारी क्षति हुई। इस भीषण बाढ़ के प्रभाव में यहाँ की सभी बस्तियाँ विनष्ट हो गयीं। कई स्थानों पर बाढ़ के अवशेष मिलते हैं।

(2) गतिहीनता–कुछ इतिहासकारों के अनुसार इस संस्कृति का पतन अचानक नहीं हुआ, परन्तु धीरे-धीरे यह बढ़ता गया और बाद में इसका अन्त हो गया। ए. एस. अल्तेकर और सुधाकर चट्टोपाध्याय इनके समर्थक हैं। उनके अनुसार एक लम्बे समय तक आर्य और सिन्धु सभ्यता के निर्माता साथ-साथ रहे। रंगपुर, लोथल, रोपड़ से प्राप्त अवशेषों से इस बात की पुष्टि होती है। यहाँ ऊपरी स्तरों से मिले अवशेषों में मिश्रण दिखाई देता है। इन विद्वानों का मानना है कि गुजरात, राजस्थान, मालवा और दक्षिण की अन्य सभ्यताओं की चपेट में आकर यह सभ्यता धीरे-धीरे विनाश की ओर अग्रसर होने लगी। 2300 ई. पू. तक सिन्धु घाटी की सभ्यता में ताम्र पाषाण युगीन संस्कृति के लक्षण दिखाई देते हैं। परन्तु 1700 ई. पू. के उपरांत इसमें गतिहीनता आ जाती है।

(3) आर्यों का हमला–अनेक विद्वानों का मानना है कि इस सभ्यता का अन्त आर्यों के आक्रमण के कारण हुआ। इस आक्रमण के अवशेष कई स्थानों पर मिलते हैं। उत्तरी बिलोचिस्तान में राजा गुण्डई के विनष्ट होने के चिह्न मिले हैं। दक्षिणी बिलोचिस्तान में शाही टक्य के कब्रिस्तान में ताँबे की कुछ मोहरें मिली हैं जो पश्चिमी एशिया की मोहरों के अनुरूप हैं। इसकी तिथि 1800 ई. पू. है। मुण्डिगन में भी इस तरह की मोहरें प्राप्त हुई हैं। इस तरह हड़प्पा संस्कृति का सम्बन्ध ईरान आदि संस्कृतियों से दिखाई देता है। हड़प्पा में एक पशु की आकृति के सिर वाला कांसे का पिन मिला

है। यवन के समय के मृद्भाण्डों में भी बदलाव दिखाई देता है। इन सब बातों से ज्ञात होता है कि संस्कृतियों का सम्मिश्रण इसी समय शुरू हो गया था। नई संस्कृति की तिथि ई. पू. 1750 है। इस प्रकार निश्चित ही किसी विदेशी शक्ति (आर्यों) का समावेश इस सभ्यता में हो गया था।

इस सभ्यता के पतन के बारे में विभिन्न साहित्यिक साक्ष्य भी प्राप्त हुए हैं। ऋग्वेद में इन्द्र को नगरों को विनष्ट करने वाला कहा गया है। लोगों का विचार है कि आर्य अग्नि की पूजा इसलिए करते थे, क्योंकि उन्होंने शत्रु के नगरों को विनष्ट किया था। विनष्ट नगरों का वर्णन तैत्तरीय ब्राह्मण (2, 4, 6, 8) में भी प्राप्त होता है। आर्य इन लोगों को वस्यु, अनार्य और दास नामों से बुलाते थे। आर्यों के हमले में यह लोग पूर्वरूप से नष्ट हो गये।

(4) नदी के मार्ग में बदलाव—कतिपय इतिहासकारों के अनुसार सिन्धु नदी ने अपना मार्ग परिवर्तित किया था। इसके कारण लोगों को जल की कठिनाई होने लगी। पेय जल के साथ-साथ कृषि में भी कठिनाई पैदा होने लगी। इसी कारण इन्होंने वस्तियों को छोड़ दिया तथा सैन्धव से रहने वाले लोग अन्य जगहों पर जाकर रहने लगे।

(5) भूचाल—कुछ अवशेषों से पता चलता है कि कई स्थानों पर भीषण भूकम्प आया था। भूकम्प के कारण अनेक बस्तियाँ विनष्ट हो गयी और धीरे-धीरे यहाँ उजाड़ बन गया।

(6) भीषण अकाल—कई विद्वानों का मत है कि कुछ स्थानों पर पड़ने वाले भीषण अकाल भी इस सभ्यता के विनाश का मुख्य कारण बना। सैन्धव क्षेत्र के अनेक स्थानों पर वर्षा नहीं हुई, जिससे खेती नहीं हो सकी और वहाँ भूखमरी मच गई। इस अकाल के कारण अत्यधिक व्यक्तियों की मृत्यु हो गयी और कई व्यक्तियों ने इस स्थान का त्याग कर दिया।

पूर्व में किये गये विवेचनों के अध्ययन से पता चलता है कि इस सभ्यता के अन्त के निम्न कारण हैं। लेकिन इसमें कौन-सा ठीक है, दावे के साथ नहीं कहा जा सकता। प्राप्त प्रमाणों से यह निष्कर्ष निकाला जा सकता है कि इस सभ्यता के पतन का कोई एक कारण नहीं था। इस विकसित सभ्यता के पतन में अनेक कारणों का योगदान था। कई स्थलों की वस्तियों के नष्ट होने का प्रमुख कारण बाढ़, आक्रमण, भूचाल और अकाल था। इस प्रकार यह सभ्यता धीरे-धीरे नष्ट हो गयी।

हड़प्पा

हड़प्पा सभ्यता का उदय 2700-2000 ई.पू. में हुआ था जो संसार की प्राचीन सभ्यताओं में एक है। यह सिन्धु नदी की सहायक रावी नदी के तट पर स्थित गांव

है। यह पाकिस्तान के पूर्वी क्षेत्र में साहिवाल शहर के पश्चिम-दक्षिण पश्चिमी दिशा में स्थित है। यह गांव कई टीलों पर बसा हुआ है, जिनकी 1921 से हो रही खुदाई से सिंधु सभ्यता (जिसे हड़प्पा सभ्यता भी कहते हैं, क्योंकि यह पुरानी सभ्यता के ऐतिहासिक अवशेषों की पहचान का पहला स्थान है) के एक विशाल नगर का पता चला। आकार में हड़प्पा 644 कि.मी. दक्षिण-पश्चिम में स्थित मोहनजोदड़ो के बाद दूसरे स्थान पर है। इस जगह पर ईंटों के चोरी हो जाने के कारण इसका भारी मात्रा में नुकसान हुआ है। परन्तु बस्ती का आकार मोहनजोदड़ो के समान ही मालूम होता है। इसके पश्चिमी सिरे पर एक दुर्ग था और पूर्वी सिरे पर खांचेदार संरचना में बस्ती थी। मिट्टी की ईंटों से क़िलेबंद दुर्ग के बाहरी हिस्से पर पकी हुई ईंटों का पलस्तर था और निश्चित दूरी पर बुर्ज़ बने हुए थे। दुर्ग व नदी के बीच में कामगारों के बैरकनुमा खंड थे और उसके साथ ही एक क्रम में ईंटों से बने वृत्ताकार फ़र्श थे, जिनका इस्तेमाल अनाज कूटने के लिए किया जाता था तथा दो समूहों में 12 हवादार कमरे थे, जो अनाज रखने के काम आते थे। समूची संरचना में दुर्ग की प्रमुखता से नदी के आसपास के क्षेत्र में होने वाली खाद्यान्न आपूर्ति पर सीधे प्रशासनिक नियंत्रण का संकेत मिलता है। पत्थर, इमारती लकड़ी और धातु सहित कच्चे माल को हड़प्पा उत्तर और पश्चिम के पर्वतीय क्षेत्रों से प्राप्त करता था।

हड़प्पा युगीन संस्कृतियाँ

जिन संस्कृतियों की प्रगति हड़प्पा संस्कृति के विनाश के बाद में हुई, वे हड़प्पा युग की संस्कृतियों की श्रेणी में आती हैं। हड़प्पा संस्कृति के पतन की विभिन्न विशेषताओं से युक्त अनेक संस्कृतियों का जन्म हुआ। खास तौर पर राजस्थान, सिन्ध, हरियाणा, पंजाव, गुजरात और पश्चिमी उत्तर प्रदेश में इनका विकास मिलता है। संक्षेप में इन संस्कृतियों की विवेचना निम्न प्रकार है—

(1) मालवा की संस्कृति—चम्बल की घाटी में नागदा, नर्मदा, घाटी में महेश्वर और नावदाटोली की खुदाई से इस संस्कृति के अवशेष मिले हैं यहाँ के मृद्‌भाण्डों की लाल सतह पर काले रंग की चित्रकारी है। यहां पर पत्थर के छोटे फलक भी बड़ी संख्या में मिले हैं। ये लोग वर्गाकार, गोल अथवा आयताकार झोंपड़ियों में निवास करते थे। इनकी दीवारें बांस की पट्टियों पर मिट्टी का लेपकर बनायी जाती थीं। अनाज रखने के लिए मटकों का प्रयोग किया जाता था जो इन झोंपड़ियों में मिले हैं।

यहां रहने वाले लोगों का मुख्य भोजन काफी समय तक गेहूँ रहा। आगे चलकर ये चावल, मसूर, मूंग, मटर और खेसरी का भी इस्तेमाल करते थे। अनाज के साथ गाय, बैल, सुअर, भेड़, बकरी आदि के मांस का भी इस्तेमाल करते थे। ये लोग भी तांबे के

हथियारों का इस्तेमाल करते थे। तांबे से कुल्हाड़ी, मछली मारने के हुक, छल्ले आदि बनाये जाते थे। तांबे से आभूषण भी बनाये जाते थे। उल्लेखनीय है कि इस संस्कृति में अपने शवों को मृद्भाण्डों में रखकर दफनाते थे।

(2) राजस्थान की संस्कृति—आहड़ अथवा बनास संस्कृतियों का जन्म दक्षिणी राजस्थान में हुआ जो हड़प्पा युग की संस्कृतियों में से एक है। इस संस्कृति का सबसे पहले उत्खनन आहड़ नामक स्थान पर किया गया, इसलिए इसे आहड़ संस्कृति के नाम से जानते हैं। इस संस्कृति के अनेक अवशेष बनास नदी की घाटी में प्राप्त हुए हैं, अतः इसको बनास संस्कृति के नाम से भी पुकारा जाता है। इस संस्कृति का विकास लगभग 2000 ई. पू. के आसपास हुआ। इस संस्कृति के अवशेष गिलुंट नामक स्थान से भी प्राप्त किए हैं। आहड़ से काले और लाल रंग के मृद्भाण्ड मिले हैं जिनके ऊपर सफेद चित्रकारी है। चित्तौड़गढ़, भीलवाड़ा और मन्दसौर में भी इस तरह के भाण्ड मिले हैं। इनसे मिलते-जुलते मृद्भाण्ड नर्मदा के तट पर नावदाटोली, तापी नदी के तट पर और प्रकाश नदी पर मिले हैं। इस सभ्यता के अन्तर्गत भवनों का निर्माण पत्थरों एवं कच्ची मिट्टी आदि से किया जाता था। छत बाँस के ऊपर मिट्टी डालकर बनाई जाती थी। इन भवनों के फर्श को लेपे जाने के लिये पीली और काली मिट्टी का प्रयोग किया जाता था। यहां निवास करने वाले व्यक्ति चूल्हे, तंदूर आदि का प्रयोग करते थे। इन स्थानों पर तांबे के औजार बहुतायत में मिले हैं। वे ताँबे से विभिन्न प्रकार के उपकरण जैसे चाकू, चूड़ियाँ, सलाइयाँ, अंगूठियाँ आदि बनाते थे। खेती और पशुपालन इन संस्कृतियों के लोगों का प्रमुख व्यवसाय था।

(3) पूर्व की संस्कृतियां—पूर्वी भारत में हड़प्पा काल की संस्कृतियों के प्रमाण भी प्राप्त हुए हैं। पश्चिमी बंगाल में वीरभूम, बर्दवान, मिदनापुर एवं बांकुरा आदि स्थानों से ताम्र पाषाण कालीन संस्कृति के अवशेष प्राप्त हुए हैं। यहाँ कुछ स्थलों की खुदाई भी हुई है। इन लोगों का प्रमुख व्यवसाय चावल उगाना था। बिहार के दो स्थानों सोनपुर एवं चिरंद में हडिड्यों, पत्थरों के औजारों के साथ-साथ मिट्टी और सरकंडे से बने घरों के अवशेष प्राप्त हुए हैं। ये लोग कृषि में चना, मूंग, गेहूँ और चावल आदि का उत्पादन करते थे। मिट्टी के लाल और काले रंग के बर्तन भी इन्हीं लोगों द्वारा बनाये जाते थे।

(4) दक्षिण भारत की संस्कृति—हड़प्पा काल की संस्कृतियों के प्रमाण भारत के अनेक दक्षिणी राज्यों में मिले हैं। महाराष्ट्र में नेवासा, हायमाबाद, नासिक, इनाम गाँव, सीने गाँव, जोखे चंदोही आदि से इस काल की संस्कृतियों के अवशेष मिले हैं। ये संस्कृति आहड़ और मालवा संस्कृति से प्रभावित हैं। 1400 ई. पू. से 1000 ई. पू. के मध्य एक विशिष्ट संस्कृति का जन्म हुआ जिसे **'जोखे संस्कृति'** के नाम से जानते हैं। मकानों की दीवारों

का निर्माण गारे और मिट्टी से इन लोगों के द्वारा किया जाता था तथा उनके बीच-बीच में लकड़ी के डंडों का प्रयोग किया जाता था और मकानों की छतों का निर्माण फूंस द्वारा किया जाता था। चाक की मदद से अनेक बर्तनों का निर्माण करते थे। वहां से छोटे-छोटे पत्थरों के हथियार भी प्राप्त हुए हैं। ये लोग तांबे के हथियारों का भी उपयोग करते थे। तांबे से ये लोग चूड़ियां, छोटे बर्तन, सलाइयां, छेनियां, छूरे, रथ, सांड, घोड़े, हाथी आदि के खिलौने बनाते थे। यहाँ के लोग गेहूँ, जौ, मसूर, मटर, बेर, पटसन आदि की खेती करते थे। इन लोगों द्वारा कृषि में चावल का उत्पादन काफी कम मात्रा में किया जाता था। अनेक तरह के जानवरों को पालना इन लोगों का प्रमुख शौक था।

रायपुर दोआब, तमिलनाडु और आन्ध्र प्रदेश में हड़प्पा काल की संस्कृतियों के प्रमाण भी प्राप्त हुए हैं। इस संस्कृति की तिथि 2300 ई. पू. से 900 ई. पू. निश्चित की गई है। रायपुर दोआब में संस्कृति का विकास कई चरणों में हुआ। यहां के लोग अपने मकान चौकोर बनाते थे। दीवारें बांस से बनायी जाती थीं और इन पर मिट्टी का लेप कर दिया जाता था। मकान के फर्श पर चूने का लेप किया गया है। यहां मिट्टी के बर्तनों तथा पत्थर के बने औजारों के प्रमाण भी मिले हैं। ये लोग बकरी तथा भेड़ पालन के साथ-साथ बाजरा तथा चने की खेती का कार्य भी करते थे।

(5) गंगा घाटी की संस्कृति–गंगा घाट की संस्कृति भी हड़प्पा काल की संस्कृतियों में मुख्य स्थान रखती है। इस सम्बन्ध में उत्खनन द्वारा पाए गए हस्तिनापुर और अतिरंजी खेड़ा की संस्कृति प्रमुख है। इस संस्कृति का विकास लगभग 2500 ई. पू. के आसपास हुआ। ये लोग भी तांबे के हथियारों का इस्तेमाल करते थे। ये तांबा राजस्थान से लाते थे। वे तांबे से कुल्हाड़ियाँ, भाले, तलवारें आदि बनाते थे। इन स्थलों से मिट्टी के बर्तन भी प्राप्त हुए हैं। इन लोगों ने काले और लाल रंग की मिट्टी का निर्माण किया। कुछ विद्वानों का अनुमान है कि उन्होंने चित्रित मिट्टी के पालिशदार बर्तन बनाये एवं लोहे का भी इस्तेमाल किया। इसलिए इस क्षेत्र को संस्कृति के लौह युगीन संस्कृतियों की जननी माना जाता है। इन लोगों ने कृषि कार्य में चावल का उत्पादन किया।

प्रमुख नगर

मोहनजोदड़ो

मोहनजोदड़ो पाकिस्तान के दक्षिण भाग के सिंध प्रांत में सिंधु नदी के दाहिने तट पर स्थित है। खुदाई से पहले इस स्थान को मृतकों के टीले नाम से सम्बोधित

किया जाता था। मोहनजोदड़ो के पुरातात्विक महत्त्व की पहचान सबसे पहले 1922 में हुई और इसके बाद की खुदाई से पता चला कि इन टीलों में सिंधु घाटी सभ्यता के सबसे बड़े नगर के अवशेष विद्यमान हैं। लगभग 5 कि.मी. परिधि वाले नगर के आकार व इसके अवशेषों की सापेक्षिक समृद्धि और इसमें पाई गई वस्तुओं के कारण इसे सामान्यतः एक विशाल राज्य की राजधानी माना जाता है।

आधुनिक दौर में वास्तुकला की बारीकियों के कोई साक्ष्य नहीं प्राप्त हुए हैं, परन्तु यह आशा की जा सकती है कि यह विनष्ट इमारती लकड़ी के काम तक ही सीमित रहा हो। पाषाण शिल्प भी दुर्लभ है; लेकिन कुछ भग्न अवशेष मिले हैं, जिनमें दाढ़ीयुक्त मानव का सिर और कंधा शामिल हैं, जिसका बड़ा सिर और नीचा ललाट, सिकुड़ी और कुछ-कुछ दंभी आंखें हैं, भौंहों के गिर्द एक पट्टिका और बाएं कंधे पर तीन तहों में एक चादर खुदी है, जिसमें पहले लाल रंग भरा गया था। सौन्दर्य एवं शिल्प कला की दृष्टि से इस शहर की विशेष उल्लेखनीय जो ढ़ेरों कंगन पहने होने के साथ-साथ पूर्णतः कांस्य की बनी एक प्रसिद्ध युवा नर्तकी की प्रतिमा है। मिट्टी से बनी अनेकानेक वस्तुओं में अभिव्यक्तिपूर्ण सांडों और भैंसों की छोटी, लेकिन सशक्त प्रतिकृतियां हैं। भव्य शीश अलंकरण पहने नारी मूर्तियां मिलती हैं और बहुतायत में हास्य बोध दर्शाने वाली मोटे-छोटे पेट वाली महिलाओं व पुरुषों की प्रतिमाएं भी मिली हैं।

मोहनजोदड़ो में शिल्प उत्पादन कार्यों में तांबा/कांसा पिघलाने और ढालने; शंख की चूड़ियां व कड़छियां; पत्थर के चूरे के कंगन; पत्थर के मनके; मिट्टी के रोग़नदार पात्र; सोने व चांदी की मुहरें; मिट्टी के बर्तन और कपड़ा आदि का उत्पादन किया जाता था।

आधुनिक दौर में मोहनजोदड़ो से सिन्धु नदी तीन कि.मी. दूर है तथा यहां प्राप्त हुये प्रमाणों के आधार पर ऐसा लगता है कि यह आज की तरह पहले भी कृत्रिम अवरोधों के द्वारा नदी से सुरक्षित था। आश्चर्यजनक नियमितता के साथ इसका अभिन्यास एक दर्जन खंडों या 'द्वीपों' जैसा किया गया था, जिसमें से प्रत्येक उत्तर से दक्षिण में 384 मीटर और पूर्व से पश्चिम में 228 मीटर का था और यह सीधी या तीखे कोणों पर काटने वाली गलियों द्वारा विभाजित था। पश्चिम दिशा में स्थित केंद्रीय खंड को मिट्टी और मिट्टी से बनी ईंटों द्वारा कृत्रिम रूप से 6 से 16 मीटर की प्रभावशाली ऊंचाई थी और इसे पक्की ईंटों से बनी वर्गाकार मीनारों से एक सीमा तक सुरक्षित बनाया गया था। इन भवनों में चारों तरफ से बरामदों से घिरा हुआ एक सुन्दर तालाब या स्नानागार है जो कि एक ऊंचे शिखर पर निर्मित है, एक विशाल आवासीय संरचना, एक विशाल गोदाम

और मार्गयुक्त कम-से-कम दो सभागार शामिल हैं। इस प्रकार यह पता चलता है कि इस दुर्ग में इस स्थल के धार्मिक केन्द्र स्थित थे। निचले नगर में काफ़ी बड़े प्रांगण युक्त मकान थे, जो खासी संख्या के मध्यम वर्ग के परिचायक हैं। अधिकांश मकानों में छोटे स्नानागार थे और गलियों की भांति उनमें भी नालियां और मलनिकास के ज़रिये थे। ईंटों से बनी सीढ़ियों से कम-से-कम एक ऊपरी मंज़िल या एक समतल आवास योग्य छत का पता चलता है। दीवारों पर मूलतः मिट्टी का पलस्तर था, जो निःसंदेह ईंटों में मौजूद लवणों के हानिकारक प्रभाव को कम करने के लिए था, तापमान और नमी के परिवर्तन होने पर यह भवन को क्षति पहुंचाते हैं।

लोथल

लोथल विशेष रूप से सिन्धु घाटी सभ्यता का मुख्य स्थान, साबरमती नदी की एक सहायक धारा के समीप नीचे मैदान पर निर्मित बस्ती गुजरात राज्य में खम्भात की खाड़ी के पश्चिम में है। प्रतीत होता है कि यह 'वस्तुओं के संग्राहक और परिवहन केंद्र' की भूमिका निभाता था। इसका अभिन्यास भिन्न है : यह स्थल लगभग चौकोर है, उत्तर-दक्षिण दिशा में इसकी लंबाई 360 मीटर और पूर्व-पश्चिमी दिशा में 210 मीटर है। यह ईंटों की एक विशालकाय दीवार से घिरा हुआ था। इस विशाल दीवार की भूमिका में अब तक उचित स्रोत नहीं प्राप्त हुए हैं। दक्षिण-पूर्वी चौथाई हिस्सा ईंटों के विशाल चबूतरे की शक्ल में हैं, जो मिट्टी भरकर बनाया गया है और जिसकी ऊंचाई लगभग चार मीटर है। इस क़िले या दुर्ग पर कुछ और छोटे चबूतरे थे, जिनमें एक-दूसरे को काटते गलियारे बने हुए थे। यह मोहनजोदड़ो के गोदामों की याद दिलाता है, जिसका आयाम 48 × 42 मीटर है। इस खंड के पीछे सार्वजनिक नाली से जुड़े 12 स्नानागारों की क़तार सहित अन्य भवन स्थित थे। अनेक भवनों का निर्माण नीचे बने शहरों में था, जिसमें निवास करने वाले शंख तथा धातु के शिल्पकार थे। निचले शहर में मनके बनाने का एक अलग स्थान भी मिला है। प्रमुख मार्ग उत्तर से दक्षिण को जाता था।

पूर्वी किनारे पर 219 × 37 मीटर का ईंटों से निर्मित एक बड़ा थाला था। इसकी 4.5 मीटर की दीवार वर्तमान समय में भी है। थाले के एक छोर पर एक छोटा जलकपाट या निकास था, जिसे बंद करने की व्यवस्था थी। यहां खुदाई करने वाले इस नतीज़े पर पहुंचे हैं कि यह थाला एक बंदरगाह था और निकटस्थ मुहाने से एक कृत्रिम नहर के ज़रिये जहाज़ वहां तक पहुंचते थे। जल निकास द्वार से पानी के नियंत्रित बहाव द्वारा इसे कीचड़ से मुक्त रखा जाता था। यह विचार सर्वमान्य नहीं है; एक अन्य विचार के अनुसार, यह पेयजल या कृषि कार्य के लिए जल का स्रोत

था। इस स्थान पर एक कब्रिस्तान भी प्राप्त हुआ है जो दीवार की परिधि के बाहर पश्चिम में है।

कालीबंगा

प्राचीन स्थानों में से कालीबंगा सिन्धु घाटी सभ्यता भी एक है। इस स्थान की खोज भारतीय पुरातात्विक सर्वेक्षण विभाग के निदेशक ए. घोष के द्वारा की गई। यहां हड़प्पा-पूर्व और हड़प्पा, दोनों के अवशेष मिले हैं; और यहां दो सभ्यताओं के बीच के संक्रमण को देखा जा सकता है। हालांकि हड़प्पा-पूर्व संस्कृति में तांबे का उपयोग होता था और मिट्टी के बर्तन बनाए जाते थे, लेकिन उनकी कोई लेखन पद्धति नहीं थी और इसके अवशेषों में सुव्यवस्थित अभिन्यास और पक्की ईंटों के उपयोग का अभाव है, जो बाद के हड़प्पा स्थलों में पाया जाता है। यहां के हड़प्पाकालीन अवशेषों में एक क़ब्रिस्तान और संरक्षित दुर्ग भी शामिल है।

भारत में लौह युग

लोहे के आविष्कार ने विश्व की प्राचीनतम सभ्यताओं के विकास के संदर्भ में व्यापक परिवर्तन किया। संसार में लोहे का आविष्कार 200 ई. पू. के आसपास माना जाता है, परन्तु भारत में लोहे का उपयोग नदी घाटी सभ्यताओं के समय से ही आरम्भ हो गया था, क्योंकि वहाँ जंगलों को साफ करने की जरूरत थी। लोहे के आविष्कार के साथ सभ्यता में विकास तेजी से होने लगा। सीमित क्षेत्रों ने धीरे-धीरे बढ़कर साम्राज्य का रूप धारण कर लिया। इस युग की प्रमुख संस्कृतियां निम्नलिखित हैं–

(1) चित्रित धूसर भाण्ड संस्कृति–मुख्य रूप से इस संस्कृति का विकास सिन्धु गंगा क्षेत्र एवं ऊपरी गंगा घाटी में हुआ। इस संस्कृति के हस्तिनापुर, रोपड़ सरदारगढ़, कम्पिल, आलमगीपुर, गंधार प्रदेश आदि मुख्य स्थल हैं। यहाँ के लोगों ने चित्रित भूरे रंग के मृद्भाण्ड का इस्तेमाल किया। इन स्थलों की खुदाई से मिट्टी से निर्मित मटके, पक्की मिट्टी के तबे, पत्थर की मूर्तियाँ, कांच, सीप और हाथी दांत आदि अनेक वस्तुएं प्राप्त हुई हैं। स्पष्ट है ये लोग इन वस्तुओं का निर्माण करते थे। इस काल में तांबे का इस्तेमाल कम हो गया।

(2) पूर्वी भारत की संस्कृतियाँ–लौह-यंत्र उपयोग करने वाली इन संस्कृतियों के अवशेष मध्य निम्न गंगा घाटी में प्राप्त हुए हैं। गंगा घाटी में इसके अवशेष चिरंद और सोनपुर में एवं अजय घाटी में पांटु रानार ढीबी और महिषादल से प्राप्त हुए हैं। महिषादल से प्राप्त अवशेषों की कार्बन-14 तिथि ई. पू. 750 से 700 आती है। इन

संस्कृतियों के लोग पाषाण, तांबे और लोहे के औजारों का इस्तेमाल करते थे। इनके बर्तन काली-लाल मिट्टी के थे।

(3) मध्य भारत की संस्कृति—हालांकि इस संस्कृति के लोगों ने भी लोहे का उपयोग करना प्रारम्भ कर दिया था, लेकिन इस बारे में पर्याप्त प्रमाण नहीं मिलते हैं। इस संस्कृति के अवशेष नागदा एवं एरण से प्राप्त हुए हैं। यहाँ लोहे के आविष्कार के बावजूद ताम्र औजारों का इस्तेमाल जारी रहा। यहाँ तक कि लोग पत्थर की भी वस्तुएं बनाते थे। पत्थर के हथौड़े, मूसल और लोहे की वस्तुओं को तेज करने के औजार बनाए जाते थे। लोहे के बने चाकू, छुरी, चम्मच, कुल्हाड़ी, कील, तीर एवं ताले आदि प्राप्त हुए हैं। ये बर्तन काली और लाल मिट्टी के बने हुए हैं। इस संस्कृति की तिथि लगभग 800 ई. पू. स्वीकार की गयी है।

(4) दक्षिण भारत की संस्कृति—बहुत दिनों तक दक्षिण भारत में महापाषाणीय संस्कृति जारी रही। यहाँ के कई स्थलों से महापाषाणों के साथ-साथ लोहे की वस्तुएं भी प्राप्त हुई हैं। इसका प्रसिद्ध उदाहरण हल्लूर है। ये लोग भी पाषाण एवं लोहे की वस्तुएं इस्तेमाल करते थे।

महापाषाणीय संस्कृति

विशेष रूप से दक्षिण भारत में कावेरी की घाटी में विशालकाय पत्थरों से ढकी कब्रें प्राप्त हुई हैं। इनसे सम्बन्धित संस्कृति को महापाषाणीय संस्कृति कहते हैं। इसका उदय नवपाषाणकाल के उपरांत हुआ।

यह संस्कृति दक्कन के पठार एवं प्रायद्वीपीय भाग में मिलती है। इनके निवास स्थान कर्नाटक में ब्रह्मगिरी, मास्की, पिक्कहल, संगमकल्लु और हल्लुर में प्राप्त हुए हैं। तमिलनाडु में नागार्जुनकोंड, केमरपल्लि, चेलंप्क आदि स्थानों में मिले हैं। तमिलनाडु में उरैपुर, पुनरत्तूर, पेयमपल्लि आदि स्थानों से इनके अवशेष मिले हैं। केरल के पोरकालम नामक स्थान से भी महापाषाण मिले हैं।

उत्खनन द्वारा पाए गए अवशेषों के अध्ययन से पता चलता है कि ये लोग पहाड़ी टीलों पर गुफाओं में रहते थे। इन स्थानों के समीप तालाब, जलाशय आदि होते थे। चावल इनका मुख्य भोजन था। ये लोग शिकार से भी मनोरंजन करते थे। इस संस्कृति के लोगों की बस्तियों का पता तो नहीं है परन्तु कब्रें दूर से दिखाई देती हैं। इन कब्रों में मनुष्य अस्थिपंजर के अलावा मिट्टी के बर्तन और लोहे की वस्तुएं भी मिली हैं। भारत के पूर्वी और उत्तर पश्चिमी क्षेत्रों में भी महापाषाण (Megaliths) प्राप्त होते हैं।

8

वैदिककालीन सभ्यता

ऋग्वैदिक काल

[illegible] द्वारा लिखित ऋग्वेद नामक पुस्तक से इस काल के बारे में विस्तार से जानकारी मिलती है। ऋग्वैदिक काल के बारे में ऐसा प्रमाण मिला है कि शायद इस काल के लोग स्थायी जीवन व्यतीत नहीं करते थे। ऋग्वेद के अध्ययन से भी ऐसा लगता है कि आर्थिक, सामाजिक, कूटनीतिक और यहाँ तक कि धार्मिक जीवन में भी कबायली संगठन प्रभावी था। इस काल के जन-जीवन के वातावरण में युद्धों, हमलों एवं जनसंहार का बोलबाला था। जातियों के आंतरिक तथा अंतर्जातीय युद्धों के अनेक उदाहरण इस संहिता में यहाँ-वहाँ बिखरे हुए हैं। स्वयं दशराज्ञ युद्ध इसका प्रत्यक्ष प्रमाण है। प्रकीर्ण उल्लेखों से ज्ञात होता है कि इस युद्ध में दस नहीं बल्कि तीस से भी अधिक राजाओं ने भाग लिया था। इस तरह की सर्वव्यापी युद्धरतता से एक निष्कर्ष यह निकाला जा सकता है कि वे लोग कोई विशेष स्थायी जीवन-यापन नहीं कर रहे थे। इसकी पुष्टि जीवन के अन्य पहुलओं के पर्यवेक्षण से भी हो जाती है।

वैदिक कालीन भारत में कृषि का विकास क्रमिक गति से हो रहा था। विभिन्न साक्ष्यों से पता चलता है कि प्रारम्भिक काल में कृषि प्रमुख व्यवसाय के रूप में नहीं थी। इस बात की पुष्टि ऋग्वैदिक देवकुल में देवियों के स्थान से भी हो जाती है क्योंकि इससे देवताओं की तुलना में उन्हें नगण्य ही माना गया है। इन्द्राणि, रोदसी, श्रद्धा, धृति आदि सभी को कोई विशेष महत्ता नहीं दी गई है, यहाँ तक कि अदिति

तथा ऊषा जैसी तथाकथित महत्त्वपूर्ण देवियों का उल्लेख भी आदर के साथ नहीं हुआ है। इस काल में यह कहा जा सकता है कि पशुचारण ही लोगों का प्रधान धंधा था तथा इस काल के अंत में कृषि का आगमन हो चुका था, जो संभवतः अनार्य लोगों से संपर्क के कारण हुआ होगा। शायद इसी कारण ऋग्वैदिक आर्य इसे विजित लोगों के धंधे की संज्ञा दी है। चूँकि ऋग्वैदिक अर्थव्यवस्था के उपरोक्त सर्वेक्षण से सिर्फ निर्वाह-अर्थव्यवस्था का ही आभास मिलता है, अतएव उसकी तार्कित परिणति सुगठित कबायली सामाजिक संगठन ही था। समाज में ऐसा विभाजन दृष्टिगोचर नहीं होता कि एक खास वर्ग उत्पादक है एवं दूसरा उत्पादन का नियंत्रणकर्ता। परवर्तीकालीन पुरुष सूक्त के आधार पर ऋग्वैदिक काल के शुरू से ब्राह्मण, क्षत्रिय, वैश्य तथा शूद्र रूपी चातुर्वर्ण्य समाज की कल्पना भी की गई। इस सूक्त में इन चारों वर्णों की उत्पत्ति आदि पुरुष के भिन्न-भिन्न अंगों से बतलाई गई है। यह तो वर्ण-व्यवस्था का अर्थ उत्पादन-पद्धति द्वारा सर्जित एक ऐसी सामाजिक संरचना से लगाया जाए, जिसमें पुरोहित तथा कुलीन वर्गीय योद्धाओं के रूप में ऊंची श्रेणियों के लोग उत्पादन के नियंत्रणकर्ता एवं अधिशेष उत्पादन के संग्रहकर्ता थे, एवं निम्न श्रेणी में आने वाले किसान, कारीगर, कृषि श्रमिक आदि ही उत्पादन का कार्य करते थे, तो इस तरह का चित्र ऋग्वेद में दृष्टिगोचर नहीं होता। कबायली समाजों में भोजन के उत्पादक या संग्रहकर्ता ही उसके भोक्ता भी होते हैं—इन समाजों में बिचौलियों का कोई स्थान नहीं होता।

ऋग्वेद में **जन, विश्, गण, व्रात, सार्ध** आदि जिन इकाइयों का उल्लेख है, वे सभी भाईचारे वाले सिद्धांत पर आधारित थीं और कबायली संगठन की ओर संकेत करती हैं। **जन** तथा विश् की तुलना में **गण** कोई महत्त्वपूर्ण उत्पादन इकाई नहीं थी। ऋग्वैदिक लोग एक जगह से दूसरी जगह जाते थे और इस प्रवासी प्रक्रिया में वे अपने पशु-संपदा को भी लेकर चलते होंगे। यही कारण है कि **विश्** को आधार मानकर अनेक उपसर्ग जोड़कर, उदाहरण के तौर पर **आ-विश्, उपविश्, नि-विश्, प्र-विश्, पुनर-विश्** आदि अभिव्यक्तियों के द्वारा लोगों का एक स्थान से दूसरे स्थान पर प्रवेश, पुनः प्रवेश संस्थापन, आदि का उल्लेख ऋग्वेद में प्रायः मिलता है। परवर्तीकालीन वर्ण-व्यवस्था के चिह्न भी दृष्टिगोचर नहीं होते—यह बात इस वर्णन से स्पष्ट होती है कि सिर्फ इतना ही नहीं है कि तथाकथित निम्नवर्ग अर्थात् शूद्रों पर किसी तरह की अपात्रताएँ नहीं लगाई गई थीं, बल्कि समाज के प्रति एक सकारात्मक दृष्टिकोण अपनाया गया था। कोई भी विशेषाधिकार-संपन्न वर्ग न था—यहाँ तक कि **राजन्** भी संपूर्ण कबीले के अन्य लोगों के समान ही था—**यों व सेनानीर्महतो गणस्य राजा वातस्य प्रथमो बभूव।**

कबीले के प्रतिनिधि तथा विशेष गुण सम्पन्न होने के कारण युद्ध के बाद जिस धन की प्राप्ति होती थी, उसका अधिक भाग पुरोहितों तथा मुखिया को मिलता था। इस समय भी वर्ण व्यवस्था थी। परवर्ती कालीन वर्ण-समाज की तुलना में मुख्य विभेद यह था कि अधिशेष उत्पादन के अभाव में कबायली समाज में वर्ग-भेद की परिस्थितियों का उदय हो सका। कबीले के मुखिए से ओहदों की विभिन्नता का आभास होता है। किंतु कबीलों के सामान्य लोगों के श्रम पर रहने वाले उच्च वर्गों का उल्लेख विशद स्तर पर दृष्टिगोचर नहीं होता शायद ऐसे वर्ण-समाज की रूपरेखा देखी जा सकती है। ऐसा प्रतीत होता है कि इस उल्लेख के माध्यम से वर्ण-समाज को कर्मकांडीय तथा सैद्धांतिक अनुसमर्थन प्रदान किया जा रहा था। ऋग्वैदिक समाज में 'दास' तथा 'दस्यु' का उल्लेख भी नितांत ही जरूरी है। क्योंकि इनके साथ आर्यों के संघर्ष के पर्याप्त वर्णन हैं। दस्यु आर्यों के भारत आगम के समय यहाँ के मूल निवासी थे। पाश्चात्य विद्वानों की भी यही धारणा रही है कि ये अनार्य जातियाँ इस भू-भाग की आदि निवासी थीं, जिनके घोर विरोध एवं अदम्य उत्साह की वजह से आर्यों को अनेक अवसरों पर कठिनाइयों का सामना करना पड़ा और दैवी मदद से ही वे उनका मुकाबला करने में सफल हो सके। किंतु दास तथा दस्युओं को 'अनार्य' श्रेणी में रखना समस्या का अत्यंत सरलीकरण प्रतीत होता है। हो सकता है कि ये लोग आर्यों के विभिन्न दलों के प्रतिनिधि हों और कुछ सांस्कृतिक तथा सैद्धांतिक मतभेदों के कारण दास करार कर दिए गए हों। उदाहरण के तौर पर यदु तथा तुर्वश जातियाँ निस्संदेह आर्य पंचमानुषों में गिनी जाती थीं लेकिन इन्हें भी एक जगह 'दास' कहा गया है। ऋग्वेद के दो महत्त्वपूर्ण नायकों—दिवोदास तथा सुदास के नामों की ध्वनियाँ भी कुछ कम महत्त्वपूर्ण नहीं हैं। भाषा शास्त्र की दृष्टि से शम्बर, शुष्ण, तुग्र वेतसु, चुमुरि, अर्बुद जैसे दास नेताओं के नाम अनार्य नहीं प्रतीत होते। दास लोगों के विषय में कहा गया है कि वे न अग्नि के हविर्दान करते थे और न ही इन्द्र-वरुण के पक्षपाती थे। दस्यु भी अदेवयु (देवताओं में श्रव न रखनेवाले), **अब्रह्मन** (वेदों को न मानने वाले), **अयज्वन्** (यज्ञ न करने वाले) बताए गए हैं। इसी प्रकार **अनासः** (नासिका रहित अर्थात् चपटी नाक वाले) तथा **मृध्रवाचः** (कटु-वाणी वाले—इसका इस्तेमाल आर्यों के एक अन्य शत्रु, अर्थात् पणियों के लिए भी किया गया है) जैसे विशेषणों के आधार पर दस्युओं को आर्यों से भिन्न जाति तथा सांस्कृतिक पृष्ठभूमि का बताया गया है। ऋग्वेद इस बात की पुष्टि करता है कि इस समय में दासों से नहीं अपितु दस्युओं से आर्य जाति को अधिक खतरा था। दस्यु हत्या का उल्लेख कहीं अधिक हुआ है। आर्यों के हृदय इनके प्रति डर एवं घृणा के भाव से आच्छादित

रहते थे। एक स्थल पर तो इन्हें **अमानुष** की संज्ञा दी गई है। संक्षेप में यह कहा जा सकता है कि दास तथा दस्यु भारत की आदिम अनार्य जाति ही नहीं बल्कि आर्यों के ही अंश हो सकते हैं, जो विभिन्न समयों में भारत आए और जो सांस्कृतिक भिन्नताएँ रखते थे।

ऋग्वैदिक काल में कूटनीतिक संगठन के कबायली स्वरूप की पुष्टि सभी समिति तथा विदथ जैसी संस्थाओं के स्वरूप तथा कार्यप्रणाली के विवेचन के आधार पर भी की जा सकती है। यद्यपि समिति का उल्लेख सिर्फ परवर्ती मंडलों में ही हुआ, सभा का वर्णन न तो मूल भाग में मिलता है। किंतु, सभा, समिति तथा विदथ के संबंध में जो थोड़े-से भी विवरण प्राप्त हैं, उनसे लगता है कि इन विभिन्न संस्थानों में संपूर्ण कबीले के सामाजिक, आर्थिक तथा धार्मिक मामलों पर चर्चा होती थी। ऋग्वेदकालीन धार्मिक जीवन एवं उस समय के लोगों की सैद्धांतिक मान्यताएँ तत्कालीन भौतिक जीवन से अत्यधिक प्रभावित थीं। अतः यह स्वाभाविक ही है कि इस क्षेत्र में भी कबायली विशेषताएँ दृष्टिगोचर हों। ऊपर आर्थिक तथा सामाजिक जीवन के संदर्भ में कहा गया था कि पशुचारण उनका प्रमुख धंधा था और पितृ-प्रधान समाज था। इसी संदर्भ में एक पहलू और इंगित किया गया था—ऋग्वैदिक देवकुल में देवियों की नगण्यता। चूंकि पशुचरण के लिए लोगों को जगह-जगह जाना पड़ता था, अतः उनके ये अभियान प्राकृतिक शक्तियों से अत्यधिक प्रभावित थे। संभवतः यही कारण है कि जहाँ ऋग्वैदिक देवकुल में अनेक देवताओं का स्थान मिला है, वहाँ ये सभी देवता प्राकृतिक शक्तियों के सूचक भी हैं।

सूर्य, अग्नि, द्यौस, मरुत्, वायु और यहाँ तक कि इन्द्र, वरुण, मित्र, विष्णु आदि भी प्राकृतिक शक्ति के गुणों को भी स्वतंत्र देवत्व प्रदान कर दिया जाता था। उदाहरणार्थ, सवितृ तथा विवस्वान् मूलतः सूर्य के विशेषण थे किंतु बाद में स्वयं सूर्य देवता बना दिए गए। ऋग्वेद में प्राप्त एक अवधारणा, जो विशेष रूप से उस काल के लोगों की सैद्धांतिक मान्यताओं की ओर संकेत करती है, ऋत की है प्राच्यविद्या के आरंभिक चरणों में विन्टरनिट्ज, मैकडॉनेल, कीथ अथद सभी ने **ऋत** की व्याख्या 'सृष्टि की नियमितता', 'भौतिक तथा नैतिक व्यवस्था', 'अंतरिक्षीय तथा नैतिक व्यवस्था; आदि रूपों में की है। किंतु वास्तव में यह तो इस अवधारणा का एक ही पहलू है। इस संदर्भ में एक दृष्टव्य विवरण यह है कि ऋग्वेद के मंत्र दृष्टाओं ने **ऋत** के ह्रास पर आँसू बहाए हैं और उसके पुनरुत्थान की कामनाएँ प्रकट की हैं। उत्तर वैदिक काल के साहित्य में तो **ऋत**पूर्ण रूप से लुप्त ही हो चुका था। अगर ऋत का अर्थ सिर्फ भौतिक, नैतिक या अंतरिक्षीय व्यवस्था मात्र होता तो उसके ह्रास पर आँसू

न बहाए जाते। ऋग्वेद में 24 ऐसे श्लोक हैं, जिनमें यह कहा गया है कि **ऋत** के द्वारा लोगों की गाएँ जल, उनका भोजन, उनकी भौतिक समृद्धि एवं जीवनयापन के अन्य साधन प्राप्त होते थे। अर्थात् ऋत समस्त भौतिक साधनों का प्रदाता था। **वरुण** को **ऋतस्य गोपा** कहा गया है। उसके आदेशों के उल्लंघन पर उसके आक्रोश का पर्याप्त वर्णन है। ऋत के वास्तविक अर्थ को समझने के लिए अक्ष (पासा) के साथ उसके संबंध की चर्चा भी अनुचित न होगी। कहा गया है कि पासा खेल कर **ऋत** की रक्षा तथा स्थापना होती है। यहाँ प्रतीक के माध्यम से इस बात पर बल दिया गया कि जिस प्रकार पासे को मुट्ठी के बंद करके नहीं रखा जा सकता और सभी के सामने खुले हाथों से फेंका जाता है, उसी प्रकार संपत्ति की सामूहिकता के द्वारा न्याय तथा ऋत की स्थापना होती है। सारांश यह है कि ऋग्वेद में प्राप्य ऋत की अवधारणा तत्कालीन **प्राक्-वर्गीय** (Pre-Class) समाज और कबायली जीवन के अनुरूप थी और जब कालांतर में समाज वर्णों तथा वर्गों में विभाजित हो गया और लोगों में लालच, ईर्ष्या, स्वार्थ अथवा लूट की भावना ने घर कर लिया तो ऋत का ह्रास हो गया—तभी वरुण की महत्ता का भी पतन हुआ। यदि हम ऋग्वैदिक काल के कबाइली जीवन पर ध्यान दें तो इस समय की आसुरी प्रवृत्तियों के साधन तथा देवी देवता भी सादय माने जा सकते हैं। कृत्या, निऋति, यातुधान, ससरपरी, आदि इसी प्रकार की अपकारी शक्तियाँ थीं। अनेकों जादू-टोनों का भी वर्णन मिलता है। अज, शिग्रु, कश्यप, गौतम, कौशिक, माण्डूक्य, मत्स्य आदि जातियां तथा व्यक्तियों के नामों से **गणचिह्नात्मक** (टोटम संबंधी) आस्थाओं के प्रचलन का आभास मिलता है। एक स्थान पर तो स्वयं प्रजापति की कल्पना भी कूर्म के रूप में की गई है, अथर्ववेद में भी इस तरह के अनेकों उल्लेख हैं। यह एक सामान्य ज्ञान की बात है कि कबायली धार्मिक जीवन की विशेषताओं में टोटम विश्वास, पूर्वज पूजा, भूत-प्रेत आदि में विश्वास, जादू-टोना, प्रतीक पूजा, आदि प्रमुख हैं। इस समय बहुदेववाद के स्थान पर ईश्वर की एक सत्ता के प्रभाव भी मिलते हैं।

उत्तर वैदिक काल

इस काल का तथाकथित कूटनीतिक इतिहास एक कथात्मक परंपरा है और किसी प्रकार के पुरातात्त्विक साक्ष्य से पुष्ट नहीं है, लेकिन तब भी सामाजिक, आर्थिक एवं कूटनीतिक क्षेत्रों में एक ऐसे ढांचे का प्रादुर्भाव हुआ, जो छोटे मोटे परिवर्तनों के साथ सदियों तक चला। इस काल में विकसित होने वाले ढांचे की प्रमुख विशेषताएँ थीं—कृषि प्रधान अर्थव्यवस्था, कबायली संरचना में दरार न पड़ना और वर्णव्यवस्था

का जन्म एवं क्षेत्रगत साम्राज्यों का उदय। तकनीकी विकास की दृष्टि से यही वह काल है, जबकि उत्तरी भारत में लौह युग की शुरुआत हुई। यद्यपि लोहे ने तत्काल ही ताम्र-कांस्य का स्थान नहीं ले लिया होगा, फिर भी यह विकास का एक ऐसा कदम था, जिसमें जीवन के विभिन्न पहलुओं को प्रभावित करने की अपार क्षमता थी। लोहे के अर्थ में **श्याम अयस् या कृष्ण अयस्** के अनेक उल्लेख उत्तर वैदिक साहित्य में मिलता हैं। शुरू में कोसांबी जैसे विद्वानों ने लोहे के क्रांतिकारी योगदान पर पहली बार बल दिया, लेकिन इस आरंभिक उत्साह में कालांतर में ढील न आ गई। ऐसा प्रतीत होता है कि लौह तकनीक का प्रयोग शुरू में युद्धास्त्रों के लिए और फिर धीरे-धीरे कृषि तथा अन्य आर्थिक गतिविधियों में होने लगा। इस तरह का अनुमान संभवतः सिर्फ इसी आधार पर लगाया गया है अब तक प्राप्य लौह उपकरणों में युद्धास्त्रों की ही प्रधानता है। यदि विभिन्न उत्खननों से प्राप्त लोहे की वस्तुओं का **स्तरविन्यासात्मक** (Stratigraphic) वितरण-संबंधी ब्यौरा प्राप्त होता तो निश्चित रूप से इसकी जानकारी करने में और अधिक सरलता होती।

इस काल में मानव जीवन पर कृषि के विकास के परिणामस्वरूप परिवर्तन आने लगा था। चित्रित धूसर एवं उत्तरी काली पॉलिश मृद्भांड पुरातात्त्विक संस्कृतियों से, जिन्हें हम विभिन्न सीमाओं के बावजूद उत्तर वैदिक काल की कृतियाँ बता चुके हैं, लोगों के स्थायी जीवन की पुष्टि होती है। यद्यपि अथर्ववेद में मवेशियों की वृद्धि के लिए अनेक प्रार्थनाएँ हैं, किंतु उत्तरवैदिक काल में कृषि ही लोगों का प्रमुख धंधा था। शतपथ ब्राह्मण में तो जुताई से संबंधित कर्मकांडों पर एक पूरा-का-पूरा अध्याय है। बीज बोना, कटाई, गहराई आदि का भी उसमें उल्लेख है। इस काल के हल इतने विशाल होते थे कि उनमें 4 से लेकर 24 बैल तक जोत दिए जाते थे। हड्डियों जैसे सख्त खदिर तथा कत्था से निर्मित फाल का वर्णन हमें प्राप्त है। यद्यपि पुरातात्त्विक साक्ष्य उपलब्ध नहीं हैं, किंतु इस काल के साहित्य में तो **प्रवीरवन्त** या **पवीरव** का भी उल्लेख है। **दात्र** या **सृणि** अर्थात् दराँती के कतिपय अवशेष तो उत्खननों में भी मिले हैं। ऋग्वेद की तुलना में उत्तर वैदिक साहित्य में विभिन्न अनाजों का वर्णन है।

प्राकृतिक गोबर-खाद और ऋतुओं के ज्ञान का कृषि-प्रक्रिया में उपयोग भी तत्कालीन विकसित कृषि प्रणाली का द्योतक है यद्यपि उत्पादन की मात्रा का अनुमान लगाना असंभव है, किंतु चूँकि समाज में स्पष्टतः ब्राह्मण तथा क्षत्रिय जैसे अनुपादी वर्गों का उदय हो चुका था, अतः यह निष्कर्ष निकाला जा सकता है कि कृषक अपनी जरूरत से कहीं अधिक उत्पादन करने की न सिर्फ क्षमता रखते थे, बल्कि उन्हें अपने निर्वाह से भी अधिक उत्पादन करना पड़ता था। कृषि के अतिरिक्त, विभिन्न प्रकार

के शिल्पों का उदय भी उत्तर वैदिककालीन अर्थव्यवस्था की अन्य विशेषता थी। इन विभिन्न व्यवसायों के अनेक विवरण हमें **पुरुषमेध** के विवेचन में मिलते हैं जिनमें धातु के शोधक, रथकार, बढ़ई, चर्मकार, स्वर्णकार, कुम्हार, व्यापारी आदि उल्लेखनीय हैं। ब्राह्मण ग्रंथों में श्रेष्ठी का भी उल्लेख है, किंतु बुद्धकालीन **सेट्ठियों** से उनकी तुलना व्यर्थ है। राजसूय यज्ञ के दौरान, **रत्नहवींषि** अनुष्ठान के समय जब राजा **तक्षण** तथा **रथकार** के भी घर जाता था, तब भी श्रेष्णियों को 'रत्निन' का दर्जा प्राप्त न था।

इस समय की व्यवस्था विभिन्न प्रकार की सामाजिक वर्ग व्यवस्थाओं में विभक्त थी। अर्थात् वर्ग इस तरह बंटे थे कि ब्राह्मण तथा क्षत्रिय अनुत्पादी होते हुए भी विशेषाधिकार-सम्पन्न थे, क्योंकि वे ही उत्पादन के नियंत्रणकर्ता थे। वैश्य तथा शूद्र निम्न वर्ग के थे और वे उत्पादन के लिए उत्तरदायी थे। इन वर्णों के पारस्परिक संबंधों पर दृष्टिपात कर लेना अनुचित न होगा। यद्यपि ब्राह्मण तथा क्षत्रिय दोनों ही विशेषाधिकार-संपन्न वर्ग के थे, किन्तु फिर भी उनमें आपस में तनाव की स्थितियों की झलक दृष्टिगोचर होती है। उत्तर वैदिक साहित्य में ब्रह्म तथा क्षत्र एवं मित्र वरुण के जिस द्वंद्व का उल्लेख है, वह ब्राह्मणों तथा क्षत्रियों के पारस्परिक मनमुटाव का ही सूचक है। हालांकि इस बात से इंकार नहीं किया जा सकता कि निजी स्वार्थों को दृष्टिगत करके वे कभी-कभी आपस में सांठ-गांठ भी कर लेते होंगे। अब यहां प्रश्न यह उठता है कि किस कारण से आपस में संघर्ष करते थे? इसके जवाब में यही कहा जा सकता है कि शायद यह समाज में प्रथम स्थान प्राप्त करने की लालसा का संघर्ष था।

ऋग्वेदकालीन धार्मिक जीवन की भाँति उत्तर वैदिक काल के लोगों की धार्मिक आस्थाएँ तथा गतिविधियाँ भी तत्कालीन भौतिक पृष्ठभूमि से कुछ कम प्रभावित न थी। इस युग में एक ओर तो ब्राह्मणों द्वारा प्रतिपादित तथा पोषित यज्ञ अनुष्ठान तथा कर्मकांडीय व्यवस्था थी, तो दूसरी ओर इसके विरुद्ध उठाई गई उपनिषदों की आवाज। यों तो यज्ञादि का आभास ऋग्वेद में भी मिलता है किंतु एक स्वतंत्र पंथ के रूप में इसका विकास इसी युग में हुआ। चूँकि ब्राह्मण एक अनुत्पादी वर्ग था, अतः अपने को विशेषाधिकार संपन्न वर्ग बनाए रखने के लिए यह जरूरी हो गया कि वे लोगों के मस्तिष्क पर अपनी धार्मिक श्रेष्ठता की छाप बनाए रखे। जिस प्रकार कर्मकांड का विकास इस युग में दृष्टिगोचर होता है, उसमें ब्राह्मणों का स्वार्थ निहित था। शुरू में तो क्षत्रियों ने भी इस पंथ को बनाए रखने में ही अपना हित समझा--इसके दो कारण थे। एक तो जैसा कि ऊपर कहा जा चुका है, ब्राह्मण तथा क्षत्रिय दोनों ही अधिशेष उत्पादन के हथियाने में रुचि रखते थे। इस युग के महत्त्वपूर्ण यज्ञों जैसे

अश्वमेध, वाजपेय, राजसूय, आदि का विस्तृत अध्ययन करने से पता चलता है कि मूलतः इनका उद्देश्य कृषि-उत्पादन को बढ़ाना था। वाजपेय तो खाद्य तथा पान से संबंधित था ही, अश्वमेध तथा राजसूय भी, जो कि तथाकथित कूटनीतिक शक्ति के द्योतक माने जाते हैं, यदि उनका ऐतिहासिक विश्लेषण किया जाए तो स्पष्ट होता है कि इन यज्ञों के कूटिनीतिक उद्देश्य खाद्यान्न उत्पादन ही था, जो कि भूमि की उर्वरता तथा प्रजनन शक्ति की प्रतीक था। वाजपेय यज्ञ में ऐसी क्रियाओं के संबंध में बृहदारण्यक उपनिषद् तथा वाजसनेयी संहिता में महत्त्वपूर्ण उल्लेख है। राजसूय यज्ञ में भी संपूर्ण वर्ष के दौरान चलने वाले अनुष्ठानों का अंत ऐसे यज्ञ से होता था, जिसकी अध्यक्षता **इन्द्रशुनासीर** अर्थात् हलयुक्त इन्द्र करता था और जिसका उद्देश्य 'पस्त प्रजनन शक्ति को पुनः जाग्रत करना होता था'। अगर राजसूय राजा के सिंहासनारोहण से संबंधित होता तो केवल एक बार होना चाहिए था, लेकिन वह तो हर साल चलता रहता था। जिस प्रकार आद्य तथा **प्राक्वर्णी समाज** में भोजन एकत्र करने के कार्य को सुगम बनाने के लिए जादुई कर्मकांड ने ले लिया था, जो विशेषाधिकार-संपन्न वर्ग ही कर सकता था। स्त्रियों द्वारा कर्मकांडीय व्यवस्था का समर्थन करने का दूसरा कारण यह था कि इनके माध्यम से वे आर्य सभ्यता की सीमा पर रहने वाले अनार्य प्रमुखों के बीच अपना प्रभुत्व बढ़ा पाते थे। अथर्ववेद एवं पंचविंश ब्राह्मण में गद्य के व्रात्य मुखिया को वैदिक समाज में प्रवेश देने के लिए विशाल कर्मकांड का आयोजन किया गया है। इसी प्रकार निषादों के मुखिया को वैदिक अनुष्ठानों में स्थान दिया गया है। राजसूय यज्ञ के दौरान जिन लगभग एक दर्जन रत्निनों के घर राजा जाता था, उनमें से चार स्त्रियाँ होती थीं। यह इस बात की ओर संकेत करता है कि अनार्य जातियों के **मातृकुलीय** रिवाजों को नजरअंदाज नहीं किया गया था।

इस समय कर्मकाण्डों की अतिशयता के कारण व्यक्ति की मानसिक स्वतंत्रता लगभग समाप्त हो रही थी, परिणामतः विभिन्न प्रकार के प्रतिरोधों का जन्म हुआ। ऋग्वेद में कुछ जगहों पर **ब्रह्मद्विष** अर्थात् वेद से घृणा करने वालों का उल्लेख किया गया है। यहाँ वेदों की आराधना करने वालों को स्वार्थी पुरोहित के रूप में वर्णित किया गया है। उपनिषदीय विचारकों ने यज्ञादि अनुष्ठानों को ऐसी कमजोर नौका बताया है, जिसके द्वारा यह भवसागर पार नहीं किया जा सकता। उन्होंने इस उद्देश्य के लिए इंसान को जीवन के चक्र से मोक्ष दिलाने के लिए ज्ञान मार्ग का प्रतिपादन किया। यह ज्ञान मार्ग था **ब्रह्मन्** तथा आत्मन् के बीच अद्वैत भाव का अनुभव करना। चूँकि कबायली संगठन में दरार पड़ चुकी थी तथा वर्णव्यवस्था का आविर्भाव हो चुका था।

महाजनपदों का प्रादुर्भाव

वैदिक साहित्य महाजनपद काल से सम्बन्धित जानकारी के प्रमुख स्रोत हैं। इन साहित्यों में इस समय की सामाजिक संरचना, धार्मिक जीवन, कृषि तथा तत्कालीन आर्थिक स्थिति के विषय में पर्याप्त जानकारी मिलती है। ऋग्वेद एवं अथर्ववेद की संहिताओं, पूर्ववर्ती ब्राह्मणों एवं उपनिषदों से विभिन्न जनों के जीवन एवं संगठन के विषय में जानकारी प्राप्त होती है। इन साहित्यों से जन से जनपद के विकास की प्रक्रिया एवं प्रारंभिक अवस्थाओं में जनपदीय जीवन की झांकी मिलती है। बौद्ध साहित्य में भी जनपद काल की स्थितियों का अच्छा चित्रण मिलता है। अंगुत्तर निकाय में सोलह महाजनपदों एवं क्षेत्रविस्तार के निमित्त काशी, कोशल एवं मगध जनपदों के कूटनीतिक संघर्षों का वर्णन है, जो जनपदीय जीवन में ऐसी नवीन प्रवृत्तियों के उदय का परिचायक है इस समय मगध का प्रभाव बहुत अधिक था। अखिल भारतीय साम्राज्य की स्थापना भी इसी महाजनपद के नेतृत्व में हुई।

उत्तर वैदिक युग में हुए आर्थिक परिवर्तनों के कारण ऋग्वेदीय कबायली जनजीवन में दरार का पड़ना और क्षेत्रीयता की भावना का जागरण होना स्वाभाविक था। पशुचारण से कृषि की ओर अग्रसर होना, जिसके पर्याप्त प्रमाण उत्तर वैदिक साहित्य और कतिपय पुरातात्त्विक अवशेषों में मिलते हैं, अपने आप में एक ऐसी प्रक्रिया थी, जिसके परिणामस्वरूप गंगा घाटी के निवासियों के जीवन के स्थायित्व का पुट आ गया। छोटे-छोटे कबीले 'राज्य' बनते जा रहे थे और 'साम्राज्य' का लक्ष्य भी कुछ दूर नहीं था। बुद्ध के समय तक पहुँचते-पहुँचते 'जन' का काफ़ी रूपांतरण हो चुका था और जनपदों का जन्म हो गया था। महाजनपदों के विषय में जानकारी के प्रमुख स्रोतों के रूप में बौद्ध तथा जैन साहित्य की भी महत्त्वपूर्ण भूमिका है। इस समय के महाजनपद मुख्यतया तीन प्रकार के थे--

1. कुछ जनों में पहले संयोग हुआ और उसके बाद उसका जनपद के रूप में विकास हुआ। जैसे—पांचाल।
2. कई जन अधिक शक्तिशाली जनों के द्वारा विजित होने के बाद, उन्हीं में मिला लिए गए। जैसे—अज।
3. कुछ जनों अथवा कबीलों ने अकेले ही जनपद की अवस्था प्राप्त कर ली। जैसे--मत्स्य, चेदि, काशी, कोशल आदि।

इन जनपदों का स्वतंत्र न होकर कई संस्थाओं के विकास का परिणाम था। लगभग ईसा पूर्व 700 तक लोहे का इस्तेमाल पहले से अधिक होने लगा था और

इससे बनाए जाने वाले औजारों से कृषि एवं अन्य उत्पादन के साधनों में प्रगति हुई थी। एक बात स्पष्ट है कि दलदली इलाका होने के बावजूद 600 ईसा पूर्व के सभी प्रसिद्ध नगर गंगा-यमुना नदियों के आस-पास ही बस गए। इसके कई कारण थे। जैसे—गंगा स्वयं ही एक महत्त्वपूर्ण व्यापारिक मार्ग थी और इसके द्वारा समुद्र तक आसानी से पहुँचा जा सकता था। बिहार में मगध और अंग में कच्चे लोहे का पर्याप्त भंडार था और गंगा ऐसे स्थानों से होकर गुजरती थी। एक बार इन खानों का मार्ग मालूम होने पर आर्यों के लिए हिमालय की नीचे की श्रेणियों से मगध की ओर जंगल साफ करते हुए मुड़ना सरल हो गया।

प्रमुख महाजनपद

कुछ प्रमुख महाजनपदों के बारे में संक्षिप्त जानकारी निम्न प्रकार दी गई है—

(1) मत्स्य—मत्स्य जनपद आधुनिक जयपुर क्षेत्र के आस-पास था। विराट नामक संस्थापक पर इसकी राजधानी विराटनगर थी। साहित्यिक स्रोतों में 'अपर मत्स्य', 'वीर मत्स्य' आदि जो उल्लेख आए हैं, वे संभवतः मूल राज्य की शाखाएँ हों। मत्स्य प्रदेश कभी चेदि जनपद के अधीन था।

(2) चेदि—प्राचीन काल में चेदि महाजनपद यमुना नदी के किनारे पर स्थित था। इसकी सीमा कुरु महाजनपद के साथ जुड़ी हुई थी। आधुनिक बुंदेलखंड का इलाका ही प्राचीन महाजनपद था। कलिंग (उड़ीसा) में जिस चेदि वंश का राजा खरवेल था, वह संभवतः इसी चेदि प्रदेश की शाखा ने ही स्थापित किया होगा।

(3) कम्बोज—कम्बोज प्रदेश उत्तरपथ में ही स्थित था। आधुनिक काल के राजोरी और हजारा के जिलों में प्राचीन काम्बोज सीमित था। काम्बोज में पहले तो शासन की बागडोर राजा के हाथ में होती थी किन्तु कौटिल्य के समय यह एक संघराज्य बन गया था।

(4) अवन्ति—पश्चिमी भारत में अवंति जनपद प्रमुख था। आधुनिक मालवा व मध्य प्रदेश के कुछ भागों से मिलकर अवंति जनपद बना था। प्राचीन समय में अवंति के दो भाग थे—उत्तरी अवंति जिसकी राजधानी उज्जैन थी और दक्षिणी अवंति जिसका प्रमुख नगर महिष्मती था। वर्धमान महावीर एवं गौतम बुद्ध के समय में, महाराज चंड प्रद्योत अवंति के राजा थे। अवंति बौद्ध धर्म का प्रसिद्ध केंद्र था। अनेक बौद्ध थेर तथा थेरी यहाँ बौद्ध धर्म का पालन व प्रचार करने में रत थे। पुराणों के अनुरूप चंड प्रद्योत शक्तिशाली राजा था। उसके समय में अवंति का वत्स, मगध एवं कोमल के साथ युद्ध हुआ था। मगध सम्राट शिशुनाग ने अवंति को जीतकर

अपने राज्य में मिला लिया। अवंति राज्य का पर्याप्त आर्थिक महत्त्व रहा है क्योंकि अनेक व्यापार मार्ग इस प्रदेश से होकर गुजरते थे।

(5) गांधार—गांधार महाजनपद आधुनिक पेशावर एवं रावलपिंडी के इलाके में स्थित था। इसकी राजधानी तक्षशिला प्राचीन काल में विद्या तथा व्यापार का प्रसिद्ध केंद्र थी। ईसा पूर्व छठी शताब्दी में गांधार में पुष्कर सारिन राज्य करता था। उसने अवंति के साथ युद्ध किया और चंड प्रद्योत को हराया। मगध के साथ उसके संबंध अच्छे थे। वहाँ उसने अपना राजदूत एवं बिंबिसार के नाम पत्र भी भेजा था।

(6) अश्मक—अंगुत्तर निकास में अश्मक जनपद का भी वर्णन है। इसकी राजधानी पोतना थी। यह जनपद गोदावरी नदी के किनारे पर स्थित था। अश्मक और मूलक प्रदेश एक दूसरे के पड़ौसी थे। दोनों ही इक्ष्वाकु वंश के क्षत्रिय थे। दीर्घ निकाय के 'महागोविंद सुन' में इस बात का उल्लेख है कि रेणु नामक सम्राट के ब्राह्मण पुरोहित महागोविंद ने अपने साम्राज्य को सात अलग-अलग राज्यों में बाँटा था। इनमें से एक अश्मक भी था। अश्मक की पहचान के संबंध में एक संभावना यह भी हो सकती है कि वह सिंधु नदी की निम्न घाटी या मुहाने पर स्थिति ऐस्सकेलॉय ही हो, जिसका उल्लेख यूनानी लेखकों ने किया है और जो सिकंदर के हमला के समय भी मौजूद थे। इस संबंध में एक और तथ्य द्रष्टव्य है—बौद्ध साहित्य में अश्मक सहित जिन 16 महाजनपदों का उल्लेख है, उनमें से सभी 15 उत्तरी भारत के हैं।

(7) वज्जि—मगध के उत्तर की ओर वज्जि संघ स्थित था। यह संघ आठ कुलों के संयोग से बना और इनमें तीन कुल प्रमुख थे—विदेह, वज्जि एवं लिच्छवि। विदेह कुल की राजधानी वैशाली थी। इसमें तीन जिलों का उल्लेख है जो कदाचित तीन कुलों के प्रमुख क्षेत्र थे। उस संघ में लिच्छवि कुल का खास उल्लेख है। महावस्तु से ज्ञात होता है कि गौतम बुद्ध लिच्छवियों के निमंत्रण पर वैशाली गए थे। बौद्ध साहित्य लिच्छवियों के सामाजिक व कूटनीतिक जीवन पर प्रकाश डालता है। लिच्छवियों का आंतरिक संगठन अच्छा था और गौतम बुद्ध के विचार में लिच्छवि गण इसी कारण अजेय था। इस एकता के भंग होने पर लिच्छवि राज्य पर मगध अथवा अन्य कोई राज्य विजय कर सकता था।

(8) मल्ल—सोलह महाजनपदों का विवरण देते हुए अंगुत्तर निकाय में मल्ल राष्ट्र का उल्लेख आया है। इसके दो भाग थे जिसमें एक की राजधानी कुशीनगर और दूसरे की पावा थी। कुशीनगर में ही महात्मा बुद्ध ने निर्वाण प्राप्त किया था। मल्ल राज्य में पहले शासन की बागडोर राजा के हाथ में होती थी किंतु कालांतर में वहां

गणराज्य की स्थापना हुई। मल्ल राष्ट्र में भी जैन एवं बौद्ध धर्म बड़े व्यापक रूप से फैला। महात्मा बुद्ध के महापरिनिर्वाण के उपरांत ही मल्ल राष्ट्र ने अपनी स्वतंत्रता खो दी। मगध ने इस पर विजय प्राप्त करके अपने राज्य में मिला लिया।

(9) अंग—यह महाजनपद जिसकी राजधानी चंपा थी, उल्लेख पालि साहित्य में मिलता है। आधुनिक भागलपुर व मुंगेर का इलाका प्राचीन अंगदेश में शामिल था। गौतम बुद्ध के समय में अंग और मगध जनपदों में सदा युद्ध की हालत बनी रहती थी। कुछ समय के लिए मगध अंगदेश का भाग बन गया किन्तु शीघ्र ही अंग का पतन हो गया।

(10) मगध—मगध का उदय सम्प्रति बिहार के नालन्दा व उसके आसपास की भूमि में हुआ। इसकी राजधानी राजगृह थी बाद में इसकी राजधानी पाटलिपुत्र को बनाया गया। इस राज्य का संस्थापक बृहद्रथ था। उस समय यह सबसे शक्तिशाली राज्य के रूप में उभरा, क्योंकि इसका भौगोलिक वातावरण, यहाँ की भूमि, खनिज सम्पदा आदि सभी इसके अनुकूल थे। बिम्बिसार ने मगध को शक्तिशाली बनाने के लिए कई राज्यों को विजित किया।

(11) काशी—काशी जनपद की राजधानी वाराणसी थी। समय-समय पर इसके नरेशों का कोसल के साथ युद्ध हुआ। कभी विजय काशी की होती थी और कभी कोसल की। गौतम बुद्ध के समय में काशी का कूटनीतिक पराभव हो गया। यह कुछ समय तक कोसल देश का अंग था। मगध और कोसल में भी काशी को लेकर संघर्ष शुरू हो गया। अजातशत्रु के समय से काशी मगध का अंग बन गया।

(12) वत्स—वत्स जनपद आधुनिक इलाहाबाद का क्षेत्र था। कौशांबी इसकी राजधानी थी। संस्कृत साहित्य में प्रसिद्ध उदयन, जो बुद्ध का समकालीन माना जाता है, इस जनपद से संबंधित था। अवन्ति के राजा प्रद्योत के साथ उसकी शत्रुता के विषय पर अनेक मनोरंजक कथानक प्राप्त हैं, जिनमें वासवदत्ता और उदयन के प्रणय-प्रसंग खास रूप से उल्लेखनीय हैं।

(13) शूरसेन—इसकी राजधानी मथुरा थी। शूरसेन राजा अवंतिपुत्र, महात्मा बुद्ध का अनुयायी था और उसने ही अपने राज्य में बौद्ध धर्म का प्रचार करवाया। राजा के नाम से ऐसा प्रतीत होता है कि मथुरा एवं अवंति के मध्य वैवाहिक संबंध थे। पाणिनि के समय में अंधक एवं वृष्टिजन का वास-स्थान मथुरा में था। कालांतर में इन जातियों का एक पारस्परिक संघ स्थापित हुआ।

(14) कोशल—16 प्रमुख महाजनपदों में इसका प्रमुख स्थान रहा। इसका विकास काल छठी शताब्दी ईसा पूर्व रहा। इसने काशी के शक्तिशाली राज्य को अपने

राज्य में मिला लिया; और लगभग 500 ई. पू. में, राजा प्रसेनजित (पसेंदि) के शासनकाल में इसे उत्तर की चार शक्तियों में से एक (शायद सबसे शक्तिशाली) माना जाता था। कोशल उस समय गंगा नदी के मैदान के व्यापार मार्गों पर नियंत्रण रखता था। उत्तरी कोशल के वाक्य जनजाति में जन्मे बुद्ध (लगभग 563 ई. पू.) अक्सर राजधानी श्रावस्ती में उपदेश देते थे, जहां उन्होंने जीवन के अंतिम 25 वर्षों में वर्षा ऋतु का समय व्यतीत किया।

(15) पंचाल—पंचाल जनपद उत्तर वैदिक काल से ही प्रसिद्ध था। इसके दो भाग थे—उत्तर पंचाल जिसकी राजधानी अहिच्छत्र थी तथा दक्षिण पंचाल जिसकी राजधानी काम्पिल्य थी। कन्नौज का प्रसिद्ध नगर उन दिनों पंचाल प्रदेश में ही स्थित था। अधिकांशतः आधुनिक पश्चिमी उत्तर प्रदेश इसी जनपद के अंतर्गत आता था। हिमालय की तलहटी से लेकर दक्षिण में चंबल नदी तक एवं पूर्व में कोसल और पश्चिम में कुरु जनपद इसकी सीमाएँ थीं। पंचाल मूलतः एक राजतंत्र था किंतु ऐसा प्रतीत होता है कि कौटिल्य के समय तक वह एक गणराज्य हो गया था।

(16) कुरु—पंचाल के समान कुरु भी उत्तर वैदिक साहित्य में पर्याप्त ख्याति प्राप्त राज्य था। सही मायने में ब्राह्मण ग्रंथों में तो कुरु-पंचाल का जोड़ा अत्यधिक शक्तिशाली माना जाता था, जिन्होंने अनेक अश्वमेध यज्ञों का अनुष्ठान किया था। कुरु जनपद आधुनिक जिला और दक्षिण-पूर्व हरियाणा का प्रदेश था। जातकों के विचार में इसकी राजधानी इंद्रप्रस्थ थी। यादवों, भोजों, पंचालों के साथ कुरु राजाओं ने वैवाहिक संबंध स्थापित किए थे। वत्स प्रदेश में जिस राजतंत्र की स्थापना हुई वह संभवतः कुरु की ही शाखा थी। यह संभवतः उस समय हुआ होगा जब कि कुरु प्रदेश का महत्त्वपूर्ण नगर हस्तिनापुर बाढ़ में विनष्ट हो गया होगा। इसका उल्लेख पौराणिक ग्रंथों में भी मिलता है इसके साथ ही साथ इसकी पुष्टि हस्तिनापुर के उत्खननों से भी होती है।

महाजनपदों की शासन व्यवस्था

इस समय सभी महाजनपदों में पृथक्-पृथक् शासन व्यवस्था थी। जहाँ कुछ राज्यों में राजा सर्वोपरि था वहीं कुछ ऐसे भी जनपद थे जहाँ पर शासक का चुनाव जनमत पर आधारित था। ऐतरेय ब्राह्मण के विचार में पूर्व दिशा (मगध, कलिंग, अंग आदि) के जो राजा हैं, उनका साम्राज्य के लिए अभिषेक होता है और वे 'सम्राट' कहलाते हैं। दक्षिण दिशा में जो सात्वत (यादव) राज्य हैं, वहाँ का शासन 'भोज्य' है और उनके शासक 'भोज' कहे जाते हैं। पश्चिम दिशा (रुराष्ट्र, कच्छ, सौवीर आदि) का शासन स्वराज्य है और उसके शासन 'स्वराट' कहलाते हैं। उत्तर दिशा में हिमालय

के क्षेत्र में (उत्तर कुरु, उत्तर मद्र, आदि) जो राज्य हैं, वहाँ वैराज्य प्रणाली है और वहाँ के शासक 'विराट' कहलाते हैं। मध्य देश (कुरु, पंचाल, कोशल आदि) के राज्यों के शासक 'राजा' कहे जाते हैं। इस तरह ऐतरेय ब्राह्मण में, साम्राज्य, भोज्य स्वराज्य, वैराज्य और राज्य, इन पांच प्रकार की प्रणालियों का उल्लेख है। सम्राट वे शासक थे जो वंशक्रमानुगत होते हुए अपनी शक्ति के प्रसार के लिए अन्य राज्यों का मूलोच्छेद करने को तत्पर रहते थे। जरासंध आदि मगध सम्राट इसी प्रकार के थे। भोज, शायद उन राजाओं को कहते थे जो वंशक्रमानुगत न होकर कुछ निश्चित समय के लिए अपने पद पर नियुक्त थे। सात्वत यादवों (अंधक, वृष्णि, आदि) में यह प्रथा विद्यमान थी। कृष्ण संभवतः भोज अथवा संघमुख्य थे। स्वराज वे शासक थे जिनकी दशा 'समानों में ज्येष्ठ' (Primus interpares-first among the equals) की होती थी।

इन स्वराज्यों में कतिपय कुलीन श्रेणियों का शासन होता था और सब कुलों की दशा एक समान मानी जाती थी। संभवतः वैराग्य जनपद वे थे जिनमें कोई राजा नहीं होता था और जहाँ जनता अपना शासन स्वयं करती थी। कुरु-पंचाल आदि मध्यदेश के जनपद राज्य कहलाते थे और वहां प्राचीन काल की परंपरागत शासन प्रणाली विद्यमान थी। राजतंत्र—जहां राजा का पद वंशानुगत होता था—के बारे में कुछ अधिक जानकारी प्राप्त है। ऐसा प्रतीत होता है कि गंगा घाटी में अधिशेष उत्पादन तथा लौह तकनीक के आगमन से जिन बड़े-बड़े राज्यों की स्थापना हुई, उन्हें करारोपण का आदि रूप निश्चित करने का अवसर मिला और उन्होंने एक प्रकार की नौकरशाही को भी जन्म दिया। राजा की मदद के लिए नियुक्त इन पदाधिकारियों में—संग्रहीत, सूत, ग्रामणी, भागदुध, पुरोहित आदि थे। ये लोग राजा के प्रति उत्तरदायी थे और इन्हें कर से प्राप्त हुए धन में से वेतन दिया जाता था। इन्हें 'रत्निन' भी कहा जाता था। स्थानीय शासन की देखरेख एक खास मंत्री करता था। पुरोहित धार्मिक मामलों में राजा का सलाहकार होता था। सेना के प्रधान सेनानी कहलाते थे। राज्यारोहण के समय सम्पन्न किए जाने वाले विभिन्न कर्मकाण्डों का उद्देश्य था ईश्वर से ऐसी प्रार्थना करना कि वह राजा को अपने समस्त गुण प्रदान करे ताकि राजा की शक्ति में बढ़ोत्तरी हो सके।

महाजनपदों की आर्थिक स्थिति

छठी शताब्दी ई. पू. में महाजनपदों की आर्थिक दशा की जानकारी के प्रमुख पहलू व्यापार की प्रगति, सिक्कों का प्रचलन, नगरों का उत्थान हैं। इस काल में जैन

व बौद्ध साहित्य से हमें कई नगरों के उत्थान का वृत्तांत मिलता है। चंपा, कौशांबी, राजगृह, श्रावस्ती, उज्जयिनी, वैशाली, पाटलिपुत्र आदि प्रमुख नगर थे। व्यापारिक मार्गों पर स्थित नगरों की खास महत्ता थी, जैसे काम्बोज, कौशांबी, कोशल, वाराणसी आदि हैं, जो उत्तरापंथ से आकर बनारस में घोड़े बेचते थे। ई. पू. 600 में कृषि के अतिरिक्त धन प्राप्त करने के अनेक साधन थे। बौद्ध साहित्य से हमें कई प्रकार के उद्योग-धंधों के बारे में ज्ञान होता है, जैसे कि कुम्हार, रथकार, सुनार, धातुकार, बढ़ई, हाथी दांत का काम करने वाले एवं रेशम का काम करने वाले। कारीगर प्रायः श्रेणियों में संगठित थे। प्रत्येक श्रेणी का एक मुखिया होता था जिसे 'जेत्थक' कहते थे। सेट्ठी अथवा श्रेष्ठि भी श्रेणी का मुखिया होता था। श्रेष्ठि कई बार महाजन का काम करते थे और बहुधा व्यापारिक श्रेणियों के भी मुखिया होते थे।

प्रायः सभी राजा श्रेष्ठियों को बहुत आदर व सम्मान देते थे। इस तरह नगरों से कारीगर व श्रेष्ठि दो वर्ग अधिक महत्त्वपूर्ण थे। गाँवों में 'गहपतियों' का लगभग वही स्थान था जो श्रेष्ठियों का नगरों में। गाँव की उर्वरा भूमि का बड़ा भाग गृहपति (गहपति) के समीप होता था। बौद्ध साहित्य में ऐसे कई गहपतियों का उल्लेख है जिनके पास कृषि व भूमि के माध्यम से बहुत धनधान्य था। गहपति मेंदक के बारे में बौद्ध साहित्य में यह विवरण आया है कि वह सेना को वेतन देता था और गौतम बुद्ध एवं बौद्ध संघ की सेवा के लिए उसने 1,250 गायों के झुंड भेंट किए थे। इस तरह समाज में कुछ वर्ग ऐसे बने जिनके हाथ में धन का अधिक भाग था। ईसा पूर्व छठी शताब्दी तक मुद्रा-प्रणाली का भी उदय हो चुका था। लगभग संपूर्ण भारत में प्राप्त चाँदी की आहत मुदाओं के सैकड़ों पुंज मिलने और उत्खननों के दौरान भी उनकी प्राप्ति से इन मुद्राओं की संख्या सहस्रों में हो गई है।

मुद्रा के आगमन से निश्चय ही व्यापार-विनिमय में पर्याप्त सहयोग मिलता होगा। ऐसा प्रतीत होता है कि तकनीकी उपलब्धियों के कारण कृषि का उत्पादन अब कुछ **अधिशेष** (surplus) की दशा में पहुँच गया था जिसके परिणामस्वरूप राज्य की शक्ति के उदय में और मदद मिली। सामरिक रूप से शक्तिशाली तत्त्वों को इस अधिशेष उत्पादन को प्राप्त करना सरल होता होगा। इन सभी गतिविधियों ने 'जन' से 'जनपद' की प्रक्रिया में अतुलनीय भूमिका का निर्वहन किया।

बौद्ध धर्म

विभिन्न धार्मिक तथा सामाजिक जटिलताओं में जिस बौद्ध का प्रादुर्भाव गौतम बुद्ध ने किया वह कालान्तर में लोक कल्याणकारी रहा। उनका जन्म शाक्य कुल में

होने के कारण उन्हें शाक्य मुनि भी कहा जाता है। उनके पिता शुद्धोधन हिमालय की तराई में स्थिति शाक्य गणराज्य के प्रधान थे जिसकी राजधानी कपिलवस्तु थी। उनका जन्म लुंबिनी नामक वन में ईसा से 563 वर्ष पूर्व वैशाख मास की पूर्णिमा के दिन हुआ था। उनके जन्म के कुछ समय बाद ही उनकी माता की मृत्यु हो गई तथा उनका लालन-पालन उनकी मौसी और विमाता प्रजापति गौतमी ने किया। गौतम के जन्म से उनके पिता की पुत्र-प्राप्ति की इच्छा पूरी हुई थी, अतः उनका मूल नाम सिद्धार्थ रखा गया।

एक बार वे रथ पर राजमहल से बाहर घूमने के लिए निकले। रास्ते में उन्होंने तीन ऐसे दृश्य देखे जिन्होंने उनकी जीवनधारा बदल दी। उन्होंने एक बूढ़े और कमज़ोर व्यक्ति को देखा, उन्होंने एक कोढ़ी को देखा और अंत में उन्होंने एक मुर्दा देखा। इन तीन दृश्यों को देखकर गौतम का मन संसार से उचाट हो गया। 29-30 वर्ष की आयु में उन्होंने अपना घर त्याग दिया और वे सच्चे सुख की खोज में निकल पड़े। गौतम का यह गृह-त्याग 'महाभिनिष्क्रमण' कहलाता है। घर का त्याग करने के बाद गौतम ने पहले दो ब्राह्मण तपस्वियों से योग सीखा, लेकिन इससे उनकी ज्ञान-पिपासा शांत न हो सकी। इसके बाद उन्होंने उरुवेला नामक वन में 6 वर्ष तक तपस्या की। वहां पीपल के वृक्ष के नीचे ध्यानमग्न बैठे गौतम को वैशाख पूर्णिमा की रात को अचानक ऐसा लगा कि उन्हें ज्ञान प्राप्त हो गया है। तभी से वे बुद्ध के नाम से विख्यात हुए। जिस वृक्ष के नीचे गौतम को ज्ञान प्राप्त हुआ, वह 'बोध वृक्ष' कहलाया और जिस स्थान पर उन्हें ज्ञान प्राप्त हुआ, वह 'बोध गया' कहा गया।

आर्य सत्य—गौतम बुद्ध के अनुसार जीवन के प्रमुख चार आर्य सत्य निम्नवत् हैं—

1. संसार में दुःख है।
2. हर दुःख का कोई-न-कोई कारण है। मुख्य कारण है तृष्णा अर्थात् भौतिक सुखों की कभी समाप्त न होने वाली चाहत।
3. दुःखों के कारण से छुटकारा संभव है।
4. दुःखों पर विजय पाने का मार्ग है।

अष्टांगिक मार्ग—गौतम बुद्ध ने निम्नवत् अष्टांगिक मार्गों का प्रतिपादन किया—

1. सम्यक् दृष्टि : सत्य-असत्य, पाप-पुण्य, सदाचार-दुराचार में भेद करना ही सही दृष्टि है।

2. सम्यक् संकल्प : कामना और हिंसा से मुक्त होकर आत्म-कल्याण का पक्का निश्चय करना।
3. सम्यक् वाणी : सत्य, विनम्र तथा मृदु वचन बोलना तथा वाणी पर संयम रखना।
4. सम्यक् कर्म : सब कर्मों में पवित्रता रखना।
5. सम्यक् आजीविका : न्यायपूर्ण मार्ग पर चलकर अपनी जीविका का अर्जन करना।
6. सम्यक् प्रयत्न : सत्कर्मों के लिए निरंतर उद्योग करते रहना।
7. सम्यक् स्मृति : लोभ-मोह, क्रोध आदि चित्त के संतापों से बचना और श्रेष्ठ शिक्षाओं को सदा याद रखना।
8. सम्यक् समाधि : राग तथा द्वेष से रहित होकर चित्त की एकाग्रता को बनाए रखना।

गौतम बुद्ध ने आचरण के दस नियम निर्धारित किए। इन नियमों को शील कहते हैं। ये नियम निम्नवत् हैं--

1. अपरिग्रह अर्थात् वस्तुओं का संग्रह न करना।
2. अहिंसा व्रत का पालन करना।
3. कोमल शैया का त्याग
4. कामिनी-कंचन का त्याग।
5. नृत्य-गान का त्याग।
6. सदा सत्य बोलना।
7. सुगंधित पदार्थों का त्याग।
8. अस्तेय अर्थात् चोरी न करना।
9. ब्रह्मचर्य अर्थात् इन्द्रियों पर संयम रखना।
10. असमय में भोजन का त्याग।

त्रिपिटक—बौद्ध धर्म के साहित्य को 'त्रिपिटक' कहा जाता है। इसके अन्तर्गत तीन प्रकार के त्रिपिटक हैं—(1) सुतापिटक, (2) विनयपिटक (3) अभिधम्मपिटक।

सुतापिटक के निम्नवत् पांच विभाग हैं—

1. दीघ निकाय,
2. मज्झिम निकाय,
3. संयुक्त निकाय,

4. अंगुत्तर निकाय, और
5. खुद्दक निकाय।

भगवान बुद्ध की मृत्यु के बाद बौद्ध धर्म में दो मुख्य संप्रदायों का विकास हुआ। इनमें से एक था हीनयान और दूसरा था महायान।

***हीनयान* संप्रदाय** बौद्ध धर्म के प्राचीन अथवा मूल स्वरूप को महत्त्व देता है। हीनयान निवृत्ति के ऊपर अधिक बल देता है और उसकी साधना-पद्धति कठोर है। उसका पालन थोड़े-से लोगों के लिए ही संभव है।

महायान संप्रदाय सभी मनुष्यों को, गृहस्थों को भी, निर्वाण का अधिकारी बनाना चाहता है। महायान संप्रदाय में भगवान बुद्ध को परमात्मा माना जाने लगा। उसमें मूर्तिपूजा का भी प्रचलन हुआ। महायान में 'बोधिसत्व' की कल्पना प्रसूत होती है। इस सिद्धांत के अनुसार साधक स्वयं बुद्धत्व प्राप्त करने में रुचि नहीं लेता। वह अपने सभी साथियों का दुःख दूर करने में ही सच्चा निर्वाण-सुख समझता है।

जैन धर्म

ऋषभदेव ने जिस जैन धर्म का प्रवर्तन किया उसे 24वें तीर्थंकर के रूप में महावीर स्वामी ने गतिशील बनाया तथा लोक मानस में इसके प्रति जागरूकता उत्पन्न की। सारांश में जैन धर्म सभी जीवों के प्रति अहिंसा पर आधारित अनुशासित जीवन के ज़रिये आध्यात्मिक मोक्ष के मार्ग की शिक्षा देता है। अपने इतिहास के दौरान यह एक सांस्कृतिक प्रणाली बन गया, जिसने भारतीय सभ्यता के दर्शन और तर्कशास्त्र, कला और वास्तुकला, गणित, खगोलशास्त्र और ज्योतिष और साहित्य जैसे क्षेत्रों में महत्त्वपूर्ण योगदान दिया। जैन धर्म का नाम संस्कृत क्रियामूल जिन यानी 'विजयी होना' से निकला है, इसका तात्पर्य उस सात्विक युद्ध से है, जो साधकों और साधिकाओं को आवेग और दैहिक इंद्रियों से लड़ना पड़ता है, ताकि वे सर्वज्ञान तथा आत्मा की पूर्ण शुद्धि प्राप्त कर सकें, जिसे जैन धर्म में मोक्ष कहा जाता है। जिन थोड़े-से व्यक्तियों ने यह सर्वज्ञान और आत्मशुद्धि प्राप्त की है, उनमें श्रेष्ठतम को जिन (विजेता) कहा जाता है, और इस परंपरा के संघवासियों तथा आम अनुयायियों को जैन 'विजेता का अनुयायी' कहते हैं।

जैन धर्म का उद्भव लगभग सातवीं से पांचवीं सदी ई.पू. के दौरान उत्तर भारत के गंगा बेसिन में हुआ, जो उस समय गहन धार्मिक चिंतन और गतिविधियों का केंद्र था। इसी क्षेत्र में बौद्ध धर्म का भी प्रादुर्भाव हुआ था। इन नए धार्मिक परिप्रेक्ष्यों की तत्कालीन साझा विचारधाराएं, संन्यास, सामाजिक गतिविधियों, कर्मकांड और

घरेलू दोनों का त्याग व इंद्रियों पर विजय प्राप्त करके पुनर्जन्म के चक्र से छुटकारा पाने के लिए आध्यात्मिक ज्ञान प्राप्ति से संबद्ध थे। इस प्रकार वेद और कर्मकांडी ब्राह्मणवादी परंपरा को अस्वीकृत कर दिया गया। पहले जैन व्यक्तित्व, पार्श्वनाथ हैं, जिनके बारे में पर्याप्त ऐतिहासिक प्रमाण मिलते हैं। वह एक संन्यासी शिक्षक थे, जिन्होंने संभवतः सातवीं सदी ई. पू. में सांसारिक मोह के त्याग के आधार पर एक समुदाय स्थापित किया। जैन परंपरा के अनुसार, उन्हें विश्व के वर्तमान युग कल्प का 23वां तीर्थंकर माना जाता है।

तीर्थंकर, जिन्हें जिन भी कहते हैं, जैन धर्म मार्ग के पथ प्रदर्शक व संन्यासियों तथा जनसाधारण के समुदाय (तीर्थ) के संस्थापक हैं, जो पुनर्जन्म के बंधन से मुक्त हैं और इस तरह, ऐसा उदाहरण पेश करते हैं, जिसका अनुसरण सभी जैनों को करना चाहिए। इस युग के 24वें और अंतिम तीर्थंकर वर्धमान थे, जिन्हें महावीर (महान नायक) की उपाधि से जाना जाता है; जैन उन्हें सम्यक् ज्ञान, सम्यक् दर्शन (आस्था) और सम्यक् चारित्र्य (आचरण) की जैन शिक्षा के इस युग का अंतिम पथ प्रदर्शक मानते हैं, हालांकि परंपरागत रूप से इनका समय 599-527 ई.पू. माना जाता है, महावीर को बुद्ध का लगभग समकालीन माना जाना चाहिए, जिनके समय का वर्तमान शोधकर्ताओं ने पुनर्आकलन किया है, जो क़रीब एक सदी बाद फला-फूला। ये जैन धर्मग्रंथों में संरक्षित महावीर के जीवन का अनुश्रुत लेखा-जोखा उनकी जीवनी की रचना का आधार है और इससे उनके द्वारा स्थापित प्रारंभिक समुदाय के स्वरूप के बारे में कुछ निष्कर्ष निकालने में मदद मिलती है।

श्वेताम्बर-दिगंबर विभाजन को मज़बूत करने का महत्त्वपूर्ण कारण शायद महावीर की मृत्यु के बाद लंबे समय तक मौखिक रूप में हस्तांतरित शिक्षा को संहिताबद्ध करने और जैन धर्मग्रंथों में लिखकर संरक्षित करने के लिए आयोजित परिषदें रहीं। जैन इतिहास में दर्ज इन परिषदों में से एक सौराष्ट्र (आधुनिक गुजरात) में वल्लभी में 453 या 456 ई. में आयोजित अंतिम परिषद् श्वेतांबर धर्मग्रंथों को क्रमबद्ध करने के लिए उत्तरदायी थी, जो अब भी उपयोग में हैं। दिगंबर संघ इस संशोधन को इतना भ्रष्ट मानता है कि यह उसके अनुसार नियामक नहीं हो सकता। इस प्रकार की विचारधारा ही सम्प्रदाय के विकास का कारण बनी। इस काल में जैन धर्म अपने उद्गम स्थल से पश्चिम की ओर उज्जैन तक फैल गया, जहां ऐसा प्रतीत होता है इसे राजकीय संरक्षण मिला। प्रारंभिक जैन धर्म, विशेष रूप से जनसाधारण के बारे में शुरुआती पुरातत्वीय और शिलालेखीय प्रमाण मथुरा नगर से प्राप्त हुए, जो पश्चिमोत्तर व्यापार मार्ग का महत्त्वपूर्ण केंद्र था। गुप्त वंश (320-600 ई.) के

शासनकाल में हिंदुओं द्वारा सत्ता के आग्रह के समय बड़ी संख्या में जैन अनुयायी मध्य एवं पश्चिम भारत चले गए, वे वहां अपने उद्गम स्थल गंगा के बेसिन की अपेक्षा ज़्यादा मज़बूत हो गए।

शैल गुफाओं से प्राप्त पुरातात्विक साक्ष्यों से पता चलता है कि जैन भिक्षु एक जगह पर धर्म विचार हेतु अवश्य उपस्थित होते रहे हों या दिगंबर संप्रदाय की लगभग दो सहस्राब्दियों से उस क्षेत्र में (वर्तमान कर्नाटक) महत्त्वपूर्ण उपस्थिति रही है। प्रारंभिक मध्य काल में दिगंबर जैन इस क्षेत्र और पड़ोसी तमिलनाडु में सबसे ज़्यादा फले-फूले। इन शताब्दियों के दौरान दिगंबरों ने तीन मुख्य राजवंशों के प्रमुख राजाओं का संरक्षण प्राप्त किया, कर्नाटक में गंग (तीसरी और ग्यारहवीं शताब्दी); राष्ट्रकूट, जिनका राज्य गंग राज्य के एकदम उत्तर में था (आठवीं से बारहवीं शताब्दी); और कर्नाटक में होयसल (11वीं शताब्दी)। दिगंबर साधु गंग और होयसल राजवंश में उत्तराधिकार को प्रभावित करने के लिए प्रसिद्ध थे, इस तरह अनिश्चित राजनीतिक स्थिति को स्थिर करके वे जैनों के लिए राजनीतिक संरक्षण और समर्थन निश्चित करते थे। बहुतायत में प्राप्त पुरालेखीय प्रमाणों में व्यापक संरक्षण व्यवस्था का ब्यौरा है, जिसके तहत राजा, रानी, राज्यमंत्री तथा सेनापति जैन समुदाय को कर राजस्व, मंदिरों के निर्माण और रखरखाव के लिए अनुदान देते थे। इसका प्रसिद्ध उदाहरण है, 10वीं सदी में गंग सेनापति चामुंडराय द्वारा श्रवणबेलगोला में बाहुबली (स्थानीय रूप से गोमतेश्वर कहे जाने वाले; पहले तीर्थंकर ऋषभदेव के पुत्र) की विशाल मूर्ति के निर्माण की निगरानी।

दक्षिण तथा उत्तर के राजवंशों में धार्मिक विचारों में वैभिन्य समय में आता है। दलित राजवंशों से अपने शासनकाल में धार्मिक गतिविधियों में सहयोग प्रदान किया। जैसे—आठवीं सदी में वनराज और 12वीं सदी में कुमारपाल, जिनके राज्यारोहण के पीछे महान् श्वेतांबर विद्वान् और राज्यमंत्री हेमचंद्र का हाथ था।

विगत कुछ वर्गों से जैन मतावलंबी तथा सम्प्रदायों ने इस धर्म के विकास के लिए धार्मिक स्थलों तथा साहित्यों पर काफी जोर दिया है। जैन लोग एक समृद्ध सामाजिक समूह के रूप में आम कल्याण कार्यों में भी शामिल होते रहे हैं, जैसे 1980 के दशक में गुजरात में सूखा राहत, जैन विधवाओं और ग़रीबों को राहत व हत्या से बचाने के लिए बूढ़े जानवरों के आश्रय स्थलों का रखरखाव, जिसे अहिंसा का कार्य माना जाता है। प्राचीन व्यापार संपर्कों के कारण पश्चिमी भारत के कई जैन पूर्वी अफ़्रीकी देशों, विशेषकर केन्या, युगांडा में बस गए। 1960 के दशक की राजनीतिक अस्थिरता ने उन्हें पहले इंग्लैंड में बसने को बाध्य किया, जहां भारत के बाहर पहला

जैन मंदिर लीकेस्टर में निर्मित किया गया; फिर ज़्यादातर अमेरिका और कनाडा में बसने लगे, जहां उन्होंने सफलतापूर्वक अपना परंपरागत व्यापार तथा व्यावसायिक पेशा चलाया। अपनी पहचान बनाए रखने की तीव्र इच्छा के कारण उन्होंने 1970 एवं 1980 के दशकों के दौरान जैन समाज (यूरोप) और उत्तरी अमेरिका में *फ़ेडरेशन ऑफ जैन एसोसिएशंस* जैसे व्यापक संगठनों की स्थापना की। *जैन डाइजेस्ट* और *जैन स्पिरिट* जैसे नियमित अंग्रेज़ी भाषा के प्रकाशनों के द्वारा इस धर्म के आदर्शों विचारों, आधारीय महत्त्व के विषय में मात्र भारत में ही नहीं प्रत्युत् विदेशों में भी इसका सहजता से प्रचार-प्रसार हो रहा है।

जैनों ने अनुश्रुत इतिहास का अपना वृत्तांत विकसित किया, जिसे '63 विख्यात व्यक्तियों के कार्य' *(डीड्ज़ ऑफ़ द 63 इलस्ट्रियस मेन)* या पश्चिमी विद्वानों द्वारा 'वैश्विक इतिहास' कहा जाता है। इनमें निस्संदेह 24 तीर्थंकर सबसे महत्त्वपूर्ण हैं, जो परिपूर्ण मानव हैं और समय-समय पर जैन धर्म के मार्ग की शिक्षा व इसे मूर्त रूप देते रहे हैं। इनके कुछ नारयक हिंदू धर्म में भी पाए जाते हैं; मुख्य रूप से कृष्ण, जिन्हें जैन 22वें तीर्थंकर अरिष्टनेमि का चचेरा भाई मानते हैं और महानायक राम, जिन्हें उनकी कहानी के 16 प्रमुख पुनर्व्याख्यानों में पवित्र अहिंसक जैन बताया गया है। ऐसे महत्त्वपूर्ण हिंदू व्यक्तियों को शामिल और पुनः परिभाषित करके जैन आसपास के हिंदू जगत का हिस्सा तथा भिन्न स्वरूप, दोनों बने रहने में सफल रहे।

जैन धर्म ने इस सिद्धान्त वाक्य पर विशेष बल देता है कि धर्म की सर्वोच्च पराकाष्ठा आध्यात्मिकता है। इस धर्म का लक्ष्य जीव की शुद्धि तथा लोक कल्याणकारी मूल्यों की स्थापना करना है। यह तभी हो सकता है, जब आत्मा सतत मोक्ष और सांसारिक मोह से निस्पृहता की स्थिति में हो। यथार्थ की जैन अवधारणा जटिल है। इसकी विशेषता उत्पत्ति, परिवर्तन व क्षय है, जो सहज स्थायित्व (हिंदुओं के लिए) और अस्थायित्व (बौद्धों के लिए) के विपरीत है। विश्व शाश्वत और 'अज' (किसी के द्वारा निर्मित नहीं) हैं। इसके कारक पांच द्रव्य हैं: आत्मा, पदार्थ, अंतरिक्ष, गति के सिद्धांत और गति संरोध व दिगंबरों के लिए, समय। ये भी शाश्वत और अविनाशी हैं, लेकिन इनकी स्थितियां लगातार बदलती रहती हैं। जैन यथार्थ का निर्माण जीव (आत्मा, जीवित द्रव्य) और अजीव (आत्मा रहित, निर्जीव द्रव्य) द्वारा होता है। जीव के अलावा सभी निर्जीव हैं; चार तत्त्वों (पृथ्वी, जल, अग्नि और वायु) में भी आत्मा का निवास है। जीव की अनिवार्य विशेषताएं हैं। चेतना, सुख और वीर्य (ऊर्जा)। जीव निराकार व लिंगरहित होता है और इंद्रियों से इसका प्रत्यक्ष आभास नहीं होता। ब्रह्मांड की तरह इसकी उत्पत्ति और समाप्ति (विनाश) का कोई निश्चित बिंदु नहीं है। आत्मा जिस शरीर में प्रवेश करती

है, उसका आयाम ले लेती है, लेकिन यह उस शरीर के समरूप नहीं होती। मृत्यु पर यह उस अंतिम भौतिक काया का आधार धारण करती है, जिसमें इसका निवास है। जैन धर्म का मानना है कि कार्य-कारण के सम्बन्ध की प्रबलता ही कार्य के परिणाम को निश्चित करती है। स्वभाव से सभी आत्माएं पवित्र होती हैं, उनमें अनंत ज्ञान, सुख और शक्ति होती है; लेकिन इन क्षमताओं को आत्मा के संपर्क में आने वाले पदार्थ हर समय कुंठित करते रहते हैं। इस प्रकार आत्मा की मुक्ति को कर्मों का संचयन अवरुद्ध करता है। ये कर्म मनुष्य के कार्यों से उत्पन्न उपादान के अंश हैं, ये स्वयं को आत्मा से जोड़ लेते हैं और परिणामस्वरूप उसको कई जन्मों द्वारा भौतिक शरीर से बांध देते हैं, जो ज्ञान प्राप्ति में बाधक बनता है।

जैनों का मानना है कि समय अनंत और आकारविहीन है। इसकी तुलना 12 तीलियों (अरों) वाले चक्र से की जाती है, जो कल्प के बराबर हैं, छह आरोही चाप और छह अवरोही चाप बनाते हैं। आरोही चाप में मनुष्य के ज्ञान, आयु, क़द (गुणवत्ता) और हर्ष में वृद्धि होती है, जबकि अवरोही चाप में उनका ह्रास होता है। ये दोनों आवर्तक जुड़कर समय के चक्र का एक चक्कर बनाते हैं, जिसे एक कल्प कहा जाता है। ये कल्प आदि या अंत के बिना चलते रहते हैं।

जैन धर्म के अनुसार, साधु का शारीरिक और मानसिक अनुशासन यानी सर्वज्ञान और इस प्रकार मोक्ष प्राप्त करने का साधन 'योग' है। योग यथार्थ के सही ज्ञान, तीर्थंकरों की शिक्षा में आस्था और शुद्ध आचरण का परिवर्धन है; इस तरह यह तीन रत्नों (रत्नत्रय) सही ज्ञान, आस्था और सही आचरण क्रमशः सम्यक् ज्ञान, सम्यक् दर्शन तथा सम्यक् चरित्र से घनिष्ठ रूप से संबद्ध है। ये तीन रत्न जैन सिद्धांत और नीतिशास्त्र संबंधी अवस्थिति का आधार बनाते हैं। सम्यक् ज्ञान, दर्शन और चरित्र एक साथ परिवर्द्धित किए जाने चाहिए; इनमें से कोई भी दूसरे की अनुपस्थिति में प्राप्त नहीं किया जा सकता है। सम्यक् दर्शन शांति, अनासक्ति, दया और जन्म का गर्व, रूप, धन, विद्वता, पराक्रम और प्रसिद्धि के परित्याग का रास्ता दिखाता है, लेकिन तभी जब इसका अनुसरण सम्यक् चरित्र से किया जाए। लेकिन सम्यक् ज्ञान के बिना कोई अच्छा आचरण नहीं किया जा सकता, यही अहम् और परम के बीच के भेद को स्पष्ट करता है। धर्मग्रंथों का ज्ञान अंतर्ज्ञान से अलग है। आस्था और आचरण के बिना ज्ञान व्यर्थ है। मन के शुद्धिकरण के बिना कड़ा संयम केवल शारीरिक यातना है। जैन धर्म का मानना है कि किसी भी दशा में सम्यक् चरित्र का अनुपालन करना ही होगा। वास्तविकता तो यह है कि बिना साधु बने किसी भी दशा में सम्यक् चरित्र का पूर्णतः अनुपालन असम्भव है।

मूर्तिपूजक श्वेतांबरों के स्थानकवासियों और तेरापंथियों के लिए हर समय मुखवस्त्रिका धारण करना अनिवार्य है। वरिष्ठ गुरु द्वारा दीक्षा के बाद साधु को निम्न महाव्रतों को अवश्य पालन करना चाहिएः किसी जीव को चोट न पहुंचाना, झूठ न बोलना, चोरी न करना, संभोग न करना और निजी संपत्ति एकत्र न करना। दिगंबरों में पूर्ण मुनि इसी प्रकार महाव्रतों का पालन करते हैं, लेकिन संपत्ति न रखने की शपथ की कठोर व्याख्या के अनुसार नग्न रहते हैं। निम्न स्तर के दिगंबर मुनि लंगोट पहनते हैं और अपने पास 1.3 मीटर से कम लंबे कपड़े का एक टुकड़ा रखते हैं। दिगंबर मुनि मोर पंख का चंवर और एक जलतुंबी का उपयोग करते हैं और दिन में केवल एक बार आहार ग्रहण करते हैं। वे जैन संघ परंपरा की अपनी व्याख्या को श्वेताम्बर की तुलना में प्राचीन प्रतिमान के ज्यादा अनुरूप मानते हैं। सभी जैन साधकों के लिए तीन गुप्तियों (विचार, वाणी और कर्म में संयम) और पांच समितियों (आचरण के बारे में एक प्रकार की सतर्कता) का पालन आवश्यक है। संघीय अनुष्ठान का एक ज़रूरी और नियमित हिस्सा है, 'आवश्यक' (छः अनिवार्य कर्म), जिनका आचरण वैसे तो प्रतिदिन लेकिन आनुष्ठानिक तिथिपत्र के महत्त्वपूर्ण काल में ज़रूर किया जाता है। ये हैं—धैर्य; तीर्थंकरों, गुरुओं और धर्मग्रंथों का आदर; पाप की स्वीकारोक्ति; पापपूर्ण गतिविधियों से दूर रहने का संकल्प और 'देह को महत्त्व न देना', यानी ध्यान की मुद्रा में खड़े या बैठे रहना।

गुरु की श्रेष्ठ महत्ता का भी इसमें प्रतिपादन किया गया है। इस धर्म के अनुसार, गुरु साधक के संयमों के स्वरूप, उनके आचरण की अवधि व उनकी कठोरता का सावधानीपूर्वक नियमन करता है और उनके आध्यात्मिक विकास, संयम बरतने की क्षमता तथा उस अवधि में आध्यात्मिक विकास में इन्होंने किस प्रकार सहायता दी, यह समझने की उनकी क्षमता की निगरानी करता है। मुनि के कठोर संयम की सैद्धांतिक परिणति 'सल्लेखन' क्रिया है, जिसमें वह कंटीली घास के बिस्तर पर एक करवट लेटा रहता है, हिलता-डुलता नहीं और न ही भोजन करता है। आनुष्ठानिक उपवास की यह क्रिया अनासक्ति का चरम है, जिसके द्वारा अपनी आत्मा के हित में वह शरीर त्याग देता है। जैन विचारधारा इसे परम आत्मनियंत्रण की सकारात्मक क्रिया मानती है, जिसमें आवेग की कोई भूमिका नहीं और इसे 'बेवकूफ़ी की मौत' या आत्महत्या से अलग करती है। प्राचीन और मध्यकालीन समय में 'सल्लेखन' का व्यापक अनुसरण होता था, परन्तु वर्तमान परिवर्तित परिस्थिति में इसके स्वरूप में भी परिवर्तन हो रहा है।

जहाँ तक दीक्षा देने की बात है तो श्वेतांबर और दिगंबर, दोनों साध्वियों को दीक्षा की अनुमति देते हैं; श्वेताम्बर समुदाय में साध्वियों की संख्या साधकों से क़रीब तिगुनी है। अक्सर आध्यात्मिक ज्ञान की प्राप्ति करने के बावजूद विद्वान जैन साध्वियों का दर्जा साधकों की तुलना में छोटा होता है। उन्हें परंपरा और धार्मिक अनुबंध के तहत साधुओं की बात माननी होती है, जिसके कारण उन पर मानसिक दबाव बढ़ता है।

यही कारण है कि दिगंबर जैन धर्म में चीवर धारण करने वाली साध्वियां संन्यास मार्ग पर गंभीरता से आगे बढ़ने के लिए पुरुष-रूप में पुनर्जन्म की आवश्यकता स्वीकारती हैं (जिसके लिए उनके समुदाय में नग्नता को ज़रूरी माना गया है)।

पुरुष को आठ प्राथमिक व्यावहारिक गुणों (भिन्नता के बावजूद आमतौर पर इसमें मांस, मदिरा, शहद, ऐसे फल या कंद, जिनमें जीवों का वास माना जाता है और रात के समय भोजन न करना शामिल है) और 12 व्रत, पांच अणुव्रत, तीन गुणव्रत और चार शिक्षाव्रत का पालन अनिवार्य है। अणुव्रत (लघुव्रत) में घोर हिंसा, असत्य और चोरी से परहेज़, अपनी पत्नी से संतुष्टि और सीमित संपत्ति रखना शामिल है। अन्य व्रत-समूह पूरक स्वभाव के हैं, जिनका उद्देश्य अणुव्रत को सुदृढ़ बनाना और उनकी रक्षा करना है। इनमें अनावश्यक यात्रा, हानिकारक गतिविधियों और सुख की खोज से बचना; उपवास और पथ्य नियंत्रण; साधुओं, गरीबों और साथी धर्मावलंबियों को उपहार व सेवा प्रदान करना शामिल है। जनसाधारण के लिए नियमित अंतराल में 'आवश्यक' का पालन करना जरूरी है।

इसके अनुसार व्यापार से लेकर आधार तथ्य समस्त व्यावहारिक जीवन में ठोस तथा निर्वहनीय तरीके से जीवन यापन करना है। साथ ही धार्मिक मामलों, विशेषकर अहिंसा के प्रति पवित्र और गंभीर दृष्टिकोण होना चाहिए। जैन मानते हैं कि उपवास या धर्मार्थ कार्यों के लिए धन के दान से प्राप्त पुण्यों से न केवल व्यक्ति मोक्ष के मार्ग पर कुछ और आगे बढ़ेगा, बल्कि उसकी वर्तमान भौतिक स्थिति भी सुधरेगी। इससे जैन जनसाधारण की अति समृद्धि और मुनियों व साध्वियों के आत्मत्याग के बीच स्पष्ट विषमता समझी जा सकती है। आज तक जैन धर्म में जन्म और विवाह जैसे आयोजनों के लिए कोई विशिष्ट जीवनचक्र-संबंधी अनुष्ठान विकसित करने का प्रयास नहीं किया गया, हालांकि नौवीं शताब्दी में दिगंबर साधुओं ने इसके नियम बनाने के प्रयास किए थे।